*Official History of New Zealand
in the Second World War
1939–45*

United States troops arriving at the gates of Oflag 79 at Brunswick on 12 April 1945

*Official History of New Zealand
in the Second World War 1939–45*

PRISONERS OF WAR

by

W. WYNNE MASON

WAR HISTORY BRANCH
DEPARTMENT OF INTERNAL AFFAIRS
WELLINGTON, NEW ZEALAND

The Naval & Military Press Ltd

The Naval & Military Press Ltd
Unit 10 Ridgewood Industrial Park,
Uckfield, East Sussex,
TN22 5QE England
Tel: +44 (0) 1825 749494
Fax: +44 (0) 1825 765701
www.naval-military-press.com
www.military-genealogy.com
www.militarymaproom.com

In reprinting in facsimile from the original, any imperfections are inevitably reproduced and the quality may fall short of modern type and cartographic standards.

Foreword

IN the First World War New Zealand troops fought in Egypt, on Gallipoli, in Palestine, in France and Belgium. Twenty-five men were taken prisoner on Gallipoli, 12 in Egypt, 464 in France or Belgium. None of the few hundred New Zealanders who served in the Royal Navy and in the Royal Flying Corps became prisoners.

In the Second World War our troops fought in Greece, Crete, Egypt, Libya, Cyrenaica, Tripolitania, Tunisia, Italy and in the Pacific, and 8348 were taken prisoner. Our sailors served in the Royal Navy, the Royal New Zealand Navy, and the Merchant Navy in every sea and 194 became prisoners or were interned. Our airmen, in the Royal Air Force and the Royal New Zealand Air Force, fought in every one of the great campaigns waged by the Western Allies; 575 were captured and 23 interned.

The reasons for this remarkable difference are clear and should be put on record.

Between 1914 and 1918 our troops were involved in no disasters. The attack on Gallipoli failed, and in a skilful, unmolested evacuation no one was left behind. There had been two periods of very heavy fighting, the fortnight after the landing and the final effort in August 1915. In each we had been on the offensive, when few prisoners are ever lost. There were no tanks to overrun the units which devotedly and at great cost beat off the great Turkish counter-attacks at Chunuk Bair. In France the New Zealand Division was almost always employed in attacks and in holding the line. A few prisoners were lost in trench raids, and a company of the Entrenching Battalion ran out of ammunition and was captured in the German offensive in April 1918. The British Official History remarks that this was the biggest loss of New Zealand prisoners during the war.

Far different were the circumstances in the Second World War. The 2nd Division shared in one disaster after another, from April 1941 until the tide was checked at Alam Halfa in September 1942 and turned at Alamein on 23 October of that year.

In Greece 1856 prisoners were lost, 242 of them wounded. Nearly half were from the reinforcement companies stranded at Kalamata. The others were lost through transport breaking down or being destroyed, through missing their way, or being left behind after reaching the beaches. For a month after the evacuation the Aegean was dotted with parties escaping in caiques and rowing boats, to Turkey or out of the frying pan into Crete. Hundreds of men wandered in Greece for months; some eventually reached Egypt, some perished; the remainder were captured in ones and twos.

In Crete 2180 men were taken prisoner, 488 of them wounded. Only a few score were captured in the fighting; the others reached Sfakia and were left there under orders to capitulate when it was decided to attempt no more evacuations. Several hundred broke away into the hills. Two hundred of these reached Egypt; the remainder were picked up during the next two years.

In the Libyan battles of November–December 1941, 2042 were captured, including 206 wounded. Most of the others were taken when 6 Brigade and 20 Battalion of 4 Brigade were overrun by tanks. We had few and weak anti-tank guns and our tanks were outnumbered and outmatched. The pattern was always the same. It was necessary to hold the positions, captured with the bayonet in costly night attacks, on Sidi Rezegh and Belhamed. It was impossible to dig deeper than two feet. The Germans acted deliberately, concentrating forty to fifty tanks, followed by one or two battalions of infantry, on a chosen sector. They advanced slowly, lashing the ground with continuous fire. Our few anti-tank gunners, with their little two-pounders, fought till struck down. There was no instance of a gun being abandoned. Meantime the infantry fired steadily with Brens and rifles and mortars, forcing the tanks to remain closed down and keeping the enemy infantry at a distance. But when the anti-tank guns were knocked out the panzers closed. Invulnerable to small-arms fire or mortars, they moved right on to our positions and the only choices were to surrender or die uselessly. Most of these attacks lasted from one to two hours, but the result was always the same. I went over these stark battlefields a few months later and saw the cartridge cases round every fire pit, the piles of mortar shells, the wrecked guns, and the rifles marking the shallow graves. Often the Germans had marked the graves with rough crosses. It was a sombre and unforgettable scene.

During the same campaign 5 Brigade Headquarters and some attached troops at Sidi Azeiz were attacked by 40 tanks, with guns and infantry, and after the seven guns had been knocked out, Brigadier Hargest and seven hundred men were overrun in the same way and had to surrender.

The men captured on these disastrous days had fought splendidly in attack after attack and had lost half their numbers before the end. The morale of the Division was never higher than at this time, yet it was the hard fate of these soldiers to be taken helplessly.

Seven months later, during the most desperate and dangerous months of the war, the Division made its great move from Syria and again plunged into a series of disasters. Almost surrounded at Minqar Qaim, it broke through the encircling forces, leaving two hundred men whose trucks had been wrecked to be taken helplessly in the morning. A fortnight later 4 and 5 Brigades, in a magnificent night attack, carried the Ruweisat Ridge, only to meet disaster in exactly the same way as at Sidi Rezegh and Belhamed. Fourth Brigade, down to half strength through casualties, was overrun by the tank and infantry counter-attack that had become the accustomed sequel to the unsupported but invariably successful night attacks which our infantry in those days had to deliver. In 5 Brigade 22 Battalion, moving in support and actually passing through a German armoured division, was overrun at dawn by the tanks of the same division attacking from the rear. A week later 6 Brigade, having taken its objective by an equally splendid feat of arms, met the same evil fate. That was the last of the disasters. In these three actions 1819 men were taken prisoner, 231 of them wounded.

It is impossible to blame the men who surrendered on these ghastly occasions. I know of no case in which further resistance was possible. The blows could not be evaded and the stage was reached in each case when they could no longer be resisted. What one man said in a report written after he had escaped—' I had thought of death or wounds, but never of surrender, yet there it was '—could have been said by all.

During the remainder of the war very few prisoners were lost: 178, including 30 wounded, in Africa, 225, including 35 wounded, in Italy; all the result of the minor misfortunes that occur in the most victorious campaigns.

Our airmen prisoners were those shot down over enemy territory. A few evaded capture who came down in occupied countries and had the good fortune to find friends quickly. For most there was no chance of escape.

Most of the sailors were captured with their ships, merchant ships—no warship surrendered. For them also there was no alternative, unless useless suicide is an alternative.

So it came about that over nine thousand New Zealanders spent years of their lives as inmates of enemy prison camps. The great majority of these men were volunteers; it was they and their contemporaries who died or were wounded or, in a few cases, escaped scatheless, who bore the brunt of the years of disaster, and in so doing gained time for the raising of the armies and air fleets of the victorious years. Among them were very many who, with better fortune, would have attained high rank.

As prisoners they endured years of uncertainty, privation and frustration. They unremittingly continued the struggle in every way that courage, pride, and ingenuity could suggest. Some escaped in almost incredible exploits, others continuously strove to escape or unselfishly helped those better equipped. In every camp they bore up against adversity, defied and deceived their guards, maintained discipline, soldierly spirit and pride of race. Only a very few failed.

I saw those who came out of Germany after the war ended. They were thin and strained, but they carried themselves as soldiers and as men who knew that they had acquitted themselves as men in a long and bitter ordeal. I was proud that I had served with them in the hard years.

This volume relates their experience as prisoners, and in doing so records an honourable chapter in New Zealand's history.

H. K. KIPPENBERGER,
Editor-in-Chief,
New Zealand War Histories

Author's Preface

THIS book is an attempt to set down an accurate, objective, and impartial account of captivity as it affected New Zealanders in the Second World War. Effort has therefore been concentrated on the checking of evidence and the avoidance of facile generalisation; on an impersonal presentation of the facts as they emerge; and on the achievement of a perspective and balance which might be fair not only to the author's compatriots and comrades but to former enemies as well.

A good many unofficial accounts of individual experiences during captivity and of escapes have already been published. But conditions varied a very great deal in different places and at different periods of the war; and individual accounts which often depict only certain exceptional aspects of life in captivity give only a fragment of the whole picture. It is this whole picture which the author has tried to achieve, in the form not of a vague impression but rather of a mosaic built up from a multitude of individual experiences.

It is obvious that an account of the life of prisoners of war and civilian internees from capture to repatriation will tell little of a country's military achievements. But the fact that nine thousand or so New Zealanders were living in enemy territory for periods of up to five years is an aspect of our participation in the Second World War which cannot be ignored. People should be able to get an idea of what happened to their countrymen when they were captured; how the event of capture affected their lives and those of their next-of-kin; what it was possible to do to help them during the war; and what were their needs for rehabilitation.

Apart from the accounts of escapes,[1] the story is on the whole an undramatic one. It tells how thousands of men, many of them at first mentally stunned after their capture and sometimes physically broken after their detention in transit camps, gradually organised themselves into civilised communities on hostile soil. Though such a theme does not lend itself to heroics, it contains some fine

---

[1] The total number of New Zealand prisoners who escaped from captivity was approximately 718, including 110 who made their way to Switzerland. Of these, approximately 236 were from German hands, approximately 480 from Italian hands, and 2 from Japanese hands. The countries from which the original successful breaks were made were: Greece 44 (approx), Crete 150 (approx), Libya 25 (approx), Italy 455, Germany 12, Austria 27, France 2 (civilians), Hong Kong 2.

examples of courage and self-sacrifice; and daring, determination, and endurance find their place in the narratives of many of those who escaped. Much of the subject matter of this book, therefore, belongs more properly to social than to military history, though what is described arises from the events of war. The last are briefly stated as a framework in which to sketch the community life of thousands of men, and some women, behind barbed wire in enemy countries.

G. M. Trevelyan once wrote that 'the sum total of social history . . . could only be mastered if we knew the biographies of all the millions of men, women and children who have lived. . . .' and that the 'generalisations which are the stock in trade of the social historian must necessarily be based on a small number of particular instances, which are assumed to be typical, but which cannot be the whole of the complicated truth'. Because the events described in this book are more recent, and because modern records are more voluminous, it has been possible to select those instances which are likely to be the most reliable, and to check doubtful ones with others of the same time and place. Quite often there are not just a few instances but dozens, of fairly certain authenticity, dealing with the same topic, time, and place.

This is not to claim that the book gives the whole story in complete detail. It is obvious that an exhaustive record of more than nine thousand captives, split into hundreds of groups, which lived for up to five years under a bewildering variety of conditions in many different parts of Europe and the Far East, and often moving from place to place, would demand not one but some dozens of volumes of this size. It has therefore been necessary to select from this vast mass of experience that part which is common to the majority of the people concerned. Priority has been given to conditions in camps where large numbers of our people were detained. For the same reason, an effort has been made to avoid devoting too much space to exceptional aspects of life in captivity and over-emphasizing cases of unusual ill-treatment. It has been thought necessary, however, to include some reference to more exceptional sides of the life, in order to give an idea of what an almost infinite variety of experience there was. Since our people usually shared most stages of their captivity with large numbers of other British Commonwealth captives, the conditions for British captives in general have often been given as a background against which to set the individual experiences of New Zealanders.

Many ex-captives may find their own particular experience not set down in detail. It is inevitable also that not every creditable

AUTHOR'S PREFACE

exploit can be described, if only because some of them are not recorded. Only successful escapes[1] have been mentioned, unless an unsuccessful attempt had something particularly noteworthy about it. Only those whose capture had been recorded in some way have been regarded as within the scope of this history. 'Evaders', who avoided capture but eventually got back from enemy territory, are excluded. In general, people who helped our escapers, and sometimes even villages where they were helped, are purposely not named lest even now they suffer any harm from having once helped British soldiers.

It early became clear to the author that the best way to make intelligible what was selected from this enormous mass of widely varying experience was to fit it into a chronological framework, presenting it stage by stage against a background of events. Each chapter therefore coincides broadly with a period of the war, either in Europe or the Far East. Nearly all begin with a brief account of the main events likely to affect prisoners of war and internees, and go on to give in more detail events which led up to capture, those immediately following, treatment of wounded and interrogation. At this point there is often a subdivision according to the category—Navy, Army, Air Force, or civilian—to which the captive or group of captives belonged, and an attempt is made to trace the journey of each group of captives as far as their first permanent camp. Permanent camps are dealt with in geographical groups according to the country in which they were situated, subdivided according to the categories of captives. The concluding sections of each chapter deal with negotiations and relief work on behalf of those in captivity, and each chapter ends with a brief general summary which attempts to draw together all the threads of the period covered.

For this history there did not exist anything comparable to the War Diaries that are available as basic source material for those portions of an official war history which deal with campaigns. There were periodic reports on permanent prisoner-of-war and internment camps, such as those of the representatives of the Protecting Power and the International Red Cross Committee. But these covered only one aspect of the narrative and, even for that, provided only a skeleton which needed to be filled out with material from individual eye-witness accounts. No useful purpose would be served by trying to record either in this Preface or in footnotes to the text the multitude of documents used, but a summary is given below of the principal sources of these, divided roughly

---

[1]The names of those who received awards, together with others whose escapes seemed sufficiently noteworthy, have been mentioned either in the text or in footnotes.

into (*a*) those which provided the skeleton, and (*b*) those which filled it out:

(*a*)
1. Records of captures, transfers, deaths, etc. (Base Records, Wellington).
2. Correspondence and various documents on all aspects of captivity (Prime Minister's Department, Wellington; Army, Navy, and Air Departments, Wellington; New Zealand House, London; Directorate of Prisoners of War, War Office, London).
3. Documents and minutes of the Imperial Prisoners of War Committee.
4. Various reports, documents, and lists (Military Intelligence Branch, War Office, London).
5. Prisoner-of-war camp histories (Air Ministry, London).
6. Reports on camps by representatives of Protecting Powers.
7. Reports on camps by representatives of the International Red Cross Committee.
8. Report of the International Red Cross Committee on its activities during the Second World War.
9. Official History of the War Organisation of the British Red Cross Society and the Order of St. John.
10. Papers and reports of the Joint Council of the New Zealand Red Cross Society and the Order of St. John.
11. Various captured enemy documents.
12. War diaries of No. 1 NZ Repatriation Unit and of 2 NZEF (UK).

(*b*)
13. Reports of interviews with ex-captives (New Zealand War Archives).
14. Narratives of escape or eye-witness accounts by ex-prisoners of war (New Zealand War Archives).
15. Private diaries of ex-prisoners of war and ex-internees.
16. Questionnaires filled in by ex-prisoners of war and ex-internees.
17. Correspondence between the author and ex-prisoners of war and ex-internees.
18. Interrogation reports of all escapers (Military Intelligence Branch, War Office, London).
19. Interrogation reports of selected prisoners of war on liberation (Military Intelligence Branch, War Office, London).
20. Evidence on War Crimes and court proceedings of War Crimes Trials (Judge Advocate General's Branch, War Office, London).
21. Official narrative of Air Force escapes (Air Ministry, London).
22. Various joint compilations and publications by ex-prisoners of war and ex-internees.
23. Books and unpublished manuscripts by individual ex-prisoners of war and ex-internees.

AUTHOR'S PREFACE

The author has carefully sifted material available in category (b). Where possible, the contributor has been interviewed in order to gain a better idea of his reliability; diaries written on the spot have been given more credence than more polished narratives and impressions written some time after the event. Occasionally this eye-witness material has tended to conflict with official reports, and one version has had to be modified in the light of others.

The collection and thorough processing of the considerable mass of material available on New Zealand prisoners of war and internees alone could have kept a research team occupied for several years. For one person, it has been a question of using what is most ready to hand and in most convenient form. There are gaps which might have been filled by further research and for some of the topics covered better material might possibly have been found. Some errors in matters of detail have already been pointed out and corrected, but the author realises that in a work of this nature and size there may be others. There is reason to hope that they are few and that the overall picture is a true one. The author's thanks go to all those, too numerous to mention here, who by checking portions of the book helped towards this end; in particular, his thanks go to Brigadier W. H. B. Bull, OBE, NZMC, Mr K. W. Fraser, Vice-President of the New Zealand Returned Servicemen's Association, Mr R. H. Johnston and the New Zealand Prisoners of War Association, who checked the complete text, and to Mr E. N. Hogben, who read the proofs and gave much valuable comment and advice.

An impersonal presentation was the one least likely to distort the picture, but the impressions of individuals are introduced where, in the light of all other information, they seem to be fair commentary or at least typical statements of the point of view of the captives. The author has also tried to take into account the point of view of the captors, and to weigh one viewpoint against the other. It is sometimes complained that in official histories objectivity and perhaps even complete accuracy are sacrificed to expediency. There is no foundation for such criticism here. In writing this book the author has had the fullest support in constantly striving to determine the facts of captivity and to present them in a balanced account.

LONDON
15 March 1953

Contents

	Page
FOREWORD	v
AUTHOR'S PREFACE	ix
INTRODUCTION	xxiii

Chapter 1: THE BEGINNINGS OF THE WAR IN WESTERN EUROPE
(September 1939–May 1940)

I : *Early Air Force Prisoners*	1
II : *Civilians in Europe*	6
III : *Protection of the Interests of Prisoners of War and Civilians in Enemy Hands*	7
IV : *Organisation of Relief for Prisoners of War and Civilian Internees*	12
V : *Enemy Aliens in New Zealand*	15

Chapter 2: FROM THE FALL OF FRANCE TO THE OFFENSIVE IN THE MIDDLE EAST (May 1940–March 1941)

I : *Prisoners of War captured in Europe in 1940*	20
II : *Servicemen and Civilians captured at Sea*	35
III : *The First Battles in the Middle East*	39
IV : *Protection of the Interests of Prisoners of War and Civilians*	41
V : *Work of Relief Organisations*	44
VI : *Germans and Italians interned in New Zealand*	49

Chapter 3: THE CAMPAIGNS OF GREECE AND CRETE
(April–October 1941)

I : *The Greek Campaign and Prisoners in Greece*	53
II : *The Crete Campaign—Prisoners in Greece and Germany*	60
III : *Civilians in Europe*	93
IV : *Protection of the Interests of Prisoners of War and Civilians*	95
V : *Relief Work*	99

CONTENTS

Page

Chapter 4: THE SECOND LIBYAN CAMPAIGN AND AFTER
(November 1941–June 1942)

I: *The Desert Campaign of 1941—Prisoners in Italian Hands* 104
II: *Prisoners in Germany* 126
III: *Civilians in Europe* 145
IV: *Protection of the Interests of Prisoners of War and Civilians* 146
V: *Relief Work* 150

Chapter 5: THE FIRST PHASE OF THE WAR AGAINST JAPAN
(December 1941–May 1942)

I: *Japanese Victories* 159
II: *Early Prisoner-of-war Camps in the Far East* 167
III: *Protection of the Interests of Prisoners of War and Civilians* 184
IV: *Relief Supplies for the Far East* 186

Chapter 6: TURNING POINT OF THE WAR IN EUROPE AND IN
NORTH AFRICA (June 1942–July 1943)

I: *The North African Campaigns of 1942–43—Prisoners in Italian Hands* 190
II: *Escapers in Greece* 227
III: *Prisoners of War in Germany* 233
IV: *Civilians in Europe* 255
V: *Protection of the Interests of Prisoners of War and Civilians* 256
VI: *Relief Work* 262
VII: *Enemy Aliens in New Zealand* 265

Chapter 7: THE ITALIAN ARMISTICE (July–December 1943)

I: *Events preceding and immediately following the Italian Armistice* 274
II: *Transit and Permanent Camps in Germany and Austria* 291
III: *Escapes from Italy after the Armistice* 301
IV: *New Zealanders captured in the Italian and Aegean Campaigns* 317
V: *Protection of the Interests of Prisoners of War and Civilians* 319
VI: *Relief Work* 322

Chapter 8: THE MIDDLE PHASE OF THE WAR AGAINST JAPAN
(June 1942–December 1944)

I: *The Turn of the Tide in the Far East* 325
II: *Prisoner-of-war and Civilian Internment Camps* 326

CONTENTS

		Page
III :	*Protection of the Interests of Prisoners of War and Civilians*	350
IV :	*Relief Supplies for the Far East*	353
V :	*Japanese Prisoners of War in New Zealand*	356

Chapter 9 : THE YEAR OF THE ALLIED INVASION OF WESTERN EUROPE (January–December 1944)

I :	*The Events of 1944 and German Camps from late 1943 onwards*	364
II :	*The War in Italy in 1944 and Escapes to Allied Lines*	410
III :	*Reception of Ex-prisoners of War in Italy*	430
IV :	*Escaped Prisoners in Switzerland*	434
V :	*Civilians in Europe*	438
VI :	*Protection of the Interests of Prisoners of War and Civilians*	439
VII :	*Relief Work*	442.
VIII :	*Enemy Aliens in New Zealand*	444

Chapter 10 : THE LAST MONTHS OF THE WAR IN EUROPE (January–May 1945)

I :	*Movements of Prisoners and Liberation in Germany*	449
II :	*Last Escapes to Allied Lines in Italy*	472
III :	*Release and Evacuation of Camps in Austria*	476
IV :	*Evacuation of Prisoners released by Russian Forces*	480
V :	*Protection of the Interests of Prisoners of War and Civilians*	484
VI :	*Relief Work*	486
VII :	*Enemy Aliens in New Zealand*	488

Chapter 11 : THE RECEPTION OF LIBERATED PRISONERS IN THE UNITED KINGDOM AND THEIR REPATRIATION   492

Chapter 12 : LIBERATION IN THE FAR EAST AND REPATRIATION (January–September 1945)

I :	*The Last Months of Hostilities and the Capitulation*	506
II :	*Recovery and Evacuation after the Armistice*	510
III :	*Protection of the Interests of Prisoners of War and Civilians*	518
IV :	*Relief Work in the Far East*	520
V :	*Japanese Prisoners of War in New Zealand*	520

CONCLUSION   524

List of Illustrations

Frontispiece

United States troops arriving at the gates of Oflag 79 at Brunswick on 12 April 1945 — *I. McD. Matheson*

Following page 126

The guard tower of Stalag 383 — *R. H. Blanchard*

Prisoners from Greece and Crete leaving Kokkinia Hospital for Germany, 1941 — *A. J. Spence*

British prisoners of war marching back from Sfakia to Galatas, Crete — *from a German publication*

'Shellfire Wadi', near Sidi Rezegh — *P. Curtis collection*

The compound at Bardia, 1941 — *British Official*

After three months in the main transit camp at Benghazi, 1942 — *H. R. Dixon*

Delousing in Campo PG 57, Gruppignano — *M. Lee Hill*

Lined up for rations, Campo PG 57, 1942 — *W. A. Weakley*

Blowers heating up a meal, Stalag IIIA, Luckenwalde — *J. H. Wilkinson collection*

Play acting in Campo PG 52, Chiavari, 1942

Inside an Italian working camp on the Austrian border—from a sketch by *A. G. Douglas*

Campo PG 57, Gruppignano, in April 1943—from a sketch by *A. G. Douglas*

Ready for evacuation from Italy to Germany, September 1943 — *M. Lee Hill*

To Germany in a cattle truck — *M. Lee Hill*

Mess queue for British civilian internees in Ilag VIII, Tost, Germany — *International Red Cross*

Working party, Stalag XXA, Thorn, Poland, 1941 — *International Red Cross*

Following page 142

Interrogation camp—Dulag Luft, Oberursel — *J. M. Garrett collection*

Living quarters for a working camp in Germany—from a sketch by *A. G. Douglas*

A village in the Sudetenland — *E. C. Cottrell collection*

LIST OF ILLUSTRATIONS

Following page 142

'Barbed-wire fever'—a cartoon by *J. Welch*	
Between the barracks of Stalag VIIIA at Görlitz	*F. Crandle collection*
A barrack interior at Stalag VIIIA	*F. Crandle collection*
Christmas Eve 1943 inside the perimeter wire, Stalag 383, Bavaria	*R. H. Blanchard*
Half of Stalag 383 from the sentry box on the north side	*R. H. Blanchard*
Stalag 383—Winter in Germany, 1943–44	*R. H. Blanchard*
Stalag 383—The restlessness of spring	*R. H. Blanchard*
Stalag 383—Mud after the thaw	*R. H. Blanchard*
Stalag 383—Hut interior at night	*R. H. Blanchard*
Stalag 383—'At the tables'	*A. H. Kyle collection*
Stalag 357 at Fallingbostel—Ablution stand for a group of over 1000 men	*J. M. Garrett collection*
Stalag 357—Dividing up swede peelings from the German mess	*J. M. Garrett collection*
Stalag XVIIIA at Wolfsberg, Austria—An Anzac Day parade in 1943	*J. Ledgerwood collection*
Stalag XVIIIA—The shoemakers' shop	*J. Ledgerwood collection*
Shakespeare played at Oflag VIIB, at Eichstaett	*G. R. Cowie collection*
Oflag VIIB—Another play	*G. R. Cowie collection*
The handicrafts section of an arts and crafts exhibition at Stalag 383	*R. H. Blanchard*

Following page 322

Manacles used by the Germans on Allied prisoners of war as a reprisal for British action in tying the hands of German prisoners taken in the Dieppe raid	
Hut interior at Stalag 383	*A. J. Spence*
Lunch from Red Cross parcels	*R. H. Blanchard*
A hut scene after transfer from Italy to Germany, drawn by *A. G. Douglas* during captivity	
A cartoon on escaping, drawn by *J. Welch*	
The punishment fortress of Campo PG 5, Gavi, Italy	*C. N. Armstrong collection*
Brigadier James Hargest in his disguise as a French railwayman	*permission Michael Joseph Ltd*
Passo Moro, over which some of the escapers from Italian camps crossed into Switzerland	*P. W. Bates collection*

LIST OF ILLUSTRATIONS

Following page 322

A Swiss frontier post	*D. J. Gibbs collection*
Escaped prisoners' footwear after reaching Switzerland	
	P. W. Bates collection
Men from Stalag 383 at Etehausen during the forced march south	
	R. H. Blanchard
A rest during a forced march	*M. Lee Hill*
Liberated prisoners waiting to be flown from Landshut airstrip to the United Kingdom	*R. H. Blanchard collection*
C. B. Burdekin, OBE, head of the prisoner-of-war welfare section of New Zealand House, London	
Prisoners of war repatriated from Italy in May 1942 reading mail at Maadi	*NZ Army, M. D. Elias*
At Cracow, in Poland, before being transported by the Russians to Odessa	*W. A. Weakley*
Reception at 2 NZEF (UK) Reception Group, a cartoon by *J. Welch*	
Outside the sergeants' mess at the Reception Group Wing at Folkestone	*R. H. Blanchard*

Following page 338

On the *Andes* on the voyage home	*R. H. Blanchard*
Home again	*NZ Army, F. A. Marriott*
A Japanese press officer at Shanghai Internment Camp	
	from a Japanese propaganda paper
The Argyll Street Camp, Hong Kong	*International Red Cross*
Selarang Barracks, Singapore, crowded by the Japanese with 17,000 prisoners of war because they had refused to sign pledges not to escape	*Australian War Memorial*
Four scenes in Selarang Barracks	*A. H. Harding collection*
Changi Jail, Singapore	*Australian War Memorial*
Women's quarters inside the crypt of Changi Jail—painted by *Gladys Tompkins* during captivity	
Prisoners of war working on a hillside in Japan	*M. Menzies collection*
Unloading sick prisoners from sampans at Chungkai—a painting by *J. B. Chalker*	
The Kwei Noi River, seen from a northbound train, Thailand, in October 1945	*Australian War Memorial*
Hospital ward—Thailand Railway, painted by *Murray Griffin*	
A trestle bridge on the Burma-Thailand Railway	
	Australian War Memorial

LIST OF ILLUSTRATIONS

Following page 338

Malnutrition case from Hong Kong on a hospital ship
The Far East Prisoner of War Social Club

A German internee in New Zealand   *NZ Army, F. A. Marriott*

Japanese prisoners of war in the Wairarapa, New Zealand
Dept Internal Affairs, John Pascoe

PRISONER-OF-WAR LOSSES IN 2ND N.Z.E.F. (Middle East and Mediterranean) — KILLED IN ACTION

Year	Dates	Operation/Location	Prisoners of War	Killed in Action	Phase
1940	3 Dec – 14 Jan 1941	WESTERN DESERT 'A'	nil	8	Advance
1941	6 Apr – 30 Apr	GREECE	(242) 1856	261	Withdrawals
	30 Apr – 2 Jun	CRETE	(525) 2180	671	"
	18 Nov – 14 Feb 1942	WESTERN DESERT 'B'	(206) 2042	879	"
1942	20 Jun – 31 Aug	WESTERN DESERT 'C'	(231) 1819	822	"
	1 Sep – 22 Oct	WESTERN DESERT 'D'	(16) 90	78	"
	23 Oct – 21 Nov	WESTERN DESERT 'E'	(3) 41	380	Alamein
	22 Nov – 14 Jan 1943	WESTERN DESERT 'F'	(2) 15	56	
1943	15 Jan – 2 Feb	WESTERN DESERT 'G'	(nil) 1	22	
	3 Feb – 19 Mar	WESTERN DESERT 'H'	nil	19	
	20 Mar – 18 Apr	TUNISIA I (Mareth Line)	(1) 6	214	
	19 Apr – 13 May	TUNISIA II (Enfidaville)	(8) 25	154	
	18 Sep – 11 Nov	AEGEAN (Leros & Levita)	(1) 22	3	
	12 Nov – 31 Jan 1944	ITALY I (Sangro)	(16) 100	399	
1944	1 Feb – 10 Apr	ITALY II (Cassino)	(7) 49	339	
	11 Apr – 16 Jun	ITALY III (to Rome)	(nil) 3	115	
	17 Jun – 24 Aug	ITALY IV (Florence)	(4) 31	298	
	25 Aug – 26 Oct	ITALY V (Gothic Line)	(8) 23	224	
	27 Oct – 10 Mar 1945	ITALY VI (Faenza)	(nil) 19	193	
1945	1 Apr – 2 May	ITALY VII (Senio to Trieste)	nil	242	

Prisoners of War

Wounded and prisoner of war (includes those who died of wounds while prisoners of war)

NZMS 101

R. E. OWEN Government Printer, Wellington — DRAWN BY LANDS AND SURVEY DEPT., N.Z.

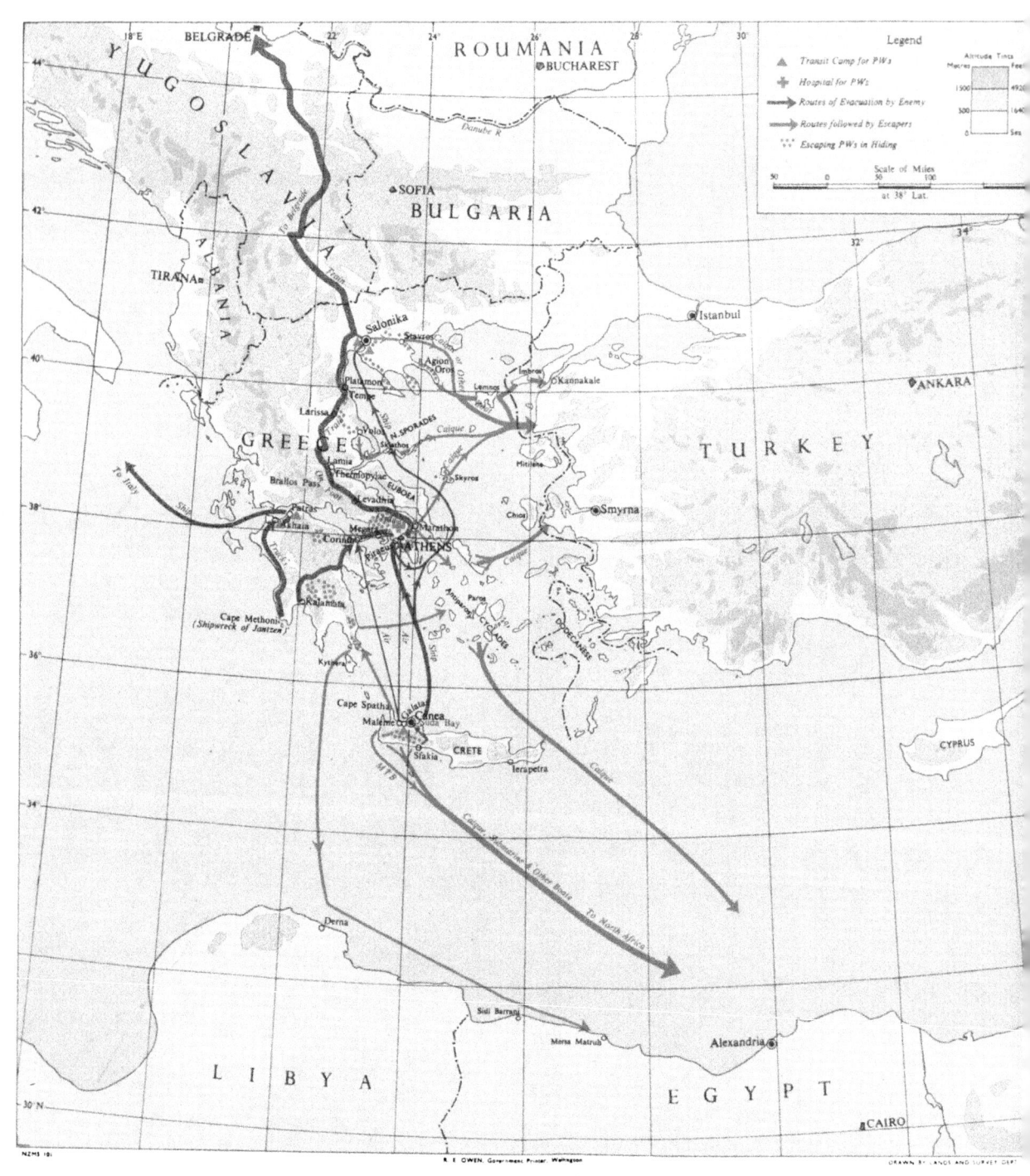

Greece and Crete: Escape Routes and Routes of Evacuation by Enemy

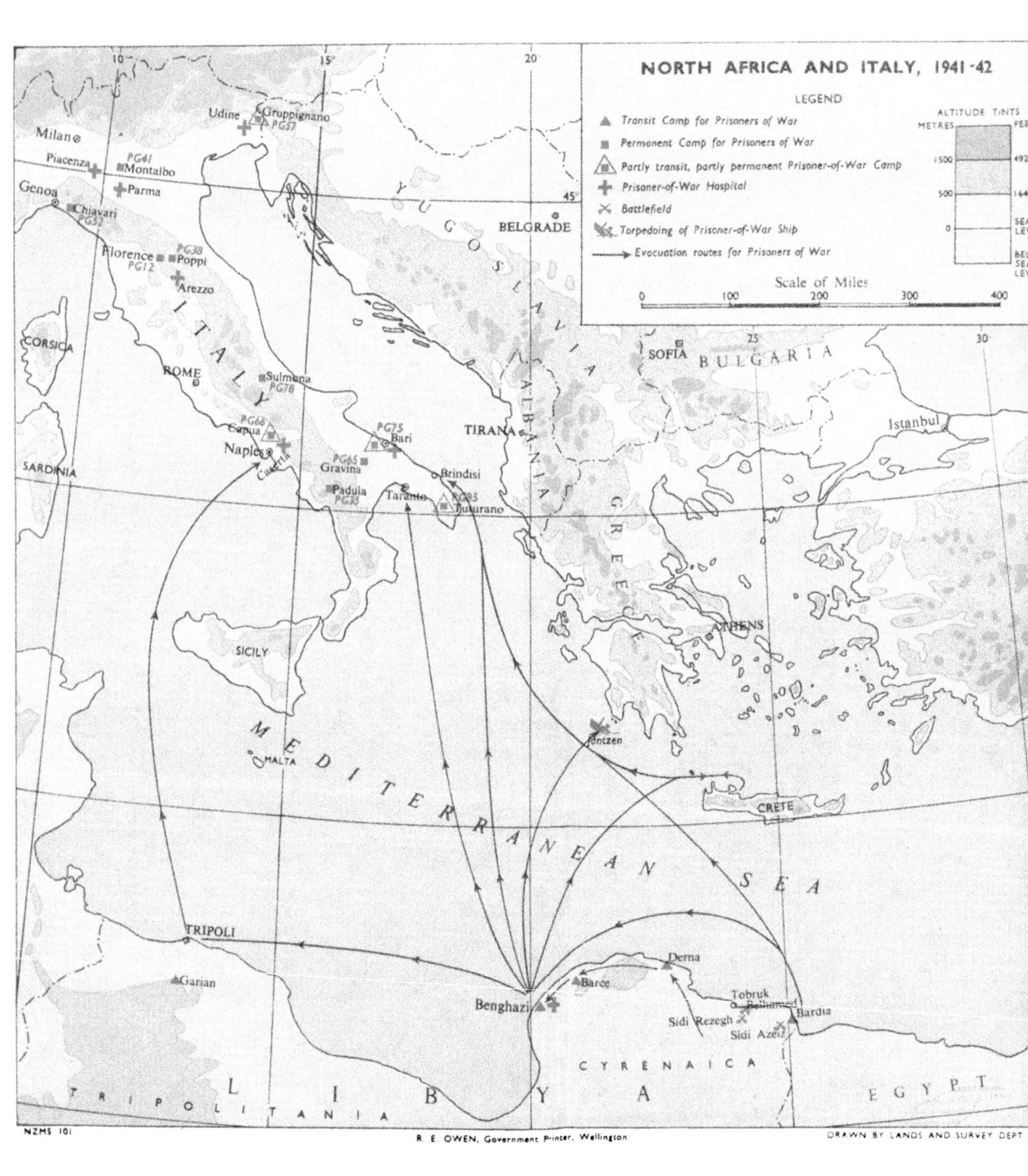

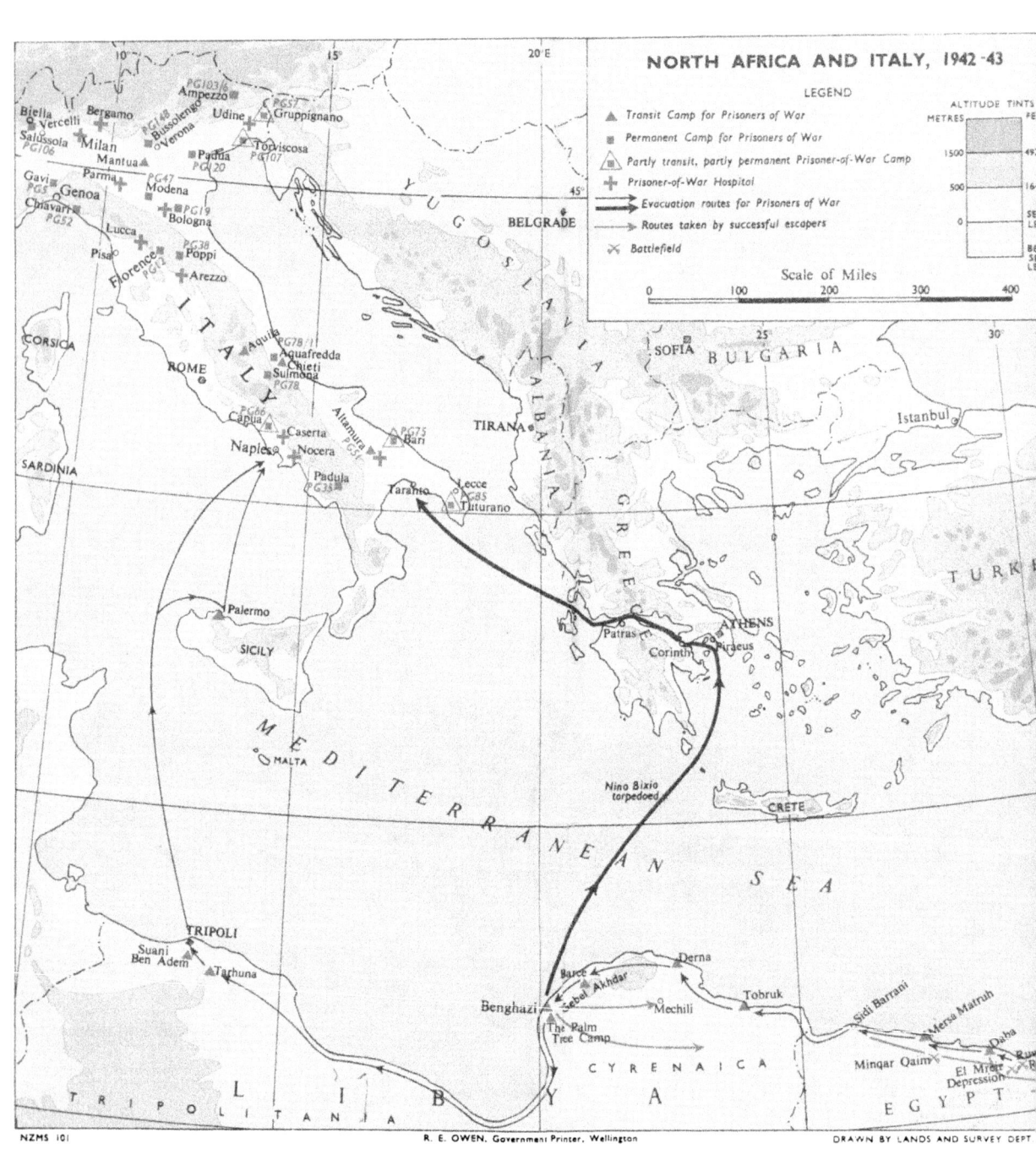

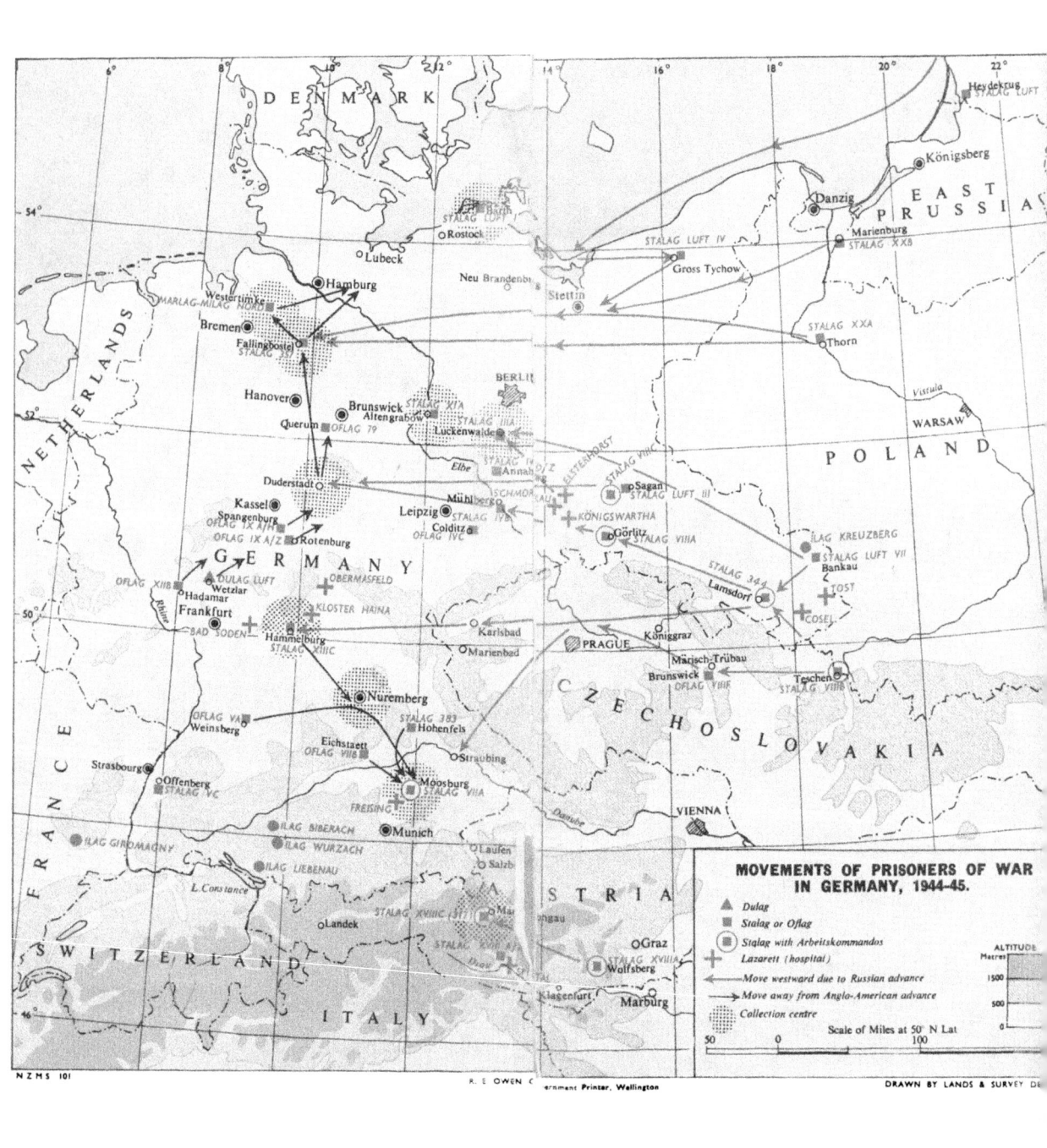

Introduction

THERE comes a stage in battle when the members of one side who are still alive, if unable to withdraw, are either incapacitated by wounds, or weaponless, or opposed by incomparably superior force. To avoid a purposeless death they have no alternative but to make some gesture of surrender and throw themselves on the mercy of their enemies. Since, in normal circumstances, no soldier desires to be a prisoner in enemy hands, almost all of those who are captured have surrendered only on finding themselves in one or other of these hopeless situations. To the Western mind of today there is nothing inherently dishonourable in such a choice of action. But this point of view and the enhanced status of captives which it implies have only become widely accepted comparatively recently.

Until the latter half of the nineteenth century the soldiers of a beaten army who surrendered to the enemy had no generally recognised rights. Their treatment in ancient times was at the whim of the victorious commander or of the person into whose power they passed. If they were not slaughtered, they became more often than not mere chattels in the possession of enemy citizens, and their subsequent life was likely to be one of servitude in an enemy country. Indeed, even those of the civilian population of a defeated country who fell without resistance into the hands of the enemy often shared the fate of the troops who had striven unsuccessfully to defend them.

History, however, provides plenty of examples of humane treatment of captives taken in battle both by their immediate captors and by their later masters, no less than of consideration of the local inhabitants by invading enemy forces. Philosophers and religious teachers have at various times been able to influence their rulers against both the ill-treatment of defenceless civilians and the brutal discipline and bad living conditions endured by war captives, practices which might otherwise have gone on being accepted as normal. But it is only over the centuries that there has slowly spread acceptance of the idea that a soldier disarmed and taken prisoner is a defenceless human being with a claim to protection against further violence and ill-treatment; and that, moreover, he is entitled, during his temporary detention, to treatment comparable to that of soldiers of the country in which he is detained. It is less than a hundred years ago that this claim began to receive international recognition.

INTRODUCTION

The first Geneva Convention of 1864, which followed the humanitarian efforts of Henri Dunant and the Geneva Committee of which he was the moving spirit, protected only the sick and wounded of opposing armed forces. Similar provision for the protection and relief of prisoners of war was the next step in the Committee's plans for helping the victims of war. But it was not until 1899, in the Hague Convention dealing with the laws and customs of war on land, that the major powers agreed that prisoners 'must be humanely treated'[1] and set down in detail the manner in which this undertaking should be carried out. As slightly amended at the Hague Conference of 1907, this was the authority for the treatment of prisoners in the First World War. For the first time, an international convention with safeguards for prisoners of war against neglect and ill-treatment was applied on a large scale and became widely known.

Approximately a decade after the end of this first world conflict these safeguards were again reviewed. The result was a separate Convention dealing entirely with prisoners of war, signed in Geneva in 1929 by 47 countries.[2] The 97 articles of this Convention covered broadly almost every contingency then thought likely to arise during captivity; and their observance according to a liberal interpretation would have ensured the welfare of prisoners of war from almost every aspect. Thus, some ten years before the events described in this book, a stage had been reached where a considerable part of the world had accepted not only the principle that prisoners should be humanely treated, but the detailed standards of conduct towards them which such an undertaking implied. Paradoxically, the Second World War produced some of the worst examples of the ill-treatment and neglect of prisoners that have been recorded.

For the protection of civilians in enemy or enemy-occupied territory during hostilities there existed at the outbreak of the Second World War only the draft for an international agreement similar to that for prisoners of war. This draft had been approved by the fifteenth International Conference of Red Cross Societies in Tokyo in 1934, and a diplomatic conference to secure governmental agreement to a treaty in these terms was to have been held in 1940. Instead, the International Red Cross Committee had, on the outbreak of war, to invite belligerents either to accept the draft convention or to treat enemy civilians in their hands along the lines laid down by the 1929 Convention for prisoners of war. Both Britain and Germany agreed to the latter alternative, and this was

---

[1] Annex on *Regulations respecting the Laws and Customs of War on Land*, Section I, Chapter 2, Article 4.
[2] The British Minister in Berne signed on behalf of New Zealand.

the basis adopted for the treatment of civilian internees in New Zealand.

Two agencies were recognised which might assist in the protection of those regarded as being covered by the Prisoners of War Convention of 1929: the 'Protecting Power' and the International Red Cross Committee. The Protecting Power, a neutral government accepted as representing the interests of one belligerent state within the territories of another, was authorised to send either diplomatic personnel or specially appointed delegates to visit all places of internment. These representatives could have conversations in private with prisoners of war and could receive complaints from them. In general they were to act as intermediaries between the prisoners and the camp authorities, and they were to mediate in the settlement of disputes between belligerents regarding the provisions of the Prisoners of War Convention.

The International Red Cross Committee was concerned mainly with the organisation of a central agency for the exchange between the belligerent powers of information regarding their respective captives, and with the distribution of relief supplies to them. But it was also stipulated in the 1929 Convention that there should be no restriction on their engaging in other humanitarian tasks on behalf of prisoners of war, including the visiting of camps and the conduct of negotiations with the governments of belligerent powers.

The outbreak of war in 1939 found the International Red Cross Committee well prepared. As far back as September 1938 it had planned in minute detail the conversion of its organisation to a war footing. Adequate premises and staff for the future central information agency had been arranged; the text of the Notes to be sent to belligerent powers offering its services had been drafted; its future delegates had been selected. By mid-September 1939 the Committee had moved its augmented staff into a large building formerly used by the League of Nations and had set to work.

It is probable that few people of the countries which became involved in the Second World War knew in these early stages anything of the arrangements made to protect their compatriots who fell into enemy hands. In the First World War only 500 New Zealand servicemen had been taken prisoner, and the problems of their protection and relief had not become widely known. Nearly every one of the 9000-odd New Zealanders held captive in the Second World War will say that the last thing to which he had given any thought was the possibility of being captured. A few had heard of the Geneva Prisoners of War Convention of 1929, but the vast majority knew nothing of its provisions. To many of them it came as a pleasant surprise to find the extent to which their

INTRODUCTION

safety and welfare were protected. It goes without saying that before long nearly all these men had more than a nodding acquaintance with the international law governing their position. It is also true that many thousands of their relatives and friends soon heard of the Geneva Convention and learnt something of the protection it gave. Even with this protection the story of captivity in the war of 1939–45 is at times grim and sombre. The fate of many of those who were without it gives some idea of the terrible story this might have been had protection not existed at all. Those who laboured over the centuries to achieve it have earned the gratitude of humanity.

CHAPTER 1

The Beginnings of the War in Western Europe
(September 1939–May 1940)

I: *Early Air Force Prisoners*

NEW ZEALAND entered the war against Nazi Germany on the same day as the United Kingdom, and some of the New Zealanders at that time serving with the Armed Forces in Britain[1] were in action almost immediately. One of the first military tasks of the war was air reconnaissance of the German Fleet and its bases on the shores of the North Sea and the Baltic, followed by aerial attack where practicable to prevent the exit of raiders and so help to reduce the dangers to our shipping. On 5 September 1939 a New Zealand officer was piloting an Anson on such a mission near Dogger Bank. He was unlucky enough to have his plane shot down into the North Sea, and recovered consciousness in time to find the attacking German seaplane preparing to land on the water close by. The only survivor, he was picked up and flown to a Luftwaffe hospital on the island of Norderney, where he '. . . was very well treated . . . . and found the German officers and men good scouts, but all the same [he] was pretty dashed lonely and the fact that [he had] lost [his] crew of three did not help matters . . . .' He had good reason for feeling lonely, for he was at the time the only Royal Air Force officer in enemy hands.

In this first month of our participation in the war the German organisation for dealing with prisoners was still in its infancy. For the handful of British prisoners there were as yet no separate camps. Accordingly, after ten days the captured airman was removed to a dark cell in a German detention barracks at Wesermunde, where he was taken each day to the local hospital. It appears that in this early stage guards were a little uncertain how to treat prisoners of war, especially officers; and in the absence of detailed instructions or knowledge of the international law regulating such treatment, some tended to treat them as civilian

---

[1] These comprised New Zealand officers in the Royal Navy recruited over a number of years; some New Zealanders serving with the British Army; Air Force officers to the number of about 80 recruited with both short- and long-term commissions, including those of the flight organised to take the first Wellington bombers out to New Zealand.

criminals. After a hungry and generally unpleasant three weeks at Wesermunde, the New Zealander was taken some sixty miles east to Itzehoe. Here, in a camp for Polish officers, he and some other captured Royal Air Force personnel lived under reasonably good conditions. The camp was 'quite comfortable' and there was ample space for exercise. But it was rapidly filling up with Polish prisoners, and after a week or so this comparatively pleasant interlude was cut short.

The number of British prisoners steadily grew, and in mid-October all British officers were moved to the high country north of Kassel. There they were housed in a twelfth-century castle perched on a rocky hill, which overlooked the village of Elbersdorf on one side and Spangenburg on the other. Built of grey stone, with a clock-tower and small turret, and surrounded by a deep moat with a drawbridge, this first British 'camp' could have been a castle from one of Grimm's fairy tales. Originally a hunting lodge, it had housed prisoners in the Thirty Years' War, but prior to 1939 had been used as a hostel for agricultural students, the interior having been renovated so that it conformed in some degree to modern standards.

By December 1939 this 'camp', known as Oflag IXA,[1] contained some thirteen officers and the same number of non-commissioned officers and other ranks. Although, in their opinion, their treatment left a lot to be desired, it is clear that relations with the German commandant were quite amicable. Rations appear to have been rather inadequate, though officers could sometimes purchase extra food through the canteen. Requests for other canteen supplies, ranging from suitcases to wine for 'celebrations', seem also to have been met. Other ranks without pay found the food insufficient, and the arrival therefore in November of gift parcels of food and other immediate necessities from the War Organisation of the British Red Cross and the Order of St. John was very welcome. Time was killed by playing cards, reading such books in English as could be got hold of, and walking when permitted in a fenced-off exercise area. The airmen found the confinement in the castle irksome, as many hundreds more were to find it as the war progressed. By the end of the year it had been decided that Air Force prisoners were to be in the charge of the Luftwaffe, which would be entirely responsible for their custody and interrogation. The Luftwaffe would build special camps for the purpose, but

---

[1] German prisoner-of-war camps were numbered according to the military area in which they were located, e.g., Oflag IXA Spangenburg was in *Wehrkreis* IX. Oflag was an abbreviation for *Offizier-lager*, or officers' camp. The letters 'A', 'B', etc., served to indicate different officers' camps in the same area.

would meanwhile take over certain accommodation from the Wehrmacht.[1]

In the first month of the war the German Army authorities had set up a temporary Off-Dulag,[2] or officers' transit camp, on the site of a former poultry farm at Oberursel, a suburb four miles out of Frankfurt-on-Main. Here the farm buildings were used as administrative quarters and a two-storied house known as the 'Stone-house', formerly for farm pupils, was set aside for the prisoners. The first officers to be held here, some Frenchmen, were moved away to permanent quarters in December, and the Luftwaffe took over the camp site. It was renamed 'Dulag Luft', a name by which it became notorious among Allied airmen over the next five years as the main German Air Force interrogation centre and transit camp. The first arrivals were a small advance party of British and French on 15 December from the old castle at Spangenburg. The latter was to be cleared of Air Force prisoners as soon as practicable, but this was delayed by the influx at Oberursel resulting from the German successes in Norway and France. The new camp compared favourably, in some respects, with Spangenburg. An RAF officer wrote:

> The setting is not so romantic but the place is modern, warm and clean. The bathing arrangements are V.G.—hot water at any time—and I can get my morning shower which I have missed so much to date. The food is much better.

The Luftwaffe seemed out to show that airmen (even enemy airmen) were worthy of higher standards of treatment than those normal to the Wehrmacht. But concealed microphones had been installed in the living quarters, and the comfort may have had the additional object of encouraging prisoners to relax and talk. As the 'Stone-house' was difficult to guard, it had the additional drawback for prisoners that their cubicle windows were fitted with iron bars and that they were locked in from 10 p.m. until 6 a.m., with only an hour's exercise twice a day outside the building.

In April 1940 the prisoners, whose numbers had grown to 35, were transferred to three newly erected wooden huts across the road. This came as a pleasant relief from the strictly guarded 'Stone-house', which was now reserved for housing prisoners during their interrogation period and for storing records. Each of the two new sleeping huts contained small rooms for two heated by stoves, its own washroom and showers with plenty of hot water, a boiler room, lavatories, and even a sitting room after the guards originally housed in each barrack had been moved elsewhere. The third barrack comprised a large dining room with a stage, two

---

[1] German Army.
[2] Abbreviation of German *Offizierdurchgangslager*.

other small officers' messrooms, kitchen, canteen, parcels store, clothing store, and a room for those of the advance party who had become part of the permanent staff of the camp. It contained in fact most of the amenities necessary for the treatment of prisoners according to the Geneva Prisoners of War Convention of 1929. But the Germans found it impossible to mass produce amenities like these when, later in the war, they had to find permanent accommodation for tens of thousands of prisoners from France, from Greece and Crete, from the air offensive on Germany, and from Italy.

It soon became obvious that a large percentage of all Air Force personnel taken prisoner would require medical attention. As additional evidence of their adherence to humane and civilised standards of treatment towards Allied airmen, the Luftwaffe requisitioned part of the nearby Hohemark hospital, 65 beds of which were from then on reserved for wounded prisoners. At the same time a number of private rooms were set aside, ' . . . where high-ranking Allied prisoners of war could be interrogated in circumstances which the Germans considered appropriate to their rank.'[1] The comfortable quartering of high-ranking officers in the Hohemark hospital, the convivial parties arranged for them, and the trips into the countryside on which they were taken, were apparently designed to create an impression of friendliness and hospitality in the minds of newly-arrived prisoners, which would help to lull their suspicions and break down their reserve. Medical requirements seem to have been subordinated to those serving an obvious opportunity for interrogation and propaganda. Only the lightly wounded were catered for, the more serious cases being treated in regular military hospitals and not sent to Hohemark until in the convalescent stage. The Hohemark hospital rapidly became a hotbed of activity for the spies and 'stool-pigeons'[2] which the German camp staff began to use as part of their interrogation scheme.

In this early stage of the war little thought had yet been given by the German High Command to the systematic appreciation of statements made by captured airmen, nor in fact to the whole business of prisoner-of-war interrogation. To quote a German report:[3]

---

[1]From an Air Ministry report on German interrogation methods.
[2]'Stool-pigeon' (in prisoner-of-war slang 'stooge'). Here used to mean a German masquerading as an Allied airman (or other serviceman) or an Allied traitor placed among Allied prisoners of war by the Germans for gaining information of use to German Intelligence.
[3]*Prisoner interrogation and documents evaluation and their intelligence value to the Higher Command*, by the Director of *Auswertestelle West*, 1945 (Translation).

Prisoner-of-war interrogation was organised on a very small scale, without a clear line which was to be followed or definite aims, not to mention a theory or method. The information which was assembled frequently only served to satisfy the desire for sensational news and the detective story romanticism on the part of those on the distribution list.

This was borne out by what is known of the first commanding officer of Dulag Luft, 'whose qualifications for the job consisted of an ability to speak some French.' The same report also blames the 'amateurish manner' in which 'unsuitable persons' attempted to carry out a preliminary interrogation near the place of capture, with results detrimental to later questioning. It was found necessary for the German High Command to issue an order in October 1939 forbidding such interrogation of Air Force prisoners and the 'souveniring' of equipment and prisoners' personal effects which often accompanied it. The report goes on to refer to the impossibility of segregating Allied airmen or preventing them from conversing while on their way to the interrogation centre, and so improvising a story or boosting each other's morale. The first installation of microphones in the barracks of Dulag Luft also apparently bore little fruit, as 'the voices of 50 prisoners produced nothing but a hopeless din in the headphones'. But, whatever may have been thought of the shortcomings of the interrogation centre in its early stages, a system was soon established by which all Air Force prisoners were transported to Oberursel after capture and put through an interrogation routine before being released to a permanent camp. The staff thus gradually became specialists in interrogation on Air Force matters, and as time went on a formidable organisation was built up under the control of the Intelligence Section of the Luftwaffe operations staff.

Letters from prisoners indicate that the Germans in control of Spangenburg and Oberursel were, in the earliest stages, not only 'correct' in their treatment but also perhaps even kindly. An officer wrote, when he was leaving Spangenburg, 'The General came up to say goodbye to us, which was a very nice gesture. I have told you before we liked him very much . . . .' On his arrival at Oberursel, the same officer wrote, 'The C.O. and 2nd in Command both appear very nice and speak English.' At this period of the war, confident in their country's military strength already demonstrated in Poland, German prison-camp officers could perhaps afford to be 'nice'. The British blockade had not yet taken effect, nor had extreme Nazi influence made itself felt among prison-camp staffs. Enemies tend to be more gentlemanly at the beginning of a struggle than after it has become a matter of life or death. On the prisoners' side there is evidence in these first weeks of something akin to a schoolboy holiday spirit, as yet unaware of the dreary years ahead and revelling a little in relief from responsibility and former routine. With the approach of Christmas these high spirits were tempered with nostalgic thoughts of home and anxiety about mail, mingled with vague hopes of a possible exchange of prisoners and the first ideas about escape.

II: *Civilians in Europe*

It is not known how many New Zealand civilians were on the Continent at the outbreak of war, either in Germany or in countries likely to come under German control. A good many were able to leave before the invasion of Poland, but some chose to stay even after the German entry into the Low Countries and France. Their position became officially known only as inquiries concerning them reached the Government in New Zealand or the High Commissioner's Office in London. Of the numerous inquiries some sixty related to people who had been born in New Zealand or who had acquired New Zealand citizenship. Most of them were people living in the islands of Jersey and Guernsey. But there were nurses, teachers, evangelists, and art students temporarily working in France and Holland, as well as others who had settled there. There were also smaller numbers in Poland, Denmark, and in Germany itself.

No immediate wholesale rounding up of British civilians took place in Germany or Poland, and only a few hundred who might constitute a danger if left at liberty were interned up to the end of October 1939. Some of those seeking repatriation were able to make their way to England after hostilities had begun.[1] For those who had not arrived in England the usual practice was to initiate a 'whereabouts and welfare' inquiry[2] through the Protecting Power. This was a lengthy process, the inquiry going through the British Foreign Office to the United States Embassy in Berlin and so eventually to the locality where the person was living. Often news would not be received for some months, especially if the person was one of those not interned.

For the latter the most urgent problem was financial assistance. Many were living on pensions or other income derived from England or New Zealand. When these payments ceased, these people, especially those who were unable to earn a living locally on account of their age or their nationality, were almost destitute. To relieve urgent distress in such cases as came to their notice, the

---

[1] The same applied to German nationals in England. Only a comparatively small number were immediately interned, and up till April 1940 small parties of them were returning to Germany through Belgium and Holland.

[2] The phrase used by the United States Embassy in Berlin. Inquiries were also made through the International Red Cross Committee.

United States Embassy in Berlin made small advances, which the British Government, and later the New Zealand Government, undertook to refund. Through the same channel relatives and friends in England or New Zealand could send remittances (limited by Trading with the Enemy legislation to £10 sterling a month) on application to the Trading with the Enemy Branch in the United Kingdom or to the United States Consul in Wellington. Beyond the arrangement of financial assistance, little could be done except to open the way for some direct communication with relatives. In December 1939 it became possible to send 25-word family messages through the International Red Cross Committee.[1]

For those interned, not only was communication much simpler[2] but relief in kind, including contributions from relatives, could be sent by New Zealand House in London through the British Red Cross[3] in much the same way as for prisoners of war.

III: *Protection of the Interests of Prisoners of War and Civilians in Enemy Hands*

It had been arranged beforehand that if and when war broke out, the United States should assume the responsibility of protecting the interests of British subjects in Germany. Although there existed international treaties for the protection of prisoners of war, it was not known whether the Nazi Government would accept responsibility for the actions of a previous German Government in signing or ratifying them. Early in September the United States Ambassador in Berlin made approaches to the German Foreign Office in order to determine to what extent Germany was prepared to honour these treaties. By 19 September he was able to quote a German Foreign Office official as saying that, ' . . . as Germany had adhered to the Geneva Convention of July 17th 1929, relative to the treatment of prisoners of war (*Reichs Gesetzblatt II* April 30th 1934), the German Government would be governed accordingly'. Britain had already given an assurance that she intended to abide by the terms of this Convention. Thus the rights of British prisoners in Germany were guaranteed on paper at least.

One of the first tasks of the United States Embassy staff, as representative of the power protecting British interests, was to trace British civilians in German territory, ascertain their condition, and

---

[1] The scheme had been first used by the International Red Cross Committee in the Spanish Civil War. The first messages from Germany were sent in December 1939 and the first from the United Kingdom in February 1940.
[2] It was practically the same as that for prisoners of war.
[3] For the sake of brevity and the avoidance of confusion with other war organisations, the War Organisation of the British Red Cross and the Order of St. John of Jerusalem is henceforward referred to in the text as the British Red Cross, the abbreviation adopted in the discussions of the Imperial Prisoners of War Committee.

if necessary arrange financial assistance for them. From the beginning it had to deal with a constant stream of requests for this kind of action. In addition, as soon as the existence of an internment camp was heard of, one of the Embassy staff in Berlin or a member of the consular staff elsewhere in Germany was sent to investigate and report fully and candidly on the conditions he found. One of the earliest of these reports drew attention to defects in the civilian internment camp at Wülsburg, Ilag XIII.[1]

> It may appear picturesque, but the fact is that the Wülsburg Castle is an old and run-down building which presents a dilapidated appearance. . . . In my opinion the camp is overcrowded. . . . The air is bad, the light is bad, there is no space for a man to put his things. . . . In bad weather the situation is in my opinion next to unbearable. . . .

This system of inspection and reporting kept the British Government informed on the unsatisfactory aspects of German treatment so that the appropriate protest could be made.

Immediately after the outbreak of war the International Red Cross Committee placed itself at the service of all belligerent governments, ' . . . to contribute in a humanitarian way, in its traditional role and with all its resources, towards lessening the evils brought by war.'[2] At a time when national hatreds were aroused, it was able as a long-established neutral and impartial body to remind leaders of belligerent states of their treaty obligations and of considerations of humanity towards their fellow human beings even though enemies. In pursuit of these objects it proposed to organise:

(1) a Central Agency for information about prisoners of war, with which it invited Information Bureaux[3] to get in touch,
(2) the exchange of sick and wounded prisoners, and of medical personnel,
(3) the forwarding of letters and parcels,
(4) the co-ordination of unofficial relief measures.

So far as civilians in enemy hands were concerned, it invited the belligerents to abide by the Tokyo Draft of 1934.[4] It also reminded belligerents of the special position of medical personnel during hostilities. At the same time the Committee wrote to national Red Cross societies to inform them of its appeal to the belligerent governments, and to request their co-operation both in drawing their governments' attention to humanitarian considerations

---

[1] Ilag (*Interniertenlager*), camp for internees.
[2] Letter to all belligerent powers from IRCC (signed by M. Max Huber), dated 2 September 1939.
[3] Set up by belligerent powers under Article 77 of the Geneva Prisoners of War Convention.
[4] See Introduction, p. xxiv.

and in themselves facilitating the exchange through the Central Agency of news regarding war victims.

As soon as possible the Committee sent special missions to Germany, France and Poland, and permanent delegations to Great Britain, Egypt and the Argentine,[1] as the latter countries were less easily reached from Geneva. Besides organising a base for future operations and arranging for liaison with the Central Agency at Geneva, the first task of these missions was to visit prisoners' camps. These visits were usually entrusted to doctors, as, '. . . . Knowing just how much trained men can endure without undue risk, medical practitioners are less easily impressed than laymen by apparent deficiencies not detrimental to health. On the other hand they are able to recognise defects which would escape the inexperienced eye.'[2] Similar visits to civilian internment camps, the securing of information through national Red Cross societies regarding non-interned civilians, and the arranging of 25-word family messages through the British and German Red Cross organisations were also part of their duties.

The Central Agency[3] for information about prisoners of war was opened in the Palais du Conseil-General at Geneva on 14 September, formal notification of its establishment being sent to the governments concerned and contact made with the bodies doing similar work in those countries. Three days later the first requests for information regarding prisoners of war were received and passed on by International Red Cross delegates, and the Central Agency began the card-indexes, files, and correspondence which developed into the enormous record system for which it became well known.[4]

Prisoners of war information bureaux were set up in London and Berlin, and from the latter official lists of British prisoners and their particulars were eventually transmitted to the United States Embassy and the Central Agency in Geneva. But as the Geneva Prisoners of War Convention specified that addresses as well as other particulars were to be given, compilation of the lists was held up until the prisoners reached permanent camps. In the meantime the only information obtainable came in reports from the International Red Cross Committee, based on what its own delegates or the local German Red Cross and other bodies had been able to ascertain, or in the prisoner of war's own letters. It sometimes happened that mail from a prisoner in enemy hands reached his

---

[1] The Argentine delegation was to be the base for South America.
[2] Report of the IRCC on its activities during the war of 1939–45, Vol. I, p. 66.
[3] As laid down in Article 79 of the Geneva Prisoners of War Convention, 1929.
[4] Up to 30 June 1947 the correspondence alone amounted to:
                Inward   59,000,000 pieces
                Outward 61,000,000 pieces

friends or relatives before the two enemy governments were able to communicate officially concerning his capture.

Thus the first report about a missing New Zealand airman came over the German radio a few days after his capture. Many such notifications were broadcast in the years following, usually in the 'Lord Haw-Haw' and similar sessions,[1] to induce friends and relatives to listen to interpolated propaganda. But the Air Ministry took no official cognizance of these early messages about captured airmen, and their distrust was later justified when many were proved inaccurate or out of date. The next information usually arrived about six weeks later in the form of a letter from the man himself. But although this was accepted by the Air Ministry for practical purposes, it was still not regarded as official confirmation of capture. It was not until about eight weeks after capture that the Central Agency of the International Red Cross was able, in answer to an inquiry, to supply authentic information regarding a man's condition and location. This aspect of the prisoner-of-war problem was kept constantly under review by governments and service ministries, and means were found later to make some reduction in the time taken.[2]

It had been early decided in the United Kingdom that, following the precedent set in 1914–18, the Army authorities should have the task of dealing with enemy prisoners and civilian internees. By reason of the experience it gained in these matters, the Prisoners of War Branch of the War Office became the body best qualified to advise generally on anything to do not only with enemy prisoners in our hands but also our own in enemy hands. However, as matters relating to Navy and Air Force prisoners often needed the expert opinion of their own services, as the Home Office had to be consulted about civilians, as Treasury opinion was necessary on financial matters, and as the Foreign Office was the channel of communication with the Protecting Power, an inter-departmental committee with representatives of these departments was set up in 1940. This committee dealt primarily with financial questions. It held its first meeting in May 1940 and continued until May 1941, when it became a sub-committee of a newly-formed Inter-governmental Committee on Prisoners of War.

Meanwhile, in the first days of the war, British Commonwealth civilians in enemy-occupied territory were an urgent claim on the energies of the Foreign Office. The latter accepted the responsibility[3] for making inquiries about them through the United States

---

[1] Broadcasts in English over the German radio during the war by a British subject working for the enemy under the radio name of 'Lord Haw-Haw'.
[2] See Chapter 3, p. 98.
[3] The British Red Cross also undertook inquiries through the International Red Cross Committee representatives in enemy countries.

Ambassador in Berlin. In addition to individual inquiries, the Foreign Office was also concerned with the broad questions of repatriation and internment, with the arrangement of funds for those without means of support, and with arranging for messages and letters from relatives to reach those in the German-occupied portion of the Continent. In this it was often merely acting on requests from the Home Office or the Dominion governments concerned, and serving as the channel of communication (through the Protecting Power) with the German Government. But the Foreign Office also accepted the responsibility for determining the international implications of all messages sent through it to enemy powers. And in order to assist the co-ordination of Allied strategy, New Zealand adopted from the first the principle of communicating with the enemy only through the Foreign Office, though this principle was not formally stated until November 1941.[1]

The departmental arrangements in New Zealand followed the pattern of those in the United Kingdom. The Army was the service branch made responsible for the custody of enemy nationals in New Zealand. Partly through this experience and partly through direct contact with the British War Office by means of the New Zealand Military Liaison Officer in London, it became the main advisory body on all matters relating to the treatment of prisoners of war and of interned civilians. The Prime Minister's Department at first handled in detail all inquiries regarding New Zealand missing and captured personnel, but as the task grew it became merely the co-ordinating body in this field, as it became in all others relating to the country's war activities. It kept in close touch with the British Government through the Dominions Office in the interests of consistency of action within the Commonwealth.

Many of the inquiries concerning civilians in enemy territory or missing servicemen came in the first instance to the High Commissioner's Office in London, and many others, which could be more easily dealt with in England, were referred there from New Zealand. In London information was gathered through diplomatic and Red Cross channels, and passed on to those requesting it. Arrangements were also made in London for the translation of money gifts into relief in kind. This was done through the British Red Cross, which was at that stage the only body empowered to send parcels to prisoners of war and civilian internees. The High Commissioner's Office in London, by thus acting as an intermediary between the agencies in closest contact with New Zealanders in enemy hands and their relatives and friends, was able to keep a constant eye on their interests.

---

[1] Minutes of meeting of the Imperial Prisoners of War Committee held on 5 November 1941, para (5).

IV: *Organisation of Relief for Prisoners of War and Civilian Internees*

At the beginning of the war British nationals in German hands depended almost entirely on the British Red Cross for all the little comforts that made life in captivity more bearable; later they were to depend on its relief supplies very largely for the essential elements of their survival. The British Red Cross Society and the Order of St. John of Jerusalem had acted jointly in carrying out relief for prisoners of war, missing, and wounded in the 1914–18 War, and the War Organisation then set up had remained alive in the inter-war period in the form of a committee which cared for the disabled. Acting on this experience of the First World War, it formed in September 1939 an Emergency Committee, which organised a Prisoners of War, Wounded, and Missing Department. This Department was approved by the British service authorities in October as the body through which parcels might be sent to British prisoners of war. It began its work, including the packing of parcels, in St. James's Palace, which the King had placed at its disposal as a headquarters.

The Department's original plan of relief for each prisoner comprised an 'initial parcel' containing personal clothing and necessities for the period immediately after capture; three eleven-pound food parcels each fortnight; an eleven-pound 'personal parcel' every quarter in which relatives could send articles and medical comforts; and bread parcels, though these were soon discontinued because of the time taken in transit. All parcels were at this stage addressed to individual prisoners[1] in accordance with Article 37[2] of the Geneva Prisoners of War Convention, and so could not be sent off until the British Red Cross had received notification from the War Office of the prisoner's place of detention. However, in October 1939, at the request of the Air Ministry, some initial parcels were sent off to Geneva by air, for distribution to captured airmen as soon as the International Red Cross Committee should learn their locations. They were followed by food, invalid comforts and warm clothing, including some personal kit, and the first of them reached the prisoners within a month. This was the beginning of a service which was to continue until the end of the war, though later on parcels usually took very much longer to arrive. As the war progressed, the British Red Cross parcel service became a vital factor in the health and welfare of all British subjects in enemy lands.

---
[1] Collective consignments as envisaged in Articles 43 and 78 were not started until later in the war.
[2] Article 37 reads: 'Prisoners of war shall be authorised to receive individually postal parcels containing foodstuffs and other articles intended for consumption or clothing. The parcels shall be delivered to the addressees and a receipt given.'

Early in the war the British Government stipulated that all food parcels should be sent through the British Red Cross, which devoted considerable effort to devising an optimum content for a standard parcel.[1] It is laid down in Article 11 of the 1929 Geneva Convention that 'the food ration of prisoners of war shall be equivalent in quality and quantity to that of depot troops.' But it was taken for granted that, even if this provision were adhered to, differences between the prisoners' own normal diet and that of the nation holding them might justify making the despatch of food parcels a first priority. The first letters from prisoners in Germany, especially other ranks, left no doubt of their need for supplementary food.

The remainder of the British Red Cross relief plans quickly took practical shape. An Invalid Comforts Section was set up in October to provide medical supplies and invalid foods for sick and wounded prisoners. A reserve of greatcoats was established at Geneva, to be sent on by the International Red Cross Committee to each newly-captured prisoner, and an initial parcel[2] was sent as soon as the name and location of the prisoner was received. Relatives were then asked to let the British Red Cross have any items of clothing that they wished to send. If nothing was forthcoming, another parcel[3] containing clothing and toilet necessities was sent off. Limited by the British Government to one every three months, these parcels, some of which contained gifts from relatives, were the beginning of what came to be known later as 'next-of-kin parcels'. From December 1939 these were all sent through the British Red Cross, for the postal censorship authorities asked the latter to undertake the examination of all parcels from relatives. Cigarettes and tobacco too could only be sent 'under Red Cross label', and so were at first included in every food parcel. Although the original relief plans included books to enable men to study while in captivity, transport difficulties delayed their despatch. But early in 1940 an attempt was being made to determine the precise educational needs of each camp so that a scheme could be worked out to cater for all.[4]

No serious difficulty arose at this stage over the transport of all these parcels: the General Post Office accepted them for transmission by post, and they were shipped to Ostend and through neutral Belgium into Germany. At the beginning of the war,

---

[1] The estimated number of British prisoners before the battle in France was 1500 from all Commonwealth countries. Even when prisoners were as few as this, the items were analysed by a dietitian and approved by Lord Dawson of Penn as comprising the right proportions of starch, protein and sugar to keep a man in health.
[2] Contents of an initial parcel: vest, pants, shirt, scarf, pyjamas, jersey, balaclava, socks (3 pairs), mittens, handkerchiefs (4), boots or blanket.
[3] Contents of the second parcel: vest, pants, shirt, pyjamas, slippers, braces, socks (2 pairs), towels (2), handkerchiefs (2), boots or blanket.
[4] From the beginning of the war the World Alliance of YMCAs, the IRCC, and other bodies in Switzerland all sent books to prisoners of war and civilian internees.

therefore, the maintenance of a steady flow of relief to prisoners of war in Germany was as simple as it had been through Holland in the First World War. But the events of succeeding months made it necessary to provide relief on a scale not before experienced nor foreseen. Moreover the German occupation of the Continent so complicated the transportation of these relief consignments that it created a supply problem of major proportions.

In New Zealand the Joint Council of the Red Cross and the Order of St. John of Jerusalem,[1] which had been in existence since 1934, followed the example set by the equivalent joint body in England. It formed a War Committee soon after the outbreak of war along the lines of the War Organisation formed by the Red Cross Society and the Order of St. John of Jerusalem in England. In November 1939 it cabled the British organisation for advice on how it could best assist. To help co-ordinate the national war effort and to prevent waste and overlapping, the Patriotic Purposes Emergency Regulations (introduced by the New Zealand Government in October 1939) had placed the raising and spending of all funds for patriotic purposes in the hands of a national advisory body.[2] The National Patriotic Fund Board, in whose hands was placed the administration of all moneys raised under this scheme, appointed the Joint Council one of its collecting agents. It also appointed it the sole agent for expending funds on behalf of sick and wounded, prisoners of war, and civilians in distress as a result of hostile action. Although no organised campaign for funds was launched until May 1940, some sixty cases of clothing were forwarded to overseas Red Cross organisations for the relief of refugees on the Continent and evacuees to the United Kingdom, and some parcels were also sent for prisoners of war.

Considerable detail has been given in order to show that from the first a number of governmental and other agencies were watching over the welfare of those in captivity and taking steps to ensure that relief supplies reached them. There was also the problem of coping with the requests of their relatives and friends. Prisoners and internees were at times worried about their own situation; but many of their relatives and friends, especially those on the other side of the world from the war theatres, were in a more or less constant state of anxiety. Many of them felt they could visualise the life of their son or husband on active service, but his possible fate as a prisoner was, in the early stages of the war, something unknown and frightening. For relatives the initial shock of receiving a 'missing' notification (however tactfully

---

[1] For the sake of brevity this will be referred to in the text as the New Zealand Joint Council, or simply the Joint Council.
[2] With eleven provincial branches.

worded) often gave way to a period of mingled depression and hope, during which they tried every expedient to get information. People wrote to the 'Red Cross', to their Member of Parliament, to the High Commissioner in London, to the Prime Minister in Wellington. Often all that could be done was to send a sympathetic and reassuring answer, for it was at first some time before any definite information could be given, owing to the long delays in official notifications of capture. Relatives and friends of a civilian in an enemy country had a similar period of anxiety in the early days of the war, until welfare reports came through from either the Protecting Power or the International Red Cross Committee.

Official news that a man was a prisoner of war and in good health did something to relieve the anxiety of relatives about his safety, but could not prevent further anxiety about his future welfare. Relatives and friends often pictured him as continually hungry, cold, and comfortless; and they wanted to know what food, clothes, books, tobacco and money they could send. Knowledge that the British Red Cross was catering for his immediate needs, though reassuring, did not weaken their desire to make their own personal contributions, or at least to do something practical to help. As the war progressed, the Joint Council harnessed this desire to the war relief effort, by inviting relatives and friends to help on local committees and parcel packing organisations. Such work often had a value beyond the number of man-hours supplied towards war relief. For many of those who took part felt less despondent and frustrated once they became engaged in practical tasks which they knew would be of use in bringing help to their own men in captivity.

V: *Enemy Aliens in New Zealand*

At the same time as she was safeguarding the interests of her own men and women abroad, New Zealand was engaged in securing herself against danger from enemy aliens within her own shores. In view of the potentially dangerous international situation in 1938, the New Zealand Government had in that year empowered the already existing Organisation for National Security to take such preliminary steps as would not leave the country unprepared in the event of war with Germany. This organisation, which comprised representatives of the Services, of the Department of Internal Affairs, of the Police and of other interested departments, set up committees to cover various aspects of the national emergency which hostilities would create. Among these was an Aliens Committee for deciding how to deal with enemy nationals living in New Zealand and her dependencies, so as to safeguard the interests of the country without contravening either international agreements or humane standards of conduct. As a result of the Alien Control Emergency Regulations 1939, all aliens (to the number of 9000) had to register with the police. The latter kept up-to-date lists of their names and whereabouts, and had little difficulty in a small population like that of New Zealand in keeping track of their activities and opinions.

The interest of the police in aliens had begun much earlier. In February 1934, for example, the Auckland police were keeping a watch on the activities of the Auckland German Club, where it was known that a Nazi group had grown active under the encouragement of successive German consuls with Nazi sympathies. By August 1939 the necessity for internment was being investigated, but it had been decided as a matter of policy to take into custody only those aliens with pronounced anti-British views, whose liberty would probably constitute a public danger. Arrangements were by then in hand for the arrest and detention by the police, on an order from the Attorney-General, of any persons whose records or whose open hostility warranted it. They were to be handed over to military authorities in twelve convenient centres throughout the Dominion, the Army being thereafter responsible for their custody both in transit and during internment. Although there were 786 Germans in New Zealand and 535 in Samoa, it was not anticipated at the time that the number interned would be more than fifty, and it was decided to set up a single central internment camp.

In the 1914–18 War the treatment of interned aliens by New Zealand, as a matter involving her relations with another state, had been laid down by the British Government. In October 1939[1] the New Zealand Government, although by then possessing full power of independent action in this field, decided in the absence of any other precedent to use the British Government's proposed course of action as a working basis for their own. The United Kingdom, in the spirit of the Tokyo Draft,[2] was referring all doubtful Germans and Austrians to special tribunals to determine whether in the interests of national security they should be interned, or subjected to special restrictions, or left at liberty. If they were to be interned, they were to be placed in special camps apart from prisoners of war.

---

[1] The period following the First World War had seen a speeding-up of the evolution of the Dominions as self-governing states responsible for their external affairs no less than their internal administration. In 1931 they were given recognition as sovereign states in British constitutional as well as international law by the Statute of Westminster. Although New Zealand declined to ratify it, she was forced in time to follow the example of her more nationally conscious sister Dominions. New Zealand's ratification took place at the end of 1947.

[2] See Introduction, p. xxiv.

In order to centralise the transmitting to Germany of information regarding Germans anywhere in the Commonwealth through one channel, namely the Prisoner-of-War Information Bureau in London, Commonwealth governments were asked to submit details of any action taken regarding enemy aliens. By 25 November New Zealand was able to report that the German consular staff of eleven had left for Germany, that 19 others were also on their way to their countries of permanent residence, and that up to that time no Germans in New Zealand had been arrested or interned. So far as Samoa and the Island Dependencies were concerned no Germans had left; but 14 were interned in Samoa, 29 (including two women) had been released on parole, and a further 15, including the president and secretary of the former Samoan Nazi Party, were coming to New Zealand for internment. The property of internees was to be vested in a Custodian of Enemy Property and ' the utmost consideration was being given to their comfort and social needs.'[1] Details had been given to the Swiss Consul as the representative of the Protecting Power for German interests in New Zealand.

Somes Island had been the site of New Zealand's camp for civilian internees in the 1914–18 War, and it was again selected for this purpose in 1939. Situated in Wellington Harbour at some distance from the mainland on every side, its 120 acres of high grassland planted with trees contained a number of buildings easily adaptable to the needs of an internment camp. The island was taken over by the Army authorities, and the first batch of German internees was landed by ferry boat on 23 December 1939.

No women or children were interned there and the treatment of the men who were was based on the Geneva Prisoners of War Convention of 1929, camp standing orders consisting largely of extracts from it. Everything within reason was done for the comfort and welfare of those interned. They had single or double cubicles, bedding which included a kapok mattress, five blankets, sheets and pillowcases, and ample bathrooms. They were given plenty of excellent food, the same in fact as that prepared for the camp staff, and generous free issues of good clothing. They shared a canteen with the camp staff and were supplied with additional comforts by the Salvation Army, the Society of Friends, the New Zealand Red Cross Society, and also by individual wellwishers. From the same sources they received books and from the New Zealand YMCA games and recreational material, including two billiard tables. They enjoyed freedom to move over the whole of

---

[1] Government official statement released in Wellington on 28 November 1939.

the island from 6 a.m. to 8 p.m., with permission to fish and bathe; the privilege of six visitors once a week; ample provision for letters and parcels. On one occasion during the summer of 1939–40 the camp commandant, 'to alleviate the monotony of life on the island', even arranged a launch trip round Wellington Harbour. But although this was at the expense of the internees, it was not considered advisable to repeat it.

Despite all this it needs little imagination to see that being interned was a matter of some inconvenience and resentment for many of those taken to Somes Island. The more politically minded succeeded to some extent during the early days in organising a campaign aimed at wearing down the camp commandant and the guards by pin-pricking annoyances. This was to develop into open insolence as the war progressed and the news of German successes became known.

* * * * *

The period covered by this chapter, referred to variously as 'The Phony War' or 'The Twilight War', was filled with suspense and uncertainty for many of those whose lives had become entangled in the war. Prisoners in enemy hands were wondering whether the whole conflict might not soon finish, and so relieve them of doubts about whether to attempt an escape and about the correct course of their actions in general during captivity. Civilians in enemy countries were often surprised at the moderation of their treatment, and those in internment camps were wondering whether they might not soon be released to their homes. Next-of-kin were solicitous for news and filled with anxiety about quite often exaggerated hardships which they visualised their captive relatives enduring. They had not yet realised what long years of captivity and separation lay ahead. Governments and service departments were uncertain whether they should commit themselves to large-scale organisation for dealing with possible large future batches of prisoners. The International Red Cross Committee[1] and the national Red Cross war organisations, whose purpose it was to deal with emergencies such as war, and with specific problems arising from it such as alleviating the lot of prisoners, went ahead and set up the machinery blueprinted for them. The main burden of the early relief work for Commonwealth captives fell on the British Red Cross. But though this body was pressing for expansion and campaigning for more funds in the first six months of the war, there were many who did not then realise the importance of the work for prisoners and internees on which it had embarked. There

---

[1] The IRCC had set up a 'Commission for Work in Wartime' in September 1938.

were, moreover, few who foresaw the scale[1] on which this work would increase before the war was finally over. In the remaining months of 1940 all this hesitation at home was to give way before the certainty of a long and bitter struggle. For those in German hands, their hopes of early release dispelled, there remained only the vague possibility of escape or the bleak prospect of years of helpless captivity in an enemy country amid the restrictions and shortages of a long war.

---

[1] Before the evacuation of Dunkirk there were some 1500 in enemy hands; the total number of British Commonwealth prisoners who fell into enemy hands was over 300,000.

CHAPTER 2

From the Fall of France to the Offensive in the Middle East

(May 1940–March 1941)

I: Prisoners of War captured in Europe in 1940

THE lull that followed the first air raids and naval actions of the autumn of 1939 gave way in the spring of 1940 to the unforeseen series of events in Europe which changed the whole aspect of the war. In April, after the leaflet raids over north-west Germany, came the ill-fated Allied expedition to Norway. In May the German land offensive through the Low Countries ended with the fall of France and the evacuation of the British Expeditionary Force. In August and September the British air victory over the Luftwaffe narrowly averted a land Battle of Britain. The respite thus afforded gave Britain a chance to reorganise her forces, and in the months that followed she began the strategic bombing of Germany which was to continue until the end of the war.

Small numbers of New Zealanders in the Royal Navy, the British Army, and the Royal Air Force took part in all these operations. Some were members of the crews of naval vessels or Fleet Air Arm planes. Others were with British Army units in the land operations on the Continent. New Zealand airmen took part in the Norway expedition; in the fighter patrols and close-support bombing of the land battle for France and in the fighter screen over Dunkirk; in the fighter defence of Britain and the bombing of the German invasion ports; and later in the long-range bombing of Germany itself. The heavy fighting and the Allied withdrawals brought a new flood of prisoners into German hands. It was almost inevitable that a proportion of the New Zealanders in action should be among them, and by the end of 1940 the number of our servicemen prisoners in Europe had risen to fifty or more, the majority of them airmen.

Some airmen who crashed or baled out on to enemy territory were able to evade immediate capture. A few of these made their way back to England, usually with the help of local inhabitants in enemy-occupied countries. The rest, after dodging about in a game of hide-and-seek with the occupation forces, usually fell into the hands of German troops, collaborators, or the Gestapo. A good many airmen were however picked up by enemy troops where they landed,[1] or in the immediate neighbourhood. German military personnel had detailed instructions for dealing with crashed Allied aircraft. They were to 'remove' the airman from the wreck, if necessary 'rescue' them and extinguish fires, prevent them destroying equipment and documents, segregate them one from the other, put a guard on the aircraft and the prisoners, and finally inform the nearest German Air Field command so that the latter could take over. All Wehrmacht units and police in the vicinity of the crashed aircraft were to maintain increased vigilance in order to round up any of the crew who might have evaded capture. As soon as possible the Air Field command staff took over guard duties on both prisoners and all captured equipment, and then sent on particulars of the prisoners by teleprinter to Dulag Luft at Oberursel. It was forbidden, under pain of court martial for 'sabotage of the Defence of the Reich', for members of the Wehrmacht to take away the personal property of prisoners of war. This was less out of respect for the right of a prisoner to his possessions than because of their possible value to the interrogation centre. After a search for escape materials, the entire personal property of each prisoner was taken over by the German Air Field Headquarters, which kept it in a separate envelope and issued a receipt.

Within twenty-four hours fit prisoners were supposed to be despatched in third-class train accommodation to the interrogation centre at Oberursel.[2] On the journey they were to be prevented as far as possible from communicating with each other, an adequate scale of guards being laid down to ensure this. If immediate despatch was not possible, prisoners were to be accommodated overnight at the local military headquarters, where there could be better surveillance than at a local police station. Thus, on paper, security was very high. In practice, however, human weakness and sympathy defeated many of the aims behind these strict and detailed orders. A New Zealand officer records that he was 'well treated by an Austrian officer who knew English—he went as far as to [advise us] not to be forced to say anything as the Germans could not [force us to speak], and if bullied or shouted at to stand on one's dignity as a British officer.'

---

[1] After the arrival of German forces in North Africa, some of the British airmen shot down in that theatre of war who fell into the hands of German troops were flown to Germany. A New Zealand warrant officer had this experience in March 1941.
[2] From these and similar journeys from Dulag Luft to permanent camps attempts at escape were made from time to time, though no ultimately successful escape of this type is recorded.

Wounded prisoners were sent immediately to the nearest German Air Force hospital if hospital treatment was necessary; otherwise their wounds were usually quite adequately treated by the nearest unit medical officer. Sometimes in cases of urgency it was necessary to place a captured airman in the nearest German Navy or Army hospital, but the Luftwaffe saw to it that he was transferred to one of its own hospitals as soon as his physical condition permitted. At all types of military hospital the treatment seems to have been as good and as expert as that given to the German wounded there. A New Zealand warrant officer writes:

> Taken to Zuiderziekenhuis Luftwaffe hospital in Rotterdam and X-rayed. Found to have broken vertebra, and received good treatment for over a month, especially from Dutch staff who had been taken over with the hospital. German doctors applied treatment prescribed by Dutch (civilian) doctor who arrived before them at the crash. . . .

As soon as the wounded prisoner was well enough he was transferred to Hohemark,[1] where

> Medical service [was] indifferent, but only slight or convalescent cases were taken. Food and quarters excellent, walks every day for those able. . . . [Staff] augmented by volunteer R.A.F. personnel with some experience obtained good results.

Medical skill was, it appears, not necessarily the main recommendation for appointment to the staff of Hohemark. At one period the administration tried German nurses who could speak good English, the idea being that they could extract military information from a prisoner while nursing him. His reserve was apparently to be broken down by a combination of comfortable and relaxing surroundings, services demanding his gratitude, and feminine appeal. The experiment was not a success. It was abandoned for want of sufficient results, the official explanation being that the nurses used were not of a 'suitable' type. It is not clear whether this referred to their inability to make the required impression on their patients or to their being themselves susceptible and sympathetic enough to forget about interrogating them. After a short time they were all replaced by elderly male medical orderlies.

The Germans themselves characterised the accommodation and food at Hohemark as 'on a peace-time basis'. They came to the conclusion that for most prisoners of war a stay at the hospital was 'a real holiday compared with what they had gone through from the time they took off on their last mission'. In spite of these efforts to make the prisoner more comfortable and so more friendly and less vigilant, the results of hospital interrogation appear to

---

[1] The hospital attached to the interrogation centre and transit camp at Oberursel. See p. 4.

have been meagre. Those in command of the Oberursel interrogation centre were by no means pleased with the amount of intelligence which came to them from this source, but for the time being they had no remedy to suggest.

Though now housed in a separate building at the Oberursel camp and building up extensive records, the interrogation centre had not yet attained the machine-like efficiency of its later periods.[1] The staff was still small—five interrogators only—and the 'pressure' does not seem to have been applied anything like as seriously as it was in the middle and later years of the war. On their arrival prisoners were certainly placed in solitary confinement, but in what are described by various prisoners of this period as 'good quarters' or 'a quite comfortable small room'. And the treatment there seems to have been reasonable, at all events by comparison with the experiences of those who passed through in subsequent periods. The whole atmosphere seems to have been in complete contrast to that which was later to earn the Oberursel 'cooler' such a sinister reputation.

The first step in the interrogation was the presentation of a long list of questions on a form marked with a Red Cross.[2] This the prisoner was asked to fill in ' in order to facilitate sending particulars regarding his capture through the Red Cross to his relatives.' In some such vein the interrogator endeavoured by friendly chat over a cigarette (for which purpose he received a special daily allowance) to persuade the prisoner to give the required answers. It seems that the idea of the 'Red Cross form' was derived from Article 77 of the 1929 Geneva Prisoners of War Convention. This charges all belligerents with prompt notification of captures together with 'all particulars of identity', and gives a list of the latter which should be noted down (' as far as possible and subject to the provisions of Article 5'):

. . . the regimental number, names and surnames, date and place of birth, rank and *unit* of the prisoner, the surname of the father and name of the mother, the address of the person to be notified in the case of accident, wounds, dates and places of capture, of internment, of wounds, of death, together with *all other important particulars.*[3]

The last phrase coupled with the unfortunate reference to 'unit' no doubt provided a pretext for the German interpolation in their questionnaire of several additions[4] designed to obtain intelligence

---

[1] Interrogation of the former German commandant and other staff of the interrogation centre showed that 'business-like' methods were not introduced until November 1941.
[2] The 'Red Cross' marking was omitted from later forms.
[3] Italics are the author's.
[4] The additions were: Service; profession; religion; whether married; number of children; pay; when, where, and by whom shot down; squadron; group; command station and its number; letters and number of aircraft; state of health; particulars of crew.

for the High Command. And the fact that the clause quoted above was to be read in conjunction with Article 5 (which exonerated the prisoner from stating anything other than his name, rank, and number) was glossed over. Very few airmen fell completely for this ruse, as some of the questions were quite blatant in their attack on security; but there were also very few who gave only their name, rank, and number.

After the business of the Red Cross form there followed the interrogation proper a day or so later. Armed with all the details of the prisoner's private and service background which the interrogation centre Documents and Records Section had been able to piece together, the interrogator attempted to engage the prisoner in apparently innocent conversation, and at the same time to impress him with a display of the information already possessed by German Intelligence. An officer prisoner who was interrogated by the camp commandant describes him as 'most charming', and goes on to say that he 'talked mainly of the East Indies, told me who I was and where I came from in England, target, etc.' The next step was to surprise the prisoner into making comments on operational matters and possibly also on those relating to politics and morale. For this the German interrogation officers adopted a friendly approach, especially in the early part of the war, as it gave the lie to the picture of the 'brutal Hun' built up by Allied publicity in the mind of the young airman. Moreover this method was invariably used with officers, as they sometimes felt bound to converse out of courtesy after treatment which was most hospitable even by ordinary standards, let alone those of an enemy in time of war. Another officer who was also interrogated by the camp commandant mentions that he 'chatted amiably for half an hour, producing cigarettes and liqueurs', and that 'towards the end of the conversation he briefly commiserated my sad fate and then casually asked' questions on operations. Apparently the 'friendly approach' in this form did not always achieve the expected results, for it underwent considerable modification later.

As soon as the interrogation process was completed the prisoner was released from his cell, given back his personal possessions, and sent into the transit camp or 'overflow' across the road to await despatch to a permanent camp. Here his creature comforts were lavishly attended to—showers, clothes, good meals—his stay varying from a few days to three months according to whether or not it was thought that any further information might be extracted from him. For in the compound the Germans endeavoured by means of stool-pigeons and microphones concealed in some of the rooms to glean further scraps of intelligence. In the early stages of the war a good many Allied prisoners were caught off their guard by the set-up at Oberursel and unwittingly gave away much valuable information.

The number of Allied prisoners who yielded to the blandishments of the Germans and agreed to spy on their comrades was happily small, and their success was in the German view very limited. There were a few who belonged to the Mosley Party or held other political views which made them susceptible to German propaganda, but most were ordinary men of 'commonplace' background. They were used mainly in the early days as camp staff in the Oberursel 'overflow' and in the Hohemark hospital. Their main assignments were to check up on identifications of units, to gather information on politics or morale, and to give warning of any impending attempt at escape. Although the Germans paid them for their services, they admit that their neglect of stool-pigeons caused the latter to be less effective and often led to their discovery. Once it became known that the compound contained these 'stooges', their value was largely gone, for security measures were taken by the prisoners against careless talk, and most of the few traitors were forced to desist through fear of discovery and consequent retribution.

A New Zealand officer describes the Dulag Luft of this period as a 'German show camp'. Another calls it 'a model camp' and goes on to say that 'after six months' previous experience in rather bad conditions as a prisoner of war this was absolute luxury.' Huts containing separate rooms for two or three beds with sheets and pillowcases, plenty of space, and even sports fields seemed indeed palatial after the makeshift accommodation experienced by many prisoners while being escorted back.

The fall of France in the summer of 1940 brought such a large influx of prisoners to Dulag Luft that the thousands of French were segregated in a separate compound for the first time. In the British compound the Germans interfered with the prisoners' daily life as little as possible, two roll-calls a day by a Luftwaffe officer being almost their only intrusions. The internal organisation of the camp was left to the senior British officer, who was also the official channel for communication with the German camp commandant, the International Red Cross Committee and the Protecting Power. The various camp activities—canteen, clothing, entertainments, sports—were run by officers or NCOs whom he appointed. Every officer contributed to a camp fund which financed the purchase of food for the messes, the orderlies' pay, and the pocket-money issued to new prisoners to buy toilet necessities from the canteen on their arrival. The sick were treated by a German medical orderly in a medical

P.O.W.—4

inspection room, the nearby Hohemark hospital being available for anything serious. A civilian dentist in Oberursel did the dental work.

Red Cross food parcels had been available from the opening of the camp, but were in short supply during the period following the fall of France until new supply routes were established. This break in supplies unfortunately coincided with the cutting down of prisoner-of-war rations to the scale allowed to German civilians. All Red Cross food was pooled to ensure that new arrivals should share equally with those who had been in the camp some time. The Germans, although bound by the Geneva Prisoners of War Convention to supply prisoners with clothing and footwear,[1] would issue no clothing except to those whose uniforms were lost or in rags. Moreover they insisted on rigid control of the issue of Air Force uniforms sent by the Air Ministry through the International Red Cross Committee, on the grounds that surplus clothing might be used to assist escape. Nevertheless the camp clothing officer was able to see that each newly-arrived prisoner did not have to go about dressed in a manner damaging to his self-respect and to the prestige of the Royal Air Force.

Prisoners at Dulag Luft were allowed to go for walks on parole in the countryside with a small German guard and to use for sports a field adjoining the barrack area on the south side, which had been enclosed by a six-foot barbed-wire fence. Sports equipment distributed through the International Red Cross Committee made it possible to play a variety of games, and permission was given for early morning swimming during the summer of 1940 in the Oberursel public open-air swimming bath. Educational books sent by the British Red Cross and by the World Alliance of YMCAs through Geneva enabled the studious to pass the time profitably. Many took the obvious opportunity to teach themselves foreign languages, and others to study topics related to their own civilian jobs. There was as yet very little ordinary reading matter. Once a week a variety show or a revue was produced on the small stage in the main messroom, the Germans permitting the hire of local costumes on condition that they were not used for escaping. On Sunday the same messroom was used for religious services conducted by the prisoners, though Roman Catholics were occasionally allowed to attend Mass in Oberursel. As several New Zealand ex-prisoners who were there in this period expressed it, the treatment was ' very

---

[1] Article 12 states:
    Clothing, underwear and footwear shall be supplied to prisoners of war by the Detaining Power. The regular replacement and repair of such articles shall be assured. . . .

reasonable indeed'. A delegate of the International Red Cross Committee gave it a glowing report:

This camp is the best of its kind visited in Germany. A well regulated, clean and nice camp. In addition to the physical comforts provided, an endeavour is made to alleviate the mental depression present in persons in confinement.

It is said that the morale of prisoners at Dulag Luft was very high, partly as a result of the spirit of comradeship and solidarity established by some of its earliest inmates. Doubtless an adequate supply of material goods fairly distributed must share the credit, as it did in most prisoner-of-war camps. There can be little doubt that the sensible policy adopted by the senior British officer at an early stage did much to obviate possible later causes of grievance. His aim was to create among those in the camp a cohesion based on mutual confidence, which if not quite that of a service unit, would at least present a solid front in the presence of the enemy. Thus there was a common mess for senior and junior officers; a communal pool of all camp food supplies from which all ranks received the same food; a communal pool of clothing from which only those in real need of it were supplied. The minimising of the privileges of rank, a scrupulously fair distribution of available goods, a friendly welcome to new prisoners coupled with a few words of advice, all helped to weld the prisoners into a community united against the enemy outside the wire. When it came to a question of escape or any other action, co-operation might then be assured.

It was sometimes imagined that discipline and co-operation inside a prisoner-of-war camp could be taken for granted, since prisoners of war were still servicemen and would give, even after capture, unquestioning obedience to their senior officers. But capture often produced a considerable loosening of the bonds that gave a service unit its discipline and morale. In the first place it was only too obvious that those really in command were no longer the senior officers but the enemy guards, since they were the only ones with the means of enforcing their authority. Secondly, senior officer prisoners might not always have the qualities necessary to make a successful prisoner-of-war camp leader. To inspire confidence a leader had to show that he was completely unselfish about food and personal comfort. He had to ensure that everyone in the camp always received a fair share of everything, taking a firm line if necessary with those of no matter what rank who tried to get more than their share. He had to be indefatigable in negotiating with the enemy to improve conditions in the camp and to protect its inmates from ill-treatment. Finally he had to bear hunger, cold, and other discomforts cheerfully, and by this example and other means help maintain the morale of his fellow prisoners.

In the maintenance of morale news of the war and of the outside world was a considerable factor. In Dulag Luft this was made easy when early in 1941 the Germans installed a radio receiver. All the European and American programmes could be heard, and the senior British officer saw to it that news bulletins were made available to the camp at large. In this period of disasters there was nothing in the German news bulletins that might have given logical grounds for belief in a final Allied victory. In spite of this, most officers and men maintained in their speech and attitude the proposition that Britain always wins the last battle; and apparently such illogical stubbornness usually left the German guards in baffled amazement.

By virtue of its role as an information-collecting agency and as part of the security organisation of the Luftwaffe Intelligence Branch, Dulag Luft was in this period saddled with the censorship of the incoming and outgoing mail for all Air Force prisoners in Germany. It was not until later, when numbers increased and this additional burden proved too great to cope with, that the duties were placed elsewhere. Besides this the transit camp had to look after its own security by ensuring that nobody escaped. From the first, the German security system attached importance to the examination of parcels entering a camp. But the volume of parcels received by British prisoners made thorough searching of them impossible without the employment of enormous staffs. Conscientious as some of the searchers were, the sheer necessity for clearing space to admit new deliveries prevented the strict examination of everything; and the searchers, especially Wehrmacht personnel not belonging to the security branch, were by no means all conscientious. Thus food and tobacco tins were at first all opened and often emptied, but later those from Red Cross sources received no examination[1] and many others but a cursory one. Clothing parcels were usually checked for civilian shirts, ties, and other garments, but the German examiner could often be persuaded to let some pass. Games parcels were searched for escape aids, and all books had to be read for anti-Nazi views as well as for possible assistance to would-be escapers. While much was found by the German censorship staff, a good deal got past them.

If in the earlier part of 1940 the Germans had not yet got down to anti-escape measures in earnest, neither had the prisoners got down to the business of escaping. Spring had brought the leaflet raids and speculation whether the whole war in the West might

---

[1] Red Cross societies, the British Red Cross, the Joint Council, and the International Red Cross Committee were scrupulous in seeing that safe delivery of their consignments was not prejudiced by any breach of censorship regulations. They never used them to convey contraband articles.

not just peter out. And if so what was the use of trying to escape? With autumn came the realisation of a long war ahead, and escape took on a new meaning. A committee was formed and schemes were thought out. In all but the most temporary transit camps the first escape schemes were as a rule based on tunnelling, and three tunnels were commenced in Dulag Luft in this period. One of them was successfully completed in May 1941, when 18 officers got away. They were all recaptured within a short period, but the break was doubtless a shock to the German staff of Dulag Luft. From then on camp staff, selected from ' men inclined to accept imprisonment passively ',[1] were the only prisoners retained in the camp for any length of time, and likely escapers especially were quickly passed on to permanent camps.

Although the German High Command had decided at the end of 1939 to construct special permanent camps for Air Force prisoners, none had been completed up to the middle of 1940. From Dulag Luft, therefore, prisoners were still being sent on to camps where there was a mixture both of arms of the service and also of nationalities, although the latter were by now usually in separate compounds. Officers went to Oflag IXA at Spangenburg, already described, and other ranks to Stalag XIIA at Limburg, not far north-west of Oberursel, or to Stalag VIIIB at Lamsdorf in Silesia.

In this period the accommodation at Spangenburg[2] had been increased by the addition of a group of half-timbered buildings in the village below the castle, these being known as the *Unterlager* (Lower camp) and the castle as the *Oberlager* (Upper camp). Before this expansion the Upper camp had become very overcrowded—a phase which usually preceded any addition to living space for prisoners of war. British other ranks acting as orderlies for the camp were particularly cramped. To make matters worse the plumbing in the old castle, having deteriorated badly during the winter, was still being repaired well on into the summer. This meant having tub baths instead of showers, carrying buckets of water instead of turning on taps, and other inconveniences which brought life in the castle to some extent back to its medieval pattern. Partly because of this and partly because of the defective ventilation from small windows through which there penetrated only narrow shafts of sunshine, the whole place had become damp. And the dark, grey stone walls, the concrete floors, and the clammy air combined to create a depressing atmosphere except on very sunny days.

It may be imagined, therefore, that in spite of a general prisoner-of-war prejudice against having to move, many were not unwilling

---
[1] The phrase is that used in the British Air Ministry *Camp History of Dulag Luft*.
[2] In this period its designation changed from Oflag IXA to Oflag IXA/H.

to be transferred to the village. But even there the old-fashioned buildings had to be closed for a period while renovations were done, including the installation of steam-heating, which fortunately was functioning in both camps by the winter of 1940. The transfer of the remaining French officers made the camp an entirely British one, Navy and Royal Air Force officers remaining in the castle and Army officers going down to the *Unterlager*. But though the space was ample for a time, convalescents discharged from hospitals and a steady flow of airmen brought the numbers up to about 300 in each camp by the end of the year.

The amenities of the castle were improving with the passage of time. The Germans had been persuaded to allow the use of a small piece of ground near the castle as a football 'kick-about' area. A gymnasium attached to the castle had been made available. Two plots of ground had been set aside for the prisoners to cultivate. A pleasant, medieval-style room served as library, which by numerous consignments of books from England and Geneva soon possessed an excellent stock. German daily newspapers and illustrated periodicals were delivered to the camp regularly. Musical instruments could also be bought, and an orchestra had been built up. Walks in the neighbourhood for officers on parole not to escape[1] were permitted twice a week, but the commandant insisted on guards 'to protect prisoners against possible insults from German civilians'. Some officers protested that they were prepared to take the risk of anything the German population might do; others complained that the imposition of guards under such circumstances was a slur on the honour of the officer who had given his parole. But no amount of argument was of any avail. 'No guard—no walks' was the German standpoint, and it remained so in most German camps throughout the war.

The camp at Limburg, Stalag XIIA, was a convenient dumping-ground for other ranks from Dulag Luft, being no more than 25 miles away. As far as can be ascertained, however, most Dominion personnel found their way to Stalag VIIIB at Lamsdorf, not far from Breslau in Silesia, a two-day journey by cattle-truck. It is described by a visitor as a 'classically' typical prisoner-of war camp.

At this stage of its history it already boasted sixty barracks laid out in long rows with 'streets' between on a huge area of sandy flat. Its population counted some 3000 Poles and 8000 British, with 6000 of the latter out in working detachments. The barracks,

---

[1] The giving of parole by British officers had been forbidden by an Army Council Instruction of 15 February 1940 and similar Navy and Air Force instructions. But the practice of giving a temporary parole for exercise, recreation, and medical treatment was recognised when a new order was promulgated in early 1942.

in which they were locked at night, were of a type that had become standard in prison camps for other ranks. Each half-barrack held three-tier wooden bunks for 180 men and additional space for tables and forms; and between the two halves there was a small concrete personal ablutions room and a similar one for washing clothes. Hot or cold showers were organised by the Germans in a separate building. There was at this stage no canteen, and in any case no pay was received except by those on working parties.[1] There were practically no facilities for indoor recreation and entertainment, even if lighting and heating had been adequate for their enjoyment; so that resort was had to organised sing-songs to relieve the dullness. The camp's sole redeeming feature was the space within the perimeter where prisoners might exercise. A New Zealand prisoner captured at sea, who had been in the holds of two ships and through three transit camps, describes it as 'the worst camp we had so far experienced in every way.'

It is apparent that without relief supplies from Red Cross and other sources it would be difficult for such a camp to be bearable over a length of time. Even when food parcels arrived there were no facilities for cooking the contents, other than crude stoves made by the prisoners themselves. Nevertheless there seems little doubt that neither the discomfort of the camp nor the arrogant harshness of the guards after the Dunkirk evacuation quenched the spirit of the inmates. Their resiliency and adaptability in those first dark months were something on which in later years, with the aid of all the relief supplies poured in from outside, the camp population was able to build up a position of moral superiority over its guards.

By July 1940 the first permanent camp for Air Force prisoners of war in Germany was ready for occupation. The site which had been chosen was near the town of Barth, on a small peninsula jutting out into the Baltic almost due south of Copenhagen. It consisted of a few single-storied wooden barracks clustered together on a sandy flat, not much more than five feet above sea-level. Twenty-one officers sent from Dulag Luft, Oberursel, in July 1940 were the first to occupy the two officers' barracks. They were joined by parties from Oflag IXA/H, Spangenburg, and later by further parties from Dulag Luft, to make a total complement of about 200 in which were members of each of the Commonwealth Air Forces as well as of the Fleet Air Arm. At the same time NCOs transferred from Stalag XIIA, Limburg, and from Stalag VIIIB, Lamsdorf,

---

[1] 70 pfennigs a day, at pre-war rates of exchange about 11d. (1 Reichsmark = 100 pfennigs) 'In the industries and trades prisoners of war received 60 per cent of the rate paid to civilian workers. In agriculture prisoners of war received a very small daily wage, but they were fed and lodged by their employer.'—IRCC Report on Activities during Second World War, Vol. I, p. 287. (See also note 3 on p. 85.)

together with parties from Dulag Luft—a total of some 500—occupied three similar barracks in a separate compound. All the barracks were subdivided into small rooms and each contained a kitchen where Red Cross food could be cooked. Sanitary and washing facilities were included in each officers' barrack, but those for NCOs were in a separate building. An extension to one of the officers' barracks was used as a messroom.

A senior prisoner in each compound became responsible for internal organisation and for dealing with the German camp administration. On the whole prisoners were allowed to administer their own affairs, the Germans conducting an occasional search or inspection of barracks and holding two roll-calls daily. The latter were at first rather perfunctory counts, but in November 1940, following several escapes, they became individual roll-calls and remained so for nearly eighteen months. The prisoners' organisation was similar to that already described for Dulag Luft. To pay for fresh vegetables and other communal purchases made through the canteen for both officers and NCOs, and to provide the latter with funds for minor expenses, all officers paid a levy proportionate to their rank into a camp fund. Such a practice became almost universal in camps containing both officers and other ranks, and was later extended to provide for other ranks of the same country or unit in another camp. In Barth financial assistance of this type was provided for merchant seamen's camps. The Geneva Prisoners of War Convention provides for a percentage of canteen receipts to be set aside for the establishment of a camp welfare fund. The German camp administration took 10 per cent of the value of all canteen sales, but it does not appear to have been used on behalf of the prisoners. Sick prisoners were cared for reasonably well, in spite of meagre medical supplies, by a German medical officer and German orderlies in a sick-bay situated in a *Vorlager*[1] outside the compounds. Serious cases were sent to nearby hospitals, and dental work was done by a Luftwaffe dentist who visited the camp weekly.

In the first few months only a few Red Cross food parcels addressed to individuals captured before May 1940 arrived at the camp, October bringing the first consignment to the senior British officer. Though this was still too small for a full distribution, quantities received gradually increased until, half-way through 1941, full weekly distributions became possible.[2] But it was a hungry period as the German rations,[3] although supplemented by small amounts of fresh vegetables purchased from the canteen, were

---

[1] A fenced-off area between the prisoners' compounds and the camp entrance, containing German administrative and living quarters.
[2] By this time the breakdown in deliveries due to the fall of France had been repaired by the establishment of the new route round the coast of Spain.
[3] Estimated at the time as about 1500 calories a head daily.

insufficient to meet the rigours of a German winter; and even these were reduced when the supplies of Red Cross food became regular. Nevertheless by then the camp escape committee was able to reserve a certain amount of food for use by escapers.

It was not until about six months after capture that a prisoner's first quarterly clothing parcel arrived. Up to the time when bulk supplies of British uniform began to arrive in May 1941, the Germans issued captured French, Belgian, and Polish uniforms and other clothing to any prisoner who needed it. This captured uniform was naturally not a satisfactory substitute, and the arrival of RAF battle dress enabled those temporarily without proper uniforms to take pride once again in their personal appearance.

Although there was a sports field in an adjacent compound, shortages of guards forced the Germans to curtail its use to about twice a week. With this restriction, the shortage of food and the lack of equipment, not much sport was played in the first year, except a little soccer and some ice-hockey on a home-made rink. Autumn 1940 brought a great demand for books, and a small library was formed from private contributions. As time went on this was supplemented by parcels sent through the International Red Cross Committee and by the purchase through the canteen of continental editions in English. In the winter one or two educational classes were started in spite of a lack of books and writing materials, there having been practically none at all in the first six months. An RAF staff duties course petered out through lack of interest. Such a fate befell most prisoner-of-war courses on service matters and was probably due to the remoteness, for a serviceman behind enemy barbed wire, of any opportunity to apply them. Courses in escape work, practical techniques, languages, or contract bridge were by comparison consistently attended. A pantomime for Christmas 1940 set going a series of theatrical and, later on, musical performances with instruments bought out of camp funds. A German padre held regular church services for the NCOs, officers taking their own services, until the arrival in mid-1941 of an officer of the New Zealand Church Army who thereafter acted as padre.

The first ideas about escape brought from Spangenburg and Oberursel were followed up intensively at Barth, which by its nearness to the Swedish coast seemed almost an answer to an escaper's prayer. In addition there were working parties, compulsory for aircraftsmen and voluntary for NCOs; and from a farm, a fish-packing factory, or a flourmill escape was at first relatively easy. Indeed the escape record of Stalag Luft I[1] for the first nine

---

[1] Stalag Luft was the original name of the camp, but the number I was added later to distinguish it from other Air Force camps. The title Stalag Luft I is used here to avoid confusion.

months of its existence shows considerable activity. Besides a number of unsuccessful tunnel schemes, thirteen officers broke out of the camp and twelve NCOs were able to get away from working parties. This was enough to keep any set of camp guards on their toes. But German security was for some time not highly developed, and had escape planning, control and security not been at a similar stage of development many more attempts might have succeeded. The efficient camp departments which were built up later to deal in almost professional fashion with disguise, forged papers, photographs, food, maps, compasses, and other gadgets were as yet non-existent. Such work had to be shouldered by the individual, or at most a handful of associates. Not until the summer of 1941 were the foundations laid of the first of such large escape organisations.

The anti-escape defences of Stalag Luft I consisted of a double barbed-wire fence eight feet high with concertina wire in the six-foot space between, corner sentry-towers with searchlights and machine guns, a sentry patrol outside the fence, which was lit at 20-yard intervals, a warning wire 15 feet inside the fence, a dog patrol in the compound at night, and some attempt at control of persons and vehicles passing through the gate. The pattern was typical of German prisoner-of-war camps. In February 1941 the security (Abwehr) officer was given two assistants to keep an eye on the compounds and to control searches. Their nickname of 'ferrets', given as a result of their frequent crawling under the barracks, stuck to Abwehr personnel for the rest of the war. The Abwehr were also mainly responsible for the examination of parcels entering the camp as they were at Dulag Luft, and were often similarly swamped into inefficiency by the magnitude of that task. For the same reason they were often dilatory about the searching of new arrivals and of the barracks. But the first discovery of a tunnel at Barth in January 1941 brought a thorough ransack of the offending barrack, lasting a week and involving the evacuation of the occupants, the tearing down of wallpaper, and the emptying of mattresses. Then began a kind of search blitz culminating in searches on 28 successive days in May 1941, but gradually petering out in the summer.

At first attempted escape was punished by five days in a cell for a first offence, ten for a second and so on, with normal rations and Red Cross food, the escaper being later returned to his compound or perhaps sent to a camp such as Colditz.[1] But escape activity

---

[1] Oflag IVC, Colditz, was a camp for troublesome prisoners (later for prospective hostages too), officially no different from any other except for being more difficult to escape from. In fact it was a comfortless old fortress, and the staff was less 'correct' and the treatment considerably harsher than at other camps.

assumed such proportions that the attitude of some German camp commandants became much more severe, and exasperation sometimes drove them into imposing reprisals on the whole camp. At Barth measures such as short-clipping prisoners' heads and a month of successive daily searches, although within the letter of the Geneva Convention, were in intention reprisals and therefore a contravention of its spirit. The rights of a would-be escaper under international law were often similarly circumvented by the imposition of long sentences for trumped-up charges based on the German civil code. ' Sabotage of the Reich ' was often the excuse for getting rid of a persistent escaper with a sentence of several months' duration.[1]

II : *Servicemen and Civilians captured at Sea*

Besides those who fell into enemy hands in the course of land and air operations, a number of British Commonwealth subjects were captured at sea. German U-boats and surface raiders had begun their attacks on British merchant shipping in the first week of the war, and by the latter part of 1940 German marauding craft had penetrated into most of the sea-routes of the British Commonwealth. On 25 November of that year it was known that the MV *Port Hobart* on her way to New Zealand from the United Kingdom had been attacked by an enemy raider. Nothing more was heard of her until a British warship reported sighting and picking up two empty boats belonging to the sunken vessel. It was however some time before anything became known of the fate of those on board, among whom were a number of New Zealanders, both passengers and crew. Slowly the news trickled through in personal letters from occupied Europe and in welfare reports from the International Red Cross Committee. The *Port Hobart* had been sighted in the Caribbean Sea by the German pocket battleship *Admiral Scheer*, which immediately gave chase and fired a warning shell, forcing her to heave to. A boarding party from the *Admiral Scheer* then took off her complement and laid explosive charges inside her.

After some three months at sea, during which they were several times transferred from one ship to another, the captured passengers and crew were eventually landed on 1 March 1941 at Bordeaux, where they were placed in a transit camp at St. Médard en Jalles, known as Frontstalag 221. Conditions at this camp, which appears to have been a reception camp for personnel captured at sea, were described by a New Zealand member of the crew of the

---

[1] Articles 50 and 54 of the 1929 Geneva Convention made escape by a prisoner of war punishable only by ' disciplinary punishment ', limited to 30 days' imprisonment.

Port Hobart as 'terrible', and he speaks of a 'lack of adequate food, clothing and sanitation.' These impressions are corroborated by other men of similar status who came for the first time into contact with the watery soup and the crude sanitary facilities so well known later in many German prisoner-of-war camps. The living quarters consisted of rough wooden barracks, in each of which a hundred men slept, ate and passed their time. Each barrack contained a hundred bunks but four forms only and no tables. On the other hand, two New Zealand women passengers, who had had three months at sea under very difficult and trying conditions, were 'well treated but had practically no clothing'.[1] The latter predicament resulted from the circumstances of their capture and from the lack of any replacements on the raiders. To enable them to remedy this discomfort and to buy a few extras, the United States Consul at Bordeaux had advanced sums of money to the civilian passengers and smaller sums to the merchant seamen. One of the worst aspects of treatment in St. Médard appears to have been the considerable delay before permission was given to write letters. There was an interval of several months before either first letters or International Red Cross 'capture-cards'[2] reached their destinations.

Two days after the attack in the Caribbean just described, two German raiders in the Pacific made their presence felt in waters uncomfortably close to New Zealand. In the early morning of 27 November 1940 the MV *Rangitane*, bound for England with (among other passengers) a number of recruits for the Royal Navy and the Royal Air Force, was intercepted when only about four hundred miles from Auckland by the German surface raiders *Orion* and *Komet*. The *Orion* shelled and damaged her, took off her complement by launch, and then sank her by torpedoes and gunfire. Wounded brought on to the *Orion* received immediate medical treatment and the women were very well cared for. But the bulk of the prisoners, after a cursory interrogation, were housed below decks in rather dirty, overcrowded, and unbearably hot storerooms next to the engine-room. Accommodation on the *Komet* was even worse, and rations were of the poorest.

At the end of a week or so they all had the unpleasant experience for some days of being unwilling passengers on enemy vessels

---

[1] The seven New Zealand women from the *Port Hobart* were accommodated in a refugee camp at Eysines, some three miles from St. Médard. Here they remained for three weeks under reasonable conditions, except for very poor food and sanitation.
[2] By Article 36 of the 1929 Geneva Convention each prisoner was entitled within a week of his 'arrival in camp' to send a postcard to his relatives informing them of his capture and the state of his health. This postcard became known as the 'capture-card'. In May 1940 the IRCC persuaded the German authorities to allow another 'capture-card' to be sent direct to their Central Agency at Geneva.

going into action. Captives in such a position are not only helpless in the face of physical danger, but they are torn between a patriotic desire for the enemy attack to miscarry and a hope that they themselves may escape injury. Just before Christmas 1940 the civilians and some of the servicemen from the *Komet* were relieved from further trials of this kind by being put ashore at Emirau Island in the Bismarck Archipelago. A little later all those on the *Orion* were transferred to the German merchantman *Ermland* in the North Pacific. Leisurely cruising, with the majority of the captives in the hold, brought them round the Horn to the South Atlantic. Here overcrowding was aggravated by picking up a further 400 assorted prisoners from ships sunk by the pocket battleship *Admiral Scheer*, though the prisoners were allowed on deck for a good many hours each day. They were then taken northwards to Bordeaux, where after a four months' voyage they joined the survivors from the *Port Hobart* and other ships at Frontstalag 221.

In early April, about a fortnight after their arrival there, the whole batch of 'saved from the sea' then at St. Médard were sent off to Germany. Civilian passengers and officers travelled in third-class carriages, but most of the others except the women[1] had an uncomfortable five-day journey in cattle-trucks, followed by an 11-kilometre march which brought them, filthy and many of them none too fit, to the gates of the huge Stalag XB at Sandbostel, near Bremen. After a two-hours' wait in pouring rain they were allowed to pass through. Inside was a population of 25,000 prisoners of all nationalities housed in overcrowded, drab, ill-lit wooden barracks, laid out in long rows with 'streets' between. Food was as bad as it had been at Bordeaux, if not worse; clothing issued consisted of dirty garments previously worn by other prisoners. Sanitary conditions were bad and medical supplies poor. The newly-arrived servicemen were forced to work digging a rifle range, but received some compensation in the form of a slightly higher scale of rations. Their stay at Sandbostel was comparatively short, and by the middle of the year they had been sent to their appropriate permanent camps.[2] Members of the Merchant Navy, however, including several New Zealanders from a number of different merchantmen, were to remain in a separate 'Navy' compound until the middle of 1942.

Two members of the Merchant Marine escaped while on the way to Germany from Bordeaux on the night of 3 April. They jumped from the train as it was passing through a cutting at night. Being still in occupied France, they made their way south and

---
[1] The British women, now nine in number, made this trip in a lorry.
[2] Most of the Air Force trainees went to Stalag VIIIB at Lamsdorf, passing through Dulag Luft for interrogation en route.

crossed the border into Vichy territory. One of them, a New Zealander, Bernard Cooper, succeeded in getting free of the Marseilles police and reaching Spain. After 52 days in an unsavoury political prison and another 32 in a concentration camp, he made his way to Madrid and eventually to Gibraltar, reaching England in January 1942.

The civilians from St. Médard, including the women, were kept at Sandbostel for a short while before being sent off to internment camps. By that time several such camps for civilians had been established. For, although the Germans in the first months of war had allowed the repatriation to England of a good many British women from Germany and Poland,[1] most of the men, married or single, had had to remain. Of the British women who stayed none had been interned up to March 1940, but most of the British Commonwealth male subjects (married or single) had been brought to Ilag XIII at Wülsburg[2] before the end of 1939.

Mention has already been made of this old converted convent enclosing a large park-like area, where prisoners of war had been housed in 1914–18. In its early days it had only 142 inmates (mainly British) in dormitories of twenty to thirty beds. The main worries of the inmates at first concerned lack of mail from their families or the financial position of their wives if still on German soil. But by June 1940 the invasion of the Low Countries and the Norwegian campaign had crowded the camp out with Belgians, Dutch and Norwegians, besides the original British, Egyptians and French—a total of 972 men. Three-tier bunks took the place of beds in the packed dormitories, which had always been used for eating as well as sleeping. In succeeding months the numbers increased and the camp became still worse: lack of proper sanitation, insufficient heating, insufficient water, no soap, and food, as a visitor put it, 'just enough'. Life was difficult for the internees, and the control of such a heterogeneous mass of civilians under such conditions doubly so.

The German occupation of large areas of Western Europe in the spring and summer of 1940 had brought further numbers of British and Commonwealth civilians into enemy hands. The Low Countries being no longer neutral, the repatriation of civilians was much more difficult, quite apart from the German unwillingness to arrange further exchanges. While men of military age appear to have been interned almost immediately, British women in France, Holland,

---

[1] 1611 British and Commonwealth persons were repatriated before the frontiers were closed on 5–7 September 1939. A further 539 were repatriated between then and the end of February 1940.—IRCC *Revue*, April 1940, p. 304.

[2] See page 8. The camp was originally called Stalag XIIIA and then Zweiglager (branch camp) XIIIA to distinguish it from a prisoner-of-war camp of the same number.

and Denmark seem to have gone on living for the first few months at their former addresses. Students, teachers, evangelists, nurses, wives—some of them remained uninterned for the rest of the war; others were interned about the end of the year either in France or Germany. For those at liberty, financial assistance up to £10 sterling a month was available through the United States consulates everywhere except in the Channel Islands. And these people were able to communicate with the outside world either by means of the 25-word messages that could be exchanged through the International Red Cross Committee, or by using a communications scheme operated for a time on their behalf by Thomas Cook and Son.

III : *The First Battles in the Middle East*

On 10 June 1940 as resistance in France was crumbling, Mussolini brought Italy into the war on the side of his Axis partner. Before the end of the year his forces had pushed across the Libyan border into Egypt as the thin British garrisons withdrew; and, using Albania as a base, they had made a bid for ascendancy in the Balkans by attacking Greece. By December not only had the Greeks unceremoniously pushed them back into Albania, but the British counter-attack was driving the desert army helter-skelter across Cyrenaica, with thousands of Italian troops pouring back into Egypt as prisoners. Royal Air Force and Fleet Air Arm units co-operated in these first battles of the Middle East, and some of their crew, including a few New Zealanders, had the misfortune to fall into enemy hands. Whether captured in Albania or Libya, whether officers or NCOs, these airmen found themselves sooner or later brought to Sulmona[1] in Italy, at that time the only prisoner-of-war camp for British and French on the Italian mainland.

The camp itself was a few kilometres from the town of Sulmona in a beautiful valley up among the Abruzzi, near a village with the romantic name of Fonte d'Amore. The camp had been used for Austrian prisoners in 1917. Concrete barracks on a sloping terrain contained dormitories with twenty or so double-tiered bunks for other ranks, but for officers there were small rooms for two with tables and cupboards. There was a spacious sick-bay with an Italian medical officer in charge. Patients had hot showers once a week, and abundance of good food—for the officers the same as that for the Italian officers' mess. If an officer prisoner was short of clothes, the *Unione Militare*[2] would come and measure him for a uniform. There were armchairs in the officers' mess, and tablecloths and glassware; attached to the mess was a gymnasium and games room.

---
[1] About four hours' journey from Rome on the Pescara railway.
[2] Suppliers of clothing to the Italian forces.

Out of doors there were gardening facilities and Sunday walks up into the mountains. There was every courtesy from the Italians, who were clearly doing everything possible to make the monotony of what seemed to them the unnatural life of a prisoner-of-war camp more bearable.

At the time of the entry of Italy into the war very few New Zealand civilians were in that country, and none were interned. The difficulties that arose concerned the provision of means of subsistence for a student at Genoa and the New Zealand-born widow of an Italian at Rome. As happened in Germany, those deriving an income from New Zealand suddenly found themselves without funds. Great Britain had accepted responsibility for British-born widows of enemy subjects, and New Zealand followed this example on 19 June 1940 when she agreed that:

. . . the fund held by United States Government should be expended in same manner and on same conditions in respect destitute persons normally domiciled in New Zealand as is being done on behalf of H.M. Government in United Kingdom.[1]

After the necessary arrangements for repayment had been made, money was thus made available through the Protecting Power.

Besides those who fell into the hands of enemy belligerent states there were a few, almost always airmen, who were forced while on military operations to land on the territory of a neutral country. Such men had under international law to be treated as military internees and so kept until the end of hostilities. One of our naval airmen operating over Norway in September 1940 had to make a forced landing in Sweden and was detained by the police for questioning, being billeted meanwhile in a hotel. His identity established, he was transported to an internment camp at Falun, 100 miles north-west of Stockholm. There he was well fed and generally well treated, his pay and any special wants being attended to by the British Legation in Stockholm.

In November and December of the same year during operations in the Mediterranean, two New Zealand RAF pilots were forced down on French North African territory.[2] They were similarly interned at Aumale in Algeria for similar reasons, though their treatment was by no means so hospitable, and improvements were largely due to the efforts of the United States Consul in Algiers. The internees were strictly guarded, but one New Zealand NCO[3] was able to escape by way of the roof of the internment building and make his way (with native help) some distance west before being recaptured.

---

[1] Cable from Prime Minister to New Zealand High Commissioner, London.
[2] At that time under the control of the neutral Vichy Government.
[3] F/Sgt C. Belcher.

IV: *Protection of the Interests of Prisoners of War and Civilian Internees*

It will be seen from these glimpses of the life of our people in enemy and neutral countries, either as prisoners of war or internees or civilians at liberty, that the problem of watching over their interests had in 1940 suddenly become one of major importance. The rapid spread of the conflict and the increase in the numbers of those in enemy hands[1] necessitated greater efforts on their behalf and made relief work for them much more complicated. Those external relief agencies whose initial efforts were outlined in the preceding chapter found their work suddenly increased out of all proportion. Not only had they to cope with this emergency, but they had to make long-term plans for relief in what was now recognised as a world war whose dimensions had already in some respects eclipsed those of its predecessor.

The United States of America continued to represent the interests of British Commonwealth countries in Germany: her representatives continued inspections of internment camps, making special inquiries on our behalf, and conveying to the German Foreign Office protests and other communications from the British Government. On Italy's entry into the war the United States became our Protecting Power in Italy as well. The increase in the number of camps to be visited and the enormous number of inquiries for information regarding individuals both interned and at liberty threw a heavy burden of work on the United States diplomatic and consular staffs.

It was perhaps as well, therefore, that their work to some extent overlapped that of the International Red Cross Committee. Both agencies carried out camp inspections, forwarded lists of prisoners, and generally tried to see that the Geneva Prisoners of War Convention was observed. Sometimes a United States consular official and an International Red Cross delegate would carry out a camp inspection together, though their impressions were of course conveyed in separate reports; and points that were perhaps missed by one visitor were noticed by the other. Apart from the improvements achieved on the spot, there seems little doubt that the right of inspection was one of the greatest safeguards of the welfare of the inmates of these camps. As the International Red Cross Committee saw it, 'some infringements of the elementary laws of humanity are too grave for a state, even though it has little concern for the respect of such laws, to dare expose before the eyes of neutral witnesses'.[2]

---

[1] By the end of the French campaign Germany had claimed over 3,000,000 prisoners, many more than she took in the whole of the First World War.
[2] IRCC Report on Activities during the Second World War, Vol. I, p. 222.

A detaining power might sometimes indulge in considerable window-dressing before an inspection in order to favourably impress a visitor. But the effect of this was often counterbalanced by a discussion with the prisoners' representative. What is now known of certain camps where no neutral visitors were permitted is convincing evidence that inspection put an effective brake on any tendency toward neglect and ill-treatment.

The work of the International Red Cross Committee in Geneva which saw most rapid expansion in 1940 was that of the Central Agency for information. By July it had a staff of 1400 (1200 of them voluntary) and by August it was sometimes handling 50,000 letters a day. In addition to the transmitting of official lists of prisoners and internees between belligerents by photostat copies, the Central Agency had its own file for each individual. From this a card-index[1] was kept up to date with the latest information so as to answer inquiries without delay. 'Capture-cards' were often sent to Geneva first and gave notification long before the official lists from Berlin were made up. Telegraphic communication of this news to London after June 1940 was often the first word received there, and in the case of Air Force personnel was averaging about fourteen days after capture. Inquiries were legion, sometimes as many as twenty-one for the same person, each inquiry often a letter of several pages. A large staff of linguists, retired officials, and teachers were taxed to their utmost simply to read and mark this flood of correspondence for those who wrote the replies. In addition there were the numerous letters destined for those interned, which had to be reduced to 25-word messages before being sent on.

The Committee itself did not have the financial resources to supply relief in kind to the mass of war victims resulting from the European blitzkreig of 1940. After the breakdown in communications in June 1940, it bought on behalf of the British Red Cross many tons of Swiss food to bridge the gap in supplies sent from England. But it concentrated mainly on collating requests from prisoners in the camps, sending these to their national Red Cross societies, and facilitating the despatch of whatever relief supplies the latter sent. The transport, storage, and distribution of the food, medicine, and clothing sent to British Commonwealth prisoners alone became an enormous task for its relief department. Besides the large-scale undertakings involved inside Switzerland, it necessitated the setting-up of offices in Lisbon and Marseilles which were in effect large shipping and forwarding agencies.

The Committee had from the first interested itself in spiritual and intellectual help for prisoners of war and civilian internees, and

---

[1] By July 1940 alone there were 700,000 names indexed.

when numbers were small had taken upon itself to send books to the camps in Germany. In the spring of 1940 when this was no longer practicable, it began the co-ordination of this type of relief through various religious and lay organisations which had hitherto all been active on their own accounts. It presided over an 'Advisory Committee on Reading Matter for Prisoners', which centralised the activities of six such organisations[1] and to which the appropriate requests from camp leaders were passed on. Economic and censorship restrictions had made it a more difficult task than in 1914–18, and this centralisation of effort made the best use of available resources.

Besides these tasks the Committee, by virtue of its recognised neutral status and the expert knowledge it had accumulated through visits to camps and through correspondence with camp leaders, accomplished a great deal by negotiating with belligerents for reciprocal improvements in conditions. It played a leading part in fostering the agreement for setting up the Mixed Medical Commission[2] in Germany, which in June 1940 began examining sick and wounded with a view to the repatriation of those incapable of again taking up arms. It negotiated too in such matters as free postage for the mail of civilian internees, exchange of correspondence between prisoners, and the fixing of pay and upkeep allowances in prisoner-of-war camps. These many and varied war activities placed a heavy strain on the modest financial resources of the Committee and necessitated an appeal to governments and national Red Cross societies.[3] Although the Committee had to resort to a voluntary collection in Switzerland to balance its 1940 budget, the appeal met with a progressively increasing response as the war went on and as the indispensable nature of its relief work for those in enemy countries came to be realised.

In England the prisoner-of-war branch of the War Office also expanded considerably during this period, becoming the Directorate of Prisoners of War. The Inter-departmental Committee[4] on

---

[1] The organisations were: The World Alliance of YMCAs, the International Bureau of Education, the Ecumenical Commission for Assistance to Prisoners of War, the European Student Relief Fund, the International Federation of Library Associations, the Swiss Catholic Mission for Prisoners of War. The relief included the sending of school and university textbooks, periodicals, articles for use in religious services, artists' materials, games and sporting gear.

[2] Article 69 of the 1929 Geneva Convention provides for the appointment of Mixed Medical Commissions of three members (two neutral and one appointed by the detaining power) to examine sick and wounded with a view to their repatriation.

[3] The New Zealand National Patriotic Fund sent a first contribution of £500 in December 1940. From 1 September 1939 to 31 December 1946 the IRCC spent 55 million Swiss francs on war work, of which governments and other agencies contributed 27 million; a special Relief Department for dealing with relief supplies cost 15 million, all raised by national contributions.

[4] See p. 10.

prisoners of war and civilian internees met regularly. It was concerned primarily with financial matters such as fixing the rates of exchange for prisoner-of-war pay in enemy countries,[1] and limiting the use of British currency on goods sent to prisoner-of-war camps. Nevertheless the more pressing general problems relating to prisoners of war in Germany—such as the supply of relief food—came in for full discussion; and general policy had often to be thrashed out before financial detail could be settled. Moreover, as the Committee dealt also with problems relating to the custody of enemy prisoners, of whom some were being accommodated in Canada by January 1941 and others were likely to be transferred to Australia, South Africa and India, Commonwealth governments became involved in its work. The necessity for some central body to lay down general policy on all prisoner-of-war matters[2] concerning the British Commonwealth gradually came to be recognised; and early in 1941 an inter-governmental committee was set up under the chairmanship of the financial secretary to the War Office. Two sub-committees were to attend to detail:

Sub-Committee A, to deal with general questions,
Sub-Committee B, to deal with financial questions, thereby superseding the Inter-departmental Committee.[3]

Commonwealth governments were to be represented on the new main committee and Sub-Committee A.[4] Through the High Commissioner's Office and the service liaison offices in London, the New Zealand Government was kept in touch with any arrangements being made on behalf of British Commonwealth prisoners and internees. The information was passed on to relatives and others interested in New Zealand by the service branches concerned, or by the Department of Internal Affairs in the case of inquiries relating to civilians.

V: *Work of Relief Organisations*

Throughout the period under review the British Red Cross was still almost alone in supplying and organising the sending of relief in kind to Commonwealth prisoners of war and internees. The increase in numbers resulting from the land operations of 1940 had a profound effect on its work. It involved a huge expansion of output, necessitating the training of new staff and the establishment

---

[1] The rates agreed on finally with enemy governments were:
Germany   15 RM = £1
Italy   72 lire = £1

[2] A similar body for civilians was not set up until 1944, though Dominion governments were consulted when necessary.

[3] The 'United Kingdom Departments of State concerned' were, however, to be represented on the inter-governmental committee.—Army Council memorandum of 23 June 1941.

[4] By July 1941 they had representatives on Sub-Committee B as well.

of new packing centres at a time when the bombing of Britain began seriously to affect the whole life of the country.

With thousands now to cater for instead of hundreds, it was essential that the best use should be made of the funds and the forwarding space available. As a first step, further attention was devoted to determining the optimum content of food parcels from all points of view. Nutrition, packing space, keeping quality, the lack of cooking facilities in camps, and the satisfaction of requests from camp leaders were all taken into account. This work became the responsibility of a special committee, comprising not only representatives of the relevant departments of the British Red Cross but also dietetic advisers from the War Office and the Ministry of Food. Average diets were worked out from the camp ration scales and menus reported by the Protecting Power and International Red Cross Committee representatives. Food parcels were then planned, which when added to the camp rations would produce a satisfactory diet in calories, vitamins, and other essential food constituents.

Rationing and cost too began to play a part for the first time. As time went on it was found that the amount of food sent could be reduced. After some experiment it was cut down in August 1940 to one 11-pound parcel each week, which remained standard for the rest of the war. The value of ten shillings a parcel[1] fixed in early 1940 was not however reduced, as it was felt that anything lower would not give sufficient nutritive value; and even rising costs in the later war years were not allowed to interfere with this. In October 1940 the British Board of Customs and Excise allowed dutiable goods for prisoner-of-war parcels to be purchased duty free, thus helping to offset the increasing prices. In January 1941 the Canadian Red Cross began shipping small quantities of its own food parcels direct to the distribution route. This was the beginning of a form of Commonwealth aid which was to greatly relieve the strain on Britain's home food resources. To cater for the many sick and wounded, quantities of invalid food to supplement their diet, together with medical and surgical supplies, were sent to Geneva and to camp infirmaries and hospitals.

The increased numbers confirmed the impracticability of addressing food parcels to individuals. With the notification machinery on both sides in its formative stage, it took considerable time for all names of prisoners and their locations to come through; and the sorting-out process in Germany made camp addresses quickly out of date. There resulted a great deal of inequality of distribution, which with a primary necessity like food was the cause of much ill-feeling, for not all camps had adopted the principle of pooling.[2]

---

[1] This cost included food, soap, cigarettes and tobacco, packing materials and freight.
[2] For similar reasons a ban had been placed on the *sending* of food *by* private individuals.

In August 1940 the practice was begun of consigning food parcels in bulk to the International Red Cross Committee which, by keeping in close touch with the present and probable future situation at camps, could ensure a prompt and adequate distribution.

Clothing had now become a serious problem. Early in 1940 the matter of clothing for prisoners had been under consideration by service departments, for the German supply under Article 12[1] of the Geneva Prisoners of War Convention had been found inadequate if the prisoner was to maintain his morale and self-respect. An attempt had been made to negotiate an agreement by which the prisoner's country of origin would supply his uniform, as it was felt that the supplying of large numbers of prisoners with appropriate uniforms might prove embarrassing to both sides. In the meantime service departments had begun to supply uniforms for other rank prisoners to the British Red Cross for onward transmission, officer prisoners having to pay for their own. Faced now with catering for an additional forty-odd thousand, the War Office supplied this number of greatcoats and battle dress in bulk;[2] and these were despatched by the British Red Cross before the end of the year, together with smaller quantities of clothing for sailors and airmen. In addition the British Red Cross supplied and sent 24,000 sets of underclothing and other articles similar to the contents of an 'initial parcel.'[3] This emergency coped with, it was obvious that the British Red Cross could not continue to finance such a project. After inter-departmental conferences early in 1941, it was decided that it should be responsible only for the provision of socks and toilet articles; uniform, underclothing, and blankets were to become the responsibility of the service departments.[4]

The examination, repacking, and despatch of 'personal' parcels from next-of-kin also began to develop into a task of alarming size; but after inter-departmental discussion it was felt that this could still be most economically undertaken by the British Red Cross. Accordingly a special Next-of-kin Section was set up at St. James's Palace to maintain card-indexes for all prisoners and next-of-kin, and to send the latter the necessary instructions, labels, and documents. At the same time a Next-of-kin Parcels Centre was established at Finsbury Circus to examine and re-pack all the parcels sent in. By the end of December a highly efficient organisation had been evolved with a staff of 65, and some 41,000 parcels had been dealt with and sent off.

---

[1] See p. 26, note 1.
[2] At a cost of £206,000.
[3] See Chapter 1. The cost was £85,000.
[4] A supply of uniforms alone for two years for 50,000 was budgeted at £692,007.

The problem of finding someone to act as next-of-kin in the United Kingdom for the sending of parcels to Dominion prisoners was solved in New Zealand's case by giving the task to Mr. C. B. Burdekin, OBE, of the High Commissioner's Office in London. The arrangement was to supply regular parcels for those without next-of-kin in the United Kingdom, and to make up the weight in any parcel sent in by next-of-kin or friends which was short of the maximum allowed. Any articles so provided were purchased by the New Zealand War Services Association,[1] reimbursed by the National Patriotic Fund, and the New Zealand Joint Council's representative in London was consulted when necessary on matters of policy. The parcels were packed at the New Zealand Forces Club in Charing Cross Road, and on 7 December 1940 the first parcel was despatched.

In August, too, there was established the 'permit' system by which anyone could send cigarettes and tobacco through an English firm which held the required government permit to export in this way. Many New Zealanders were thus able to receive parcels from friends or relatives in the United Kingdom. The British Red Cross as a permit holder continued to send also on its own account cigarettes and tobacco in bulk, and no longer included them in food parcels. As from March 1941 cigarettes and tobacco were also sent each month by the New Zealand War Services Association through a London firm, with whom the arrangements were made by the High Commissioner's Office. In a similar way members of the public could now send books, music, games, cards, and sports equipment. And in the late autumn of 1940, after the more urgent matters of food, clothing, and invalid comforts were well in hand, a new Fiction and Games Section[2] of the British Red Cross made itself responsible for regular consignments of lighter books and material for indoor recreation.[3] It began the task of selecting and despatching books for building up camp libraries to satisfy all tastes.

The despatch from England of educational books and correspondence courses for prisoners of war had been postponed. The former, it was felt, might prejudice the despatch of urgently needed food parcels. The latter might restrict correspondence with relatives and might impose a strain on British censorship if German and Italian prisoners were granted similar privileges. By the end of the year, however, the Educational Books Section of the British Red Cross was reorganised and transferred to the New Bodleian Library

---

[1] Formed in London in November 1939. This Association, the Joint Council, the National Patriotic Fund Board, and the High Commissioner's Office co-operated in all matters relating to relief for New Zealand prisoners of war and interned civilians.
[2] Called at first the Indoor Recreations Section.
[3] The New Zealand Joint Council reimbursed the British Red Cross for this service from the National Patriotic Fund at the rate of 5s. a year for each New Zealand prisoner of war.

at Oxford, to cater for the large response to the questionnaire regarding study sent to camps early in 1940 and for the needs of the thousands of new prisoners. It aimed at enabling the prisoner of war to spend the enforced leisure of captivity in fitting himself by study for peacetime work after his release. Besides satisfying individual requests for books and courses, it helped the organisation of educational facilities in the camps and made arrangements for prisoners to sit examinations there which would further qualify them in their chosen vocations. Under the chairmanship of the Master of Balliol College, Oxford, the section's advisory committee in 1941 persuaded more and more educational bodies and professional institutions to provide study facilities and to recognise examinations held in prisoner-of-war camps.

The invasion of Belgium by the Germans in May 1940 caused the abandonment of the Ostend–overland route for relief consignments and the establishment of a new one to French ports, overland through France to Switzerland, and so on to Germany. A month later the collapse of France put an end to this too, and considering the uncertainty then prevailing in England regarding the future of the war it is not surprising that for a month and a half no despatches were sent off by the General Post Office. By 24 July the best that could be arranged for bulk consignments was a complicated route to Lisbon, through Portugal, Spain, Vichy France, to the International Red Cross Committee in Switzerland, and so to camps.[1] Gift parcels from friends and relatives were able to avoid the most difficult stage of this route, as they could simply be sent through any neutral country.

It was soon realised that, owing to the time now taken and the interruptions in transit, needs would have to be estimated if possible some time in advance; and to secure smooth delivery, reserves would have to be built up at nodal points all along the route. For, although between 500,000 and 600,000 parcels were shipped by the end of the year, the many rail changes and the slowness of the new route prevented sufficient deliveries to camps and caused a vast accumulation at Lisbon. A British Red Cross official was sent there to investigate and succeeded in chartering a Portuguese vessel to go to Marseilles, whence the International Red Cross Committee guaranteed transport to Geneva. With the consent of the British postal authorities, a relief shipment sailed on 22 December. This temporary expedient to relieve the bottleneck at Lisbon was soon recognised as the only practical route. Four more ships sailed in

---

[1] The gap in supplies thus created was partly met by purchase of bulk food in Switzerland and Balkan neutrals. But this was not before there had been a period of acute shortage of food in camps, resulting in much concern among next-of-kin and demands for the right to send personal parcels of food.

January 1941 and by April Lisbon was clear of parcels, with three ships on a regular run to maintain the flow.[1] By mid-1941 camps in Germany were getting regular and adequate supplies.

There was at this stage little point in attempting to organise relief in New Zealand when the necessary machinery was already so well established in England. The Joint Council kept in touch with its British counterpart, passing on such information as might help next-of-kin and friends in communicating with a prisoner or in sending gifts to him.[2] By an arrangement made with the British Red Cross in May 1940, the National Patriotic Fund was to meet the cost of the food and clothing sent to New Zealanders.[3] In May, too, the Joint Council launched an appeal for funds in New Zealand which in just over a month realised more than £500,000, some of which was immediately donated to the British Red Cross in recognition of the work it was doing.[4]

VI: *Germans and Italians interned in New Zealand*

Reference has already been made to the New Zealand Government's decision to intern a number of Germans and Austrians whom it was thought unwise either to leave at liberty or to repatriate. The entry of Italy into the war entailed further security measures, this time involving Italians living in New Zealand, some of whom it seemed desirable to intern. In June 1940, partly to allay public uneasiness, special alien tribunals were set up, on the pattern of those in the United Kingdom, to examine police evidence concerning aliens and to decide what precautionary action should be taken in each case. The small Italian communities scattered throughout New Zealand, most of them engaged in fishing or farming, were found to contain a number of Fascist Party members. A branch of the party had been set up in New Zealand in 1927 and had been fostered by the Italian consulate. By 1941 it had been found necessary to detain on Somes Island some 86 men, of ages ranging from 22 to 63 years, and grouped broadly as 58 Germans or Aus-

---

[1] In fact there was established a steamship service under a neutral flag between Lisbon and Marseilles. The crews were neutral and the ships bore the Red Cross emblem and carried an IRCC convoy agent. The ships were chartered by the national Red Cross societies and running costs were apportioned.

[2] The Joint Council, besides being in direct postal communication with the British Red Cross, had a liaison officer in London, Colonel B. Myers, CMG.

[3] At that stage the annual cost for one prisoner of war was:
        Food   £41 12s.
        Clothing   £7

[4] £10,000 was paid in June to the Lord Mayor of London's appeal for the British Red Cross.

trians, 25 Italians, a Norwegian, a Pole, and a Russian.[1] No women or children were ever interned.[2]

It has been shown that from the first the authorities in New Zealand were resolved to be above any possible reproach in their treatment of enemy nationals; and it is clear that every effort was made subsequently to minimise the discomforts of those interned. The originally high standard of the internment camp diet was more than maintained, and we hear from an International Red Cross visitor that 'Italians make as much as 75% of their own meals. They make spaghetti with eggs and flour, go fishing and smoke their fish in a special shack put up on the beach.' To guard against undernourishment each internee was given half a pint of fresh milk a day, exclusive of that used in cooking.

Camp routine appears not to have been too hard to bear. Four hours were set aside each morning for camp duties: cleaning out rooms, airing bedding, and cultivating vegetable gardens. This done, the internees were free to apportion their time as they wished. For their convenience there were dining rooms and restrooms where continuous fires burned; a piano in the guard hut could be used whenever desired; tennis and bowls were available, and for winter use there was a long hut with facilities for deck tennis, table tennis, quoits, and other indoor games; and each barrack had a small library of fifty novels, in addition to the main camp library. Two-thirds of a long hut was set aside for 'manual work', where the Italians in particular 'do excellent work with shells, make plaster statuettes, wooden toys, models of ships and pretty inlaid tables.'[3] The remainder of this hut housed the school, where languages and other subjects were studied, books being supplied by Victoria University College, the National Library Service, and the Protecting Power for German interests. In addition there was a general workshop hut, with barber, watchmaker, and the main library. The clothing provided seems to have given no cause for complaint.[4] The canteen sold tobacco, cigars and cigarettes, chocolate, condensed milk, biscuits, wine, beer, and soap, at prices from five to ten per cent lower than the retail price in Wellington. One bottle of beer a day and one bottle of wine a week was the allow-

---

[1] Of the Germans twelve were naturalised and two were 'Germans but not identified as such'; of the Austrians one was naturalised; of the Italians eight were naturalised.
[2] Two German women were held at Point Halswell in Wellington for a short period in 1940, but were released and repatriated through Japan.
[3] Report of the IRCC delegate. This work was not allowed to be sold, nor were any arrangements made for the internees to do paid work. On the other hand, all their creature comforts were amply provided for, and many of the internees had independent means, amounting in some cases to £4 or £5 a week.
[4] The clothing provided included for each man: woollen pullover, woollen underpants, woollen vests, flannel pyjamas, military boots (2 pairs), serge suit. To quote the IRCC report, 'All these articles are of good quality, especially the suits.'

ance. The visiting International Red Cross delegate was hardly exaggerating when he summed up conditions by saying that 'the treatment generally' was 'excellent'. It was indeed a far cry from the lack of adequate food and clothing, the overcrowding, and the general squalor of the camps at Bordeaux, Sandbostel, and Wülsburg during the same period.[1]

* * * * *

The events of the war referred to at the beginning of this chapter had made Germany the master of the western continental Europe, with Britain left struggling to preserve the integrity of her shores. In the exultation of victory many Germans thought the defeat of Britain only a matter of time—and not a very long time at that. Such a situation might well breed arrogance towards the prisoners of enemy countries already defeated or about to be so, and an inclination to disregard treaty obligations in respect of them.

In May 1940, before the French collapse, an International Red Cross delegate was able to say:

> A great effort is being made everywhere in Germany to lodge the hundreds of thousands of prisoners. . . . The authorities show a fine spirit of understanding. . . .

The fact that comfortless old fortresses and tents were sometimes used for accommodation, that food was 'just sufficient', and that there were always delays in arranging for mail might perhaps be excused in an undertaking of the size necessary to cope with the huge influx of prisoners. But in the months that followed the capitulation of France, there is a good deal of evidence of uncompromising refusal by German camp guards to be in any way restricted in their conduct towards the enemy soldiers who were in their power. There were reprisals for refusal by other ranks to work overtime—withholding of mail and standing to attention for hours on end; there were transfers of prisoners' representatives for 'inciting complaints'; there were long delays before officer prisoners received their pay and other ranks their working wages; there was high-handed action regarding the disposal and distribution of relief supplies sent to camp leaders. As the year drew on, with Britain not only holding out but hitting back, many of the earlier abuses were corrected. The right of prisoners to lay complaints with inspecting officials was grudgingly conceded; the ever-growing stream of British mail and relief supplies was allowed to enter more freely; and in general the traditional German attitude of being *korrekt* in the observance of paper agreements reasserted itself, perhaps because the permanent rank and file of German

---
[1] For a description of St. Médard, Bordeaux, see pp. 35-6; for Stalag XB, Sandbostel, p. 37; for Ilag XIII, Wülsburg, pp. 8 and 38.

officialdom was temporarily saved from that complete dictation by the Nazi Party which a final victory might have imposed.

Against the oppressive weight of German restrictions and the harshness resulting from a tendency on the part of some German guards to exploit to the utmost their power as captors, the British prisoner in time found weapons. There was his own native stubbornness which left him unmoved after torrents of screaming abuse; there was his sense of humour which made him laugh at his misfortunes and brought the sting of ridicule to the enemy's raw spots; there was the cheering news of the Battle of Britain brought in by newly-captured prisoners; there were the gifts of food, clothing, and other comforts which restored his physical energy and gave him a sense of pride in belonging to the country which had sent them; there was the organisation of escapes and anti-propaganda measures which made him feel he was carrying on the fight in some small way. On their side, governments and relief agencies immediately shouldered the burden of supplying him with the extra food and clothing necessary to keep him in health and good heart, until such time as he would be again free to make his contribution to the nation's economy. And lastly, his next-of-kin were at pains to follow the special postal regulations for sending the letters and parcels from home which would bring him the best mental comfort of all.

The beauty of the Italian scene and the volatile lightheartedness of many of its people brightened the first months for prisoners in Italy. Moreover, the Italians were eager to show their civilised attitude towards their fellow-beings, even though prisoners—perhaps especially to the British. In those days of few prisoners it was no great strain on their economy to treat British officers much as they did their own, and to reduce considerably for British other ranks the wide gap that existed between the traditional standards of living of their own officers and other ranks. Then, too, the surrender of their armies in East Africa and the later British successes in Cyrenaica placed a mass of Italians in British hands which far exceeded the number of prisoners they had any prospect of taking. Whatever the value of international conventions, treatment of prisoners tends to be reciprocal; and the nation with a preponderance in numbers captured is placed in a favourable bargaining position. Whether or not such considerations had any restraining influence on the Fascist Government, it seems that many Italians were only too willing to show friendliness to their British 'guests'. Many next-of-kin in New Zealand felt happier when they heard that their sons or husbands were prisoners of the Italians and not in German hands; and it is clear that in the early stage at least their attitude was justified.

CHAPTER 3

The Campaigns of Greece and Crete
(April – October 1941)

I: *The Greek Campaign and Prisoners in Greece*

EARLY in 1941 it was decided to send a British Commonwealth force to help Greece against German invasion from the north. This decision was to involve the 2nd New Zealand Division in a major fighting role for the first time. The experience was to be a short one. The first New Zealanders of the Greek expedition arrived in Piraeus Harbour on 7 March; on 28 April the last of them to take part in the planned evacuation were taken off by sea. In the three weeks that followed its first actions the Division was engaged in a rapid succession of defensive and rearguard actions, delaying the enemy advance and covering its own withdrawal southward. At Mount Olympus, Servia and Platamon, at Tempe and Elasson, at Thermopylae, at Thebes, at Corinth and on the Peloponnese, and almost up to the evacuation beaches themselves, units of the Division were engaged in holding advanced forces of the enemy in check.

A military withdrawal is difficult to accomplish without numbers of troops being left wounded or cut off, especially if the withdrawal has to be carried out rapidly. In a retreat through Greece of some 300 miles in the space of three weeks, over difficult terrain and harassed by the enemy air force, it is perhaps surprising that the numbers left behind were not higher. Besides those captured in action, a few wounded in each engagement missed being brought out, and those cut off in the north had to try and improvise some means of getting away. A number of stragglers did not reach the evacuation areas in time to be taken off, and at some places the evacuation machinery broke down. Of the New Zealanders who remained behind, 1856 fell into German hands as prisoners of war.

By far the greatest number of these were captured near Kalamata,[1] in the southern Peloponnese, where a large number of British Commonwealth reinforcements and base troops from Voula (near Athens) had been moved ready for evacuation. Some 10,000 men

---
[1] The total number captured there according to a German estimate was about 7000. The number of New Zealanders taken was approximately 800.

had collected under cover around the port of Kalamata by 27 April and their evacuation was planned for the 29th. In the early evening of that day German forces, having penetrated the approaches to the area, were able to take possession of the town and seafront. Somehow a counter-attack was organised, and in a brief action marked by one or two feats of great individual gallantry[1] our forces cleared the town of the invaders, inflicted considerable casualties on the enemy, and took some prisoners. When the warships arrived for the evacuation, however, they had time to take on board only a few hundred before withdrawing in accordance with newly-received orders. Ammunition was at a low ebb and many of the troops were unarmed; the Germans were reinforcing ready to renew their attack, and a conference of the senior officers therefore decided to cease further resistance in the early hours of the following morning. This left but little darkness for anyone to escape to the hills through the surrounding German posts. A few succeeded in getting clean away; a number of others stayed in the neighbourhood only to be rounded up in the next few days; most were too tired or bewildered to realise that this was the best opportunity they would have to escape.

When the German forces re-entered the area, their prisoners were liberated and their former captors marched to a holding area in a field on the outskirts of the town. The Germans are reported as having been 'courteous and fair', though lack of shelter made the holding paddock unbearably hot during the day and water supply proved a problem. Their medical officers assisted our own to establish in the town hall an emergency dressing station for the 250-odd British wounded.[2] Within two days all prisoners except these were entrained for Corinth, which had become the prisoner-of-war collecting centre for southern Greece.

In the early stages of the evacuation from Greece about 500 New Zealand sick and wounded, with five medical officers of 1 NZ General Hospital and 40 orderlies, had been moved from a walking-wounded hospital established at Voula to an olive grove on the westerly side of Megara. Their numbers were swollen by the addition of the New Zealand Mobile Dental Unit, the YMCA, Pay Unit, Postal Unit, and various reinforcements from our base at Voula. Some were evacuated on the night of 25–26 April, but the beachmaster at Megara ordered the remainder to proceed to the Peloponnese for evacuation from one of the southern ports.

---

[1] For his part in this action Sgt J. D. Hinton (20 Bn) won the VC.
[2] Maj G. H. Thomson, NZMC, states: 'I was put in the care of the Medical Officer with the German column . . . . he was an excellent man as was their Commandant and they both helped me to the utmost of their capacity during the following three weeks . . . . I have no comment of an adverse nature to make regarding our treatment by the combatant troops at Kalamata.' They were later transported to Kokkinia hospital, arriving on 16 May.

Ambulances sent ahead with patients unable to walk became caught up in the attack on the Corinth bridge by German parachutists, as did the walking wounded following them; and the rest of the party fell into German hands a little later. A good many other New Zealanders were picked up near the evacuation beaches, on islands to which they had made their way, and even on the caiques[1] and launches by which they were preparing to continue their journeys. The action at the Corinth Canal which followed the landing of the German parachutists accounted for further captures, many of them wounded.

For all these prisoners in southern Greece the German evacuation plan was the same: to the collection centre at Corinth, thence to Salonika en route for Austria and Germany. Those captured in the north—at Thermopylae or south of Tempe, for example—would go direct to Salonika, passing sometimes through staging camps at Lamia and Larissa. While awaiting transport to a collection centre they might be held in a field, an empty cottage, a schoolhouse or a cemetery. The Germans put many prisoners immediately to work, and men found themselves in a variety of places ranging from a slaughterhouse or a stables to a German quartermaster's store. There does not seem to have been much looting from prisoners— a practice frowned upon by the German officers, though their troops could offer to buy a prisoner's possessions and often paid a good price. Such interrogation as was done was very perfunctory. No effort was made to insist on answers that were not forthcoming, and sometimes the whole matter was disposed of in friendly conversation amid an atmosphere of the greatest good humour. A victorious army sweeping all before it had perhaps no time to niggle over detail and could afford to be magnanimous. But the interrogations later in the year of captured escapers and evaders, to discover who had helped them and where they had been hiding, were severe and intensive.

The help given by the German medical corps at Kalamata in looking after our wounded was no isolated instance. Reports show that treatment by German medical officers was good and that their conduct generally was correct and humane. It is true that some of our wounded might have had to wait in improvised lock-ups for a day or so with their original field dressings before evacuation, and that there were sometimes delays (at the peak period for casualties) while German wounded were treated first. But in general it seems that serious cases were evacuated as soon as possible to Greek hospitals, where our own medical officers were given facilities to treat them. At Corinth they were taken first to

---

[1] Greek fishing vessel with sail and usually auxiliary engine.

an emergency Greek hospital in a converted schoolhouse; but on 27 April the New Zealand medical officers from Megara were allowed to set up a temporary British hospital in two of the city's hotels, largely as a result of the efforts of a Greek Red Cross worker.[1]

After a fortnight there all patients and staff were moved by ambulance to Piraeus, where the remnants of 5 Australian General Hospital were receiving all British wounded and sick. They had been moved by the Germans to an imposing four-storied, five-block, white stone building standing bathed in sunshine on an area of open wasteland at the foot of the hills behind Piraeus Harbour, and about half a mile above the cluster of houses that made up Nea Kokkinia village. Here British, Australian, and New Zealand medical officers and orderlies were coping with 500-odd cases brought in from emergency dressing stations, using the fairly complete facilities of the Australians and what the Greek Red Cross could supply. Many of our prisoners of war owe limb and life to the operations performed in Kokkinia hospital and to the medical care which followed. To keep enough beds clear for new patients, a walking-wounded and convalescent camp was established in some old Greek barracks below the hospital on the outskirts of Nea Kokkinia.

At the beginning of June, when the influx of wounded from Crete began to arrive by plane, some of the staff were allowed to organise another emergency hospital in the heart of Athens. They were given the large Polytechnic School building with space for 700 beds, and adequate medical facilities appear to have been set up in a very short time. The Germans seem to have left us a fairly free hand at both hospitals. But in both, in spite of help from the Greeks and Red Cross funds, the shortage of food proved a very great difficulty and, especially in dysentery cases, the patients' greatest hurdle to recovery.

Meanwhile the transit camp at Corinth had become filled to overflowing with captured Allied troops, mixed with some 4000 Italians (former prisoners of the Greeks), whom the Germans decided should remain under guard. By 6 May nearly 8000 Australians, British, Cypriots, New Zealanders (1000) and Palestinians, some 350 of them officers, were packed into a sandy area of about 15 acres near the aerodrome on the outskirts of the city.[2] Inside the camp perimeter were some old, verminous, Greek stone barracks

---

[1] Miss Ariadne Massautti commandeered the hotels, persuaded the Germans to allow the transfer there of captured medical personnel, organised the Greek Red Cross sisters and VADs to work there, arranged for supplies of all kinds, and generally set an example of cheerfulness and energy. She was awarded the George Medal for her efforts.
[2] There were also 1100 Yugoslavs. Dr. Brunel, the IRCC delegate, gives the total in the camp (excluding Italians) as 12,000.

and wooden sheds with inadequate ventilation. There was no bed except the cold stone floor, and no blankets beyond what men had brought with them or could in some way lay hands on. A quart of water from one of two primitive wells was the daily allowance for drinking and washing. A huge open-trench latrine over 200 yards long was the only concession to sanitation, and with heat and flies completing a vicious circle, the spread of dysentery was rapid. The camp guards were frequently changed as German units were moved: paratroops, followed by Austrians, then young SS troops, and finally older men unfit for front-line service, who proved to be the most reasonable. There was at times some rough work with rifle butts and a good deal of unnecessary shooting, with resultant casualties in the compound.

Senior officers had a constant struggle to wring something approaching adequate rations from successive German commandants, some at least outwardly courteous but none very concerned about the welfare of a large mob of prisoners. Dried or salt fish, lentils or rice, a little oil, and a hard army biscuit[1] or one-ninth of a loaf of bread, with a very little sugar or honey, were a typical day's rations, the whole estimated at about 800 calories. But it was possible to supplement this to a limited extent. Gifts from the Greek Red Cross[2] of whole sheep and other foods helped to thicken the camp soups. A Greek market allowed to operate inside the camp supplied those who still possessed drachmae. Other ranks sent out on working parties, to the Piraeus aerodrome for example, did not want for whatever the generous Greek population could make available to them, and some of these were able to help out their less fortunate officers. Nevertheless, after a week or two many within the camp began to have the 'black-outs'[3] which were to become a common experience in prisoner-of-war camps short of food; and men acquired the habit of hanging about the camp perimeter in the hope that a friendly Greek might throw them something to eat.

Food soon became a main topic of conversation—the beginning of a preoccupation with diet which was later in Germany to become for many prisoners of war an obsession. Material conditions being thoroughly wretched, men sought escape from their environment not only in memories of good food but also in recalling what they were doing in New Zealand a year back, and perhaps the soldier

---

[1] About 5 ins by 5 ins and about half an inch thick, very like some of our dog biscuits in appearance and flavour.

[2] Besides its own resources, the Greek Red Cross was being supplied with funds by the International Red Cross Committee to expend for British Commonwealth prisoners of war.

[3] Feeling of faintness (actual fainting in extreme cases) on suddenly standing up or other sudden bodily action; attributed by medical officers in prison camps to lack of sufficient nourishment, and also sometimes to prolonged inactivity.

who dreamt one night he was returning to New Zealand on a luxury liner was typical. Escapism took another form when there began to circulate those wild prison-camp rumours, ranging at this stage from the entry of the United States into the war to a promise by Mr. Churchill to have all prisoners released within seven days. Captured chaplains and YMCA secretaries co-operated in organising open-air church services and evening concerts, and for a time a kind of revivalist enthusiasm seems to have swept the camp. Men's pent-up emotions found relief in the mass singing of the popular tune 'There'll Always be an England', when the National Anthem had been banned by the German camp authorities.

The coming and going of Greek vendors in and out of the camp in the first weeks gave many of the Palestinians and Cypriots an easy opportunity to get away, and other prisoners were also able to make a break before German security was tightened up. One New Zealander[1] made his way to Salonika, travelling at times under the coaches of troop trains. He spent a week and a half in Salonika, alternately sheltering with Greek families and spending the night in the streets, as the Germans had announced that Greeks helping British troops would be shot. After hiding for a while in a village some 30 miles to the north, he made his way with the aid of Greek police and civilians to the Agion Oros (Mount Athos) peninsula.[2] Here he was helped with a boat which took him to the island of Imbros, where a party of escapers had collected. Another boat took the party on to Turkey, whence the Turkish authorities returned them to Allied hands over the borders of Syria. It is difficult to say how many prisoners broke out from the Corinth transit camp, as there is no official record of many who temporarily regained their liberty but were recaptured. But this account may be taken as typical of the experiences of some thousands of Allied troops at that time at liberty in Greece.

During the first fortnight of May Dr. Brunel, the International Red Cross delegate, was able to visit the camp three times, bringing quantities of medicines and toilet articles. The rations began to improve in both quantity and quality, and more Red Cross food began to make its way into the camp. Prisoners were allowed to go bathing in parties in the Gulf of Corinth, a concession which made the problem of personal cleanliness much easier to solve. Even so a medical inspection in early June found 20 per cent of the camp infested with lice. The Germans allowed each prisoner to send off

---

[1] Tpr A. Connelly (Div Cav), mentioned in despatches.
[2] Agion Oros (Holy Mountain) is the name given to the Athos Peninsula which contains many Greek Orthodox monasteries. The most easterly of the three south-pointing fingers of northern Greece, it was used by many escapers as an embarkation point in attempts to reach Turkey by boat.

a first capture-card and several letters. However, the improvement in conditions received a setback towards the end of May. There had been much speculation in the camp from 20 May onwards concerning a noticeable increase in air activity, particularly on the large numbers of troop-carriers passing overhead. This speculation was set at rest about a week later, when some naval prisoners from Crete began to arrive, and when the German commandant closed the camp market, cut down the rations, and generally toughened up discipline as a reprisal for alleged ill-treatment of German parachutists on Crete by the British. Two days later the charge was admitted to be baseless. On 3 June considerable numbers of prisoners started to arrive from Crete, and a day or so later prisoners began to move from Corinth to swell the stream of captured Allied humanity now flowing north through Salonika and Yugoslavia to prisoner-of-war camps in Austria, Germany, and Poland.

In the early hours of 5 June the first party of some hundreds, including most of the officers, marched the eight miles to connect with the train on the other side of the Corinth Canal. After some weeks of comparative inactivity and poor food, many found such a march, carrying all their belongings, a strenuous one. But the 25-mile trek which followed the train journey to Gravia (near Levadhia), over the hot, dusty shingle of the 4000-foot Brallos Pass, left everyone exhausted. They had been warned beforehand that any man falling out would have to discard all his gear, an order which made them angry and determined. No one fell out on this party, though two of a later party died on the road. A few had the daring to break from the dusty line of march, ducking into the scrub by the roadside, and the good luck to remain undiscovered, until nightfall enabled them to get clean away. Near Lamia, on the other side of the pass, the prisoners were packed into cattle-trucks and carried north to Salonika,[1] where they were marched through the crowded streets to the prison barracks. They were spared more than a day or so in this place, and then, again pushed into cattle-trucks, they began their long journey north to Germany.[2] In the week that followed, the exodus from Corinth continued, and the evacuation was reported to be complete by 11 June. Some parties went through to Germany almost immediately, but numbers of men had to remain at Salonika to work for the Germans and to endure for some time longer conditions similar to those they had already experienced in other German transit camps in Greece.

---

[1] There was one other break in the line of a mile or so near Platamon.
[2] Subsequent parties had very similar experiences, except that many were able to get food and drink from friendly Greeks who were waiting along the route, at great risk to themselves from some of the German guards. Many of the later parties stayed some time in Salonika transit camp.

II : *The Crete Campaign—Prisoners in Greece and Germany*

Three weeks after the British evacuation from Greece those British, Australian, and New Zealand troops who were put ashore on the island of Crete had, together with the small British garrison, to defend it from invasion. With barely time to recover from fatigue, to regroup, and to take up defensive positions with the inadequate weapons available, these troops had to deal with a full-scale airborne attack. Preceded by bombing, the first units of the German air invasion force, previously assembled on the Greek mainland, landed on the island on 20 May. The invaders were superior in weapons and were in complete control of the air. Fortunately the Royal Navy made the situation less hopeless by destroying or dispersing the seaborne landing force. The enemy on Crete were at first more than held in some desperate fighting; but once their bridgehead had been strongly reinforced, the British forces were driven back in a series of defensive actions and withdrawals. There was little time for a carefully planned sea evacuation such as that from Greece, and naval losses left fewer ships available. Under such circumstances it was inevitable that many would be left behind, and after the last warship had pulled away from its position off Sfakia in the early morning of 1 June 1941, a large number of our troops still remained ashore.

Of this number some 520 New Zealand wounded had been taken prisoner either on the battlefield or in the first-aid posts and hospitals cut off from possible evacuation by the German advance.[1] Apart from other odd groups similarly cut off all along the north-western sector of the island and a few stragglers on the withdrawal routes south, most of those captured were taken near the beach at Sfakia. As in Greece, not all who remained behind fell into enemy hands, and many did so only after a considerable period of liberty. A few made their way in various craft direct to North Africa; many went into hiding on the island and were undiscovered by the enemy for up to two years. Some of the latter got boats and reached Greece or one of the islands of the Aegean, and many of these were able to make good their escape to Turkey or Libya. Nevertheless the great majority of those not evacuated were rounded up by the German forces. In all 2180 of the New Zealanders in Crete became prisoners of war—the largest number to be captured in any single campaign in New Zealand's history.

Some of these had been taken prisoner near Maleme as early as

---

[1] The figure 520 includes those who died of wounds in captivity. A good many walking wounded were able to make their way to the evacuation beach and were among the first to embark on each evacuation night.

21 May. After a brief search for arms they were immediately made to work on the airfield, dragging away wreckage and unloading planes,[1] carrying wounded and burying dead. Even had they known that the Geneva Convention exempted them from such work —and most prisoners had barely heard of it—their protests at this stage would have availed them little.[2] The German invasion troops had suffered heavy losses and were desperately trying to maintain their bridgehead: they were certainly in no mood to discuss the niceties of international law. A YMCA secretary was forced at rifle point to carry containers of ammunition; a chaplain was put to digging graves alongside the airfield, others to filling in shell holes and sandbagging gun emplacements. Among those pressed into service were walking wounded and dysentery cases. Some worked there for several days under fire from our own artillery and occasional bombing, suffering casualties as a result. No rations were issued and prisoners were left to find their own food.

Those who managed to avoid being thus commandeered for forced labour on the airfield were taken to a holding area near Maleme on the western bank of the Tavronitis River. This the Germans had established early in the battle for captures in the Maleme sector. There they were searched, and all papers, steel helmets, possible weapons, and occasionally valuables were taken. The Germans seem to have wasted little time in interrogation.[3] One New Zealand officer who had commanded Greeks received an intensive questioning, but it was usually a cursory affair, mixed with conversation on such propaganda lines as, 'Why come so far to fight for England?'[4] In the early stages of the battle for Crete the disorganisation of the German forces probably precluded immediate interrogation; and the speed of the German advance once it got under way superseded any tactical advantage that interrogation might normally be expected to give. So far as it concerned information of strategical or political value, the German Army does not appear to have developed interrogation much beyond the type of thing quoted above and the 'Red Cross form'[5] which

---

[1] Prisoners captured in the German thrust into Libya at this period were being similarly forced to unload 'bombs, food and petrol from JU 52's', and protests had been made through the Foreign Office.—War Office Directorate of Prisoners of War report for week ending 5 July 1941.
[2] According to evidence supplied in the trial of General Student for war crimes, three men who did so were immediately taken aside and shot.
[3] One or two German soldiers demanded, under threat of shooting, information regarding minefields ahead, but this does not fall into the category of what is usually understood by interrogation.
[4] Similar questions or expressions of surprise at the Dominions' having sent expeditionary forces to aid Britain were the experience of many other prisoners both at this and at later stages of the war.
[5] See Chapter 2, p. 23.

was issued later at the transit camp. In general, beside the interrogation methods of the Luftwaffe, even in this early period, those of the Wehrmacht look rather like the work of amateurs.

At the holding area near Maleme, as at the airfield, there was no attempt to provide rations, and for the first few days there was some kicking and other rough treatment from nervy and ill-tempered guards. The Germans claimed to have found some of their men horribly mutilated and suspected the British troops, though they later admitted this to be quite unjustified. Nevertheless for those captured while the rumour was current, the situation was ugly. A chaplain and some walking wounded were lined up against the outside wall of their RAP ready to be shot, and were saved only by the intervention of a German wounded officer who had been well treated. Similar timely pleas by recaptured Germans probably saved many others, and those who found themselves the prisoners of their former captives reaped the reward of their own treatment of the enemy. The front-line German troops were on the whole much better in their behaviour than some elements of the occupation force which later carried out such brutal mass executions of the Cretan civilian population.

The alleged German use of prisoners during the Crete battle as a 'screen' between themselves and British fire became in New Zealand a matter for public controversy at the time of the War Crimes trial of General Student.[1] That prisoners were placed in this unenviable situation is clearly stated by so many survivors of the 'screen', as well as by those who tried to fire through it, that it may be taken as established. That it was the German troops' intention to use them thus, much less General Student's, is not so clear. A large body of prisoners in the custody of three or four guards would inevitably have to be driven ahead of them, if it were to move at all. The reconstruction in 1946 of the motives behind the conduct of German troops and commanders in the heat of a battle fought in 1941 must have been a task fraught with great difficulty. Our own arrangements for the treatment of prisoners in the field at this stage of the war were of the haziest, and it is not impossible that enemy instructions to their lower ranks on the same topic were equally sketchy.

The average German soldier seems in fact to have been at a loss to know what to do with wounded prisoners. A New Zealand NCO found lying wounded near the crossroads at Galatas was given

---

[1] The German officer commanding the airborne invasion force in Crete. His trial as a war criminal took place in Germany during May 1946. He was found guilty of being responsible for cold-blooded shootings and for the use of prisoners in unloading warlike stores, but not for the use of prisoners as a 'screen'. He was sentenced to five years' imprisonment, but the sentence was not confirmed. See also New Zealand Official History, *Crete*.

a field dressing and then fired on after the German soldier had walked twenty yards away. But those that followed later gave him drugs and filled his empty water bottle; and next day he was taken to Maleme in an ambulance. Wounded captured near Maleme airfield were brought back to a German dressing station in a wine-cellar in Tavronitis village, and then taken on to the prisoners' holding area. A wounded officer recounts how in the cellar a German with an arm wound gave him his chair, and how he received kindly, though little, attention from German medical orderlies in the holding area. When the British withdrawal began, wounded left behind in RAPs were brought back behind the German lines in trucks. Those of our own medical officers who had remained with their wounded were given a free hand to treat and nurse them, and a German medical unit helped them with dressings, instruments, drugs and anaesthetics. The wounded in 7 General Hospital on the coast north of Galatas were 'well looked after by the Germans'. On the other hand the Suda Bay hospital, after being inspected by the enemy, was ignored for the first week. Cretans brought the patients food, and without their kindness they would have been on the way to starvation. One New Zealand dressing station in the village of Neon Khorion, about three miles from Kalivia, actually had a month's supply of food taken away by the invaders. But once the Germans had stabilised their position they did what they could to help, and some of those stationed near an Australian dressing station at Kalivia came into the wards in the evening to share their cigarettes and chat. One prisoner writes: '. . . our talks were of a friendly nature. No mentioning anything detrimental to either side. Neither side bothered about information. . . .'[1]

Although very little food was supplied, the treatment of our wounded by the German medical corps seems to have been as humane as it was within their power to be. Our own doctors speak of their correct behaviour and co-operation. From the first day the policy seems to have been to fly the badly wounded direct to Greece,[2] and British and Germans took their places in the earliest planes according to the seriousness of their condition. In little over a week all cases needing evacuation had been emplaned in Ju52s and landed at Athens, Corinth, or Larissa.[3] Thence an ambulance or truck—the journey in the latter sometimes made needlessly rough and painful by the whim of a callous driver—brought them to the hospital at Kokkinia, near Piraeus, or to the

---

[1] Statement by a wounded New Zealand sergeant.
[2] By 5 June 220 officers and 976 other ranks of the Commonwealth forces had been flown to Athens.
[3] The aircraft were not marked as ambulance planes, and at least one carrying wounded was shot down on the way to Greece.

newly set up emergency hospital in the Polytechnic School at Athens. Both were now running smoothly under the control of our own medical personnel, and although some of the wounded were beyond recovery when they arrived, hundreds of others were nursed back to health in the months that followed.

Near the southern village of Sfakia on 1 June the last scenes of the battle of Crete were being enacted. From hill positions overlooking the coast, German alpine troops began mortaring the miscellaneous remnants of the British forces below. Many of them had been without food for several days, and though most had carried their arms, ammunition was in negligible supply. It was known that no further major evacuation was possible, and to avoid purposeless loss of life orders to capitulate had been passed on to senior officers at an early morning conference. There was no alternative for the men but to abandon any thought of further resistance and destroy what weapons they could. When the Germans arrived there was a light search and a German officer gave an address on the exceptional amenities to be found in Germany's prisoner-of-war camps. The crowd of prisoners was moved uphill to a village, and in the afternoon, formed into groups of 200-odd, began the long trek back over the hills to the north.

There were no rations and little water until the end of the second day's march, and for men who started tired and hungry the going was strenuous along hot and dusty roads under a burning sun. Hurried slaking of parched mouths indiscriminately at whatever pools and streams appeared along the route, no doubt bred much of the disease which appeared later. The German guards on the whole do not seem to have been brutal, though they kept the line of march going so that all the prisoners had completed the thirty miles to the north coast by 3 June. Many fell sick by the roadside —an officer who had stuck it out sat down quietly in a doorway in Canea and died; and the exhaustion from the march no doubt helped the mounting toll of sickness among the mob of prisoners now collecting at the former 7 General Hospital area.

This had been chosen as the site for the main prisoner-of-war camp on the island. Here, on a sandy coastal area three miles west of Canea, a mass of prisoners was being herded together to form 'Dulag Kreta', better known to most of the prisoners as 'Galatos Camp'. Prior to the arrival of the long columns from Sfakia, a chaplain and one or two NCOs had succeeded in achieving reasonable order among the small numbers there, salvaging enough bivouac tents to give everyone shelter. But the masses of new arrivals swamped the available facilities, though a New Zealand hospital corporal who had established an RAP made a great effort to cope with the daily sick parade of several hundred. As they straggled in, hungry, bedraggled and weary from the march north —Australians, British, Cypriots, Greeks and New Zealanders— they lay down on any available open space under what makeshift covering from the blazing sun they could improvise. Dormitory, meal area or latrine, it was all the same—whatever arrangement gave the least effort. For water there were long queues at an old well of the type once worked by an ox. Many of the dead lay still unburied along the roads, in ditches, and among the olive groves, and an overpowering stench and buzzing bluebottles dominated the camp area. Sickness and hunger helped to bring morale to a low ebb. Many, incensed at being the victims of what seemed yet another fiasco, somewhat naturally blamed their commanders and those in charge of the general conduct of the war, and some in their bitter disappointment vowed that they were glad to be prisoners to let someone else have a turn at being muddled about to no purpose.

Gradually officers and NCOs were able to create some kind of order. By 8 June the Australians had been moved elsewhere and the 5000-odd remaining had been organised into groups (one containing 1500 New Zealanders), an area had been allocated to each, and the senior British officer with his adjutant had appointed NCOs to take charge of them. On the 9th the officers were flown to Greece, with the exception of nine who were kept for administrative and medical duties at the camp. Enough tents were salvaged to put everyone under cover in orderly rows, and shovels were obtained to enable proper latrines to be dug. The three hospital buildings, together with a few marquees, were organised by the senior medical officer as a 200-bed camp reception hospital. The poor food, overcrowding, and insanitary conditions produced a crop of scabies and dysentery.[1] These cases and others of malaria, of poliomyelitis,[2] and of woundings by trigger-happy guards kept the five hospital wards full and their staffs continually occupied.[3] After a few weeks the sick and wounded from the dressing stations near Suda, together with the medical staffs looking after them, were brought in too.

Rations were never sufficient[4] to keep men healthy, and for some weeks the guards winked at prisoners' leaving camp to get fruit

---

[1] 'During June, July and August, estimated that every prisoner of war had at least one attack, and many two of sonne dysentery.'—Lt-Col W. H. B. Bull, NZMC, *Medical Report on Prisoner of War Life in Crete*.

[2] '. . . in all some 15 cases of infantile paralysis appeared with no more deaths.'—Ibid. The first case had proved fatal.

[3] The fact that, in spite of the unhealthy conditions in the camp and the lack of facilities in the hospital, only 23 deaths are recorded from 1212 admissions is a tribute to the work of the medical staff.

[4] Approximately 1000 calories daily.

and other food nearby and allowed Cretans to bring basket-loads to the camp fence. Authorised foraging parties too were allowed to bring in rice and other supplies from British dumps. When the German food supply became more regular, prisoners' daily meals resolved themselves into a cup of porridge or rice, a cup of bean stew, and two-thirds of a pound of sometimes sour and mouldy bread. With such a meagre and monotonous diet, it is perhaps not surprising to find men boiling up bird-seed and finding it good, fighting for food at the camp fences, and scavenging in a rubbish heap for mouldy bread discarded as unfit for human consumption.

Beyond the fatigues of the camp there was little for men to do but sleep during the day, unless they had drawn a place in one of the German burial or working parties.[1] The former were avoided as hard and unpleasant work, the latter sought after for the opportunities afforded of picking up extra food. A stretch of beach included in the camp bounds became a means at once of recreation and cleanliness, and was probably the reason that the camp remained so long free of vermin. In the later stages there were improvised games of cricket. In addition to two church services daily, the chaplain organised evening concerts and debates. A wireless set smuggled in by a working party enabled him to tack a news session on to the evening service. Morale improved and the wave of fantastic rumours which swept the camp in its initial stages gave place to a more reasoned and sober view of the war.

At Dulag Kreta there was no issue of capture-cards[2] within the first week or so, and it seems doubtful whether the early nominal rolls at any rate were ever sent on by the Germans. It happened, therefore, that men got away from the camp before they were officially prisoners of war, and their activities are therefore outside the scope of this volume. Yet many were in fact several weeks in enemy hands before making a break, and the Crete escapes[3] are so numerous that they constitute a notable feature of the campaign. It is largely guesswork even to estimate the numbers who broke from captivity there, just as it is difficult to disentangle evaders from escapers among those who got back to Allied territory direct from Crete, those who made their way to Greece or one of the

---

[1] ' By arrangement with the Germans, many parties were sent to Galatos for the purpose of identifying & marking British graves.'—Lt-Col Bull, op. cit.
[2] There was an issue of field postcards on 26 June, which were sent off later from Germany after censorship. One bears the censorship stamp of Stalag VIIIB and postmark 18 October. It reached New Zealand in late December. None seem to have gone to Geneva.
[3] Over sixty New Zealand escapers got back to Alexandria by submarine. This made up the majority of our escapers, a few others having got back via Greece or the Aegean islands. A number of *evaders* (men who had successfully evaded capture) got back by these two routes and a few direct to North Africa. See also New Zealand Official War History, *Crete*, Appendix VII.

Aegean islands and got back from there, and those who were finally recaptured or had to give themselves up, too sick to continue. But as numbers of eye-witnesses speak of 'men breaking out every night', of thirty getting away in one such party and fifteen in another, it is clear that the numbers were considerable.[1] In July New Zealanders and Australians were stated to be at large all over the western end of the island, a dozen or more in many villages.

Most of the escapes took place in June and July[2] from the Galatas camp, where the prisoners were at first 'loosely guarded'. It was said to be comparatively 'easy' to crawl out at night under the wire of the compound after a sentry had passed, and under cover of darkness to make the shelter of the vineyards and olive groves across the road. Although some of the nearby fields were occasionally lit up by Very lights and raked with German machine-gun fire, no one appears to have been hit, and the risk seems to have been discounted when planning an escape. In the early days of the camp some of the prisoners were allowed out unofficially to forage for food in Canea or neighbouring villages, and some casually walked away from these outings. For most men it was the lack of food and the appalling conditions of the camp which determined them in desperation to go and live elsewhere (even if only temporarily), quite apart from whether it would be possible to escape from the island. They made for the green slopes leading to the mountains behind, and many collected in the Omolos plateau high up among the ranges. Some roamed about the hills for months, following the mule-tracks from village to village, before stumbling on a means of getting away. Others lived on among the Cretans for a year or so, unable to get a boat, and were eventually recaptured. The idea of securing a boat to escape in had been in the minds of some escapers when they left the camp. But although in the period just following the end of the planned evacuation a party of evaders had reached the coast of North Africa in an MLC,[3] and others had got away in caiques and launches, the Germans afterwards kept a close check on all such craft and on likely evacuation points along the coastline.

The Cretans were almost invariably kind and helpful. From almost every escaper the story is one of good reception at their hands. Food, civilian clothes, guides and money were given freely,

---

[1] The New Zealand officer in charge of the compound of Greeks puts the figure of escapes from his compound at close on 400.
[2] At least forty of the ultimately successful New Zealand escapers got away in June and 13 in July. On the night of 18 June alone 30 broke out of camp.
[3] A party of five officers and 154 other ranks reached the North African coast by MLC (motor landing craft) on 9 June 1941. The party included two Maori members of 2 NZEF, Pte Thompson (28 Bn) and Gnr R. P. A. Peters.

often from homes none too well stocked. Many men were nursed back to health and strength in the hill villages after arriving in a state of exhaustion from dysentery and lack of food. Here amid the pretty, grey-walled peasant cottages, the neat flower gardens, the gnarled olive and fruit trees, they had time to rest. A diet of meat and eggs, vegetables and fruit, cheese and goat's milk, with plenty of wholemeal bread and olive oil, helped their bodies to recover strength. As the weeks went by and the Germans raided the villages to look for British soldiers in hiding, to punish those whom they found harbouring them and to confiscate food and stock, the helping of escaped prisoners became a dangerous business involving much self-sacrifice on the part of local inhabitants. But food was found for them even if sometimes the Cretans themselves were hungry, and shelter was often given them at the risk of the villagers' lives and homes. The German occupation force in the western portion of the island[1] adopted a particularly brutal policy. Initial harshness had led to resistance from the Cretans, and so to raids on villages by the German troops. There were large-scale shootings, burning of houses—even of whole villages—and confiscation of everything that could be carried away. Some of the evaders and escapers may have got fat and lazy in their hill refuges, but most were thoughtful enough in the circumstances to remove themselves before harm came to their benefactors, and mindful enough of their right course of action to try and leave the island.

Meanwhile the Middle East branch of the War Office military intelligence section (MI9), established to assist British servicemen in enemy territory to escape, had plans in hand to rescue the considerable numbers at large in Greece and Crete. On the night of 17 July a British naval officer[2] was landed from a submarine and set about collecting a party of 67 British Commonwealth evaders and escapers. On the night of 27–28 July, according to the prearranged plan, another submarine[3] called; the men reached it by lifeline from the beach through rather heavy seas and were taken off to Alexandria, arriving there on 31 July. The naval officer stayed ashore to make contact with those in hiding and to organise a further party. Three weeks later, on the night of 19–20 August, another submarine[4] embarked a party of 125 escapers and evaders and brought off the naval officer.

---

[1] Italian troops occupied the eastern portion of the island, corresponding to the former province of Lasithion, east of the Lasithi Mountains, and are reputed to have treated the inhabitants reasonably well.
[2] Lt-Cdr F. G. Pool, RNR; awarded DSO for 'courage and good service during the withdrawal from Crete'.
[3] HM Submarine *Thrasher*. Only three New Zealanders came off in this party.
[4] HM Submarine *Torbay*. This party included 62 New Zealanders.

... when we reached the little bay we found we were outnumbered by those who had come to farewell us. . . . the first members prepared to go out to the waiting submarine which had appeared close inshore at a few minutes to 9 p.m. A line had been run out to the shore supported by cork floats and we were instructed to strip and make our way to the sub by grasping this line if we were unable to swim the short distance. It was a tense period before we finally pulled out—there was enough noise to attract Hitler himself to the spot on shore. . . .[1]

The submarine reached Alexandria on 22 August 1941—a successful conclusion to an operation carried out with great skill and daring.

Equally daring was the exploit of two Australians and two New Zealanders[2] who at about this time left the south-west coast in a small open boat, which they rowed and sailed with a blanket sail to Sidi Barrani in 90 hours. Many of those who missed the submarine evacuations made their way in Greek vessels to the mainland of Greece. Greeks and Cretans were leaving the coast at night from the northern tip of Cape Spatha, and many British Commonwealth soldiers hearing of this made their way there, hid in caves, and joined the boatloads. In one such party a New Zealand sergeant reached the south-east coast of the Peloponnese and began to try and obtain a boat that would get them away. After many delays, disappointments, and narrow escapes from capture by Italian soldiers, this party of 17 embarked in a caique. The uncooperative Greek crew had to be overpowered and the New Zealander took command, sailing the vessel to North Africa. After avoiding enemy air attacks and surviving bombing by our own planes on the way across the Mediterranean, they ran out of fuel 20 miles from the coast. The leader of the party went ashore in a dinghy, arranged for fuel to be sent out, returned, and sailed the caique into Alexandria.[3]

Meanwhile on Crete the German paratroops and alpine battalions had been replaced by rather irresponsible young soldiers who had arrived as a permanent force for garrison duties, including the guarding of the prison camp near Canea. There followed much indiscriminate shooting by guards, both along the fence and into the compound, with resultant casualties[4] both to our own people and to the kindly Cretans who brought along food. Bringing food to the camp was now forbidden as part of a campaign to prevent further escapes, and some of the occupation force were employed

---

[1] Narrative by a New Zealand member of the party.
[2] Ptes D. N. McQuarrie (18 Bn) and B. B. Carter (27 MG Bn). All four were awarded the MM.
[3] Sgt J. A. Redpath (19 A Tps Coy) was awarded the DCM for this exploit. The other New Zealanders in the party were: Sgt A. H. Empson (18 Bn), awarded MM, Sgt R. R. Witting (19 A Tps Coy), Sgt W. H. Bristow (18 Bn), Pte T. Shearer (20 Bn), Gnr G. E. Voyce (5 Fd Regt) and Dvr R. S. Barrow (Div Amn Coy).
[4] When a complaint was made concerning these woundings and fatalities, the German general commanding replied that the climate of Crete was affecting his soldiers' nerves.

on the task of collecting any British soldiers still at large. Those captured were punished with a week's confinement in a small enclosure, exposed all day to the sun and without any covering at night. A fairly systematic round-up was made in August and September and many were caught waiting on the coast for boats, though many others eluded the search parties by going further inland into the mountain country. But some of the enemy patrols were even getting high up into the hills. Notices were posted in villages giving warning of the death penalty for Cretans who should harbour escaped prisoners, and leaflets were dropped about the island exhorting British troops to give themselves up.[1]

To seal off the coast the Germans established daily sea and air patrols to watch for boats. But in spite of this small parties continued to get away. A British naval officer landed at the end of October to organise parties for evacuation, and after taking one party off he returned in late November for others. Through his efforts two New Zealanders[2] came off in a party on a Greek submarine at the end of November, and 28 were among a party of 86 taken off in a large Greek caique[3] about the same time.

German vigilance was intensified, and many craft noticed by their patrols were rendered useless by machine-gun fire. No further New Zealanders got away until April 1942, when a party of nine under a New Zealand sergeant stole a boat and rowed it across the Mediterranean to Derna.[4] The information concerning escapers and evaders thus brought back encouraged further rescue efforts. By this time Cairo was in wireless communication with agents on the island and arrangements were made to gather together further parties. On 25 May a fast motor torpedo boat landed near Bardia with a party of 31,[5] and a fortnight later another party of 19 was

---

[1] One such leaflet read :
SOLDIERS
of the
ROYAL BRITISH ARMY, NAVY, AIR FORCE!
There are MANY OF YOU STILL HIDING in the mountains, valleys and villages. You have to PRESENT yourself AT ONCE TO THE GERMAN TROOPS. Every OPPOSITION will be completely USELESS!
Every ATTEMPT TO FLEE will be in VAIN!
The COMMING WINTER will force you to leave the mountains.
Only soldiers who PRESENT themselves AT ONCE will be sure of a HONOURABLE AND SOLDIERLIKE CAPTIVITY OF WAR. On the contrary who is met in civil clothes will be treated as a spy.
THE COMMANDER OF KRETA

[2] Pte L. S. Rosson (19 Bn) and Dvr S. N. Loveridge (Div Sup Coln).
[3] The *Hedgehog*, commanded by Lt C. M. B. Cumberlege, RNR. He was awarded the DSO for his work during the evacuation of Greece and Crete.
[4] Sgt T. Moir (4 Fd Regt) was awarded the DCM for this escape and for his later work with 'A' Force. The other New Zealanders in the party were L-Bdr B. W. Johnston (5 Fd Regt), awarded MM, Pte G. G. Collins (20 Bn) mentioned in despatches, Dvr R. W. Rolfe (4 Res MT Coy), and Pte H. W. Gill (18 Bn).
[5] Including nine New Zealanders.

brought off in the same way.[1] On 19 June a party of eight New Zealanders was brought off 'at the last moment' by a Greek submarine.

The New Zealand sergeant who escaped in April 1942, now seconded for duty with the Middle East branch of MI9, was convinced that there were still a number of escapers and evaders in hiding on the island and obtained permission to go there to try and collect them for evacuation. He was landed in early February 1943, and on 8 May a party of 51 escapers which he had collected was brought off following a commando raid. He himself was captured[2] after having gone back to make contact with yet one more escaper. Those in the party taken off, including 14 New Zealanders, all received recognition for their 'perseverance and determination under great difficulties' and for their 'fortitude in remaining undetected for nearly two years.' This was the final rescue operation from Crete, as it was reckoned that there were few, if any, British servicemen still at large on the island.[3]

The spate of escapes from the Galatas camp in June 1941 caused a speeding up of the German evacuation programme, and a number of crowded shiploads of prisoners left Suda Bay for Greece in July and the months that followed. Some of the ships were 'incredibly filthy', and for the hundreds crammed below in the holds the quite inadequate supply of food and water, the few rudimentary latrines slung over the side of the ship, and the battening down at night made the four or five-day trip to Salonika something of a nightmare. By August, when the numbers had been greatly reduced, camp conditions were beginning to show considerable improvement—the result of weeks of constant pressure on the Germans. Showers had been installed near the hospital, some razors, blades, and soap were procured, and rations were greatly improved. But in spite of every effort by our own officers no Red Cross supplies were ever obtained, and men began to discuss whether they really existed or were just some kind of propaganda. By early October all had been embarked except a small medical staff and about 800 prisoners for working parties, some of which were transferred to Maleme to work on the airfield.

In early January 1942 the last columns were marched along the road to Suda Bay. Three hundred for whom there was no room

---

[1] There were eight New Zealanders in this party. It arrived back on 8 June 1942.
[2] He escaped again and headed for Selino with two German deserters in a motor car. But it proved impossible to rescue him, and he was recaptured and flown to Germany.
[3] The last New Zealander to escape from Crete, Dvr W. H. Swinburne, was one of those who broke out of Galatas camp in June 1941 by crawling under the wire. After vainly trying to contact a boat party, he joined a band of guerrillas in June 1942 and stayed with them until taken off on 8 September 1943.

on the small freighter in port spent a fortnight at Suda in a filthy enclosure, ankle deep in mud. Known to these unfortunates as the 'pig pen', it was for most the worst 'camp' they had to endure. But they had some compensation when, after reaching Greece, they went to a by then reasonably clean barracks at Hymettus, near Athens, where a representative of the International Red Cross Committee distributed food and cigarettes. Some of this party continued their journey in a German tramp, the *Arkadia,* on top of a hold full of figs and sultanas. When the prisoners staggered from the 'fig ship' on to the quay at Salonika under the weight of crammed haversacks, the German guard officer conducting a search expressed wonder at the amount of dried fruit that the Red Cross in Athens had given them. The remaining 160 of the party, including three stretcher cases, did not fare so well. They reached Salonika after a 17-day trip through rainstorms and snow in a small, louse-infested Greek caique, which ran out of food some days before making port. Both at Suda and at Athens, and even from the caique, a few were able to make a break to freedom, however temporary. Indeed, in late 1941 and early 1942 there were scattered British soldiers at large all over Crete and Greece, as well as in the hundred and one islands of the Aegean.

A number of those in these last shiploads were recaptured evaders and escapers, of whose experiences in Crete some account has already been given. In Greece, too, not all of those who missed the naval evacuations had been made prisoners of war, at all events not immediately. Some had made their way from the battlefield, or had ducked into hiding soon after capture, and were at liberty for months or even years either on the Greek mainland or on one of its satellite islands. Some had reached Crete in time for the fighting, others only to fall into enemy hands almost as they landed, and others still to elude the enemy a second time and make their way back to the mainland. The number of these roving groups and individuals in Greece was being constantly augmented by those who broke away from custody either during a move or while in one of the transit camps.

Not a few of these had made their break from the British hospital at Athens and that at Piraeus, and from the convalescent camp near the latter. This was an old Greek military barracks surrounded by a stone wall, inside which was a barbed-wire perimeter. The houses and gardens of Nea Kokkinia came almost up to the stone wall, which made it easy for messages and food to be thrown across. In a rectangular area of red dust and shingle stood 16 longish brick sleeping huts containing bedboards and straw palliasses, a few other buildings for camp services, and at one time marquees to take the overflow. To this camp came those sick and wounded who were considered to have sufficiently recovered, but there were also a number of fit prisoners, making up a total varying from one to two thousand. Food was at first poor, but with money subscribed by officers from their pay, augmented by donations from the Greek Red Cross, it became possible to obtain meat and eggs, and a canteen operating in the camp sold fruit, wines and milk supplied by Greek vendors. The prisoners were left pretty much to their own devices, except that working parties were required for Kokkinia hospital on the hill above.

At first men were deterred from escape by the apparent hopelessness of getting a Greek caique and the formidable alternative of a 600-mile trek to Turkey, but messages from friendly Greeks raised their hopes. In early July two New Zealanders[1] succeeded in crawling under the wire after dark and getting over the wall into one of the nearby gardens. Through the camp garbage collector they had previously arranged a rendezvous for that night with a Greek family, who took them in and gave them civilian clothes. Next day they were taken into Athens and put in touch with an underground organisation which fitted them up with proper suits of clothes and identity cards. In the subsequent weeks while trying to arrange a boat to take them away, they met a number of other escapers. After the success of the first attempt at the convalescent camp, careful plans had been made by other patients and a mass escape[2] took place one night shortly afterwards. Three check roll-calls next morning convinced the Germans that the camp security was falling down somewhere; the commandant was replaced, and guards became considerably more alert.

It is not possible in this account to deal with the varied experiences in Greece of every escaper and evader. With the exception of those who made a quick getaway,[3] most of them lived for varying periods with Greek families. Often they were passed from family to family, both for reasons of security and because there were sometimes domestic intrigues in which it might be fatal for an escaper to become involved. For the escaper life centred round the finding of some craft to take him to sea. Until he found one he had to attempt to look like one of the inhabitants without arousing gossip, and to avoid troops or the type of Greek willing to betray

---

[1] 2 Lt J. W. C. Craig and Cpl F. B. Haycock (both 22 Bn). In a party of six, they reached Alexandria by caique. Craig subsequently returned to Greece secretly to assist the Greek underground and help escaping prisoners. He was captured a second time and taken to Italy. Haycock rejoined 2 NZEF. For this escape Craig was awarded the MC and Haycock was mentioned in despatches.
[2] One estimate put the figure as high as 45; among them were further New Zealanders.
[3] Three New Zealanders who had made their way to Skyros came back in a party of 31 which reached Port Said on 25 May 1941.

him for the rewards the Germans soon offered. Although the chances of making contacts were greater in a city like Athens, many preferred the security of the hills, a lonely cave, or a remote country village.

In the early months escapers and evaders had to depend on help from Greek individuals or from the members of one of the Greek underground organisations, and as enemy security tightened, the parties which got away became smaller. A party of five (including one New Zealander)[1] made their way in a caique from near Volos, via Skiathos and the northern Sporades, to Turkey, which they reached on 11 September.

Although it is beyond the scope of this volume to attempt accounts of these improvised voyages, it can be said that they were often fraught with hazard both from the enemy and from the elements. A party of five British (including one New Zealand officer)[2] and ten Greeks set sail in a small caique from Piraeus on 3 September, with only a school atlas to guide them to North Africa. They ran out of food and water after three days, and out of fuel just south of Crete. When nearly at the end of their tether, they were picked up at night by a British destroyer and arrived in Alexandria on 10 September.

A party of six,[3] all of whom had escaped from the convalescent camp at Nea Kokkinia in early July and had since been looked after by friendly families in Athens, joined forces to secure a boat. They finally made arrangements with the Greek captain of a caique and sailed from the coast of Attica on 26 September, travelled to Antiparos and Paros, skirted Crete, and reached Alexandria on 8 October with food and fuel in hand.

A New Zealand sergeant,[4] also formerly in the convalescent camp at Nea Kokkinia, spent two months in Athens running an 'Intelligence bureau' for the collection of military information and the helping of escapers. He eventually organised a party of six escapers to go by hired motor caique to Turkey. The party sailed from Marathon on 3 October and safely reached the coast of Turkey six days later. There they managed to climb a steep cliff and were taken into custody by Turkish gendarmes.

From October onwards the Middle East branch of MI9 began to expand its activities; its strength was increased by the temporary recruitment of a number of outstanding escapers, and it began

---

[1] WO II D. B. Hill (21 Bn).
[2] Lt R. B. Sinclair (22 Bn), mentioned in despatches.
[3] There were three New Zealanders in the original party—2 Lt Craig (22 Bn), awarded MC, 2 Lt E. F. Cooper (LAD attached 5 Fd Regt), and Cpl Haycock (22 Bn). Cooper and Haycock were mentioned in despatches.
[4] Sgt D. G. MacNab (6 Fd Coy), awarded DCM. The other New Zealander in the party was Dvr J. B. Morice (Div Amn Coy).

to organise help and rescue for escapers and evaders in both Greece and Crete. Some of the operations in Crete have already been outlined. In Greece food, clothing, and blankets were dropped by air in areas known to harbour these men—Mount Tagetus, Katerini, and Mount Olympus. Agents operating caiques continued to evacuate British and Imperial servicemen, and groups of the newly-recruited successful escapers were landed on the Greek mainland to organise further assistance and escape routes.

As the result of their activities a party of 18 was evacuated by caique from the coast near Athens on 22 November, reaching Alexandria five days later.[1] After the capture of several agents and MI9 personnel, the Germans and Italians started to set traps for escapers by posing as the representatives of escape organisations. By this means they were able not only to capture a number of escapers and evaders but also to make the remainder suspicious of whoever made contact with them, and genuine MI9 agents had to carefully work out means of proving their identity. It was over five months before the next New Zealander[2] was brought out from the Athens area in a party of twenty, which left Porto Rafti under MI9 arrangements on 2 May and reached Turkey two days later.

While some fifty had been making away from the convalescent camp, escape activity had been launched also in the hospital set up in the Polytechnic School. A large marble and granite building in one of the main streets of Athens, its situation made contact with friendly Greeks comparatively easy. In mid-July two of the patients made a successful break, Greeks whipping them off to safety almost as soon as they were outside the building. A day or two later some New Zealand medical orderlies successfully broke out through a door leading on to the street, though two were wounded and immediately recaptured. The Germans apparently soon reached the conclusion that this prisoner-of-war hospital was more trouble than it was worth. It was closed down shortly after the escapes, and patients and staff were transferred to Nea Kokkinia, either to the convalescent camp or to the hospital.

It was a fortunate thing for the hundreds of our wounded in Greece that not only were there numbers of British doctors, dentists, and orderlies there to treat them, but that in the early stages there was available for prisoners of war a transit hospital as well equipped as Kokkinia. A wounded man who arrived by plane from Crete speaks of the joy of being properly washed for the first time by our own orderlies, of sheets and pyjamas. Here as elsewhere there was a struggle to get sufficient rations, and the shortage of

---

[1] New Zealanders in this party were Lt H. B. J. Sutton (18 Bn), 2 Lt N. R. Flavell (21 Bn), Sgt D. J. Stott and Gnr R. M. Morton (5 Fd Regt), and Pte A. S. R. Foote (21 Bn).
[2] Dvr E. F. Foley (4 Res MT Coy), awarded MM.

food does not seem ever to have been fully overcome. The International Red Cross delegate left funds to buy milk and special foods, the Greek Red Cross gave very generous help[1] in view of the general food scarcity, and Greek nurses visiting the wards were able to bring comfort to the patients as well as to distribute much-appreciated fruit and cigarettes. But all such visits were soon stopped on security grounds by the German staff, who kept a rigid control over rations and movements in the hospital. The Germans did not interfere with the medical treatment in the hospital, except for occasional inspections by one of their senior medical officers.

Since the hospital's hurried and crowded beginning[2] the staff had been able to develop many amenities. A canteen was established, a fund from officers' pay and a subsidy from the International Red Cross Committee funds making it possible for all ranks to buy, though high prices did not allow money to go far. Concerts were put on for the walking patients in one of the large courtyards, and after musical instruments had been obtained an impromptu dance band was able to tour the wards. Patients could write a letter a week and had a camp library to help while away the hours of recovery. As they got better they were allowed to stroll outside the buildings up to the barbed-wire fence, and stretcher cases were taken on to the roof to sunbathe. Men were able for a time to forget their hunger while lying and sitting in the Greek sunshine, reading, playing cards, and talking over the battles through which they had recently come.

During these weeks and months of recuperation, small 'escape clubs' had discussed how best a bid for freedom might be made when physical condition permitted. There were plenty of maps and compasses, for the German searches had been perfunctory only. Many attempts were made by those sufficiently recovered: cutting the wire and crawling through; hiding in the laundry van or the rubbish cart as it went out with a load. A New Zealand professional artist, then a prisoner, persuaded a Bavarian guard to pose for him while three Australians crawled through the wire behind his back. Two New Zealanders[3] climbed through the wire in daylight on 30 July, when only two guards were on duty. They

---

[1] Mme. Zannas of the Greek Red Cross was active in organising food for prisoners in Greece. At one stage the Greek Red Cross was spending 1,000,000 drachmae a month in ' sending gifts to the wounded and on the revictualling of the canteens installed by their efforts in the hospitals at Kokinia and the Polytechnic School.'— Report for June 1941 by Dr. Brunel, delegate of the IRCC in Athens.

[2] Dr. Brunel reported that the hospital held 1676 (including medical personnel) on 6 June 1941. A member of the medical staff reported that it had between 800 and 900 beds at the peak period after the battle of Crete.

[3] L-Bdr F. S. Marshall (7 A-Tk Regt) and Spr S. E. Carson (6 Fd Coy). Both men had been wounded and sent to Kokkinia hospital for treatment. Carson was mentioned in despatches.

hid in a trench 20 feet from the wire until darkness, and then made for Eleusis and eventually reached Euboea. On 27 August they bribed a Greek to take them by boat to Skyros and reached Turkey on 3 September. Only a few breaks from the hospital were successful. After the mass escape from the convalescent camp, the hospital suffered some reprisals too: no concerts, delay in the delivery of rations and in the issue of pay—the somewhat natural reactions of the German guards to the reprimand and increased guard duties which no doubt came their way.

In August and September the Germans pushed ahead with the transport north of the prisoners in hospitals and transit camps in and around Athens. For the sick and wounded this posed a difficult problem because of the breaks in the Athens–Salonika railway line over which it was necessary to march, and because of the absence of suitable rolling-stock. A typical journey by this route has been described, and parties of convalescents, some with only partially healed wounds, fared little better. In late August a large batch of sick and wounded from Kokkinia hospital were driven to Piraeus docks in large passenger buses and embarked on the Italian hospital ship *Gradisca*. Those who travelled on her for the five-day voyage to Salonika speak in glowing terms of the care and good food they received from the Italian medical officers and sisters. The rest of the convalescents went north on small cargo vessels, on which the treatment and food seem to have been reasonably good although the holds were much overcrowded.

Almost all prisoners of war captured in Greece and Crete who did not escape passed through the main transit camp at Salonika, known as Frontstalag 183, an old, disused Greek barracks on the outskirts of the town. Some stayed only twenty-four hours; others were kept there up to several months to do forced labour for the Germans. Many had already been through Galatas or Corinth and other camps, but Salonika capped them all, and in its first six months of existence earned for itself an infamous reputation.

Round a clay barrack square stood rows of old Greek wooden hutments, on the floor of which rows of men had to lie.[1] These buildings were dilapidated, thick with filth, and infested with lice, fleas and bedbugs. Swarms of flies and mosquitoes and numerous rats helped to make sleep for a newcomer almost an impossibility. The German commandant and his staff seem to have made little or no attempt to provide blankets or other bedding. At one end of

---

[1] Some of the officers had beds, which were, however, no protection against most of the varieties of vermin encountered there. Many officers preferred to lie outside at night, until indiscriminate shooting by guards made this unnecessarily risky; it was forbidden for other ranks.

almost every barrack were a water tap and four latrines, which had to suffice for the 250[1] or so prisoners who were made to occupy it.

In one corner of the compound—formed by the original high brick walls and fences of barbed-wire—were two concrete huts, which were set up as a 65-bed hospital shortly after the camp opened in May and manned by Serbian[2] doctors and orderlies. At that time there had been only some 300 British Commonwealth prisoners there, but it was realised that large numbers would arrive when the evacuation of Corinth began. Fortunately a few British medical orderlies were able to prepare a nearby two-storied hutment to accommodate a further 160 patients.

In early June the first drafts from Corinth began to arrive, most of them exhausted from their forced march over the Brallos Pass but somewhat cheered by their friendly reception from Greeks in the streets of Salonika. Many were by now an easy prey to sickness; some had reopened wounds. They kept on pouring in during the month until the camp population rose as high as 12,000. Throughout June more than 400 cases were treated daily at the camp medical inspection room.[3] Food was the worst that the prisoners had yet experienced. Daily rations comprised three-quarters of a hard Italian army biscuit, about four ounces of bread, sometimes mouldy, a pint of watery lentil soup with an occasional flavouring of horseflesh, and two hot drinks of German 'mint' tea. On this diet men soon lost weight and it is little wonder that beriberi made its appearance, though the German medical officer refused to recognise it, and cases eventually rose to as high as 600. Nor is it surprising, in view of the location of the camp in the centre of a malarious belt, that there were many cases of malaria, and the German authorities were forced to make a daily issue of ten grammes of quinine. As for disinfectants, the camp hardly ever saw them, and the only drugs available were captured supplies left by our own medical units. Although not able to help in this direction, the Greek Red Cross did splendid work in providing milk, brown bread, rice, fruit, vegetables, eggs, and cigarettes for the hospital patients—a task made by no means easy by the German commandeering of local supplies.

The lot of all those below the rank of sergeant was made the harder by having to go out to work. At the six o'clock morning roll-call everyone was usually detailed for a work-party, including many genuine cases from the sick parade. A few were given fatigues in the German quarters, but most had to do heavy physical work in the heat of Salonika—shifting wood in timber-yards,

---

[1] At one period as many as 500.
[2] There were some 1600 Serbian prisoners there at that time.
[3] The two-storied camp hospital was most admirably organised and run by Capt A. L. Cochrane (RAMC), ably assisted by Capt C. C. Cook (NZDC).

unloading heavy sacks from railway trucks at a siding, pushing along 40-gallon petrol drums at the docks, cleaning out stables and working with pick and shovel. From some of the guards in charge of working parties there seems to have been a good deal of screaming and bullying and some kicking and knocking about with rifle butts; other guards appear to have been sympathetic towards those who were obviously unable to stand the heavy labour. And being in a working party had the compensation that from some jobs men were able to come back with items of food and tobacco variously obtained. In the camp itself there was much indiscriminate shooting by some of the sentries, one New Zealander being shot dead without warning and another wounded for being allegedly too near the trip-wire inside the camp perimeter. One night a sentry threw a grenade into a barrack latrine because someone had lit a match, and three men were seriously injured.

There seems little that can be said to the credit of the German authorities at Salonika. To put the best construction on things, the conditions were the result of lack of provision and supervision by the German Higher Command,[1] whose main attentions had been diverted elsewhere. But the conditions were also the immediate result of cynical neglect and exploitation by the German line-of-communication authorities on the spot, who imposed little if any check on the acts of brutally minded guards and delayed granting permission for delegates of the International Red Cross Committee or of a neutral power to pay a visit of inspection.

In the height of the summer of 1941, although many thousands had already gone north by train, the shiploads arriving from Crete again made the camp badly overcrowded. A variety of diseases was rampant, and with the sick and wounded also coming up from Athens the camp hospital and auxiliary huts at one period held 800. By working long hours British Commonwealth medical officers and orderlies managed to cope somehow with the 3000-odd patients who passed through the hospital, and it says much for their efforts that the death-roll was kept down to 80-odd. Fortunately the amputees, blind, and other serious cases in transit from Kokkinia hospital did not have to wait more than a few days for transport on to Germany, though too many had to make the journey lying on the straw of a cattle-truck.

By the end of September the camp had been practically cleared and the few serious cases that could not be moved, together with the skeleton medical staff and a number of escapers recaptured near Salonika, were shifted to four barracks wired off in a smaller area.

---

[1] Commonwealth troops taken prisoner in Greece and Crete amounted to some 25,000, the feeding and administration of whom in a hostile country just occupied would no doubt present a considerable problem.

In early November some Red Cross food parcels were received with amazed delight. Half-way through that month the Italian hospital ship *Gradisca* arrived with nearly all of the remaining wounded from Athens, and a few days later they left by hospital train for Germany. Gradually conditions in the camp improved: some of the last inmates—mostly recaptured escapers—speak of disinfestation, of the issue of new clothing, and of going into fumigated barracks. There seems, however, to have been little improvement in the German rations, and another period of acute hunger followed when supplies of Red Cross food temporarily ran out.

From the many working parties at Salonika and from the main camp itself right up to the end of its existence, numbers of prisoners, including many New Zealanders, made breaks for freedom. Some got away and were recaptured several times, only to be finally taken off to Germany; others made their way to Turkey and eventual freedom. Two parties got out through a camp sewer. An officer[1] cut his way through a barrack backdoor and, dodging the camp searchlights, crawled through the wire and scaled a wall into the street; another party of twelve used a similar route a little later. Once in Salonika they were almost always able to rely on temporary help from Greeks, though it was not always possible to trust all civilians or police, many of whom were not unnaturally fearful of German punishment. An MI9 organisation was set up in Salonika as well as in Athens to collect parties of escapers and evaders and arrange for them to be got away by caique.

Most escapers made for Stavros or the east coast of the Agion Oros finger of the Chalcidike peninsula, the north-eastern strip of Greece being soon in German hands and policed by Bulgarians. From the coast the next step was to reach Turkey, either direct or via the island of Imbros. Many who made breaks from trains en route for Germany followed the same plans. Some navigated their own boats across the stormy waters of the northern Aegean; others persuaded Greeks to take them on trading or fishing vessels.

A party of four who met in Stavros in July 1941 bought a boat for a promised £50 and sailed it to the Turkish mainland, which they reached in early August. Of the two New Zealanders in the party, one had got away from the transit camp at Larissa and walked north;[2] the other[3] had crawled out under the barbed wire at Salonika transit camp in the early hours of one morning and had been looked after by friendly Greeks. Both made their way eventually to Stavros, where they met.

---

[1] Lt W. B. Thomas (23 Bn), awarded MC.
[2] L-Cpl W. T. W. Kerr (25 Bn), awarded DCM.
[3] Pte O. V. T. Brewer (21 Bn).

Another party of 16 which had collected on the island of Imbros was taken over to the Turkish mainland in September 1941. Three New Zealanders had all reached the island separately. They had been helped by Greek civilians and police, one of them[1] having been taken across personally by a Greek policeman for a small fee. This ex-prisoner and one of the others[2] had escaped from the train taking them to Germany, and the third had got away from the Corinth camp and made his way north on German trains.[3] All three had eventually walked to the Agion Oros peninsula, where they had been helped to get boats.

In October a New Zealander[4] and two companions rowed across the Aegean to Turkey in an open boat, a remarkable feat of daring and endurance. Two others,[5] both escapers from Salonika, who had made their way to Agion Oros, seized a boat and put to sea on 30 October when they heard of a large German patrol coming to search the area. Their party of seven made the island of Imbros and reached Turkey on 10 November. Another party of seven, including four more New Zealanders[6] from Salonika, also seized a boat about the same time, sailing to Lemnos and Imbros and reaching Turkey a day behind the others.

For a time it had not been too difficult for escaped prisoners to live undetected on the Chalcidike peninsula. One New Zealander,[7] for example, who had escaped from a working party at Salonika, spent ten weeks there trying to obtain a boat before he got away with a party of 14, which hired one and reached Turkey via Lemnos and Imbros on 2 November. But as German security increased it became more and more difficult both to remain hidden and also to get away by boat. The MI9 agents operating in the Salonika area were able to smuggle away only a few at a time. All the New Zealanders who got away after the middle of November made contact with the organisation and had their final journey arranged for them. One reached Turkey in December,[8] another in May 1942,[9] and still another in late October 1942.[10] All these men had made several attempts to get away and had shown great courage and tenacity. Most of those unable to obtain a boat or a passage fell eventually into the hands of German patrols or security police.

---

[1] Pte J. Reid (20 Bn), mentioned in despatches.
[2] Pte R. T. Blackler (19 Bn).
[3] Tpr A. Connelly (Div Cav). See p. 58.
[4] Tpr W. A. Gadsby (Div Cav).
[5] Pte J. McR. Brand (23 Bn), awarded MM, and L-Cpl W. T. F. Buchanan (23 Bn); Buchanan won the MM in Tunisia in April 1943.
[6] Sgt J. T. Donovan (21 Bn), Cpl J. Westgate (18 Bn), Ptes D. P. Gilroy and W. S. Marshall (both 27 MG Bn).
[7] Pte E. A. Howard (19 Bn), awarded MM.
[8] Pte W. A. Le Lievre (19 Bn).
[9] Lt Thomas (23 Bn). See p. 80.
[10] Pte P. R. Blunden (20 Bn), awarded MM. See p. 83, note 1.

A few who in despair tried to make their way back to southern Greece were in the main picked up by the Italian occupation forces, which since September 1941 had taken over the territory south of Olympus.[1]

The move of prisoners to Austria or Germany was for most of the British officers and men transported their first experience of travelling long distances in closed cattle-wagons. From June 1941 until April 1942 long trainload after long trainload of this human cargo travelled north on journeys lasting from five to ten days. Accounts of the experiences of various parties at different periods vary in details, but there are features common to almost all. An average of 35 officers in a wagon made it difficult for everyone to lie down; yet the numbers rose to 55 for other ranks. Biscuits and tinned meat—the only rations—seem usually to have been issued only for a four-day journey and generally on a very lean scale. The Serbian populace, however, seems to have been very generous with gifts of bread and farm produce as the trains passed through their pleasant countryside, and the Serbian Red Cross at Belgrade met many of them with hot soup, food, and cigarettes. On the longer journeys, too, there seem to have been small additional German issues, albeit rather haphazard. As the cattle-trucks had the openings barred or wired and the doors fixed to prevent escape, the lack of a supply of water and of any sanitary arrangements in them was probably the most serious hardship—the more so as many men were suffering from intestinal disorders. On occasions trucks were not opened for as long as 22 hours. Sleep was of course difficult on the hard, jolting floor of a goods-wagon, and in the summer the chilling draughts at night following the baking, sweaty heat of the day did not make it any easier. For those who travelled in winter in these cold trucks the icy temperatures encountered as the trains moved north over the ranges became something of a torture. One report by a senior officer speaks of the guards on his train as correct in their behaviour; but it is clear at least that on many trains the truck doors could have been opened more frequently. It is probable that guards were few and overworked and not over-comfortable themselves; and it may be that their omissions to attend to the physical needs of the prisoners were the result of laziness rather than of malice.

Moreover, their tempers were never improved by an escape or an attempt at it; yet in spite of threats of reprisal shootings at the outset of each journey, breaks occurred from almost every train.

---

[1] An account of the few who managed to remain at liberty and finally escaped to Allied territory is given in Chapter 6, pp. 227–33. Those recaptured by the Italians were claimed by Italy as her prisoners of war.

Though there were no such shootings, there were instances where the remaining occupants of a truck were subjected to kicking, clubbing with rifle butts, and beating with sticks. It is impossible to estimate with any accuracy the numbers who left the trains in this way. Some were recaptured only to escape from another train later. At least five New Zealanders who broke loose eventually reached Allied territory. The example which follows is typical of their experiences. In October 1941 the inmates of one truck cut a hole with smuggled tools through the wall near the sliding door, reached outside to undo the catch, and were able to open the door. Ten jumped clear before the guard began firing and signalled the train to stop. By the time it had come to a halt the escapers were in hiding well behind, ready to head for one or other of the Greek villages and so begin the second stage of their escape.[1]

The first trainload of officers was unloaded at Biberach in Bavaria on 16 June and marched to the nearby camp, Oflag VB. After the gruelling journey north following weeks in the transit camps of Greece, they arrived in Germany, as one officer put it, 'lousy, bearded, hungry, tired, and dejected'. There was apprehension about how much longer their health would survive the type of conditions under which they had been living in Greece, and dread that Germany might be even worse. Having resigned themselves to the almost continual state of disorganisation in which they had existed since capture, they were quite unprepared for their reception at the oflag. Here, after a routine search and a hot shower provided by the Germans, they went into an orderly camp, where food and friendliness were lavished on them by the occupants. They discovered with surprise that British Navy, Army, and Air Force officers had already built up an organisation capable of coping with most of the difficulties of life in a prison camp and with the idiosyncrasies of German guards. No one seemed hungry, everyone had the appearance of fairly good health, and morale was high. Hope dawned for the newcomers, and a few encouraging words of greeting from the senior British officer, Major-General V. M. Fortune,[2] acted like a tonic on morale. One of the officers present still remembers his words well enough to repeat them 'almost verbatim':

> Gentlemen. In spite of being prisoners of the enemy you are still honourable British officers. You have not disgraced yourselves nor have you been dishonoured by others whom you may think have contributed to your capture. You have not been defeated, nor has the Empire, nor will it

---

[1] Pte Blunden (20 Bn) was, so far as is known, the only New Zealander in this party to reach Allied territory.
[2] Later Sir Victor Fortune, KBE, CB, DSO.

ever. We have all suffered a few temporary reverses, but these should only serve to strengthen us for more bitter struggles before final victory is achieved. We as prisoners of war still have our duty clearly before us, we must continue the fight behind the enemy lines.

In Biberach everyone had his own eating utensils, a clean palliasse, pillowslip, and towel—luxuries indeed for the new arrivals. They were housed in modern concrete blocks, divided into separate rooms with a reasonable number in each. These contained steel-frame two-tier beds with wooden slats, of the type later well known in many German camps for officers and NCOs. The camp was free of vermin and there were good washing facilities, with hot showers at least every ten days. The German rations were much better than the prisoners from Greece had yet experienced; they were supplemented from Red Cross supplies, and the meals were properly cooked in a central kitchen. Letter-cards were regularly issued for writing home; pay in camp money (*Lagergeld*) was regularly credited. There were organised educational classes and facilities for sport and exercise. To those with fresh memories of Corinth and Salonika it all seemed like a pleasant dream. But it should not be forgotten that such a state of things was the fruit of months of hard work, good leadership, and skilful handling of the German authorities.

As further parties of officers arrived from Greece, some of the original occupants of the camp were sent to Titmoning. The health of the newcomers rapidly improved with the better food and camp conditions, though it was to take a long time to recover the two stone in weight which some had lost. A committee controlled attempts at escape, newcomers being allowed for the time being to assist but not actually to make a break. During the summer a number of such breaks were made, mainly by means of disguise or concealment on transport, and on 14 September 26 got clear through the longest tunnel that had yet been made. After each break there were the usual searches, extra parades, and minor restrictions. It was probably the considerable number of breaks from the camp, together with the closeness of Biberach to the Swiss border, that decided the Germans to transfer the officers elsewhere. In October they were moved to a large vacant camp at Warburg, where British officers from all over Germany were being collected.

Most of the officers from Crete who had been held some weeks in Salonika were finally transported to the Baltic port of Lubeck and accommodated in Oflag XC, a few kilometres out. A former German army camp, its quarters and general facilities were on a par with those at Biberach, and the canteen seems to have been much better stocked. But no well-organised British community was in occupation to welcome the newcomers and show them the ropes;[1] and no Red Cross food was available during their six weeks' stay. The greater part of the German food provided consisted of potatoes and bread, and was so meagre in quantity that loaves were often divided with the aid of a ruler to ensure that each man got an accurate share. The effect of the lean camp rations on these men who had come there after months in bad transit camps was so obvious when, in early October, they were all transferred to Warburg, that they were given double Red Cross issues there for a while to enable them to recover lost weight.

The trainloads of other ranks were distributed between the town of Marburg, on the Drau just south of the Yugoslav border, and Wolfsberg, a little to the west in Austria. By July 1941 Stalag XVIIID, at Marburg, contained nearly 4500 British Commonwealth prisoners from Greece and Crete, including 800-odd New Zealanders. Over a thousand were in tents while new buildings were being constructed. The buildings already in existence were dirty and swarming with lice and bedbugs, and the camp was, in the opinion of the senior British medical officer,[2] overcrowded beyond safety. There were shootings for breaches of discipline, by guards all too quick on the trigger. Yet many of the prisoners preferred Marburg to camps they went to later. At the beginning of September the arrival of a Red Cross consignment gave a great boost to morale, and thereafter regular supplies ensured a sufficient diet and at least some medical supplies for the camp. Moreover, although the German commandant and some of his staff were usually inefficient and unreasonable, guards were often rather easy-going, and it was comparatively simple (especially with Red Cross chocolate and cigarettes) for prisoners to persuade them to give them an outing—to the cinema, to a swimming hole, or to the local store for shopping with the 70 pfennigs[3] a day they earned on working parties.

Almost immediately after the delousing and registration which followed their arrival, a number had gone to work-camps, *Arbeitskommandos*, in the district. They were made to work on roads, on railways, in factories, clearing a building site, or on odd

---

[1] There were about fifty RAF officers transferred from Stalag Luft I and a few from Dulag Luft.
[2] Maj G. H. Thomson, NZMC, who was awarded the OBE for his continuous efforts to secure better conditions for British prisoners of war in Germany in the course of his duties as a camp medical officer.
[3] A Reichspfennig was one-hundredth of a Reichsmark. At the exchange rate agreed by Britain and Germany of £1 = 15 RM, 70 pfennigs represented just over 11d. The pay was really 1.80 RM a day, from which 1.10 RM was deducted for food, board, and camp fund thus:

Food	.80 RM
Board	.20 RM
Camp fund	.10 RM

jobs for the local council. Many were hired out to local farmers and lived well on the farms, though their hours of work were very long. Although warned strictly about fraternisation with prisoners, many of the civilians were soon on friendly terms, which in spite of the heavy penalties involved[1] sometimes ripened into intimacy. While it was in summer comparatively easy to get away from such places of work, it was difficult to go far without being caught, and the long distance to be covered on both land and sea before reaching Allied territory caused most men to regard final escape as impracticable. Nevertheless many broke camp, even if only to get a change of scene, and a few reached Hungary or the partisans in Yugoslavia.

The truckloads of prisoners not destined for Marburg found their way to Wolfsberg in south-eastern Austria. The little town is set in a broad green valley against a background of snow-capped mountains and fir-planted slopes. The camp just outside the town had originally held Belgian officers,[2] but for some months before the arrival of British prisoners had become a base camp for Belgian and French labour detachments and had been renamed Stalag XVIIIA. In order to keep the camp free from vermin, the trainloads which began to arrive from Greece at the end of June were temporarily segregated in eight large tents erected on a spare piece of ground outside the camp. They were searched, given a hot shower, their clothes were deloused, and they were registered in the camp records. Some were issued with assorted pieces of captured continental uniform, with wooden clogs, and with unfamiliar square pieces of cloth in place of socks. As fresh trainloads (sometimes a thousand strong) arrived, all fit prisoners who had been 'processed' were sent off to working camps to make room for the new arrivals. Those who remained were housed in converted brick stables, where three-tier bunks with a palliasse and a blanket had been prepared for them and rather primitive washing troughs and latrines improvised. By 21 July the camp strength included some 5500 British and Dominion prisoners, 3700 of whom had been sent on to various work detachments.

The German rations were estimated to provide about 1800–2000 calories a day[3], which when supplemented by Red Cross parcels provided an ample diet, though there were at first delays over the Red Cross issues. With good food, a clean camp, and the healthy climate of the district, the British medical officer was able to report

---

[1] Sentences of up to ten years' imprisonment (in a military prison) for the prisoner of war.
[2] At that time it was known as Oflag XVIIIB.
[3] The estimate is that of an IRCC delegate (a doctor), and would have been made before the ration cut of June 1941.

in August that, although the prisoners had arrived from Greece in a very bad condition, their health was now improving.

It did not take the British Commonwealth prisoners long to weld themselves into a strong community. An energetic 'man-of-confidence' was elected to deal with the German authorities in all matters regarding the prisoners' welfare;[1] a senior warrant officer took charge of internal discipline and administration, presiding over a committee of hut commanders. At first no one knew the rights of prisoners under the Geneva Convention, but they were quick to learn after the visits of United States consular representatives and delegates from the International Red Cross Committee. Non-commissioned officers who had unwittingly obeyed orders and gone out to work were informed of their privileges. When British battle dress arrived in September, the prisoners finally had their way over the control of its issue, though not without considerable argument. No doubt their path was made a little easier by the fact that the deputy commandant was reasonably well disposed towards them.

Gradually the amenities of the camp were improved. Some books arrived in August and gave men something to talk about other than the campaigns they had just fought, which had up till then been the subject of endless recountings, elaborations, and sometimes recriminations. A small theatre was rigged up in one of the rooms. The arrival of mail from England in September supplied the link with the outside world for which many were hungry, though men from Australia and New Zealand had to wait longer for their first letters from home. As winter drew on the cold began to cause hardship to the many with insufficient underclothing, no socks, and worn-out boots. The stables proved damp and comfortless and the promised shelter for latrines and washing troughs did not materialise. By October the German camp authorities were administering some 22,500 prisoners, whose representatives were encountering that delay in effecting promised improvements which many camp leaders elsewhere were also finding so exasperating.

Conditions in the *Arbeitskommandos* depended very largely on the character of the German NCO in command and of the employer for whom the prisoners worked, though living quarters were generally quite good. A large party working on a dam at Lavamünd was comfortably housed and enjoyed good camp facilities, including hot showers daily. Eighty men working in a brick factory lived in the well-lit and heated rooms of specially built barracks.

---

[1] The term 'man-of-confidence' is a literal translation of the French 'homme de confiance', which appears in the French text of the 1929 Geneva Prisoners of War Convention, its equivalent in the English text being 'representative'.

A party of 160 engaged on road work was lodged in a large converted house. Two hundred men working for an engineering firm had single-tier beds with three or four blankets, ample space for sport, flower and vegetable gardens—in the words of the inspecting IRCC delegate, 'a model camp'. Their hours of work varied between eight and nine and a half, with Sundays free for most, though laundry and camp fatigues took up a good deal of their free time. They were fed on the larger scale of 'heavy' civilian worker's ration,[1] together with Red Cross food from the stalag. On the other hand, with only a medical orderly in the camp and an often rather indifferent civilian doctor paying infrequent visits, injuries were sometimes badly treated and incipient illnesses neglected. There were sometimes delays in the smaller *Arbeitskommandos* in getting letter-cards, pay, and canteen facilities. And many were not used to the 'stand-over-you' type of foreman and the longer hours of work common in European countries.

Many of the later train-loads of prisoners leaving Salonika between August 1941 and April 1942, including medical officers and convalescents, travelled north as far as Silesia to Stalag VIIIB at Lamsdorf.[2] The camp had a different atmosphere from that of the days when the British Army prisoners from the campaign in France straggled wearily in and the RAF NCOs and other ranks began to arrive from Dulag Luft. To the newcomers the contrast with what they had known up till then of prisoner-of-war conditions was as striking as that experienced by the officers who had gone to Biberach. The impression made is expressed in one report thus: 'On 20 October 41 our arrival at Lamsdorf seemed to afford a glimpse of another world—a well-organised camp, food in plenty, PWs smart in new battle-dress and a high morale. . . .' As at Biberach, the progress made was largely attributable to the efforts of the camp leaders, in this case two very competent British Army warrant officers. A new German commandant appointed in 1941 seems to have been more amenable to reason than his predecessors. This is not to say that material conditions at Lamsdorf were comfortable.

Stone barracks with concrete floors each gave a floor space of about 75 yards by 12 yards, divided into two large rooms by a five-yard space containing an ablutions room and a room for washing clothes. About 350 men slept in each barrack in three-tier bunks, of which the uppermost was very close to the ceiling and the lowest within ten inches of the floor. In summer the barracks were dry and admitted plenty of light and air, but the water supply would often fail except for a few hours each day. In winter the floors

---

[1] It included, for example, 500 grammes of bread, as against the ordinary ration of 320 grammes.
[2] See pp. 30–1 for an earlier account of the camp.

were almost constantly wet from tramping feet and the barracks festooned with damp clothing. Missing windows had to be boarded up to keep out the weather; even so, the low temperatures caused layers of ice to form on the inside walls and on the floors of the ablution rooms. Five pathetic light globes in each room made winter reading almost impossible, and there was never enough fuel to supply the two or three large stoves. Latrines were of the deep-pit type, cleared at too infrequent intervals by pumping into a mobile tank, which then spread its contents over the surrounding fields[1] within 50 yards of the stalag perimeter. Nobody was allowed out of the barracks after 9 p.m., and the inside night latrine provided was quite inadequate for the numbers who had to use it. Inadequate provision for delousing new arrivals was responsible for the introduction of vermin into the camp, to which an outbreak of typhus towards the end of 1941 was thought to be attributable. Fortunately the British medical staff took prompt and effective measures, and the German camp staff were jolted into co-operation, with the result that only three deaths occurred.[2]

If the buildings and sanitation left much to be desired, their standard was very little lower than that of the German rations. Fortunately there was a stock of Red Cross food parcels sufficient for a while to issue one a week. Potatoes were cooked, and soup and hot drinks made in a central kitchen in huge boilers. One warrant officer summed up the food situation by saying, ' You could exist but not get fat '. In the sleeping barracks, to which the food was carried in large containers, there was less than half the number of tables and forms necessary to seat all the occupants, and no eating utensils were supplied.

While there was a shortage of drugs, medical facilities were it seems quite adequate, though there were the same difficulties at working camps as have been noted with Stalags XVIIIA and XVIIID —especially in a nearby coalmine *Arbeitskommando*. At the head of the prisoners' own administration was the camp leader—in this camp the elected ' man-of-confidence ', a very able British warrant officer. He appointed a representative for Red Cross supplies and correspondence, a camp sergeant-major, and a leader for each

---

[1] This method of sewage disposal was in fairly general use for prisoner-of-war camps in Germany.
[2] The delousing station was outside the camp but was operated by British Commonwealth medical orderlies from within. It was used not only for British but also for Russians. Typhus broke out in the camp on 28 November, the first six cases being from among medical orderlies working in the delousing station. On the orders of the senior British medical officer, Lt-Col Bull (NZMC), all hair was removed from the heads and bodies of the inmates of the camp within the next four days and a strenuous effort was made to rid the camp of lice. When fresh cases occurred on 6 December, Bull strongly recommended to the German authorities certain improved arrangements for isolation, disinfestation, and personal hygiene. These were accepted and put into practice. Only 18 cases of typhus occurred in the camp and only three of these proved fatal.

compound[1] (of about 1000 men), who in turn appointed his own barrack leaders.

Recreation seems to have been well organised and aided by ample equipment, thanks largely to the World Alliance of YMCAs: sports, games, theatre, arts and handicrafts, and gardening were all flourishing. Music was of a good standard, with an orchestra performing as early as 1941. After much persuasion the Germans agreed to set aside half a barrack each for a church, a theatre, and a school. The last was inadequate to accommodate all those who flocked to the language and other classes offered.

A New Zealand warrant officer who was at the camp wrote:

> The bearing of the British soldiers who were captured in France and their generosity and organisation was the biggest factor in improving morale . . . .

Most informants are agreed that an adequate supply of food from whatever source sent morale up, and lack of it caused despondency. For a while the German authorities broadcast 'Lord Haw-Haw' sessions over the camp loudspeakers in an effort to obtain converts. But the scornful laughter that greeted the more far-fetched of the broadcast statements, and the lack of any tendency on the prisoners' part to act otherwise than as the temporary detainees of a nation that would ultimately be defeated, probably influenced the authorities in later discontinuing them. Indeed the early German propaganda was so naïve, and showed so little psychological understanding of British prisoners, that many of the latter developed the habit of disbelieving on principle every statement, oral or printed, which came from enemy sources. Escape from the heart of western Europe was in this period generally considered wellnigh hopeless, though a camp organisation helped a constant succession of attempts, mostly from working camps. For many, breaking camp was merely a means of relief from an undesirable working party, as on recapture the offender was returned to stalag.

The increased British offensive air activity in 1941 consisting of fighter sweeps and bomber raids on the Continent was not carried out without losses in aircraft over the sea and over enemy territory. In 1941 the French underground organisations were assisting many shot-down airmen to evade capture and return to England. But not all had an opportunity to make contact with helpers, and others were caught after weeks of freedom. By October the number of New Zealand Air Force prisoners had risen to over a hundred. As early as July 1941 the British Air Force NCOs' and other ranks' compound at Lamsdorf was full to overflowing, and that at Stalag

---

[1] There were ten compounds, each of four barracks intended to hold about 1000 men, but in which more than 1500 were packed on occasion. At the end of 1941 the camp population (all nationalities) was about 20,000.

Luft I was also overcrowded.[1] Accordingly a hundred newly-captured Air Force NCOs were sent from Dulag Luft to Stalag IXC at Badsulza, in Thuringia, and another fifty to Stalag IIIE, at Kirchhain, on the northern borders of Saxony, numbers at the latter being increased during the summer to just short of two hundred. Badsulza was a large, crowded stalag, of the same type as Lamsdorf, for French, Belgian, and Serbian other ranks, the British Air Force personnel being placed in a separate barrack and not allowed to leave their own compound. Kirchhain comprised a wired compound enclosing four brick bungalows, which had been a pre-war youth hostel and rifle club, now shared by the British Air Force prisoners with some French. In spite of strict security measures at the latter camp, twelve men managed to break out in October; rather brutal reprisals were taken on the remainder.[2]

At Oberursel interrogation centre it was still the policy to solicit information in a smooth and plausible manner, and on release to the adjacent transit camp, to almost kill the prisoner with kindness. Thanks to adequate supplies of Red Cross food parcels, the food was good and well prepared. In the spring ski-ing parties gave place to pleasant walks in the woods. Nevertheless, by the end of the summer of 1941, 19 had made breaks from the transit camp and five from the hospital. In Stalag Luft I at Barth the spring and summer of 1941 saw regular supplies of Red Cross food coming into camp, the arrival of sports gear and books and the purchase of musical instruments, all of which gave considerable fillip to sport, educational classes, and entertainments. This period saw, besides several unsuccessful attempts, the first two Air Force escapes from Germany, two RAF officers getting to Sweden.

The officers of all three services who had been in Oflag IXA/H at Spangenburg were in February 1941 suddenly transferred to Stalag XXA, a fortress at Thorn, in Poland, as a reprisal for alleged ill-treatment of German prisoners in Canada. The castle was closed up and 60-odd convalescents from hospitals, with a few doctors and chaplains, were left in the Lower camp. At the same time 50 Air Force officers from Barth were also sent to Thorn. While the German authorities denied using reprisals and claimed to be within their rights under international law, it is clear that the conditions at Thorn could not be reconciled with the spirit of

---

[1] Although 50 officers were sent from Stalag Luft I at Barth to Stalag XXA at Thorn in February 1941, and another 50 to Oflag XC at Lubeck in July, by the end of the year there were still 230 at Barth. The NCOs' compound contained 550 as early as June 1941.
[2] Their boots were taken away and they were made to move in wooden clogs at their fastest pace at rifle point round a field for two and three-quarters hours, even though many men were physically weakened on account of the poor rations received over the previous months.

the Geneva Convention. The prisoners were housed in a fort used by the Germans in 1914–18, the greatest part of which was below ground level and flanked by a moat with sheer sides. Several escapes were attempted from the fort and one Air Force officer succeeded in reaching Sweden. Meanwhile, the German officers having been removed from the offending camp in Canada, the British returned from Thorn to Spangenburg in July,[1] both upper and lower camps becoming more overcrowded than ever. Finally, in October the officers were moved out to Warburg in conformity with the German plan of assembling all British officers in one large camp.

The last considerable batch of those seriously sick and wounded, who had come up from Athens in the *Gradisca,* had left Salonika by hospital train in November. The train, which was properly equipped with hospital beds and orderlies in attendance in each carriage, also carried German casualties. The journey took a devious route, dropping on the way patients, both British and German, at various hospitals which specialised in certain types of sickness or wound. In German military hospitals our men seem to have received very similar treatment to that given to the German patients. Eventually they found their way to prisoner-of-war hospitals, which varied to some extent according to the attitude of the local German authorities, though most seem at this stage to have suffered from overcrowding and to have had to rely mainly on British Red Cross supplies of bandages and dressings. The 450-bed hospital, or *Lazarett,* attached to Stalag VIIIB, Lamsdorf, was equipped for almost any type of operation and fully staffed by British medical officers and orderlies. On the other hand Lazarett Dieburg (attached to Stalag IXB), to which some of our wounded were sent, was reported as having rather out-of-date equipment. Others who went to Lazarett Rottenmunster (attached to Stalag VB) were reported in September as needing Red Cross supplies of food, clothing, and blankets. The efforts of British medical officers and orderlies in hospitals and camp sick-bays to secure better treatment and comfort for sick and wounded prisoners, as well as their own care for them, are beyond praise.

The plight of the maimed, incurable, and other sick whose continuance in captivity would prejudice their chance of recovery had not been neglected. The initiative on their behalf had been taken on the outbreak of war by the International Red Cross Committee, which drew the attention of belligerent powers to the

---

[1] The German Government had by then agreed not to make further use of fortresses or penal establishments to house British prisoners of war. But Oflag IVC remained an obvious contravention of this principle.

articles[1] of the Geneva Prisoners of War Convention relating to repatriation of such cases and to the setting up of Mixed Medical Commissions to select candidates for repatriation, at the same time urging them to conclude agreements for the purpose on the model of that set out in the Annex to the Convention. This model was accepted by the British, German, and Italian governments at an early stage of the war, with the omission of the provisions for accommodating certain categories in a neutral country instead of repatriating them. Mixed Medical Commissions had been set up, and although in Italy progress was slow, by the end of March 1941 66 Germans and 1153 British Commonwealth prisoners had been passed as eligible for repatriation.[2] No agreement had been reached concerning the route to be used for the exchange, until in September the Germans suggested the use of the cross-Channel route, which they had previously opposed.[3] Arrangements went ahead smoothly until a few days before the scheduled date, and shortly after Hitler's return from the Russian front, when there was a sudden change of tone on the German side. On 6 October the German radio broadcast that they would not agree to repatriation except on the basis of numerical equality. Britain refused to accept these new terms, and the whole scheme had to be abandoned. It appears now that the German volte-face was due to the personal intervention of Ribbentrop; and it is thought that the advance public interest shown in the British press and radio encouraged the Germans at the last moment to raise their price and so commit this 'flagrant breach of faith'.[4] For the amputees, the blind, the cot-cases, who had been so near to deliverance, it was a heartbreaking experience. Though they were kept for some time at Rouen,[5] nothing further eventuated. It was probably this first sad failure which gave birth to a distrustful attitude towards repatriation among prisoners in Germany. Even among those selected in later years to go home, many remained sceptical until they were actually on the repatriation ship.

III: *Civilians in Europe*

The breakdown of this first effort at repatriation in October 1941, which was to have been the prelude to further exchanges of servicemen and civilians, wrecked all immediate hopes for negotia-

---

[1] Articles 68 and 74.
[2] In addition 35 Germans and 700 British Commonwealth protected personnel were selected including a few New Zealanders. Britain had also agreed to include a number of German civilian women and children in the transport leaving from her port.
[3] Dieppe was to have been the port of exchange.
[4] For this reason most careful preparations were made in each later repatriation operation to avoid publicity until it was an accomplished fact.
[5] The Rouen party included several score without one, two or three limbs, all of whom were returned to Lamsdorf.

tion in this field. At the end of 1940, or early in 1941, a good many of the British Commonwealth civilians in occupied Europe were placed in internment camps. The German occupation force made use of French camps for the purpose. New Zealand men, for example, in France on business at the outbreak of war or working for the War Graves Commission, were taken to La Grande Caserne, St. Denis, on the outskirts of Paris. This was a huge old-fashioned barracks, with part of the grounds enclosed by barbed wire to allow space for exercise.

Overcrowding in Ilag XIII at Wülsburg having made conditions steadily worse, in October 1941 the German authorities transferred the British internees to a camp at Tost, not far from Lamsdorf, in Silesia. Known as Ilag VIII, it already held over 1000 British internees, including 200 of the crew of the SS *Orama*. They were housed in a group of large institution-like buildings of brick and concrete. Many were still short of clothing, though their needs in food and tobacco were being well catered for by supplies from the British Red Cross. As early as the end of 1940 there had been a well-organised education system and a camp orchestra. In spite of this, about a quarter of the internees expressed a desire for paid work to relieve the demoralising boredom of internment camp routine, and a start had been made by the employment of a few in forestry work.

Some of the women were interned at the end of 1940 in a French camp at Besançon, Doubs, renamed Frontstalag 142. Of those who had come under its control by February, 2400 were crowded into the Vauban barracks and 500 old and sick into the St. Jacques hospital. A thousand of those originally interned had already been liberated and several hundreds more were to follow. In June the British internees were transferred to Vittel, a French watering place near Epinal, Vosges. This 'camp', although given the forbidding label Frontstalag 121, consisted of first-class hotels and later accommodated families as well as single persons of either sex. From Vittel a young New Zealander, Miss Olga Marks, and two British women were able to escape in August 1941, making their way to Switzerland and eventually to England in January 1942.

Other women were taken to Germany, where they were accommodated in a spacious old convent at Liebenau, near Lake Constance in Wurtemburg. Those captured at sea who had been temporarily held at Sandbostel were also brought to Ilag Liebenau. Here they seem to have been 'well situated and kindly treated'. There was at first the same shortage of clothing and other necessities which was evident in other internment camps, though a fortunate few always seemed to have been able to move with a large amount of their personal belongings.

IV: *Protection of the Interests of Prisoners of War and Civilians*

The creation of new internment camps for civilians as well as additional prisoner-of-war camps for British Commonwealth soldiers captured in Greece and Crete,[1] involved a further increase in the work of visiting representatives of the United States diplomatic staff and of the International Red Cross Committee. The German authorities limited the latter to three visits a year for each camp, in view of the fact that there were also visits from the Protecting Power, the World Alliance of YMCAs, and from German inspectors. The Germans apparently found this aspect of their adherence to the Convention something of a nuisance.

The criticisms of the delegates, the text of the reports, and the conclusions of the covering letters did not always suit the camp commandants, or the Ministry of Foreign Affairs. There was a certain tension from time to time. . . .[2]

Moreover, the existence of so-called 'transit camps' where, as has been seen, conditions were usually primitive, was not reported by the German authorities until some time after their establishment; and a visit of inspection was arranged only as a result of long negotiation. Yet prisoners were kept for months at Salonika and at Galatas, the latter camp receiving no visit of inspection during the whole of its seven to eight months' existence.[3]

Not only was the circuit of camp visits enlarged, but welfare matters were constantly cropping up which entailed negotiation with the detaining power. Whereas it was the usual practice of the inspecting United States consular official merely to record complaints and criticisms for transmission to the government of the detainees, the International Red Cross Committee found it expedient to discuss many such matters on the spot and if possible effect a settlement there and then.[4] There were, for example, from late 1940 onwards almost continuous negotiations regarding prisoners' rations; for although they were entitled by the Convention to the rations of 'depot troops', in practice they received less than those allotted to the civilian population.[5] There was constant dispute as to whether Germany should provide clothing in addition to that sent by the British Government through Red Cross channels. It took time to persuade the German authorities to distribute chap-

---

[1] The number of British prisoners had risen to over 80,000.
[2] International Red Cross Committee Report on Activities during the 1939–45 War, Vol. I, p. 244.
[3] An International Red Cross delegation had been set up in Athens in 1940.
[4] In view of the increased expenses of the IRCC an appeal for funds was made, to which the New Zealand Government responded with a donation of £2500 in June 1941.
[5] There was a general reduction of the ration for prisoners of war in Germany on 3 June 1941.

lain prisoners among the various camps so as to give the greatest possible number of prisoners an opportunity for the practice of their religion. Neither Britain nor Germany could make up her mind to exchange information regarding the location of prisoner-of-war camps, in spite of air-raid casualties among prisoners of war on both sides of the Channel. Prisoners in working camps had to be protected as far as possible against excessive working hours, lack of proper medical attention, and inhumane conditions coupled with exposure to danger at work such as obtained in the Silesian coal mines.

The complaints on which such negotiations were based reached the International Red Cross Committee and the Protecting Power in a variety of ways. Their visiting delegates were entitled on each inspection to a private interview[1] with a 'camp leader'—the senior officer in an oflag, the 'man-of-confidence'[2] in a stalag, the senior medical officer in a hospital and often in other camps too. These camp representatives made it their business in the interview to bring to light all matters on which they were in dispute with the camp authorities. Complaints often came also in letters either from camp leaders or from individual prisoners of war; still others came in letters from prisoners' next-of-kin. If during a visit nothing could be done to settle the matter on the spot, it was communicated to the British Foreign Office so that it could be examined by the various British departments, Dominion governments and committees concerned, before a formal complaint was made to the German Ministry of Foreign Affairs.

The inter-governmental committee on prisoners of war announced by the Dominions Secretary on 30 April 1941 never met. Its Sub-Committee B[3] continued the meetings concerning pay, allowances, and other financial matters which it had begun as the Inter-departmental Committee. Sub-Committee A met once on 26 June 1941 and took note of its terms of reference:

> To consider such questions affecting policy and general administration of prisoners of war as concern more than one Government within the Empire with a view to avoiding undesirable differences of treatment.

After broaching the knotty questions of whether the Dominions should act in the custody of enemy prisoners as agents for the British Government, and whether they should canalise all their communications to enemy powers through the British Foreign Office, it adjourned for a month. But no further meeting was

---

[1] Geneva Prisoners of War Convention.
[2] See p. 87, note 1.
[3] Sub-Committee B never at any time ceased to conduct regular meetings no matter under what title it went.

called for some considerable time, as the Canadian Government, which had been in the habit of communicating direct with enemy governments through the State Department at Washington, was pressing for a revision of the whole system of committees. The present system, it claimed, mixed policy with administrative detail and allowed the committees to be swamped with a mass of British Government officials. The view of the New Zealand representatives was that the presence of the British Government experts saved time that would be lost by having to refer matters back to them, and that they had noticed no tendency on the part of the British representatives to exercise undue influence on the deliberations of any committee.

After some months agreement was reached by letter to a reconstituted committee, and on 5 November 1941 there met for the first time the Imperial Prisoners of War Committee, whose terms of reference were:

> To secure co-ordination of the action of His Majesty's Governments in regard to matters relating to prisoners of war both in our own and in enemy hands.

It consisted of the Dominion High Commissioners or their representatives[1] under the chairmanship of the Financial Secretary of the War Office, with expert departmental advisers co-opted as was thought necessary. Two sub-committees similarly constituted were to carry on the work of their predecessors. They met regularly throughout the remainder of the war and between them controlled the administration of prisoner-of-war matters within the Commonwealth. The suggestion that the British Foreign Office should act as a common channel of communication with the enemy was approved (without prejudice to the rights of the Dominions as separate signatories of the Geneva Convention) as a practical expedient to prevent the Axis governments from playing off one member of the Commonwealth against another.

One of the matters considered at the first meeting of the main Imperial Prisoners of War Committee was the notification of capture and of subsequent moves of prisoners. In addition to the official lists (with addresses)[2] sent ordinary mail by the German Government to the United States Embassy and the International Red Cross Committee, a third copy was by arrangement sent to the War Office[3] in London through the prisoner-of-war post. After the fall of France in June 1940, the transmission of all these lists to London

---
[1] The main Committee met only three times and High Commissioners were present in person at only one of these meetings. It also included a representative for India.
[2] See above pp. 9–10.
[3] The Prisoners of War Information Bureau of the War Office passed all relevant information on to the New Zealand High Commissioner's Office in London.

was subject to severe delays owing to the interruption of mail services which has already been noticed. It was arranged, therefore, that the International Red Cross Committee would telegraph to the War Office in London short particulars as soon as the list reached Geneva. For the same reasons this arrangement was later extended to New Zealand and other Commonwealth countries, telegrams being sent to New Zealand Base headquarters in Cairo for checking and onward transmission,[1] and also to the prisoner's home country in answer to a special inquiry.

For some time this proved the quickest route for information. But the subsequent speeding up of the prisoner-of-war post by flying it from Stuttgart to Lisbon, and from Lisbon to London, meant that a postcard from a prisoner often reached his next-of-kin before official notification of his capture, owing to the time taken to assemble official lists in Berlin. The receipt of personal mail and of answers from Geneva to cabled inquiries before any official casualty notice caused many next-of-kin in New Zealand to be highly critical of governmental channels of communication; and so long were the delays in notification of prisoners from the Greece and Crete campaigns, that many relatives spent money on reply-paid cables to Geneva. There were on 1 October 1941 still 2400 missing servicemen unaccounted for.[2] As a result of many representations on the matter, the New Zealand Government investigated the possibility of appointing a liaison officer to work with the International Red Cross Committee in Geneva in facilitating the transmission of New Zealand names. The Committee, while pointing out that only neutrals were eligible for appointment to its staff, suggested the visit of a New Zealand Red Cross representative to Geneva to see at first hand the working of the Central Agency for Information. Meanwhile it was arranged for notifications to be cabled to the Prime Minister's Department in Wellington[3] as well as to Cairo, and for the lists of New Zealand missing to be immediately sent to the International Red Cross Committee. In October, to discourage next-of-kin from continuing to spend money on cables to Geneva, the International Red Cross Committee was asked to hold replies to individual inquiries for sixty hours to give time for an official government notification to reach the inquirer's address. By the end of the year, most of the prisoners having arrived at permanent camps in Germany, their names had been notified and the current difficulty was largely solved.

---

[1] The only delay occurred in the checking of details at Cairo, which was necessary to ensure accuracy. The information was also sent to the War Office, whence it was passed to the New Zealand High Commissioner's Office in London.

[2] In general the German authorities would not include the name of a prisoner on an official list until he had reached a permanent camp. For those taken in Crete especially this was not for anything up to six months after capture.

[3] The first of these cables was sent on 10 September 1941.

V: *Relief Work*

The miserable position of prisoners at the transit camps in Greece and Crete could have been immeasurably improved if sufficient Red Cross food supplies had been on hand. The generosity of the Greek Red Cross, assisted by grants of money from the International Red Cross Committee's delegate in Athens,[1] did much to relieve the immediate wants of the sick in transit hospitals and sick-bays. But this source alone could not be expected to supply adequately the thousands of Allied soldiers who filled the camps, and an attempt was made through the International Red Cross delegation at Ankara to have food shipped from Turkey.[2] Then, in early August, rail communication was re-established with Switzerland, enabling four wagons of British Red Cross food parcels to go through to Athens. Although some were distributed at the transit camp and the hospitals in and near the capital, by the time the remainder of this consignment and the first shipload of Turkish food could be got to other camps, most of the prisoners had been moved to Germany.

Although it seemed a long time to hungry prisoners, there was a delay of only a few weeks before relief supplies of food parcels arrived at the new British camps in Germany and Austria. Sometimes there was considerable delay after their arrival in reaching agreement with the German camp authorities regarding distribution, for German ideas of control varied from camp to camp. Some camp commandants insisted on all tins being opened and their contents emptied into the prisoner's containers—usually a bowl and a mug—so that no tins, box, packing, or string should remain in the prisoner's possession. Others contented themselves with puncturing all tins, so that food could not be stored up for use in an escape. The German cut in the rations for prisoners of war in June 1941 served to emphasize the necessity for the regular supply to camps of these parcels. The end of the year saw the British Red Cross weekly output increased to 80,000 parcels, in addition to 22,500 supplied by Canada, 2500 of which were paid for by the New Zealand Joint Council from the National Patriotic Fund.[3] The amount of food available for distribution had also been increased by shiploads of bulk food from the British community in the Argentine, the first of which was sent to Lisbon in July 1941. All supplies from whatever source were checked into a bulk store in

---

[1] £5000 was sent by the British Red Cross to the IRCC delegate, Dr. Brunel, to be spent on supplementary food. Milk, fruit, and other provisions were supplied.
[2] The first shipload, consisting of 70 tons of food parcels and clothing, left Turkey about mid-October 1941. £10,000 was sent by the British Red Cross to the IRCC delegate at Ankara for the purpose.
[3] Canada's output reached 22,500 in October 1941. New Zealand's quota was increased to 4000 early in 1942. The cost was approximately 15s. each.

Geneva to form a common pool, which could be drawn upon by the International Red Cross Committee according to the demands of the various camps of both prisoners and civilian internees in Italy as well as Germany.

By the autumn of 1941 medical and invalid comforts (now standardised by the British Red Cross to a milk parcel and a special food parcel) were being distributed from Geneva in accordance with reports and requests received from camp and hospital medical officers. Besides building up an eight weeks' reserve at Geneva and a reserve in each camp and hospital, the plan was to send off weekly supplies on a fixed scale.[1] Braille appliances and training material were sent for the blind; hearing aids for the deaf, many of whom were elderly civilian internees; and dental materials according to the requests of captured dental officers. British doctors and dentists had to rely to a very great extent on these supplies received through Geneva from the British Red Cross.

With the large increase in the number of New Zealand prisoners resulting from the campaigns in Greece and Crete, it was obvious that some of the services undertaken for New Zealanders by the British Red Cross would soon entail a very considerable extra volume of work. It was obvious also that the bulk of it should be shouldered by some New Zealand organisation. But although there was in London a representative of the New Zealand Joint Council, Colonel B. Myers, he had no staff for dealing with the administrative task involved. Accordingly a special Prisoners of War Section of the High Commissioner's Office was set up under Mr. C. B. Burdekin to expand the work which had already begun in arranging for the sending of a small number of 'personal parcels' and packages of tobacco. Colonel Myers continued to act in an advisory capacity. In July the section began to handle all inquiries sent to the British Red Cross concerning New Zealanders.

To answer similar inquiries in New Zealand the Joint Council had in May already set up a Prisoners of War Inquiry Office, which was organised to give next-of-kin and friends additional information and advice concerning a prisoner's welfare after government notification of his capture had been received. Shortly after the middle of the year depots were set up at the four main centres for censoring and repacking quarterly next-of-kin parcels, following the methods used by the British Red Cross in conjunction with the censorship authorities in England, and the first batch left New Zealand towards the end of September.

---

[1] Invalid comforts were sent on a scale of 50 parcels to a thousand men in a camp, and 17 for each 50 beds in a hospital. Each of these groups also received one unit of medical supplies.

Meanwhile, owing to the extra time a prisoner would have to wait for his first parcel if it were sent from New Zealand, it had been arranged for the Prisoners of War Section of the High Commissioner's Office in London to pack and send an initial parcel. Moreover, since it often was some time before a prisoner's permanent camp address was known, and as the International Red Cross Committee was unable to undertake the enormous task of redirection, it was arranged that parcels from New Zealand should be sent to the section in London for this purpose. To accommodate the large volume of parcels which would have to be handled,[1] extra premises were secured in Charing Cross Road. The Prisoners of War Section in London continued to arrange for monthly supplies of tobacco and cigarettes to be sent to each New Zealand prisoner, in addition to those already being sent in bulk through Geneva. It was felt that the needs for all British Commonwealth prisoners in books, games, music, sport, gardening, and education were being adequately catered for on a camp basis by the British Red Cross.

* * * * *

While the general behaviour of the German medical corps towards prisoners in Greece and Crete was entirely humane, the same cannot be said of the treatment meted out either by some of their paratroops under the stress of battle or by some of those who took over the control of transit camps. The starvation which led to beriberi at Salonika, the beatings and other ill-treatment during transport to Germany, the indiscriminate shootings on Crete, are all examples of that ruthless subordination of humanity to expediency, of means to ends, with which the Nazi leaders succeeded in infecting a good number of their subordinate commanders.

The increasingly overt hostility of the United States, confirmed by the mid-Atlantic meeting of Churchill and Roosevelt in August 1941, and the surprise of the Russian counter-offensive in September dispelled the German optimism of the summer, based on hopes of a quick victory in the East and a new onslaught in the West before America was ready. By late autumn the German leaders knew that they were launched on a long and exhausting struggle. While committed to being *korrekt* in their observance of the Geneva Convention,[2] it became the policy of the Nazi Government to use their prisoners to the utmost and to make them as little of a drain on the national economy as possible. As many as could be used were pushed out into farm work, coalmining, factory work, and

---

[1] The number of parcels handled rose from seven in December 1940 to 801 in October 1941.
[2] Hitler made a pronouncement to this effect in 1939.

any unskilled tasks that would free Germans for a more active part in the war effort. On the other hand, to conserve Germany's national resources, expenditure of materials for prisoner-of-war accommodation was kept as low as possible; lighting, heating, and feeding were reduced to the lowest possible scale, and their canteens were so depleted as to be little more than tokens. Some attempts were made to employ prisoners on military work, but the vigilance of British camp leaders and the action of visiting neutral inspectors forced such projects to be abandoned. Under pressure of this kind many of the worse defects of the prisoner-of-war camps were remedied. On occasion, however, the Germans were prepared to completely ignore the Convention, as their demand for a numerically equal exchange at Dieppe and their reprisals on the British officers sent to Poland clearly showed. Indeed, considering the Nazi Government's record of cynical disregard for pacts and treaties, it is remarkable that the Prisoners of War Convention survived the first three years of the war, when Germany held so many of our men prisoners and we held so few of hers.

Used to an iron discipline which repressed the slightest deviation from an order once given, the average German prisoner-of-war camp guard failed to understand how British soldiers could question the orders of his superiors. Still less could he understand how prisoners could want to disobey camp orders by trying to escape. However, seeing that the British prisoners were incorrigible in the matter, security measures must be enforced to prevent them: locking up the barracks at night, restricting the issue of clothing so that none could be used for making civilian clothes, meticulous examination of all parcels arriving by post. Although it took the German authorities some time to realise that an uncomfortable camp and harsh discipline often provided the incentive to escape, propaganda to convert the prisoner to the German way of thinking was thought worth while from the start. We find anti-Semitic pamphlets distributed at Stalag IXC, and others at Dulag Luft on atrocities committed by the Poles. For general distribution to camps there was a small four-page newspaper in English—*The Camp*—which in the autumn of 1941 was pointing out to its as yet 'unenlightened' British readers the solidarity of Germany and Italy and the exploitation of the 'Anglo-Saxons' by 'world Jewry'.[1] Over the camp radio loudspeakers came the voice of 'Lord Haw-Haw' expatiating on British losses and difficulties in England. Camp leaders took a firm line in combating such propaganda, and so effectively did they build up a resistance to these German advances that both printed and broadcast propaganda

---

[1] Further details of this paper and its method and contents are given in later chapters.

became for the vast majority of British prisoners matter for derision, often lifting morale rather than lowering it.

Those who passed through Greece and Crete had been cheered by the fearlessness of most of the inhabitants, their sterling loyalty to the Allied cause, and their generous help to British prisoners, often in defiance of German disapproval. Yet it is hard for men to remain cheerful when they know they are rapidly losing weight, and when their bodily craving for nourishment keeps them thinking constantly of the next miserable meal. No other single factor seems to have restored morale so much as the issue of Red Cross food. Some prisoners of war, like the man who wrote in his diary for June 1941 that he could not agree with his friend's prediction that they would be 'home by Christmas' but that Christmas 1942 would be a reasonable hope, seem now to have been touchingly optimistic. But for most people in the heart of an enemy country during a war, cut off from the world by barbed wire and a double censorship, a realistic viewpoint is neither easy nor satisfying. For non-working prisoners, unless they were engaged on some camp duty or escape work (and not everybody could be), the days could become just 'plain boring'. And the mood of many in this situation varied between acute depression and wild optimism, according to the food supply, a favourable turn to the war, or news from home.

The losses in prisoners of the New Zealand Division in the period from April to June 1941 gave rise in the Dominion to a widespread interest in the position of captured servicemen, and brought the authorities face to face with the problem of organising help for them on a large scale. In leading next-of-kin through the maze of labels, coupons, and lists of prohibited articles which had to be tackled each time a personal parcel was sent, and in generally interpreting the prisoner-of-war situation to relatives, the Joint Council Inquiry Office and its local branches served a most useful purpose. The decision to pack and send food parcels for prisoners gave New Zealand the opportunity to make her most appropriate contribution to the pool of relief supplies now coming from British communities in various parts of the world. The welfare of British prisoners and the custody of enemy prisoners had both become problems for the whole Commonwealth, a fact of which the practical outcome was the setting up in London of the Imperial Prisoners of War Committee. For the rest of the war its two sub-committees of British and Dominion representatives were responsible for settling the vast number of administrative problems relating to British Commonwealth prisoners of war.

CHAPTER 4

The Second Libyan Campaign and After
(November 1941 – June 1942)

I: *The Desert Campaign of 1941—Prisoners in Italian Hands*

LESS than six months after the end of the campaign in Crete the British Western Desert Force, now the Eighth Army, again took the initiative in North Africa. As part of this force the New Zealand Division, reformed and re-equipped, crossed the border into Libya on 19 November ready to play a full part for the first time in desert warfare. The initial successes of the campaign in eastern Cyrenaica could not be exploited because of the unfavourable outcome of the great tank battle around the Sidi Rezegh area. The plan to destroy the enemy armour failed, and British losses in tanks and guns left some of our detached forces a prey to enemy armoured columns. Whereas the Greece and Crete campaigns had culminated in fairly controlled withdrawals from stubbornly defended positions, the Libyan campaign of November 1941 developed into a bewildering alternation of attack and defence with a possible front on every point of the compass.

The result was a complicated tangle of captures, escapes, recaptures, and liberations. General von Ravenstein, commanding part of Rommel's armour, fell into the hands of three of 21 NZ Battalion's Intelligence Section near Point 175. The headquarters of 5 NZ Brigade Group, isolated on an airfield near Bardia, was swept up by Rommel's mobile column. Captured Italian prisoners were liberated when German tanks surrounded their captors. A thousand-odd British prisoners were freed when Bardia was retaken. So difficult was it to tell whether a column of vehicles was British or enemy, that newly-captured prisoners were sometimes able to drive away in enemy trucks and make their way back to our lines.

Most of the New Zealanders captured were infantry and supporting elements whose positions had been overrun by German tanks. An infantryman's diary of events at Sidi Rezegh on 30 November tells a typical story of capture in the desert:

I look again through the loop-hole on my side and I can scarcely believe my eyes. The sun has set and through the moonlit dusk two hundred yards in front of me scores of men from all directions are walking in among the German tanks, their hands raised above their heads. . . . A minute or two and tanks are rumbling through and in our lines, men rising from their possies and surrendering. . . .

A warrant officer of the same battalion mentions that the attached artillery was out of shells and that the supply line was cut; an attached machine-gunner states simply that 'both machine-guns were silenced'. Such a situation made resistance to a tank attack hopeless, and indeed suicidal.

With appropriate alterations in time and place, this is in general the story of most of the other groups of army prisoners taken in the campaign of November 1941. The overrunning of the headquarters and attached troops of 5 Brigade by a tank column from Bardia on 27 November has already been mentioned; an already weakened 21 Battalion met a similar fate at Point 175 on the 29th; 24 and 26 Battalions were cut to pieces at Sidi Rezegh on the 30th; and on 1 December a German armoured attack on Belhamed practically destroyed 20 Battalion. Almost the entire medical services of the Division, grouped together and left unprotected south of Zaafran, had fallen into enemy hands on 28 November. Our assumption that, in view of their protection by the Geneva Convention, medical personnel would not be taken prisoner did not prevent many of them being transported back to the Axis base areas and later to Italy. The German armour had reaped a good harvest among the widely spread units of the Division. Less than a fortnight after the three brigade groups had crossed the Libyan border, 2578 of their number were killed or wounded and another 2042 were prisoners in the transit camps or hospitals of Bardia, Derna, and Benghazi. The remnants of 4 and 6 Brigades made their way back to Egypt, and three battalions of the 5th remained in the field with an improvised headquarters.

After a brief search for arms, most prisoners were almost immediately herded back along the enemy's line of communication. Some had only a short distance to go, others a march of four hours before they reached trucks to take them on to a staging compound in the enemy rear areas. Both on the march and in enemy transport it was sometimes the misfortune of prisoners to be bombed and machine-gunned by our own planes. At the staging compounds they were usually handed over to Italian line-of-communication troops, often with expressions of regret from the escorting guards of the Afrika Korps. The majority of these makeshift 'cages' were just wired-in pieces of open desert, on which prisoners had to spend a cold night, with a blanket among three or more and little or no food and water, before going on next day. Some parties were made by the Germans to work temporarily at supply dumps, but while there they seem to have been treated generously with food and cigarettes. The German front-line soldiers appear to have been instructed against looting from prisoners, for they were in general scrupulous in avoiding it; but it is clear that no such scruples weighed with many of the Italian guards.

Although only a few of those taken seem to have undergone interrogation, there were some Italian and German interrogators (mainly the latter) at the staging camps. The Italians collected large quantities of photographs and personal papers for examination. The German methods ranged from getting into casual conversation in the prison compound to shouting and screaming and threatening with a revolver (fired over the prisoner's head or near his feet), or even with a machine gun. Almost every soldier had had it impressed upon his memory that if captured, no matter what he was asked, he must give only his name, rank, and number; that the German interrogators had to resort to methods of intimidation indicates that few of our men gave away information.

Although few official instructions on what to do in the event of capture were given out in the Greece and Crete campaigns, the matter was not neglected in the preparations for the desert campaign of 1941. An instruction from GHQ Middle East had been passed on to almost every man, and maps of enemy countries and other escape aids had been distributed on as wide a scale as possible. The instructions emphasized the warning concerning name, rank, and number mentioned above, and the importance of trying to escape. Lack of cover in the desert made the initial concealment necessary for an escape very difficult; and this, combined with heat, lack of water, and heavy going underfoot made a long journey back to our lines a tremendous feat of physical endurance. Some succeeded in evading capture, like the machine-gunner at Sidi Rezegh on 30 November who feigned death and crawled away in the darkness to reach our lines the same night, but many others who tried lying low in a similar way were discovered.

The capture on 28 November of the New Zealand medical centre containing a thousand of our wounded and the majority of the medical personnel of the Division was a serious blow. It prevented our evacuating any more of our casualties, and meant that unless the dressing stations were recaptured the lightly wounded combatant troops would be taken west by the enemy as prisoners of war. The medical personnel were at first thought to be exempt from this treatment, but at midday on 2 December some 200 of them were taken off by the Italians on the pretence of forming a base hospital in the back areas.[1] Realising that the

---

[1] A Note from the British Government to the Italian Government on 11 September 1941 had given Italy the right to retain British medical personnel and chaplains if they were needed to attend to British prisoners.

same might happen at any time to the rest of the occupants of the centre, a party of 31 lightly wounded and medical personnel made a successful break-out by truck that night; another party of 20 did the same at midday on 4 December. Both parties reached Allied lines safely.[1]

The evacuation by truck of prisoners taken in the area near Tobruk followed the main coastal road through Derna and Barce to the main transit camp at Benghazi. This journey took two days or considerably longer according to the transport available and the time spent at one or other of the many staging places along the route. Most of these were wired enclosures in open ground of the type already described, sometimes equipped with Italian bivouac tents for shelter, primitive sanitation, and a little bedding. Rather heavy rain during this period made most of these temporary camping grounds quagmires, thus completing the discomfort occasioned by cold nights with very little bed covering. By way of contrast Derna was pleasantly situated, had tidy rows of big square tents with plaited mat floors and an ample water supply, and seems to have been properly organised beforehand. At all these staging camps there were hard rations of tinned meat and biscuits.

Prisoners taken in the Bardia–Sollum area were marched or transported into Bardia. Here the accommodation consisted for other ranks of a stony compound near the coast, enclosed by a wall but practically devoid of other shelter, and for officers an adjacent barn-like shed with a fenced-in area for exercise. The nights were cold and sometimes wet as well, and as many as six other ranks slept together to spin out their blankets and to keep each other warm. In the weeks that followed they rigged up primitive shelters with old blankets, stones, and pieces of corrugated iron. Proper sanitary arrangements were non-existent and dysentery cases soon made their appearance. Water had to be brought to the compound in barrels: fresh water for drinking but only sea water for washing. Food—coffee, macaroni or rice, bread or biscuits—was of quite good quality, but only enough to keep men alive, and ' not enough body in it to give [them] . . . much strength'. After a week a large party of the more senior officers, including Brigadier Hargest,[2] was moved away at night to Benghazi on a submarine which had just arrived with fresh water and petrol. The other officers followed soon after in other submarines but went direct to Italy. Although the evacuation of small parties by submarine went on

---

[1] The first party (2 December) was under the command of Lt-Col G. Dittmer, CO 28 (Maori) Battalion, and the second party under Lt-Col Kippenberger, CO 20 Battalion.
[2] Brig J. Hargest, CBE, DSO and bar, MC, m.i.d.; Member of Parliament for Invercargill 1931–35, Awarua 1935–44; born Gore, 4 Sep 1891; farmer; served 1 NZEF 1914–20, commanded 2 Bn Otago Regt, 1918; comd 5 NZ Inf Bde May 1940–Nov 1941; p.w. 27 Nov 1941; escaped Mar 1943; killed in action, France, 12 Aug 1944.

almost until the town was recaptured, and 60-odd sick went off in a German hospital ship, a thousand men finally remained to be liberated. They passed the month of December in acute discomfort and suspense, sharing with the beleaguered garrison the short commons, the Allied bombs, and the uncertainty whether or not they would be evacuated.

The main enemy collecting centre at Sidi Hussein outside Benghazi had been in use for some time. Airmen shot down in Libya and troops captured during or since the enemy counter-thrust to the Egyptian border in April made up a total of several hundreds by September 1941. At that date the camp was suddenly cleared. A small number remained in North Africa as a working party for the Germans, but most were taken by truck to Tarhuna, near Tripoli, whence after a short stay in military barracks they were shipped to Italy. When in November 1941, as a result of the British offensive, unexpected thousands of British troops fell into enemy hands, the German policy of speedy evacuation by truck to the rear soon filled Benghazi transit camp to overflowing. By 5 December it held behind barbed wire some 6000 British Commonwealth troops—Australians, Indians, New Zealanders, South Africans (including negroes), and men from the United Kingdom. The facilities were quite inadequate for such numbers, and improvements were neglected, seemingly in the hope that the prisoners would quickly move on to Italy.

The main compound, a large area of sandy ground, contained several barracks and sheds for motor transport; an overflow compound alongside it contained only Italian groundsheet bivouac tents. Over 700 had to jam into each draughty, unlighted shed at night, the majority sleeping on the concrete floor after the few camp beds were occupied. The lack of bedding is typified by three men who shared a blanket, a greatcoat, and a groundsheet; many had still less. In the daytime the men milled about in the space between the barrack huts. There were long queues for the few small taps: beards grew for lack of shaving facilities, and most men, unable to wash properly, had not had their clothes off since going into action two or three weeks before. The long trenches serving as latrines soon became cesspools and clouds of flies spread dysentery.

A dreary diet of half a pound of bread, a little macaroni soup, and a little tinned meat was issued daily through the camp staff of South Africans appointed by the Italian commandant. By mid-December men were experiencing the 'blackouts' through lack of nourishment which have already been noticed in the transit camps of Greece and Crete; and many had adopted a policy of lying down as much as possible to conserve their strength. An occasional issue of a lemon and a few cigarettes did little to alleviate the situation. Tempers began to fray under the boring routine of waiting all day to queue up with an empty meat-tin for the next meagre issue of food. Both with each other and with the Italian troops, some men traded for food at fantastic prices such of their valuables as had survived various searches: wristlet watches, rings, or fountain pens for small quantities of cigarettes or loaves of bread. Besides the all-important topic of food, thoughts and conversation turned on the possibility of rescue by our advancing forces and the alternative of transportation to Italy. Rumours of the British advance and the nightly sound of bombs on Benghazi helped to maintain morale, which to judge by the enthusiastic evening sing-songs seems to have been high in spite of the conditions. Almost every night men got out from the compound, planning to hide up and wait for Allied liberation, but most of them were recaptured.

In early December a first draft of 2000-odd had marched down to the docks, bound, as the guards enthusiastically put it, for 'bella Italia'—an aesthetic rapture which brought little response among the prisoners. They sailed from Benghazi packed in the holds of a merchant ship, and in the next few days several smaller drafts followed. By the 20th the camp still held some 1500 prisoners, but had been cleared of almost everything else, in anticipation of the arrival of British forces. Hopes of liberation ran high among the prisoners. When no rations were forthcoming the camp store was ransacked for what it would yield. A false march down to the docks and back to camp heightened the prisoners' suspense and made it look as if this last evacuation would indeed prove impossible. But next day they were marched off and packed into the holds of a German cargo ship, which left for Tripoli the same night.

A few prisoners made last-minute escapes from the line of march to the docks, diving up alleyways or dodging inside ruined buildings. One New Zealander[1] hid in a cement heap and finally emerged with cement bags over his head and legs, to stroll easily out of the town as an Arab. Senussi fed and concealed him five miles out until it was safe to return. Another[2] simply hid with two companions in a ruined hotel, where they carefully rationed out their remaining food and lay low. They had only to wait in hiding for three days, for on Christmas Eve British armoured cars were in the town, and that night they had a celebration dinner with their rescuers.

The party of 1500 from Benghazi reached Tripoli on 23 December. A train was ready to take them to a temporary camp at Garian

---
[1] Sgt P. A. McConchie (20 Bn).
[2] Sgt C. C. McDonald (20 Bn).

and they were packed into goods-trucks, in which, the engine having broken down, they spent a miserable night huddled together for warmth. The next day they completed their journey with an exhausting 14-kilometre march into the hills, in the course of which fatigue, sickness, and lack of food caused many to fall out by the side of the steep hill road. That night they were housed in old Italian concrete barracks and given hard rations and a blanket. And here they spent a cold and unpleasant three days in spite of a small tot of cognac, cigarettes, and additional food on Christmas Day. The year's end saw them packed into the cold iron holds of the same freighter, bound for Italy 'and exile', as one man puts it in his diary. A foul three-day trip amid the reek of seasickness and dysentery brought them to Naples. After intolerable muddling and delay came the relief of getting ashore and the joy of a hot shower while clothes were being disinfested. They were the last of this large haul of prisoners from North Africa to pass through Naples.

Statements by eye-witnesses, both medical and combatant, indicate that the treatment of our wounded on the battlefield by the Germans was as good as conditions allowed. In the Italian field hospital at Bardia there seems to have been no discrimination between patients of whatever nationality, though general overcrowding lowered the standard of care. The Italian nursing nuns in the Torelli hospital at Benghazi made up in kindness to prisoner patients what was lacking in medical treatment and hospital equipment. Many of the patients in the hospital were liberated when Benghazi was recaptured.

Apart from the few who were transported from Bardia by submarine, the bulk of the prisoners from North Africa had left Benghazi or Tripoli direct for Italy in Axis cargo or passenger vessels or in Italian warships. Crammed into the holds and battened down at nights, they had been rushed across the Mediterranean and were just as relieved as the Italian guards and crew to reach Taranto or Brindisi in safety, though many prisoners had vaguely nursed wild hopes of a dramatic naval rescue during the crossing. One of the ships paid an unexpected call to Crete, where a party of 250-odd spent a week or so at the then comparatively empty Galatas camp before going on to Taranto.

On 8 December a large draft of 2100 had left on the *Jantzen*, an 8000-ton cargo vessel, with rations sufficient for the 36-hour dash across to Italy. In the middle of the next afternoon, just off Cape Methoni, near Pilos on the south-west coast of the Greek Peloponnese, she was struck by a torpedo in one of the forward holds. Five hundred or more of the prisoners packed there were killed, and the hatchboards falling in with men lying on them killed others as they crashed below. As soon as they had recovered from the shock of the explosion, men rushed to the decks up ropes or still usable ladders. The rugged coastline of Greece could be seen a mile or two away with heavy seas breaking on it, lashed by a bitterly cold wind.

The Italian captain and crew had taken themselves off in two of the three lifeboats, the other having capsized in launching, and some of the men jumped overboard in an attempt to swim to the shore. Nine New Zealanders reached one of the boats, which eventually made a nearby uninhabited island where they spent the night, and they were taken over to the mainland next day. Fifteen got away on a raft they had managed to launch, but more than half of these died of exposure. Meanwhile a German naval engineer had taken control of the ship, explaining to those on board that the engines would still go and that there was a good chance of reaching safety. He ordered everybody aft in order to keep the weight off the damaged bow and organised rescue parties to bring up to the officers' quarters the injured from the lower decks. Although the wind and sea were still strong, the ship was brought in stern first and beached about 5 p.m. broadside on to an open piece of coast. In spite of the bitter cold many now swam the remaining fifty yards to the shore, and when darkness fell many others made their way to safety along ropes secured to the rocks. Next day dawned fine, and those still on board came off in the remaining lifeboat or on stretchers slung to the ropes. A check made later showed that a little over two-thirds of the British prisoners had survived, the remainder (including 44 New Zealanders) having perished either in the explosion or in the events which followed.

The survivors, many of whom had lost clothes and boots, spent a wretched winter in primitive and ill-provided transit camps on the Peloponnese, now under Italian control. They lived successively in empty buildings near the scene of the wreck, in the cells of an old Turkish fort at Pilos, and in Italian bivouac tents erected in a small area at Akhaia, on the route to Patras. The last became known to the prisoners as 'Dysentery Acre', on account of the prevalence of the disease among them at the camp and the thick mud resulting from persistent rain and snow. Food consisted of the normal kind of Italian army rations, though the quantity was insufficient in cold weather to satisfy the needs of men who had been on limited rations for some time. The nearest water supply was the pump of a Greek household several fields away. After a fortnight the Italians issued boots and greatcoats for those without them. Much sickness (some of it fatal), the squalid living conditions, and a good deal of unnecessary regimentation by Italian officers left an indelible imprint on the memories of those who endured the short stay at this 'camp'.

At the end of December the prisoners were taken north to Patras. Here they lived in the old, verminous concrete huts of a transit camp near the shore, formerly used by the Greeks for Italian prisoners. After a month the Italian guard, whose almost sole consideration was to prevent anyone escaping, allowed the prisoners out of the huts for a set time each day. Two New Zealanders who tried to escape received a brutal beating up and a spell in a civilian jail in chains. During February the camp was cleared in small drafts to Italy, the men travelling on Italian transports under the most favourable conditions they had yet encountered during captivity.

Most of the early shiploads of prisoners from North Africa had disembarked at Naples and, after disinfestation there, had been taken to the prisoner-of-war camp at Capua. Later shiploads had disembarked at Brindisi and gone to a transit camp at Tuturano, some miles inland; others had disembarked at Taranto or Bari, to be accommodated at a camp on the outskirts of the latter. And so at the beginning of 1942 almost all the able-bodied New Zealanders taken in the Second Libyan Campaign found themselves in prison camps in southern Italy. Some of the senior officers had gone to Sulmona (Campo PG 78)[1] and the sick and wounded were in hospitals in Caserta and Bari. The bulk of the prisoners, however, were in Campo PG 66[2] at Capua, in Campo PG 85 at Tuturano, or in Campo PG 75 at Bari, each of them near a port with a disinfesting plant. They were all temporary camps intended for holding prisoners until 'disinfestation and sorting' had been carried out. But it is doubtful whether either process ever reached finality in any of them, and a 'temporary' stay might sometimes extend to several months.

Campo PG 66, on a flat stretch of ground on the outskirts of Capua, had been in use as a prisoner-of-war camp since early 1941, when a medical officer reported favourably on its food, water supply and sanitation, and the men stated that they were being 'well taken care of.' Though overcrowding at the end of 1941 stultified such amenities as were provided, conditions were an improvement for most prisoners. Other ranks lived 18 to a tent (made of Italian groundsheets), slept on duck-boards with straw palliasses and two Italian blankets each, and had regular though not always sufficient

---

[1] Campo (or Campo PG) is short for *Campo concentramento di prigioneri di guerra*, permanent camp. The camps were originally known by their place names, and numbers were not introduced until early 1942.
[2] *Campo disinfestazione e smistamento*, quarantine camp.

rations. An area of about five acres gave adequate space for exercise, though the continued wet winter weather converted it into a quagmire. Hot showers and barbers were available, and an issue of clothing, though poor in quality, satisfied an urgent need.[1] The whole set-up was comparative luxury after the rigours of being herded about North Africa; an eye-witness records that those who had been longest in transit appeared much more pinched and weary than the others.

Soon after their arrival most parties of prisoners had the experience of their first Red Cross food parcel since capture. 'What a scene! . . . We cheered, clapped one another on the back, and went temporarily crackers. . . .'[2] There was a canteen, too, which in return for camp pay chits sold fruit, cigarettes, and other small goods but was quite inadequate in size for a camp of 2000-odd. And as in most camps which had not had time to become fully organised, there were muddles and anomalies in issues and enormous queues whether for rations, canteen goods, or Italian clothing. When Red Cross supplies ran out, food again became the prime preoccupation of men's minds, and the more obsessed haunted the rubbish heaps for cabbage leaves and other scraps which they could carry off and boil up. Men passed the time between meals reading whatever printed matter they had in their pockets, writing letter-cards home, and swopping stories of their capture and subsequent experiences, especially when an occasional issue of wine warmed the blood and loosened the tongue.

Many made their first acquaintance with one of the more annoying features of prison-camp routine—counting the prisoners. This sounds a simple procedure, but to arrive at an accurate total for hundreds of uncooperative prisoners—or a total which would at any rate tally with the records—often took several counts and much time, to the exasperation of prisoners as well as of guards. One man's diary contains the entry: 'Got checked and checked and checked till we nearly went screwy. . . .' Even when prisoners had not planned to upset the count by double-covering[3] and other ruses, accuracy and speed of counting among prison-camp guards were rare qualities. At Capua there were three counts a day, each of which went on in all weathers until the counters were satisfied. The cold and wet of January 1942 made particularly trying the long hours spent by prisoners standing in the mud covered off in threes while an Italian passed slowly along intoning the foreign numerals.

---

[1] It consisted of cotton underpants, cotton shirt, belt, cap, handkerchief, and two squares of calico in place of socks.
[2] From a diary kept by a New Zealand private at Campo PG 66.
[3] A system by which, on a roll-call parade, a rear rank one (or even two) less in number than a front rank could be made to appear to be covering the latter man for man. It usually involved slight sideways movements by rear rank men during the count.

Then followed further delay while the counting staff met to grapple with the arithmetical problems involved in reaching a final result. Towards the end of the month the numbers were decreased as trainloads of prisoners were sent north, and by early February most of the New Zealanders had been transferred to Campo PG 52 at Chiavari, or to Campo PG 57 at Gruppignano.

Many transports from North Africa went to Brindisi or Taranto, and prisoners who disembarked at these ports, after going through a disinfesting centre, were taken to the camp at Tuturano. Accommodation here was totally inadequate. Whereas the officer prisoners were housed in wooden huts, other ranks were herded into an adjacent piece of ground turned by rain and the tramping of a thousand men into a sea of mud, on which they had to erect Italian bivouac tents.[1] Officer prisoners were given a camp bed each; other ranks received a heap of straw and two fibre blankets. There was a concrete washing place and latrine in the officers' compound; the whole of the other ranks had to manage with two small tubs for ablutions and a trench three feet deep for a latrine. Though the air was bracing, wet weather culminating in snow and the prevalence of intestinal disorders helped to make living conditions trying. Nevertheless, as one medical officer put it, the 'morale of [the] men seemed to thrive on it'. The British senior warrant officer maintained a smartness and discipline which was an obvious contrast to the comportment of the camp guards; and the Australian bugler who added a patriotic tune to each call unbeknown to the Italians raised the spirits of the whole camp in a different way.

The food consisted of the Italian army ration of bread, macaroni or rice, and other staple items, with the addition of a little fresh fruit and vegetables for those ranks who could pay for the extras.[2] Those with pay credits were also able to buy cigarettes, a few toilet necessities, some packs of cards, and Italian newspapers. There developed an alternating routine of card-playing and walking up and down to keep warm, with breaks for meals and periods in bed. A week before Christmas the English and South African officers were sent to permanent camps in the north, and in early January the New Zealand officers left for Campo PG 38 near Arezzo.

Other ranks were also sent off to permanent camps in the new year. At the same time the authorities' decision to build more wooden huts began to bear fruit, and these were under construction when the shipwrecked party arrived from Greece in March. Though they were housed in barracks, the ill-luck of this unfortunate group held. They arrived in time for a 60 per cent cut in prisoner-of-

---
[1] These consisted of Italian groundsheets buttoned together.
[2] Officers received the pay of Italian officers of equivalent rank; other ranks received one lira a day.

war rations on 13 March, and shortly afterwards they had an outbreak of meningitis which caused several deaths and kept them at Tuturano in quarantine until May. There were instances during this period of prisoners being tied to trees as punishment for attempted escape or disobedience of Italian orders. On the other hand, from the Italian civilian population there were many examples of friendly behaviour, including surreptitious gifts of food. The issue in April of the first Red Cross food parcel produced, as might be expected, a tremendous effect.

All were like children on a Christmas morn eager to see what each parcel contained . . . [that night] sleep was out of the question. The camp was one continued buzz from end to end with chaps conversing on the sole topic—the parcels.[1]

In early May some Indians were sent out on the first working party, and a few days later the majority left for Campo PG 65 at Gravina, where further working parties were planned.

The first inrush from North Africa had soon filled Tuturano, and some smaller drafts arriving at Brindisi or Taranto were sent to a similar camp on the outskirts of Bari. This also was a 'temporary' camp, though some prisoners remained in it for four months or more. Here also the few wooden huts were allotted to officers, and other ranks were put into a bare field with bivouac tents and a heap of straw. Representations were made to the Italian authorities to have these men brought under cover in view of their small numbers (about sixty), but this was not permitted until snow was lying on the ground. The small, flimsy wooden huts, entirely without heating, were grossly overcrowded and the exercise area very cramped. Indeed, the whole compound measured only one hundred yards by twenty, and it was only after many weeks that an outside walk once a week was allowed. Food was on the Italian army scales applying in most camps,[2] but prisoners' accounts

---

[1] From a diary kept by a New Zealand soldier—one of the shipwrecked party.
[2] Italian ration scales for prisoners of war (grammes daily):

	Officers	Other Ranks (non-working)	Other Ranks (working)
Bread	150	200	400
Macaroni or rice	66	66	120
Fat	10	13	13
Sugar	16	15	15
Cheese (cooking)	10	10	10
Cheese (table)	when available	30	43
Meat	14	34	34
Tomato puree	15	15	15
Egg	(1 a month)	. .	. .
Peas and beans	15	30	30
Coffee substitute	7	7	7

Officers were sometimes able to buy green vegetables, small amounts of salted fish, fresh and dried fruit, wine and cakes; other ranks only occasionally. Estimated calorific values, based on a report by Lt-Col A. A. Tennent, NZMC, on repatriation in April 1942, for the three columns above, taking into account possible extras, are 780, 1081, and 1821.

indicate that they were seldom able to obtain their full ration. Personal belongings were looted by the guards, especially on one occasion in March when a search followed the discovery of an escape tunnel. Some cases of striking prisoners and handcuffing with wire occurred. There were instances of wild shooting by sentries, probably due more to temperamental instability than to malice, but sufficiently dangerous to wound some of the prisoners. Appeals to authority proved of little use; both the camp commandant and the general commanding the military district were hostile. They not only condoned but encouraged ill-treatment, and both were later tried by War Crimes tribunals for a shooting incident in which a British officer was killed, the general being sentenced to death for his part in the affair.

Those transferred to other camps were not slow in reporting these matters and in early 1942 Bari had achieved sufficient notoriety to demand urgent investigation by a neutral observer.[1] The lot of prisoners, especially of officers, would have been considerably worse if it had not been for one or two of the junior Italian officers who were well-disposed towards the British. Through their efforts 'canteen' supplies came into the camp, including such things as dried fruits, jam and cakes. A senior medical officer estimated the value of the additional food bought in this way at an average of 500 calories a day for each officer. Besides food, the supply of toilet necessities, playing-cards, and Continental editions of authors in English did much to make life more tolerable and relieve the irritation of confinement in such a cramped space. The day passed mainly in domestic chores, card games and reading, with lecturettes in the evenings to give variety. After two or three months some issues of Red Cross food (although on a low scale) did much to restore flagging energies, which medical officers ascribed to a 'decline in general health.' Nobody was able to break out of the camp during this period, a first tunnel project in March having come to an abortive end. But the discovery of the tunnel probably hastened the transfer of prisoners, and no one in the parties which left for permanent camps or for repatriation was sorry to see the last of Bari.

In early January about forty New Zealand officers were moved from Bari and assembled with their fellow countrymen from Tuturano,[2] and a few English, South Africans and Rhodesians, at Campo PG 38 just outside the village of Poppi, in a rather remote

---

[1] No inspection was allowed until 13 May 1942, when a member of the Swiss Legation in Rome visited the camp.
[2] The numbers rose to about 90 officers (mostly New Zealanders) and 25 other ranks (mostly South Africans).

part of the Arno valley. Accommodation consisted of a white, four-storied convent building—the Villa Ascensione—set picturesquely among cypresses high on the slope of a hill. In addition to being fenced around with barbed wire, it had been redecorated and fitted with showers and modern kitchen equipment. The furnishings included very comfortable beds and bedding and even bedside cupboards and carpets. The messroom gleamed with white table-cloths and new china and cutlery, and Italian sergeant interpreters were on hand to supervise the mess-waiters at meals. A courteous commandant greeted new arrivals as his guests; and it was clear that pains had been taken to provide a welcome and comfort suitable for British officers.

After a day or two it was also clear that this high standard of attention, with the best will in the world, could not be kept up. Moreover there were material defects beneath the façade of renovation. The fuel supply was inadequate for keeping the building warm, and the rations, though of good quality, were sufficient only to keep everyone perpetually hungry. It was difficult to get Red Cross and other supplies owing to the isolated situation of the camp, especially in winter when the only road to the village below was inaccessible to all but foot traffic. Critical news from the Far East and the bitter cold helped to cast a gloom over this period, though the obviously ridiculous claims and stories of heroism appearing in the Fascist press provided material for countering depression. There was, too, a strong sense of solidarity among the prisoners, no doubt helped by the initial decision of the senior British officer to let the camp be run as an officers' mess by a democratically elected committee, which had to answer for its actions at monthly meetings of the whole camp.

From the spring of 1942 onwards the supply of Red Cross food parcels, together with the extras that it was found could be bought in addition to the basic ration, provided everyone with an ample diet. Prisoners were able to supplement this with vegetables and fruit grown in the plots of the convent garden, which they were allowed to cultivate under the supervision of an Italian officer, who not only took a friendly interest but contributed seeds from his own agricultural estate. After some preliminary delay a canteen enabled prisoners to buy fruit, sweets, cigarettes, and wine (often at exorbitant prices), as well as toilet articles, shirts, pyjamas, and other items of clothing that were badly needed. In time, too, the purchase of plenty of books in English, and music and the hire of a piano gave increased scope for recreation and entertainment, which had hitherto been confined to card games, chess, lectures, and learning to read the Italian newspapers.

An attempted escape opened the eyes of the Italian camp staff to another side of their guests' make-up, but though more cautious they remained well-disposed. As the May sun brightened and warmed the beautiful Italian countryside, the 'Villa' became rather like an officers' rest camp, with the day spent reading in a deck-chair or sketching, or walking (with guards) in the surrounding hills or playing basketball and deck tennis, and the evening in sipping wine over cards, chess, or music. The carefree Italian atmosphere became infectious and time lost its meaning; for anything that could not be fitted into one day could always be left till the morrow. *Domani è un altro giorno.*

The New Zealand officers who went to Campo PG 35 about two months after the Poppi draft had a somewhat similar experience. A large medieval monastery building at Padula, in a beautiful valley south-east of Salerno in southern Italy, was converted into accommodation for officer prisoners, the first batch of whom went into residence on 22 March 1942. A high-ceilinged monks' refectory became the officers' mess and served also for entertainments, and there was a two-acre area in grass to provide a playing field, walking space and gardens.

After a preliminary period of food shortage, it was soon found that some members of the camp staff were willing to act as middlemen for the purchase of black-market goods. By May hams, poultry, cheese, eggs, and large amounts of condensed milk were being smuggled into the mess, to say nothing of private transactions. So that with the Red Cross food parcels which had arrived towards the end of April, the late spring became a period of plenty. Clothing could be ordered from a visiting tailor. The camp soon had a well-stocked library and the lectures and classes common to most camps. There was no difficulty in providing talent for a variety of good entertainment from the 400-odd officers and 140-odd other ranks to which the camp strength had risen by the middle of the year.

There were a few New Zealanders in other officers' camps—Montalbo, Sulmona, and Vincigliata. Campo PG 41 at Montalbo was a fourteenth-century castle near Piacenza, converted into a camp for British officers without losing the defects in heating, sanitation, and water supply which by modern standards such buildings possess. It had held British prisoners, together with a number of Greeks, since September 1941, and though extra purchases of food were possible, the Italian camp staff was hostile and amenities were only slowly developed. Campo PG 12, a castle-like villa at Vincigliata on a hill above Florence, housed all the captured British generals and brigadiers (including two New Zealanders[1]) in quarters suitable to their rank. A close watch was kept on their activities in order to prevent the escape of such valuable prisoners. But they were allowed to keep hens, rabbits, and a vegetable garden, to indulge in hobbies, to have books and gramophone records, and to take daily walks under strong guard in the surrounding countryside.

Campo PG 78 at Sulmona has already been described in its earlier period, and a report by a medical officer repatriated in April 1942 confirmed that the ' general conduct and appointments of the camp' surpassed any other in Italy. Although during the first year of its existence camp security had tightened up, and although during the winter there was a shortage of fuel and of Red Cross food, the amenities for officers and NCOs remained comparable to those described at Poppi, except that the larger numbers at Sulmona gave more scope for entertainments.[2] For other ranks the quarters had become overcrowded and lacked comfort, though they were compensated by additional rations. The ration cut in March caused most camps (even that of the generals) to depend for an adequate diet on the arrival of Red Cross food parcels. Sulmona was no exception, for there was little black-market food obtainable in the area, and for junior officers at all events the regular messing charge of 21 lire a day left too little in their pay accounts to buy at the enhanced prices.[3]

The majority of the New Zealand other rank prisoners[4] were transferred in early February 1942 to a camp 16 kilometres from Chiavari in the hills north of the Italian Riviera, between Genoa and La Spezia. Campo PG 52 comprised an area of five acres in a valley among terraced and wooded hillsides, fenced in by barbed wire and containing some forty jerry-built huts of one or two stories,[5] some of which were found to leak and let in the cold winter air. Inside were two-decked wooden bunks, each with a straw palliasse, a pillow, three blankets and, to the surprise of the prisoners, two calico sheets. There was no heating in the huts and rather poor lighting, and the perforated pipes at the ablution stand provided trickles of water quite insufficient for washing as we know it, so that it was some time before body lice were eliminated. Nevertheless some found the conditions better than those at Capua.

---

[1] Brigadiers R. Miles and J. Hargest. They and one or two others were kept in a villa near Sulmona until transferred to Campo PG 12 in the spring of 1942.
[2] 1678 all ranks on 23 April 1942.
[3] This was the messing charge as in January 1942. The pay of a British second-lieutenant in Italian hands was 750 lire a month. After deducting a messing charge of 630 lire a month, this left 120 lire for all other purchases and incidental expenses.
[4] Between 700 and 800. By mid-1942 there were about 950 out of a camp total of 2700, the remainder being mainly South Africans and United Kingdom troops.
[5] A prisoner's diary describes the huts thus: ' Some wooden, made from what we think were large packing-cases, and some pre-fabricated, type of Gibraltar board. . . .'

The commandant, an elderly Italian colonel, seems to have been fair and genuinely interested in the welfare of the prisoners in his charge. Internal administration of the camp was in the hands of the senior warrant officer, assisted by an office staff and other NCOs in subordinate positions.

Food supplied in the first period of the camp's existence was considered a great improvement on that at Capua. But satisfaction with the rations was shortlived, for the 60 per cent cut imposed in March brought back the food shortages, and a prisoner wrote resignedly that everyone was 'constantly semi-hungry, but that [was] a permanent feature of prisoner-of-war life.' Some Red Cross supplies had arrived in mid-February, but deliveries were irregular owing to the difficulty of access to the camp and to the shortage of Italian transport. There was evidence of considerable pilferage of parcel mail for prisoners. One man who kept a careful check received a total of three and a half food parcels in the period January to April 1942. This was insufficient to stop men thinking about food (if indeed many prisoners of war ever did stop), and there developed a craze for collecting and writing down recipes for tasty dishes which would be prepared and eaten when the collector was again in a position to procure the ingredients. A canteen was available to sell onions, dried fruit, some tobacco and wine, and fresh fruit in season, but the facilities were adequate for about 150 men only instead of the 3000 which the camp soon held; and the pay of one lira a day[1] restricted what could be bought at the high prices ruling. Hunger, besides making men thinner and hollow-cheeked and weak enough to faint on occasions, also made them bad-tempered and suspicious of the staff of the cookhouse from which food was issued to each hut. An Easter Sunday diary entry indicates the state of irritability which sometimes prevailed:

> Have been nearly crazy today for lack of something to do; if ever there was a lazier, more useless, hungry, and at times hopelessly boring life than that of a prisoner of war in a foreign country, I cannot imagine what or where it could be . . . waiting for our third and last check parade, then drearily to bed with hunger gnawing at our stomachs.

The urgent need for an occupation, for physical and mental activity during captivity, was soon realised. Working parties carrying shingle from the riverbed and doing other odd jobs about the camp once a week hardly provided sufficient opportunity to satisfy the needs of active young men. A committee was set up in February to organise entertainment, but with the lack of material it had to fall back on lectures, quiz sessions, euchre evenings, and improvised concerts.

---

[1] 1.25 lire for NCOs.

Lectures were given on subjects ranging from fox-hunting to diamond mining, and some men kept full notes of what they heard in exercise books bought at the canteen. Numbers of men experienced a return of religious fervour or perhaps turned to religion seriously for the first time in their lives, and a full programme of services was carried out. Classes and study groups (on farming for example) soon sprang up; and later, as books and materials were obtained, a small library, a drama society, and an art circle were formed. A useful art that flourished in Campo 52 was the making of a variety of articles by re-shaping used food-tins—' tin-bashing' as it came to be known; there and in other camps it kept some prisoners occupied and interested for the rest of their captivity. Many huts clubbed together and bought the Italian daily newspapers and *Tempo* or other illustrated journals, which though known to be full of propaganda helped men to maintain some touch with the world outside the wire. Camp and hut lotteries provided another interesting way of making use of the coupons issued in lieu of money. In time sufficient instruments were bought for an orchestra, and concerts were given in the large 'mess-hut', originally built for messing but far too small for the purpose and so used for recreation.

Walks outside the camp under guard were started in March, and many men derived pleasure and inward solace from the beautiful north Italian landscape in spring flower and from the friendliness of the civilians they encountered. One man writes, after the long dreary winter months, of calm starlit evenings with fireflies showing their fascinating lights, and the nightingale's lonely song. Another, seeing a lovely Italian girl through the wire, recalls how long it is since he spoke to a woman. The arrival of New Zealand mail in April brought back a sense of reality and gave our men a new incentive to fill up and send off the cards and letter-forms issued to them. On Anzac Day a service and march past made many remember past occasions and reawakened in them a feeling of corporate and national pride that they could still turn on a smart parade if necessary.

A break out had been attempted as early as February, but the would-be escapers were caught and punished, together with the hut commanders, by a short period of solitary confinement. Though discipline was easy and punishments on the whole light, an erratic outburst was always liable to occur, and one day two prisoners were flogged for 'insolence' by the Carabinieri[1] attached to the camp. A party of New Zealanders worked during the winter on an escape

---

[1] *Carabinieri reali*, royal guard—a type of Italian police. Each of the larger prisoner-of-war camps had carabinieri attached for security purposes—searching, investigating escapes, and keeping a check on the other Italian guards.

tunnel, but in mid-June, when it was almost ready for use, it was discovered.

A number of New Zealanders went straight from Capua to Campo PG 57 at Gruppignano, near Udine in north-east Italy, which had at first held mainly Australians. The camp stood on the flat ground of a river plain surrounded by the distant, snow-capped Dolomites—a large area enclosed by barbed wire and planned for division into compounds as expansion took place. For administrative purposes, accommodation, and food the camp was organised at this period into two compounds, each with its own cookhouse and orderly room serving about 800 men. An Italian colonel of carabinieri, a stern disciplinarian with dictatorial methods, controlled the camp. Though it was run more efficiently than many other Italian camps, pinpricking regulations and some brutal punishments[1] made it clear that this was not due to feelings of humanity or goodwill.

Double-walled wooden huts about 80 feet long on concrete foundations held two-tier wooden bunks in batches of eight. Only enough fuel for three to four hours' heating each night was available, and one double and one single blanket was a meagre enough allowance to combat the winter wind off the mountains. A recreation hut had been in use up till the end of 1941, but the large influx of prisoners in early 1942[2] (including some 400 New Zealanders) made necessary its use for accommodation. Water was plentiful, there were proper ablutions outside the huts and adequate latrines, but the poor drainage system was to be a source of trouble later. Hot baths were irregular and there was the usual difficulty in getting rid of lice.

The camp food was much the same as it was in other camps and suffered from the same ration cut. Red Cross food and fifty cigarettes were distributed weekly while supplies lasted. The Italians seldom failed to issue the standard tobacco ration, equivalent to five cigarettes daily. Normal Italian clothing issues were made, but when in early spring Red Cross clothing arrived (as it did about this time at most camps in Italy) Italian garments had to be returned. Many private parcels began to arrive pilfered and there were long delays in the censorship of letters. A camp welfare committee, set up according to Article 43[3] of the Geneva Prisoners of War Convention to deal with these and other matters relating to the men's

---

[1] Besides numerous handcuffings and long and rigorous treatment in the camp cells, two New Zealanders were shot dead and two were wounded in this camp.
[2] By June 1942 the camp strength had risen to 1500, including some 450 New Zealanders.
[3] 'In any locality where there may be prisoners of war they shall be authorised to appoint representatives to represent them before the military authorities and the Protecting Powers. . . . in the event of the prisoners deciding to organise among themselves a system of mutual aid, such organisation shall be one of the functions of the prisoners' representatives.'

welfare, was disbanded in February 1942 by the commandant, who would thenceforth treat only with the senior British NCO. No neutral inspector visited the camp in the first two and a half months of 1942, and special permission had to be got for a letter to Geneva, which even if permitted was subject to censorship and a delay of up to three months.

Educational classes flourished in much the same way as at Chiavari, though entertainments were hampered by lack of a proper hut and equipment. A New Zealander writes of studying surveying and sitting examinations under an Australian sergeant; another writes of 'all trades and professions' being taught. Red Cross consignments made possible the formation of a library, a large number of the books having been selected for their educational value. Accordions and mouth-organs helped to provide the music in the concerts that were held by each hut. In one respect Gruppignano was better off than Chiavari: the large area where the check parades were held was available for sport—baseball, cricket, soccer and volleyball—although wet weather made it too muddy to use. Much of the problem of recreation in summer was solved if there was space for physical play, and space for others to watch.

The last of the shipwrecked party left Tuturano in early May for Campo PG 65, which had been established in March at Gravina, about thirty miles inland from Bari. It was surrounded by a countryside divided into huge fields of wheat and oats, and the city of Altamura could be seen in the distance. Large new barrack buildings of white stone, roofed with red tiles or slates, were divided into seven or eight bays, each holding twenty or so two-tier bunks. Quarters were roomy and designed so as to be cool and airy in the hot summer months. Although all the camp buildings had not been completed, there were well-built ablutions and latrines, served with a good water supply, and a proper infirmary. As in other permanent camps the sheets on the beds were the biggest surprise to new arrivals. Like Gruppignano, the camp was organised by groups of huts into 'compounds', each holding about a thousand men.[1] It was an immense improvement in living conditions for the harassed party from Greece, most of whom were still suffering from the privations they had endured, a hundred of them badly enough to be put on extra rations for a while by the Italians. Basking in the southern Italian sunshine one of the party wrote, 'At last we are settled.'

At this stage work other than camp fatigues was not compulsory for prisoners of war in Italy. Men were invited to put in their

---

[1] The camp was designed eventually to hold 8000 men. On 12 May 1942 it held some 3150, including 387 New Zealanders.

names for farm work or casual labour in the neighbourhood of the camp, the double rations for workers being held out as a bait. A first batch of volunteer farm workers left Gravina towards the end of May; and as the harvest time drew nearer further parties were sent off. Those remaining in camp began to organise recreations: carving chess sets, bringing out a single-copy camp newspaper, practising on newly acquired musical instruments, and many improvised pastimes we have already noted in other camps. At the beginning of September they went north to join the other New Zealanders at Gruppignano.

Although many sick and wounded prisoners remained in Libya in field dressing stations and hospitals and were ultimately recaptured during the British advance, others were transported by hospital ship to Italy. A good number of these went to the large hospital at Caserta, just outside Naples. Some of the buildings were surrounded by barbed wire so that they could accommodate prisoners of war, not only those who arrived by hospital ship, but those ill enough to warrant their evacuation from a camp in the neighbourhood. Officer prisoners occupied the third floor of a stone building, and other ranks some two-storied wooden barracks. The situation of the hospital was pleasant, with plenty of sun and fresh air.

Men speak of being well treated in Caserta hospital, and a repatriated medical officer reported that the Italian doctors were doing their best for the prisoners. The food was much better than that received in camps; even so, Red Cross supplies greatly helped to speed the patients' recovery. From December onwards three British medical officers worked in the hospital, assisted by British medical orderlies, though the supply of instruments was meagre and they had to rely a great deal on Red Cross parcels of medicaments. They were able to make improvements in sanitation, in the washing of patients, and in other aspects of nursing which had up till then been largely neglected.

The same conditions obtained in other hospitals which had prisoner patients in this period, though there are indications of considerable neglect of prisoners and shortage of food in Bari hospital. Repatriated medical officers also criticised the medical treatment available in camps, which was often rigidly controlled by a not very competent Italian and suffered from a shortage of drugs. Some officers' camps[1] held large numbers of captured medical officers and chaplains for several months before their transfer to hospitals or to other ranks' camps where their services could be of more use.

---

[1] Notably Campo PG 35 at Padula and Campo PG 38 at Poppi, so far as New Zealanders were concerned.

Many of these officers had applied to the Italian authorities, some through the Swiss Legation, for repatriation. Since September 1941 a Mixed Medical Commission had been at work in Italy examining cases nominated for inclusion in a future exchange of prisoners; similar commissions were working on Italian cases in the United Kingdom and the Middle East. Towards the end of the year an agreement had been reached between the United Kingdom and Italy that either power could detain any protected personnel whose services were required to care for their fellow countrymen who were prisoners. The right of medical personnel to repatriation, instead of resting on the individual's wish, had become a matter for decision by the detaining power. Only the four most senior medical officers and a handful of orderlies were selected from the large numbers of New Zealand medical personnel in Italy in spite of their not being used to any great extent to care for the comparatively small number of British prisoners in Italian hands.[1]

Late in March 1942 the Italian authorities informed the selected sick and wounded and protected personnel, then scattered in various camps throughout Italy, that they were to be exchanged. There was much congratulation of the fortunate ones and raising of hopes among the others. The 129 repatriates were assembled in Bari and embarked and sailed on Easter Saturday (4 April) on the hospital ship *Gradisca*. On 7 April she was anchored in Smyrna Harbour a few hundred yards from the *Llandovery Castle*, which had arrived from Alexandria with 919 Italians. Next day the exchange took place under arrangements made by International Red Cross delegates with the Turkish military authorities, the transfers being made on a ferry-boat in mid-harbour with the aid of pontoons moored to the two ships.

Treatment on the Italian hospital ship had been excellent, and a warm welcome awaited this first batch of repatriates on the *Llandovery Castle*. There was another more formal welcome to the party when it arrived at Alexandria on the 11th. A journey by hospital train brought them to Cairo, where they dispersed, the disabled New Zealanders going to 1 NZ General Hospital and the protected personnel to appropriate camps. During the train journey there was a distribution of comforts by women of the British Red Cross and an interrogation by Intelligence officers.

For the first time men who had been prisoners in Italian hands were able to give to the Allied world a full and uncensored account

---

[1] The numbers of British prisoners repatriated were:
        Sick and wounded   60 (including 3 NZ amputees)
        Protected personnel   69 (including 27 NZMC)
A British request to include those who had been held at hospitals in Greece (in an area which had been handed over by the Germans to Italian occupation troops) was not agreed to by the German Government.

of life in their prisoner-of-war camps and to draw some general picture of life in Italy. Many felt it their duty to try and get something done about the defects of prisoner-of-war camps they had seen, and letters delivered to the International Red Cross delegates on the hospital ships were followed later by numerous reports dealing with prison-camp diet, sanitation, and other matters. Much valuable data on which to base relief work was thus made available.

II: *Prisoners in Germany*

While the campaign had been raging in the Western Desert, those captured in Greece and Crete had been making the best of their first winter in Germany. In October 1941 nearly all the New Zealand Army officer prisoners, and a good number from the Air Force as well, had gone to Oflag VIB. This camp at Dössel, near Warburg, Bavaria, had been previously occupied by civilian workers but vacated so that all British officers in Germany could be brought together. It was soon crowded out with 2500 British officers and 450 orderlies, and although the commandant was sympathetic and tried to make improvements from time to time, some of his subordinates were uncooperative, and living conditions remained unsatisfactory during the whole of the camp's existence. International Red Cross Committee delegates described it as ' the worst camp we have seen in Germany '.

It was situated on a high, desolate, and exposed area—a space of about twenty acres containing a number of old wooden hutments, haphazardly arranged and in a bad state of repair through leaking roofs and walls. There were no proper paths, with the exception of one central roadway, and wet weather turned the remainder of the camp area into a quagmire. The hutments were alive with rats and mice, and beds and bedding were dirty and flea-infested. As rooms held from 16 to 52 officers in two-tier beds—12 to 16 in a space of about 21 feet by 12 feet—it is not surprising that ' It was literally impossible to remain in one spot for more than a few seconds without being in someone's road.'[1] Most prisoners experienced something similar to this in the course of their captivity, but the other defects of Warburg made it especially hard to bear. Water supply was inadequate and uncertain in operation, ablutions and showers were far too few, and latrines discharged into three open cesspools inside the camp which flooded and overflowed in bad weather and never ceased to spread an overpowering stench. All were locked in the crowded huts from dusk till daylight, the entrance space and passages to each hut containing buckets for use

---

[1] Quoted from a New Zealand officer's diary.

The guard tower of Stalag 383

PRISONERS FROM GREECE AND CRETE LEAVING
KOKKINIA HOSPITAL FOR GERMANY, 1941

British prisoners of war marching back from Sfakia to Galatas, in Crete

'Shellfire Wadi', near Sidi Rezegh, where New Zealand Medical units and wounded were held captive for eight days, 1941

THE COMPOUND AT BARDIA, 1941

AFTER THREE MONTHS IN THE MAIN TRANSIT CAMP AT BENGHAZI, 1942

DELOUSING IN CAMPO PG 57, GRUPPIGNANO

LINED UP FOR RATIONS, CAMPO PG 57, 1942

BLOWERS HEATING UP A MEAL, STALAG IIIA, LUCKENWALDE

PLAY ACTING IN CAMPO PG 52, CHIAVARI, 1942

Two characters from 'The Importance of Being Earnest'

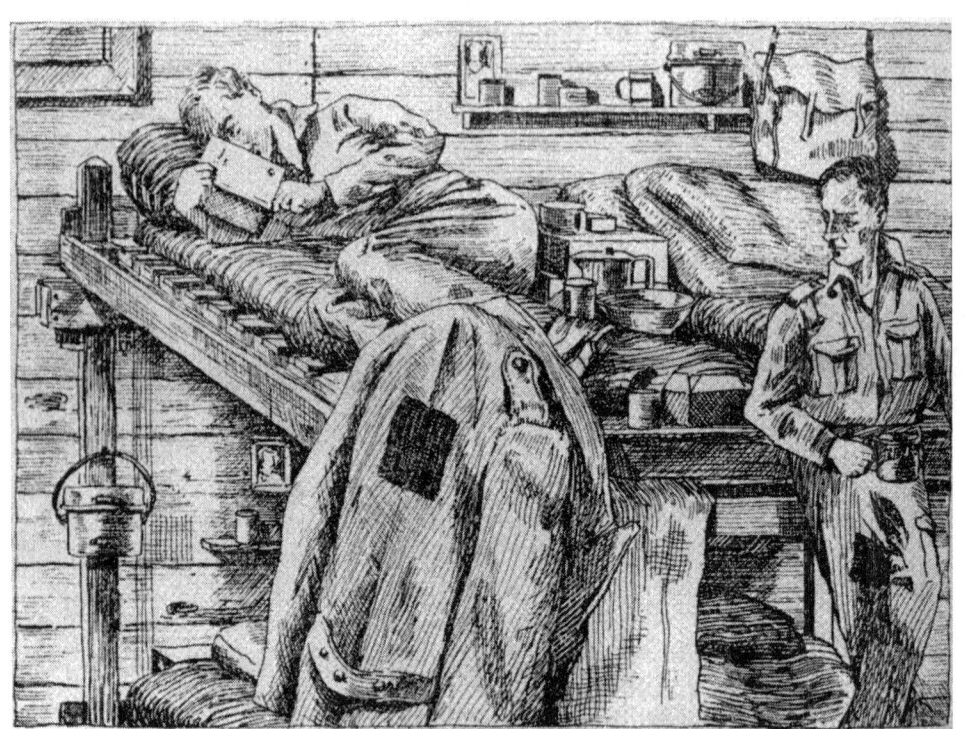

INSIDE AN ITALIAN WORKING CAMP ON THE AUSTRIAN BORDER—from a sketch by *A. G. Douglas*

CAMPO PG 57, GRUPPIGNANO, IN APRIL 1943
—from a sketch by *A. G. Douglas*

READY FOR EVACUATION FROM ITALY TO
GERMANY, SEPTEMBER 1943

TO GERMANY IN A CATTLE TRUCK

MESS QUEUE FOR BRITISH CIVILIAN INTERNEES
IN ILAG VIII, TOST, GERMANY

WORKING PARTY, STALAG XXA, THORN, POLAND, 1941

as night latrines. Only half the huts had electric light; the remainder were lit by carbide hurricane lamps for which there was always difficulty in getting fuel. Each room had a stove but insufficient fuel. The blanket allowance was at first only one for each man, and rigid German control allowed too little clothing from Red Cross sources to be distributed to the orderlies. The prospect for the winter was not encouraging.

The camp was visited soon after its establishment by International Red Cross delegates and representatives of the American Embassy, who recommended to the German Foreign Office that a thousand officers should be immediately moved away. As a result, the German authorities began the construction of ten new brick buildings and promised to move some hundreds of officers in the new year. The German rations were on the same meagre scale allotted to other camps, but fortunately for the health of the prisoners Red Cross food parcels poured in, the camp reserve in December standing at 18,000. Although the camp infirmary held 84 in December, including some cases of diphtheria, an International Red Cross inspector remarked in the same month how fit most of the prisoners looked, even the jaundice and beriberi cases from Greece and Crete being much improved. There was at least plenty of space for outdoor recreation: three netball courts and a football ground were soon in operation when the mud had been treated with clinker, and the winter saw an ice-skating rink in use. Books and other recreational material had been brought from other camps, and the library soon had 4000 books. An orchestra playing during meals 'helped to drown the noise of 500 men consuming soup'. The theatre enthusiasts produced a hilarious Christmas pantomime 'Citronella', which one man described as a 'riot of fun and forgetfulness'. As winter set in with very low temperatures, ice and snow alternating with longer periods of rain and slush, organised recreation was almost essential to men who had to spend long periods indoors, especially as 'practically all subjects of conversation (had by then) been well thrashed out'.

Fortunately a large camp of officers provided 'a galaxy of talent in all fields from church to vaudeville, from football to poker';[1] and the exchange of ideas among several thousands of men from the Commonwealth and from many European countries was a lively stimulus to mental activity in general. There was an orchestra which gave regular symphony concerts; three dance bands—'hot', 'sweet', and 'gypsy'; educational courses on a variety of subjects (including even lessons in Maori), and a scheme for advice on post-war careers; a theatre company which produced everything from

---

[1] Quoted from an officer's diary.

revues to straight plays, with woman-impersonators such that an oldish major ' could hardly restrain himself from going to the stage-door after the show'. A few enthusiasts experimented at New Year with an alcoholic beverage made from sugar and dried fruit, the effects of which possibly surprised the brewers for several ended up in the cells. To compensate for the very cold weather there was ice-hockey. When something was in short supply there was always a chance that it might be bartered for at Foodacco Ltd., the camp exchange market which dealt in everything from cigarettes and food to old clothes. And when the news was bad from the Eastern Front there were often long and heavy RAF raids to listen to—a reassurance that Britain was not yet beaten. The winter might have been an uncomfortable one, but no one could have called it dull.

By February vermin had been more or less eliminated, extra heating stoves had been installed, and each man had two blankets, one a Red Cross issue. Two hundred and fifty senior officers and some orderlies had been transferred to Spangenburg, reopened to receive them, and the Germans had stated that no further British officers were to come to Warburg. In mid-April the new buildings were still not completed, little or no improvement had been made in lighting, washing and sanitary arrangements, and the coal issue had been stopped. The meat ration had been cut from 300 to 230 grammes weekly on the pretext that prisoners received too many food parcels, although the issue fell in winter to about half a parcel a week. Later the camp dental officer reported a deterioration of teeth in the camp owing to lack of fresh vegetables and animal fats in the diet. There had been delays in the censorship of mail, and parcels had arrived at the camp rifled.

None of these things were allowed by the administrative officers of the camp to go unnoticed, and there was continuous pressure on the German staff as well as complaints to neutral observers. Morale was very high and junior officers lost no opportunity of baiting the German staff, especially the Abwehr personnel, and especially on *appel* when there was delay in being dismissed. There was at these times a certain carefree schoolboy hilarity which irritated the serious-minded German beyond self-control, as it was usually intended to. The cells were nearly always full of officers charged with offences ranging from an ' insult to the German Reich ' on the Christmas menu card to ' blowing slowly the nose ' or ' shouting an undisciplined remark '[1] at a German sentry on parade. There

---

[1] The quotations are from the German promulgation notices of sentences awarded by the commandant.

was little or no brutality and sentences were of comparatively short duration, though some officers were constantly being crimed.

From the first days of the camp there were numerous attempts at escape. Many got out through tunnels, which included one from a punishment cell; others on transport going out the gate or by crawling under the wire. But though two officers almost reached the Swiss border, nobody was completely successful. The guards were kept continually on the alert: searches of barracks were continually being carried out, often with ruthless disregard for personal property, while prisoners were made to stand about outside; and minor collective punishments were imposed, such as slowing up the delivery of mail or parcels and closing the theatre. Sometimes the commandant was probably justified,[1] if, for instance, attempts to escape had created so much extra work that he had not enough fresh guards to supervise the activities in question. In the last month or two of the camp's existence escape activity was on an unprecedented scale, culminating on the night of 31 August in the 'evacuation' of 20 officers by scaling ladders, after the fusing of the camp lights. It must have been with some relief that the German camp staff saw the last of the British officers go in September.

The control of some 2500 British officers and orderlies bent on demanding their full rights and giving as much trouble as possible was a great deal for the OKW to expect of any one camp commandant. The theory has been advanced that the Germans expected at this stage that the winning of the war would soon be an accomplished fact, which would obviate the necessity for any further moves of prisoners. At all events it was only in August 1942, when the chance of victory in the Middle East seemed to have vanished, that they began to disband Warburg. Senior officers had already been transferred to Spangenburg in January. They were divided between the Schloss (Upper camp) and Elbersdorf (Lower camp), where they carried on most of the activities that the stimulating community at Warburg had brought to life, though on a smaller and more limited scale.

In an established camp like Stalag VIIIB at Lamsdorf there had been little change. The British camp population had risen to between five and six thousand in the stalag and upwards of thirteen thousand out at work in the *Arbeitskommandos,* and of all these nearly two thousand were New Zealanders. The German policy of expending as little as possible on the maintenance of prisoners

---

[1] This is not to be taken as condoning collective punishment as such, which was clearly a breach of the 1929 Geneva Convention, but merely as giving a practical reason why the Germans were sometimes forced to take action whose results could be construed as collective punishment.

continued. There were still overcrowded barracks, the interior of which, as one sergeant wrote, 'put[s] you in mind of a laundry and a second-hand shop in one.' Broken windows were not repaired and had to be boarded up to keep out the weather; expended light-globes were not replaced; taps that got out of order remained so indefinitely. There never had been an issue of eating utensils to the prisoners at Lamsdorf; in fact table knives in their possession on arrival had been confiscated. Most had made their own from pieces of wood or empty tins. Though the outbreak of typhus in December 1941 should have been a warning, there was still irregularity in the provision of hot showers, some men having to wait as long as three months for their turn; and it was not until the spring of 1942 that a ten-day roster was established.

Rations continued to be on the same exiguous scale,[1] and the breakdown in the supplies of Red Cross food parcels during the bitter winter of 1941–42 was keenly felt,[2] more especially as all tins were punctured at issue and nothing could therefore be saved. Even when Red Cross food was on hand there were difficulties in cooking it. The camp cookhouse produced only hot soup and cooked potatoes, and for a while cooking inside the barracks on the heating stoves was forbidden. But 'kriegie'[3] ingenuity produced the jam-tin stove and the blower, and though officious guards at first kicked them over, prisoners' persistence won this argument as it did many others. Over the control of Red Cross clothing they were not so successful. At first the Germans had decided that an issue should only be made to those going out to a working camp; and for those already in working camps there were varying interpretations by German NCOs in charge, including one according to which no new garment was issued except in return for an old one, even though many of the men coming straight from capture had only the few garments they stood up in. The quashing of this absurdity and also of a German attempt to charge prisoners for the new garments issued were among the points gained by the British NCO in charge of Red Cross supplies at the stalag, who succeeded by the end of 1941 in getting a new outfit for every man in the camp. Nevertheless, as in other camps at this period of the war, the Germans retained a strict control over all issues of clothing and blankets, and were reluctant to allow a prisoner of war to retain his old clothes as a working suit.

---

[1] Those doing heavy work were entitled to between 400 and 600 grammes of extra meat, but the IRCC delegation noticed that from 1942 onwards 'PW were only given part of the extra rations allowed to civilians engaged in similar work.'—IRCC Report on Activities, Vol. I, p. 335.
[2] The camp doctors estimated an average loss of weight of 8 per cent over this period.
[3] Corruption in prisoner-of-war slang of the German *Kriegsgefangener*, prisoner of war.

Most of the annoying controls in camps, including this one, were aimed at the prevention of escape. And though there were some German commandants who liberally interpreted the regulations governing such matters, the latter were usually applied in every pinpricking detail. Several senior New Zealand NCOs at Lamsdorf said that the difference between German discipline and ours was that they had more rules to break, and that they were more sensitive concerning their rank and the 'honour of the Reich'. These considerations and the existence of a few brutal and martinet types in their forces, as in our own, explain most of the 'incidents' that occurred with camp guards. The German reverence for higher orders, too, caused many of the German camp staff to reject openly the provisions of the Geneva Convention, where these might be taken to conflict with their instructions from 'above'.

There was at Lamsdorf[1] a large number of NCOs of the rank of corporal and over and therefore exempt under the Convention from work. Much argument took place over German efforts to get these prisoners out to work. The German authorities suspected, not without good reason, that some of those claiming NCO rank had merely assumed it for the duration of their captivity, giving themselves 'stalag promotion' in order to avoid having to work; and it was not easy to distinguish these from genuine NCOs. Pressure on the whole group took various forms: threats, long parades out in the cold, restriction of clothing issue to those going out on working parties. Finally it was decided that if NCOs were not to work they must exercise instead; they were therefore marched round the sports field and drilled for two hours each morning and made to play games each afternoon. There were not of course enough German guards to supervise the scheme adequately, and the whole thing became rather farcical. It was discontinued for three months when the winter weather forbade it, and thereafter NCOs were excused drill provided they attended educational classes. The latter, which had begun in September 1941, were now receiving German encouragement. They were developed to embrace 63 subjects, with a team of 41 trained instructors and nearly a thousand men attending daily. Plans were also in hand to extend the scheme to the working camps. The German was realising that by giving prisoners the opportunity to study he could avoid much of the extra work which arose from their seeking other more troublesome outlets for their energies.

As many as could be got out to work were sent to coal mines, sugar-beet factories, aerodrome construction jobs, and other work

---

[1] The same problem arose at most other stalags.

in the neighbourhood.[1] In early April a party of Australians and New Zealanders were sent to a coal mine at Oerhingen, near Gleiwitz. The living quarters were right at the mine-shaft and conditions were very primitive. Prisoners were made to work three shifts, so that with men in the same barrack coming in from or going out to the mine through the night, barrack lights were never off during the night. At first the German civilian 'bosses' were apt to shout at the prisoners and to make free with pick-handles, and the civilian miners who worked alongside the prisoners were inclined to adopt bullying tactics as well. There were a number of fights down in the mine and resultant complaints to the commandant, but the civilians came quickly to realise that British prisoners were not to be trifled with. The latter soon developed a technique to cope with the situation. A civilian 'boss' shouting at a prisoner was dealt with by the prisoners' throwing down all tools and giving an answering storm of words if not physical violence; a civilian miner who was objectionable was given a thrashing; and in the end there was rather friendly admiration for the prisoners who could defy the hectoring overseers, of whom everyone else stood in dread. Nevertheless, an appreciable number of prisoners were going sick in order to avoid the dangerous and unpleasant conditions below, which resulted from German haste to extract coal quickly at all costs. A few prisoners refused flatly to go down the mine, preferring a term in jail.

Without Red Cross food parcels and camp concerts, boxing tournaments and other sports, this unpleasant existence would have been hard to bear. Boils, a common complaint among prisoners of war, became particularly prevalent. Sickness gave several an opportunity to get back to stalag, though many others who were sick were ordered out to work by the German doctor or the commandant, whose decision as to whether a prisoner was fit enough to work was final. One man comments in his diary that, despite what is laid down in the Geneva Convention, 'they make their own rules'. At many of the *Arbeitskommandos* remote from stalag and infrequently visited by neutral inspectors, treatment of prisoners depended very largely on the type and disposition of the local German commandant, often merely of corporal's rank.

While the British section of the stalag at Lamsdorf was already a large, properly organised camp at the time of the influx of prisoners from Greece and Crete, it will be remembered that for those who went to camps in Austria the accommodation was makeshift in the extreme. Conditions in Stalag XVIIID at Marburg at the end of October, as described by visitors from the United States

---

[1] There were in March 1942 more than 260 *Arbeitskommandos* dependent on Stalag VIIIB.

Embassy and the International Red Cross Committee, were deplorable. The inspectors found dilapidated barracks with most of the rooms unheatable, primitive wash-places and latrines in an open yard exposed to the weather, the usual insufficiency of food (made good by Red Cross parcels) and refusal by the Germans to make a full distribution of clothing that had arrived from Geneva. Factors like these, with 'everything in disorder and badly organised', led them to report that the camp was a real danger to the health of prisoners.

Some improvement had been made in the sick-bay, where in July British doctors had found patients of all types lying on bare beds without blankets. Palliasses and two blankets were secured for them, treatment was properly organised with the help of medicines from Geneva, and by August the ordinary scale of rations on which the sick had to exist was supplemented by Red Cross food and parcels of medical comforts. Fortunately those whose condition warranted sending them to the civilian hospital in Marburg received good treatment there at the hands of the Yugoslav doctors and nurses.

By the end of the year men were starting to receive both letters and clothing parcels from next-of-kin. Music and theatre productions, which had received some encouragement from the Germans, and an increasing supply of books were providing prisoners with some of the necessary mental distraction. Outdoor recreation was limited, for there was room in the cramped camp area for a basketball court only. In spite of these improvements, however, the stalag remained a bad one. There was an outbreak of typhus in early 1942 similar to that which occurred in other large camps. As in the other camps, Russians were the chief victims, but compounds of other nationalities were in quarantine for some time to prevent the spread of the disease. By the beginning of June all remaining British prisoners[1] had been moved from Marburg, those liable for work to working detachments, and non-working NCOs, medical personnel, and those unfit for work to Stalag XVIIIB at Spittal-on-the-Drau. So far as British prisoners were concerned, the stalag had been 'dissolved, because it did not reach the standard of other main camps in the Salzburg district.'[2]

Many of the men coming from Greece had been in the stalag only a day or so before being sent out to a working detachment, and those who had a longer stay were not sorry when they were finally moved out to work. The farming or *Landwirtschaft*[3]

---

[1] At this stage about 400. The stalag had under its control about 3550 British prisoners, including about 400 New Zealanders.
[2] Quoted from the Swiss representatives' report of 1 June 1942.
[3] Designated by the letter L and the number of the detachment.

Arbeitskommandos were preferable to most others, and there seems to have been a tendency to transfer British and especially Dominion prisoners from industrial work-camps[1] to the farms. Though the hours of work on farms were much longer—sometimes fifteen or sixteen as against eight to ten hours daily—quarters were often warmer and more comfortable, and there was invariably more food to eat. Prisoners were in fact usually given the same as the civilian workers. They had in addition their Red Cross food, and were often able to acquire eggs and other farm produce. It was a life where New Zealanders at any rate felt at home, though many from New Zealand towns made their first close acquaintance with cows and other farm animals; and those from New Zealand farms encountered unfamiliar traditional European methods. Though hours were very long, they were no longer than those worked by the Austrian men and women, the work could be as strenuous as one liked to make it, and the outdoor life kept the men tanned and fit. There was, moreover, a certain amount of freedom to move about, and the civilian farm people were on the whole quite friendly after the first barriers had been broken down.

Although the great majority were on farms, other New Zealanders worked with picks and shovels on roads or canals and in quarries. Most of these small working parties[2] had reasonably comfortable sleeping accommodation but primitive washing and sanitary arrangements. They did not have the recreational facilities of the stalag but their day was on the whole more interesting. At some of the working camps the guards insisted on impounding the prisoners' trousers and boots each night to prevent attempts to escape. In spite of this and the lock-up and guarding precautions, numbers of prisoners were able to make a break from their camps, though most were recaptured after a short period of liberty and few thought it was possible to reach Allied territory. The nearest neutral state was Hungary, and in early December 1941 a New Zealander and an Australian who had got away from a farm succeeded in crossing the border next day. They were picked up by the Hungarian police, who placed them in an internment camp. There they met other escaped British prisoners and were later to be joined by more. The only other escape procedure regarded as practical was to cross into Yugoslavia and join one of the bands of partisans which had been formed since the country was overrun by the German forces in April 1941. A New Zealand corporal,[3]

---

[1] Designated by GW (*Gewerbe*) and the number of the detachment.
[2] The commonest size for *Arbeitskommandos* was about 30–40; there were sometimes a dozen or less on a group of small farms and sometimes several hundred on a large construction job.
[3] Cpl J. Denvir (20 Bn), awarded DCM and Soviet Medal for Valour. A fuller account of his work with the partisans is given later.

who had already been free for a while in September, succeeded in getting away with two companions during a heavy fall of snow. Later in the month he was in the hills near Ljubliana, armed and being trained as a guerrilla.

In the other Austrian camp containing a large number of New Zealanders—Stalag XVIIIA at Wolfsberg—the Germans made little improvement in this period. At the end of 1941 the British compound still contained only the original three converted stables, which were still too crowded to allow any space for indoor recreation. There were too few tables and seats to accommodate all the occupants.[1] Stoves were fitted in time to provide winter heating; but for some time only a certain proportion of the prisoners had more than one blanket, and although a large reserve of clothing had arrived from Geneva, the Germans placed every obstacle in the way of its issue, so that everyone was short of warm underclothing and socks. The lighting was bad enough to make reading virtually impossible, and even the few ineffectual lamps installed were switched off at dark because there were no blackout fittings for the stable windows. There was no interference with the issue of one Red Cross food parcel a week, but an International Red Cross visitor reported that the commandant thought the British prisoners received too many parcels and had therefore decided to cut down their rations. The general impression recorded at this time was that British prisoners were not being treated as well as prisoners of other nationalities.

In December and January the camp had an outbreak of typhus, which was then epidemic in prisoner-of-war camps throughout Germany, having broken out among Russian prisoners and spread to camps containing other nationalities.[2] The British compound was placed in quarantine, which made conditions still more difficult. One of the occupants wrote: ' 850 of us cooped up in a run a hundred yards by a hundred yards for nearly two months . . . a horrible nightmare.' Another mentioned the foul, insanitary conditions and the lack of any water supply for two days. But the period of quarantine had the advantage that the camp population was practically fixed and undisturbed by the German camp staff; it could thus devote itself unreservedly to organising recreation and

---

[1] There were under the camp's control about 22,500 prisoners, of whom 5000 were British, including 800 New Zealanders. In the stalag there were about 4300, of whom 800–900 were British. The camp held also French, Belgians, and Russians.

[2] The first cases in prisoner-of-war camps in Germany were noticed in November 1941. It was thought to have been brought from Russia, where it was apparently endemic, and to have been encouraged by the ravages of war, movements of population, and disorganisation of sanitary services. According to a report by a medical officer working on behalf of the International Red Cross Committee, it ' accompanies tragically all the great upsets of human history ' and finds especially fertile ground among the dirty, half-starved, lousy populations of prisoner-of-war camps.

other activities. Outdoor sports in the restricted space, card tournaments and other indoor games, lectures and educational courses, and even a camp newspaper were all well started. The early improvised concerts were developed into a Christmas Cinderella pantomime, which seems to have been the first choice for an end-of-year entertainment in many camps. Two months of freedom from searches also proved an invaluable opportunity to form an escape committee, to work out possible plans for the spring, and to collect and make all sorts of escape aids.

By March prophylactic measures had the typhus under control and the quarantine was off. But the British prisoners' accommodation had become more overcrowded than ever. One stable had been given up to Russians, of whom great numbers[1] were at this time being freighted back to Germany under appalling conditions to become virtually slave workers. There was no change in the washing facilities, which had always been insufficient and exposed to the weather; the number of hot showers was restricted to one every three weeks; and the latrines were little better than when the first complaints had been made. There was still the shortage of underclothing and boots, though numbers of personal parcels had reached the camp. In spite of the arrival of books, the organised recreation already mentioned, and the provision of a small recreation room, the 'spirit of the prisoners' according to a Swiss visitor was 'certainly not as high as in other camps'. The German loudspeakers daily blared forth their special news bulletins of further successes on the Eastern Front, sandwiched between full-throated renderings of *Wir fahren gegen England* and other martial music. It is not surprising that many prisoners, despite their outward unconcern, felt sick at heart and wondered what the outcome would be.

The large numbers of prisoners in the working camps attached to Stalag XVIIIA did not have so much time to think. By the time they had done their nine and a half or ten and a half hours' work (even longer on the farms), got back to their camps and done their chores, they had little time or energy left for anything but food and sleep. There were nearly two hundred New Zealanders among the hundreds working on the large dam at Lavamünd, some fifty at Klagenfurt on building work, other parties on roadmaking, railway maintenance, or at sawmills, and dozens of small parties on the many farms in the Stiermark-Kärnten area within the stalag's control.

Living quarters were usually situated on the outskirts of a town—wooden huts with crude washing and latrine arrangements,

---

[1] Estimated in December 1941 at 500,000.

though in the winter of 1941 and the spring of 1942 something was done to improve them. Rations were those of a civilian heavy worker and there were no difficulties about getting Red Cross food parcels. In the autumn of 1941 the men's clothing had been in a bad state, many still having only the old French uniform issued on their arrival from Greece; and though, after pressure, the clothing from Geneva was issued in the following months, spring still saw a shortage of underclothing and boots. A large camp like Lavamünd was fortunate enough to have a British medical officer attached to it, but many others had to rely on local German doctors, often unwilling or perhaps unable to make regular and frequent visits, and sometimes quite unfeeling in the application of such medical skill as they possessed.

Until November or December 1941 many of these small camps had no books or games at all; a few had a pack or two of cards or a football, or a few musical instruments they had saved for and bought. Almost everyone took a keen interest in his mail: the two letters and two cards[1] he wrote each month, the cigarette parcels from New Zealand House, and especially the letters and personal parcels from next-of-kin in New Zealand, which were beginning to arrive by the end of the year. In a few *Arbeitskommandos* almost all free time was occupied in camp fatigues, and in the winter at any rate the bad light precluded much reading. By the spring, however, the *Arbeitskommandos* were receiving parcels of books on loan from stalag, several had their own orchestras and concert parties, and many were given facilities for outdoor games and river swimming. The adjustment to strenuous physical labour seems to have been achieved, and surplus energy was finding its outlet for some in serious reading and plans for study in the coming winter.

For others there was an absorbing outlet in escape. Few made the attempt from the stalag, but there were many attempted escapes from working camps during what was known to prisoners as the 'spring handicap'. It was not very difficult to get away from a working party, pick up a cache of food and civilian clothing, and make across country. The objectives at this period were Switzerland or Hungary, or the partisan-held hill territory in Yugoslavia. In spite of the sparseness of frontier guards at this stage of the war, there were few successes. For those caught the punishment was usually three weeks in solitary confinement on bread and water, followed by a period at one of the ' disciplinaire' *Arbeitskommandos,* which had been created to discourage prisoners who broke the rules. At these there was usually heavy pick-and-shovel work,

---
[1] Increased by the end of 1941 to two letters and four cards monthly. Most belligerents had agreed on this figure by December 1940.

living conditions were often inferior to those at other working camps, and guards were encouraged to be 'tougher'. The result was that many would-be escapers resolved to try again at the first opportunity, and those at the 'disciplinaire' camps gave so much trouble to the guards that the latter sometimes bribed them with concessions or even black-market goods in order to make things easier for themselves.

Although the bulk of New Zealand prisoners in Germany were in the Silesian or Austrian camps just described, there were always a hundred or two scattered about in a number of other camps in both Germany and Poland. At Moosburg, in Bavaria, there were in Stalag VIIA a few New Zealand Army prisoners from Greece and a few Air Force NCOs, adding yet another to the collection of Allied nationalities at this huge camp. Mention has already been made of the Air Force prisoners in Stalag IXC at Badsulza; and apart from them there were Army prisoners who were continually being discharged from the hospitals in *Wehrkreis* IX.[1] There were New Zealanders working at farm *Arbeitskommandos* attached to Stalag XIIIC at Hammelburg, 50 miles east of Frankfurt-on-Main.

A rather larger number of prisoners from Greece had gone to Thorn, in Poland, and were housed in one of the series of forts making up Stalag XXA, where in February 1941 some British officers had been sent as a reprisal. Conditions at these camps did not differ materially from those already described, except that in Poland there was evidence of harsher treatment by guards, including a number of fatal shooting incidents. As a result of British representations through neutral channels, Germany agreed later in the year to notify immediately by telegraph all such violent deaths and also to discontinue the use of fortresses and penal establishments as quarters for British prisoners.

Besides the groups already mentioned, there were sick and disabled men in various hospitals, and medical and dental personnel who were still more scattered. There was a New Zealand dental officer in Ilag VIII at Tost, where over a thousand British civilian men were interned, only a handful of whom were New Zealanders. And sometimes transferred medical or dental staff found themselves the only New Zealanders in their new camp, like the two doctors and the medical orderly[2] who volunteered to go and treat an outbreak of typhus at a Russian camp at Neuhammer, near Stalag VIIIB, Lamsdorf.

[1] Hospitals in this military area containing New Zealanders included Obermasfeld (attached to Stalag IXC), Stadroda (attached to Stalag IXC), Dieburg (attached to Stalag IXB).
[2] Capt H. M. Foreman, Capt E. Stevenson-Wright and Pte J. Butler, all NZMC. The two officers were both awarded the MBE, and Butler the BEM, for this and for outstanding services to their fellow prisoners of war during captivity. Foreman and Butler both developed typhus fever but recovered.

All the Army prisoners referred to in the foregoing account of German camps had been prisoners since the middle of 1941, with the exception of recaptured escapers and a few who had evaded capture for some months. There was no fresh intake of prisoners for Germany as a result of the Libyan campaign, since British Commonwealth troops taken there, though nearly all captured by German forces, were placed in the custody of the Italian Government and by 1942 were in camps in Italy.[1] It was otherwise with airmen prisoners, of whom there had been a steady intake since the outbreak of war, consistent with Britain's continual harassing of Germany from the air. The last months of 1941 saw the Royal Air Force bombing German-occupied ports and bases on the Atlantic coast; and in 1942 the stepping up of the bombing offensive on Germany's communications and factories was carried out. For the first time raids took place involving more than a thousand planes. This intensification of the air war by the RAF brought about a rapid increase in the number of airmen prisoners in Germany.[2]

In November 1941 the Luftwaffe appointed a new commandant for the interrogation centre and transit camp at Oberursel. This may reasonably be attributed to a renewed effort to protect Germany from air attacks, and possibly also to dissatisfaction with the results of interrogation so far achieved. The centre was supplied with all the necessary materials and manpower and underwent a business-like reorganisation. Evaluation of documents, preparation of RAF squadron histories, interpretation of photographs, compilation of technical data, and a number of other adjuncts of interrogation were delegated to small sections of specialists. The number of interrogators was increased, and they were classified into mere 'receptionists', who were discouraged from going beyond the 'Red Cross' form, and those versed in what the commandant referred to as the 'fine art of interrogation'. Even the latter specialised—on bombers, fighters, or flak for example. About this time the centre assumed the name *Auswertestelle West* (Evaluation Centre for the West), a new block of 50 solitary confinement cells was built—the 'cooler'—and there was a toughening up in methods.

On reaching Oberursel railway station prisoners had a short journey by tram or a thirty minutes' march to the camp, where they were lined up outside the reception hut—the old 'Stone-house'. The escorting guard then handed them over, together with their personal effects, and the 'reception' staff got to work verifying

---

[1] A few airmen prisoners captured by Germans in Libya were flown to Germany. Others taken by the Italians went to Italy, where their experiences were almost identical with those of captured Army personnel.
[2] New Zealand airmen prisoners rose by 105 in the period November 1941 to May 1942.

the details of each prisoner previously notified over the teleprinter. Officers were asked to step forward and their crews to take their places alongside them, 'to ensure that they would not be separated, and to allow them to go to the same camp'.[1] They were all given a 'strip' search for weapons, escape aids, and personal property; they were photographed and fingerprinted. Finally they were escorted away to solitary confinement in wooden, soundproof cells fitted with microphones[2] and containing nothing but a bare minimum of furniture. The introduction to prison-camp life was as severe as the Germans could make it within the limits allowed by the Geneva Convention, and perhaps slightly beyond.

Within the next twenty-four hours each prisoner was visited by a German 'receptionist', whose task it was to persuade him to complete the so-called 'Red Cross form'. At the same time he tried to assess from a psychological viewpoint the suitability of the newly-arrived prisoner for further interrogation. On the back of the 'Red Cross form' he might note, 'heavy smoker', or 'very secure', or 'susceptible to flattery', so that the interrogation officer who dealt with this prisoner would have some guide as to the best kind of approach. To soften the prisoner's resistance he might point out that as soon as his interrogation was over he would be free to go to a comfortable permanent camp—the sooner the better for everybody.

Living conditions at this stage of the prisoner's progress were bad enough to amount almost to inhumane treatment. The cells, though bigger certainly than those in a German military prison, were no more than 13 ft by 10 ft by 6 ft 6 in; they contained nothing but a bed, a wooden stool, and two blankets; they were grimy, ill-ventilated, and always evil-smelling; they had no facilities for washing or shaving; they contained no reading or writing materials; and they were sometimes heated to an unbearable degree if it was felt necessary to add to the inmate's discomfort. The only breaks in the monotony and loneliness were meals brought three times a day: bread, jam, and coffee; soup; bread and water. Living conditions were in fact designed to lower morale and to produce acute mental depression.

At first interrogations were made in these cells, but it was soon found that better results came from transferring the prisoner to a comfortable, sometimes opulently furnished, room complete with maps and diagrams, the contrast in surroundings helping to throw him off his balance. Previously primed with all relevant

---

[1] This ruse, which often caught men unawares, obviously simplified the checking of information obtained in later interrogations.
[2] There were two microphones in each cell, linked to a listening post next to the commandant's office.

information about the prisoner, the interrogation officer met him with a smile and an invitation to sit down (invariably facing the light), and began a friendly conversation on some innocent topic—sport or home and family—to prove he was a human being.

The ice once broken, he led on to the question of proof that the prisoner was in fact an Allied airman and not a saboteur or spy. The answers to a few queries, he would point out, could settle the thing and facilitate his transfer to a permanent camp; on the other hand failure to satisfy the interrogator might cause the latter reluctantly to hand him on to the Gestapo as a suspect. If recalcitrant, the prisoner was after a time transferred back to the squalor of his cell 'to think it over'. On his return after a few days he was often 'at least willing to start a conversation'.

The more the prisoner talked the longer he was retained for interrogation, though he might be occasionally granted small privileges (such as a wash or a shave) by way of reward; and although the average stay was two to three days, solitary confinement with intermittent questioning might if necessary go on for a month. During this period he might receive treatment ranging from simple neglect to mild third degree, involving minimal rations, the withholding of facilities for keeping clean and tidy, refusal of tobacco and books and of Red Cross supplies of any kind, overheating of the cell—'sweat-box' tactics—and constant switching on and off of the light to prevent sleep. At the same time no opportunity was lost of pointing out that all this would cease as soon as the interrogation had been satisfactorily concluded. Thus, although the Germans were *korrekt* to the extent that physical violence was rare and never employed as a policy, to quote the commandant, 'no amount of solitary confinement, privation, and psychological blackmail was considered excessive'. Only when the prisoner was given up as 'stubborn' or 'exhausted of information' was he released from his cell to the transit camp.

Slightly wounded prisoners were treated in the same way as those who were unharmed. Severely wounded were put into single rooms at Hohemark hospital and interrogated there, but the same tactics could not be applied. The commandant complained:

. . . the Interrogation Officer could not carry out the interrogation as forcibly because of his own feelings towards the state of the P/W's health, added to which the prisoner had no desire to be moved from the hospital where he felt he was particularly comfortable. He had everything he needed: care, medical treatment, a decent bed and good food.

On one occasion a German interrogation officer, who had been sick, was put while convalescent in the same room with a prisoner of war and was thus able to achieve 'good results', but chance did not allow the employment of such a ruse very frequently. It was found better practice, if the prisoner's wounds were not too serious and he had recovered in a day or two, to transfer him to a cell at the interrogation centre, where the contrast in his surroundings 'in most cases brought quick results'. Hohemark was thus enabled to continue its propaganda role of showing 'a contented group living under model conditions' capable of impressing newcomers with the German 'comradeship of Knights of the Air'.[1]

The transit camp, Dulag Luft, also maintained its former standard of comfort and the stool-pigeons used by the Germans continued in residence, though RAF crews were now being thoroughly warned about the enemy's methods of interrogation, and the traps of Dulag Luft were being explained to them in England by escapers who had got home.

As a contrast to the semi-luxury of Oberursel, conditions at the small camp at Kirchhain had, since the escape already mentioned, become more grimly uncomfortable than ever. The wooden clogs issued to replace confiscated boots were the only footwear allowed, even after a Red Cross consignment of clothing had arrived in December 1941. Rigid control was exercised by a large camp guard over the amount of clothing in each man's possession and the issue of Red Cross food. In spite of this all the prisoners co-operated in the digging of a tunnel begun in January 1942, and 52 of them got out on the night of 11 May—just before the final evacuation of the camp to Sagan. They were all recaptured within ten days, but they raised a considerable hue and cry in the area.

In mid-1941 Stalag Luft I at Barth had had a new commandant, who had been responsible for many of the improvements mentioned in the last chapter, and who (in the words of a New Zealand warrant officer) was 'ever ready to help making life in the camp a bit more bearable'. On the other hand he was well aware of the need for security, and prisoners were locked inside their barracks from dusk until morning. Fortunately, before the onset in the Baltic of the bitter winter of 1941–42, many had received parcels of warm clothing from New Zealand House, and there was on hand a plentiful supply of food parcels. Sports gear had arrived, the stock of books was increasing, and mail, though irregular, was sometimes coming in fairly quick time. In the winter an ice-skating rink gave a great deal of amusement and helped everyone to keep fit, and in the spring regular football matches were held. The spring, too, with the rumour of a

---

[1] The quotations in this section are from a captured report on *Auswertestelle West* by the German commandant.

INTERROGATION CAMP—DULAG LUFT, OBERURSEL

Living quarters for a working camp from a sketch by *A. G. Douglas*

A village in the Sudetenland where a British working party was quartered

'I dunno George—sometimes I wonder if this life isn't leaving its mark on us!' This cartoon by *J. Welch* exaggerates a general fear of 'barbed-wire fever'

BETWEEN THE BARRACKS OF STALAG VIIIA AT GÖRLITZ, EAST OF DRESDEN

A BARRACK INTERIOR AT STALAG VIIIA

CHRISTMAS EVE 1943 INSIDE THE PERIMETER WIRE,
STALAG 383, BAVARIA

HALF OF STALAG 383 FROM THE SENTRY BOX ON THE
NORTH SIDE
This shows the type of hut and layout common to many German camps

STALAG 383—SNOW, SLUSH AND SLEET
Winter in Germany, 1943–44

STALAG 383—THE RESTLESSNESS OF SPRING

STALAG 383—MUD AFTER THE THAW

STALAG 383—
HUT INTERIOR AT NIGHT

STALAG 383—'AT THE TABLES'
A miniature Monte Carlo, with cigarettes as currency

STALAG 357 AT FALLINGBOSTEL
Ablution stand for a group of over 1000 men

STALAG 357   Dividing up swede peelings from the German mess.
Each man represents a barrack of eighty prisoners and stands in front
of the cardboard boxes into which their share is put

Stalág XVIIIA at Wolfsberg, Austria— An Anzac Day parade in 1943

STALAG XVIIIA The shoemakers' shop

SHAKESPEARE PLAYED AT OFLAG VIIB, AT EICHSTAETT

OFLAG VIIB—ANOTHER PLAY

The handicrafts section of an arts and crafts exhibition at Stalag 383

move brought a further crop of attempts at escape, which continued until late April 1942,[1] by which time the evacuation of the camp was nearly complete.

Stalag Luft I at Barth had not proved large enough to accommodate all British air force prisoners, and its situation on the Baltic had encouraged attempts at escape. There had also been numerous breaks by airmen from camps under Wehrmacht control, and two NCOs from Badsulza had reached England via France. Accordingly the Luftwaffe decided to assemble all Air Force prisoners in a new camp at Sagan, in Lower Silesia, 80 miles south-east of Berlin. Prefabricated wooden huts were erected in a clearing at the edge of an area of pine afforestation, about a mile from the town of Sagan. There were at the beginning two compounds, one for officers and another for NCOs and airmen, known later as the East and Centre compounds respectively. In April 1942 some three or four hundred officers arrived in the East compound from Barth, from Lubeck, from Warburg and from Spangenburg; and from then on these were supplemented by batches from Dulag Luft. At the same time Lamsdorf, Badsulza, and Kirchhain were practically cleared of all NCOs and airmen, who were brought to the Centre compound; these were supplemented in the same way. By the end of May the camp strength had leapt to over 2000 all ranks.

It seems likely that the Luftwaffe hoped in this new camp to combine security with contentment: to make the camp escape-proof, to provide better amenities than most other camps, and to disarm prisoners' antagonism and suspicion by a show of friendliness. There were all the usual camp defences,[2] with the addition of ground microphones to detect digging. There was a full staff of security personnel (Abwehr), who clad in their dark-blue overalls spent their day crawling under barracks, peeping in windows, eavesdropping, and generally keeping a watch on what the prisoners were doing. Searches of barracks were laid down in camp orders for every second day, though in practice this became every month. At the same time the Luftwaffe guards brought from Barth were schooled in a certain superficial friendliness and courtesy to officers, and were characterised in some letters from prisoners as 'reasonable'. The commandant himself hoped by these tactics 'to gain influence over the prisoners' and also an 'advantage in dealing with the Protecting Power.'[3]

---

[1]Up till this time 46 had broken out of the camp from 37 different attempts, excluding another 48 tunnel projects. All were recaptured within a short time of their breakout, except two who reached Sweden.
[2]See account of Stalag Luft I on p. 34.
[3]The quotations are from the report of the court martial of the commandant and others following the mass break of March 1944.

The officers' barracks were subdivided into rooms, which at first held from two to six but were later more crowded; other ranks' barracks consisted each of two large rooms with double-tier bunks to hold sixty, though this figure was later increased to eighty. Officers' barracks each contained cooking facilities, a washroom and latrines; those for other ranks contained only a small stove and an improvised night latrine, the cookhouse proper, washing facilities and latrines being in separate buildings. There was a sports field which, though a little small, enabled football, cricket, and baseball to be played. Educational classes were soon organised, many books having been brought from Barth and elsewhere; and plays, concerts, and revues were soon being produced by an active theatre group, who received plenty of assistance from the Germans by way of hired costumes and stage accessories. For most of the other ranks from Wehrmacht camps conditions at Sagan were a considerable improvement; and for a large number of all ranks from smaller camps it was good to see new faces and to exchange news and ideas with a larger number of men.

No time was wasted in putting escape schemes into action. Soon after the first arrivals in April there were successful breaks from the camp by walking through the main gates in disguise and by negotiating the wire. German vigilance was increased and an anti-escape ditch was dug to a depth of seven feet just inside the perimeter. When a favourable opportunity occurred at dusk one evening in early June, three officers[1] entered the ditch and dug their way out from the side nearest the wire. Sealing up the tunnel behind them and poking through to the surface for air as they went, they gained their temporary freedom the same night. Five days later they were arrested near Stettin. Although none of these early attempts was completely successful, a large camp organisation was being built up on foundations which had been laid at Barth, to control escape activity and to assist all approved schemes with expert planning, escape aids, and provision against discovery by the German camp staff.

In this period a few more New Zealand airmen were forced down in neutral territory and interned. By the end of 1941 there were four detained in Algeria, four in unoccupied France, and one in Eire. In December 1941 those who had been interned at Aumale in French North Africa had been transferred to a camp at Laghouat, in a healthy locality on the edge of the Sahara 200 miles south of Algiers. The camp soon held between three and four hundred servicemen, mostly from naval vessels. Difficult

---

[1] The New Zealander in the party was Flt/Lt H. W. Lamond, RAF.

relations with the Vichy Government had made alleviation of the conditions of internees in Algeria a slow matter. The new camp, however, was an improvement, and food and clothing parcels received through the Red Cross relieved their two major wants.

The airmen in unoccupied France were interned at Saint-Hippolyte-du-Fort, about 52 kilometers from Nîmes (Gard), where between three and four hundred were collected, including many recaptured escapers. Quarters were reasonably comfortable, rations, the same as for French civilians, but clothing was very short; treatment was, on the whole, fairly good. In mid-March, however, they were all transferred to Fort de la Revere, not far from Nice, where all military internees in unoccupied France were being assembled. This proved to be a depressing old fortress, very overcrowded and short of water. For those forced down in Eire, the British internment camp near Kildare was adjacent to that for Germans detained under similar circumstances. Though strongly guarded it was comfortable, there was plenty of good food, and treatment was excellent.

III: *Civilians in Europe*

As Red Cross supplies became better established the position of civilian internees in Europe became physically more tolerable, and the organisation of recreation did much for a while to ease their psychological burdens. In Paris the old flea-ridden St. Denis barracks and some thin-walled new hutments were still crowded with a thousand or more British male internees.[1] But Red Cross food made their otherwise sparse diet a healthy one, and a good library, theatre, and sports field provided recreation. Clothing was still very short and men were worried over the financial position of their relatives outside the camp, in view of the entry into the war of the United States, which had hitherto made the relief payments to uninterned civilians.[2] The position of the men at Tost (Ilag VIII) was similar. New Zealand members of the Merchant Navy, of whom the number had increased steadily, were still in a special compound (Milag) at Sandbostel, which had improved somewhat since the appointment of a new commandant. They were treated as civilian internees and not compelled to work. The needs of all New Zealanders at these camps were carefully watched by the Prisoners of War Section of the High Commissioner's Office in London.

The interests of women internees were just as carefully watched. The British interned community at Vittel was still comfortably

---

[1] Considered by the internees' representative to be 500–700 too many.
[2] The new Protecting Power, Switzerland, carried on these payments.

housed in imposing-looking hotels and had been reduced to about 2400 people by the release of women over sixty, men over seventy-five, and children under sixteen. Provision for recreation included the local theatre, as well as a park containing seven tennis courts and other sporting facilities. The interned women at Liebenau were also 'well fed and comfortably housed'[1] and were receiving quantities of material to be made into clothing, of which they were short.

There was a suggestion towards the end of 1941 that Australian and New Zealand women were to be released and allowed to live together in Berlin,[2] a change which most of the women concerned did not relish. The view of the New Zealand Government was that this step should not be taken unless it would be to their advantage and was in accordance with their wishes. For they would be unable, in their proposed new status, to receive relief parcels, they might find difficulty in obtaining suitable living quarters, and their monthly allowance of 150 Reichmarks (£10) might be insufficient to keep them. It was suggested to the German Government in early April 1942, however, that if it was prepared to permit their repatriation the New Zealand Government would do the same for German women in New Zealand. In the meantime two New Zealand women who were agreeable had been released, one to live with relatives in Holland and the other to live in Paris, as she had been doing before the war.

IV: *Protection of the Interests of Prisoners of War and Civilians*

The machinery of negotiation on behalf of prisoners of war had now assumed the form which, broadly, it retained for the remainder of the war. In London the Imperial Prisoners of War Committee co-ordinated the views of the British and Dominion governments on prisoner-of-war matters as they arose; the British service Ministries, especially the War Office, worked out the details of their application; and the Foreign Office communicated them to the Protecting Power for action or transmission to the German Government. The British Home Office similarly co-ordinated matters relating to civilian internees, and they were similarly communicated.

Besides making representations on our behalf the Protecting Power, as well as the International Red Cross Committee, acted as our informants on conditions in prisoner-of-war and internment camps. There were other sources of information—prisoners' letters, accounts by escapers or repatriates, sometimes giving aspects not

---

[1] Quoted from a letter sent by a New Zealand woman internee at Liebenau.
[2] No German women were interned in New Zealand, and this was thought to be a reciprocal move by the German Government.

obvious to a visiting inspector; but the reports of the experienced observers of the United States Embassy and the International Red Cross Committee remained, on the whole, the most thorough and reliable. Many of the letters of complaint written by camp leaders, even though addressed to these neutral agencies, were not being sent on by the detaining power but merely marked 'not necessary' or 'not of interest'; so that the three-monthly visits, although felt to be infrequent enough, were essential even to gain an uncensored version of the prisoners' view of the situation. When in December 1941 the United States became a belligerent, Switzerland took over her duties as Protecting Power for British interests in both Germany and Italy.

As the result of our losses in the Libyan campaign, considerable numbers of British and Imperial prisoners were for the first time transported across the Mediterranean for detention in Italy. The torpedoing of the *Jantzen,* though so far the only such incident involving New Zealanders, was not the first occasion on which ships conveying prisoners had been lost or damaged at sea; and in February 1942 the International Red Cross Committee was led to propose to the belligerents safety measures for minimising these dangers. It suggested the use of sea transport only for imperative reasons, a special recognition signal for ships carrying prisoners of war, and adequate provision of lifebelts and boats; if possible these ships were to sail in the company of other vessels capable of picking up survivors. But practical difficulties in the way of these measures and dangers of their abuse prevented any basis of agreement being reached.

Reference has already been made to the agreement reached between the British and Italian governments regarding the treatment of protected personnel, and especially regarding their repatriation.[1] The German Government maintained that the 1929 Sick and Wounded Convention[2] gave them the right to decide which protected personnel were to be repatriated on the grounds that their services were not required for the care of their fellow prisoners; and the rather loose wording of the relevant Articles in this Convention certainly made such an interpretation possible. There was thus little action that could be taken other than insisting that protected personnel should receive the extra letter-cards and walks on parole[3] to which their status entitled them, and establishing

---

[1] See p. 125.
[2] Convention for the Relief of the Sick and Wounded in Armies in the Field, signed at Geneva in 1929.
[3] They were entitled by bilateral agreements between belligerents to twice the number of letters and cards given to ordinary prisoners. The number was fixed with the Italian Government in December 1941 as two letters and two cards a week.

with detaining authorities the identity of British protected personnel in their hands, by forwarding lists and Red Cross identity certificates to those who had lost them.

Notification of capture had during this period begun to operate smoothly and expeditiously, and it was decided not to send any one to Geneva to report on the working of the system. Instead of the International Red Cross cables going direct to New Zealand, however, they were sent to the High Commissioner's Office in London, whence they were sent on to Wellington, any corrections being cabled later. This involved a delay of only a few hours and effected a considerable saving in cable costs.[1] The International Red Cross Committee had arranged with the Italians for the *Ufficio Prigioneri di Guerra* in Rome to telegraph all captures to the Central agency in Geneva, which passed them simultaneously to London and to their delegation in Cairo so that they could inform the military authorities there. Only twenty-four hours elapsed from the time the message left Geneva until it had been checked by our Army Records and was ready to send on to New Zealand. This plan worked with the same efficiency that had been attained in notifications from Germany, but Italian notice of transfers to permanent camps was unsatisfactory 'owing to the notorious inadequacy of the information given by the Italian military authorities' to the Bureau in Rome. In addition the Vatican City broadcast lists of the names of prisoners of war and also transmitted by wireless through the papal delegate in Australia short messages between prisoners and their next-of-kin. By May 1942 over 6000 New Zealanders had been officially notified as prisoners of war.

Pay for our officers and other ranks while in enemy hands had from an early stage of the war been the subject of much discussion in Sub-Committee B of the Imperial Prisoners of War Committee and of the exchange of a considerable number of notes between the British and both the German and Italian governments. Article 23 of the Geneva Prisoners of War Convention of 1929 laid it down that officer prisoners were entitled to receive in captivity the pay of their equivalent rank in the army of the detaining power, provided this did not exceed the rate paid by their own country. In Italy the rates paid were high compared with those in Germany (though not as high as the British), and it was found that there was often an insufficient balance left in officers' home accounts to provide

---

[1] A saving of 5s 7d a word.

for their dependants, or even to pay necessary expenses such as subscriptions and insurance premiums.¹

As reciprocal free messing had been agreed to, and as the amenities provided by Italy in 1940 and early 1941 were good, it was felt that extra pocket-money was not needed there. The British Government accordingly suggested a considerable reduction in rates of pay for officers of all three services.² A corresponding reduction of the pay granted to the large numbers of Italian officers in British hands would also effect considerable saving in public expenditure. For the same reasons, and also because so little could be bought in German canteens, a similar suggestion was made to the German Government. Both countries in reply indicated their willingness for a reduction in the rates paid to British officers in their hands but not in those paid to their own prisoners in British hands. As messing in Germany was free and their rates were not greatly in excess of our own, it was decided to let the suggestion to Germany drop.

The problem in Italy was more difficult. It was soon established that in Campo PG 78 at Sulmona officers had always had to pay not only for their food and fuel but also for all mess equipment and replacements. A steady rise in prices had raised an officer's mess bill from 420 lire (about £5 14s.) in August 1941 to 630 lire (about £8 15s.) in January 1942.³ Furthermore, the slowness in arrival of tobacco and clothing parcels and the breakdown in the deliveries of food parcels often necessitated local purchases over and above this amount. The same position obtained in other camps in early 1942. Many officers would not buy the extra fruit and sweets that would to some extent have compensated for the meagre diet supplied by the Italians, for fear of exhausting their pay balances through the exorbitant prices charged. In order to relieve their position it was found necessary at Campo PG 38, Poppi, for example, to agree at a mess meeting that messing charges

---

¹The comparative rates of pay for officers were:

	Italian (basic ?)	German (basic ?)	British (basic)	New Zealand (inclusive)
Second-Lieutenant	£10 8s 4d	£4 16s	£16	£24 15s
Lieutenant	£13 3s 11d	£5 8s		£26 5s
Captain	£15 5s 7d	£6 8s		£31 10s
Major	£18 1s 2d	£7 4s		£41 5s
Lieutenant-Colonel	£19 8s 11d	£8 0s		£57 10s

At these rates a second-lieutenant prisoner in Italy would have only £5 10s a month left in his home account. The Italian Government had agreed in principle to remittances of pay to the prisoner's home country, but no definite arrangements had been made.
²The rates suggested were: Subalterns, £3 a month; Captains, £4 a month; Majors and over, £5 a month. It should be noted that both in Germany and Italy pay took the form not of local currency but of coupons redeemable at a prisoner-of-war camp canteen.
³It will be seen that the exchange rate of 72 lire to the £ sterling was no longer realistic.

should be on a sliding scale proportionate to rank. In May Sub-Committee B agreed that a messing allowance of three shillings a day should be credited to the home account of each British Commonwealth officer in Italy.

No provision was made in the Geneva Convention of 1929 for the pay of other rank prisoners, but merely for their remuneration for any work they did for the detaining power. In Germany full advantage was taken of this, and in order to secure the necessary funds for essential canteen purchases such as tooth powder, or for airmail charges, the prisoners were forced to work, even if as NCOs they were exempt. The net pay for most work in Germany was 0·70 Reichmarks (about 11d) daily, though special rates were paid for some special types of work; and this was thought to be adequate for out-of-pocket expenses. For those in Italian hands an agreement had been made with the Italian Government for advances of pocket-money, as distinct from earnings,[1] commencing from 1 October 1941 at the rate of seven lire (1s 11d) a week to corporals and below and ten lire (2s 9d) a week to those over this rank. A proposal for similar reciprocal rates had been made to the German Government in June 1941, but the latter had rejected it on the ground that the rates were too low. As they had, however, agreed in principle to the remittance home of prisoners' credit balances, a second proposal with higher rates was made to them. The pay for those in Italian hands seemed on the face of it to be sufficient in view of the fact that the Italian Government was supplying food, clothing, and tobacco. In point of fact, as has been seen, these were all on an inadequate scale, and additional funds in the period at the end of 1941 and beginning of 1942, before the flow of relief parcels properly began, would have made things a good deal easier.

V: *Relief Work*

The organisation of relief supplies for prisoners of war and civilian internees had by 1942 become stabilised. Although the Italian ration for prisoners of war was bulkier than that received by those in German hands, analysis showed that it was even more deficient than the latter in certain essential nutritive elements.[2] Accordingly, the need for food parcels on the same scale was early recognised by the British Red Cross in the United Kingdom, and the extra quantities were despatched to Geneva for distribution to Italian camps. At the end of 1941, too, New Zealand had begun to contribute in

---

[1] At this stage almost no British prisoners in Italy were employed on outside jobs, but merely on camp or construction fatigue work.
[2] Calcium, vitamin A, animal protein, riboflavin.

kind to the pool of relief food for prisoners at the rate of three thousand parcels a week. The parcels were standardised and contained chiefly the cheese, milk, honey, and meat that are the staple products of a pastoral country, though the contents were planned dietetically in the same manner as those packed in other countries. The packing was done by teams of voluntary women workers organised by the Joint Council and the whole scheme was paid for by the National Patriotic Fund. By the middle of 1942 these parcels were being sent overseas at the rate of six thousand a week.

The British Red Cross Middle East Commission had arranged through the International Red Cross Committee for food parcels paid for privately to be sent to individual prisoners of war. They were paid for either by friends and regimental comrades, or out of regimental funds, or out of funds made available by the National Patriotic Fund Commissioner in the Middle East. Sub-Committee B of the Imperial Prisoners of War Committee had already decided to discourage the sending of private food parcels, as being unfair to those who did not receive them and unnecessarily clogging up the mail services. In addition many were not arriving or were arriving in a badly pilfered condition, especially in Italy, and after the end of 1942 no more were being sent from the Middle East.

The first quarterly next-of-kin parcels[1] packed and censored at the Joint Council depots left New Zealand at the end of September 1941. As they were expected to take upwards of five months to reach the prisoner-of-war camps (well over six months after capture), authority was given in November for the depatch of a second parcel from the Charing Cross Road packing centre in London. Free initial parcels[2] containing necessities for those newly captured continued to be sent from London as soon as reliable information was received of a prisoner's camp address. In addition there were a number of prisoners and internees with next-of-kin in the United Kingdom, all of whose parcels were sent from London.[3] If no next-of-kin were forthcoming either there or in New Zealand, or if next-of-kin could not pay for the parcels, the National Patriotic Fund supplied them or contributed to their cost. Parcels sent in weighing less than the permitted eleven pounds were brought up to

---

[1] See above pp. 13, 46, and 100.
[2] The cost of these initial parcels to the National Patriotic Fund for the period 1 November 1941 to 4 March 1942 was £5905, of which £5470 was expended on the contents and £435 on administration. The contents were: shirt, vest, underpants, pyjamas, two pairs socks, two handkerchiefs, pullover, balaclava, gloves, towel, soap, safety razor, four blades, shaving brush, shaving stick, toothbrush, toothpaste, boot polish, bootlaces, comb, two pencils, 1¼ lb. slab chocolate.

Later parcels substituted for some of these articles the following: hairbrush, nailbrush, bootbrush, 'hussif', pipe and pouch (in every fifth parcel), slippers, gym shoes, kitbags. Items left out would include winter wear when the parcel was expected to arrive in summer.

[3] There were about 250 such cases as at March 1942.

full weight by including chocolate or woollen garments, paid for out of the same fund.

It was obviously uneconomical to send books and courses from New Zealand, except those published there, for which there was a special demand. Instead, our per capita contributions to the British Red Cross Indoor Recreations Fund[1] were continued. By December 1941 some 71,000 books had been sent to camps from this source, and a reserve had been established at Geneva to provide for new camps. Great care was devoted to the selection of the right proportions of lighter novels and Westerns and of the more solid reading to which a large number of prisoners' tastes were turning. The co-ordinating 'Advisory Committee' set up by the International Red Cross Committee at Geneva[2] continued to control the distribution of all these books.

The distribution of material for games and sports, music, and other entertainment was supervised by the World Alliance of YMCAs in conjunction with the International Red Cross Committee at Geneva. Special parcels of games[3] were made up for working parties of various sizes. By the end of 1941 eight camps had each been supplied with 14 instruments to make up an orchestra, in addition to hundreds of mouth-organs, ukuleles, and other single instruments. Gramophones and records, sets of sports equipment and team clothing, flower and vegetable seeds were among other types of recreational consignments.

The work of the Educational Books Section set up at the New Bodleian in Oxford soon began to bear fruit. Requests for books and study courses reaching the New Zealand Prisoners of War Section in London were referred to the specialists at the New Bodleian. Italian censorship regulations forbade study courses, but over 3500 had been sent to Germany by the end of 1942; and in addition to the many study books sent from England, a reserve of 50,000 was established at Geneva so that time might be saved in delivery. At Oflag VIB educational activity had been organised as a 'university' with six faculties and twenty sub-divisions, the language branch alone catering for instruction in 22 languages. A similar type of organisation was later found to be suitable in other officers' camps.

Although the stalags did not have as much free time nor as many highly qualified instructors, the organisation at Stalag VIIIB already mentioned indicates what could be done. Examinations had at first been thought impracticable, but an agreement on the matter had

---

[1] Formerly called 'Fiction and Games' Fund.
[2] See p. 43.
[3] As an indication of the quantities involved, over 15,000 packs of cards were sent by the end of 1941.

been reached with Germany by autumn 1941,[1] the machinery had been arranged through the External Registrar of the University of London, and by the middle of 1942 the first results had been announced. It was now possible for men not only to occupy their time usefully in captivity with study, but also to qualify themselves academically for whatever career they intended to pursue in the post-war period.

The monthly despatch by the New Zealand House Prisoners of War Section of two hundred cigarettes or eight ounces of tobacco for every prisoner or internee was now done directly from the tobacco companies, who were supplied with the required names and camp addresses.[2] The British Red Cross bulk supplies of tobacco and cigarettes were now handled in the same way. In addition to regular consignments of medical supplies and invalid comforts, a braille letter service for blind prisoners[3] was established towards the end of 1941, and about the same time material for the manufacture of artificial limbs was sent to Switzerland to be made up on the measurements of Swiss orthopaedists, who had been given permission to visit amputation cases in the camps. The despatch of all these relief supplies from England had to be carefully watched[4] in order that the enemy should not escape his responsibility for feeding and caring medically for prisoners of war; and the real needs of prisoners, together with the propaganda effect of British goods in Germany, were constantly being weighed against any possible economic advantage achieved by the enemy.

* * * * *

In this period the war was extended so as to involve the greater part of the world. At the end of 1941 Japan had begun her aggressive sweep southwards and eastwards, which by May 1942 had brought almost all of South-East Asia into her hands. The United States had declared war immediately following the Japanese attack, and in January 1942, 26 nations (henceforth the United Nations) had pledged themselves to employ their ' full resources, military or economic ' against the three Axis powers. Russia had gained herself breathing space by her winter counter-offensive, followed by further efforts in the spring at Leningrad and the Black Sea. And during the last months of 1941 the British had made their second thrust into Libya, rather neutralised by a German

---

[1] Italy never permitted either study courses or examinations.
[2] The cost to the National Patriotic Fund of this service for the quarterly period 1 January to 31 March 1942 was £3210.
[3] Assembled first in Obermasfeld hospital and later in Kloster Haina.
[4] By the Ministry of Economic Warfare.

counter-thrust which by May 1942 had regained much lost ground and ended in a stabilised position at Gazala. So far from being near a decision, the war had reached a secondary and more intense stage, described by the Germans as 'total war'.

In these circumstances Germany probably decided, as her labour force needed no immediate reinforcements other than those pouring in from the Russian front and the millions of foreign workers already available in occupied Europe, that Italy should take her share of looking after the troublesome British. At all events it seems clear that Italy had not expected to receive British prisoners in anything like the numbers that arrived at her southern ports in November and December 1941. There was a lack of camps, and the disinfestation centres near Naples, Brindisi and Bari, intended for moderate numbers of the Italian armed forces returning from overseas service, were far too small to cope with the shiploads of prisoners which were marched into them. Improvised accommodation was very crude, and the position became serious on account of the length of time prisoners were kept in overcrowded and unhealthy conditions through lack of permanent camps to which they might be sent. It is fairly safe to say that at this stage Italian intentions towards British prisoners were humane if not kindly. But shortage of materials, the over-centralisation which necessitated the reference of a vast number of matters to 'Rome', and a tendency on the part of some camp staffs to postpone action even on matters of urgency combined to prolong situations in no way complying with the humane provisions of the Geneva Convention, in spite of the eagerness of most Italians to show that they accepted its provisions and that they treated their prisoners in a civilised way.

Perhaps a certain natural dilatoriness was linked to a desire for the creation of an artistically perfect plan before taking any action; the plan was usually excellent, but the interim chaos before it was executed, or even worked out, was allowed to take care of itself. Thus there could be no pay credits issued to the officers at Campo PG 38 until an elaborate system had been detailed and fine-looking account books headed up, though officers were meanwhile prevented from buying the clothing and toilet articles they needed. Bulk Red Cross consignments had to be sent to Milan, where a new Italian distributing depot was set up, in spite of the International Red Cross Committee having all the machinery for sending direct to camps. No parcels of any kind could be sent to camps until they were all given numbers at the end of January 1942, though men were hungry and short of cigarettes and clothing. All mail had to be sent to a central censorship office at Rome before going on to its camp address; and from Campo 57 at any rate, letters which arrived uncensored were sent back to Rome. The effects of bureaucratic control were sometimes mitigated by a reasonable attitude on the part of the local camp administrative staff; but where the latter were intractable or worse, there resulted much real hardship, especially among other rank prisoners, which could easily have been avoided.

The interest of carabinieri in the guarding of prisoners and their presence on many of the camp staffs threw a great emphasis on security measures. At the camps and during all moves there was a large proportion of guards to those guarded. Censorship of mail, carried out in Rome, was more strict than in Germany. At one stage there was a prohibition on receiving playing cards, at another on printed music, and there were unpredictable bans on books, presumably through fear that they might be used for messages that might conceivably convey undesirable information. Though the average Italian officer did not greatly care about such matters, still less the soldier, constant police supervision saw that in general these strict regulations were adhered to. The severe punishments awarded by Italian military authorities to camp staffs after successful escapes were a measure of the importance attached to their prevention.

After the somewhat chaotic conditions and the exceptional cold of the winter, men began in the spring sunshine to adapt themselves better to their new environment and to understand better the temperament of their guards. Though by our standards technically backward in their sanitation and their medical facilities, there was little doubt of their respect for the Red Cross and what it stood for, and for the Church in all its manifestations. There was little doubt too of their desire to be friendly and of their lack of interest in a war with Britain. Many commandants of permanent camps did what they could to improve them, and in some, tolerable conditions were soon achieved. Prisoners who had at first wondered what sort of a future their captivity held in store for them, felt after a few months in Italy that they knew how to secure fairly civilised treatment in Italian hands.

Those in Germany had by the end of this period been prisoners for about a year. For them, under the lean conditions provided by the German authorities, the winter had been a severe one, made all the harder by a shortage of Red Cross supplies. Though this was in part due to difficult winter transport conditions in Germany, the chief cause was a breakdown in shipping both between England and Lisbon and between Lisbon and Marseilles. Of the ships on the latter run one had gone aground and another had suffered a breakdown in machinery, so that there was an accumulation at Lisbon of a million parcels. The importance of maintaining the shipping service from Lisbon to Marseilles was recognised in the establishment during April 1942 by the International Red Cross Committee of a distinct organisation for buying and chartering vessels to carry relief supplies.

There was, however, no certainty that new consignments of clothing would have been promptly distributed, even had they arrived before the winter. The German attitude was that, in view of the conditions of total war, they were entitled to consider bulk clothing and footwear from Red Cross consignments as part of their own issues. The distribution of battle dress, underclothing, and boots sent from the United Kingdom was therefore controlled almost as strictly as if it were being supplied by the German Quartermaster-General. In spite of all its efforts, the International Red Cross Committee was never able to obtain full recognition of the right of prisoners to consider clothing and footwear from relief consignments as supplementary to the issues due to them from the detaining power.[1]

Blankets were treated similarly; in some camps the issue was reduced to one per man. There was in this period an acute shortage of bedding and warm clothing in German-occupied Europe, aggravated by the winter campaign in Russia. German leaders were moreover keenly alive to the effects of well-clothed and well-fed British on the morale of the ill-provided civilians among whom the prisoners worked and travelled. It is probable that this consideration, as well as that of preventing escape, was behind the prisoners' low ration scale and the restrictive orders regarding the issue of clothing.

It is generally recognised that Red Cross supplies of food and smart new clothing had much to do with raising prisoners' morale, both by helping to maintain their bodily and mental health and also by giving them a sense of independence of the enemy for their basic everyday needs. In this respect British prisoners appear to have been better off than those of other nationalities, and even than many German civilians. Their living quarters, however, still remained crude and overcrowded. And just as a period of food shortage gave rise to the hobbies of planning menus and collecting cooking recipes, so many men turned, after months of living in sub-standard accommodation, to planning the ideal home they would live in after the war. The Cinderella pantomimes common in the camps at Christmas also seemed to strike a sympathetic chord.

Hopes of early liberation held by many of those taken in Greece and Crete were seen to be illusory as Christmas 1941 saw the war still no nearer conclusion, and most men had begun to adapt themselves

---

[1] It did, however, arrange for a double issue of underclothing.

to the circumstances of prisoner-of-war camps. They had already had experience of the closely communal life of the services, though a prisoner-of-war camp was a wider and harder school than a regimental mess. As prisoners they were learning not to obey all orders implicitly but to consider them first in the light of their own and their country's advantage. Whereas their regimental duties had previously given them plenty to do, in captivity those who did not work had to devise occupations for filling in the long waking hours. Accommodation and weather and shortage of materials did not always make it easy to study. But though at first any book would do, as time went on there was a keener demand for the more solid type of reading and an increased interest in serious study both for its own sake and with a view to sitting examinations.

Those who had chosen escape as their main activity gradually developed a technique and even a routine: transfer to a suitable work-camp, break out in the spring, move at night or in disguise by day, make for a neutral border or partisan-held territory, or try to contact an underground organisation. On recapture there would be two or three weeks in solitary confinement, followed by a period at a 'disciplinaire' work-camp, and then perhaps an opportunity to try again in the autumn or the next spring. In some of the officers' and NCOs' camps the business of escape was becoming highly organised and controlled, for much more skill and planning were necessary there to achieve successes on account of the fewer opportunities offering and the stricter security measures employed by the guards.

During this period the number of New Zealanders notified as prisoners of war and internees rose to over six thousand. Dealing with the mass of inquiries concerning the capture, camp addresses, and welfare of such a substantial number of people in many different countries imposed considerable strain on the agencies involved. Official notifications from Geneva still went first to the Prime Minister's Department, whence they were distributed to the appropriate service branches; the Casualty Section of Base Records was kept especially busy as most of the new notifications were of Army personnel. The four Inquiry Offices, run by the Joint Council and financed from the National Patriotic Fund, had to expand their staffs to cope with the increasing tasks of keeping next-of-kin informed on welfare matters and of running the machinery for the despatch of relief supplies from New Zealand.

Besides the keeping of a personal file for each prisoner of war and the maintenance of card-indexes, there was a first letter to each next-of-kin following a prisoner's capture, explaining what could be done for him, particularly in the way of sending parcels. There often followed a good deal of correspondence and sometimes personal interviews for those living near an Inquiry Office. In November 1941 the Joint Council issued free to next-of-kin a pamphlet giving translated extracts from the *Revue* of the International Red Cross, including reports by neutral delegates on various camps and also extracts from prisoners' letters sent in by recipients as of general interest. In February a Prisoners of War Relatives' Association, formed on the model of a United Kingdom organisation of the same name to assist prisoners' relatives and keep them informed, brought out its own news sheet. Three organisations in Britain already had similar publications and the British Red Cross brought out a fourth in May 1942. There was no lack of information for next-of-kin either in New Zealand or in the United Kingdom. It was suggested that the publication of letters and reports showing favourable treatment, while intended to reassure relatives, might weaken morale and encourage the attitude that getting captured was not a bad thing after all. But the more unpleasant aspects of prisoner-of-war camps were also publicised, though not prominently enough to create anxiety.

For the rest, the new airmail letter services via Lisbon and the Atlantic, both to and from camps, meant that next-of-kin were more closely in touch with prisoners, and permission in March 1942 to send home photographs made them seem still closer. The preparation of the thousands of quarterly next-of-kin parcels and the packing of the weekly three thousand food parcels became minor industries. Hundreds of women did voluntary work in the food-packing centre at Wellington and the four next-of-kin parcel centres as a contribution to the war effort. Indeed the portion of the war effort relating to prisoner-of-war relief was costing all those concerned some £50 a prisoner per annum and was using up a large number of man-hours. Prisoners and internees now made up well over one-ninth[1] of the New Zealanders serving overseas, and the preservation of their safety and welfare had become a task of considerable national importance.

---

[1] As at May 1942 there were roughly 53,000 New Zealanders on active service overseas, including over 6300 prisoners of war.—*Statement of Strengths and Losses in the Armed Services and Mercantile Marine in the 1939-45 War*, War History Branch, 1948.

CHAPTER 5

The First Phase of the War Against Japan
(December 1941 – May 1942)

I: *Japanese Victories*

ON 7 December 1941, when British Commonwealth troops were fully engaged in a desperate struggle with the German and Italian forces in Libya, the third member of the Axis, Japan, announced hostilities against the United States by her attack on the American fleet in Pearl Harbour. Within four days the United States had declared war on the three Axis countries, and Britain was at war with Japan. Japan wasted no time. The previous July she had walked into Indo-China. Now, landing a seaborne force in Thailand near the Malayan border on 8 December, she began her attack south and two days later had taken the Kota Bharu airfield in the north-eastern corner of Malaya. The same day her air forces sank the two battleships, *Prince of Wales* and *Repulse*. Immediately she swept across Thailand, to sever the Malay peninsula and drive north into Lower Burma and south to link with her seaborne forces. Meanwhile she had landed in North Borneo and the Philippines; her troops had crossed the Kowloon border to attack Hong Kong; and with the Allied fleet for the time being crippled, her warships were able to range unmolested as far east as the Gilbert Islands, which she occupied on 11 December.

The weeks and months that followed brought a series of disasters for the British Commonwealth and United States forces. Hong Kong fell on 25 December after a 14-day attack; Kuching, the capital of Sarawak, was taken about the same time; Manila, in the Philippines, fell on 2 January 1942, and soon only the Bataan Peninsula and the island of Corregidor remained as a centre of American resistance there. The British forces in Malaya were unable to hold the Japanese southward drive, and on 15 February, a week after Japanese troops had come across from the mainland, Singapore surrendered. Overpowering the remaining British and Dutch naval forces in the Java Sea, the Japanese swept south and east to the Dutch East Indies: Java capitulated on 9 March, and by the 20th Japan was not only in possession of the two main islands of Java and Sumatra, but was moving eastward to complete her occupation of the Dutch group. In Burma Rangoon fell in the same month to the Japanese northern spearhead; and by June 1942, six months after her first attack, with Mandalay and the Andaman Islands in her hands and the last American resistance quenched on Corregidor, Japan was in undisturbed possession of the whole of South-East Asia and the north-western Pacific.

At the time when these areas were overrun by the Japanese forces they contained between three and four hundred New Zealanders.[1] Some of these were serving with the Royal Navy and the Royal Air Force, and there was a handful of New Zealand Army personnel. More than two-thirds, however, were civilians—missionaries, business officials, surveyors, engineers, journalists, nurses, teachers. Though mainly in Malaya, Burma, Hong Kong and parts of China, they were scattered over almost the whole of the south-east Asian archipelago and as far north as the islands of Japan itself. They formed only a small proportion of the British white population, just as our servicemen in the Far East were only a small proportion of the British forces in that vast region; but in most of the Japanese detention camps and internment centres of the Far East there were at one time or another some of our people. And New Zealanders can be said to have shared, with much larger numbers of other Commonwealth, American, and Dutch people, most of the experiences of prisoners of war and civilian internees in the areas of Asia and the Pacific occupied by the Japanese.

Just before the Japanese attack there were 24 New Zealanders on various islands of the Gilbert, Ellice and Ocean Groups, either as civilian radio operators or as 2 NZEF personnel on coastwatching duty. It was clearly one of the first objectives of the Japanese assault to occupy these points and capture the means of communication they afforded to the Allies. Thus there were Japanese transports off Makin Island in the Gilberts on the morning of 9 December, and in the next few days Japanese landing parties took possession of this and the other almost undefended islands of

---

[1] The difficulty in reaching an exact figure lies in deciding exactly who were New Zealand nationals. On the one hand a number of people of New Zealand origin had been away from New Zealand either in the Colonial Service or in the service of some foreign business concern long enough to have almost lost touch with their country of birth. On the other hand there were people not of New Zealand origin who by marriage or previous domicile appeared to have sufficient association with the country to be looked after by the New Zealand authorities. The Missing and Prisoners of War Agency gives the following figures for New Zealanders:

Civilians interned in the Pacific (including 52 in Volunteer Defence Forces)	214
Merchant Navy	51
Navy	52
NZEF	7
Air Force	53
	377

the group. Some of the posts kept transmitting information until the last moment and those who were not surprised were able to destroy their codes and equipment. On Tarawa in October 1942, 17 New Zealand coastwatchers were executed by the Japanese; seven others captured in December 1941—three from Makin, three from Little Makin, and one from Abaiang, all in the Gilbert Group —survived the war as prisoners in Japan.

Treatment by the enemy of those they had allowed to survive does not seem to have been unduly bad at this stage: there was strict supervision accompanied by a good deal of threatening behaviour, as well as jeering and some attempt to degrade the white prisoners in the eyes of the natives. 'This is the Imperial Navy's grand advance! You are now prisoners of the Emperor of Nippon', one party was told. Only the radio operators were interrogated, and those not very intensively, though they had a somewhat more thorough questioning after reaching Japan. They were all transferred north-west on Japanese transports and warships, and in early January 1942 disembarked at Yokohama, among the first prisoners to arrive in Japan.

On the Asian mainland the first people to be affected were those in China. At the time of 'Pearl Harbour Day' (as it came to be known to the internees) there were in various parts of China a number of European missionaries, mostly British and American. Though the Japanese invasion of the mainland—the 'China incident' —had taken place three years before, the mission stations had kept going in spite of the immediate dangers from bombing and later annoyances and restrictions from the Japanese occupation forces. The Japanese had landed in October 1938 to the north of Hong Kong, Canton had fallen almost immediately, and in the course of the next few months European missionaries and others, though free within their residential compounds, became a good deal restricted by the Japanese occupation forces in their activities outside.

The majority of them (some forty) were in the Shanghai area, and there were two other smaller groups, one near Peking and the other near Canton. On 8 December 1941 the International Settlement at Shanghai was occupied by the Japanese, and shortly afterwards they published a proclamation in the newspapers and over the radio ordering all enemy subjects to register with their consular authorities within a stated period. Full particulars were taken of each person in return for the issue of an identification card. Some families were confined to their homes for the first ten days, and a few who were working for the Chinese authorities, and so suspected of political activities or of having special knowledge, were taken away immediately for detention and intensive interrogation. But for the most part British civilians were soon allowed to go freely about the city and to carry on with their occupations. The greater number of them were not interned until early 1943, and the older people not until 1944.

Mission stations in outlying districts some little distance from main cities were allowed to continue their work, but Japanese military guards were posted to them to exercise supervision over their activities and to indicate that the Japanese Government had confiscated all British property. Restrictions were placed on the amounts of food and medicine which missions could purchase, and the number of Chinese workers which they could employ was reduced. Much was done towards making the mission communities self-supporting by growing fruit, nuts, and vegetables, and by rearing stock inside the mission compounds; and help was usually given by local Chinese villagers. For the most part the Japanese guards did not interfere inside the compounds, but there were exceptions, especially when guards had been drinking saki. At Kong Chuen, near Canton, much unnecessary victimisation was endured from a self-important young guard officer, who took the mission books and anything else he fancied, rode his horse through a hospital corridor, and conducted mock bayonet practice in front of the hospital several times a week. On the other hand the director of this mission records that from other Japanese soldiers they experienced 'good-will and friendliness' and received help with their mail arrangements and goods permits. This is a pattern of contradictory behaviour on the part of the Japanese which was the common experience of most British people who fell into their hands.

The only other British Commonwealth subjects to feel immediately the effects of Japanese hostilities were those unfortunate enough to be either in Thailand, in the path of the Japanese advance by land, or else in Japan itself. The latter were the object of immediate attention by the Japanese police. A New Zealander resident in Tokyo, where he was teaching English, found four policemen waiting for him on his return from work, and was bundled off to a police cell in a small nearby township. From there he was taken to Yokohama Prison, where he was to remain for questioning at intervals during several months.

British people employed in mines, plantations, and other concerns in Thailand were for the most part rounded up with their families by Thai police in the day or two following the commencement of hostilities. One New Zealand surveyor was in a party of 27 civilians handed over to the Japanese and transported to Kampong Toh, where they were kept under guard in the main living rooms of two bungalows. On the night of 13 December 1941 a party of

Japanese troops arrived from the front with eight Indian prisoners, whom they put with the civilians in one of the bungalows. Some time later two hand grenades were thrown into the living room of this bungalow, a machine gun was fired up through the floor, and a number of Japanese soldiers burst into the room, fired at the occupants, and then set about bayoneting them. Thirteen were killed as a result of this and of further shooting next morning, and all but eight of the others lost their lives trying to get away through the jungle. The New Zealander, though wounded in the legs and head, was able with help to make off into the jungle, but after some ten days was recaptured by Thai police and taken to Bangkok.

The New Zealanders in Hong Kong consisted of a few naval personnel (mainly signals), a few nurses at the military hospital, and a number of civilians, some of whom were serving with the Hong Kong Volunteer Defence Force. Hong Kong was attacked from the air on the same day as Pearl Harbour, and this was followed shortly afterwards by artillery fire and infantry attacks which penetrated the outer defences of the area of the colony on the mainland. The island of Victoria held out for three weeks, but the Governor had to surrender to superior forces on 25 December. Disarmed troops and volunteers were marched, laden with what belongings and food they could gather together, into the city, where Chinese had been ordered into the streets to see the British disgrace. The prisoners were accommodated in some damaged wooden huts in a dirty area at North Point reserved for Chinese refugees. Naval men were for the most part assembled at the dockyard and later taken across to the Kowloon side, where the Shamshuipo Barracks, already damaged and looted, were being used as the main prisoner-of-war collecting centre for the Hong Kong area. Medical staffs in hospitals were allowed to carry on their work and the wounded there were mostly unmolested, though in one auxiliary emergency hospital many of the patients and some of the hospital staff were massacred. Some of the wounded outside the hospitals were left to die without food or medical aid, and medical search parties were forbidden.

Civilians not taken while fighting with the Defence Force were sooner or later assembled at what became known as the Stanley Internment Camp—a large area on a narrow neck of the Stanley Peninsula, the south-east corner of Victoria Island. The whole area had been fought over and was in a very damaged and disordered condition when all the internable men, women, and children of the colony were herded together there in January 1942. Only an exceptional few, such as a New Zealand woman[1] in charge of a

---

[1] Mrs M. A. Jennings, Superintendent of the Taipo Rural Home and Orphanage.

rural home and orphanage near Kowloon, were allowed to continue their work and live outside the camp.

By the end of 1941 the Japanese invasions of the Philippines and Borneo were well advanced. Kuching, in Sarawak, surrendered on 24 December; and in the Philippines Manila, having been declared an open city after the American withdrawal to Bataan, was taken over by the Japanese on 2 January 1942. In Sarawak not all civilians were immediately interned, some being allowed to live normally in their own houses for some four months. On the other hand a New Zealander who held an administrative post with the Sarawak Government was immediately arrested and kept under guard until a general internment camp had been set up in Kuching. In the Philippines civilians were taken in early January to the newly set up internment camp at Santo Tomas University.

After the first Japanese drive south from Thailand in December 1941, fighting continued in Malaya during the early weeks of 1942, with the British Commonwealth forces staging delaying actions and withdrawing to the south. Finally on 30 January the land forces were evacuated to Singapore Island, secure in the thought that there would be some respite for weary troops as the Japanese would not have sufficient landing craft to cross the Straits of Johore in large numbers. Shortly afterwards (8–9 February) the Japanese brought over 18 battalions with tanks and artillery in one night. Resistance continued until by 15 February the essential services of the city had been so severely damaged as to decide General Percival to capitulate.

During the next day or so members of the armed forces were marched to the Changi military area on a small promontory 15 miles outside the city. Among them were a number of New Zealanders—engineers, surveyors, miners, civil servants and others who had joined the Federated Malay States Volunteer Force, as well as men serving with regular British Army units in Malaya—though they made up only a small proportion of the 60,000-odd moved to Changi. At the same time a proclamation ordered all British civilians to assemble at various points in the city, whence they were moved, mostly on foot, the men to the 'Karikal' camp at Katong, some six miles out, or to the Joo Chiat police station, the women to a camp near the Roxy Cinema. There were a number of New Zealanders among those who went to 'Karikal', including some members of the Volunteer Force who had managed to get rid of their uniforms before capture.

As in Hong Kong, the fall of which also marked the termination of a campaign, there was practically no attempt at interrogation, though a New Zealander who lived beside the sea in Singapore was subjected to some hours of severe questioning concerning local fortifications. The wounded were left in charge of the British medical authorities, but were before long all moved to accommodation in the Changi area no matter what their condition, many, including some leg-wound cases, being forced to walk the whole fifteen miles. As in Hong Kong, too, there were some instances of the killing of wounded, especially badly wounded in the field, and there was a massacre at one hospital in which many patients and hospital staff were bayoneted, and altogether 250 lost their lives.

Many people were able to get away from Singapore by sea in the days prior to the capitulation. But, owing to the almost complete Japanese domination of the sea and air in the Banka Straits and generally to the east of Sumatra, many of the ships were bombed and sunk and others were forced to surrender because they had women and children aboard. Those survivors who managed to get ashore on Singkep, Banka, or other islands, or on Sumatra itself, were sooner or later rounded up in the course of the Japanese conquest of the Dutch East Indies. Only those who lost no time in continuing their voyage on to Australia or to Ceylon were spared the ordeal of captivity in Japanese hands. One New Zealand naval officer[1] serving on HMS *Grasshopper*, which left Singapore on 13 February in company with HMS *Dragonfly*, bringing away civilians and servicemen, was among those who made Singkep Island after both ships had been destroyed by Japanese bombing. Later he reached Sumatra and then sailed with a party for Ceylon in a native prau, only to be picked up by three Japanese tankers in early April and brought back to Singapore.

There were four New Zealanders among the servicemen taken off on the Fairmile 310 on the same night. She was attacked twice and then ran on to a shoal off the Seven Brothers group of islands, everyone getting ashore. Three of the New Zealanders set sail with a Javanese for Batavia but were never heard of again; malaria and other diseases killed 19 other officers and men. The survivors (including one New Zealander)[2] were taken to Singkep and later to Changi Camp at Singapore.

At the end of February, in order to clear the way for the military occupation of Sumatra, Java, and Celebes, the Japanese fleet brought to action the remaining British, American, and Dutch naval vessels in Dutch East Indian waters. There were New Zealanders among the complements of the cruiser *Exeter* and the destroyer *Encounter*, both of which were sunk on 1 March, and on the *Stronghold*, sunk next day in the Timor Sea. The survivors were picked up by

---

[1] Lt R. A. Holloway, RNZNVR.
[2] Able Seaman H. R. Oldnall.

Japanese naval vessels, transferred to captured Dutch merchant or hospital ships, and taken on to Macassar in Celebes. There they were given accommodation in old Dutch barracks, and though some were transported to Japan, many remained in camps near Macassar until their liberation.

Japanese paratroops attacked Medan in north-eastern Sumatra on 13 February, and the Allied land defences proved insufficient to stem the Japanese advance. In face of the rapid progress of the enemy, RAF fighter and bomber squadrons operating from Medan and Palembang respectively, together with other servicemen, were evacuated to Java after a few days, some getting away from their stations just before the Japanese occupied them. Attempts at evacuation continued until the capital, Padang, on the west coast, fell on 17 March. There the Japanese captured, as well as a large number of Dutch, approximately 1200 British servicemen awaiting transport to Java. The majority of them were from Singapore, and the New Zealanders among them were either naval or air force personnel. The naval personnel were survivors from the complements of ships sunk during the evacuation from Singapore, and the Air Force personnel either evacuees from Singapore or members of the squadrons stationed on Sumatra who were unable to be evacuated in the earlier drafts to Java.

Naval and Air Force officers were taken by truck to Medan and transported back to Singapore almost immediately; some of them were interrogated on their arrival there. There seems to have been little attempt to interrogate the remainder, for whom a camp was set up in some Dutch military barracks. Wounded who happened to be in hospital at the time of the Japanese invasion were looked after by the Dutch, but others not so fortunate suffered neglect.

The Royal Air Force squadrons evacuated from Sumatra continued to operate from north-western Java until Japanese landings on 28 February forced them farther south. Some units were still able to continue, but others were moved to Tjilatjap, on the south coast, to await evacuation to Australia. Japanese attacks on shipping prevented any large-scale evacuation after 4 March. On the 8th the Dutch forces capitulated, and some RAF units were ordered to the Tasik Malaja airfield to await the arrival of the Japanese. Of the remainder many hid up in bush country near Garoet in the hope of evacuation. But although some got away in locally obtained craft and reached near enough to Australia to be picked up and taken on by flying boat, the majority were captured by the Japanese occupation forces over the next few weeks. Some were apprehended and handed over by Javanese native police; and some suffered beatings and other ill-treatment according to the whim of the commander of the Japanese unit in the area. A few, too, were given a fairly severe interrogation if they were suspected of being guerrillas or of knowing Air Force dispositions and plans. Soon after capture they were assembled in temporary camps at Garoet, Tasik Malaja, Tjilatjap, and other centres near the places of capture.

II: *Early Prisoner-of-war Camps in the Far East*

After a few days of makeshift accommodation and good treatment in Yokohama, the New Zealand coastwatchers and radio operators captured in the Gilbert Islands were taken south to the island of Shikoku, in the north of which lay the newly formed Zentsuji prisoner-of-war camp. This was the first to be established in Japan, and conditions there were originally fairly satisfactory. Prisoners were housed in what were formerly Japanese military barracks, equipped with ablution and sanitary facilities of a kind. There was no heating, however, and though the party arrived at the camp in the middle of a cold Japanese January, the allowance of blankets was small. Later there were small stoves for officers' quarters and braziers for those of the other ranks. Soup, rice, and bread were the usual items in the daily diet, all in insufficient quantities, but supplemented occasionally with fish and very occasionally with meat. Such a spartan regime was considered normal for the Japanese troops, who tended to pride themselves on living ' uncomfortably' as it made them ' strong '. There is evidence that at this stage the Japanese commandant was reasonable and doing the best he could for the prisoners.

A few hours after the arrival of the New Zealanders several hundred Americans from Guam Island were brought in, and from then on the numbers continued increasing, so that the camp was never anything else than overcrowded. It was several weeks before the civilians from Guam were sent to an internment camp at Kobe and it became possible for the remainder to be organised into groups under the internal administration of American officers and NCOs. Accommodation worked out for other ranks at 32 to a small room (about 700 square feet in area), eight men sleeping on about 21 feet of bedboard. Some American medical officers, in spite of the lack of equipment and drugs, were able to organise a sick-bay, where patients received better and more food, including a special quality of white rice and a small amount of milk; and their representations to the Japanese had some effect in improving the general camp rations. The Japanese issued a certain amount of used army clothing, ranging from winter overcoats to underclothing. There was also an issue of some thirty Japanese cigarettes a week during the first months of the camp's existence. A canteen contained nothing edible but sold pens, pencils, drawing books, slide-rules, and a few toilet articles. Other ranks received ten sen a day which could be spent in this way.

It was not long before lectures and classes began to be held, including classes in Japanese organised by the camp authorities and classes in radio organised by the prisoners. Sunday evening entertainments were held in an empty barrack: the first was a showing of Japanese films illustrating their successes in the Pacific, but later ones were concerts arranged by the prisoners. Some books sent from the former American Embassy in Tokyo formed the nucleus of a library. For the rest, recreation took the form of cards and other indoor games, and drawing and handicrafts with improvised materials. A Japanese interpreter was present as censor at all entertainments as well as religious services.

The first working party went out about the middle of February and began clearing a piece of mountainside of scrub and boulders and making it ready for agriculture. From that time on parties were regularly supplied by the camp for this purpose, the daily wages being up to 70 sen. Though the tools were mainly primitive hoe-like grubbers, the work does not seem to have been too arduous (in the earlier stages), and men enjoyed the excursion through the pretty surrounding countryside and up the nearby mountain.

In the first months there were no arrangements about sending mail, but Japanese radio technicians came to the camp in March 1942 and made recordings of one and a half minute messages from prisoners to their next-of-kin, and these were later transmitted from Radio Tokyo. They were received clearly in New Zealand the same month and were the first and for some time the only news to reach relatives there. News for prisoners had to be gleaned from Japanese English-language newspapers and from new arrivals, the latter unfortunately only too often confirming the successes reported in the Japanese press. Prisoners' thoughts were for the most part concentrated on their own rather miserable surroundings, and it became a popular hobby to plan one's ideal home in order to escape from the drabness of one's present accommodation. The meagre diet gave rise to endless discussions on food, together with the compilation of collections of ideal recipes. The whole of this was probably some kind of psychological release of the individual from the repression and regimentation of a prisoner-of-war camp, and has already been noted in Italy and Germany.

The camp was run according to the strict Japanese Army discipline. Precise instructions covered all aspects of camp routine including roll-call in Japanese, filling all ash trays with water, correct folding and alignment of all kit, and seeing that all sleeping men were covered with their blankets. Offences were usually punished on the spot by the culprit having his face slapped (a normal punishment in the Japanese Army) for a length of time depending on the seriousness of the offence. Many British prisoners were to experience this treatment before the end of the war, and though there was occasional injury to eardrums, the punishment lay rather in the humiliation. As one man put it, 'The injury was greater to our dignity than to our persons'. Before long the Japanese insisted on all prisoners in the camp signing a promise not to escape, and those who refused were given a period in the camp cells. It was decided by the senior officer, after a great deal of argument among the prisoners, that such a document would be signed under duress and as such would not be binding; and most of the camp signed. Those who had been put in the cells for not signing were out again in something under a fortnight, none the worse for their experience. But in this respect, as in many others, it is clear that Zentsuji was better off and more humanely administered than the vast majority of other Japanese prisoner-of-war camps.

A New Zealand naval officer,[1] wounded and captured during the taking of Shanghai by the Japanese, was, after treatment at the hospital, placed in a camp near Woosung village at the mouth of the Whangpoo River. The camp had formerly been an army barracks, and though very dirty on their arrival was soon made habitable by the British prisoners, of whom there were a few dozen, and the American civilian internees, of whom there were over a thousand. The British Residents' Association, the Swiss Consul, and the International Red Cross delegate were able to help the camp with food parcels, clothing, medicines, and even stoves and fuel in the winter. There was a recreation ground and two vegetable gardens, and conditions could be said on the whole to be fairly tolerable.

The dirty, shell-damaged huts of the North Point Camp on the island at Hong Kong were used to accommodate captured service personnel, including members of the Hong Kong Volunteer Defence Force. The damaged huts were repaired and the camp was cleaned up; but the Japanese had used the place as mule lines, and this combined with its neglected surroundings brought clouds of flies. At first, too, there was no provision for sanitation, but as the camp was on the sea's edge this was not too difficult to remedy. Food was on a fairly generous scale, as permission was given to take supplies from British Army dumps and also to receive parcels from friends outside. An inadequate water supply, however, which

---

[1] Lt S. Polkinghorn, RNR, awarded DSC for his action with the 300-ton gunboat *Petrel* on 8 December 1941.

limited each man's ration to a bottle a day, helped to make life in this overcrowded camp more difficult. Spare time passed in thinking out plans for an escape by boat or in attending the lectures and classes that usually began at a very early stage in all the camps containing British prisoners of war. Although North Point was used as a prisoner-of-war camp until October 1942, a great number of the British personnel were moved across to Shamshuipo in the first month or two after their capture.[1]

At Shamshuipo a large flat area reclaimed from the harbour at Kowloon and laid out as a British military camp, with brick barracks and other amenities, provided the Japanese with a ready-made prisoner-of-war camp to accommodate several thousand men. But the barracks had been badly damaged by bombing and later were completely looted and stripped of all wooden fittings. For the first few months there was neither lighting nor heating, though the Japanese did supply firewood for cooking. Food provided by the Japanese consisted mainly of rice, with low-grade Chinese green vegetables, a little fish, and occasionally a very small portion of meat. But after a time the latter items ceased, and for a good part of 1942 the prisoners had to exist on a diet consisting of little more than rice and water, with resultant malnutrition and the diseases that go with it.

In the early months of 1942 the guarding of this large, crowded camp was not always perfect, and a number of prisoners (mainly Chinese) were able to slip through the wire into the outskirts of the town. For white prisoners, however, the difficulty of concealment in a city of Asiatics made it more practicable to attempt the hazardous method of leaving the camp by boat. A New Zealand pilot officer[2] and two British Army officers broke through the triple barbed-wire fence to the seafront at 1 a.m. on 2 February and jumped aboard a sampan, which they had bribed a local Chinese to sail past the breakwater at this hour. When Japanese guards opened fire they took to the water and swam for twenty minutes across Laichikok Bay. They then eluded a Japanese patrol while crossing a brilliantly lit road, and walked on for some hours well into the surrounding hills. The party kept heading north, hiding by day and travelling by night over hills and through swampy valleys, and ekeing out their scanty food supply. They were attacked by two different parties of Chinese bandits, and on one occasion were beaten up and robbed of their valuables but were finally released.

---

[1] Naval prisoners were transferred to North Point from Shamshuipo in January 1942, but were moved again in April, the officers to Argyll Street and the other ranks back to Shamshuipo.
[2] Plt Off E. D. Crossley, awarded MC for this exploit.

Seven days after their break-out they reached a South China guerrilla band, which looked after them and gave them guides to take them through the Japanese garrison posts to the regular Chinese forces. After crossing the Canton–Kowloon railway, they made their way from village to village until they met regular Chinese forces on 18 February. They reached Kunming after a complicated journey by river, rail and lorry, and were finally flown to Calcutta on 1 April. Only one other New Zealander[1] and fewer than fifty British (excluding Indians) succeeded in escaping from Japanese hands during the whole war.

At Japanese camps successful break-outs were followed by reprisals on the rest of the inmates; and Shamshuipo was no exception. Besides punishment of the leader and possibly the other members of the group to which the escaper belonged, there were increased restrictions of movement and reduction in both the quantity and quality of rations for the whole camp. At Shamshuipo the guards were tightened up and eventually part of the perimeter wire was electrified. The Japanese were so suspicious of any gathering of prisoners that they forbade the holding of educational classes, which had thenceforward to be carried on surreptitiously.

In April 1942 most of the officers were transferred to an officers' camp in the Argyll Street Barracks, though a small number of them remained to help with the internal administration of the 5000-odd prisoners who remained in Shamshuipo. In May the Japanese decided to require all prisoners to sign a pledge not to escape, similar to that exacted at Zentsuji. At Shamshuipo there was a parade of all prisoners to enable the signing to be done en masse, and the Japanese guard mounted machine guns for the occasion. At first the senior officer refused to admit that such an action was possible for British troops. But a few signatures had already been obtained in private by the Japanese, and it was learned that the officers at Argyll Street had signed 'under duress'. Thereafter the majority of the camp signed the form, the few who maintained their refusal being taken away in a truck to the Japanese Kempetai barracks. The Kempetai were the equivalent of the German Gestapo, and men who spent a period of detention in their hands, with the tortures and deprivations that accompanied it, usually came back to their camp physical wrecks, if they came back at all. The knowledge that their escape might result in their nearest sleeping companions undergoing such punishment did much to deter men from making attempts. While there were always some who considered that an escape did not justify the reprisals it brought

---

[1] Lt R. B. Goodwin, RNZNVR, see page 347.

on the camp, there were others willing to support any attempt that had a reasonable chance of success.

On the island there was established, besides the North Point prisoner-of-war camp and the Bowen Road hospital for sick and wounded prisoners, the Stanley Internment Camp for civilians. Reference has already been made to this last camp and to the confusion that resulted there from suddenly throwing together in a war-damaged area, regardless of sex or age, practically the whole white civilian population of Hong Kong, the British portion of which alone amounted to some 2500 people.[1] The area was nevertheless the best available, and is described by one New Zealand ex-internee as 'ideal for the purpose'. It comprised 50 acres of the grounds of the former civil prison on a promontory cooled in the summer by sea breezes, though cold in winter during the period of internment owing to the complete lack of heating. The area enclosed by barbed wire contained European and Indian prison warders' quarters, a Chinese boys' residential college and several bungalows, as well as three recreation grounds, a bowling green, and a good deal of hilly, unoccupied land.

Even after the accommodation had been properly allocated, the buildings were overcrowded by European standards and contained only about half enough beds. This shortage was made good by improvising with boards and old wooden doors, but washing and lavatory accommodation remained inadequate. Fortunately for the internees there was a hospital within the grounds, though it was handicapped by shortage of equipment and drugs; two dentists among the camp personnel were hampered by similar shortages. There were clinics in each group of buildings for the treatment of minor ailments. The administration of the whole camp was carried out by the Colonial Secretary and a small staff, assisted by a camp council and block committees.

The food received from the Japanese consisted mainly of rice, vegetables, and peanut oil in varying quantities, relieved in this early stage by a small ration of meat and bread, occasional fish, and small amounts of tea, sugar and salt. It was cooked in communal kitchens, one for each group of buildings. The diet was never adequate for Europeans, and continued lack of essential elements resulted in progressive malnutrition. It was possible to buy tobacco and cigarettes from the Japanese, but only in insufficient quantities, and a black market sprang up through which it was possible to obtain supplies at exorbitant prices. A similar black market for food enabled those who had the money, or could give cheques, to buy

---

[1] Approximately 1000 men, 1200 women and 300 children, some twenty of whom were New Zealanders.

eggs, sugar, onions, and oil. Apart from all this the canteen at times sold bran, soya beans, peanuts, and a few other items of food.

Recreational facilities abounded in Stanley Camp. Although two playing fields were converted into gardens, which themselves provided a healthful and useful occupation, there still remained another for football and softball, as well as the bowling green. In the daylight hours the internees had the freedom of the whole camp to walk in or otherwise occupy themselves, including the use of a sea beach at certain hours in summer. Hong Kong University professors and other teachers organised lectures and classes on a wide variety of subjects and also a school for the children in the camp. Books brought in by various internees made possible the formation of small, moderately well-stocked libraries. Four pianos were brought in, there were concerts and plays, and in general fair scope for musical and artistic talent. The Japanese allowed normal religious services. Apart from such recreational activities many people found an occupation in various camp duties—administrative work, cookhouse fatigues (which carried an extra half ration as a reward), cutting up firewood, mending clothing, and keeping the camp clean. A number were employed on the prevention of mosquito breeding and so of malaria, a task only partly accomplished as the internees were not allowed to extend their work outside the perimeter wire.

Two parties attempted to get away from the camp in the first month, one succeeding and the members of the other being imprisoned. Owing to the Japanese policy of reprisals on those remaining and the fact that these would involve the old people, women and children, it was generally considered 'unethical' to attempt to escape. In spite of a number of face-slappings for breaches of their regulations, somewhat rougher treatment of black marketeers, and attempts to enforce bowing (in lieu of a salute), the Japanese do not seem to have interfered much with life inside the compound. A Japanese-sponsored newspaper in English, the *Hong Kong News,* enabled readers to gain some idea of the war situation by reading between the lines. There were the usual series of rumours which beset prisoner-of-war and internment camps at most stages of their history. These the camp administrative authorities attempted to combat because of their ultimately bad effect on morale when they proved false.

Some of the prisoners of war taken in the Malayan campaign remained in temporary places of detention, such as Pudu Jail at Kuala Lumpur, for several months. But the bulk of them—some fifty to sixty thousand[1]—were concentrated at the Changi garrison area in the eastern corner of the island, about 18 miles from the city.

---

[1] New Zealanders numbered only about fifty.

The area had been well equipped in peacetime with modern buildings to accommodate several regiments, and contained married officers' bungalows, blocks of flats for married other ranks, barracks for single men. Clearly these could not solve the problem of permanent quarters for several divisions, and men's opinions of their quarters in Changi vary according to how well or how badly they fared in the allocation of areas and buildings. A naval officer, one of 18 in a married officer's three-roomed bungalow, calls it 'very comfortable by later standards'. An officer in the volunteers, as one of 128 in a somewhat larger two-storied bungalow, speaks of having 'only enough space each to lie down in at night'. Non-commissioned officers, among 500 allocated to a small three-storied building, comment only that they slept on the concrete with approximately one blanket among six men and that the building had neither light nor water. A large number had to camp in the open until they could acquire by some means the materials to build themselves shelters. Washing and sanitary arrangements would have been inadequate in any case for such large numbers, but the damage to buildings and water supply aggravated these deficiencies and recourse had to be had to water wells and pit latrines.

For the first weeks the Japanese, having placed a barrier of guards across the peninsula, seem to have interfered little with the internal running of this large prisoner-of-war area. One New Zealander comments, 'We never saw a Jap those days, except during searches and parades for visiting Japanese officers'. Later, however, when Changi had been divided into wired sub-areas and prisoners sorted and redistributed, the Japanese posted Sikh guards to patrol these boundaries, and they were a source of considerable trouble and friction. The organisation of the camp personnel into brigade messes, all under the control of an 'Administrative Group', provided more efficient means of co-ordinating dealings with the Japanese, of maintaining order and health, and of passing the time, than would have been possible with smaller, scattered units. A medical organisation was able through insistence on proper sanitation and other precautionary measures to prevent much disease, though lack of disinfectants, drugs, and equipment made it impossible to prevent malaria and dysentery or to provide adequately for the sick. The hospital was at first located in bombed buildings, without lights or running water or adequate sanitation and only such bedding, drugs, and dressings as had been smuggled in with the original patients, who had numbered between two and three thousand. After six months or so running water was obtainable in some of the camp buildings, and electric lighting a month or two later; and gradually the worst of the deficiencies in medical and nursing equipment were remedied, for the most part by improvisation.

For the first two or three weeks men lived on tinned army rations and biscuits, which they had brought in to Changi amongst their kit, or on other stores obtained by foraging parties. At this period these parties were allowed to push a cart or an abandoned lorry into the town and bring back supplies. This practice was soon stopped, as it led to undesirable contact with the civilian population of Singapore; and in any case stocks of such things as chilled meat from a cold storage company's premises soon gave out. The Japanese began to deliver rations regularly: a pound or so of rice a man, some green vegetables, and very small quantities of salt, sugar, tea, cooking fats, jams, and occasionally dried fish. One man described the rations at the beginning as 'ample' though short of fish and meat; but others found a diet composed mainly of rice hard to get used to. To make matters worse, the quantity of rice soon considerably decreased, and the lack of protein and certain vitamins in the diet, combined with its overall insufficiency, led to general loss of weight among the prisoners and later to deficiency diseases. One New Zealand officer's weight fell from 10st. 8lb. to 9 stone in the first three months, and remained at the latter figure until he left the camp. Coconuts, occasional tinned fish, toffee, and *gula malacca* (sugar substitute) from the canteen, once it had been established, provided some small supplement. Apart from this, green vegetables such as spinach and even tapioca were grown inside the camp area. But attempts to supply additional protein by keeping pigs had to be abandoned owing to 'lack of fattening material'; and a similar project for keeping poultry was able to provide only sufficient birds for the hospital.

The canteen supplied tobacco: some locally made cigarettes and cheroots and some tobacco from Java were available to those who had the money to buy them. Sometimes men had to eke out their supplies with dried paw-paw leaves; but it seems that some kind of a smoke was nearly always available. Apart from tobacco the canteen sold notebooks and playing cards, toothbrushes and razor-blades. For clothing most men had to manage for the whole period of their captivity with what they originally brought into their first prisoner-of-war camp. A minority received an issue of one garment or another from the Japanese, but for the rest it was a matter of patching or improvising new garments from any kind of material which came to hand. Fortunately the weather in South-East Asia obviated the necessity of wearing anything but the minimum of clothing considered necessary for decency.

There was no lack of opportunity for recreation at Changi. Individuals had brought in what amounted collectively to a fair-sized library of books, and these, together with others that were found in deserted houses and barracks in the Changi area, were exchanged at book depots. Permission was given by the Japanese, too, to bring in a number of textbooks from the city in order to establish a 'University'. Among such large numbers there was a considerable variety of knowledge and talent, and excellent classes covering a wide curriculum were started—a feast of educational activity which those who were later transferred from Changi to other camps never again tasted. Entertainments included plays, vaudeville shows, and serious music. For the athletic there were cricket, football and boxing, though poor food and a consequent decline in physical condition soon dissuaded many from taking part. Some found an almost full-time occupation in 'pottering', doing useful odd jobs and gardening. Religious worship was not restricted and services were held regularly.

From the first the Japanese had daily fatigue groups of prisoners clearing up the damaged areas of Singapore city, and in a very short time they began to draft men out on permanent working parties. Some of our men went to Bukom Island, where they were set to work clearing debris and were relentlessly kept at it by Japanese guards, who did not hesitate to administer a beating-up at any sign of slackening or insubordination. Others went to dig pits for the storage of drums of petrol among the rubber plantations at Woodlands. Others still went to Blakang Mati Island to load and unload bombs and to dig underground tunnels for their storage. At these working camps the men were quartered in cement barracks or attap huts, tightly packed or comparatively well off for space according to whatever was available. They were allowed to carry out their own internal administration, but only under close supervision by the Japanese. They worked for eight or more hours daily for thirteen and a half days out of fourteen, and in some camps were allowed no educational classes and no recreation except gardening. Their diet, consisting mainly of rice and vegetables, was insufficient to maintain their health under such hard conditions, and there were many cases of malaria and sporadic outbreaks of beriberi.

One of the first reactions of prisoners of war in their early captivity is to think out some way of escaping. But for those at Changi their distance from the nearest Allied-held territory, their white skins which easily picked them out in a coloured population, the execution of recaptured escapers and severe reprisals on any other prisoners who might be implicated, combined to make such attempts too costly except in special circumstances. Men's thoughts turned instead to their future liberation, about which a surprising number held the optimistic view that it would probably take only some six months to a year. The only newspapers available were

Japanese-sponsored publications in English, such as the *Syonan Shimbun (Singapore Times)* which gave full accounts of Japanese victories and the progress of the Axis forces in general. But neither this propaganda nor the brutal Japanese punishments for minor offences broke men's morale. The result of beatings with sheathed swords or rifle butts or pick-handles, of kickings, of standing to attention in the hot sun for hours on end, was to make the prisoners despise their guards as uncivilised rather than to be intimidated by them. Almost from the beginning a concealed radio gave them the headlines of the news from the British point of view and so discredited exaggerated Japanese claims. When food became desperately short, thoughts were concentrated on diet and on means of improving it. But the vast majority of men seem to have remained cheerful, and what one informant calls 'the fellowship of good friends' prevented temporary depression from becoming chronic.

Civilians at Singapore, who had been made to walk seven miles with their baggage in the heat of the day to the Karikal camp, had another similar forced march two weeks or so later, when they and those from the other three temporary camps were all transferred to Changi Jail. At Karikal, the home and outbuildings of an Indian merchant, together with the adjacent houses and convent, proved inadequate to house all the internees sent there, and sanitary, cooking, and water services were equally deficient. Changi Jail, a former penitentiary for Asiatic criminals, besides being better equipped, no doubt provided far fewer security problems to the Japanese than the miscellaneous collection of buildings at Karikal.

It was built to hold only 600 Asiatic civil prisoners in single cells, but into this accommodation, together with the workshops and some other quarters, went some 2800 civilians including 400-odd women and children. Three or four men occupied each cell, allowing a lying space roughly 27 inches wide for each man; they slept either on the concrete slab originally intended for the prisoner or on either side of it. Others slept on the grating outside the cells. The lighting of the building functioned more or less normally, though expended electric lamps were hardly ever replaced. The prison building being only five years old, washing and sanitary facilities were satisfactory though also very overcrowded; and shortage of water made it necessary to use boreholes instead of the proper prison latrines.

The internal administration of the camp was in the hands of elected block committees, which in turn elected representatives to a central camp committee. The women and children, who occupied a special block, had their own committee and their own representative for liaison with the Japanese camp commandant. Although described by an interned lawyer as a 'very complex democratic organisation', it seems by and large to have given satisfaction to the camp as a whole. In each block there was a clinic run by one of the interned doctors, and a central camp hospital was organised for more serious cases. Both doctors and dentists are generally reported as having given exceptionally good service to the internees in spite of lack of equipment and necessary drugs.

For the first few months the Japanese supplied only some 13 to 15 ounces of rice daily, together with small quantities of other food. The internees supplemented this with tinned stuff, a quantity of which had been laid in by each of the four original camps and brought to Changi when all their occupants were transferred there. Those with funds were able to purchase from the camp 'shop' small amounts of food brought in by the fatigue party which went out of camp to collect the rations. In this way, eggs, coconuts, palm-oil, *gula malacca,* and sweets became available to help break the monotony of rice meals. Local cigarettes, cheroots, and tobacco were obtained in the same way, the occasional Japanese issues being quite inadequate for most smokers. Food was cooked in the prison kitchen and distributed to sections of the camp in large tubs. Even with the extras mentioned above, the diet had such serious deficiencies, notably in proteins, fats, and vitamin B complex, that it was insufficient to maintain health. By the middle of 1942 most of the internees had lost weight, there were signs of weakness and swellings typical of nutritional oedema, and ten cases of beriberi were recorded. Fortunately for all the internees there were among them a large number of medical practitioners, who formed a 'Medical Reference Committee' to keep a close watch on the camp diet and hygiene. Over the period of internment this committee was able to do a great deal to prevent the incidence of disease.

Every internee had to take his share in the running of the camp, either in an administrative capacity or by doing a turn of cookhouse or sanitary fatigues, collecting the camp rations, or gathering firewood for the camp kitchen. Spare-time recreation provided little difficulty: the internees were able to obtain a considerable number of books and sufficient musical instruments to set up an orchestra. All manner of educational classes were established, there were regular concerts and plays, and individuals were able to pursue their own favourite handicraft or other artistic occupation, although often with improvised materials. Some of the more energetic played cricket, football, and other sports in the early days, but as in the Changi prisoner-of-war area the later lack of a sufficient diet made it inadvisable for people to undertake anything too strenuous. Religious services were allowed, but only with guards in attendance. In the early period the internees were allowed to go under guard on one afternoon a month to bathe in the sea, and for a while they were allowed to walk outside the prison within a wire perimeter on two evenings every week.

The Japanese guards were outside the prison quarters except for searches, inspections, and roll-calls, but they kept a close control over everything that went on within. As in most Japanese camps, there were very severe restrictions on smoking and strict instructions concerning bowing by the internees to all Japanese guards. Failure to observe these regulations brought an immediate 'indiscriminate bashing' (in the words of one of the victims)—beating and kicking similar to that administered to prisoners of war for the same offences. For anything more serious there was solitary confinement as well. But this sort of treatment does not seem to have undermined most people's morale or their (at the time) somewhat irrational belief that their captors would be finally defeated. Against this optimistic background the internees met their captivity with various degrees of impatience or equanimity, perhaps epitomised by the man who described his state of mind as one of 'resigned exasperation'.

The main internment camp in the Philippines, and that to which nearly all the New Zealand internees[1] went, was the Santo Tomas University, the buildings of which lie in spacious grounds just outside Manila. For a few days the internees were without beds, bedding or mosquito nets, until the Japanese authorities allowed these to be brought out to the camp. In spite of the size of the buildings the 3300 men, women, and children who in January 1942 found themselves obliged to live there experienced bad overcrowding in the sleeping quarters, and still worse in eating, washing and sanitary facilities, with which the buildings were not of course equipped on anything like the necessary scale. A camp committee of seven American and three British internees became responsible for organisation and negotiation with the Japanese. Medical internees soon realised that immediate measures should be taken to minimise disease, and a hospital was set up to deal with the sickness which it would be impossible to prevent entirely.

Many people had brought in a supply of tinned food when first transported to the camp. When this was exhausted they had to manage on what could be obtained from the Filipino Red Cross and what their former Filipino servants or staff brought to the gates of the camp, as for the first six months the Japanese supplied them with no rations. They were able to obtain fruit, eggs, and vegetables

---

[1] There were some twenty New Zealanders interned in the Philippines.

through a canteen, if still in possession of sufficient money to buy them. There was plenty of recreation, and educational classes for adults as well as children were well organised. Attempted escapes were punished by the Japanese with extreme severity, and breaches of their regulations brought reductions in the amount of food allowed into the camp or in the hours during which the internees were allowed to move about the grounds. Members of religious orders, of whom there were two or three New Zealanders in the Philippines, were not interned for the first two and a half years but allowed to stay in their own quarters. They were given a red armband, were made to understand that they were on parole, and were allowed out for medical attention, for the conducting of religious services, and sometimes even for shopping.

Some of the servicemen captured in Java had to remain in temporary camps for weeks before being moved to a more permanent camp. At Serang in North Java, for example, 800 men, including wounded and survivors from sunken vessels, were crowded into a native cinema, where they slept on the stone floor, lived on a daily ration of a handful of rice and some bread, together with water from a disused well, and had only the most primitive improvised sanitary and washing facilities. In the south numbers of prisoners were held at a school in Garoet or in temporary quarters on one of the aerodromes. Parties of prisoners were set to work on most of the latter making them serviceable for the Japanese and later unloading stores and ammunition; they remained there until the job was finished or their labour was more urgently required elsewhere.

The prisoner-of-war camp at Bandoeng was located in the barracks formerly used by Dutch infantry units. As it soon contained several thousand prisoners of different nationalities, each national group was organised by one of its senior officers, and in the early stages the administrative control of the whole camp was entrusted to the senior medical officer.[1] This officer and the officer in command of the British group succeeded at the outset in exacting from the Japanese certain standards of treatment, which remained in force almost throughout the camp's history and made conditions there better, in the opinion of most prisoners, than they were in most other Japanese prisoner-of-war camps. The medical and dental care of the prisoners at Bandoeng was assured by a large number of medical and dental officers, though there was the usual difficulty in getting drugs and equipment as most of it had been confiscated by the Japanese. A hospital was set up in the camp, but serious cases were evacuated to the Tjimahi hospital nine miles away.

---

[1] Lt-Col E. E. Dunlop, AAMC

The ration of food at Bandoeng consisted mainly of rice and dried potatoes, with some green vegetables and a small quantity of meat.[1] Though better than that at many other camps, especially in later periods, this ration had the deficiency in protein, fats, and vitamins (especially the B complex) already noted in the diet supplied in other Japanese camps, and after a few months proved a similar source of malnutrition and deficiency diseases. Fortunately the Japanese began to pay both officers and men, and it became possible to establish a camp fund through which purchases of eggs, yeast, and a type of bean rich in vitamin B complex were made. Besides being used for patients in the camp hospital, these extra supplies were sufficient to make a full camp distribution. For a while each man received an egg a day, and it became possible for various sections of the camp to open 'cafés' where those with extra money could buy odd meals, ranging from coffee and a biscuit to eggs and bacon or steak, eggs and chips. Once the camp fund had been established the canteen was excellently supplied: 'one could order anything from a choice steak and the onions to go with it, to a pot of gilt paint and crayons for the Art School, and get them', was the summing up of one of the inmates at this period.[2]

The senior officers in Bandoeng camp appear to have set from the beginning a high standard of camp discipline and morale. Besides insistence on tidiness and cleanliness and general obedience to camp orders, this usually involved the provision of mental recreation to take the place of the work and leisure activity that would have been the normal routine of those on active service before their capture. At Bandoeng the educational classes, the library, and the theatre productions appear to have all been very good. Religious services for all denominations were held in the camp theatre. A daily newspaper entitled *Mark Time* was typed and displayed on the camp notice-boards: besides items of news and commentaries it contained results of raffles, advertisements of concerts, local gossip, and illustrations. A more elaborate monthly edition contained original articles, stories, and verse.

The news in the local Malay-language newspaper consisted largely of Japanese claims of military successes, sometimes patently exaggerated, especially in the numbers of ships sunk and aircraft shot down. There were, however, in the camp a number of concealed wireless sets, on which various men listened in regularly and reported the news to senior officers. It was considered advisable, in order to avoid discovery of the sets by the Japanese, not to publish this

---

[1] Estimated at 2000 calories daily by Lt-Col Dunlop, 'Medical Experiences in Japanese Captivity', in *British Medical Journal*, 5 October 1946.
[2] Flt Lt R. D. Millar, DFM, *Narrative of personal experiences. . . in the Far East* (RNZAF Historical Records Section).

news to the camp generally but to allow most of it to circulate indirectly without mentioning its source.

The working parties from Bandoeng consisted mainly of daily labour gangs for unloading railway trucks, moving ammunition and bombs, and clearing up debris. The Japanese discipline was strict, often illogical and sometimes brutal. Clipping of the hair to a length of one centimetre, numbering and giving all military orders in Japanese, saluting all Japanese ranks: failure to observe such regulations brought a beating which varied from a few cursory blows on the head with a closed fist to a full-dress affair lasting an hour or two, at the end of which the gashes, lacerations, bruises, and possibly internal injuries sustained by the victim often necessitated his admission to hospital. One or two who attempted to break camp were publicly executed.

Most prisoners in the Dutch East Indies seem to have experienced a large number of different prisoner-of-war camps, being almost continually transferred from one to another both on Java and on other Dutch islands. Some New Zealanders went to the Boei Glodok native jail at Batavia, where they were packed in with half or less than half the allocation of space formerly allowed by the Dutch for native civil prisoners. When the first parties arrived there in March 1942 there was barely room to lie down, and the 'cells were infested with vicious, smelly bugs, flies in the daytime and mosquitos at night.' Prisoners from this jail were at that time clearing away debris and repairing damage to the civil airport a few miles away. Gradually conditions were improved: prisoners were allowed to sleep on improvised beds in the jail yard; the food, which had consisted mainly of maggoty rice, became somewhat better, though not good enough to prevent the onset of deficiency diseases; concerts were allowed once a week and other forms of recreation began to be organised.

As Batavia was the port of departure for many of the working groups leaving for other parts of Japanese-occupied territory, this jail and the former barracks of a Dutch cycle battalion, which had become known as the 'Cycle Camp', were frequently being packed to overflowing by such drafts of men, and knew some respite only after each draft had embarked. A good many New Zealanders passed through the Cycle Camp, where accommodation and food were better than in the jail. The Japanese staff of the camp, however, achieved a reputation for harshness and brutality, and beatings of the type described elsewhere became commonplace.

Apart from the Navy and Air Force officers transported almost immediately to Singapore, the majority of the other prisoners taken in Sumatra remained in the camp at Padang until May 1942. They were housed in army barracks and had high wooden benches to sleep on. Here, too, the diet consisted mainly of rice, with a little vegetable and dried fish. A New Zealand able seaman (speaking in retrospect) states that he could not complain of his treatment there and that the guards 'seemed to be in a jovial mood' because the war was going so well for them. No doubt Padang was a pleasant contrast to the labour camps in other parts of Sumatra or in Burma to which many of the inmates later went.

Civilians captured by the Japanese at sea while attempting to escape from Singapore, and others who reached Banka Island by lifeboat from their sunken ships, were roughly handled by their Japanese captors. Men, women, and children were herded into coolie quarters in a native *kampong,* where they slept on sloping concrete platforms so tightly packed that their bodies touched. They were fed on dirty, badly-cooked rice and hot water, and their guards were, in the words of a New Zealand nurse, 'rough, ruthless, and bombastic'. They were shipped across to Sumatra and accommodated, together with some hundreds of Dutch women and children, in two small streets of houses in Palembang. Thirty internees had to live in each small house, originally built for a married couple and one child. The septic tanks were not able to cope with these numbers, and there was a constant struggle to avoid insanitary conditions harmful to health. The water supply functioned only for an hour or so at 2 a.m., and cooking arrangements had to be improvised. For the first six months, however, a bullock-cart was allowed to bring extras into the camp, and although so badly overcrowded, these people were better off in this makeshift 'camp' than under the appalling conditions they had later to endure.

Most of the New Zealand naval personnel captured in the Java or Timor Seas following action with the Japanese fleet spent the first few months of their captivity in former Dutch barracks at Macassar, in Celebes. The buildings were solid and clean, but many of the men, whose only clothing after their rescue from the sea was a pair of shorts, had to make the best of sleeping thus clad on bare concrete floors. There was no shortage of water, but the latrines were open ditches with no precautions to prevent the spread of fly-carried disease. The food consisted almost entirely of rice and a little dried fish, nearly always inadequate in quantity. The Japanese supplied the prisoners with the bare minimum of clothing and no footwear, in spite of their almost complete lack of both on arrival. One New Zealand able seaman received two cotton singlets and two pairs of cotton shorts during the whole three and a half years of his captivity. But the more enterprising of the prisoners found illicit means of obtaining clothing and other things, such as tobacco, while on working parties in the town.

The prisoners had a library of books obtained from the town, and at first they were allowed sports and occasional concerts; but as time went on more and more restrictions were placed on gatherings and the playing of musical instruments. Most of the prisoners were in any case forced to do hard manual labour during the hours of daylight for seven days a week, with perhaps half a dozen holidays a year. Discipline was very severe and enforced by the type of beating with clubs, wet ropes, and even iron bars already mentioned, but probably more frequent and more brutal in Macassar than elsewhere. As in other Japanese camps, the punishment for recaptured escapers was torture and beheading. After the first such incident the camp's occupants were divided into groups of ten, the remainder of whom were to die if one of their number tried to escape. The lengthy record of Japanese savagery towards their captives from December 1941 until the end of the war in the Far East is so well-spread geographically that it is not always easy to pick out the worse from the better camps. But the records of the prisoners tend to show that living conditions, the ruthless use of human beings as slave labour, licence for sadistically minded guards to beat and torture their captives, both individually and in mass, were in Macassar almost continually at their worst.

III: *Protection of the Interests of Prisoners of War and Civilian Internees*

A few days after the outbreak of the war in the Far East the Imperial Prisoners of War Committee held a special meeting in London to examine the position of prisoners taken during hostilities with Japan. The latter was bound by the Hague Convention of 1907, and had signed the Prisoners of War Convention of 1929 but had never ratified it.[1] The International Red Cross Committee had written immediately after the announcement of hostilities to Great Britain, the United States and Japan, inviting their *de facto* reciprocal observance of the Convention and requesting them to forward all information regarding prisoners of war to the Central Agency in Geneva. By 7 January 1942 a reply had been sent to the British Minister at Berne intimating that the British Government agreed in principle with the proposal of the Committee. At the same time a communication was sent to the Japanese Government through the Argentine Government,[2] informing the Japanese that the United

---

[1] Japan had also signed the Convention of 1929 relating to the treatment of sick and wounded in the field and had ratified it except for one minor point.
[2] At this stage the Argentine Government had consented to act as the Protecting Power for the interests of the United Kingdom, Canadian, Australian, and New Zealand subjects in Japan, and the Swiss Government for those in the various occupied territories.

Kingdom, Canada, Australia, and New Zealand were observing the provisions of the 1929 Convention and asking for an assurance that the Japanese would do the same. It was specifically mentioned in this communication that for reasons of practical convenience it was proposed that the application of Articles 11 and 12 relating to food and clothing should take into account the national and racial customs of both sides. To this request the Japanese Government replied that, while not bound by the Convention, they would ' observe its terms *mutatis mutandis*[1] in respect of English, Canadian, Australian, New Zealand and Indian prisoners of war '; they would moreover take account of national and racial customs (on a basis of reciprocity) when supplying prisoners of war with food and clothing. So far as civilians were concerned, Japan agreed to apply the provisions of the 1929 Prisoners of War Convention *mutatis mutandis* and not to subject them against their will to manual labour.

These replies, though delayed,[2] gave grounds for hope that treatment of our prisoners by Japan would be at least as humane as that of Italy and Germany, and that similar facilities for the protection of their interests and for the supply of relief would be granted. As the months passed these hopes were belied. It is true that the Japanese set up a Prisoners of War Information Bureau in Tokyo (*Huryojohokyoku*) in January 1942, but even in late March the only information it gave concerned the numbers of prisoners of war held in various places; and next-of-kin had to be content with fragments of information gleaned from various sources concerning their British relatives in the Far East. By mid-April the Japanese announced that they were preparing a list of 28,000 names of prisoners of war, which would be sent on the ship going to Lourenço Marques for the exchange of diplomatic personnel arranged to take place later in the year. But by the end of 1942 casualty lists from the Japanese were far from complete, and a good many of the captives held by them were never notified at all.

The same difficulties were encountered by the neutral agencies working on behalf of British prisoners of war and civilians in Japan or in Japanese-occupied territory. In Japan the International Red Cross Committee's delegate at Tokyo[3] was approved in January 1942; but the Japanese distrust of all foreigners who were not nationals of a power allied to Japan made the work of

---

[1] This was taken by the British Government to imply that the Japanese, though not bound by the letter of the Convention, would nevertheless live up to its spirit.
[2] They were not received until February 1942. Meanwhile there had been constant approaches to the Japanese Government by the IRCC's representative in Tokyo and also a second formal communication from the Committee.
[3] Dr Paravicini, a Swiss national who had lived for some twenty years in Japan.

this representative and that of the Protecting Power most difficult. In occupied territory the only delegates who were recognised were those at Shanghai and Hong Kong,[1] the former beginning work in April and the latter in June 1942. Disturbing news received in February from a civilian refugee about atrocities committed by Japanese troops in Hong Kong gave rise to increasing concern for the future of captives in their hands; and information from various sources indicated that most of the provisions of the Geneva Convention were being openly flouted by the Japanese military authorities. In April the British Government, which strictly observed the provisions of the Geneva Convention with regard to the Japanese prisoners and internees, was considering whether or not to take some measures of reciprocity, particularly in respect of the withholding of information and the refusal of visits of neutral inspectors; but only certain special privileges, such as permission to attend cinemas, were withdrawn. It was thought advisable to give the Japanese no pretext for making their treatment of British nationals any worse. By May Japan had agreed in principle to the establishment of a mail service, and there were indications that she might in future prove more tractable.

IV: *Relief Supplies for the Far East*

At the end of December 1941 the British Red Cross had made tentative plans for the shipment to British nationals in the Far East of relief supplies similar to those regularly despatched to Europe. It was proposed to send a neutral ship with supplies obtained in Australia and New Zealand from an Australian port, and the International Red Cross Committee was asked to try to organise a shipping line. By February the food supplies[2] had been arranged and a neutral ship was ready to sail as soon as the Japanese should supply a safe conduct. All the negotiations for the use of 'Red Cross ships', however, fell through, and the Japanese refused to allow relief supplies to come by any other means than on the exchange ships bringing back Japanese diplomatic personnel. There was nothing left but for the British Red Cross to arrange to have as much food and medical supplies at Lourenço Marques as the ship returning to Japanese territory would carry.

The value of such large and well-selected consignments when and if they eventually reached the prisoners made it worth while to send them, but the immediate problems in the camps requiring urgent relief, some idea of which has been given earlier in this chapter, had to be met as best they could by those on the spot.

---

[1] The delegate in Shanghai was Dr Egle and in Hong Kong Dr Zindel.
[2] New Zealand's offered contribution consisted of 70,000 tins of meat, butter, jam, chocolate, and coffee and milk.

The work of the neutral committee of the World Alliance of YMCAs in Tokyo in supplying recreational material has already been mentioned. But when the International Red Cross Committee's delegate in Shanghai tried to organise a relief service for prisoners of war at the beginning of 1942 he was flatly refused, the Japanese authorities claiming that the prisoners 'lacked nothing'. He was able to organise supplies, however, through the local residents. The first relief for those in Hong Kong had to be organised in the same way, since it was May before Dr Egle from Shanghai was allowed to visit Hong Kong, and no permanent delegate arrived until June. The delegate at Singapore was informed at first that the services of a representative of the International Red Cross Committee were not required either for prisoners of war or civilians; and the supply of relief there also had to be organised privately. In the Philippines, in the Dutch East Indies and in Borneo, the same conditions applied: the Japanese refused to recognise delegates and neutral officials, and anything that was done had to be informal and indirect. It was always hoped that in time these restrictions would be relaxed. But the course of the war was to make the Japanese more suspicious than ever of foreigners and to make work on behalf of prisoners and internees a source of personal danger to those who attempted it. Moreover the inflated prices which resulted from the Japanese occupation made it more and more difficult to finance the private purchase of relief.

* * * * *

The rise of Japan to be one of the great powers of the twentieth century resulted from her wholesale adoption of the technology and many of the social and political institutions of the West. The fact that she had emerged from centuries of isolation less than a hundred years before emphasized the almost miraculous speed with which she had adapted Western ideas to her own needs, and showed that such a people possessed at least the intelligence and industry of Europeans. Her military technique had been proved efficient, and her industrial products, if not always considered so durable, were convincing reproductions of their European counterparts. It was tempting to draw the conclusion that she had become completely 'westernised' in outlook. Her interest in Red Cross matters seemed indicative of a humanitarianism analogous to that of the West. Even the horrifying events of the 'China incident' tended to be regarded as exceptional to a war between two Asiatic peoples with a long tradition of mutual antagonism, and not as a warning of what might happen in hostilities between Japan and a Western power. Public opinion was quite unprepared for the type of outlook created among the men of the Japanese armed forces by their Samurai training.

The traditions of the Imperial Japanese Army established the principle that the military honour of a soldier forbade his surrender to the enemy; and the military regulations promulgated by the Japanese Minister of War in January 1942 reaffirmed the idea and made it enforceable. The training manual of each branch of the service contained the paragraph: 'Those becoming prisoners of war will suffer the death penalty'. Combat instructions found in a captured notebook contained the following advice:

When you are temporarily knocked unconscious by a blow and fall into enemy hands, quickly attack, escape, or commit suicide.

When you faint due to wounds quickly commit suicide the moment consciousness is regained.

When a Japanese soldier left his family to join a combatant unit a farewell ceremony was carried out in accordance with funeral rites; and after his departure he was regarded by his family as dead unless he should return as a conqueror. Since notification of his capture involved disgrace for his family, few captured Japanese desired it.

In view of these considerations, the attitude of Japanese troops to their captives was hardly likely to be other than one of contempt. Since prisoners were little better than dead men, their living conditions were of no importance and the notification of their capture to their relatives unnecessary. In any case, not only were the rations issued to the Japanese soldier inferior in quality and quantity to those issued to the Allied forces, but his discipline was severe and brutal by comparison. British captives were, moreover, members of a detested enemy nation, which in the past had been patronising and superior, and whose loss of face should be made apparent to the peoples of the East which Japan was in the process of liberating and incorporating in a 'Greater East Asia Co-prosperity Sphere'. It was small wonder that the Japanese authorities took little interest in the transmission of information concerning captives. Their callous neglect of wounded prisoners and their murder of some of them were the logical consequence of their military code. The beatings into unconsciousness, the mass punishments in the presence of an arch-offender before his more frightful torture in private, the bayoneting to death and the beheading of recaptured escapers all become explicable in terms of their own severe discipline. And while some such cases might have had their origin in the sadistic complex of an individual guard, the major incidents of this type were all enacted with a purpose and the attitude of those responsible was, it seems, more one of amused indifference than of sadistic enjoyment.

While there can be no doubt of the extreme savagery of these incidents, any more than of the rapings and massacres following

Japanese victories, it would be easy by dwelling on them to give a false impression of their place in the overall picture of captivity under the Japanese. The accounts of War Crimes trials, by their very nature, seldom tell the whole story. To balance the picture it is necessary to detail the living conditions in a fair sample of camps and to recount the sometimes surprising amenities and recreational facilities that captives were able to improvise. Although violent physical ill-treatment was all too common, the most widespread ill-effects of captivity in the Far East seem to have resulted from lack of proper food and medical supplies. But in this field, too, the prisoners themselves and their medical officers did much to mitigate Japanese neglect, often without the knowledge of their guards. To those who organised these aspects of camp life must go much of the credit for the maintenance of morale.

In early May the Battle of the Coral Sea brought a sharp check to the hitherto scarcely unhampered eastward advance of the Japanese forces; and the Battle of Midway at the beginning of June put an end to their plans of conquest for the time being. The check became a turning point and the wave of Japanese aggression began slowly to recede westwards. But at this stage there was for British prisoners of war in the Far East no indication of Japan's ultimate defeat, beyond the news brought in by new prisoners and fragmentary information gleaned from surreptitious listening on a secret radio or snatched conversations with friendly natives. Their guards showed no sign of relenting in their treatment; they were in fact entering on the period to which belong the worst examples of Japanese neglect and ill-treatment of European captives.

CHAPTER 6

Turning Point of the War in Europe and in North Africa

(June 1942—July 1943)

I: *The North African Campaigns of 1942-43—Prisoners in Italian Hands*

TO prisoners of war in Europe hearing enemy broadcasts and anxiously scanning enemy newspapers to try to follow the trend of the war, the months of 1942 until autumn brought news of disaster after disaster to the Allied cause, even allowing for the distortions and exaggerations of enemy propaganda. Yet by the end of the year the whole complexion of things had changed, the initiative was with the Allies, and as the first half of 1943 brought to light new successes (glossed over in the enemy press, but impossible to hide completely), prisoners began to realise that the Allies were, as one man put it in a letter, 'starting on the home run'.

The early disasters in the Far East have already been mentioned. Yet by the end of 1942 the United States forces had stabilised the situation in the Pacific, and during 1943 the Japanese were dealt some heavy blows at sea. On the Russian front Sebastopol fell in July 1942 and the Germans entered Stalingrad in September; and the losses of the British raid on Dieppe, although it created a diversion in August, seemed a bad augury for the success of a second front. Yet by November the Russian forces were on the offensive and the new year brought them enormous gains in territory, together with the annihilation of large German and Italian forces. In North Africa a German offensive launched in late May gathered momentum in June and forced Eighth Army to withdraw hurriedly to the Egyptian border; then followed the fall of Tobruk and the retreat to Alamein, in spite of some delaying actions. Yet not only did the line hold at Alamein, but in October the British attacked and broke the Axis forces and during the next four months pursued them across Libya into Tunisia. The landing of Allied forces in French North Africa in November prevented their further retreat to the west, and in the first half of 1943 attacks from this quarter and from the south-east by Eighth Army put an end to enemy resistance on the African Continent.

The New Zealand Division was again heavily involved in the North African fighting and, especially in the struggle to hold the enemy at Alamein in July, suffered losses almost as severe as those of the previous November. Nor was the intense air activity in support of the ground forces maintained without losses, and more than half of the New Zealand airmen serving with the RAF who fell into Italian hands did so in North Africa during this period.[1] Of the two thousand or so 2 NZEF personnel taken prisoner, about a hundred were captured south of Matruh in the first stand by the Division after its hasty return from Syria, and in its break-out from encirclement at Minqar Qaim. But the vast majority were lost in actions on the Alamein Line in July.

The first of these was an attack on the western end of Ruweisat Ridge by 4 and 5 Brigades, which found themselves on the morning of 15 July in possession of their objective but, as our own tanks did not come up, completely at the mercy of the enemy armour: 22 Battalion was overrun almost immediately, and so by evening were 19 and 20 Battalions. The incidents of capture were a recapitulation of Belhamed and Sidi Rezegh. An infantryman's diary tells the story:

> The tanks having knocked out our guns, came rumbling and clanking towards us with nothing to stop them. Their machine guns were going all the time at anyone they saw moving, while behind them were German infantry and more tanks. We could do nothing, but kept hoping that some of our own tanks would turn up to the rescue; alas we were alone in the desert. A big Mark IV was only about seventy yards off me by this time . . . I only had a rifle and had seen two pounder shells bouncing off the tanks . . . .

As on previous occasions no one had visualised being captured, least of all after a successful attack. It came as a shock to see our men with their hands up, and one man puts it, 'I think we all felt rather silly and self-conscious'.

A week later almost the same thing happened to the infantry of 6 Brigade. In a night attack they captured the eastern portion of the El Mreir depression, only to be sacrificed to enemy armour in the morning; Brigade Headquarters, 24, 25, and 26 Battalions suffered heavily. Some 1700 New Zealanders were taken prisoner in these two engagements—a sad and undeserved fate for troops

---

[1] Some forty New Zealand airmen fell into Italian hands, of whom over twenty were taken in the second half of 1942.

who had played a notable part in the defence of Egypt and had faithfully carried out their orders.

Patrol activity in August accounted for another 50-odd prisoners, and a harassing movement on Rommel's withdrawal from his September attack for still another 90-odd. From the beginning of October 1942 until the end of fighting in North Africa in May 1943, however, we lost only another ninety or so prisoners. Moreover, from the Battle of Alamein in late October 1942 until the end of the war in Europe—from all the subsequent fighting in Libya, Tunisia, and Italy—the Division's losses in prisoners were fewer than 350, as compared with over 8000 in the preceding period of the war. If the number of prisoners taken in land fighting can be used as an indication, the battle of Alamein was clearly the turning point of the fighting in the West.

In holding up the German advance after the fall of Tobruk, the New Zealand Division had been encircled at Minqar Qaim near Mersa Matruh. A night attack with the bayonet during the breakout from this position was the cause of much high feeling among the encircling German forces. A party of 92 New Zealanders who were left grounded there and were captured in the morning received rough handling, and perhaps owed their lives to the intervention of a senior German officer. They were lined up, stripped of everything except uniform and greatcoat, and told after a long harangue that they would be shot as a reprisal for the tactics of the New Zealanders on the previous night.[1] Eventually, however,

---

[1] The following account of this incident by Capt J. Ayto (NZ Div Sigs) appears in the Divisional Signals' history:

'About 9 a.m. the group comprised approximately eighty New Zealanders, two British officers from an armoured unit and a Canadian air force pilot. At this point the Commandant of the Panzer Division came forward with his Intelligence Officer as interpreter and then the New Zealanders were instructed to leave all their kit on the side of the hill and form up in three ranks. The Divisional Commander then said: " Tonight you New Zealanders fought us and didn't fight fair. You shot prisoners and bayoneted wounded and now we will show you that we can be just as hard as you." We were then searched one by one and had everything, even handkerchiefs, taken from us except the clothes we were wearing. We were then formed up in another position and some of the German NCOs fitted the butts to their machine-guns. It looked as though we were to be shot. One of the British officers, who was not concerned in this, went up to the Divisional Commander and spoke to him in German. I was able to ask him later what he said and he said that he told the German commander that he thought it would be a mistake to start shooting prisoners as from then on there would be no prisoners taken by either side. He was roundly told off for his interference. Whether this had any effect, or whether the whole thing was designed to frighten us I don't know, but we were told we would be left standing in three ranks all day as a punishment. At this stage four or five men were taken away to bury the dead at the point where the breakthrough had taken place the night before. . . .

' The main group was left standing in the sun, the only relief occurring when a party was required to bury some of the dead and the wounded who had died on the spot. These tasks were given to those most affected by standing in the sun and in most need of relief. A little after midday the German supply column arrived. We were lucky in that the opportunity had to be taken to send us back and so we were spared the rest of the day standing in the sun. We were not allowed to take anything with us except our paybooks—not even water.'

after a conference with their senior officer, the Germans in charge of the prisoners announced that they had been reprieved. Meanwhile they had been standing in the heat of the sun for some hours without food or water, while sentries with tommy guns forced back into line anyone who tried to fall out or lie down. On the other hand a badly wounded officer, after an immediate anti-tetanus injection, was removed to a main dressing station where two German surgeons ' saved [his] life and deplored the war '. From the time of his capture he encountered no hostility, but rather an attitude of ' Just too bad, but you're in the bag '.

Even those captured 18 days later at Ruweisat Ridge met with some signs of a carry-over of the hard feelings after Minqar Qaim. Some were asked expressly whether they had taken part in the Minqar Qaim action. Whether from this cause or not, although there was no brutality, the experiences of prisoners from the moment of their capture at Ruweisat until their arrival in a back area were unpleasant enough. Men of 18 and 19 Battalions, after a search for arms, were herded back a mile or two to a holding area, where there was a count and officers were taken off for interrogation. The march back then continued until late that night, by which time all had raging thirsts and a number had collapsed;[1] but there was no food and almost no water that night nor was there any until, completely exhausted, they reached transport later the next morning. Men of 22 Battalion were marched back 15 miles through the heat of the day before being picked up by lorries. Those taken at El Mreir on the morning of 22 July had a similar exhausting march back to a plateau, where they were left in the blazing sun without food or water. A soldier's diary runs:

> A scorching sun beat down on the shimmering rock. To lie was unbearable. To stand and feel the barely discernible breeze from the sea was impossible for more than a few seconds. Our legs were too weak to bear the weight of our bodies . . . . Chaps were offering watches for a cup of water.

Eventually transport came and took them to the prisoner-of-war cage at Daba.

Some were able to escape during the herding back from Ruweisat, and many walking wounded who had been left by the Germans unattended at RAPs were able to set out for the British lines under cover of darkness. Many felt that the wearying marches back without food or water were intended to make sure that no one was in a fit state to regain his freedom by walking away.

---

[1] Although the Germans had threatened to shoot any who fell out, in point of fact they brought them back on a truck.

At El Mreir the 6th Brigade commander[1] took off his badges of rank and, playing the part of a medical orderly, helped with the wounded for a day, then feigned death and made his way back after nightfall. He was captured again shortly afterwards in early September, and though he made a temporary break for freedom he was picked up by a German vehicle while making his way back across the desert. Many others who had made a break were picked up similarly by armoured-car patrols or lone vehicles. It is difficult to say how many escaped during this early transit stage. Many men simply rejoined their units, and the incidents of their escape were left to chance to record.

There was a more serious attempt at interrogation than there had been in the campaign of the previous November, though still nothing like the systematic process to which captured airmen were subjected in Germany. Officers were questioned at German formation headquarters, many of all ranks by German interrogators at Daba and by Italians at Mersa Matruh, from which point back the lines of communication were manned by Italian forces. Some of the wounded were interrogated at the various dressing stations they passed through. Papers and paybooks were examined and questions were asked mainly with a view to unit identification; but though there was some angry shouting at times, there appears to have been little or no attempt to obtain information by intimidation or violence.

The leaving of some of the wounded on the battlefield at Ruweisat without attention has already been referred to. It happened at more than one place on this occasion and was probably the cause of many deaths that could have been avoided by immediate medical attention, however makeshift. But the Germans appear to have had a large number of their own casualties to treat, with only very limited medical supplies. The delay in treatment of prisoners seems to have been limited to sixteen hours at the most—long enough, certainly, to be fatal for many cases. Treatment at the dressing stations farther back seems to have been adequate and humane. In later battles during this period seriously wounded prisoners seem to have been attended to promptly, and even lightly wounded to have been segregated and treated at the first headquarters on the way back. There were hospitals at Matruh and at Tobruk, though with limited facilities, and most of the serious cases were evacuated to Italy by hospital ship from these points.

The first stop for transport bringing back prisoners was the British cage at Daba, now in German hands—a piece of the desert

---

[1] Brig G. H. Clifton; awarded a second bar to his DSO for his continued attempts to escape during captivity and his final successful break in March 1945.

enclosed by barbed wire. To men parched and some almost insensible from the exhaustion of their twenty-mile trek across the desert, the cool evening sea breeze restored some life. Officers and men were separated, there was usually another search, and an issue of half a mug of water and a few ounces of biscuit. Most men had no hunger, some had not even the necessary saliva to masticate food; for the most part they lay on the soft sand of the pen and tried to sleep. Many knew that this would be their best chance of escape—barely thirty miles from their own lines—but few had the physical resources to attempt it. One New Zealand officer,[1] however, got away and, after gamely plodding alone for three days across the scorching desert, reached our lines in a state of exhaustion.

From a night bivouac near Sidi Barrani six British officer prisoners, including one New Zealander,[2] were able to get away unseen in the early hours of 12 July. They hid for two days in the old Italian positions south-east of the town. They then seized an Italian vehicle and, overpowering the two Italians in charge of it, left them with some food and drove off by the coast road to the east. By picking up water, petrol, and other necessities from derelict trucks en route, they made their way to the Alamein positions and eventually came through to a British armoured detachment, waving a white towel.

From Daba back to Benghazi prisoners were taken in large Italian trucks, sometimes in trailers, and often packed so tightly that it was only possible to stand. The journey by the coastal road took some four or five days, with stops at night wherever there was a barbed-wire pen to hold the prisoners. There was some kicking and the use of rifle butts by Italian guards, and the ration of biscuit and bully beef was all too little; but after the tortures of thirst during the first two days of captivity, men felt that so long as there was a reasonable amount of water they had something to be thankful for. The more fortunate were allowed to swim at Sollum or to wallow at a water point en route.

The compound at Mersa Matruh in Italian hands was the first place where thirsts were really slaked, and men were then able to take more interest in the dry rations that were issued. Some were interrogated here and, as at almost every staging point, there was a search; not many valuables remained in the possession of prisoners by the end of the journey. As at other staging camps, most men had only shirt and shorts to sleep in.

---

[1] Capt R. R. T. Young (22 Bn).
[2] Lt J. D. K. Logan (Div Cav).

Tobruk's large prisoner-of-war compound was on the escarpment at the edge of the aerodrome. A prisoner gives his first impression on debussing:

> Seen through clouds of racing dust it seemed a hopeless confusion, shanties, blanket-huts, tin shelters and tents all higgelty-piggelty and strung together with string and rope. There was a babel of tongues and a confusion of outlandish figures and dresses—South African Blacks, Indians, Gurkas, Siamese, Springboks, Tommies and Kiwis were living together, cheek-by-jowl. All conventional values were gone. The private no longer deferred to his officer nor black man to white.

The coloured troops were forced to work on the docks during the day, and while doing so were able to acquire not only extra food but firewood, groundsheets, blankets, and other things of high value to a prisoner of war. Their standard of living was higher than the average, and many of our men benefited by generous gifts from them. At night wood fires lit up the polyglot encampment and gave it an exotic atmosphere; and the gabble of foreign voices, some musical, some harsh, recalled to some men's imaginations stories they had read of Asiatic bands of freebooters. There was the usual issue of dry rations, and men lay down to sleep on the dust where they could. RAF raids made the nights broken, but though shell splinters fell among the prisoners the bombs were further away. In the morning there would be an issue of water and a convoy of trucks full of prisoners would move off.

There were further staging camps at Derna and Barce, with groundsheet tents at the former and huts at the latter. At Derna an Italian commandant with 'reprisal mania' kept the prisoners short of water, allowed guards to loot and bully, and generally kept conditions as uncivilised as possible. At Barce a well-disposed commandant did all he could to provide them with necessities and to see the sick properly cared for. From Derna most of the officers were flown to Lecce, in Italy.

The end of their journey brought most of the other ranks to a camp a few kilometres south-east of Benghazi in a small stony wadi with steep sides, about 50 yards wide and 350 yards long. An oasis thickly planted with tall, shady date palms, it became known to the prisoners as the 'Palm Tree camp'.[1] There were two main compounds, one for Free French and coloured troops and the other for British, the latter an area of about two and a half acres, which soon held over a thousand prisoners and a little later 2600. Within the wire there were buildings for a cookhouse, storehouse and orderly room; there were also bivouac

---

[1] This name embodies the main idea of a number of popular variants, 'The Palm Grove', 'The Palms', etc.

groundsheets for about 500 men, numbers of which were grouped together to form makeshift shelters somewhat after the fashion of sprawling bedouin tents.

Barbed-wire fences lined the tops of the gully sides, and the guards 'looked down on [the prisoners] as though it was a bear pit'. There was no sand and men slept on stones or hard rock with a top layer of dirt, many without coat or groundsheet; during the camp's most crowded period 'you could hardly step between the bodies' at night. Fleas and mosquitoes helped to make rest difficult. Latrines were dug on the slopes, but space was limited and there were always too few; in time the sewage seeped down into the central sleeping and eating area and a constant stench hung about the windless wadi. The place was partly redeemed by a plentiful supply of water from a spring, and there were even cold showers of a kind.

The food compared favourably with that of other transit camps: in the morning sweetened black substitute coffee, a quarter pound of tinned meat and more than half a pound of bread of inferior quality, and at night a cup of rice stew and half a lemon. Men brought some variety into their daily meals by cooking up the various elements of the ration, until the commandant placed a ban on fires to prevent the camp buildings disappearing as fuel. The one cookhouse which served the whole camp was difficult to control; unguarded rations quickly disappeared and others were sold at exorbitant prices, for under such circumstances money and treasure lose their value by comparison with food.[1] Most men derived too little nourishment from the diet and became weak and listless. A great number soon had dysentery, spread by the swarms of flies, and there were never-ending queues for the latrines day and night. It was fortunate that there were British doctors at the camp to do what they could with the limited medical supplies for the hundreds of cases of digestive disorders and desert sores which daily lined up for treatment.

There were a number of books which circulated by a system of barter, and a few men had packs of cards or made them from cigarette cartons. Some made draughtboards, and chessmen from green dates or the rubber fittings of a steel helmet. Men talked over their capture and experiences in this campaign or in others. Some were bitter about their capture: 'It's hardly worth fighting for people who use you as an anti-tank weapon.' Others were more philosophical: 'Not having a clear perspective of the whole show, I shall not attempt to judge'. Apart from those on the war, there were endless discussions on food and

---

[1] Prices quoted for 12 ounces of jam : 10s, 50–60 piastres, a good wrist watch, or a signet ring. Forty cigarettes brought similar prices.

the possibilities of escape. Rumours swept the camp periodically about a British breakthrough or the interception by the Royal Navy of ships taking prisoners across to Italy. At night some men found it possible, while gazing at the brilliant stars and moon through waving palm-fronds, to forget the filth and misery of the camp and substitute a romantic picture of happier circumstances.

There were no lights on the perimeter of the Palm Tree camp, and several men got away in the dusk but were recaptured in a few days. Two New Zealanders clung underneath the daily wood truck as it went out the gate,[1] and thereafter there was some competition to go out in the same way; but the next two who attempted it were caught and chained to the camp gates for a night, though the guards who released them gave them cigarettes and grapes. Security was tightened up and sentries became quick on the trigger, sometimes no doubt made jittery through prisoners rattling the wire or throwing stones at it. There was some firing into the compound as well as along the perimeter, and at least one of our men was shot through the thigh while lying asleep.

In early August after over a fortnight in the camp, commanders of the groups into which the men had organised themselves decided, on the assumption of a lengthy stay, to try to secure better rations and amenities from the Italian commandant, who was described as 'easy-going' and not ill disposed to the British. But ten days later the camp was suddenly cleared and the prisoners transported by truck, 600 to a waiting ship and the rest next day to the main Benghazi prisoner-of-war collection centre.

The influx of prisoners following the fall of Tobruk and the swift Axis advance had extended the collection centre just outside Benghazi into an enormous encampment spread over a rectangular area covering 25 acres or so of the adjoining desert. By August 1942, when most of our men went there, drafts to Italy had reduced its population from 15,000 to about 10,000 prisoners, but over the whole area a mass of low bivouac tents still spread into the distance. The prisoners were segregated to some extent according to nationality and colour into huge pens. The thousand or so New Zealanders, with some others from the Palm camp, were almost immediately crowded into a small, well-used, and therefore dirty and (as it turned out) lousy compound, where drafts were held before being embarked for Italy. Transfer of some of these to another pen eased the overcrowding, but it was nearly a month before a ship was available.

---

[1] Sgts H. P. Campbell (19 Bn) and G. G. Cleverley (25 Bn). They were free for five days before recapture.

Many of those in the camp had been there since the fall of Tobruk, had plenty of gear, and had made themselves as comfortable as circumstances allowed. Most of our men had the clothes they stood in when captured and various implements and odd garments they had since been able to acquire while moving about. At Benghazi there was much trading 'over the wire', both with the Italian guards for food and with the coloured troops who worked at the docks and brought back firewood, food, and cigarettes. Cigarettes (of which there was an issue of ten to fifteen a week) became the medium of exchange between prisoners for such transactions,[1] as in so many other prisoner-of-war communities, and indeed among some civilian populations as the war brought enemy governments tumbling and enemy currencies soaring to ruin. Some prisoners at Benghazi went into business buying food from the sick and selling it later at a profit to men hungry from a working party; but most were good comrades enough to reject the idea of profit-making and to make exchanges at the ruling values.

Food varied in different compounds and at different times, but in general there was a small tin of meat, half a loaf of poor bread and six ounces of British biscuits, a small amount of sugar and substitute coffee, and some rice every few days. For food-rationing purposes men were formed into groups of fifty, as they were for water, which was issued to individuals from German cans[2] filled by an itinerant water truck twice daily. No cooked meal was supplied, nor even hot water, and men set to work in syndicates to build stoves from stones, mud and old tins, to acquire firewood and to plan their own cooked menus. Hours of ingenious endeavour were spent devising and carrying out dozens of ways of serving the never-varying 'bully and biscuit' as rissoles, pies, and stews. Besides making the food more palatable, all this domestic activity had the virtue of helping to occupy men's minds and to prevent them from brooding on their present miseries.

Indeed, as time went on there was little in the situation to keep men cheerful. The nights began to cool and there was no hope of blankets or clothing from the Italian quartermaster's store. Sandstorms and rain found out the inadequate little bivouacs. Men were lousy, but did not have the water to wash properly and so wore as little as possible during the day, spending part of it delousing by hand the garments they were not wearing. Dysentery

---

[1] Prices quoted: two biscuits for one cigarette, 10 oz loaf of bread for ten cigarettes; one tin of meat for eight; blanket or overcoat for 30–40; toothbrush (later boiled) for two; eight sheets of paper for three; bundle of wood for two or three. Italian guards sold food for watches and signet rings.
[2] Six German cans to fifty men daily: about two quarts a man.

began to make its appearance and soon spread from the open latrines, which in one compound began to overflow and form a small lake. Besides the dysentery cases all were losing weight; many became lethargic through malnutrition and experienced the blackouts and rheumaticky pains common to such a bodily state. In their low condition men's nerves frayed easily under the strain of their cramped existence, and quarrels sometimes flared up quickly. A fortunate few of the sick were taken to Benghazi hospital, where they were well looked after, but there was no space there for many others who were ill enough to warrant admission.

Those who troubled to write about their situation drew a picture of this kind:

. . . unshaven, lousy, dirty, old ragged clothes hanging from bones, with our little improvised tin-can mugs, wooden spoons, bits of stick and wire.[1]

Yet even in these primitive conditions some order and internal organisation were created. Anti-social acts were kept down as far as possible by the senior warrant officer, who dealt out summary justice as in a regimental orderly room, and punished thieving, for example, by depriving the culprit of rations for twenty-four hours. In the various compounds lectures and concerts, and later an arts and crafts exhibition, were arranged to make the best use of what little recreational material there was. A South African padre held inspiring devotional services. Apart from this, men organised themselves into small living-groups—consisting often of regimental comrades or friends in civilian life—for mutual self-help and the division of the daily tasks; and they made their own pastimes with games of chess or cards and the exchange of whatever books they had with them. Without some such order and comradeship life at Benghazi would have been indeed nasty and brutish.

When the Benghazi pen had been reopened following the recapture of the town by Rommel's forces in January 1942, there had been a number of escapes. On one occasion a New Zealander[2] had knocked the guard unconscious and opened his compound gate to let out all those inside. Though some of them were recaptured in the course of their journey to the east, he himself, with the help of food, water, and shelter from Senussi, and later alone in an Arab disguise, had got through to the British lines north of Mechili in April.

By the latter half of 1942 all the compounds were well guarded by machine-gun posts, sentries and patrols, which made a break-out very difficult. Beyond the perimeter fence there was little

---

[1] From the diary of a New Zealand soldier.
[2] Dvr O. Martin (4 Res MT Coy), awarded MM for his 'courage and perseverance'.

or no cover, and most men were in no physical state to commence a cross-desert trek; the few who attempted it were quickly recaptured. One or two men succeeded in escaping from the Torelli hospital. In late September two patients, a New Zealand sapper[1] and a British Army infantryman, let themselves down from an upper story in the early hours of the morning while the sentry was asleep. They slipped into the Arab quarters of the town and were hidden and helped by the Senussi[2] from then on. They headed south-east, staying at night in an Arab camp where they were supplied with food and shelter. Dodging enemy columns and keeping on with determination, they made their way south to Gebel Akhdar, where they were finally picked up by an LRDG[3] patrol 18 days after leaving hospital.

Most of the drafts which left Benghazi by ship contained men of various Commonwealth units. Some 600 of those who moved in the first batch from the Palm Tree camp were shipped almost immediately in August, and another party went on 8 September. Then followed a long gap in the transport schedule, occasioned no doubt by dangers to shipping in the Mediterranean from the RAF and British submarines; and with rumours of a British success, men who had begun to wonder about their chances of survival set their hopes on rescue by Eighth Army. In October the Italians moved a large number of South African and British troops to Tarhuna and other camps near Tripoli, but most of the remaining New Zealanders were left to be taken over to Italy by sea. In early November there were signs that Benghazi was being evacuated in some haste, by the middle of the month the last party from the main camp had gone, and on the 16th patients from the hospital who could be moved were taken off in an Italian hospital ship. A few managed to hide up, and remained with the seriously ill and a few medical personnel until the town was occupied by British forces.

A certain number of New Zealanders had been taken in the parties of South African and British Army prisoners transported overland into Tripolitania.[4] After a three-day journey by truck they were housed in a concrete barracks at Tarhuna, 20 miles south-east of Tripoli. This had been in use as a prisoner-of-war transit camp during the Libyan campaign of the previous year, though only a few New Zealanders had been held there. Many

---

[1] Spr W. A. Gregory (NZE), awarded MM for this exploit.
[2] Throughout the Western Desert campaigns the Senussi gave assistance to British escapers and evaders in spite of Italian reprisals, including many hundreds of hangings and shootings. Some of them operated as agents under a French officer attached to MI9.
[3] Long Range Desert Group.
[4] A few New Zealanders captured during our later advance into Tripolitania were also held in and about Tripoli for a short period.

of those sent there in 1942 were suffering from dysentery or 'Gyppy tummy' and most were in a weakened state after their spell in Benghazi. Tarhuna would have been much worse if it had not been for an Italian officer interpreter, who did what he could towards improving conditions, ensuring regular issues of food and cigarettes, and even supplying clothing to combat the increasing cold of November nights. After three weeks our men were moved to Suani Ben Adem, a camp close to the port of Tripoli which had achieved an infamous reputation in the preceding months. Here, in this open space of one and a half acres packed with 1500 men, were cases of dysentery, scurvy, beriberi, desert sores, and septic bites from the lice and fleas with which the sand of the area teemed. Only the worst cases were taken to hospital, and many died there or later in Italy or on the trip over. After a week the New Zealanders crossed to Naples in the holds of a ship under foul and insanitary conditions similar to those of previous drafts.

Almost all officers were flown from one of the North African airfields to Italy, most of them landing at Lecce, where they were given temporary accommodation before going north to the transit camp at Bari. The drafts of other ranks from the Benghazi collection centre were packed tightly into the holds of the limited number of merchant ships available. In one ship 350 were crowded down below on the steel deck of a hold measuring about sixty feet by forty. There was no room for all to stretch out, and most men took off their boots as it was impossible to move without treading on someone's body. The convoys usually sailed straight to Piraeus, thence through the Corinth Canal to Patras, and across the Adriatic to Taranto. After four or more days and nights of the hot, humid atmosphere below decks, the innumerable lice that swarmed from body to body, and the meagre dry rations,[1] many men, some of them suffering from dysentery, arrived ashore at Taranto in poor shape: A diary entry reads:

> We had touched bed-rock. I am sure that as a body the men were in the lightest condition they ever reached .... We presented an appalling spectacle ... lousy animated bags of bones draped in torn and greasy rags.

Here their hair was shaved off, they were given hot showers, and their tattered clothes were put through a fumigator at a large naval barracks. The process seems to have been carried out quite efficiently. Rations were issued, and the men were taken across the harbour by launch to a waiting train.

Those who had left by the first draft in mid-August were not so fortunate. They too were packed into the holds of a cargo

---
[1] One shipload of prisoners discovered a hold full of food on the deck below them, and so at least did not suffer from hunger on the voyage.

vessel, the *Nino Bixio*. On their second day out the ship was hit by two torpedoes, one of which exploded in a hold full of prisoners, causing dreadful carnage. Though there was little panic on board, a few of the Italian complement as well as prisoners jumped overboard. Some of these perished almost immediately; others reached rafts and drifted about the Mediterranean for weeks without food and water. A New Zealand survivor of one such voyage, who was picked up and taken to Benghazi hospital where he recovered, told a grim story of deprivation and death. As it turned out, the *Nino Bixio* did not sink but was taken in tow by an Italian destroyer. The injured were brought up on deck and attended to by three medical officers, whose prompt and energetic services saved much further loss of life. When Navarino, in southern Greece, was reached the dead were buried, the remainder were put ashore, and those fit enough were shipped to Bari after a short stay at Corinth. This fresh disaster to a ship carrying prisoners of war cost the lives of 118 New Zealanders.

In late August the survivors marched into Campo PG 75 at Bari, which was then being used as one of the main transit camps for British prisoners from North Africa, and was receiving nearly all our officers who had not gone to hospital and a good number of our other ranks as well. The unsavoury reputation for brutality and general ill-treatment achieved by this camp in the first few months of its history had resulted in a change of commandant at the end of March, though the previous holder of the post had remained as guard commander. The new commandant had been quite favourably disposed towards the prisoners, and there had been just sufficient time to set the camp more or less to rights and to transfer all those who knew it at its worst before the first visit of a delegate from the Swiss Legation on 13 May 1942. On this occasion 'no complaints were made . . . by the internees';[1] but it is clear from the evidence accumulated by the War Crimes Commission that had the visit been allowed a month or two earlier or later there would have been no lack of them. When the camp numbers had risen sharply in June and July 1942, the new commandant was unfortunately replaced by two more senior officers, one of whom, in charge of the officer prisoners, proved particularly difficult to deal with. And the general commanding the area, a quick-tempered, highly excitable little man with anti-British feelings, remained to influence the camp during its whole history.

In 1941 work had been begun on the construction of stone barracks which were eventually to replace the original wooden huts. These were of a standard Italian military barrack design and

---

[1] Many of these were recaptured escapers and others just brought over from Greece.

were to hold 200 officers and 2500 men. Progress was slow and the new buildings were by no means completed by June 1942, when there occurred the large influx of prisoners from North Africa resulting from the fall of Tobruk and the military events mentioned above. Eight of the new barracks were, however, put into use and soon contained some 450 in each, with sleeping accommodation in two-tier bunks so close to one another that there was just room to pass. Many of the other rank prisoners who were pouring in, as many as two thousand arriving in one day, were packed into the orchard area and given the usual Italian groundsheet tents and heaps of straw. Others, still more unfortunate, were herded together and kept for a week or two in a dry canal bed just outside the camp, without hut, tent, or any other protection from the weather, and with no proper sanitation. One of these men when asked to describe Bari camp understandably replied that there was 'nothing [there] which could properly be called a camp at all'. The over-crowding was excused on the grounds that Bari was a transit camp only; yet some prisoners of war remained there for seven months.

The scale of food rations differed little from that mentioned in the account of this camp at an earlier period, except that there was half as much meat and a little more cheese. It seems doubtful if even this meagre amount of food was supplied in full, for several officers describe their diet as consisting to all intents and purposes of a small loaf and two servings of skilly daily, with a tiny piece of meat once a week. For this and the extra fruit and vegetables supplied for their messing, officers had to pay approximately four shillings a day.[1] From a canteen those able to pay the prices could buy irregular supplies of dried and fresh fruit and occasional cakes. Issues of Red Cross parcels were similarly irregular and inadequate.[2]

Many men had not recovered from the dysentery and other complaints contracted in North African transit camps, and most had been weakened by a lengthy period on short rations. There was a general prevalence of lethargy and cases of fainting on long roll-call parades; a ten-minute walk was the limit of most men's physical effort. Medical officers, although given space for a sick-bay, had little gear or medical supplies with which to treat the sick; one of them speaks of medical facilities in this period as being 'almost non-existent'. To make matters worse, lice

---

[1] Daily rations cost three to four lire, and fruit and vegetables ten lire, a total of 13 to 14 lire.
[2] Over four weeks of this period an officer records the following issues: an eighth, a quarter, and a half, a total of less than one complete parcel. Others record less.

infestation was common owing to the absence of proper delousing arrangements, and a shortage of water caused the latrines (normally adequate) to become stagnant. There were several unsuccessful attempts at escape,[1] followed by brutal treatment with rifle butts and wire manacles and mass reprisals in the form of withholding Red Cross supplies. With few books and only what makeshift recreations men could devise, Bari camp had few good words said about it by those who knew it in the summer of 1942.

In September most of the New Zealand officers were sent to Sulmona, and shortly afterwards numbers of our other ranks moved north to Gruppignano. Heavy rain in October made it necessary for other ranks who were in tents to be moved into the barracks, thus making the latter more overcrowded than at any previous period. More other ranks were transferred elsewhere, however, and of the New Zealanders only some thirty remained as part of the permanent staff of the camp doing cookhouse and other duties. There was little change in the food and no issue of Red Cross parcels for one period of 13 weeks.

In the New Year conditions began to improve. Issues of Red Cross food became more frequent, and plenty of hot water was available from the cookhouse for drinks. Italian uniforms marked with a yellow band, as well as underclothing and socks sent through the Red Cross, were issued to those who needed them. Each man had three blankets and sheets, though the latter were later withdrawn from other ranks as they were not being supplied to Italian prisoners in British hands. Pay was received regularly and mail started to arrive fairly well. Besides occupying themselves with indoor games and various arts and crafts, prisoners had organised lectures on accountancy and other subjects and classes in Italian and other languages. There was a weekly lecture on current events and a camp news sheet with items of topical interest. As the weather became warmer and sunnier in late February, men were able to divest themselves of their clothing and set about disinfestation in earnest. A New Zealand sergeant wrote, ' Things seem to be improving all the time '. At the end of February the camp was visited by a papal nuncio, who insisted on reading complaints written by officers relating to past treatment in the camp. Five days later 2300 prisoners were transferred to other camps, leaving only the permanent staff of 139 and some Greeks. Most of the New Zealanders were transferred to Campo PG 85 at Tuturano, ready to be sent out to work, and Bari became a kind of base camp for neighbouring work detachments.

---

[1] A few succeeded in breaking out of the camp but were recaptured after a few days at large.

Some of the drafts from Benghazi which arrived at Taranto during September were sent after disinfestation to a new camp three miles north-west of Altamura. It was on a gentle slope in the middle of a plateau of parched and stony land, but the barrenness of the compound was relieved by a shady almond grove which cut across one corner. Like Bari, this camp was only half finished: an administration block and latrines were built, but the only accommodation for the thousand or more prisoners consisted of the groundsheet bivouacs standard in Italian transit camps.[1] Although the amount of food was very small, it was all of excellent quality by contrast with what had been issued at Benghazi, especially the bread, cheese, and fresh vegetables. With this diet, the crystal-clear water and the fresh upland air, men's digestive complaints began to clear up and their appetites if possible to increase. After three or four days one Red Cross food parcel was issued to roughly each ten men, much to their delight and amazement, for in two hungry months spent in North Africa since their capture they had almost forgotten that milk, butter, jam, chocolate, and other such foods existed.

Fortunately the New Zealanders and Australians were moved before the rains made the camp into a sea of mud. During their stay the mild autumn 'enfolded [them] with sweet peacefulness',[2] and the pleasant Italian vistas helped to restore mental calm after the upheaval and strain they had hitherto experienced. The guards were easygoing and, apart from interminable roll-call parades, interfered little in the prisoners' daily lives. There was a general urge for mental occupation, which bore fruit in classes in languages and in informal lectures and debates under the only almond tree inside the compound. At night open-air concerts in the improvised parade ground gave men a chance to let off pent-up emotion in the community singing of sentimental and patriotic songs. In early October our men were moved north to Gruppigano by train—a crowded and uncomfortable two-day journey through the smiling Italian countryside.

Some of the last shiploads to leave Benghazi in November were sent after arrival at Taranto to Campo PG 85 at Tuturano, which earlier in the year had temporarily held some of our prisoners captured in the previous desert campaign. The camp had been enlarged by the erection of more wooden huts, and a small additional overflow compound had been added. Originally intended as a transit camp, it developed during this period into a base camp for working parties in the neighbourhood; and

---

[1] Five or six months later there were still no huts, though the foundations had been laid.
[2] Quoted from the diary of a New Zealand soldier.

although many of the first arrivals were sent north to permanent camps, others were retained, and some were sent from other camps for work among the almond and olive groves, the vineyards and the farms of southern Italy.

To the new arrivals from Benghazi in November the camp was 'like heaven'. They were shown to a bunk in a reasonably comfortable hut and issued with a palliasse and two blankets, some Red Cross food and fifty cigarettes. After a week they received a new British battle dress and an old Italian uniform as a change.[1] Letters and cards for writing home and five Italian cigarettes were given out regularly. There were drawbacks: the huts were still infested with lice and fleas, and the Italian non-worker's ration was insufficient to build up their lost strength, so that there were still cases of dysentery and a prevalence of giddiness following exertion. But the Italian doctor did what he could with the scanty medical supplies at his disposal, and there seems to have been a general disposition on the part of the camp authorities to do their best for the prisoners.

In March 1943 there were nearly 5000 on the camp strength (including 300–400 New Zealanders), of whom 1700 were already out in work detachments and many others preparing to go. The large numbers in the main camp marred the efficiency of many camp services, and numbers of prisoners were again sleeping in tents. Heavy rains made crowded tent life very trying, and a Swiss Legation inspector who happened to arrive at this period mentioned that 'tents were leaking and looked most uncomfortable', and that there were 'large lakes all over the place.' In many men's minds there arose a conflict about accepting a place in a working party: one man described it as 'trying to decide which comes first, duty to one's self or to one's country.' Those who went out to work received double rations, were given preference for Red Cross supplies, and had at least the illusion of greater freedom; but, they reasoned, working for the enemy must be helping his war effort. In the upshot they had no say in the matter, for when the supply of volunteers ran out the Italians simply detailed parties by name. Some New Zealanders were sent to farming camps in the neighbourhood, and in May 200 went to a new work-camp at Aquafredda, attached to Campo PG 78 at Sulmona.

One party of fifty were sent in April to a large estate specialising in viniculture. They were billeted in a large storeroom and were employed for nine hours daily on general farm labour,

---

[1] Stocks soon ran out, and later arrivals received only old Italian uniforms and Yugoslav coats. A Swiss inspector reported in March 1943: '. . . the outfit of the men is quite terrible to look at.'

working in parties of from six to fifteen men, with a guard and a civilian overseer. Most of the guards were easygoing and work was not too strenuous. Pay was at the rate of four lire a day, and went in cigarettes and toilet articles bought for them in the local village by the guard commander. Double rations, extra fruit and vegetables smuggled in from the farm, and exercise in the open air soon made them all very fit, and brought their bodily condition up to what it had been before capture.

Most of the shiploads of prisoners leaving from Tripoli at the end of 1942 were disembarked at Naples and sent to the camp at Capua, a few miles away. At the beginning of the year, when a number of New Zealand other ranks had spent some weeks in it, Campo PG 66 had possessed tent accommodation only. But in its new character of partly transit and partly permanent camp, it now had eight stone and twelve wooden barracks in one of its compounds and further barracks under construction in others. In general, tents were used only for prisoners in transit, though these sometimes comprised a very large proportion of the camp population, which rose on occasions to 8000 officers and men. The camp now took in an area about one and a half miles long by over 500 yards wide.

Our own men passed through in one of the comparatively empty periods of the camp and were housed in barracks. There was a good stock of Red Cross food parcels, though not enough clothing. The canteen sold fruit and toilet articles and there was a kitchen garden at the disposal of the prisoners. As Capua had previously been regarded as a transit camp, not many books or other recreational material had been sent there; but officers received Italian newspapers and other periodicals and organised lectures and classes. It was generally agreed that, although the completion of the barrack buildings was taking an unconscionable time, the commandant and his administrative staff were doing their best for the prisoners. After three or four weeks there most of our other ranks were moved north to Gruppignano, to join other New Zealanders from Bari, Tuturano and Altamura, as well as many taken in the previous campaign.

Except for a few captured at Minqar Qaim, who had arrived at Bari in early July and had gone with a number of South Africans and British Army officers to a camp at Chieti, all the New Zealand officers at Bari were sent in September to Sulmona. Officers who had been at Campo PG 78 for some time were living in comparatively comfortable quarters with ' good hired civilian furniture and proper beds '; but the new arrivals were put into large huts with concrete floors and given sailcloth stretchers and one wooden stool each. At this period many of the brick buildings were getting into a bad state of repair and were very crowded,[1] especially the accommodation for other ranks, some of whom had to sleep on the floor until March 1943. There was, too, the difficulty experienced in many Italian prisoner-of-war camps during the summer months that the water supply either failed or had to be restricted to a few hours each day.

On the other hand Sulmona had a regular canteen where fruit, jam, sweets, and cigarettes could be bought, although at excessive prices. There was now a football ground on which nearly everyone could get at least one game a week; and over the long period of its existence the camp had built up a good theatre organisation which produced some very good entertainments. In October, following their plan of segregating Dominion prisoners into camps of their own, the Italian authorities transferred the New Zealand officers to the new camp at Modena.

About forty of the New Zealand officers captured in the desert campaign of November 1941 remained at the monastery camp at Padula for the summer of 1942 before going on to Modena. The thriving black market which had provided such large additions to the diet (and the cost of living) suddenly collapsed after a raid by carabinieri and a full-scale inquiry involving many of the camp's administrative staff. The new commandant (for such inquiries were almost always the prelude to a change of command) was a colonel of carabinieri and considerably more strict than his predecessor. The discovery of an escape tunnel was followed by the closing of all the ground-floor sleeping rooms and consequent overcrowding elsewhere. The perimeter barbed wire was heavily guarded and equipped with searchlights and numerous machine-gun posts. Nevertheless in September a successful tunnel enabled a party of thirteen to break out, including two New Zealanders;[2] and with a little more luck the remaining 18 of the escape team would have got away too next day but the tunnel was discovered. The first party were all recaptured within three weeks and were shortly afterwards sent to Campo PG 5.

Both Padula and Poppi for many months had large numbers of medical officers and padres, far in excess of camp requirements; but it was not until July 1942, after the large increase in the numbers of prisoners and camps in Italy, that they were moved to hospitals or other ranks' camps where their services were needed.[3] Finally in October all but a few of the New Zealand officers were sent north to join their countrymen at Modena.

---
[1] Camp strength rose to about 2000 in this period.
[2] Lt J. W. C. Craig and Sgt J. A. Redpath. Redpath had assumed the rank of lieutenant when taken prisoner so that he could continue to work with Craig.
[3] Medical officers from Padula were sent to Lucca hospital.

The amenities of Campo PG 38 at Poppi, which in early 1942 held between 80 and 90 New Zealand officers and a few other ranks, remained good throughout its history, owing to a well-disposed Italian staff. The orderlies received workers' rations of bread (400 grammes) and the officers more than that supplied in most other officers' camps (200 instead of 150 grammes). Although the summer brought difficulties in the water supply, outdoor exercise and a plentiful supply of Red Cross food, together with fresh fruit and vegetables, made everyone healthy and fit. And the now regular arrival of mail[1] and parcels set at rest many of the worries that arise when contact is lost with those at home.

The Italian staff was alert to discover any activity on the part of the prisoners which might lead to an escape. Besides searches by carabinieri, the camp guards and interpreters were frequently in and out of the living quarters, and with the small numbers in the camp it was not difficult for them to detect anything suspicious. In July, however, a bold and hastily improvised attempt by two New Zealand officers[2] gave them their freedom for three weeks. They lowered themselves at dusk one evening from an upper story on a rope made from sheets tied together, having first been swung clear of an intervening barbed-wire fence by assisting officers operating inside the building. The sentry who fired at them had a faulty rifle, and in the darkness and sudden downpour of rain which quickly followed they were able to elude the numerous guards and dogs which went off in pursuit. Keeping to the hills they reached La Spezia, but were there apprehended by carabinieri and sent back to camp. Soon afterwards they were transferred to Campo PG 5, which was then receiving prisoners who had attemped to escape or had committed other breaches of discipline. In October all the remaining New Zealand officers were transferred to Campo PG 47 at Modena.

This was a new camp, both in the sense that it now housed prisoners of war for the first time and also in that it consisted of buildings completed only in 1942. They were stone barracks of the standard Italian horseshoe-shaped bungalow type, well adapted to the hot weather which predominates in the district for most of the year, though not so easily heated in winter. Bathrooms, lavatories, and shower-rooms were lavishly faced with marble, the kitchen was well fitted up with modern equipment, and there was a comfortable, well-equipped infirmary. By the end of the year the camp held about 900 officers and 200 other

---

[1] Letters were arriving from New Zealand airmail in 16 weeks on the average.
[2] Lts C. N. Armstrong (22 Bn) and A. Yeoman (21 Bn).

ranks,[1] of whom 217 officers and 20 other ranks were New Zealanders, and almost the whole of the remainder South Africans.

Food, well cooked and abundant, included large amounts of fresh vegetables; there were plenty of Red Cross food and medical comforts parcels on hand; and there was a well-stocked canteen selling a variety of articles from good watches to vermouth and other wines. The internal running of the camp was left almost entirely to the prisoners of war and was very highly organised. A library was built up from books brought from other camps, together with some local purchases and, later, books from private and Red Cross parcels. An educational scheme was soon in action, embracing classes on a wide diversity of subjects, conducted by members of various professions, including specialist teachers and university lecturers. A small stage was erected in the canteen, where an active theatre group produced a Christmas pantomime and thereafter a succession of musical and other shows. A large clay area in between the barracks provided ample space for basketball, teniquoit, even football and baseball matches, and a full-scale sports meeting. For those uninterested in games there were boxing, wrestling, and other forms of physical training, or daily walks along the roads through the pleasant countryside. In the sunny and healthy climate of the area and the stimulating atmosphere of a large group with plenty of ideas to exchange, there was no reason at Modena for physical or mental stagnation.

This all seemed too good to last, and indeed, following escape attempts by several officers in the new year (one of whom was successful in reaching Switzerland), the Italian commandant became reluctant to listen to any complaint or grant any request, whether about lighting or heating or any other matter, on the assumption that it might relate to future escape activity. Air Force officers had their uniforms taken away on the grounds that they might be used for civilian disguise. Books arrived from the censor with their covers ripped off (later merely slashed open) in case articles might be hidden in them. There were early morning searches by carabinieri of prisoners' personal effects, and regular testing of each barrack floor for tunnels, before which literally everything in the barrack had to be moved outside. During these inspections the ground outside the barrack was covered with an array of beds, stools, and the heterogeneous collections of improvised furniture and other property which prisoners acquire. Though many found these evictions irksome, they had the merit of being the occasion for 'spring-cleaning' which might otherwise have taken place only at much longer intervals.

---
[1] The ratio of orderlies allowed in Italian camps for officers was one in four, though in practice it was generally lower.

There were other annoying measures, categorised by the Italian authorities as 'reprisals' for treatment of Italians in British hands. Red patches were sewn on prisoners' clothing; rings and other valuables were confiscated. In January the officers' messing charges were raised by a 'maintenance charge' of 8·60 lire a day, to pay for the hire of the property and furniture being used. Not only was this charge made retrospective to the beginning of July 1942, but the whole of the arrears (some 1500 lire a head) was to be deducted from each officer's account in one lump sum. Most of these reprisal measures were common to other camps, though in most other officers' camps the amount of 'maintenance' arrears was at least spread over a period of some months.

Although a communication from the senior officers regarding these excessive charges was forwarded to the Swiss Legation in Rome, communications complaining of other matters, and in particular of conditions in the transit camps of North Africa, were held up indefinitely. In this, as in many other camps, the only way of ensuring delivery of such communications was to wait for the visit of a delegate and put them in his hands. In the spring of 1943, following another escape from the camp, there was a new commandant who proved more reasonable; and thereafter administrative arrangements ran more smoothly.

It took some time for matters to straighten out between the Italian authorities of Campo PG 5 at Gavi and those officers and other ranks who were transferred there in June 1942 and subsequently. The camp was described by repatriates as an 'officers' punishment camp' or 'bad boys' camp', but though the Italian military authorities would admit that *pericolosi* were sent to it, they claimed that it differed from other camps only in that it was more difficult to escape from. Certainly camp security was taken seriously, for at one period 180 officer and 50 other rank prisoners[1] were guarded by 14 Italian officers and 240 other ranks, including several carabinieri.

The 'camp' was an old castle, situated on a hill overlooking the village of Gavi, about twenty miles north-east of Genoa. Formerly used as a civil jail for criminals, its use for that purpose had been discontinued, according to some reports, because it proved too damp and unhealthy in the winter. Officers slept eight or ten to a cell twenty feet long by twelve wide, with one small barred window and one faint electric light. Like most buildings of its type it was woefully short of latrines and poorly off for water; there was no exercise space except the castle courtyards at restricted times, and even the use of the messroom was denied the prisoners.

---

[1] This remained roughly the camp strength. By December 1942 there were twelve New Zealanders at Campo PG 5.

Indeed the restrictions for the first six weeks amounted to ill-treatment: there were no letters or cards for writing home, no means of obtaining cigarettes or necessary toilet articles, no Red Cross food parcels, no walks outside the camp. A Swiss representative, who had heard of the camp's existence only by chance, visited it at the end of July, from which time some of the defects began to be remedied. But there were numerous attempts at escape, each with an adverse effect on the camp conditions and each followed by the withdrawal at least temporarily of concessions already granted.

In March 1943 the 'Generals' camp'[1] at Villa Vincigliata—Campo PG 12—was the scene of one of the most notable escapes of the war. It was notable not so much for its execution, which was matched by many other examples of clever planning and determination, but because the actual break-out was made by two generals, an air vice-marshal and three brigadiers, all above the age of most other men who attempted such exploits, and because two of the brigadiers[2] succeeded in reaching Switzerland.[3]

There had been several unsuccessful attempts to escape from the villa by one or two of the officers in the spring and summer of 1942. Finally in September entry was gained to a disused and sealed-up chapel, from which a tunnel leading into the outer garden was begun. All the officers and other ranks in the camp assisted in some way in the tunnelling and other preparations for this attempt. On a wet evening—29 March 1943—the six men went out through the completed tunnel, and by 9.30 p.m. four were on their way to the railway station to catch a night train to Milan, and the two generals had set off to walk to the Swiss border. The latter and two of the others had the misfortune to be recaptured; but the two New Zealand brigadiers travelled by train to Como, and at half past ten on the evening following the break-out they crawled through the frontier wire near Chiasso into Switzerland.

Later in the year, separately and each with the assistance of the French Resistance Movement, they reached the borders of Spain. Brigadier Hargest was able to make his way to the British consulate in Barcelona and was flown to England in December. Brigadier Miles[4] lost his life in Spain in this last stage of a game attempt to reach Allied territory.

---

[1] There were at this stage in the camp one lieutenant-general, three major-generals, one air vice-marshal, eight brigadiers, two junior officers, and 14 other ranks.
[2] Brigadiers R. Miles and J. Hargest, both of 2 NZEF.
[3] Of the 1500 attempts at escape from Italy before the armistice known to British Military Intelligence only three (including these two) are on their records as having got clear of Italy.
[4] Brig R. Miles, CBE, DSO and bar, MC, ED, m.i.d.; born Springston, 10 Dec 1892; Regular soldier; NZ Fd Arty 1914–19; CRA 2 NZ Div 1940–41; comd 2 NZEF (UK) 1940; wounded and p.w. 1 Dec 1941; died, Spain, 20 Oct 1943.

Only a comparatively small number of New Zealand other ranks were employed as orderlies in officers' camps in Italy,[1] the majority of them having gone to Chiavari or Gruppignano, or later to one of the many work-camps established throughout the country. By the summer the large camp near Chiavari, which then held some 950 New Zealanders, had considerably improved. Besides the large mess hut which was available for concerts and other recreation, gravel paths had been laid down between the huts, a hot-shower unit had been installed (though hot showers stopped in the spring through lack of fuel), and sanitation and water supply had been improved, though the latter was still liable to fail. The food rations remained on the same slender scale, but Red Cross food parcels began to arrive more frequently. Private parcels of clothing and cigarettes also began to arrive abundantly, and the camp which had had to rely largely on the regular issue of five Italian cigarettes became flush with English ones. Some of those with large quantities of cigarettes spent a good deal of time gambling with them; and the demand for such amusements was so great that a kind of gambling alley was set up where most of the better known games of chance were played.

Many spent much of their time cooking up tasty dishes made from the contents of their food parcels, on a great variety of miniature stoves made from empty tins. It was forbidden to use these inside the huts (as it was in other camps), but the commandant set aside an area in the compound where cooking might be carried out. An International Red Cross Committee delegate describes the scene thus:

> This is a characteristic picture of Camp 52—little groups of men crouching round a mess tin and giving the most serious attention to the cooking of their 'supplement' in their own little 'kitchen'. The question of fuel for these hearths, however, presents constant difficulties because wood is scarce and the prisoners find in their search for chance combustibles a scource of distraction and interest.

The shortage of fuel no doubt brought about the evolution of the 'blower', a circular fan adaptation which had the effect of a blacksmith's bellows. Owing to insufficient facilities and fuel for cooking Red Cross food in both Italy and Germany, the 'blower' played an important part in the feeding of great numbers of prisoners of war. So keen was the interest at Campo PG 52 that in July a contest was held to determine how quickly a certain quantity of water could be boiled on one of these contrivances.

The results of hobbies practised in the camp to fill in time were shown at an exhibition of arts and crafts in August. Beside

---

[1] In December 1942 there were at Modena 20 New Zealand other ranks out of 200, although more than one-fifth of the officers in the camp were New Zealanders.

numerous models, there were etchings and paintings, sculpture and tapestry work, and a great variety of utility articles, from the stoves mentioned above to spoons and teapots, slippers, knitted scarves and socks, and attaché cases. Such exhibitions were characteristic of prisoner-of-war camps in both Italy and Germany, especially non-working camps, where some form of practical manual activity helped many to get through the long hours of otherwise enforced idleness.

Though the camp space did not allow the playing of any large-scale sports, a boxing tournament excited a good deal of interest. Walks under escort outside the camp, swimming parties to the river, and a life inside the camp spent almost entirely in the open air and sunshine helped to restore men to good physical condition. The library, a full programme of educational classes, music and the theatre provided mental activity. A bulletin of 'news from home' compiled from New Zealand letters, which were beginning to take only two and a half months in transit, was circulated—an idea which had been put into practice in other camps too. Although the morale of the camp seems to have been high, there were many who were not sorry to be among the 700 selected in July[1] for farm work, with its prospects of seeing more of the country and getting better food. Parties began to leave in September for Campo PG 107—a work camp—and many others were sent to Campo PG 57 preparatory to being drafted to work. By the new year there was only a handful of New Zealanders left at Chiavari.

By September 1942, owing to transfers from other camps, the largest number of New Zealand prisoners in Italy had been concentrated in Campo PG 57 at Gruppignano.[2] In July the camp had held only 1600, including some 450 New Zealanders, and the new intake made necessary the opening up of a third compound for which the huts had recently been completed. From then on the numbers rapidly increased until in March 1943 the camp held nearly 4500 (including 1800 New Zealanders) even after some had been sent off to work-camps. Although new sleeping barracks and other necessary buildings were put up, the accommodation never kept pace with the numbers arriving, and in spite of the use of recreation barracks as sleeping quarters the camp became very overcrowded.

---

[1] In July the camp held some 950 New Zealanders.
[2] As at 30 September there were in the camp 1000 New Zealanders and 1200 Australians out of a total of some 2500. The largest transfers were from Campo PG 65 at Gravina, where the party of 300–400 from the shipwrecked *Jantzen* had been held, and from Campo PG 51 at Altamura, where a large number of new arrivals from Africa had gone.

Nevertheless most of the new arrivals at Campo PG 57, which had been represented to them by Italians as the 'best camp in Italy', felt that it satisfied at least some of their expectations. One of the shipwrecked party from the *Jantzen* notes that the camp had 'a good administrative staff' and that the 'rackets' in food experienced in previous camps were 'minimised'. Others in the party from Altamura who had been captured at Alamein mention the contrast between themselves—'lousy, bony and ragged'—and their fellow countrymen taken in the previous campaign—'cosy, clean, plump, and well-dressed in full British battle dress'; and the terms used, though perhaps somewhat exaggerated, express a contrast that was real. The newcomers mention the gifts of food and clothing they received, and the 'fine spirit which existed throughout that camp'. Another man who had spent his previous period of captivity in transit-camp tents was impressed with the 'neat huts': and another still, who had been in Greece at Salonika, Larissa, and Patras, thought it the 'best place [he] had been at for any period since [he] was first captured'.

By July 1942 a large number of the new sleeping huts with plenty of light and fresh air had been completed (as well as four intended for recreation), the sanitation had been made more efficient, and the water supply improved. Each of the compounds had its own kitchen, latrines, ablutions, and place for washing clothes, and was controlled by a senior prisoner NCO with a small staff. There were plenty of Red Cross food parcels on hand, and those who had lost weight in transit camps began to replace it rapidly. The canteen was well stocked and parcels of tobacco were beginning to arrive freely from New Zealand House and private sources. Letter mail from New Zealand itself was taking only two and a half months.

A small library of educational books had been built up and there was a large variety of general reading matter. All kinds of classes had been arranged, though among our men those in agriculture, accountancy, and languages seem to have had the greatest following. There were art, music, and drama groups; and individuals filled in their time with a variety of crafts, from knitting and crocheting to wood-carving and making objects from tin. For some time those who had wished had been able to cultivate flower and vegetable gardens within the camp bounds, seeds having originally been provided by the camp authorities. The arrival in the summer of 1942 of some cases of sports material sent by the World Alliance of YMCAs enabled full use to be made of the large area available for sport, and baseball, soccer, cricket, volley-ball, and deck tennis all had their following.

The Italian commandant, of whom some mention has already been made, prided himself on maintaining strict 'discipline'. For not standing to attention at the lowering or hoisting of the huge Italian flag at the camp gates, for not saluting an Italian officer, for talking during check parade, or for not wearing sufficient clothing near the perimeter fence (apparently considered an incitement to indecent assault) the punishment was 30 days in solitary confinement. Some claim that the commandant kept the cells almost always full as a matter of policy, and that they were emptied to some extent only during the visit of a neutral delegate or of a papal representative, or on the occasion of some happy event in the Italian royal family. Nor was brutality discouraged among his subordinates: the camp has a record of handcuffing, 'beating-up', and shootings and woundings at least as bad as that at Bari. And although one of the New Zealanders killed there was shot dead while cutting the wire for an escape, another who walked across the trip-wire in broad daylight in his pyjamas was obviously at the time mentally unbalanced and could easily have been apprehended.

The perimeter defences of the camp were exceptional: a squared barbed-wire fence 17 feet high, followed by a double concertina obstacle, and then a high double-apron fence of barbed wire with concertina wire under each apron. The whole length was lit by powerful arc-lights at close intervals and manned by frequent machine-gun posts, as well as by moving sentries. The commandant took pride in the fact that no one had been able to escape. On the night of 29 October, however, 19 Australians and New Zealanders broke out of the camp through a tunnel planned by two senior warrant officers. The tunnel—about 150 feet long—had been dug over a period of months, with great attention to secrecy even from the other prisoners in the camp; for it was found by experience that, especially in a large mixed camp, even if there was no one of doubtful loyalty, there were always some who through various kinds of indiscretion could not be relied on.

There was consternation among the Italian staff when the break-out was discovered at roll-call on the following morning, and there followed a hue and cry involving large numbers of troops in the district. Most of the escapers made their way across country in pairs, some heading for Switzerland and others for Yugoslavia, but all were recaptured in five days. Some of them spent long periods in the cells, part of the time in chains, and on release were housed in a special barrack and subjected for a while to special checks every two hours. The rest of the camp, too, came in for its share of what was described by a Protecting Power representative as ' severe control and surveillance '. Searches similar to those described in connection with Campo PG 47 at Modena, involving the complete evacuation of each barrack and the taking up of sections of the flooring, occurred every week regardless of the weather. The prisoners were sometimes called out to check parade at past midnight. When taxed by a neutral delegate with the illegality of such treatment under international law, the commandant gave the arrogant reply that he proposed to continue it until he was satisfied that the prisoners were no longer secretly planning to escape.

Fortunately the winter turned out to be mild. Although the allowance of blankets was sufficient, there were few heating stoves in the barracks and only enough fuel to keep them going for about two hours each evening. Conditions in the cells were especially severe in winter, as they were not heated in any way, and prisoners slept on bare boards with one blanket only. Supplies of Red Cross food parcels failed owing to the breakdown in the transport arrangements through southern France, and the International Red Cross Committee warned all camps to issue at the rate of half a parcel a week as from 1 December. Some men who had not sufficiently recovered from previous privations broke down in health as a result of this additional food shortage; there were a good many cases of beriberi and a disproportionate number of deaths both in the camp and in the local hospital.

In February the supply of parcels again became ample, day after day of sunny weather made possible almost unlimited sport and sunbathing, and most of the camp population became physically fit. When medical inspections were held to determine who were fit enough to go out on a work-party, few were rejected. Because of a lack of volunteers for these labour camps a party of 300 had been detailed in October,[1] and a ballot for another party had been held in December. From then on parties began to leave for work on various construction jobs in the district, mainly with pick and shovel; and in the spring and summer of 1943 considerable numbers left Campo PG 57 for agricultural work, both in the neighbourhood of Gruppignano and as far afield as the upper reaches of the Po in north-western Italy.

Unlike Nazi Germany, Fascist Italy did not immediately employ British prisoners of war as an auxiliary labour force, although she was perfectly entitled to do so under international law. Instead British prisoners merely did their own camp fatigues, or work necessary for the erection of additional barracks in

---

[1] This party had no medical inspection, and several had later to be returned as unfit for work.

their camp, or an occasional odd job in the locality that did not involve sleeping away from their quarters. The reasons for this are not clear. But it was probably the strain on prison-camp accommodation in the summer of 1942, combined with German encouragement, which brought about the formation of work detachments living apart from but still under the administration of the main camp. There is some evidence that German officers experienced in the organisation of work by prisoners of war and in the running of work detachments visited Italy at this period in an advisory capacity, for Germany had been employing prisoners for some two and a half years. At first the detachments were small (about 50-odd) and were employed mostly at farms and vineyards, especially at harvest time, though some were employed on the construction of new prisoner-of-war camps. In late 1942, however, the Fascist Government began to realise the value of such a reserve of unskilled labour for engineering and industrial projects as well as farming, particularly when the drain on their own manpower became heavier. But by the time the Italian authorities had really got round to organising the employment of the masses of fit men held in their prisoner-of-war camps on work useful to the Italian economy, and had begun to set up completely independent work-camps in the areas where they were most needed, the regime was collapsing and with it the whole Italian war effort.

The first of the independent work-camps set up in Italy was Campo PG 107 at Torviscosa. In September 1942 a large party was transferred from Chiavari; in October another 300 were sent off from Gruppignano; and by the end of the year further parties from these two camps had brought the total of the new camp to a thousand, over 600 of them New Zealanders and the remainder South Africans. In the spring more men were transferred to the strength of Campo PG 107, but almost all went to its sub-camps, some of which were a considerable distance from Torviscosa.

The town, and the prisoner-of-war camp about a mile away, were situated in low-lying swamp country in a plain that lies at the extreme northern end of the Adriatic. It was about twenty miles from the sea, with Udine about fifteen miles to the north, and, beyond, the Julian and Venetian Alps. There was a large factory in the town for the manufacture of cellulose fabrics from cane that was grown on land reclaimed from swamp. Prisoners of war were used in the task of draining and levelling the swamp area, constructing roads through it, and later cutting the cane and preparing it for despatch to the factory. They were paid by the company at the rate of three lire a day,[1] in addition to their normal pay from the Italian Army authorities, and received double the normal ration of bread and macaroni and extra cheese.

The camp itself comprised an area of about 200 by 100 yards, and contained ten brick sleeping huts besides cookhouse, infirmary, showers, and recreation huts. One of the last had for a long time to be used as extra sleeping accommodation owing to the overcrowding in those originally intended as dormitories. Beds consisted of long shelves three tiers high, allowing a space of a little over six feet by two and a half feet for each man and his possessions. There was a good water supply, though the ablution benches were not protected against bad weather, and rain also converted the camp area into something like the ground of a pigsty. There were no heaters in the sleeping barracks, and there was an almost continual shortage of fuel for cooking and heating in other buildings.

After an early morning drink of coffee substitute, the men were counted out the gate by 7.15 a.m. and marched along the road to the fields where they worked. They were organised in parties of a hundred under a foreman and three or four overseers, and worked with pick, shovel, and wheelbarrow at first, digging drains or small canals and levelling off the areas so drained. Winter working hours were 8 a.m. to 12 p.m. and 1 p.m. to 3 p.m., but in summer the hours were increased to ten. The prisoners were not overworked, but each had to wear a metal disc with a number on it so that he could be reported by the overseers if necessary. As it turned out the latter were found to be only too willing to do an illicit trade in food and wine for cigarettes and soap, and to retail items of news they had heard over the BBC. There was little hope of escape from the fields, as the area was well ringed by guards and thoroughly searched when the party lined up to return to camp.

As many of the men first drafted from Campo PG 57 were still suffering from their initial period of undernourishment, the decision of the original camp commandant to restrict the issue of Red Cross food parcels to one every three weeks almost produced a camp strike. What the leaders of the New Zealand party finally decided to do was to go out to the fields but refuse to work when they got there. This resulted in the company blaming the military authorities for managing the prisoners badly; and as there was already no love lost between the directors of the business and the Army, the commandant was replaced and the

---

[1] This rate was laid down for working camps by the Italian Ministry of War, and raised to 4·50 lire as from 1 February 1943.

prisoners thereafter received one parcel a week so long as supplies lasted. The new commandant seems to have been 'a very fair man', and he did what he could to look after the welfare of the prisoners.

Mail began to arrive from New Zealand in about two months in 1943, and clothing parcels, although taking longer, were coming in well; so that with cigarette parcels from London and private food parcels from the Middle East, the inmates of Campo PG 107 did quite well for relief supplies. Work on the swamp area played havoc with clothes and at first there was a shortage, but ample consignments from the International Red Cross Committee in 1943 remedied this. They were not so well off for sporting and other recreational material as other camps, though in the spring they were able to play soccer and baseball and to open a proper library. In the winter they had had concerts, including one devoted to Maori songs and hakas. But as the Swiss representative pointed out, they did not have so much time for sport as in non-working camps. It was symptomatic of working camps, too, that the need for mental distraction was not so great; for, in the camp leader's words, 'the majority vastly preferred work with all its fatigue to inaction in a camp'.

The seven sub-camps of Campo PG 107 formed in the spring of 1943 were smaller parties employed on agricultural labour. Campo PG 107/4, for example, on a state farm at San Dona di Piave on the Adriatic coast north of Venice, consisted of 50 New Zealanders employed on haymaking, weeding, and digging. Their quarters were cramped though quite comfortable, and they did well for food on the farm, after the same fashion as their compatriots at farm *Arbeitskommandos* in Germany. In such small groups it was possible to obtain concessions from the guards by organised going slow at work, concerted action of a kind that would be hard to organise in a large camp containing men of different nationalities.

In mid-December another offshoot of Campo PG 57 was formed by the transfer of some 250 New Zealanders to a new working camp near Bussolengo, about twenty miles north of Verona. They were employed on pick-and-shovel labour in the building of a canal, which was part of a large hydro-electric scheme using the waters of the Adige River. The river itself ran just below the camp and, together with far-stretching fields of grape-vines and orchards, provided the camp with a view of unusual beauty. Prisoners worked in squads of 25 and were engaged in filling trucks with spoil for most of their working day. This was six hours in winter and nine in summer, though a New Year decree made eight hours the minimum working day for all Italian workmen as well as for prisoners of war.

To house the prisoners new stone barracks had been built, containing three-tier wooden shelf-bunks similar to those at Torviscosa; cookhouse, ablutions, messroom, canteen, infirmary, and detention cells were in a separate block. The canteen was well stocked, and there were occasionally extra issues of wine, as at Christmas when the prisoners were allowed four days for celebrations. Though mail, both inward and outward, took longer in a work detachment than in one of the main camps, consignments of Red Cross food and clothing arrived fairly well at Bussolengo. A neutral inspector remarked that, apart from the satisfaction of the extra worker's rations, the men at such working camps seemed happier.

A smaller party of New Zealanders, together with South Africans, had gone to work under similar conditions on almost identical work at Campo PG 129 near Macerata, not long before the draft left for Bussolengo. In the spring Campo PG 148 became a base for small agricultural working camps in the district, in much the same way as Campo PG 107. At the same time about a hundred more New Zealanders went from Gruppignano to Campo PG 120, newly formed in the neighbourhood of Padua for similar farm work, with eight detachments. About 150 others went still farther afield to the neighbourhood of Vercelli, 50 miles north-east of Turin, where a new series of over twenty labour detachments, given the base number 106,[1] was being set up. At Arro (Salussola) Campo PG 106/20 provided labour from among some eighty New Zealanders and twenty Australians for five nearby rice farms on the Piedmont plains. The prisoners were housed on their return from work in a disused cow-byre, where they were plagued by swarms of mosquitoes. As at many of the other work detachments on farms, the improvised sleeping quarters were very crowded, and the sole source of water was a pump and trough. At most of them, too, there were long delays in the arrival of Red Cross supplies and in sending on mail that had gone to their previous camp at Gruppignano. The bad living conditions produced sit-down strikes at more than one of these camps, one occurring on the day of a Swiss delegate's visit. There was little attempt to escape at this stage, most men realising that the end of the war for Italy was near, and that when it came opportunities would be much more favourable.

In the spring the Italians began to use prisoner-of-war labour for pick-and-shovel work on the roads in more remote districts.

---

[1] Nearly all the New Zealanders were at Campo PG 106/19 and Campo PG 106/20.

New Zealanders at Campo PG 103/6 near Ampezzo and at Campo PG 103/7 near La Maina, among the Dolomites, were engaged in the construction of new roads for a hydro-electric scheme. Prisoners' letters speak enthusiastically of the magnificent air and fine mountain scenery at their new situation. Both camps seem to have had sympathetic commandants and to have given the prisoners good food. The quarters of the camp at Ampezzo though rough were adequate, and the compound had space for a basketball court. One of the hundred New Zealanders who lived there from May to September 1943 sums up their four or five months working in the mountains as ' that period of our P.O.W. existence when good living conditions, an able camp leader and a sympathetic Italian Commandant made life for us more or less tolerable.' It is not the first example of a camp in which good conditions coincided with the presence of a capable leader. The latter had to be scrupulously fair to all his fellow prisoners, energetic in looking after their interests, and able to handle the enemy guards with firmness and tact.

Mention has already been made of the party of 200 New Zealand prisoners transferred from Tuturano in May 1943 to Campo PG 78/1 at Aquafredda, in the hills to the north-east of Sulmona but near enough to come under Campo PG 78 for administration. The camp was 2000 feet up among the Abruzzi; the work was making a road with picks and shovels and carrying rails and posts connected with the operation of a stone quarry. The buildings were clean and new, but there were at first only poor rations and no stock of Red Cross food parcels. As these supplies came to hand, illicit trading with guards and civilians made it possible for the prisoners to supplement their diet. And whatever the drawbacks of navvying and roughing it among the Italian mountains, a good many of the men had reason later to be thankful for being in a place remote from a main camp and in the high country away from a town. For when the armistice came they were in a most favourable situation to reach the Allied lines, and large numbers of them were able to regain their liberty.

The seriously wounded and sick from hospitals at Matruh, Tobruk, and Benghazi received good treatment on the hospital ships which brought them to Italy, some landing at Reggio di Calabria and going on to Caserta hospital, others at Bari and going to the hospital there. Together with some of the survivors of shipwrecks and the sick from existing prisoner-of-war camps in Italy, they made a total of British prisoner patients far in excess of the hospital accommodation available for them. Although rooms and sometimes wards were set aside in Italian military hospitals to accommodate them, the need for further space necessitated the setting up of special hospitals for prisoners of war at Bergamo and Lucca in July 1942, and later at Bologna, Altamura, and Nocera. At the same time most of the surplus British medical officers and chaplains were transferred from officers' camps to the newly opened hospitals, or to those already established which had set aside portions for prisoners of war.

The overcrowding at Caserta hospital in the latter half of 1942 caused a considerable falling off in food and medical attention, though men still spoke of being well treated and, theoretically at any rate, they were on the same rations as the Italian patients.[1] There were at the hospital 15 captured British medical officers who worked under trying conditions, as their actions were under constant supervision by the Italian medical staff, who if necessary could overrule them. In November 1942, in spite of the transfer of over 400 British prisoner patients to Bologna and Nocera, there still remained 1300 or more. Many others were moved on in the month following and Caserta came to be regarded as a 'clearing hospital', some patients passing on after two or three weeks, though others stayed for several months.

Bari military hospital had imposing new buildings set in beautiful gardens, three wards being allocated to prisoners. Here also, in spite of a fine-looking ration scale, there was a severe shortage of food, made all the worse by the complete absence, at least up till May 1942, of any Red Cross food parcels. There had been armed sentries in the wards and excessive restrictions on the use of latrines and washrooms, though conditions had improved later in the year. By contrast, in the wing of Parma hospital reserved for British prisoners, run mainly by Italian nuns, the patients were well treated and had plenty of food and cigarettes, though much of the latter were Red Cross supplies. The military hospital at Morigi di Piacenza had two wards set aside for prisoners, where although there were shortages at first, conditions by 1943 were pronounced 'first-class'. Sick prisoners from Campo PG 57 at Gruppignano were sent to the Ospedale Vescovile in Udine, the converted upper floor of an ecclesiastical seminary. Sometimes where numbers were few, patients would go to the military or civilian hospital in the nearest town of any size, those from Campo PG 38 at Poppi going to Arezzo.

---

[1] The military hospital daily ration scale given to a Swiss representative in May 1942 was:

Bread	400 grammes	Vegetables	800 grammes
Meat	400 grammes	Salad	150 grammes
or Poultry	500 grammes	Fruit	200 grammes
or Fish	300 grammes	Wine	¼ litre

It is clear from accounts by prisoners of war in Italian hospitals during 1942, and from their dependence on food from Red Cross parcels, that they received only a fraction of this ration.

Of the new hospitals for prisoners of war only, Ospedale PG 201 at Bergamo opened in mid-July in what had been an old people's home. It was a huge, modern building with excellent equipment, and though not all of it was given up to the prisoner-of-war hospital, there was space for separate wards for officers, severely wounded, lightly wounded, and sick. By the end of the year there were over 300 patients, mostly from Bari and Caserta. All treatment was by British medical officers and orderlies, though under Italian control, and there were Sisters of Mercy attached for domestic duties. Plenty of Red Cross supplies enabled a high standard of diet to be maintained.

At Lucca, Ospedale PG 202 was also opened in July 1942. Once a civilian hospital, it soon held 530 prisoner patients with 13 British doctors and 104 orderlies to look after them. The hospital was fairly well equipped and supplied with drugs, and the Italian medical staff did their best for the patients. Although the British medical officers were at first hampered in their duties by the same supervision on the part of some local Italian medical officers that we have seen elsewhere, they gradually took over most of the surgery and curative treatment, with beneficial results to the patients. Cures were greatly helped by the addition of Red Cross food to the diet. Red Cross supplies of books and games helped prisoners to pass the time more easily while they were inmates of the hospital, and supplies of British uniforms and underclothing enabled them to be discharged properly clad.

Castel San Pietro military hospital at Bologna, established in a large school building among pleasant fields and vineyards and renamed Ospedale PG 203 when set aside for prisoners, was similarly well equipped, and the treatment and food for the 450-odd patients in January 1943 gave no ground for complaint. A smaller hospital for prisoners was established at Piacenza in an old palace belonging formerly to the Alberoni family. By January 1943 it held some sixty wounded British prisoners, who were looked after by an Italian medical staff assisted by nuns.

One of the chief discomforts suffered by prisoners of war in hospitals in the early days of 1942 had been insufficient heating in the wards. Constant pressure by our own medical officers as well as neutral inspectors had some effect, and a Swiss report notes in January 1943 that Bologna hospital was if anything rather overheated. For clothing many of the earlier patients had to be content with a shirt, though proper hospital suits were later issued to them. Mail was very slow in reaching almost all the hospitals, chiefly due to delay in readdressing; and sometimes the accumulation of months arrived all at once. Some hospitals had to rely on the nearest camp for their Red Cross supplies, and arrangements for regular consignments often took some time. For tobacco and recreational material all the hospitals had mainly to rely on such supplies, though playing cards and language textbooks were often bought for them locally. British chaplains did useful work at many of the hospitals in organising concerts, talks, and other entertainments. Apart from these, men spent their time in yarning, playing bridge, reading, and studying languages.

Owing to the lack of provision for either artificial limbs or re-education centres for disabled prisoners, and to the crowded state of the hospitals, many amputees and other disabled men were discharged as soon as their wounds were healed and sent off to a camp. Most of these men and other serious cases had their names sent forward by our medical officers for submission to the Mixed Medical Commission. After the first repatriation operation in April 1942 the Commission had continued with the examination of cases brought to its notice. Unfortunately, owing to occasional arbitrary action by some local camp authorities, a number of repatriable prisoners were sometimes not permitted to see the Commission despite energetic protests.[1]

Negotiations with Italy for a further exchange of prisoners dragged on through the latter half of 1942 without definite results. British proposals regarding a scale for the retention of protected personnel met with the Italian argument that it would be unfair to lay down a hard and fast scale regardless of climate and other factors, and that the number should be related to the amount of medical and dental work to be done in the particular area. On the other hand an Italian request that prisoners so mutilated as to be obviously incapable of further employment in the armed forces should be repatriated without the formality of an examination was at first rejected, as it was felt that such cases would all come before the Commission and be disposed of immediately. In December there was a considerable interchange of telegrams, and by March agreement had been reached on most of the main points. About the same time the Vatican, whose delegate had during his Christmas visits seen in the prisoner-of-war camps and hospitals of Italy cases of blindness, mutilation, tuberculosis and beriberi, expressed concern that their repatriation had been so long delayed and asked both countries to do what they could to hasten it.

Eventually in early April 1943 the men selected in Italy were notified, and after hearty and sometimes hilarious farewells from their fellow prisoners who were remaining, those bound for Smyrna and the Middle East left to assemble in Ospedale PG 204 at Altamura, and those bound for Lisbon and the United Kingdom

---

[1] Article 70 of the Geneva Convention of 1929 gave any prisoner the right to go before the Commission if he makes such a request to the camp medical officer.

in Ospedale 202 at Lucca. About 150 sick and wounded (including 44 New Zealanders) left Bari on 10 April on the Italian hospital ship *Gradisca,* on board which as on the previous occasion they were very well treated. The exchange for 1211 Italians took place in Smyrna Harbour on 19 April under the supervision of the IRCC delegates. The British hospital ships *Talamba* and *Tairea* brought our repatriates back to Alexandria after three days at sea spent, to quote one repatriate, in ' eating, drinking, and talking [their] heads off '. A hospital train supplied with every comfort and Red Cross amenity took them from the disembarkation port to Cairo. The United Kingdom party went by train from Italy to Lisbon, where they embarked on the British hospital ship *Newfoundland* on 18 April, arriving in England on the 23rd. Among the 300-odd British sick and wounded and 130 protected personnel were the former Senior Chaplain[1] and 14 other New Zealanders with next-of-kin in the United Kingdom.

The *Talamba* and *Tairea* returned with the *Cap Saint Jacques* to Smyrna on 9 May for the second flight, with 400 Italian sick and wounded and 2000-odd protected personnel. They brought back to Alexandria on 13 May some 150 British sick and wounded (including twelve New Zealanders) and 350 protected personnel (including 96 New Zealanders). Some NZASC transport drivers attached to medical units were fortunate enough to secure inclusion in both these flights. A third party exchanged at Smyrna on 2 June consisted of 2676 Italians and 430-odd British (140 sick and wounded and 290 protected personnel), some of whom had been passed by the Commission in Italy during a supplementary tour made after the commencement of the operations for the first flight. In this last party, which disembarked at Alexandria on 6 June, were four New Zealand sick and six protected personnel. Even after this large repatriation movement, involving the exchange of some 1630 British for upwards of 5700 Italians, there still remained in Italy a number of prisoners with amputations and eye injuries, as well as cases of tuberculosis and other diseases giving grounds for repatriation. Negotiations began almost immediately for a further exchange in the autumn, just too late, as it turned out, to avoid getting caught up with the march of events.

II: *Escapers in Greece*

Reference was made in the chapter on the Greece and Crete campaigns to the number of British troops who remained at large in Greece[2] during its occupation first by the Germans and

---
[1] Rt. Rev. G. V. Gerard, CBE, MC, m.i.d.
[2] See pp. 72–5 and 80–2. The subsequent history of those at large in Crete, being shorter and unconnected with Italians, was dealt with in that chapter. See pp. 66–72.

later by the Italians. It was seen that a good many were able to make their escape to neutral Turkey or to Allied territory by boat within a month or two of the end of the campaigns; others had the misfortune to be recaptured within the same period, or if they had previously evaded capture, to be made prisoners for the first time. Some of these again escaped before being sent to Germany; added to a core of evaders who had been at large since the remnants of the Allied forces had disintegrated after the end of the sea evacuation, they made up a considerable number who remained 'loose' in Greece for a year or more after April 1941, and a few even until the British liberation of Greece in 1944.

Although in the days following the cessation of fighting in Greece many of our men, like some of the evaders from the action at Corinth Canal, were able to live more or less openly (even in uniform for a short time), it was not long before enemy efforts to round up British Commonwealth soldiers forced them into the hills. In the latter months of 1941 they were broadly in three areas: the hills of the Peloponnese; the hills behind Megara and Athens, with some men hidden among the populations of Athens and Piraeus; the hills and coast of the Chalcidike peninsula and its three fingers east of Salonika, together with odd ones who had returned west and got as far south as the Larissa plain. In the southern Peloponnese were evaders from the British forces not evacuated, together with others who had made their way from Crete either in launches or by rowing, as one New Zealander and an Australian did. In the northern Peloponnese and the hills behind Megara were evaders from the Corinth action, remnants left behind from the evacuation or survivors from the evacuation ship *Nea Hellas* which blew up near the shore, and escapers from the Corinth and Athens prisoner-of-war camps. There were many of the latter, too, living in Athens as civilians among the Greeks, helped by the Greek underground and waiting for the opportunity to get away by boat. Almost all those in the north were escapers from Salonika transit camp or from the trains taking them to Germany, though a few had made their way up from the south hoping to get overland to Turkey. Some, disappointed in this hope and also in that of being taken off by boat from the coast east of Salonika, trekked on foot down the eastern hills in the hope of finding better luck at Volos or a more southern port. Lastly there were a few on various islands of the Sporades and Cyclades groups in the Aegean who had accomplished the first stage of the journey to Turkey or North Africa and were awaiting the opportunity to complete it.

Without the active help of the Greek population these men could not have remained at large for long. Greek families fed them from their own increasingly scanty food supplies, fitted them out with civilian clothes and, when the cold of winter approached, either sheltered them temporarily in their own homes or provided them with blankets and other necessities to enable them to live in a cave or an improvised hut. Many an escaped prisoner who had contracted malaria owed his life to the care of a friendly Greek family which looked after him until he was well enough to move on. Some who spent the bitter winter cold of 1941 and early 1942 above the snowline, were able to do so only because of the food and other generous help they received from Greek shepherds and other hill people. Sometimes these brave and simple village folk were able to smuggle parties of prisoners away to Turkey or guide them to Athens, where better arrangements could be made for them. An underground organisation with its headquarters in Athens supplied those who came to its notice with everyday necessities as well as money, and where possible reimbursed Greeks who were feeding and helping British soldiers.

Of the escapers who reached the Middle East, a good number volunteered to go back and help extricate their comrades still seeking a way out, and a few (including four New Zealanders)[1] were selected for an organisation known as 'A' Force.[2] Under one scheme, members of 'A' Force were landed on an island and made their way to Greece with money and stores to aid the Greek underground in its work of sabotage, helping prisoners, and generally resisting the occupation. They stayed on the mainland to collect a party of prisoners and then returned with them to their island base to be evacuated. Two of the New Zealanders (Craig and Redpath) were caught during one of these trips in January 1942 by a large Italian launch patrol, and after a period in noisome island prisons and a lengthy interrogation, were sent to Bari as prisoners of war.

In spite of such setbacks aid from the Middle East continued, and the Italian occupation forces became alarmed by the increasing activities of bands of armed Greek partisans which had begun operating from the hills in the summer of 1941. Knowing that the Greek underground had active support from the British, they launched a campaign in 1942 to round up all British soldiers who were at large and to punish Greeks who had sheltered and aided them. Rewards of food for the betrayal of a British

---

[1] Lt J. W. C. Craig and Sgts A. H. Empson, T. Moir, and J. A. Redpath.
[2] In the rescue of escapers 'A' Force worked in conjunction with the Middle East branch of MI9.

soldier were offered to the now starving Greeks, where the German forces had during their occupation offered money. Stool-pigeons (some of them Greek-speaking Italians) were planted among the Greek population, and even men posing as escaped British soldiers. Pressure was brought on the Greek police[1] to assist the occupation forces; and Italian patrols of soldiers and carabinieri (sometimes in civilian clothes) were continually active. Besides the sacrifice of sharing their meagre food supplies with one or more British soldiers, a Greek family, if suspected, often had their house searched or pillaged; if caught, they were sent to one or other of the horrible concentration camps which had been set up in Greece. Yet Greek help, though much more cautious in the later stages, continued until the end of the occupation; and 'the vast majority of the Greek population, even under circumstances of extreme hardship, repudiated all collaboration'.[2]

The few Greeks who gave way to greed or fear of starvation were responsible for the capture of many British soldiers who had been at large. During 1942 some of our men had to give themselves up through illness and shortage of food, but many others were betrayed. One New Zealander was sold by the mayor of a small village for four and a half pounds of flour. Most of those taken at this stage were in civilian clothes and therefore not recognised by the Italian authorities as prisoners of war. After passing through various local jails, some extremely dirty and crowded, they were usually taken to the huge Averoff civil prison at Athens.

This prison was largely run by the Italian authorities, though there was a German section for their own deserters and some political prisoners. It was of the traditional type: courtyards leading into a five-storied building with rows of iron partitions and cells. Conditions had at first been universally bad, but in early 1942 under a new commandant they began to improve. Some of the cells became reasonably comfortable, there were showers, and at intervals the British received Red Cross food parcels. Certainly the Italian ration of bread and thin soup was little enough to live on, and many of the 1200 or so Greek political prisoners had to be helped with parcels sent in to them by relatives and friends. Some of these people were awaiting trial for having sheltered British soldiers.

---

[1] The Greek police were in general only too willing to help British soldiers, but were later forced to arrest them if they were betrayed by a 'Quisling' Greek. Those who did not ran the risk of being denounced by the same man and sent to concentration camps. Many were.
[2] Report on Greece by the Supreme Allied Commander, Mediterranean, to the Combined Chiefs of Staff, 1949.

One or two New Zealanders and others attempted to escape but were caught and given a period in the dungeons. These, as their name implied, were below ground, dark, filthy and wet. There was no semblance of a latrine, but once in a dungeon the prisoner was allowed out only at the caprice of his guard until his sentence—sometimes of a month or more—was up. After several weeks cooped up in these vile conditions men emerged broken, lousy, and covered with scabies which had turned into running sores. Many of the British who had passed through Averoff were interrogated, some as many as twenty times, often to the accompaniment of beatings up by carabinieri, to persuade them to disclose the names of Greeks who had helped them and the whereabouts of other British soldiers. Some had been tried by an Italian military court, usually on charges of espionage, sabotage, or armed insurrection. Some were sentenced to death,[1] others to long terms of imprisonment. A New Zealander who had been condemned to death in October 1942 had his sentence commuted later to 30 years' imprisonment, and was sent off to Bari and later to a penitentiary at Sulmona to serve it.[2]

Some went from Averoff straight to Patras to await shipment to Italy; others to the Italian-run concentration camps at Xilocastron or Larissa. They travelled under very strong guard, nearly always handcuffed, sometimes in pairs. The concentration camp near Larissa was, in the summer of 1942, crowded with Greek political prisoners, including women and children put there, after confiscation of their property, because one of the family was fighting with the partisans. The fenced-in area covered eight acres or more, on which were some buildings, dirty and infested with lice. Some of the British prisoners who had been sentenced to long terms of imprisonment for 'sabotage' or 'espionage' were in a main compound with the Greeks, but the 'less dangerous' prisoners of war were in a small compound of their own. The camp food was far too meagre to maintain health, and it was fortunate that the Greek Red Cross and occasionally the International Red Cross delegate were able to visit the camp and distribute food and clothing. Many Greeks who did not receive any gifts of food from outside simply died of malnutrition, just as their fellow countrymen died in the streets of Athens from the same cause. The internal guards of the camp carried three-foot rubber whips to enforce discipline. On one occasion in the midsummer of 1942 a New Zealand private soldier and a British

---

[1] Only one death sentence was carried out on a New Zealand soldier at Averoff.
[2] He and another New Zealander under a 16-year sentence awarded in Greece were liberated, together with other British prisoners, when British officers from Campo PG 78 opened up the penitentiary after the Italian Armistice.

officer, who were caught while attempting to escape, were tied to posts and given 40 lashes each before a parade of the whole camp, while some of the guards shouted their applause. Both men were nearly unconscious at the end of it and had to have medical treatment.

Eventually all the prisoners of war were sent to Patras, where they were housed in the cells of an Italian artillery barracks. Though rations were poor, treatment was more humane, and one New Zealander who had a spell in the Patras hospital received nothing but kindness and friendliness from the Italians there. In 1942, when these parties of former escapers and evaders were being transported to Italy, the waters of the southern Adriatic were becoming increasingly hazardous for Italian shipping. One of the ships taking prisoners across to Italy was sunk in January 1943, a New Zealand officer losing his life.[1] The other New Zealanders went to prisoner-of-war camps in Italy, and found life easy after the hardships of living in hungry Greece or being confined in noisome prisons by the occupation forces.

Although in 1942 few got away from Greece (compared with the numbers who succeeded in 1941) and many fell into the hands of the occupation forces, some remained hidden by the Greeks for periods up to three and a half years. Hunted and often half starving, they held on in the hope of gaining contact with an escape organisation and, as the war took a more and more favourable turn, of seeing the occupation forces go. The activity of 'A' Force increased and it developed into a clandestine military mission on Greek soil, recruiting helpers from among the escapers and evaders who knew the language, the geography, the people, and the whereabouts of many of the British soldiers in hiding. Two New Zealanders,[2] one an escaper from a train going north from Corinth and the other an evader, were able to get in touch with this military mission in early 1943. They stayed on to work with it until the following year, helping to organise the evacuation of parties of escapers and evaders.

One New Zealand soldier,[3] who was among those evacuated in August 1943 on a caique arranged by the British Military

---

[1] The only other New Zealander on the ship was Cpl F. I. A. Woollams (19 Bn). He had evaded capture in Greece for 18 months, survived the torpedoing, and after some months in Italy as a prisoner of war he got away from Campo P.G 78/1 at the time of the armistice. He reached Allied lines at Palmoli on 7 November 1943. For his attempts to escape he was mentioned in despatches.

[2] WO II L. N. Northover (19 Bn) escaped from a train in June 1941 and worked for the British Military Mission from March 1943 to August 1944. Sgt R. A. Hooper (1 NZ Gen Hosp) evaded capture and worked for the British Military Mission from April 1943 to January 1944. Both were awarded the MM.

[3] Pte R. J. Nielsen (19 Bn).

Mission, had evaded capture after the action at Corinth bridge and had been sheltered and fed by Greek shepherds north of Megara. Later he had moved to Athens and, in spite of a short spell in Averoff jail, had contrived to live as a Greek in a house there until he made contact with the escape organisation.

Another had made two escapes from the Galatas camp on Crete, had reached the Peloponnese in a caique, and was helped there by Greek villagers. After a series of narrow escapes from Italian troops and pro-Axis collaborators, he lived for eight months in late 1942 and early 1943 in a small hiding-place under a flagstone in the floor of the cottage whose occupants had befriended him. His food was lowered down to him, and when the light was good enough he passed the time by reading a Greek child's primer. When he was at length rescued by the British Military Mission and smuggled away to Turkey on a caique in June 1943, he had temporarily lost the use of his legs and was in a very weak physical condition.[1]

In 1944 there still remained in Greece and the islands of the Aegean a few Commonwealth troops who, though unable to make good their escape, were determined not to be captured. Some had been wary of having anything to do with an escape organisation, as the occupation authorities had quite early begun to plant bogus 'agents' who promised to help British soldiers but betrayed those who unsuspectingly took them for what they claimed to be. Nevertheless the military mission continued to get away small parties in early 1944. In September it evacuated a New Zealander[2] who had lived for three years and four months on the island of Kythera.

Finally, in October, when the Axis occupation of Greece came to an end, the British Military Mission was able to unearth those with whom it had previously been unable to make contact, and the men who had stuck it out for the whole period of the occupation were at last evacuated to Allied territory.

III: *Prisoners of War in Germany*

While this period saw the British prisoner-of-war population in Italy increase by many thousands,[3] in Germany, apart from those captured in the Dieppe and other raids on the French coast, there were practically no new Army prisoners, only a steady trickle of naval personnel, and larger numbers of airmen. So far as prisoner-of-war camps for Army personnel are concerned the period was one of sorting out, of tightening up security,

---
[1] Sigmn F. Amos (Div Sigs), awarded MM for his 'unflagging determination to escape'.
[2] Pte I. C. Curley (22 Bn).
[3] The increase of New Zealanders in Italian hands was approximately 2000.

and of reprisals, coupled with some co-ordinated attempts by Axis powers to use prisoners as a lever for influencing Allied conduct of the war.

It will be remembered that the two sections of Oflag IXA/H at Spangenburg were reopened for senior officers in February 1942. At first there were only about 250[1] in the Upper and Lower camps, but by April the numbers had risen to nearly 480, and although the German Foreign Office denied that the camp had yet reached capacity, Swiss representatives reported both sections as overcrowded. Even after the transfer of the 45 Air Force personnel to Stalag Luft III at the end of the month and four Navy and Merchant Navy officers to Marlag-Milag Nord, the numbers continued at the excessive figure of about 450. As might have been expected after the move from Warburg, mail was slow in arriving, books and recreational facilities were rather short, and it took some time before adequate areas were agreed upon to enable outdoor games to be played. However, parole walks were arranged, permission was given to use a local sports field twice a week, and the floor of the moat in the Upper camp was used for rockeries, vegetable gardens, walking paths, a cricket pitch, deck tennis and other games. By July the prisoners in the Upper camp had done sufficient art and craft work to hold what was described by the Swiss representative as a 'fine exhibition'. On the other hand the overcrowding at the Lower camp precluded the use of any rooms for recreation and made it difficult for prisoners to do any serious reading.

The German camp authorities were described by the prisoners to an International Red Cross representative as 'strict but correct'. There were, however, a number of matters on which the two senior British officers were continually pressing them for satisfaction. Canteens, although they existed, had practically no stocks, in spite of an issue of weak beer every ten days; but this was of general application throughout Germany, and was part of the economy measures taken by the German authorities in conformity with the principle of 'total war'. The same was true of the fuel for cooking, which had been cut by 45 per cent in mid-1942, and of the very poor lighting supplied by a local village power station.

The German Foreign Office, in reply to a complaint about dental work, stated that 'owing to the raw material position' it was no longer possible to allow prisoners to have dentures made[2] except when the lack of them would cause a breakdown in their

---

[1] The numbers included between 40 and 50 New Zealanders, mostly from Oflag VIB but four from Oflag IVC and seven from Stalag XXA. The camp contained most of the senior officers in Germany.
[2] Previously they could be made for any prisoner who applied for them, at his expense.

health. There were protracted negotiations before prisoners were allowed to remit pay balances home to England. As a result of many requests for the surplus of 35 chaplains to be transferred to other camps, five only were transferred in September, and the German authorities seemed from the first loath to accede to this request. In one reply on the subject they claimed that 'frequently there is no wish among prisoners of war for spiritual care', and in another regarding an individual transfer, that the chaplain in question was not able 'to produce a propitious effect upon his comrades' but that 'his demeanour even evoked a certain unrest'.

There seems to have been some attempt on the part of the Germans at this stage to impose collective stoppage of privileges and to offer to reintroduce them only if parole were given regarding their use. This the senior British officers strenuously opposed. Mail, both outward and inward, was stopped from the beginning of August. Finally, at the end of September, doctors, chaplains, '*grand-blessés*',[1] and those of Irish birth were moved to Rotenburg, and the remainder of the camp was subjected to rigorous restrictions on the orders of the High Command as a reprisal for alleged ill-treatment of German officer prisoners en route to South Africa. Not only were the officers denied the use of all books (except bibles) and other collectively owned property, but their private effects were confiscated and they were without soap, towels, razors, toothbrushes, knives and forks. Their badges of rank, decorations and other insignia were removed and they were denied the services of any orderlies. It goes without saying that the order was not taken lying down by the camp leaders, but it was not revoked until two months later in spite of letters of complaint and exchanges of government notes. Strange as it must have seemed to the German authorities, it occasioned a great deal of good humour in the camp, not the least part of which resulted from a beard-growing competition. Swiss delegates who visited the camp during the reprisal period commented, 'The spirit is splendid'. Their report goes on to say:

> The sight of nearly four hundred bearded officers in plain uniforms is of course shocking, but the air of manliness and dignity with which they bear themselves makes a great impression on everybody.

The new year was comparatively peaceful after the turmoil of the reprisal period, and though many of the drawbacks of the camp remained, mail improved a little and it was at least possible to eat, sleep, and indulge in recreation in a more or less civilised fashion.

---

[1]There had been over 50 amputees and other seriously wounded in the camp.

The camp to which those doctors and others who were to be exempt from the reprisals had been sent in September was only ten miles away, at Rotenburg on the River Fulda. When Oflag VIB at Warburg split up in August and September 1942,[1] the Air Force officers were sent to Schubin in Silesia, the junior and younger officers to Eichstaett in southern Bavaria, and the 'over thirty-fives', together with repatriable cases, to what became known as Oflag IXA/Z[2] at Rotenburg. In order to make room for the doctors, chaplains, '*grand-blessés*', and others from Spangenburg, 120 of those who had come from Warburg were sent off to the Upper and Lower camps from which the former had come.[3] The camp at Rotenburg was a former girls' school, a large, fairly modern stone building of classrooms and cubicles, equipped with central heating. Though the latter advantage was largely nullified by the small coal ration, for those coming from Warburg the place was comfortable indeed. Food consisted of the normal inadequate German rations but was supplemented by ample Red Cross supplies. Contrary to the procedure at Warburg and other camps, all meals were prepared in a central kitchen and served in a common dining room.

The building was in the middle of a lovely countryside, into which walks on parole were arranged with the German authorities. For a while these made up for the limited space in the camp for outdoor exercise—an area no more than fifty yards square. By the new year, however, the school gymnasium was in use, and cinema shows, a theatre, and a good library provided plenty of indoor recreation. Unfortunately the camp became more and more crowded; and, as at Spangenburg, classes became difficult to hold (though there was plenty of coaching), and men trying to study found it hard to concentrate. In April there were 33 medical officers and 20 chaplains in the camp—a decrease on the earlier numbers of each. Though they had applied for work in other camps, no action was taken to transfer them; and there were some hints from the Germans that they caused too much trouble in camps with their complaints about conditions and refusal to allow sick men to go out to work. There was some tunnelling and other escape activity in Rotenburg, but as might have been expected, the thoughts of large numbers of unemployed protected personnel and disabled men turned mainly towards hopes of repatriation.

---

[1] The figures were: 445 all ranks to Oflag IXA/Z, Rotenburg; 413 all ranks to Oflag XXIB, Schubin; 1860 all ranks to Oflag VIIB, Eichstaett. See map facing p. 355.
[2] The Z stood for *Zweiglager*, branch camp.
[3] This left about 350 officers and 70–80 other ranks at Rotenburg, including 30–40 New Zealanders.

In September 1942 the 1800 or so younger and more junior officers[1] at Warburg were moved by train to Eichstaett. Their reputation for escaping and generally defying authority apparently went ahead of them, for not only were their boots taken away at night during the train journey, but they were subjected to a most thorough search on arrival, and in the new camp they encountered stricter regulations than ever before. As with most strict regulations, the human weaknesses of those who had to carry them out soon brought about their relaxation.

The camp was an old cavalry barracks, built some forty years previously and set in a beautiful Bavarian countryside of meadow, trees, and hills. Prisoners were housed in one of the original three-storied barracks on the slope of a hill, and in eight or so new concrete army huts on the flat below. The former was fairly comfortable and was served by tarsealed paths; the latter were surrounded by mud in winter, were damp and ill-ventilated, and had only carbide lamps instead of electric lighting. Men captured during the Dieppe raid were already in the camp, and the accommodation was from the first very overcrowded in its sleeping quarters, ablutions, and sanitary installations. As might be expected where accommodation was limited and of varying quality, there was some ill-feeling at times about its allocation. The cold of the winter of 1942 combined with the very small German coal ration to produce considerable ill-health among many of those in the lower barracks; and there was such a serious outcrop of chilblains, rheumatics, and bronchial troubles that the senior medical officer ordered a general issue of malt and cod-liver oil and submitted a strongly condemnatory report concerning the accommodation. Eventually in mid-1943 the German authorities moved 120 officers to another camp.

Oflag VIIB had fine grounds, including gardens, a sports field, and two tennis courts for the use of the prisoners. In a short time the camp had an active theatre group, and the German camp authorities had arranged cinema shows. When weather permitted there were parole walks into the Bavarian countryside, and as winter approached an ice-skating rink was prepared. A large part of the library from Oflag VIB—some 11,000 to 12,000 books—came to Eichstaett. The potential resources of the camp for recreation were thus very great indeed.

The slowness in the censorship of books and other parcels militated against the full exploitation of these possibilities, and even letter mail was held up for long periods.[2] Indeed, the whole

---

[1] These numbers included New Zealand, Australian, and United Kingdom officers.
[2] At the beginning of November 1942 one estimate gives the number of letters to be censored as 20,000.

German camp staff was more than usually security minded and the commandant very regimental; so that in spite of an ample supply of Red Cross food and other supplies and reasonably comfortable quarters, most of the camp arrangements were at first hampered by a mass of petty restrictions. It took some eighty minutes to read out the salient points only of camp standing orders on two special parades of the prisoners. At first all tins of food from Red Cross parcels had their contents emptied into containers, but as this procedure resulted in the issue of approximately four parcels in 35 minutes, it was soon abandoned. On one occasion a roll-call was delayed for an hour and a half on account of fog, apparently on the assumption that prisoners might try to escape if it were held. On another occasion the commandant inspected officer prisoners' dress and made some critical comments. On such occasions appropriate retorts or any other flippancies and laughter were frowned upon and often resulted in minor collective punishment, such as stopping prisoners' tea for two days.

In November, when the first five prisoners escaped, there was a roll-call lasting five hours the following day, and two more that night which took up another two hours or so. After three weeks the roll-calls settled down to three a day until June 1943, when 65 got out through a tunnel and another five-hour roll-call was held to discover the identity of the escapers. They were all recaptured within a short time and confined in the nearby Willibaldsburg castle, some of the camp entertainments being banned as a punishment.

At the roll-call on 8 October, to their bewilderment 107 officers and 20 other ranks taken prisoner at Dieppe were fallen out and marched to the castle, where their hands were tied with rope and remained so for twelve hours daily. This, it was explained by the German authorities, was a reprisal for British ill-treatment of German prisoners at the time of the Dieppe raid and also during the commando raid on Sark. The commandant was at pains to explain that he was acting on orders from the High Command and that the binding was done in the most humane way possible; many of the German camp staff gave obvious indications that they disliked the whole affair.

Three days after the first announcement came a second that, as German prisoners in England were now being bound, the reprisal would now apply to three times the present numbers. Accordingly the last thirty or so in each group on roll-call parade were marched off and placed in handcuffs, which had by then been substituted for the original rope; there were, therefore, finally 321 officers and 60 other ranks in handcuffs, including a number of New

Zealanders. In spite of there being a medical officer in constant attendance, the camp leader reported to the Swiss Legation that the treatment was 'having serious effects on mental and physical health'. Indeed, by 18 October several of those originally shackled had been replaced because of illness or calloused wrists, and one officer wrote in his diary that the Germans were 'quite sympathetic and a little disgusted about it all'.

As time went on conditions were considerably relaxed for the shackled prisoners. The original tight handcuffs were replaced by police fetters with a fairly comfortable length of chain between them. The Dieppe prisoners had all been moved down to the barrack block occupied by the other victims, and although this was at first wired off from the rest of the camp and subjected to a strict guard, those in handcuffs were later allowed to move about the camp freely and to attend lectures and entertainments. Meanwhile prisoners had found that the handcuffs could be opened with a nail, and a good many began taking them off while not under observation by guards. The guards themselves had begun the practice of simply leaving the right number of manacles in each room, instead of seeing that they were put on. By April some of the shackled prisoners were playing 'baseball in the mornings and hockey in the afternoons',[1] though for obvious reasons such developments could not be mentioned in the prisoners' letters.

Eichstaett was not the only camp where shackling was imposed. There were prisoners from Dieppe at Stalag VIIIB, at the newly formed camp for NCOs at Hohenfels, and a handful at Stalag IXC; they were all subjected to it. When the number to whom the order applied was trebled, the other British prisoners in these camps took their share of the reprisals. On 9 October in Stalag VIIIB at Lamsdorf, some 1500 British and Canadians had their hands tied with pieces of Red Cross string 18 inches in length—apparently a misinterpretation of an order specifying 18 inches of play between the hands. This was bad enough for those concerned, who four days later included another 800 of the camp strength.[2] But it seemed as if the German camp authorities seized the opportunity to work off old scores. The issue of Red Cross food parcels, cigarettes, and regular mail was discontinued, and shortly afterwards all sports, concerts, and educational classes were forbidden until further notice. With only the poor German rations to exist on, an acute shortage of blankets and no allowance of fuel to combat the increasing cold, conditions in the stalag became as hard as they had ever been.

Moreover, fortified by the uncompromising attitude of the High

---

[1] Mentioned in report by Swiss representative on his visit to the camp on 25 April 1943.
[2] The camp strength at this time included about 21,000 British (1800 New Zealanders) of whom some 6000–7000 were in the stalag itself.

Command, German camp staff were now disclaiming any obligations under the Geneva or any other convention, and openly talking of the continuance of collective punishments, no matter what appeals were made. There was some kicking and bayonet prodding of bound men by one or two sadistic guards, and those found with loosened bonds or smoking inside the barracks were subjected to rather brutal punishments.[1] After six weeks handcuffs with the proper length of chain were substituted for the string, and representations through neutral agencies had most of the collective restrictions removed.

The period preceding the shackling had been one of strained relations between the prisoners and the German staff. It had been signalised by many lively disputes concerning the handling of Red Cross supplies and the conditions of work, and also by numerous escape break-outs from the stalag and from *Arbeitskommandos*. The medical officers of the stalag complained vigorously about the system of puncturing all tins of Red Cross food before issue, on the grounds that it involved a waste of food, or alternatively, danger to the health of prisoners if they ate the food after the tins had remained punctured for some time. There were individual refusals to work the long hours demanded at some *Arbeitskommandos*, there were heated disputes about sending sick men out to work, and there were some refusals by a whole gang to work until an issue of Red Cross food had been made. The prisoners could always rely on the support of the prisoner-of-war doctor or padre, if they had one at their work-camp, and many of the camp leaders of working gangs had daily, and often trying, struggles with the local guard officer to secure better terms for the men they represented. To add to the worries of guards and commandants the summer brought a crop of break-outs from working camps; even at the stalag several parties got out by cutting through the wire, and a tunnel nearing completion was found in September. So far from being subdued by the imminence of defeat that might be indicated by the war news in the summer of 1942, the British prisoners seemed to be making more trouble than ever.

The fact was that by the summer of 1942 the prisoners had got their life at Lamsdorf pretty well organised. There were normally ample supplies of Red Cross food parcels to keep the men healthy and vigorous, although the issue had again to be reduced to half a parcel a week in the winter of 1942–43. Private clothing and tobacco parcels were coming into the camp quite plentifully. Those in need of medical and dental treatment were well catered for

---

[1] Several hours with wrists shackled and held up tightly behind the back, nose and toes touching a wall.

in the camp infirmary, which carried plentiful stocks of Red Cross materials. Half a barrack had been set aside as a church, suitably furnished and decorated, and the religious needs of the camp were thus catered for. The camp school which operated in the other half of this barrack had several thousands on its roll and ran a continuous series of classes from 9 a.m. until the closing of the barrack at night. A camp newspaper, printed in Oppeln on paper supplied by the World Alliance of YMCAs, published its first number in January 1943. Although a fire in September 1942 destroyed the large camp library, together with a good deal of other recreational material, large relief supplies were soon arriving to replace the loss. There was a camp theatre and five musical combinations of varying types, including a pipe band. There were vegetable and flower gardens for the horticulturally minded, with any amount of seeds from Red Cross sources. The organisation of sport had reached a phase where series of international cricket and football matches and boxing and all-in wrestling tournaments were being staged.

The prohibition of these activities for any length of time was a considerable hardship to men living amid the depressing surroundings of this large, crowded camp. The lifting of the ban on them did much to relieve what would have otherwise been a dismal winter. In spite of repeated protests concerning the withdrawal of all blankets supplied by the German Army,[1] the camp authorities were not able to supply any more, and the camp leader had to make a redistribution of the Red Cross blankets in the stalag so that everyone possessed at least two, either Red Cross or privately owned. The British Government was equally adamant about not sending further relief supplies of blankets and so enabling Germany to escape another of her obligations towards prisoners of war. The High Command had already instructed camps to cut down the rations for prisoners if they were receiving Red Cross food parcels.[2] Their failure to supply

---

[1] The Germans were at this stage very short of blankets and allowed each prisoner at most two (usually well-worn), whether his own or issued by the OKW. At Stalag VIIIB before September 1942 they had even withdrawn all their own blankets and allowed prisoners to retain only those which were privately owned or sent through the Red Cross. When late in 1942 a request from Stalag VIIIB for 5000 blankets, backed by the International Red Cross Committee, was referred to the War Office, the latter declined to accede to it. For it was felt that if the blankets were sent the Germans would almost certainly withdraw those they had issued, and thus escape responsibility for supplying British prisoners with adequate bedding.

[2] A comparison of the cut and normal weekly rations is shown in the following table:

	Cut	Normal
Bread	2250 grammes	2250 grammes
Meat	260 grammes	300 grammes
Fat	135 grammes	205 grammes
Cheese	60 grammes	62·5 grammes
Flour	100 grammes	160 grammes
Sugar	140 grammes	175 grammes
Jam	140 grammes	140 grammes

clothing has already been remarked upon, together with their unwillingness to allow British clothing to be issued except on a strictly limited scale. Although all these restrictions were partly justified by the contention that surplus blankets, food, and clothing were used by prisoners in escaping, the attempt to rely on British relief was also a measure of the shortages in Germany, and the restrictions a result of their fear that civilians would see that enemy prisoners of war were better off than they were.

If some of the *Arbeitskommandos* were quartered in reasonable comfort, though somewhat crowded, and were employed by firms who thought it good policy to treat their workers with consideration, others lived under bad conditions and relied upon relief supplies to alleviate their lot. Although by March 1943 50 per cent of the men in working camps had two sets of battle dress, many had had to go for a long time with one only, and for those in mines and on other heavy manual labour this one suit had, in the words of a Red Cross delegate, reached a 'deplorable state'. Many employers, too, found great difficulty in obtaining overalls for their civilian workers, let alone prisoners of war. A large number of these camps had blankets that were small and worn thin, though it must be admitted that their barracks were usually quite well heated. Many of the working camps supplied heavy workers' rations, but others depended on supplies of Red Cross food from stalag to maintain a sufficient diet. Owing to transport difficulties deliveries from Lamsdorf were usually only every three months, and it was not until 1943 that a sufficient stock was built up there to make it possible to deliver enough to last three months. In 1943 two whole barracks at Lamsdorf were set aside for relief supplies, and a senior warrant officer and a staff of 60 were handling as many as 70 railway wagon-loads a week; they once handled 30 in one day.

The majority of the *Arbeitskommandos* were in industrial areas[1] and sometimes in the centre of a town; often the compounds were rather small and sometimes the outlook was depressing. Recreation for the men in these camps was an important consideration. Lighting was often better than it was in the main stalag, but supplies of reading matter and other recreational material were naturally much more limited and slow in arriving. Moreover, space for games, whether outside or inside, depended a great deal on the local camp commandant and on the employer. The men working in a paper-mill at Krappitz were allowed to swim

---

[1] An analysis of the *Arbeitskommandos* dependent on Stalag VIIIB in September 1942, given in a report by an IRCC delegate, shows the percentage of prisoner labour employed in various classes of work: Industry, about 70 per cent; Agriculture, about 20 per cent.

in the river and given the use of a football field; at a sawmill near Oderfest the men were said to 'receive everything they need from the owner of the mill'.[1] On the other hand the owner of a sugar mill at Ratibor was 'reluctant to do much for the prisoners', and a railway workers' camp at Gleiwitz, where all water had to be carried from a distance of over 500 yards, was so bad from all points of view that a scathing report from a Swiss delegate led to its being closed down. The recreational capacities of men working from eight to twelve hours in cement factories or brickworks, hewing coal or loading barges on the River Oder, were not as great as those of non-workers confined in a compound all day long, and men working at a sugar factory during the season when the sugar-beets were being brought in had 'no time for sport'. On the other hand many *Arbeitskommandos* were able to play matches against each other, and some of the larger ones had their own concert party. Although few had canteens, most were able to have things bought for them at a local shop. British doctors working in *Arbeitskommandos* were often able to do much for the general welfare of the camp, besides attending to sickness and accidents which might, but for their presence, have gone neglected. Padres, who might if allowed have done a great deal more welfare work, although permitted to conduct funerals,[2] were greatly restricted in their movements; and as has been seen, large numbers of them remained unemployed in officers' camps.

The majority of the other New Zealand army prisoners were still in south-eastern Austria, mostly in working camps, either industrial or agricultural. In the latter half of 1942 many changes were made in the administrative set-up of the Austrian camps and their numbering. The convalescents, medical personnel, and non-working NCOs transferred to Stalag XVIIIB at Spittal-on-the-Drau when Marburg was cleared of all British prisoners were joined in September by nearly 400 British NCOs from Wolfsberg, in accordance with the German plan to segregate non-workers. Spittal was a pleasant camp in the valley of the Lower Drau below the Austrian Alps, had good accommodation and a good supply of Red Cross food and recreational material brought from Marburg. It soon became overcrowded, however, and Marburg had to be used again for the overflow. In October the British NCOs were transferred to Hohenfels in Bavaria to form, with others

---

[1] Quotations in this paragraph are from a report by a Swiss representative, August 1942.
[2] The German authorities were on the whole scrupulous in seeing that deceased British prisoners had a proper military burial. There were usually wreaths on behalf of the German guard company as well as the prisoners, a firing party, and sometimes quite an elaborate cortege. Numerous photographs were usually taken of the ceremony, of which copies could be sent home in prisoners' letters.

from Lamsdorf and elsewhere, the new NCOs' camp; the remainder went to another new camp at Wagna,[1] which now became Stalag XVIIIB. Spittal-on-the-Drau was renumbered Stalag XVIIIA/Z and became a hospital centre for medical and dental treatment and convalescence of sick prisoners from Stalag XVIIIA and camps dependent on it. The latter now included all those which had previously been administered from Marburg and Spittal, and Wolfsberg became the administrative centre for some 26,000 prisoners of all nationalities, including upwards of a thousand New Zealanders.

Not a great number of these were in the stalag, the population of which, with the exception of administrative staff, convalescents, and men awaiting repatriation, was continually changing. The British section of the camp had always suffered from crowded quarters and what are described in a neutral report[2] as 'deplorable' washing and sanitary facilities. Insufficient disinfestation had resulted in large numbers of palliasses becoming so infested with fleas and bugs as to be unusable; the water supply became totally inadequate as the result of a breakdown at the local waterworks, being for three weeks available only for one hour daily between 7 a.m. and 7 p.m.; and the septic pools into which drainage took place were too infrequently emptied, smelt badly, and attracted flies.

A new commandant appointed in July appears to have done what he could to improve matters. Three new barracks which had been building for some time were opened in September. These and the transfer of non-working NCOs did much to relieve overcrowding, so that it was no longer necessary to use the lowest of the three tiers of bunks. The installation of a new sewerage system was begun, but, mainly through shortage of materials, took until February 1943 before it was completed. It was a long time too before the water supply was made anything like adequate by means of a new well. The camp theatre, library, and educational classes were carried on, in spite of losing among the transferred NCOs many who had done most to help with them, and a sports ground was laid out. The camp had its own hospital and a dental surgery which did something to cope with the large amount of dental treatment that was required.

In general the British *Arbeitskommandos* in Austria contained a mixture of men from the United Kingdom, Australia, and New Zealand. A large number worked on farms, and most of the remainder in quarries and on roadwork, in sawmills and timber

---

[1] By February 1943 there were only 118 British prisoners (20 New Zealanders) there, and these were later transferred to Stalag XVIIIA.
[2] Report by delegate of the International Red Cross Committee of 6 August 1942.

yards, in magnesite mines, on building projects, and in various kinds of factories. Now that they were all administered from Wolfsberg, responsibility for their welfare and for the distribution of their mail, food parcels, clothing, and other supplies devolved on the chief British man-of-confidence at Stalag XVIIIA, an Australian warrant officer, who carried out a difficult administrative task with great ability. For the many small work-camps scattered over southern Austria, this centralisation was valuable in ensuring equitable distribution of relief and in checking irregularities both by local enemy guards and sometimes by the prisoners themselves.

The land workers usually had their quarters in one or two rooms of a farmhouse near their work. There was scarcely ever any running water, ablutions and latrines were usually very primitive, and the improvements in their quarters depended largely on the prisoners' own efforts. They usually had their meals on the job with their employers, and though a meal was sometimes a rushed affair[1] and sometimes eaten from a communal bowl, our men very soon adapted themselves. The hours of work were long—sometimes eleven hours a day in winter and thirteen in summer, frequently with jobs on Sundays such as feeding the horses—but prisoners in these camps were found to be in good health, thought the work 'not too tiring', and were above all in 'excellent spirits'.[2] Their day was spent largely in the open air, temporarily free from barbed wire. Most of the Austrian countryfolk after a while were finding our men, if not gluttons for work, at least decent people to have about their farms. Although some men ascribed this to the change in the trend of the war, it is clear that a good deal of real friendliness soon developed on both sides. A Red Cross delegate speaks of prisoners being 'much appreciated by their employers' and of an 'esteem and understanding that is reciprocal'.

This was not generally the case with those employed on industrial undertakings. Some of the employers treated them quite well and provided reasonable amenities in their living quarters; others did their best to exploit them to the full and had to be checked (as a result of complaints by the local man-of-confidence or one of the neutral inspectors) from overworking them, from neglecting to provide a proper standard of accommodation, and sometimes from abuse and brutality. One or two *Arbeitskommandos* which were clearly unsatisfactory were closed down as a result of complaints. The men were usually housed in barrack huts with bunks, often quite well lit and heated, sometimes with good washing facilities, but almost always with crude sanitary arrangements. Few employers

---

[1] The German authorities allowed them half an hour for the midday meal, but sometimes an employer would try to limit the time to ten minutes or so.
[2] Report of the IRCC delegate in January 1943.

were able or willing to provide working clothing, and although new German regulations allowed prisoners to have two suits of battle dress, it was some time before supplies allowed a complete distribution on this scale. At one magnesium mine where the work was particularly hard on boots most of the prisoners were in wooden clogs. It is noteworthy that at this camp bad food almost caused a rebellion. In general, working prisoners had few complaints about the food; they received heavy workers' rations and, especially in the smaller *Arbeitskommandos,* the cooking was done for them.

About a hundred New Zealanders and 250 or so other British prisoners worked until the end of the war on the building of a dam and hydro-electric plant at Lavamünd. Quarters installed near the works were at first crude and overcrowded, but later were replaced by roomy new barracks described by a neutral inspector as 'model'. The men could keep clean with daily hot showers, but most had for some time no clean uniform to change into after work. The work consisted mainly of shifting concrete from mixers to the timbering of the dam, a task which occasionally provided opportunity for sabotage by dropping tools either into the river or the wet concrete of the dam itself. Work lasted for eight and a half hours daily,[1] but was described as 'not too hard', at least in the way in which the prisoners went about it. By an arrangement with the commandant, those who wished could do an agreed amount of work daily and stop when it had been completed —usually in about five and a half hours. This 'contract system' was in use in many other *Arbeitskommandos* and was generally in favour with prisoners, provided the agreed amount of work could be kept as low as possible by the local man-of-confidence in his negotiations with the local commandant. As at other camps, the commandant sometimes sent out to work men whom the doctor had ordered to rest, and there were at first a number of accidents, at least one of which was fatal, arising from dangerous work. But with constant pressure the camp improved and in May 1943 was pronounced 'excellent' by the Swiss representative who inspected it.

The medical care of prisoners in the smaller *Arbeitskommandos* was usually in the hands of the local civilian doctor, often efficient and humane but usually with insufficient authority to prevent a callous German NCO from sending a sick man out to work. The local dentist was similarly charged with the care of prisoners' teeth, but in practice he usually did little beyond extractions (sometimes when only a filling was needed), and those with serious mouth conditions had to be sent to stalag for treatment there. As Red

---

[1] These hours, with Saturday afternoon and Sunday free, were usual in Austrian industrial *Arbeitskommandos.*

Cross supplies became available, more dentures were made for men who needed them, but as in the other camps supply never kept pace with demand.

Many men were still making breaks from *Arbeitskommandos*, but usually with little of the equipment necessary to complete their escape and with little idea beyond making for the borders of Hungary or Yugoslavia. For food and shelter it was common to call at one of the *Arbeitskommandos* encountered en route. Many men were chary of getting entangled with partisans, and the later schemes for providing would-be escapers with information, routes, contacts, clothing, and other equipment had not yet been worked out. The German security measures had moreover been increased. All escapers recaptured in Austria were sent to an interrogation centre at Landek, where they were often kept for a week or so while persistent efforts, using methods reminiscent of Oberursel, were made to find out the route taken by the escaper and where he had sheltered and been fed. From Landek they usually went to Stalag XVIIIC at Markt Pongau, where they were kept in the punishment cells for a week or two before being returned to Stalag XVIIIA to serve whatever term of punishment they might be awarded for their attempted escape. This sentence could not exceed 28 days by the terms of the Geneva Convention, but their previous periods in Landek and Markt Pongau added a good many extra weeks to their confinement.

Although many *Arbeitskommandos* were being supplied with reading matter from the stalag circulating library, they still did not have sufficient material for indoor recreation. There were seldom any organised classes, though the keener prisoners studied privately with books sent to them. One or two sympathetic German commandants arranged periodical visits to a local cinema. Football matches between different *Arbeitskommandos* had now been forbidden by the German High Command; on the other hand, many of those in the country were allowed to swim in a nearby river or lake. During this period permission was extended to the Anglican chaplain[1] from the stalag to visit working camps. In addition to purely religious duties, he was able to do a great deal of welfare work and to give essential help with various camp activities both in the stalag and the outlying kommandos.

The German guards at these isolated camps had a difficult task: to prevent the prisoners from escaping and, at the same time, see that they were living under satisfactory conditions and were not ill-treated by their employer. In its propaganda campaign concerning

---

[1] Mr J. H. Ledgerwood, YMCA secretary, acted as Anglican chaplain during his stay at Stalag XVIIIA. He was awarded the MBE for his work there.

the humane treatment of prisoners, the High Command could not afford to be embarrassed by bad examples from its own work-camps, and the stalag authorities who controlled the administration of these scattered units were described at this period as 'sympathetic and anxious to be conciliatory'. Under a new arrangement the men-of-confidence from a group of kommandos were brought on the day of a neutral inspector's visit to the most central camp of the area so that their various complaints could be heard. Some of the less competent of the local German commanders, weighed down by their responsibilities, were harsher in their discipline than they need have been—a few brutal ones were replaced after representations by the Protecting Power; but the inspecting delegates found that on the whole guards were now 'fair and correct with few exceptions'.

The Germans had never ceased their pressure on NCOs to go out on working parties, but by September 1942 they were finally resigned to allowing those who claimed exemption to go to a special camp at Hohenfels—at first Oflag IIIC and later Stalag 383. Between September and the end of 1942 over 3000 NCOs were collected there from camps all over Germany, and by April 1943 their numbers had increased to over 4000, including 320 New Zealanders.

The camp, formerly for officers, was built on a gentle slope in the middle of a piece of heavily wooded country, some miles from the nearest town. Instead of being crammed by the hundreds into unpartitioned barracks, the NCOs found themselves allocated small dormitory huts holding twelve or less, described by one of them as 'snug billets'. The camp had plenty of room for sports fields and walking space besides, and some larger barracks for theatrical shows and indoor recreation. When Red Cross food arrived in October to supplement the ordinary German prisoner-of-war ration, there was little to complain of at Hohenfels. Much effort went into constructing small stoves so that private food could be cooked when desired. By November one man was writing that he was 'fourteen pounds heavier than when he joined up'; others spoke of there being 'more freedom and less interference' and of the camp being 'far less depressing' than Lamsdorf. The winter proved to be cold, but there was sufficient coal and the men were allowed to collect wood from a nearby forest. For most of them it was the best camp they had been in.

It was to be expected that, although there were only three NCOs from Dieppe at the camp, such a large body of non-workers would be selected as suitable for the tying-and-chaining reprisal. It began on 10 October and by the 14th some 1250 had their hands tied for twelve hours each day. At first, too, they were separated from the rest of the camp and all recreational activity was stopped. Thereafter the history of the reprisals at Stalag 383 is much the same as in the other camps, except that relaxations were introduced more quickly and in the later stages men were allowed to take the shackling in rotation—a month at a time.

After the first week or two shackling interfered little with the recreational life of the camp. Many musical instruments and other material had been brought from other camps; by February several different kinds of orchestra and a choir of 500 voices were performing as occasion demanded, and a number of shows had been presented on the newly-built stage. A stalag 'university' had been organised by a former NCO of the Army Educational Corps; and classes under this scheme, together with the activities of no fewer than 56 clubs—from a debating club to a Caledonian society—enabled men to pass the winter months profitably. A first exhibition of arts and crafts was held in February, and in March, with the ground drying up, sport was in full swing. Plenty of parcels from the Red Cross and from home had made the food and clothing position of the camp secure, and men could write with conviction that they were 'well and being well-treated'.

Mention has already been made of the RAF activity connected with the land defence of Egypt and the Alamein offensive, in which twenty or so of our airmen fell into Italian hands. A number of others shot down in the Middle East and Mediterranean front fell into German hands and were transported to Germany as quickly as possible. But the majority of the 180-odd who became prisoners in Germany during this period were lost on air operations over western Europe. Here bombing attacks were being extended and fighter sweeps were reaching out to the coastal areas of France and the Low Countries. Although casualties fell somewhat during the winter, the summer of 1942 saw the New Zealand losses in prisoners average nearly twenty a month, and in each of the months of May and June 1943 more than twenty of our airmen were captured as a result of air operations over the Continent.

By this time *Auswertestelle West* had attained considerable importance and authority as a source of intelligence for the German Higher Command. The Luftwaffe claimed that the information from captured airmen (though gleaned more from the evaluation of documents captured with the prisoners than from their interrogation) was better than that obtained through any other source, including agents abroad. Police, area troops, and airfield staffs therefore co-operated by sending captured airmen to Oberursel as quickly as possible, and in taking the utmost care to ensure that every article and document from their persons or from the crashed aircraft was sent on ahead of them.

The mass of information filed at Oberursel concerning Allied air force units, airmen, and possible operational activity had now become formidable, and many prisoners were surprised by the completeness of their squadron histories and 'Who's Who'. There was little change in the procedure during interrogation, though there were some refinements. It was considered that the mental shock of capture to the young airman was not very great, and that it was necessary to lower his morale by a week or so of solitary and hungry confinement in the cells (already described) before commencing his interrogation proper. The interrogator then usually apologised for the previous treatment suffered by the prisoner and usually claimed to be an anti-Nazi, or at all events a man to whom politics and national prejudices were immaterial. Sometimes a quarrel was staged in the presence of the prisoner between his interrogator and another German who had expressed fanatical opinions likely to give offence to the British. After a friendly man-to-man talk about civilian days and home and family, came the pressure: subtle appeals to the conceited to show off their knowledge, veiled threats to the stubborn of the Gestapo and possible disappearance, sometimes to the more imaginative a carefully prepared scene with 'noises off' as of men undergoing torture or even being shot.

Though many men realised the purpose behind these threats and maintained silence, others less patient did not hesitate to give the interrogator a piece of their minds. The commandant's report mentions that some of the United States, Australian, and New Zealand airmen 'were openly recalcitrant and brought a certain native virility to their rescue in resisting the " dressing down " which followed' their refusal to talk. From the fact that the report goes on to talk of the punishments that followed, it may be deduced that the 'virility' of the expressions used on these occasions did not leave the interrogators wholly unmoved.

On the other hand the interrogators were finding their task made increasingly difficult by the instruction now being given to air crews in the probable methods that would be used to interrogate them should they fall into enemy hands, the subjects about which information would be sought, and the traps into which they might fall. Prisoners were now, without exception, unimpressed with the 'Red Cross' form, notwithstanding the quoting of the Geneva Convention to show them how necessary it was to indicate their unit. Just as prisoners came in time to disregard everything in German broadcasts and newspapers as propaganda, so numbers of airmen were convinced that the copies of the Geneva Convention they were shown at Oberursel had been falsified to suit German purposes. The Germans claimed that a large proportion of the forms continued to be filled in at least partially, but it seems unlikely that the prisoners completed the questions relating to operational matters. Prisoners' familiarity too with oral methods of interrogation entailed greater efforts and more subtle advances on the part of the interrogating officer. As time went on and pressure of work for the staff became greater, nervous tension at *Auswertestelle West* was by no means confined to the prisoners, and a special kitchen had to be installed ' to cater for the duodenals of harassed interrogators. . . .'[1]

Airmen had been well warned too of the likelihood of approaches by stool-pigeons in Dulag Luft, and so careful were they to avoid 'careless talk' and so greatly did the German information obtained in the transit camp decrease that it was decided in 1943 to abandon the use of stool-pigeons altogether. Those whose interrogation was completed were therefore not kept long at Dulag Luft. Most of the officers went to Stalag Luft III, though a number captured in late 1942 and early 1943 went to Oflag XXIB at Schubin. NCOs and other ranks went to Stalag Luft III or, as that became more crowded, to Stalag Luft I, which reopened in October 1942, or to the RAF compound at Stalag VIIIB; a few NCOs were for a time in the Army NCOs' camp, Stalag 383.

The numbers in Stalag Luft III at Sagan rose steadily until in September 1942 there were 710 officers and 1797 NCOs and other ranks[2] in the East and Centre compounds respectively. By then, too, American airmen taken prisoner were being sent to the camp. In six months the camp administration and amenities had been thoroughly organised. The East compound was under the control of the senior British officer, and the Centre compound under a British warrant officer elected to the post of compound leader by a majority vote. These two men met the German commandant periodically to settle points under dispute. The camp had ample food and clothing consigned to it by the International Red Cross Committee, and medical care was adequately provided for, though the dental officer sent to the camp—a New Zealander—was as usual greatly overworked.

Each compound had its own sports field, and so many different forms of sport were available that the standard of physical fitness in the camp was soon very high. With various kinds of ball games, boxing, fencing, and athletics in summer, and the sports field

---

[1] Air Ministry report on *Auswertestelle West*.
[2] New Zealanders in these totals were 34 officers and 100 NCOs and other ranks.

flooded for ice hockey in the winter, a neutral inspector was led to refer to the camp as 'a regular athletic training camp'. There was a library and a scheme of educational classes in both compounds; each had built a theatre[1] inside an empty barrack allotted by the Germans for the purpose and produced its own concerts and dramatic shows. All this activity was encouraged by the German authorities, who even sent an NCO to Berlin to hire costumes for plays. The two compounds were allowed to interchange their shows and to play inter-compound matches in various sports. These privileges were withheld on occasion as collective punishment for escape attempts and other breaches of discipline. Theatre and other communal expenses were met from a fund into which each officer paid one-third of his pay, and from which activities in the other ranks' compound were also financed. The NCOs on the other hand were able to supply the officers with BBC news bulletins received over their secret radio—an important factor in morale.

All this did not prevent much attention being devoted to escaping. There were a number of attempts to escape from both the officers' and the NCOs' compounds by walking out of the entrance gate disguised in German uniform; some had partial success, but all were recaptured within a short time. None of the numerous attempts at going through the gate hidden in some form of transport succeeded, and only some of those at going through or over the wire had initial success; none of the men concerned finally reached freedom. There was tunnelling, but all such projects were discovered by the German security staff, and during the winter of 1942–43 all large-scale efforts were temporarily abandoned so that the Germans might be induced to think that the prisoners had tired of the idea, and in order to prepare for the coming move to the new North compound.

The most important work was the improvement of the escape organisation. The senior British officer in the East compound ruled that assistance with escape activities was a camp duty, although no one would be ordered to do a job involving the risk of his life. In particular every officer was called upon to take his turn at watching and warning of the approach of German guards. Indeed, by means of 'duty pilots' at the entrance to the compound and by German-speaking 'contacts', so careful a check was kept on the movements of the Germans that it seems likely that the prisoners knew more of the guards' activities than the latter did of theirs. At the same time the organisation for preparing all the accessories necessary for the success of an escaper after he had broken out of the camp was

---

[1] That in the NCOs' compound seated 400 and was stated by an IRCC delegate to be the best he had seen in any camp in Germany.

elaborated and brought to a high degree of efficiency. An NCO was smuggled in from the Centre compound for a fortnight to study the organisation in order to help build up something similar when he returned. Cohesion among the NCOs could never be quite as strong, for an elected camp leader did not have the same authority as a senior officer.

In September 1942 a hundred officers and some fifteen NCOs who had volunteered as orderlies were transferred to Schubin; they and another 200 from Warburg made up the first Air Force group to go there. Another hundred officers were sent from Sagan in November, and from then on a steady stream came direct from Dulag Luft.[1] Schubin lies in a large agricultural plain in Poland, some 150 miles west of Warsaw. The camp, Oflag XXIB, had consisted in 1940 of a large girls' school with fine grounds and gardens before it was taken over to accommodate prisoners of war; and since then a number of brick barracks had been built in the grounds to accommodate more. Though the surroundings were so pleasant, those who had been used to small rooms found the verminous, unpartitioned, stalag-type barracks hard to get used to. There were the usual tiered bunks, and a table and two forms for twelve. The stove-heating was inadequate, and there was no provision for cooking private food other than what could be contrived in the open or in the washhouses.

In spite of the comparative lack of comfort, morale seems to have been high, as the camp was considered in many ways ideal for attempts at escape. It was guarded by Wehrmacht troops, who had become somewhat slack; the security officer was a rather benign professor of English; and in the neighbourhood Polish workmen, with whom no time was lost in making contact, were found to be friendly and helpful—some of them members of a Polish underground movement. Until the end of the year there were a number of attempts to escape, all unsuccessful except for one NCO who reached Sweden. There had been enough escape activity, however, to cause a tightening of the camp discipline: six roll-calls daily at times, orders to sentries to shoot any prisoner outside the barracks after 9 p.m. and even to shoot ' when surrounded by the prisoners of war ', though this was later amended by the addition of the words ' with maleficent intention '. None of these orders, nor that insisting on the saluting of all German officers regardless of rank,[2] were allowed to go unchallenged. The German commandant tried

---

[1] By the end of November there were nearly 600 officers, 56 NCOs, and 50 orderlies. Some fifty New Zealanders were in Schubin.
[2] In almost every officers' camp in Germany difficulty was at first experienced in getting the camp authorities to agree that prisoners need salute only those German officers of equal or superior rank.

to insist on his right to appoint the SBO (Senior British Officer), though this attempt was abandoned. Relations were sufficiently strained to justify the International Red Cross delegate's comment in November, 'There certainly have been difficulties in this camp.'

The 'difficulties' came to a head in the new year. A carefully planned tunnel completed in early March made possible a mass break of 33 prisoners. Though none was finally successful, this break caused large numbers of troops, police, and Home Guard to be employed for a week while the escapers were being rounded up. SS troops took over control of the camp and almost immediately evacuated the prisoners in parties of two hundred. Although the additions to Stalag Luft III were not yet ready, it was decided to use them and move all those at Schubin to Sagan rather than risk another break-out in Poland.

On 27 March 1943 the East compound at Sagan was practically cleared of British officers when 850 were moved to the North compound. A large party of officers from Schubin took their places, and thereafter both compounds received additional batches from Dulag Luft and also later from Italy. Many of those transferred to the North compound had been allowed to go there before it opened in order to help prepare the barracks for occupation and particularly to fit up the theatre. They made good use of this opportunity to note the layout of the camp and prepare for a large-scale escape. The accommodation differed little from that of the East compound and the German defences against escape were almost identical—fences, patrols inside and outside the wire, dog patrols, ground microphones to detect tunnelling. Nevertheless there were several attempts at the wire and the gate in the first month or two of the new compound's existence, and three large tunnels, which had been carefully planned, were begun simultaneously as soon as the prisoners moved in. It was through one of these that one of the largest successful mass break-outs of the war was made, a year later.

Of the ten New Zealand naval prisoners in Germany at this period, seven belonged to the Fleet Air Arm and were in Stalag Luft III, treated in the same way as if they belonged to the Royal Air Force. Six of these had been on the ill-fated *Rangitane*; one had been shot down near Mersa Matruh in September 1942 and had been taken direct to Dulag Luft. Of the three who did not belong to the Fleet Air Arm, two had been captured in Royal Navy operations off the French coast—a petty officer who seems to have been the only New Zealander in the Marlag section of the camp for naval prisoners, and a rating who after a spell in Sandbostel was moved to Stalag VIIIB to work; the third, a leading seaman, was captured on the *Port Hobart* and had since been treated as a member of the Merchant Navy. Also in the Milag section were some twenty New Zealanders belonging to the Merchant Navy.

In August 1942 Marlag-Milag Nord, which had hitherto formed a special section of the huge Stalag XB at Sandbostel, was moved to Westertimke, in the flat sandy plain between the Weser and the Elbe, where a new camp was still being built on a pine-planted area to accommodate naval prisoners and was commanded and guarded by German naval personnel. A small compound was set aside for naval officers and a larger one for petty officers and leading seamen, who as non-commissioned officers were exempt from work. The Merchant Navy compound was larger still and held over 3000 officers and seamen drawn from over twenty different nations. The organisation and discipline of this large collection of different ranks and races must have been a most difficult task, but the camp seems to have been soon running smoothly. As civilian internees these men were exempt from compulsory labour, but over 400 worked on maintenance in the camp and a few on farms outside.

Shortly after the Allied landing in French North Africa the camp for military internees at Laghouat was liberated, and the British servicemen, including the four New Zealand airmen, returned to England. The German occupation of Vichy France had taken place about a month previously, and during this period a number of interned British servicemen there, including three New Zealand airmen,[1] were able to make good their escape from Fort de la Revere near Nice and were in England in early October. Others not so fortunate fell into German hands and were later transferred to a prisoner-of-war camp in Germany. Although those shot down in Switzerland and Sweden were closely guarded, a few who came down in the Iberian peninsula were able to make their way to Gibraltar.

IV: *Civilians in Europe*

The German military occupation of Vichy France did not involve the internment of any more New Zealand civilians. In France there remained two men at St. Denis and one young woman and a married couple at Vittel. In accordance with a move by the International Red Cross Committee to have married couples and families reunited in internment, one hotel in Vittel had been set aside for families, elderly couples, and 150 men from St. Denis whose wives were at Vittel. Although the ration scale for an interned civilian was the same as that for any other and therefore less than the German

---

[1] Flt Lt M. B. Barnett, Sgts S. F. Browne, and H. T. Hickton.

civilian ration, those at Vittel were after strong representations placed on the same footing as internees in Germany.

There were in this period six New Zealanders in Ilag VIII at Tost in Silesia and six New Zealand women at Ilag Liebenau, the latter being exchanged at Istanbul in November 1942. Liebenau had the misfortune to become involved in the reprisal campaign, 80 women being locked up in one small damp room as a retaliation for internment conditions in Jamaica. In September 1942 the German authorities moved 2000 men, women, and children from the Channel Islands to internment camps in Germany. They comprised all non-permanent residents and those not born there who were between the ages of 16 and 70 years and were 'English people'. Another 350 were sent in March of the following year. The only New Zealanders affected were a married couple and an elderly woman, who were interned at Ilag Biberach, and two men who went to Ilag VII at Laufen, both camps in Bavaria.

V: *Protection of the Interests of Prisoners of War and Civilians*

It often seemed to prisoners and internees, particularly in those periods of depression with which now and again most of them appear to have been afflicted, that nothing much was being done about their requests and complaints either by Allied governments or by the neutral agencies entrusted with the task of seeing that they were properly treated. In point of fact, every piece of evidence from whatever source that indicated any departure from agreed standards of treatment was the subject of careful investigation by the War Office Directorate of Prisoners of War in conjunction with the Foreign Office, Red Cross, and other interested welfare bodies. If the sources of information were letters or interrogation reports, in fact any reports other than those of the delegates of the Protecting Power, the latter was asked to verify them before taking action. If they were found to be true and to justify a protest, the Protecting Power almost invariably made one, and in the experience of the Directorate of Prisoners of War, this usually achieved some amelioration of the conditions. On the rare occasions when no protest was made, the Protecting Power was immediately asked to make one; and if this was not considered to be strong enough, it was asked to protest in specific terms, demanding the closing of a camp or the punishment of those responsible for bad treatment. When a series of Protecting Power reports from different camps showed that one of the enemy powers was consistently ignoring some article of the Convention, a general protest was sent. Matters of sufficient importance were discussed by the Imperial Prisoners of War Committee and agreed upon by the various governments represented before action was taken. A time lag before the results of these measures were seen in camps was inevitable, and was probably the reason for the commonly held opinion among ex-prisoners of war that little was ever achieved. The deplorable conditions that could obtain in camps not subject to inspection were a measure of the solid though unspectacular achievement of this patient work of protest and negotiation.

Though not the official channel for protests and other communications between belligerents, the International Red Cross Committee played an important part in assisting the betterment of conditions through the information supplied by its visiting delegates, through its official representations to belligerent powers, and through its unofficial contacts with national Red Cross societies. The volume of its work in this field, together with the distribution of relief supplies and the forwarding of information through the Central Agency, had raised its expenditure to such an extent that by June 1942 it was running a monthly deficit of 300,000 Swiss francs. In response to an appeal addressed to all interested governments, the New Zealand War Cabinet decided in January 1943 on the payment of an annual contribution of £2000 sterling, an amount which was later to be increased.

By far the most serious matter for mediation between the belligerent powers that had so far arisen concerned the application of reprisals, and in particular that of binding or shackling prisoners. For a good many months the Allies had been conducting a publicity campaign against any actions by enemy powers, such as the German execution of hostages in France, which came under the heading of 'war atrocities'. This culminated in a solemn declaration by the Allied governments in January 1942, which was followed up in July and August of that year by preliminary steps towards the formation of a commission to deal with atrocities and their perpetrators as 'war criminals' as time should allow. It is not difficult to understand that the Axis governments concerted their propaganda to meet this situation and were alert to seize upon any Allied action which could give the slightest grounds for criticism. An atmosphere was created which was not propitious to calm negotiation, the personal interest of national leaders was aroused, and the former polite suggestions through diplomatic channels that 'reciprocal measures' might have to be taken hardened into the immediate application of reprisals.

A report of irregularities in the treatment of German officers on board the SS *Pasteur* was followed immediately by severe reprisals on the British officers at Oflag IXA/H in September.

Then, after the Dieppe raid in August, the German authorities discovered that some of their men taken prisoner by the landing forces had been bound temporarily, for security reasons, in accordance with a brigade operation order, a copy of which fell into German hands. Germany protested in terms of Article 2 of the Geneva Convention, which laid it down that prisoners 'shall at all times be humanely treated . . .', and Britain in a War Office communique published a statement that there were no general instructions for the tying of prisoners' hands and that 'any such order if it was issued will be cancelled'. Unfortunately similar tying of prisoners occurred in a commando raid on Sark in early October, and on 7 October the German Government threatened to place prisoners taken at Dieppe in irons. Britain in a declaration published next day protested that such reprisals were expressly forbidden by the Convention, but went on:

> Nevertheless should the German Government persist in their intention, His Majesty's Government will be compelled in order to protect their own prisoners of war, to take similar measures upon an equal number of enemy prisoners of war in their hands.

The tying and shackling of prisoners already described at Oflag VIIB, at Stalag VIIIB, and at Stalag 383 then followed. Britain shackled an equal number of German prisoners, and Germany shackled three times the previous number.

There was no knowing where this might end, and clearly if it was a game of numbers the advantage rested with the Germans. The situation had rapidly developed into one in which the whole question of the treatment of prisoners of war under the Geneva Convention might be jeopardised in order to satisfy the prestige of governments. Moreover there was a fear, expressed by the Australian Government, that the controversy might affect the treatment of prisoners by the other Axis powers, notably Japan. Germany gave a hint that inhumane treatment of Germans by any one of the Allied powers, Russia for example, might have repercussions on the whole body of prisoners taken by Germany irrespective of nationality. There was a good deal of public feeling in England against the shackling of German prisoners, and our men in Germany were taken aback to find that the Allied authorities had descended to reprisals. By 13 October, however, the British Government had offered to withdraw these counter-measures if Germany also desisted from shackling. The Swiss Government and the International Red Cross Committee were well aware of the seriousness of the threat to the future welfare of prisoners of war, and both offered their services in any form of mediation that might be practicable. The ordinary means of negotiation having failed, they were asked to take whatever action they thought fit.

The Swiss Minister in Berlin concentrated his efforts on the concluding of an agreement for the termination of shackling at a mutually agreed time. There were many in the German Foreign Office and High Command who would have liked to see shackling at an end, but the political leaders were adamant and difficult of approach, especially when the war turned against them. Meanwhile, in order not to exacerbate feeling, the whole matter was given as little publicity as possible. It was hoped that the large number of German prisoners captured during the Alamein offensive might have some influence, but a German reply to overtures in December talked in terms of 'confessions' by the British Government and demanded the issue by them of strict orders forbidding tying of prisoners in all circumstances. Hearing that the Germans intended to remove prisoners' shackles during Christmas week, the Swiss Government and the International Red Cross appealed on 8 December to both belligerents to continue this concession for an indefinite period afterwards. The British and Canadian Governments took the opportunity to free their prisoners from chains on 12 December and never rechained them. In Germany prisoners were freed for Christmas Day and New Year's Day and then reshackled.

Meanwhile, although Britain would not agree that tying of prisoners in the field might not be necessary from time to time under stress of circumstances, new War Office orders in February 1943 forbade the general tying up of prisoners and made it incumbent on all ranks to know and observe the terms of the Geneva Convention, especially in the treatment of prisoners immediately after capture; and these new orders were adopted by the New Zealand War Cabinet. In February there were indications that the German High Command had begun to regard shackling as symbolical of their opposition to the British view that tying of prisoners might sometimes be justified, and by March this attitude was confirmed. Some commandants began making efforts to treat shackled prisoners well, and by April 'symbolical' shackling consisted of no more than the issue of the required numbers of handcuffs in the morning at half past eight and their collection in the evening at half past seven. It was clear that German officials were seeking a way out that would save face and at the same time not inflict hardship on British prisoners.

Another reprisal measure taken by the German authorities during this period concerned prisoners' mail. Because of delays in receipt of mail by German prisoners in Canada and Australia, British prisoners in Germany were to be allowed inward and outward mail only in proportion to that being received by the former.[1] This reprisal lasted from August until October 1942, by which time the delays in our own service had been corrected. It had become clear, however, that the Germans were short of censors. As from 1943 communications to organisations or to regimental headquarters were allowed by the Germans only through the camp leader. Letter mail in Italy too suffered long hold-ups in the censor's office. And in order to avoid cluttering up the mail service any further in both countries it was found necessary to appeal to the public to cease writing to 'lonely' prisoners as penfriends—a practice which had been general in the earlier part of the war.

Reprisals so far as the Italian Government was concerned took the form of the red patches and the exorbitant additional charges for officers' messing already mentioned. As the latter was in response to an additional messing charge imposed on Italian officers in British hands, negotiations on the matter ended in April 1943 with all of the extra amount being refunded to both sets of officers concerned, and an undertaking by the Italian authorities that messing charges for British officers would be kept down to 15 lire a day.

Mention has already been made of German attempts to force NCO prisoners to work, either by declining to recognise their status and proceeding against them for refusal to work or, if their status was recognised, by withholding issues of Red Cross clothing and in other ways making their position in the stalag uncomfortable. There were sometimes complaints among the men that voluntary NCO workers occupied places in the good working camps (for they could very often nominate the *Arbeitskommandos* to which they wished to go), instead of remaining in the stalag and maintaining their right not to work at all. But in 1941 and 1942, when conditions at numbers of work-camps were bad and men, no matter how sick, were forced out to work by the use of arms, some NCOs went out to work-camps from a sense of duty in order to try and protect the men's interests. And as labour in Germany became shorter and hours of work increased, many of these camp leaders were able greatly to help the men under them. Until September 1942 those NCOs who elected to work had to sign an undertaking to do so for the duration of their captivity; after that date, however, an agreement was made whereby the work could be relinquished at any time, the same conditions being applied to German NCOs in British hands. At about that

---

[1] In some *Arbeitskommandos* outward mail was restricted to one letter and one postcard every two months.

time non-working Army NCOs, with the exception of those in administrative positions in the stalags, were moved to Stalag 383. Air Force NCOs, who had long been debarred from work owing to numerous attempts to escape, remained in Stalag VIIIB and other camps pending their transfer to special Air Force camps.

Medical orderlies who had been captured without any evidence to show that they were protected were similarly coerced, and some who persisted in their refusal to work served sentences of imprisonment, which sometimes continued even after their protected status had been established. Many who had proved their identity as members of the Medical Corps assisted in camp infirmaries, hospitals, and work-camps, but a good many others who had not been allowed to perform medical duties chose to do some other kind of work. In their efforts to extract the greatest possible labour force from the prisoner-of-war population, the German authorities would not accept a British typewritten statement concerning a soldier's protected status; and even when individual certificates were sent according to a special agreement between the two powers, they declined to deliver them unless reason could be shown why the addressee did not possess his original proof of identity. With negotiations again in progress for an exchange of protected personnel, recognition became a matter of some urgency for those who were eligible for repatriation, and by May 1943 most of the certificates had been distributed. Up till the end of this period, however, Germany had given no indication whether she would agree to a set scale for retention of protected personnel similar to that arranged between Britain and Italy; and it seemed clear that, certificates or no certificates, she intended to retain as many British medical personnel as she thought were necessary.

A large amount of the negotiations during this period dealt with repatriation of sick and wounded and of protected personnel. Although they did not bear fruit in Italy until April 1943 the negotiations were still more protracted in the case of Germany, as the bitterness arising from the reprisals made negotiation on almost anything a delicate and difficult matter. To deal more expeditiously with this particular branch of prisoner-of-war work, two Repatriation Committees were set up in London, one to handle the terms of negotiations with the enemy powers and the other to make administrative arrangements for carrying out any projected repatriation operations. The committees were separate from the Imperial Prisoners of War Committee, although provision was made for reference to the latter 'where necessary and where time permits'. Provision was also made for the co-option 'as and when required' of Dominion representatives who were omitted from the composition of Committee No. 1; in practice, however, they attended the first meeting in June 1942 and all subsequent meetings, and in September they were invited to sit as permanent members.

VI: *Relief Work*

The necessity for a considerable supplement to the diet provided for our prisoners by both Germany and Italy, if they were to maintain their health, never passed.[1] The large increase in the number of British prisoners resulting from the fall of Tobruk and the subsequent Axis advance upset the numerical calculations of those organising British relief, and made it difficult to maintain supplies at the per capita rate which had hitherto prevailed. To avoid any future surprises of this kind, it was decided to maintain a reserve of twelve weeks' supplies both in existing camps and at Geneva.[2] This created problems in storage, especially at Geneva, where it was difficult to find warehouse accommodation to house the enormous amount of relief supplies required. The main task, however, was to produce the goods, and the British Red Cross weekly target of 150,000 food parcels was temporarily increased by another 64,000 until the necessary reserves should have been built up. Included in this total were some 80,000 from Canada and (as from the beginning of 1943) 8000 from New Zealand,[3] where the packing organisation of the Joint Council had stepped up its output to cover approximately the increase in numbers of New Zealand prisoners.

While arrangements were being made to supply this increased mass of prisoners with outfits of clothing, there came a request from the camp leader at Stalag XXA in November 1942 that

---

[1] On data available to the British Red Cross up to the time of the Italian capitulation, the dietetic position in Italian camps for British prisoners was as follows:

	Italian Ration	Red Cross Parcel	Total	Full Diet
Protein (gms)	55	42	97	70
Calcium (mgms)	460	533	993	800
Iron (mgms)	10	9	19	12
Vitamin A (international units)	890	3274	4164	4000
Vitamin B (international units)	260	180	440	600
Riboflavin (mgms)	0·6	0·5	1·1	2·2
Nicotinic Acid (mgms)	9	6·1	15·1	15
Vitamin C (mgms)	7	28	35	75
Calories	1290	1551	2841	3000

The Italians also allowed the supply of fresh fruit and vegetables to the value of one lira a day.

[2] The British Red Cross estimated that in order to assure regular supplies at the standard rate it was necessary to have 29 food parcels for each prisoner somewhere on the line of transport.

[3] New Zealanders taken prisoner rose in this period to some 8500, over one-eighth of our overseas servicemen.

men in working camps should be allowed two suits instead of one. Representations by International Red Cross delegates, who had visited the mining camps and those attached to industrial projects where the work was hard on clothes, were able to convince the War Office that a change of clothing for these men was necessary both for hygienic reasons and for the sake of individual morale. Although employers were supposed to provide working clothes, in fact very few were able to procure them. It was clear that Germany was evading her obligations under the Geneva Convention in this as in other aspects of her provision for prisoners, but it was equally clear that, in the prevailing mood of her leaders, intransigence on our part would have little effect on them and would merely produce additional hardship for our own men in Germany. It seemed likely, too, that economic considerations would be outweighed by the propaganda effect of well-dressed British prisoners on German civilians. At all events 20,000 to 30,000 extra suits of battle dress were allocated for distribution as a change of clothing, under the control of the International Red Cross delegates, at certain camps where it was thought necessary. The maintenance of these additional supplies of clothing was complicated by the fact that Switzerland had objections to holding large quantities of British military uniform.

Similarly it was thought advisable to continue the despatch of medical and surgical material and invalid diets,[1] though modified according to the recommendations of repatriated medical officers and the wishes of those remaining in camp infirmaries and prisoner-of-war hospitals. The International Red Cross Orthopaedic Mission made a tour of German camps and hospitals for the purpose of examining amputees in the latter half of 1942, and returned in June 1943 to fit artificial limbs which had been made in Switzerland from British materials. With dental material supplied by the British Red Cross, the surgery at Lamsdorf was able to turn out an average of between forty and fifty artificial dentures a month, besides doing a large number of fillings—only a fraction, however, of the work necessary to restore among all the British prisoners something approaching their state of dental health before capture.

Although the Italian censorship authorities by the severity of their restrictions made the development of educational work in their camps a difficult matter, in Germany, where the authorities had begun to give it considerable encouragement, a great deal

---

[1] The weekly rate of supply in June 1943 was: Medical units, 450; invalid diets, 15,000—apart from special consignments such as cod-liver oil and malt.

was being done. By early 1943 the British Red Cross Educational Books Section had sent out over 5500 courses and well over 100,000 books. The latter were in addition to books from other sources, including private book parcels, considerable numbers of which were now coming from New Zealand, the censorship being undertaken by a newly formed section of the Joint Council's Inquiry Office. In July 1942 the first results of examinations held in camps were announced, and by the end of June 1943 nearly 500 prisoners had received their results. New Zealanders made up only some 3 per cent of this total, but it must be remembered that at this stage there was no machinery for the taking of New Zealand examinations, and the recognition of London equivalents by New Zealand bodies was, to the prisoners at any rate, problematical.

Recreational material such as general reading matter, indoor games, sporting units, and sets of team clothing reached prisoner-of-war camps in an increasing stream. Camp padres were assisted with religious books and equipment for conducting services. After some early distrust on the part of the British Ministry of Economic Warfare, seeds were sent regularly to bring to camps the pleasure of growing flowers and to make possible additions to camp diet in the form of salads and vegetables. The volume of private parcels of clothing, books, and tobacco to be handled by the New Zealand authorities increased considerably. During this period over 5500 next-of-kin parcels were sent from the packing centre of the Prisoners of War Section in London, apart from their regular monthly consignments of cigarettes and tobacco, and the number of next-of-kin parcels censored at the Joint Council inquiry offices in New Zealand increased from under 1000 a month in 1942 to upwards of 2000 in 1943.

The transport of such an increased volume of relief presented new difficulties, in addition to the temporary hold-up caused by the German occupation of Vichy France. Until the position concerning the use of the land route from Marseilles to Geneva for relief trains had been settled, no further sailings of transport from Lisbon took place. The fleet of six ships was however increased to eleven in 1943, and in the period April to August of that year brought more than six and a half million parcels from Lisbon. Transport of this mass of valuable goods through the enemy countries from Geneva seems at this stage of the war to have been less hazardous than the earlier part of its journey. Acknowledgment from camp leaders showed that in the twelve months ending August 1943 more than six and a half million food parcels, not to mention large quantities of other kinds of relief, were received in their camps, and that only a very small percentage of their consignments had been lost through pilferage or other causes.[1]

VII: *Enemy Aliens in New Zealand*

The camp for civilian internees on Somes Island described in an earlier chapter remained in use until the end of 1942. Since the entry of Japan into the war, 47 Japanese and three Thai civilians had been evacuated from various Pacific islands to New Zealand for internment. These and a further 53 German civilians, mostly merchants and planters from Samoa, Tonga, and Fiji, brought the numbers on Somes Island at the end of 1942 to 185. Some of the internees were elderly, and an attempt was made to give these men more privacy by the erection of private cubicles. The internees were left fairly free to organise their own domestic arrangements and recreation. Outside they had a tennis court and a bowling green, and they could move freely over the island except to the beaches, where however they were permitted to fish and swim under guard. Inside they had billiard tables and other indoor games, a good library, an orchestra and film shows. On the other hand, there was no opportunity on the island to earn pocket money by doing paid work, the camp was exposed to southerly storms which made winter weather conditions damp and bleak, and Wellington Harbour was rapidly becoming an important centre of naval and military activity and, therefore, highly dangerous in case of enemy attack.

At the end of January 1943 the internees were moved to a new camp on the former racecourse two miles south of Pahiatua. Here, if they could not escape the wind entirely, they were less exposed than on Somes Island. The camp was already well equipped with dormitory, mess, and hospital buildings constructed of concrete blocks, and recreation barracks and grounds were being prepared. There were wire and kapok mattresses, sheets, and up to six blankets for each internee. Food and drink were on the same liberal scale as previously, and separate menus catered for the different tastes of Germans, Italians, and Japanese. Here the internees were able to work on jobs for the completion of the camp and in vegetable gardens outside; for this work they were paid at the rate of five shillings a day. They were able also to continue their hobby of making small articles ornamented with paua shell and to sell these to certain institutions which disposed

---

[1]The losses recorded in transit between Geneva and camps in 1942 were as follows:

Food parcels	·0013 per cent
Clothing bales	·0032 per cent
Tobacco parcels	·0035 per cent
Other relief	·0016 per cent

of them on the New Zealand market. The internees were on cordial terms with the camp authorities, and there can be little doubt that the general treatment at Pahiatua was, as a neutral inspector described it, 'excellent'.

* * * * *

The Italian transit camps in North Africa were in this period even worse than those of the preceding campaign. But although there were a few vicious and anti-British commandants, there were others who did their best, and there was probably on the whole no intent to maltreat. The standards of food, clothing, sanitation, and medical care for the Italian soldier were lower than those for the British, and what passed for a temporary transit camp by their standards failed by a long way to satisfy our own. It seems likely, too, that the Italian military authorities really intended to evacuate the prisoners from North Africa to Italy almost immediately after their capture, and not to leave them rotting in filthy desert cages as they did; but Allied sea and air activity in the Mediterranean reduced sea transport to a minimum and delayed the process of evacuation so much that it spread over many months.

In the same way, on the mainland, although there were some shocking transit-camp conditions (the mass of our men did not experience the worst), the intention was on the whole to treat British prisoners well. One or two of the officers' camps provided luxuries which not even the most optimistic prisoner expected, even if at the same time they lacked some of what we regard as the most elementary necessities. There might be no adequate water supply (and most Italian prisoner-of-war camps suffered from this deficiency), but officer prisoners were seldom without wine and could often buy the more expensive varieties through their canteens. Italy is of course a wine producing country, while her agricultural population has never been accustomed to the standards of sanitary engineering that our local bodies would demand. Perhaps this and other similar anomalies are also indicative of the contrast between a Latin love of enjoyment and our more sober pursuit of health and cleanliness.

In some respects it was clear that Italy simply did not have the supplies: timber for buildings and furniture, fuel for heating, staple foods—especially meat—and warm clothing and blankets. But the climate of Italy is such that once the three winter months have been surmounted, life can be lived largely in the open air. Whatever could be supplied seems to have been made available to British prisoners. There were bed sheets for every British other rank, until it was realised that British authorities were unable to supply them for the vast numbers of Italian other ranks in their hands. On the other hand, instead of socks there were only square pieces of cotton cloth. There is little doubt that after our men were supplied with British Red Cross food, British Army clothing supplemented by parcels from home, and the cigarettes and books that came through relief channels, they were better off by far in these respects than the average Italian soldier and great numbers of Italian civilians.

This had a good deal to do with the high morale which prevailed among our men in Italian prisoner-of-war camps, together with a sunny climate and opportunities for healthy outdoor exercise both in sport and later in work on the farms and in the hills. The Italians, with few exceptions, made little attempt to depress morale or convert British prisoners to Fascism. There was a news sheet in English—*The Prisoner of War News*—a half-hearted affair after the style of *The Camp* in Germany, edited in Rome and distributed to camps. Some Italian officers, in addition to those who were kindly disposed in any case, set themselves to leave as good an impression as possible with the British who were temporarily in their custody. But the initiative in propaganda activity lay rather with the prisoners, who found it easy to work on the soldiers and civilians of a nation which was becoming more and more weary of what now seemed a futile war against Britain and America.

By the spring of 1943 the treatment of British prisoners at most of the permanent camps in Italy was such that, when allowance was made for material shortcomings remedied by relief, there was little room for serious complaint. There were still long delays in the censorship of letter mail at the central office in Rome; and the same office by withholding large numbers of books, mutilating others, and refusing to admit study courses or allow the conduct of examinations, greatly hampered the library and educational facilities which camps were trying to organise. This suspicious zeal in carrying out security measures could even extend to the inhumanity of forbidding braille material for the blind. The central military authorities which ordered the sewing of red patches on British prisoners' uniform also did little to help their own security, and a good deal to confirm the prisoners' opinion that they were hardly to be taken seriously. But these were minor annoyances, often largely mitigated by Italian camp staffs, many of whom were becoming more and more openly friendly; and this in spite of the hostility of local Fascists and occasional anti-British outbursts in the press. On the whole, prisoners in Italian camps at this stage were in good health and high spirits. The continued successes of the

Allied forces in North Africa, culminating in the Tunisian campaign, helped to enhance a feeling that they should be giving the orders rather than taking them, and to engender a feeling of exaltation that the trials of captivity might soon be over.

Although for prisoners in Germany there were no indications of approaching liberty, their morale had steadily increased until it began to give the German authorities serious concern. The latter were in a difficult position. On the one hand they needed the work done by prisoners of war in order to make up for the depletion of their civilian labour force; in early 1943 this became so acute that it was necessary to increase the hours for all workers and to recruit more prisoners for mines and other essential industries. A German official statement of this period runs:

> In view of the shortage of man-power, the fullest use (within the limits of the Convention) must be made of prisoner-of-war labour, thus obtaining maximum benefit from their capture.

On the other hand the German propaganda campaign, which was designed to present Germans as humane and 'chivalrous'[1] in their treatment of prisoners in order to give the lie to the Allied accusations about atrocities, forced them to make numerous improvements and concessions and to listen to prisoners' complaints in a way that mystified their own subordinate guards. A German report from Graz stated, 'It often happens that the guards are arrested on the strength of a British report'. A German guard NCO wrote, 'It's no wonder the British get cheeky, as the officers listen to their complaints privately, and simply send the German soldiers out of the room'.

Thus many such occurrences could be traced to the general international situation; but other underlying factors were good leadership of the prisoners in the camps concerned and high morale among the prisoners generally. Although the improved strategic position of the Allies did a good deal to strengthen and increase morale, British prisoners had from the first not only stood up to their captors but kept up what the Germans described as 'the British tradition of behaving as Herrenvolk'. A factory foreman who tried to dictate unreasonable working hours and conditions was told by a British man-of-confidence that he might be able to impose such terms on prisoners of other nations, but that he must remember he was now dealing with the British. Another detachment of British prisoners going to a new place of work had no difficulty in

---

[1] In the declaration of the German Supreme Command concerning the reprisals at Oflag IXA/H, occurred the following passage: '. . . . up to now it has always been the earnest endeavour of the German Supreme Command to treat the British POW with chivalrous consideration.'

hiring some German boys with a few pieces of chocolate to carry their luggage. Another group demanded that the Fuhrer's portrait should be removed from the dining room which had been allotted to them in the factory where they worked. Germans complained that British prisoners marched along singing 'a rude song' to the tune of *Deutschland uber Alles*. Although the extent of sabotage caused by British prisoners during work is unlikely to have been sufficient to have had any appreciable effect on the German war effort, they speak of British prisoners doing railway maintenance work so badly that they had to be taken off it for fear it might lead to the derailment of trains. They speak bitterly too of British ' swinging the lead' by having as many as 50 per cent on the sick list at one time; though it is known that this sometimes resulted in an irate guard commander picking on the really sick men to send out to work. Broadly speaking, German opinion was that the British did just enough work to avoid being penalised—an opinion which is confirmed by numerous statements of New Zealand ex-prisoners.

It is clear that the German authorities were specially concerned about the effect of such behaviour on the civilian population. In a secret report[1] the SS summed up the situation thus:

> The manner in which the British behave to the population leaves no doubt of their confidence in victory. They take every opportunity to show that they will soon be masters of Germany. This assurance of victory and self-possession does not fail to impress the people, who think they see in these qualities the symbol of British strength.

According to the German view, British prisoners on farms were ' particularly arrogant to the local population '; they acted as though they were ' lord of the manor ', were ' waited on hand and foot ', accepted no orders and did exactly as they liked. Though this is an extreme statement, ex-prisoners' own accounts make it clear that they were given a great deal of latitude. The German account goes on to complain bitterly:

> The prisoners are particularly well-treated by the womenfolk, who believe the political prophecies of the British and think it clever to ingratiate themselves.

A great number of the prisoners had taken advantage of their enforced stay in Germany to learn the language thoroughly; many could converse with fluency and seldom lost an opportunity in their speech and their manner to spread disaffection among civilians and guards.

---

[1] The quotations in this and the preceding paragraph are from a captured German secret report by the SS on internal security, dated 12 August 1943, section entitled *Herren Engländer*. The term 'British' is used here, as elsewhere in this book, to denote those from all British Commonwealth countries.

Another factor responsible in large part for the high morale of British prisoners and for their demoralising effect on some of the German populace was the good health and tidy appearance resulting from regular and complete relief supplies through Red Cross channels. A report from Görlitz complained that the British were 'undoubtedly healthier' than the average German worker but that their output was 50 per cent lower. A report from Klagenfurt reads:

> Of all the prisoners of war in this district, the British are the most respected and discussed by the local population. The reason for this lies in the smart appearance of individuals, as well as the smartness of organised units of British prisoners. The British are always decently dressed, their uniforms are always in faultless condition, they are shaved, clean, and well-fed. Their attitude is extraordinarily self-possessed, one could almost say arrogant and over-bearing. This, combined with the good impression they give of the nation, influences the German people in a way that should not be underestimated. When they march in formation, they frequently look better than our own German replacement units. You can see that the uniform they wear is of much better material than the German uniform.[1]

Prisoners were always careful to display the contents of their food parcels when going among the German public, especially those articles which were very short in Germany; and children were often given small presents of chocolate to show how much better off people were in British countries. The diary of a New Zealander in an *Arbeitskommando* at Gleiwitz shows progressive steps in the attitude of German people. In December 1942 he records: 'Civilians won't argue with you now; things have changed a lot'. In January he notes that 'guards and civilians now come and listen to what we say', and, at the same time, that a notice was posted up in the camp, warning prisoners not to spread propaganda by spoken word or by drawings or by writing. By March civilians are making a practice of saying *Guten Morgen,* children are friendly, and *Engländer* are the 'most popular prisoners'. The March entry concludes with, 'What a change in the last year!'

The German propaganda machine was bound to take some action to counteract all this, at least to restore the waning faith of civilians in the Nazi way of life, even if British prisoners appeared more hopelessly sceptical and materialist than ever. In an attempt to throw the atrocity accusation back at the Allies, the slightest departure from 'correct' treatment by the latter was seized upon and magnified. In October 1942 *Völkischer Beobachter* devoted a great part of one issue to a discussion of these incidents and a comparison with the 'correctness' of German treatment. Unfortu-

---

[1] *Herren Engländer,* Op. cit.

nately the indignation thus stirred up became a runaway horse, which carried off political leaders too. At an early stage of the 'shackling' dispute it looked as if prisoners might be used by the Axis powers as hostages for the Allied conduct of the war.[1] The hastily conceived reprisal measures, however, not only became a matter for disgust among those who had to apply them, but did much to counteract the whole propaganda campaign. At all events in the period under review they did little to lessen the goodwill towards British prisoners growing among German civilians.

As to influencing the prisoners themselves against their own country, the latter had for some time past been supplying them with much of their food, all their clothing, and most of the other main essentials of a civilised existence, and was now piling up successes against the Axis powers. Here the German Ministry of Propaganda faced a wellnigh impossible task. To a German officer who told him that the Red Cross parcels for British prisoners were sent as propaganda, a prisoner replied that at least you could eat the British propaganda. In mid-1942 the Germans had not failed to rub in the apparent hopelessness of the Allied position. The fall of Tobruk, the German advance in the East, and Germany's claim to have repulsed an invasion at Dieppe had set men wondering, but most gave no sign of it to the enemy. A year later, however, *The Camp* and Lord Haw-Haw were having a struggle to appear convincing. They began to concentrate on the denigration of Russia, both to goad their own people into greater efforts and, if possible, to engender suspicion among prisoners of their Russian allies. Thus, besides the publication of articles and photographs depicting the massacre of Poles and their burial in the 'Katyn ditch', an endeavour was made to force numbers of British officers in May 1943 to go and see the actual exhibits at the scene of the atrocity. But even if the German propaganda had not been always so blatant and obvious, the BBC news bulletins, to which most camps had access through a secret radio, would have been sufficient to nullify it.

This period was one of anxiety for next-of-kin in far-off New Zealand. Apart from earthquakes and the constant threat of Japanese invasion, there were again long delays in receiving news of sons or husbands taken prisoner, for the large numbers of new prisoners captured in North Africa again clogged the machinery of notification. Delays were always caused not only by sudden increases in numbers, but by the necessity of transportation to permanent camps, and (for the sick and wounded) by a period in hospital,

---

[1] It would no doubt have been greatly to Germany's advantage if 'Commando' methods could have been ruled out at this stage of the war. Japan, too, feared United States reprisals for the execution of American airmen shot down over Tokyo.

where things were seldom properly organised for the taking of particulars. However, the reciprocal agreement between Britain and Germany for telegraphing captures of airmen to Geneva was in this period extended to naval and army prisoners. By this means, when the numbers captured were not great and when there was no other impediment, official information reached next-of-kin on the average four or five weeks after capture. There were many sources of unofficial information: British Legation lists, capture-cards, escapers' accounts, Vatican broadcasts and lists, enemy broadcasts; and these were passed on but subject to confirmation. By a new British Army Council order of December 1942 (adopted by New Zealand War Cabinet in February 1943) prisoners were forbidden to broadcast. Information was often transmitted or received inaccurately, and in any case the use of the German radio helped enemy propaganda by encouraging the public to listen in—an aspect of the matter which most prisoners did not fully appreciate. As against the early delays in notification and the mail reprisals of 1942, there were two improvements in communication both in Italy and Germany: the institution of an airmail letter service[1] and permission to send home personal photographs taken in camp, the latter of considerable value for the morale of next-of-kin.

Repatriated men who had arrived home brought first-hand news to many families, and generally did much to allay anxiety and uncertainty about the lot of prisoners in Italy. For a time they were able to answer a great many of the questions with which parents and wives had been bombarding the Prisoners of War Section in London and the Joint Council inquiry offices in New Zealand: questions about health, living conditions, reprisals, and the delivery of mail and parcels. These organisations, like the British Red Cross, were also kept busy answering numerous questions from prisoners: about their family troubles, about births and deaths, about their non-receipt of mail, and about the dangers to New Zealand from invasion. The newsletters sent out to camps from New Zealand House in London did something to keep prisoners in touch with what was happening at home. The arrival of repatriates in New Zealand stimulated interest there in the possibility of further exchanges; but in spite of the public demand for information on this subject the Government had to preserve a strict silence, lest negotiations should be prejudiced as they had been in 1940. With the position of Italy in 1943 becoming more and more shaky, hopes were raised that there might soon be repatriation of a different kind.

---

[1] Under this scheme letters were flown from Germany to Lisbon and from Lisbon to USA, whence they were taken by sea to New Zealand.

This 'post-war' repatriation, as it came to be called, had been the subject of detailed planning by the military authorities since September 1942.[1] It was to have been a large-scale operation, for British Commonwealth prisoners in Italy had risen to a total of some 63,000.[2] By the middle of 1943 it looked as if these carefully laid plans might soon be put into effect.

---

[1] Dominions were being consulted on the subject as early as January 1942.
[2] New Zealanders made up 3500 of this total.

CHAPTER 7

The Italian Armistice

(July–December 1943)

I: *Events preceding and immediately following the Italian Armistice*

MAY 1943 saw the end of Axis resistance in North Africa and the surrender of many thousands of German and Italian troops in Tunisia. Prisoners in Italy, closely studying the Fascist press or gleaning the news from friendly guards and civilians, wondered what the next Allied move would be. Most felt that Italy's days of active warfare against the Allies were numbered. Many civilians and camp guards were making no secret of their distaste for the war, and it was clear that the latter would need little inducement to leave the forces and return to their homes. Then on 9 July came the invasion of Sicily, and with it some solid fact on which prisoners might base hopes of liberation. They began speculating on how the end would come, and plans were elaborated for taking over camps and arranging protection and supplies in case of disorder. On 25 July Mussolini resigned, the Fascist Party was dissolved, and Badoglio took over control of the country. Although it was felt that an armistice was very near, it was still hard to foresee the manner in which it would affect prisoner-of-war camps.

Meanwhile plans had been co-ordinated by British Commonwealth military authorities for the taking over of all prisoner-of-war camps in the event of an Italian armistice and for the repatriation of all British Commonwealth prisoners of war. An Armistice Commission would be set up and would have working under it a Prisoner of War Sub-Commission, which would be responsible for the administration of all liberated prisoners of war and for their final repatriation—United Kingdom and Canadian troops to the United Kingdom and all others to the Middle East. Distribution headquarters formed at convenient points would be responsible for the feeding, care of sick and wounded, and evacuation of the prisoner-of-war camps in their areas. The men would be moved to specially set-up transit camps near the ports of embarkation,[1] and would go on arrival in the United Kingdom or the Middle East to specially set-up reception camps. With four distribution points, and with

---
[1] Genoa, Naples, Brindisi, and Leghorn.

transit and reception camps planned to hold 4000–5000 each, a staff of over 6000 was required to deal with the whole 60,000 to 70,000 British Commonwealth prisoners then estimated to be in Italy. The whole plan was based on the assumption that prisoners would remain at their prisoner-of-war camps and await instructions (to be dropped by air); and to prevent any prisoners leaving, the War Office found means to convey to almost every camp in Italy an instruction to that effect.

There had been a hint in December 1942 that, in view of the impending collapse of Italy, British prisoners held there would be transferred to Germany. But, to an inquiry by the Italian ambassador to the Vatican, Mussolini had replied that there was no truth in the report. Nevertheless between 20 and 22 July 2400 prisoners[1] were transported to Germany and accommodated in Stalag IVB at Mühlberg. Men in other camps were warned at about the same time that they were soon to be moved to an unknown destination. After the fall of Mussolini, in reply to a protest by Great Britain, the Badoglio Government gave an assurance that there would be no more such transfers, at the same time explaining that those already transferred had been originally captured by the German forces.[2] Visits to prisoner-of-war camps by inspectors from the Swiss Legation had been suspended as from 14 July, and even the Badoglio Government insisted on a month's notice of a forthcoming visit of inspection. To this there was a strong complaint from Britain, for in the difficult situation that might develop it was more than usually important for neutral inspectors to be on hand to protect the interests of defenceless prisoners.

In prisoner-of-war camps, although individuals of the enemy guard companies expected an early end to the war so far as Italy was concerned and were indeed obviously keen to see their country surrender as soon as possible, disciplinary and security measures were if anything tightened up. At Campo PG 57 (strict at all times), in order to prevent individual prisoners accumulating Red Cross food, whole parcels were no longer issued but merely one-seventh to each man each day; at Campo PG 106/20 men were put in jail for not working; at several camps there were searches more thorough than had occurred for some time. The sudden news of the coup d'état and the simultaneous change of tone in all the newspapers made prisoners realise that the end could not be

---

[1] Only four New Zealanders.
[2] In point of fact most of the British prisoners held in Italy had been so captured. It is possible that if Germany was demanding the custody of all those captured by her forces, the 2400 mentioned above were sent to satisfy her; and the explanation in the Italian Note to the Foreign Office was to give colour to the idea that she had now carried out Germany's demand. On the other hand, Germany must have been well aware that a much larger number had been captured by the Afrika Korps.

far off. In some places prisoners were invited to help in the defacement of public Fascist symbols which had been ordered by the new regime. In spite of public announcements that Italy would fight on, civilians hinted that Badoglio would soon speak and all would be finished.

Most camp leaders had received the War Office instruction for prisoners to remain in their camps, and had in some made elaborate plans for taking over from the Italians and preventing disorder in the neighbourhood. In Campo PG 47 at Modena[1] the plans included taking over a nearby airfield and manning the planes, Air Force prisoners in the camp having undergone a course of instruction from one of their number conversant with enemy types of aircraft. There was in nearly every camp a reserve of Red Cross food sufficient to last a week or two. The instruction to remain inside had not been generally promulgated, and a large percentage of individuals had prepared haversacks, whatever civilian clothes they could lay hands on, maps, and other necessities for a trek in whatever direction it might be best to go in the event of trouble. Prisoners were acutely aware of the possibility of transfer to Germany and further imprisonment there under unknown conditions; but there was so little reliable information about what was happening outside that it was wellnigh impossible to decide on a definite plan of action. As time went on the atmosphere at some camps became tense; early hopes of release gave place to suspense and anxiety. Had all prisoners been able to see German troops nearby digging in at the end of August, as did those working near Bussolengo (Campo PG 148), it might not have been so difficult for them to decide what to do.

In the last two or three months before the armistice there were a good many transfers of groups of prisoners from one camp to another, and especially of other ranks to working detachments. Most of the permanent camps for British prisoners had for some time been in the central and northern provinces of Italy, and in July and August the last of those still remaining in the south were evacuated and moved north. Officers from Padula (Campo PG 35), among whom there were still a few New Zealanders, were moved during August to Campo PG 19, newly set up at Bologna, where they were joined by officers from Sulmona and more southern camps. During the month Allied bombing in southern Italy increased in preparation for the landings, and on the 20th damage to the water supply, sewage system, and buildings of Campo PG 66

---

[1] Plans had also been formulated in Campo PG 19 at Bologna and numerous others. Campo PG 47 is given as an example because it contained by far the greatest number of New Zealand officers.

at Capua necessitated its evacuation north.[1] By the end of the month Campo PG 85 at Tuturano, Campo PG 75 at Bari, and Campo PG 65 at Gravina, together with their satellite working camps, had also been moved, most of the New Zealand officers going to Modena and other ranks to Gruppignano.

The hospital patients at Nocera (Ospedale PG 206) had been transferred to Milan in mid-June and those at Altamura (Ospedale PG 204) a little later. Though moved out of the potential danger zone, their new accommodation exposed them perhaps even more to Allied air operations. A prisoner-of-war hospital (Ospedale PG 207) was set up in a school building opposite a factory in central Milan. On 13 August during a bombing raid the building was wrecked by blast, a number of prisoners losing their lives (including three New Zealand medical orderlies), and the remainder being evacuated to Ospedale PG 201 at Bergamo.

Allied troops landed at Calabria on the Italian mainland on 3 September, the day on which the armistice with Italy was secretly signed. Some camps, for example Campo PG 57, had been kept without newspapers or broadcast bulletins for some weeks, no doubt for fear of demonstrations or even organised rebellion. At most camps, however, and especially at working camps, the news leaked in and soon circulated. Men waited expectantly for the announcement of Italy's capitulation, which they hoped would set them free again after periods of up to two years in captivity. There had been some attempts at escape in July and August, but they now seemed unnecessary and even foolhardy. Work continued at the labour camps and organised recreation and sport at the base camps. With a new and almost entirely unpredictable situation imminent it was easiest to carry on with routine, which helped to take men's minds off too much speculation about the future. There was little interference with mail services: letters poured in, the censorship authorities in Rome apparently making a final effort to clear their office of the accumulation of months. Private parcels, too, arrived in large numbers, and consignments of Red Cross food were kept up, a batch of 2500 food parcels reaching Campo PG 107 as late as 10 September.

The news of the armistice reached most camps in the early evening of 8 September. In many of them excited guards were cheering as they acclaimed the end of the war, at the same time throwing away their arms and preparing to leave for their homes in civilian clothes, though this did not generally happen on a large scale until the news reached them that the Germans were

---

[1] The locations of all prisoner-of-war camps in Italy had been notified to Allied Headquarters, and steps had been taken to avoid their being attacked from the air or bombarded from the sea.

on the way to take over the camp. On the whole it was received by prisoners phlegmatically—almost with disbelief, though among them too there were some scenes of rejoicing and a good deal of toasting where wine was obtainable. A few of them got away in the confusion, some seizing the opportunity to escape, others merely to pick grapes in a nearby field or to sample the local wine. But most men went back to their games of bridge or to their unfinished snacks of supper, and at Modena the orchestra played in the open air, at last able to include the National Anthem in its programme. It was a sleepless night for prisoners in many parts of Italy, not only because of disturbing thoughts about the future, but also because of much indiscriminate shooting off of firearms, a good deal of it no doubt in celebration of the armistice.[1] Moreover, the whole deadening routine of prison-camp existence had been suddenly broken and men had to use their initiative again in thinking out actions to suit a quite unfamiliar situation. The emphasis was on 'keeping cool', especially in view of the War Office instructions not to move about. Nearly all Italian camp commandants seem to have received instructions that prisoners were to be kept in their camps until collected by Allied forces, but were to be protected from seizure by the Germans. As there were considerable German forces in the vicinity of some camps, it is not clear how this protection was to have been given. In Campo PG 47 the machine guns were faced outwards, but such a gesture was in effect about as far as the resistance of the Italian guard companies could go. Some of the better-intentioned Italians, realising this, opened the gates to allow prisoners to get away.

The failure to adopt a sufficiently realistic plan for the release and evacuation of prisoners of war in Italy had most unfortunate results in the two or three days following the armistice. Camp leaders and senior officers were faced with the responsibility of deciding whether to disobey a War Office order in what seemed a potentially dangerous and very confused situation, about which almost no reliable information could be obtained. In such an uncertain position those who decided to carry out the last British order they had received could hardly be blamed; and large numbers of officers and troops, well-disciplined in spite of years as prisoners of war, obeyed the order that was passed on to them. The order was explicit,[2] admitted no alternatives, and had not been

---

[1] A New Zealand driver, for example, camp leader of a small working camp, was invited by an Italian guard to fire off the balance of the latter's ammunition, and did so.
[2] The view has been expressed that the orders were only intended to forbid mass breakouts, in view of the reprisals it was thought might be taken. But the evidence makes it clear that the orders were meant to serve the needs of the administrative arrangements for evacuating prisoners, which, in the event of an undisturbed armistice situation, would have been all the easier if no prisoners at all had left their camps.

modified or cancelled. The gist of the message conveying the order was:

> All personnel were to stay put 'when war ends'; they were to organise themselves into military units and await orders; arms and assistance would be flown in. Officers at officers' camps were to be prepared to take command of nearby other ranks' camps.

The order had been formulated several months previously, and was on 8 September 1943 totally unrelated to the existing military situation in Italy. Nothing could have played better into the enemy's hands. The outcome was the transfer to Germany of tens of thousands of able-bodied British soldiers who might otherwise have rejoined the Allied forces.

The assumption appears to have persisted somewhere, then as earlier, that the occupation by Allied troops of Italy, or a great part of it, would follow almost immediately on the signing of an armistice. A clause in the armistice[1] provided for the handing back by the Italian Government of all prisoners of war; and their collection, care and evacuation, therefore, were merely tasks for the Armistice Commission. The admirable administrative arrangements for such an operation, already described, had been cut and dried since March 1943. They were based on a picture of tidy and orderly bodies of prisoners left in their camps (with nominal rolls prepared) during a comparatively quiet occupation of an Italy from which all disturbing elements such as the German Army had withdrawn. The introductory note to the War Office plan submitted to the British War Cabinet Post-war Planning Sub-Committee stated:

> It is not known whether on the signing of an armistice with Italy, the whole country or certain strategic points only will be occupied by Allied troops.

Yet the alternative had clearly been considered:

> If however the Badoglio Government were to fall or conclude an Armistice the Germans might be able to profit by the confusion in order to seize some prisoners, whose fate in this regard would depend on whether they were north or south of the line on which the Germans decided to stand.[2]

As it turned out, the Germans formed their line well south of any of the camps for British prisoners of war.

Moreover, the section of MI9 operating in the Mediterranean area had early appreciated that on the announcement of an armistice

---

[1] Article III of the armistice terms ran:
All prisoners or internees of the United Nations to be immediately turned over to the Allied Commander-in-Chief, and none of these may now or at any time be evacuated to Germany.
[2] Paper prepared in advance of the 26th meeting of the Imperial Prisoners of War Committee held on 8 September 1943.

with Italy the Germans would remove as many prisoners to Germany as time and communications permitted;[1] and that, whatever stipulations were made in the Italian armistice terms to prevent this, there was no guarantee that the Italian Government would be in a position to carry them out. An MI9 draft plan, based on these assumptions, made provisions for:

(*a*) The opening of the gates of prisoner-of-war camps in Italy as soon as the announcement of the armistice.[2]

(*b*) The supply by the Italian authorities to prisoners of sufficient rations to enable them to make their way to the coast.

(*c*) The dropping of pamphlets at camps as soon as the announcement of the armistice instructing them to disperse in small groups and make their way to the west coast of Italy.

(*d*) The rescue of these prisoners by light naval craft with air protection.

Suggested instructions for broadcasting to the Italian people and the text of the pamphlet to be dropped for prisoners were also drafted, and these and the draft plan were submitted to Allied Force Headquarters and to the War Office in July 1943.

By mid-August the Foreign Office was able to say that it had been made clear to the Italian Government that 'the removal of any British or Allied prisoners of war from Italy to Germany would have most serious consequences for Italy.' But this dealt only with the possible collaboration of Italy in such a removal, and clearly gave the Italian Government no practical means of preventing the Germans carrying out such a removal by force. In late August, following a meeting[3] held at Allied Force Headquarters, detailed plans and instructions were issued for the 'takeover' and repatriation of Allied prisoners of war in Italy based on the scheme propounded in March. But on 7 September the War Office signalled MI9 in the Middle East that the whole question of action with regard to prisoners of war in the event of an Italian collapse was still under consideration by the Chiefs of Staff. It is clear from all this that the possible alternatives to a peaceful handing-over of prisoner-of-war camps intact to the Allies had been brought to the notice of the highest Allied authorities well in advance of events. Yet even after the conclusion of the armistice on 3 September there appears to have been no attempt

---

[1] The importance attached by the Germans to removing prisoners in order of value was illustrated in the Western Desert. RAF personnel, specialist services of the Army and Navy, and all officers were evacuated early. When the Eighth Army reached Benghazi in 1942 only a few labour corps troops remained.
[2] It was thought by MI9 that it would be preferable if the gates were opened and liaison officers and food parachuted in on the day before the armistice announcement. But this was not mentioned in the plan submitted to AFHQ and War Office.
[3] No MI9 representative was present.

to get through to prisoners before its announcement on the 8th any alternative orders to those then in force, namely, to remain where they were until Allied troops arrived.

Most of the prisoners who obeyed these orders were collected with ease by comparatively small German detachments and sent to Germany; a large number of those whose camp leaders disobeyed them eventually reached the Allied lines or Switzerland. Thus base camps like Campo PG 47 and Campo PG 57[1] were rounded up almost intact. It was from more remote working camps such as Campo PG 107 or Campo PG 78/1, where the camp leader acted on his own initiative in bringing pressure on the Italians to allow the men to leave, or at others like Campo PG 106/20, where prisoners were released and advised to leave by one of the guards, that the greatest number of our successful escapers in this period was drawn. At many camps these releases were three or four days after the announcement of the armistice.[2] Italian camp officers seem, with a few exceptions, to have carried out their orders, namely, to keep the prisoners in camps ready to hand over to Allied troops and if necessary release them to prevent their falling into German hands. But German pressure, and occasionally Fascist leanings, undoubtedly induced a few of them to hand over their camps to the nearby German troops. In any case it would clearly not have been feasible for most Italian commandants to have prevented their camps falling into German hands by force of arms. Nearly a week after the armistice announcement a BBC transmission advised prisoners in Italy that it was their duty not to remain in camps but to make good their escape. By that time, according to the German claims, 25,000 had been entrained for Germany, and judging by eye-witness accounts of the numerous trainloads which went north in the few days after 13 September this figure is probably no exaggeration.[3]

---

[1] These two camps are mentioned because Campo PG 47 contained nearly all the New Zealand officer prisoners, and Campo PG 57 the greatest number of New Zealand other ranks.

[2] Details of the conditions relating to the release of prisoners by Italy were not finally agreed upon until 10 September 1943, the second day after the announcement of the armistice. They were, briefly, that the gates of all prisoner-of-war camps under Italian control should be opened and that prisoners should be advised to move towards the east coast and the south; or north towards Switzerland.

[3] The following are the figures (so far as they are known) showing the fate of New Zealand prisoners in Italy at the time of the armistice. Where known, British Commonwealth totals in round figures are given for comparison:

	NZ	British
Numbers in Italy at time of armistice (approximate)	3,700	70,000
Successfully escaped to Allied lines	339	12,000
Successfully escaped to Switzerland	108	5,000
Killed while at large	7	
Killed in transit north	8	
Fate unknown	6	
Transferred to Germany (approximate)	3,200	52,000

Though this is the general pattern of events, the details varied in different camps. After the announcement of the armistice in Campo PG 47 at Modena, though the guards were increased, reassuring promises were made by the Italian commandant and the British order to remain was promulgated. A number of prisoners decided to disobey it and left the camp by climbing the fence with little resistance from the guards next morning. That day at 2 p.m. the Senior British Officer, after a conference of senior officers, called the camp together and said that, in view of the uncertainties of the situation, anyone who wished to leave the camp might consider himself no longer bound by the order to remain, and he advised anyone intending to leave to go quickly. Although a few more left immediately,[1] most preferred to believe the reports of Allied landings in the north and decided to wait. They had not long to wait, for by 2.30 p.m. German troops had taken over the camp and replaced the Italian sentries on the perimeter. Campo PG 19 at Bologna had been even less fortunate. A strong German force had arrived, anticipating trouble, in the early hours of 9 September, and had opened fire when a mass break-out had been attempted. There had been several casualties and only a few had got away. The German forces had also made sure of Campo PG 5, which they had surrounded and taken over early on the same morning. Thus the three camps containing nearly all the New Zealand officers were in German hands by the afternoon of 9 September.

Near Campo PG 57, which contained some 1500 New Zealand other ranks at that time, a detachment of German troops arrived on the day of the armistice proclamation to bivouac. Next day some of the Italian guards left their posts and went home, but it was not until eight o'clock that night that the Italian commandant announced the armistice to the prisoners. He instructed them to remain quietly in the camp, assured them that there was nothing to be feared from the Germans, who were busy getting out of Italy, and promised in case of any interference that the Italian guard would defend them 'to the last'. Sentries were doubled, but a number of men got away in the early confusion. A chaplain, as the senior British rank, promulgated the British order about not leaving camp, and most men seem to have believed that British troops would soon arrive. For two days there were orders and counter-orders and many wild rumours. At one time the whole camp was preparing to leave in small groups under NCOs, to be

---

[1] The total number who got away from Modena camp has been estimated at 170, though not all of these were finally successful in escaping. The remainder were taken to Germany.

led to safety by Italian guides, but this order was cancelled. On the third day the Germans took over the camp without opposition, and on the 13th the first batches of fifty were marched under heavy guard to the Cividale railway station.

Near Campo PG 148, the working detachment at Bussolengo, a party of German troops had taken a position just across the river from the camp a week before the armistice. The camp commandant announced it at midnight on 8 September and asked the prisoners to remain quiet so as not to 'disturb the Germans opposite the camp'. But the latter had apparently already had their instructions. There was considerable noise of motor transport during the early morning and:

> At approximately 6 a.m. we saw the armoured cars and tanks coming down towards the camp, and then we had an idea we had become German prisoners again. At 8 a.m. all was quiet and a German officer informed us we were now their prisoners.[1]

They were marched off almost immediately and by the 14th were on a train bound for Germany. Several other work-camps in northern Italy were similarly handed over to the Germans. The prisoners at Campo PG 103/6, high in the Dolomites, were moved suddenly on the morning of the 9th by the Italians themselves under orders and handed over later to the Germans at Treviso.

The prisoners at Torviscosa (Campo PG 107) were sent out to work on 9 September but were recalled later to hear the camp commandant announce the armistice. They then 'settled down comfortably to await the arrival of the Allies'.[2] In the next two days, during which many guards left for their homes, the camp leader, a South African NCO, had several interviews with the camp commandant to try and persuade him to allow those who wished to leave to do so, but his request was persistently refused though always with reassurances about the safety of the men. On 11 September a hole was cut in the wire and men began to leave; guards were deserting, and shortly afterwards the camp gates were opened. About 600 left the camp and 400 remained. The latter spent a busy night trading clothing and other possessions for wine and money with civilians who flocked around and inside the camp, and some of whom stayed all night. There could be no greater contrast to the normal discipline and order of camp life. On the 15th those prisoners who still remained were visited by two German officers and the holes in the wire were temporarily sealed up, but in the following days men came and went as before to pick up their possessions or to get food. Eventually

---
[1] Diary of a New Zealand private soldier.
[2] Diary of a New Zealand private soldier.

on the 19th, carabinieri, under orders from the German authorities, packed all the remaining prisoners on to trucks and took them to Gorizia, where they handed them over to German guards.

A similar break-out was made at Aquafredda (Campo PG 78/1) when an order to return to the main camp at Sulmona was disregarded by the camp leader, a New Zealand warrant officer.[1] The men were marched out of camp and told to take to the hills in small groups. At some of the smaller work detachments, such as the satellites of Campo PG 107 and Campo PG 106, all the guards went off in the days following the armistice, leaving the prisoners free to go where they pleased.[2] Even then many men preferred to stay and wait for the arrival of Allied troops. At Campo PG 107/5, Torre di Confine, which the prisoners were free to leave on 12 September, 24 out of 50 preferred to remain and were taken over by the Germans when they arrived ten days later. Where it was practicable to bring pressure to bear on the Italian guards, as at Campo PG 107/7, La Salute, they gave way without difficulty. The great majority of the New Zealanders who escaped from Italy after the armistice were from the camps described above, where the prisoners were for one reason or another left free to move out en masse.[3]

Prisoners who had been out of their camps on the night of the armistice had been toasted and embraced in local taverns and market squares in a returning wave of open friendship towards Britain; and during the next day or so ex-prisoners were welcomed with open arms into the houses of the Italian countryfolk. Their possible reactions to escapers had always been a matter for conjecture among prisoners, but the most optimistic had not expected such enthusiasm. Those who were able to leave their camps in the following days found the bulk of the Italian population well-disposed and ready to help them with food, civilian clothing and other necessaries, especially in return for woollen blankets or underclothing, cakes of soap, and other articles hard to come by in wartime Italy. Most prisoners were pleased to remain in the neighbourhood of their camp for some days until the situation

---

[1] WO II E. May (20 Bn), who successfully reached Allied lines in October 1943. He was awarded the MBE.

[2] An exception was Campo PG 107/2, Prati Nuovi, where the employer, a Fascist, threatened to hand over the entire camp to the Germans if anyone left. He then secretly arranged with the Germans to send a strong guard and take over.

[3] The rough percentage of successful escapers among those who got away from Campo PG 78/1 at Aquafredda, where all the prisoners were able to march out, may perhaps give some idea of what the overall position might have been had all camps been evacuated immediately after the armistice announcement.

    Number who got away from camp   300
    Number who finally escaped   140

This gives roughly 47 per cent, but if the suggested rescue operations had been begun immediately the percentage could well have been higher.

became a little clearer and they could decide what it was best to do. Then the radio bulletins made it plain that the Allied attempt at a swift occupation of Italy had failed and that the process of overrunning it might take a long time.

On 15 September the Germans issued a proclamation over Rome Radio and in the Italian press:

> Anglo-American prisoners of war who escaped from prisoners' camps in Italy after the armistice are to return to the camps immediately or report without delay to the nearest German military authorities outside the 'open city' of Rome.
> All prisoners who report will be treated according to the regulations of the Geneva Convention. Those found in possession of arms or who attempt to resist capture will be treated according to martial law.
> Italians giving any aid to escaped prisoners in food, money, shelter, or in any other form, will be judged according to German military law.

Many became frightened to shelter prisoners, especially as in most districts there were Fascists, now become bold again and only too willing to denounce people to the Germans and so curry favour with the new controllers of their country. Moreover, the Germans offered a reward of 1700 lire[1] for information leading to the capture of any ex-prisoner of war; but in spite of this many Italians continued to help. Eventually on 30 September an announcement over the BBC made it clear to those prisoners still at liberty what their position and duty were, and perhaps helped to safeguard against ill-treatment those who fell into German hands. The announcement took the form of a carefully prepared Government statement:

> In His Majesty's Government's view any British prisoners of war at large in Northern Italy, if captured by the German forces, are fully entitled to all the privileges and benefits conferred on prisoners of war under the Geneva Convention of the 27th July, 1929. They are under no obligation whatever to report to the German authorities in Northern Italy and the German demand that they should do so is entirely without foundation in international law. Their clear duty in the present circumstances is to make good their escape from enemy-occupied territory in order to rejoin their own forces, and the mere fact that they have acquired arms or may resist arrest in order to carry out this duty cannot in any way affect their right to be treated in all respects as prisoners of war under the Geneva Convention if they are recaptured. Any German authority who treats such British prisoners of war otherwise than in accordance with these principles will be held by His Majesty's Governments personally responsible for his actions.

Most of the prisoners now at large had brought Red Cross food with them sufficient to last for some days, and the September weather in Italy was such that it was no great hardship to sleep

---

[1] About £20 sterling at that time.

out under hedges, in maize fields, or in the woods. A good number of men were picked up by German troops in the first few days before they had had time to acquire civilian clothing or to learn whom to trust; some of these had drunk too freely of Italian wine. Many still in battle dress managed to avoid capture by remaining inconspicuous and taking no unnecessary risks. Numbers worked with Italian countryfolk in the fields and slept in their barns or in the open and had food brought to them; some even had their laundry done for them. After the German threats of reprisals for helping escaped prisoners and the increased activity of local Fascists and German patrols, Italians had to be careful, especially in the north where the German control was more effective; and many prisoners chose to move on rather than remain to incriminate the simple friendly folk who had shown them hospitality.

Even so an escaped prisoner usually got shelter and food (if only for a night) when he knocked at a house, and many Italians, apart from the peasant farmers, actively defied the German orders. An Italian Army chaplain led a party of prisoners, which increased to eighty en route, south across the Po to safe hiding in a wood near Ravenna, and then went on himself to investigate the chances of getting through the lines.[1] A curfew was imposed after 9.30 p.m. and anyone seen out after that time was liable to be shot at. Many prisoners, however, did their travelling at night by avoiding roads and bridges and keeping to the open countryside. By 25 September the German authorities claimed to have seized about 40,000 to 50,000 ex-prisoners, though they had to admit also that many were still at large.[2]

Of the 450-odd New Zealanders who escaped at the time of the Italian armistice either to Allied lines or to Switzerland, over 80 per cent were from camps where the Italians released all the prisoners or the latter moved out in a body.[3] The remaining 20 per cent escaped by individual breaks from camps after the Germans had taken over control, by hiding up successfully inside after the

---

[1] He left instructions for them to wait a week for his return and then to continue in small parties south, and arranged for them to be fed by the local inhabitants. A great number of those in this party were successful in finally escaping. The original party was from Campo PG 120/8 at Fogolana, near Padua.

[2] An estimate by MI9 in October 1943 put the figure for British Commonwealth prisoners then at large in Italy as 'in the region of 20,000'.

[3] The following are the approximate numbers of successful New Zealand escapers from such camps:

Campo PG 78/1	140
Campo PG 107 and its satellites	135
Campo PG 106 and its satellites	75
Campo PG 120 and its satellites	30
Total	380

Germans had evacuated the prisoners, by jumping off transport taking them to Germany, or by breaking out from a transit camp just inside the Austrian border. Only a few broke out from camps under German control, but a very considerable number left the German prisoner-of-war trains before they reached Austria.

At Campo PG 148, Bussolengo, there was hardly any time between the taking over of the camp by the Germans and the moving of prisoners on the first stage of their journey to Germany. At Campo PG 57 there was little delay in moving once the Germans had assumed control. Campo PG 5 and Campo PG 47 were taken over the day after the armstice announcement, but it was three days before the first prisoners left. In that period those at Campo PG 5 had explored every means of hiding up or getting out. A number worked furiously at trying to open up the sealed entrance to an old underground passage which led to the village of Gavi. Others concentrated on preparing in the roof, cellars, latrines, and walls of the old castle hiding-places ready for instant use on the first word of evacuation. When that came 68 out of 180 prisoners hid up, the rest being taken off by train. But the German troops returned with orders to winkle out every would-be escaper, and for three days they searched the building, not scrupling to dismantle portions of it nor to use firearms and grenades when necessary. All those who had hidden were found and taken to the German transit camp at Mantua, to be entrained for Germany.

The standard type of barrack at Modena did not lend itself to the variety of hiding-place that might be possible elsewhere, and 1100 to 1200 men obsessed with the same idea, many of them examining the same possibilities, did not make concealment easy. There could be no question any longer of control such as that exercised by an escape committee. The moment there were men in one barrack exploring the roof, there would be a rush to do the same in six others; and the same applied to cupboards, tunnels, wood-piles and store-rooms. It hardly seemed possible that any of those who hid up would escape detection when the camp was searched. During a nerve-racking three days while awaiting the orders to move, much clothing and food which could obviously not be carried was given away to Italians over the camp fence, and a good deal more was destroyed on a large bonfire so that it might not fall into enemy hands, until the German guards not unnaturally stopped both these activities. On the early morning of the 12th the first parties moved out of camp to the Modena railway station, and the camp was cleared by the 14th. In spite of the obviousness of most of the hiding-places, about thirty decided to hide up—in the roofs, behind a disused door, in a slit trench covered over with leaves, and even in a large (emptied) lavatory cistern. The German search was much less thorough than expected and most of these men succeeded in getting out of the camp after it had become almost deserted.

From those camps that were taken over by German troops, all except the few who succeeded in hiding up were marched to the nearest railway station. The Germans took what precautions they could to prevent escapes—a strong guard along the route, threats before setting out of the dire consequences that would follow any attempted breaks, even a demonstration with a flame-thrower at Campo PG 57. The weather was at its hottest and men struggled along in the dust, wearing or carrying whatever possessions they could, at the pace set by the guards. Some dropped with exhaustion from the heat and the exertion and were brought along later by truck. Although it was a matter of a few miles only, the weight of the food, clothing, books, and musical instruments which some felt certain they would regret having left behind, and the awkwardness of the packages, told on men who had once been used to doing route marches many times that distance, but in suitable kit and with proper equipment. The guarding was efficient and there was little chance of breaking away. From smaller camps such as Campo PG 148 or Campo PG 5 [1] the prisoners were taken by truck to a main collection centre set up by the Germans in a commandeered sports ground at Mantua. Many of those in north-east Italy were held in smaller centres such as Palmanova before being sent to Austria by the shortest route.

A few were able to make a successful getaway by jumping from moving trucks en route to a railway station or to a transit camp. One[2] of the half dozen or so New Zealanders who were still at Campo PG 52 at the time of the armistice jumped into a ditch unnoticed while being marched to the Chiavari station. With a companion he made his way over the hills to Genoa and along the Riviera to Nice. There he made contact with an underground organisation, which made arrangements for him to go to France and so to Spain. In mid-February 1944 his party crossed the Pyrenees in deep snow and blizzards, and he eventually reached Barcelona and Gibraltar.

The evacuation of British prisoners from Italy to Austria and Germany took place by train under conditions somewhat similar to those of the evacuation from Greece nearly two years previously.

---

[1] At Campo PG 5 this applied only to those rounded up after hiding in the camp. The first party were entrained almost immediately for Austria.
[2] Pte J. S. Kennard-Davis (24 Bn) awarded MM for this exploit.

Most of the trains went north via Verona, through the Brenner Pass to Innsbruck, though a few took the more easterly Tarvisio Pass to Villach. They were almost entirely made up of cattle-trucks and closed goods-wagons with a very few third-class carriages, some of them Italian rolling-stock commandeered by the German military authorities, others returning north after having brought German troops and equipment south for the Italian campaign. Into these trucks the prisoners were packed, as many as fifty in each, though the number was reduced for officers to about thirty-five. With thirty-five it was almost impossible for everyone to lie down at once, and with fifty for everyone to sit down, even when kit has been hung on the sides and from the roof beams. The sliding doors were closed and bolted, and prisoners were left for the journey with at most two small openings in the sides of the truck for air and light, no provision for latrines, and only such food and water as they had been able to carry with them. Though most had ample Red Cross food, it did not take long for men perspiring in the 'oven-like heat',[1] to empty their water bottles; and for those with any kind of dysentery the journey was a miserable experience. Sick and disabled prisoners travelled in the same type of truck, but were placed together usually with a medical officer and under not quite such crowded conditions. There were occasional halts on the journey north, often not long enough for every truckload to be allowed out. On the longer journeys there were considerable halts at stations and sometimes meals from the German Red Cross.

From the moment they were locked inside, men in almost every truck looked about for ways out of it. Before the train bringing those from Campo PG 57 had reached the junction at Udine, some had crawled through the small windows and jumped clear, and from Udine onwards the stream of escapers continued. There were similar losses from the first trains on the main line north to the Brenner Pass. In later trains those openings that were not barred were closed with barbed wire to prevent such escapes. Nevertheless, in some of the wooden trucks[2] a hole was made near the bolt securing one of the sliding doors, a hand was put through and the door opened, leaving the whole truckload free to make a break; and several truckloads did.

Such large numbers were able to leave the early trains that these bolts were later wired, and special guards were carried at the rear of the train with machine guns mounted ready to fire along

---

[1] The phrase used in one New Zealander's eye-witness account.
[2] Numbers of the trucks were of iron, which presented an almost insoluble problem to the escaper.

the outside. It was no easy matter to jump from high up on a fast-moving train, and a suitable moment had to be chosen, preferably at night when it was going uphill and had thus somewhat slowed down. A New Zealander who escaped in this way gives his impressions after he and a companion had climbed through the hole made with pocket-knives in the end of the truck and were waiting on the couplings for a chance to jump:

> Now we're through [the station] and she's going lickety split and it [makes] you dizzy to watch the telephone poles. Say to Ted, "she's moving a bit fast, isn't she?" Ted says, "If we don't go now, mightn't get another chance." Fling off into space, hit the ground running, falling forward over embankment, falling forward and smash down in a hedge. Lie doggo expecting the works any moment and watch the carriages flicking past. Now the last with dim forms on the platform, but no shot and no alarms and just a small red light fading in the distance. . . . [1]

Some men were injured by hitting posts and other objects alongside the line after they had jumped. With guards firing along the outside of the train, and in no mood to be trifled with, it was a doubly dangerous operation. Of three officers who sawed a hole through the ceiling of their truck and jumped from the roof, one was killed and two wounded.[2] On the whole serious injuries seem to have been remarkably few and most of the train-jumpers got off with bruises and scratches.

Occasionally a break could be made from a stationary train. A New Zealand sergeant squeezed through an opening in the end door of his truck while at a station and hid under the train until the guards' attention was distracted, when he boldly walked across the platform into the country.[3] After escapes, or the discovery of a hole cut through a truck wall, the German guards were vehement in threatening severe reprisals on the occupants. But though there was some rifling of kit on the pretence of looking for cutting-tools, some rough handling with use of rifle butts, and some brandishing of firearms, there were almost no cold-blooded shootings of British prisoners.

With no German train figures (before and after the journey) available, it would be a difficult task to get anything like a true estimate of the number of prisoners who got free in this way. Although considerable, it could not have been more than a small percentage of those entrained. Many thousands had been released or left their camps and were at large. Yet by 25 September

---

[1] Account of his escape by Maj T. W. Straker.
[2] Lt J. W. C. Craig (2 NZEF) and Lt E. H. Bishop (2 NZEF) were the two officers wounded; the officer killed was an Englishman in the Royal Navy.
[3] Sgt H. P. Campbell (19 Bn), mentioned in despatches for his successful escape resulting from this break. He had previously escaped from the Palm Tree Camp in North Africa by hiding under the wood truck.

the Germans claimed to have transferred 30,000 prisoners from Italy to the Greater Reich, and by the end of October 43,000 were known to have been so transferred. British prisoners, although important, were only a part of the cargo that was being pushed north; there were also large numbers of Italian civilians and disarmed troops, and food and other material from Italian stores. The Head of the Prisoner of War Division of the German High Command insisted that the transfer of prisoners was 'not carried out systematically'; and it is clear that the whole operation was pushed through in haste in view of the unstable position in Italy, and with as few personnel as possible in view of the operational commitments of German forces in the south. That being so, and considering that a good number of the British prisoners were for most of the journey trying their hardest to escape, there were unexpectedly few atrocities.

For most of the prisoners the journey was one of acute discomfort and, for some, of real physical hardship. But it was relieved by glimpses of splendid alpine scenery, which led at least one prisoner to call the Austrian Tyrol 'the most beautiful country I have seen since leaving my own'.[1] There was interest in the difference of landscape and dwellings from those in Italy; interest too in calling out to groups of British prisoners working alongside the railway, some of whom had been in German hands since the end of the campaign in France.

II: *Transit and Permanent Camps in Germany and Austria*

Such a mass transfer was bound to set a difficult problem for the German Prisoner of War Division to find sufficient suitable accommodation in the Greater Reich. The transit camps—Stalag XVIIIC at Markt Pongau and Stalag XVIIIA/Z at Spittal-on-the-Drau, both in Austria, and Stalag VIIA at Moosburg in Bavaria—were soon crowded with men from Italy, but most prisoners were kept there only for a week or two. Some of the trainloads went right through to Görlitz (Stalag VIIIA) or to Lamsdorf (Stalag VIIIB), which were to be for many of the other ranks their permanent base camps. A large number of officers were moved to Strasbourg: some to Fort Bismarck, others to Stalag VC at Offenberg, where they were kept for some weeks and a few days respectively before going to their permanent camps—Oflag VA at Weinsberg, Oflag XIIB at Hadamar, and Oflag IXA/Z at Rotenburg. Most Air Force officers and other ranks went eventually to Stalag Luft III at Sagan.[2]

---

[1] Account by a New Zealand private of his experiences while a prisoner of war.
[2] See map facing p. 355.

Those from Campo 57 were the first large party from Italy to reach Stalag XVIIIC at Markt Pongau, which then held some 1000 prisoners of several other European nationalities. Though in a beautiful alpine setting on the left bank of the Salzach, roughly 25 miles south of Salzburg, the camp was very dirty and the barracks infested with vermin. Many prisoners, to avoid the bedbugs, preferred to sleep on the floor wrapped in their greatcoats; a number would have had to in any case as there were not enough beds to go round, nor any blankets. For the first time they tasted the typical German stalag fare—vegetable soup and 'black' bread, boiled potatoes and mint tea. There, too, they went through the registration, searching, and delousing routine already described elsewhere, but had all their spare clothing, boots, and blankets confiscated. After a fortnight or so most went north to Stalag VIIIA at Görlitz in Silesia. Several thousand British and American prisoners passed through this camp, and by mid-November only 450-odd remained.

As Görlitz rapidly filled, later drafts went from Markt Pongau to Stalag XVIIIA/Z at Spittal-on-the-Drau, and some trainloads went to this camp direct. Something has already been told of its history;[1] at this period men pronounced it 'a really good camp' especially if they had just come from Markt Pongau. From here many of our men went out to working camps in Austria, but those exempt because of rank remained in spite of German persuasion and were eventually sent back to Markt Pongau. It was here, too, that a number of the transferred officers were able to pose as other ranks and make a break after joining one of the French working parties. One New Zealand officer exchanged identities with a gunner and succeeded in making his way from a French working party over the border into Italy, and eventually to Allied territory through Yugoslavia.[2]

The greatest number of transferred prisoners passed through Stalag VIIA at Moosburg, to which camp brief reference was made in an earlier chapter.[3] This was similar to Markt Pongau in that it was cosmopolitan, overcrowded and much soiled, though it was not quite as dirty as the latter. From here there were also attempts to get out on working parties disguised as Frenchmen,

---

[1] See pp. 243–4.
[2] Capt D. J. Riddiford (6 Fd Regt), awarded MC for his efforts to escape. Most of those who thus changed their identities at Spittal were caught, as they all applied to go to a working camp near the Italian frontier. Riddiford, having carefully learnt the personal details and history of the man he was impersonating and by playing both dumb and sick at his interrogation, half convinced the German commandant that he was genuine. On discharge from hospital he wasted no time in leaving the camp in a working party dressed as a Frenchman, and with two companions was in Italy in four days.
[3] See p. 138.

but most drafts passed through too quickly to make the necessary arrangements. Some trains did not unload in Bavaria at all, but went right through to Lamsdorf to swell the numbers at Stalag VIIIB.

The bulk of the New Zealand officers—the more junior ones—went from Moosburg with a thousand or more others, mostly from Campo PG 19 and Campo PG 47, to Fort Bismarck at Strasbourg. This was a large, depressing old fortress, sunk into the slope of a hill, so that air and light reached the windows of the sleeping quarters behind it only by virtue of a deep moat. It was damp and comfortless, though the shortage of fuel for the stoves was soon made good by the prisoners from spare wooden beds and fittings. Several daring escapes were made up the moat wall and through the wire under the noses of German sentries, and one or two were able to hide up when the prisoners were later evacuated.

From Fort Bismarck junior officers and other ranks—men from the United Kingdom, South Africa, Australia and New Zealand—went to Oflag VA at Weinsberg, a small village amid the woods and healthy, fruit-growing countryside near Heilbron, in Wurtemburg. Previously occupied by French officers, it contained wooden barracks of the usual German type, divided into small rooms. The thousand or more officers[1] and 130-odd other ranks were crowded at first and the camp suffered from numerous other defects: the Germans issued only one blanket, there was such an uncertain water supply that no hot showers were available for some time, and there was insufficient fuel for the kitchen so that one meal a day had to be served cold. For a week or two until Red Cross supplies began to arrive, the camp had to exist on the German rations and what cigarettes and books men had been able to carry on their persons from Italy. The worst permanent lack of the camp was space for recreation, the only outdoor area available being a sloping and totally inadequate one between the two rows of barracks where check parades were held. The use of any open space outside the camp for sport or other recreation was forbidden by the Gauleiter of Heilbron, who also for some time prevented the prisoners from having walks on parole. In the first weeks of the camp it was not unfair to say, as the Protecting Power representative did in his report, that recreational and exercise facilities were almost non-existent.

As a result of the escapes made from the trains en route from Italy and of the escapes and barrack damages which occurred while this party of junior officers was at Fort Bismarck, the German

---

[1] New Zealanders in the camp were roughly 140 officers and 10 other ranks.

staff at Weinsberg had been braced to deal with a camp full of young desperadoes and was on the alert to restrict anything and everything that might be remotely connected with escape. Microphones had been installed in most of the rooms before the prisoners arrived, and it was not long before ground microphones for the detection of tunnelling were placed round the perimeter. It was clear that the German commandant was obsessed, as the representative of the Protecting Power pointed out, with a 'fear of escapes', and preoccupied with their prevention by every means in his power.

Censoring of letters was carried out in a 'rather narrow-minded'[1] fashion. When Red Cross supplies arrived, as they soon did, all the material in which food parcels were packed was carefully collected by the German staff, on the ground that in the hands of prisoners it might be used to assist an escape. So might almost any other article in the prisoners' possession; sets of drawing instruments, a gramophone, and sports equipment were withheld for the same reason. Not only was there at first no space for indoor recreation and only a small unsuitable area outside, but the Germans declined to supply any writing materials or wood for the construction of a theatre or even the erection of goal posts. Under these conditions the recreation essential for the wellbeing of those in a non-working camp was at first very difficult to organise. But what was felt to be the worst restriction was the packing of all prisoners inside the barracks after evening check parade—at first at 5.15 p.m. and later as early as 4.30 p.m. With strict enforcement of the blackout against air raids, this meant each night a period of five to six hours in crowded, smoke-laden, ill-lit rooms before going to bed, and a total of thirteen to fourteen hours in the barracks.

All these matters were brought to the notice of the representative of the Protecting Power when he visited the camp in October 1943 and again in January 1944. Though there were some improvements—slightly more space, for example, after the transfer of a hundred officers to another camp—the imposition of 'petty, narrow-minded regulations' continued. Some attempts at escape in the new year, in which four officers were out of the camp for a short period, made matters worse. In January the Swiss representative was obliged to say in his report that he felt the moving of all the officers to another camp to be the only solution to the problem of providing adequate treatment for them, unless the direction of Oflag VA could be entrusted to a German officer with more understanding and a 'stronger sense of responsibility'. Not long

---

[1] Reports of Protecting Power on Oflag VA.

afterwards there was a new German officer in charge of the camp and conditions began to improve.

The older and more senior and some of the sick officers from Campo PG 19 and Campo PG 47 went in October to Oflag XIIB at Hadamar, near Limburg in the Lahn valley of Nassau. About 250 such officers (including some thirty New Zealanders) and 35 other ranks made up the camp complement. French officers had previously occupied this camp, too, which comprised a large, castle-like building with very thick walls, on a hill overlooking the town. Here, by contrast, there was a good deal of space both in the bedrooms and dining room, chapel and study rooms—the best officers' camp in this respect which the Swiss inspector had seen in Germany. In addition there was central heating throughout the the whole building, adequate sanitary arrangements, and a reasonably well-equipped kitchen. The officers could use a small sports field inside the camp and could go for walks on parole. Although the German staff had the same concern about possible escapes, the officer prisoners at the camp gave the Swiss delegate who inspected it the impression of being 'quite comfortable'. In the first few weeks, however, there was an absence of Red Cross supplies of food, cigarettes, books and games, which cast a gloom similar to that which had at first prevailed at Weinsberg. When the position at Hadamar was known to the senior British officer of Oflag IXA/H he sent 600 food parcels, together with invalid parcels, cigarettes, books, games, and some clothing. This tided the camp over until its own supplies arrived from Geneva.

Later drafts of officers from Italy, including most of the sick and disabled who had been in camp infirmaries, went straight through to Lamsdorf, and after a short spell at Stalag VIIIB, formed a new officers' camp just outside Märisch-Trübau, in the eastern Sudetenland bordering on Silesia. To this camp went other officers from Stalag IVB at Mühlberg to make a total of about 1500, including some forty New Zealanders. They were housed in a pleasantly situated four-storied building (a former Czech officers' training school), which was centrally heated and reasonably well appointed in most other respects, and in some small stone barracks. There were ample reserves of Red Cross food, and apart from three mental cases the health of prisoners was good. Facilities for recreation were particularly good and included a sports ground, a gymnasium, a library and a theatre.

The New Zealand other ranks from Italy went direct or through transit camps to the industrial areas of central Germany north of the old Czechoslovakian border. Many went to Stalag VIIIA at Görlitz in Saxony, 50 miles east of Dresden, or to its working camps. A number of these were later moved to working camps attached to Stalag 344, to which others had already gone direct. A few hundred, mainly from Campo PG 103/6 and Campo PG 103/7, went from Moosburg to Stalag XIA at Altengrabow, near Magdeburg, and after a short time there moved on to *Arbeitskommando* 7001 at Halendorf, attached to Stalag XIB. Some went to Stalag IVB at Mühlberg on the Elbe, 40 miles east of Leipzig, and worked in various kommandos attached to the camps in *Wehrkreis* IV. Others, after having gone to Spittal-on-the-Drau, remained in *Wehrkreis* XVIII at one of the stalags or worked in one of the attached kommandos. A few small groups found their way to other established camps such as Stalag 383.

Stalag VIIIA, to which went a trainload of prisoners from Campo PG 57, covered over 70 acres of sloping countryside on the eastern outskirts of the town of Görlitz. One of the oldest prisoner-of-war camps in Germany, it had barracks of the same type as those at Lamsdorf and had held prisoners of several Allied European countries. When our men arrived from Italy it contained French, Belgians and Serbs, together with a number of Russians in an adjacent but carefully segregated compound. The portion of the camp allotted to the newcomers was in bad repair, with many missing doors and windows and a bad shortage of beds and palliasses. It was also infested with lice and bedbugs, and though the former were soon overcome the latter persisted. There was a very poor water supply and the usual rather primitive latrine system. But under good leadership the camp soon began to show improvement. Generous gifts of food and tobacco from the French and Belgians tided the British prisoners over a lean period until copious Red Cross supplies of all kinds began to arrive in October. In time it became possible to organise all the amenities common in other, longer-established British camp communities.

The stalag very quickly became overcrowded, and remained so until sufficient working parties were moved out to work-camps. All those below the rank of corporal underwent a rather cursory medical examination by a German doctor and were graded according to the heaviness of the work he considered they were fit to undertake. Before the end of the year hundreds of men had gone to work in coal mines or stone quarries, at sugar, glass or paper factories, on railway construction or other building work, in *Arbeitskommandos* attached to Stalag VIIIA.

Many of these had been in operation for some time, and the new arrivals from Italy went out as replacements; but some new *Arbeitskommandos* were also formed. For the most part quarters were spacious, well-heated and clean, though primitive sanitation remained a main drawback. Those who occupied large rooms in German inns were usually well off. The German rations were often cooked by women at an inn or at a factory, but more satisfactory results were usually obtained when the task was given to one or more of the prisoners. In addition to the larger portion of bread and other workers' rations which the prisoners received, eggs, vegetables, and other produce could often be obtained by bartering. Hours of work were still long and many employers refused to acknowledge the prisoner's right to a day off each week. But in late 1943 guards and civilian overseers were more reasonable in their treatment of British prisoners than they had been a year or so previously. The newcomers were agreeably surprised to be able to attend a cinema on a free Sunday morning and in the afternoon play football on a local sports field or go swimming at a bathing pool.

Some of the working parties went to camps which were sufficiently far away from Görlitz to come under the jurisdiction of another stalag. A party of 200 Australians and New Zealanders went in November to such a camp just outside Oderburg, on the Czechoslovakian border not far from Ratibor. Here there was a small, not very well appointed camp alongside three main railway lines, and the prisoners were set to work on line maintenance and alterations and also on the building of a large embankment. The work was under contract to a large German firm, whose overseers kept the prisoners at it for eleven and a half hours a day,[1] unloading and spreading spoil and levering the tip-lines into place. The German authorities saw to it that plenty of Red Cross food parcels reached the camp, as few prisoners would have stood up to the heavy work on the diet of mainly bread, potatoes, and vegetable soup which their German rations gave them.

Besides the trainloads of men who went direct to Stalag VIIIB there were others who were moved from Stalag VIIIA, including members of a working party which arrived at its place of work too early and for lack of accommodation was sent on to Lamsdorf. This huge camp, which had started to show improvement since the appointment of a new German commandant, now became still larger through the sudden influx from Italy and numbered well over 30,000, 10,000 of them in the stalag itself, with men sleeping on tables, on forms, or simply on the floor, and with other camp services similarly overcrowded. Our men from Italian camps met in the stalag many old comrades from the campaigns

---

[1] Saturday afternoon and Sunday were free, however, which was not always so at other German work-camps.

in Greece and Crete. Those who had come from Italy, more especially those from Campo PG 57, wondered at the comparative lack of discipline in this camp and at the activities that could go on inside it unknown to the enemy. They saw shackling in its last rather farcical stage when the handcuffs were issued but not put on; they met men living in the camp of whom the German office had no record or only a false one. Less easy to contemplate with detachment were the activities of a gang whose members tried for a while to improve their lot at the expense of their fellow prisoners by intimidating them with blade-razors. Sooner or later the newcomers, who had all been graded by German doctors according to the type of labour they were medically fit for, left for coal mines or other places of work in Silesia.

By December the German authorities, to cope with the overcrowding at Lamsdorf and at the same time divide the work of administering its numerous *Arbeitskommandos,* transferred administrative staff to form new base camps at Teschen and Sagan. These became known as Stalag VIIIB and Stalag VIIIC respectively, the original camp at Lamsdorf being renumbered Stalag 344. The Silesian working camps were now conveniently divided between Stalag 344 and Stalags VIIIA, B, and C, all coalmining *Arbeitskommandos* coming under Stalag VIIIB at Teschen. The latter very soon had a strength of 11,000 British Commonwealth prisoners (including nearly 1000 New Zealanders); but only a little over 200 of these were at the base camp, the remainder being spread over fifty or more *Arbeitskommandos.*

One mixed party of British Commonwealth prisoners, which included a number of New Zealanders, went to a coalmining camp (E596) at Jaworzno, just inside the Polish border. They were billeted with a reasonable amount of space at an old boarding school and were regularly supplied with Red Cross food parcels. By 5 October they were below the surface pushing trucks of coal and in a month or so were working at the coal-face. The hours were long, the mine was worked for the whole twenty-four hours by three shifts, and there was only one Sunday in four free for the prisoners. Almost all were inexperienced in mining and there were numerous accidents: fingers crushed between trucks, arms broken by falls of coal. Fortunately for the men, reports on the mines were closely studied by the various authorities responsible for the welfare of our prisoners, and a careful check was kept on them by neutral inspectors. Conditions might otherwise have been much worse.

Several groups of transferred prisoners, among them some New Zealand officers and other ranks, were sent farther north to

Wehrkreis IV. Stalag IVB at Mühlberg, which was used as an assembly centre for repatriables and as a general transit camp for Allied prisoners, also became overcrowded[1] with prisoners from Italy. Life at such a camp could be very trying, even for a short period, and prisoners' letters indicate their relief on being moved elsewhere. One man was out working at a cement works by 12 October, but others, including the officers, had longer to wait before going to a permanent camp. Other ranks went to working camps in *Wehrkreis* IV: to farm work at an *Arbeitskommando* dependent on Stalag IVA, for example, or to railway maintenance at one dependent on Stalag IVD. The stalags themselves were for the most part merely administrative headquarters for the working camps dependent on them. The New Zealand officers, with the exception of medical officers sent to working camps in *Wehrkreis* IV, went in December to Oflag VIIIF at Märisch-Trübau, which has already been described.

Some of the later trainloads, which included most of the New Zealanders from Campo PG 103/6 and Campo PG 103/7, as well as men who had been at large for a time in Italy but had been later recaptured by German troops or Fascist militia, were sent to Altengrabow, north of Magdeburg. There in Stalag XIA they remained for several weeks while waiting to go to working camps. The camp had been used for prisoners of other nationalities and was overcrowded with them when the first British troops arrived on 6 November. One result of this was interminable queues for food and everything else. The British quarters were converted stables, and the bedding was straw and two light blankets; other camp amenities were of a similarly primitive kind, and there was no provision for recreation. One man speaks in a letter of 'nothing to do or read for five weeks', and others were glad to leave such depressing conditions.

From there a large number of the New Zealanders went to *Arbeitskommando* 7001 at Halendorf, which for administrative purposes came under *Wehrkreis* XI. Here they were set to doing railway maintenance work in and around the Herman Goering Steel Works. They had good huts and conveniences and could supplement their food with extra potatoes and sugar-beet. Recreation was amply provided for by a library, a concert room, and a sports field.

Patients in Italian camp infirmaries and hospitals were among the last parties to leave for Germany, and at least some of the

---

[1] From the collapse of Italy until mid-November the camp had housed some 15,000 British.

seriously disabled went through by hospital train. They went for the most part to Lamsdorf or to Spittal, and some to the prisoner-of-war hospital near Vienna. Some, like those in Ospedale PG 201 at Bergamo, remained in Italy for a while, sufficient medical staff being kept back to look after them. Some of the doctors and orderlies transferred to Germany from the hospitals were distributed to stalags and working camps where their services were needed; numbers of others were kept idle in oflags in accordance with the deplorable German policy already noted.[1]

In July 1943, in view of the possible transfer of prisoners from Italy to Germany, it had been suggested at a meeting of the War Office Repatriation Committee that another exchange of repatriable prisoners should be arranged as soon as possible, preferably in August. This date proved impracticable, but by 6 September the Italian Government confirmed that all necessary arrangements had been made. Over 550 Italians and a few German civilians sailed for Lisbon in the *Atlantis* from England on 8 September, and over a hundred British prisoners left for the same destination by a train on the same morning. The train, however, fell into the hands of German forces and was not allowed to proceed; some of those on board were sent back to camps and others to a hospital at Treviglio. By 15 September it was realised at Lisbon that the British party was detained, and the Italians were sent to Sicily or North-West Africa until it was practicable for them to reach the Italian mainland.

In spite of British Government requests to allow our sick and wounded to reach Lisbon, or alternatively to be accommodated in Switzerland, the German authorities remained adamant. Although their Government had raised no objection to the exchange at the time it was arranged, they now refused to recognise the findings of the Italian Mixed Medical Commission, and finally stated that the men would have to be medically boarded again in Germany. Amputees and sick within sight of the homeward journey had to resign themselves to going by train to Germany, with the gloomy prospect of further years of captivity, this time in the hands of the Nazi authorities. On some men the disappointment had a depressing effect which might well have prejudiced their recovery. They were the victims of a turn of events which for many months had been the dread of all prisoners in Italy, and from which it seemed that these few had been saved at the last moment by their departure for repatriation.

---

[1] See p. 236.

III: *Escapes from Italy after the Armistice*

Of those British prisoners who had managed to avoid being taken to Germany, a few had set off immediately to reach Allied forces either in southern Italy or at the supposed invasion bridgeheads near Genoa and Venice; but the great majority, not quite sure of the best course to take, had remained in the neighbourhood of their camp or gone into the hills nearby. As soon as it became apparent that the Allied advance in the south was held up, that its future progress was uncertain, and that the risk of being rounded up by Germans or Fascists was daily increasing, many were spurred on to make their way out of enemy-occupied Italy.

There were three routes open to them. For those in northern Italy, more especially the north-west, an attempt to cross the border into Switzerland seemed to offer a better chance of freedom than a long trek south; for those in north-east Italy the Yugoslav border was nearest, and it seemed best to try to reach the Slovenian partisans, work south, and so eventually cross the Adriatic; and for those in central Italy the most obvious course was to try and work their way south through the German defensive lines and so reach an Allied outpost. These were broadly the groupings of the successful escapers, though large numbers of those from camps north of the Apennines, especially in the lower Po valley, eventually made their way south. It was unfortunate that the bulk of the New Zealand prisoners were north of the Apennines and in the north-eastern area, for the Yugoslav route proved most difficult in the months immediately following the armistice, and the route south from north-eastern Italy was long and made difficult by German and Fascist control of roads and bridges. It was unfortunate, too, that nearly half the New Zealanders were in Campo PG 57, which was transferred to Germany en bloc. This may explain why the number of New Zealand escapers from Italy was roughly 12 per cent of the total New Zealand prisoners there at the time of the armistice, whereas the overall percentage for British Commonwealth forces was double this figure.[1]

With the exception of three who were brought into France by agents in October 1944 and a few others who remained in hiding

---

[1] These calculations are based on the Return of Escapers and Evaders up to 30 June 1945, prepared by MI Branch of the War Office:

British Commonwealth escapers in Mediterranean (West) area (nearly all from Italy)	11,776
British Commonwealth escapers to Switzerland	4,916
Total	16,692
Estimated approximate total of British Commonwealth troops in Italy at the time of the armistice	70,000

The New Zealand totals were roughly 450 escapers (including those to Switzerland) out of 3700 in Italy at the time of the armistice.

or with Italian rebel bands until the end of the war, all the New Zealand escapers from working camps in north-west Italy made their way into Switzerland; these men (from satellites of Campo PG 106) made up about 70 per cent of the New Zealanders who reached that country.[1] There was, however, only a small number of New Zealanders in this area at the time of the armistice,[2] and though roughly half of these escaped, they made up only a little over two per cent of the total of British *évadés* (as they were known) in Switzerland.[3]

Numbers of Allied escaped prisoners as well as Italians made their appearance on the Swiss border almost immediately after the armistice. The British were mainly from Campo PG 62 at Bergamo,[4] which had been thrown open by the Italian camp authorities, and they reached the border near Chiasso. A first party of 70 was admitted by the Swiss frontier guards without demur, but the news that many thousands were also making their way there caused the Swiss Government to delay further parties at the frontier while they considered the consequences of admitting all and sundry.

By the Hague Convention of 1907 prisoners of war who escaped from capture into neutral territory (as distinct from uncaptured troops who entered neutral territory to avoid capture and were internable) became free men, but they were expected to leave the territory as soon as possible. A neutral power had the right to limit their liberty in so far as it was necessary for the security of the state. Prior to September 1943 only small numbers of escaped prisoners of war had made their way into Switzerland, where they were accommodated without difficulty. But after the Italian armistice the admittance of a large influx of Allied escapers and Italian refugees[5] raised a number of important issues: how they were to be fed and clothed, the possible entrance of spies and fifth columnists among genuine escapers and refugees, and, in view of there being at the time no exit from Switzerland, the threat to her neutrality of having large numbers of Allied troops at liberty in her territory. To meet these objections Britain agreed to allow sufficient food and clothing for escapers to pass through the blockade of Europe, to attest the genuineness of all British escapers, and to allow some measure of immediate military control over them other

---

[1] Another 20 per cent came from Campo 107 and its satellites north-east of Venice; the remaining 10 per cent were drawn from various camps.
[2] Estimated at 155.
[3] A total of 108 New Zealanders made their way to Switzerland after the Italian armistice, the total number of British being over 4900.
[4] One New Zealander from this camp crossed into Switzerland at Chiasso on 22 September 1943.
[5] According to a Swiss communique, about 20,000 of both categories arrived in Switzerland between 8 and 24 September 1943.

than merely assigning them a place of residence, on the understanding that details would be worked out later. This gentleman's agreement, left rather vague in spite of repeated British requests for clarification, was later to be a source of 'continual resentment, irritation and confusion'[1]—a confusion between escapers, who strictly speaking were entitled to be free men, and military internees such as airmen forced to land in Switzerland, who were, properly, held under guard in internment camps.

As soon as it was known that they would be freely admitted across the Swiss border, many of those who had been hesitating or sheltering with Italian rebels made their way in that direction. Almost all received some help on the way from Italian people—food, clothing, shelter, maps, money, information about the whereabouts of Germans and Fascists, directions as to how to reach the border, sometimes guides who took them by train or by car to a convenient place and arranged other guides to take them across. Some Italians were very frightened of reprisals, but it should be remembered that many paid later with imprisonment, confiscation or burning of their property, and death, for help given with no certainty of reward.

The Swiss border projects into Italy in four places: near Monte Rosa, near Como, near Tirano, and near Bormio. It was towards the four salients of Swiss territory thus shown on the map that the streams of escapers were directed. On 19 September the first New Zealanders arrived in Switzerland, all from the Vercelli area. An Italian took one man by train to the vicinity of Lake Lugano and showed him how to get across; two others were taken to stations on the eastern edge of Lake Maggiore and made their way over at Ponte Tresa. Four others were taken by car to Piedicavelli north of Biella and made their way to the foothills, where they were taken by guides across the mountains and into Switzerland by the Moro Pass, to the north-east of Monte Rosa in the Pennine Alps.

This last became the main route for escapers, for though the German-Fascist patrols were soon on the frontier, especially at Como, they were not yet sufficiently strong or organised to cover all the ground all the time. From the foothills north of Biella the usual route was north along the mountain range and down to Alagna in the Sesia Valley to the east; another climb and descent to Macugnaga in the Ansasca Valley to the north; then west over the 10,000-foot Moro Pass and down a glacier into Swiss territory. Many of the places on the route contained active Fascists, but with the help of guides and friendly civilians, and often under cover of darkness, they could be negotiated. One party went the whole

---

[1] Berne to Foreign Office, dated 7 June 1944.

journey in their British uniforms, and though according to the diary of one of its members, they created ' a sensation ' in the village of Alagna, they were shown an empty hut to sleep in and were able to go on their way next day.

Many parties hired mountain guides or smugglers to help them negotiate the mountainous part of their journey Some of them included Italian troops who, to avoid conscription into the Fascist militia, chose to flee the country. Many of their fellow-soldiers pursued the alternative course of going into the mountains and taking up arms against the German intruder. Some of our men spent several weeks with these armed bands, which had formed almost immediately after the armistice, in the hills of many parts of Italy. But in most of them there was a shortage of arms and a lack of organisation which decided the majority of our men to seek a way out.

During the month of September and the first half of October 1943 seventy[1] New Zealanders made their way into Switzerland, nearly all of them over the Moro Pass, and most approaching it through Alagna and Macugnaga. Extracts from one man's[2] account may serve to illustrate their experiences:

So we decided for Switzerland. That night, 16th September, by the full moon we started. . . . First night 9 p.m. to 6 a.m. we did about sixteen miles over the flooded paddocks to near the city of Biella. We could see the dome of the sanctuary[3] by moonlight. We slept in the pines and revealed ourselves to the peasants that evening to get some food. . . . We ate and paid with soap and Canadian coffee and moved on. It rained and when we ran into a civilian he persisted in us sleeping in a room where we could stay next day. We slept, but when daylight came he insisted we move out . . . we moved hurriedly. We never stopped until we were about two thousand feet up in the mountain in a dairy farmer's hayloft. We stayed till ten that night and bought some cold polenta for some coffee. . . . At ten we moved and over the hill at a good speed. At daylight we were forced to ask the way. . . . We marched till 6 p.m. without a rest until we reached a Refugio on the mountains (about 8,000 feet) . . . we met a German-speaking Tyrolese who guided us over the mountain. . . . That day we crossed to the next valley (the Sesia). We had expected to be away from roads but were only really crossing ranges between roads going up the valleys. It was there we saw the notices offering rewards for our capture and the announcement of the death penalty for harbouring us. We slept the night in a house but were ushered out well before daylight and went up the valley and over Col Turlo (about 9,000 feet), and down to our last village in Italy, Macugnaga. We were informed by an Italian who said he was forming a partisan band that the Germans stayed in the village on alternate nights and that Fascists guarded the track over the hills. . . . We slept under the pines that night. He had told us of these Fascists and their routine. They came out

---

[1] By this time there were over 2000 Allied escapers in Switzerland.
[2] Cpl D. J. Gibbs (20 Bn).
[3] A huge Catholic sanctuary built on the slopes of Mont Mucrone.

at daylight with binoculars and scanned the mountainside, which was visible to them, and if anyone was seen they would send up a patrol with bloodhounds to make a capture.

However at 1 a.m. we were woken by a cold rain. We started on an empty stomach and found our way through the village and up a track cut in the cliff face for some distance. It was raining heavily and at the end of the formed track we were lost in the rhododendron scrub. Daylight came and we looked down to the village from which pursuit might come. A belt of fog separated us and it was a great comfort to think that no scent would remain for even the most acute-nosed bloodhound. We found the track at about 6 a.m. and moved upwards. The rain changed to snow. There were mounds of stones marking what was apparently a contrabandier track. At about 2 p.m. we crossed the top. We had been told that on the other side the first two villages were Italian and the third Swiss. However we were over Moro Pass (10,400 feet) and the true position was that the border was the mountain top. Down the side a little, the two of us who were bringing up the rear saw our other two mates collected by a soldier in the blue of the Italian Army. We immediately thought of an opportunity to crown him with a boulder or put him over a cliff. Then we looked closer. . . . He was Swiss and we'd made it . . . (22 September).

In September two of our men had been able to cross over the Theodul Pass by the Matterhorn. All these men were other ranks from camps in the Vercelli area.

In November six New Zealand officers, five Army and one Air Force,[1] crossed the border. Three of them had jumped from trains on the way to Germany, two had hidden up in Campo PG 47 at Modena and got out after the Germans had left, and one had hidden in the neighbourhood of Campo PG 29 at Viano after it had been released.[2] They had spent their period at large in Italy with Italian families or with rebels in the hills. Two of those who jumped from a train remained together, and they and each of the others made their way separately to Milan and north with Italian help. They were guided over the Swiss border by Italians, three near Lake Como, one at Ponte Chiasso, and two with a smuggler beyond Lake Maggiore.

The mountain routes were almost impassable by December and German garrisons guarded the approaches to each; in the village of Macugnaga, for example, there were 300 German troops. But by this time there were also Italian underground organisations for assisting British to escape. Four New Zealand other ranks from the working camp PG 120/5 at Abano, near Padua, made contact with one such organisation operating in the Padua area. Within a few days each was taken to Milan by train and then to Como either by

---

[1] Three more New Zealand Air Force officers were successful later.
[2] From trains: Maj T. W. Straker, Capt W. G. Gray, and Lt F. E. Wilson, all while in transit from Campo PG 5 to Germany. All were mentioned in despatches for their escaping work. From Campo PG 47: Lt K. M. W. MacDonald and Fg Off K. L. Lee (RNZAF), mentioned in despatches. From Campo PG 29: Maj R. S. Orr.

train or on foot, across the lake by boat, and then over the hills to the border. Four others from Campo PG 107 at Torviscosa, who had made their way to Padua, were brought out in the same way by the same organisation.

Three men crossed the border in December at Campo Cologna, near Tirano in the Tellina Valley north of Brescia. One[1] had escaped from Campo PG 107 only to be recaptured; he cut a hole in the side of the truck taking him to Germany and jumped off near Verona. Making his way to Gorizia, he tried to cross the frontier into Yugoslavia but failed and, after some time with guerrillas, finally turned south to Padua Here he met another New Zealander from Campo PG 107 and together they made their way north to Tirano, where they were helped over the border by a smuggler. Another man from Campo PG 107 who had got as far north as Udine, turned back and made his way to Brescia and so to Tirano, crossing into Switzerland on the last day of the year.

Swiss frontier guards were waiting at most of the entrances to their country. 'They seemed to be expecting us,' runs the diary of one soldier who came over the Moro Pass. Parties arriving by that route were taken to the Swiss village of Almagell, where in the dining room of a hotel their particulars were taken and they were given a meal; later they were allotted a place to sleep on straw in a Sunday School building, and a doctor attended to raw and blistered feet or any other conditions requiring first aid. For most of them the last part of the journey had been strenuous and not a little nerve-racking, and many arrived 'all in'.[2]

From Almagell they were taken north up the Saas Fee valley to Visp, where a three-storied building was serving as a transit and sorting camp for escapers of all nationalities. Most of them had arrived over the border 'in rags and tatters' and 'in next to no footwear';[3] here they had hot showers and received new clothing from International Red Cross stocks at Geneva. A medical examination and interrogation by the Swiss for identification purposes completed the routine for each ex-prisoner. The food at this reception camp was excellent, but most men chafed under the enforced inactivity. A British headquarters for escapers was soon set up at Wil, 20 miles east of Zurich in St. Gallen, and the men were sent on there as soon as possible. After some weeks they were drafted to detachments, about 200 strong, at small country towns in the neighbouring cantons. Many of them had expected that soon after their arrival in Switzerland they would in some way be

---
[1] Pte T. Robson (25 Bn), mentioned in despatches for his escapes.
[2] Report by Maj Orr and other officers on New Zealand escapers in Switzerland, 20 October 1944.
[3] Ibid.

returned to Allied forces, and the news that they were to have an indefinite stay in that country came as a disappointment. Owing to their numbers, this enforced stay was to be not without its difficulties, and for most of them it was to last nearly a year.

Prisoners who had left their camps and were living in the plains surrounding the Gulf of Venice soon heard of armed rebels operating in the hills to the north and east of Gorizia, to which many Italian soldiers[1] were flocking to avoid conscription by the new Fascist Republic. Many prisoners made their way to them shortly after the armistice in the hope that they might thus be able to gain entry into partisan-held Yugoslavia.

The partisans in Slovenia were by late 1943 an organised and disciplined military force which had been fighting for over two years. They had survived Mussolini's offensive of May 1942 intended to destroy them, and were in full occupation of considerable areas of liberated territory. Since the arrival of a British liaison officer in April 1942 they had been recognised by the British Government, which was sending them supplies. There was as yet, however, no arrangement with them for evacuating through their territory escaped British prisoners of war, and their outposts operating in north-east Italy, seeing only the need for recruits, tried to persuade or force escaped prisoners of whatever nationality to fight with them. Most British prisoners returned west[2] when they found that instead of being helped to rejoin their own forces they were expected to join a partisan[3] band; many who had done so soon tired of fatigues and guard duties and hit-and-run fighting with a motley, ill-armed and ill-fed force, in the command of which they had no say, and whose political aims were more apparent than its military objectives.

At the beginning of October, however, when Germans and Fascists began seriously rounding up loose ex-prisoners, a number set out and joined the partisan bands, intending to shelter with them for the time being at least. One man's diary describes his first encounter with a partisan outpost in the foothills of the Julian Alps:

Arrived at a village called Castel Dobra, where we were all given a great time. One chap rushed up and kissed us all. All rebels here giving the closed fist salute . . . climbed high ridge, down a valley and up another ridge where we struck a rebel outpost. All in various kinds of

---

[1] Many thousands also formed their own bands of *rebelli*.
[2] Some were threatened with shooting by the partisans if they 'deserted', but these threats were not carried out.
[3] To avoid confusion in this section the term 'partisans' has been used to refer to the Yugoslav guerrillas and the term 'rebels' to the Italian bands formed after the German occupation, most of whom seem to have called themselves in the early stages *rebelli*.

uniforms and with all sorts of arms, covered with hand grenades—one even had a sword. Girls also armed and in uniforms. . . . Mongolian and two Serbs joined this battalion.

Men who had jumped from north-bound trains also joined the partisans, and soon there was a sprinkling from most parts of the Commonwealth and from several Allied countries. The partisan headquarters for the area had decided to set up a British camp at Caporetto; mixed platoons of British Commonwealth troops were soon formed and were being used in action against German patrols in early October.

It was at this stage (about 11 October) that two escaped British majors[1] arrived in the area and decided that British troops could be put to better use if they were extricated and brought back under British command. By the middle of the month they had ordered those with whom they made contact to cease fighting under partisan command,[2] had collected a party of 85 at Stupizza for evacuation, and were negotiating with the partisan leaders at Caporetto for a safe conduct through partisan-held Yugoslav territory to the Dalmatian coast. Partisan headquarters viewed with disfavour what they regarded as the defection of the British and were uncooperative. After a heated argument, however, they agreed to pass them on to the next command on 17 October, and this process, with much similar argument, was repeated as the ex-prisoners continued their slow journey southwards. They were usually able to arrange for a guide from village to village and sometimes an armed escort.

From command to command we were passed, spending with different units of Tito's variegated forces, sometimes a few hours, sometimes days, and on one occasion over a week. Always there were interminable discussions with the partisans, always the same difficulties in persuading them to agree to our plans. Once we were held captive for over a week, four days being spent in the open with rain falling and snow threatening. With the first winter snow on the ground they flatly refused to give us any [further] guides or escort on account of a large-scale German round-up of

---

[1] Maj E. H. Gibbon, DSO and bar (4 RTR), and Maj Ballentine, DSO (SAEC).
[2] In a report to the War Office Gibbon states that he did not stop those who wished to stay and fight, and that four stayed. He gives his reasons for persuading the men to leave:
  '(a) Half of them were in civilian clothing, which together with their boots, was in a bad state and the partisans could not supply any more.
  (b) The partisans lived by raiding local Italian villages and taking what they required, and were trying to use British troops on these raids as much as possible, for political reasons.
  (c) According to a British captain who had been engaged in fighting with the partisans, co-operation was next to impossible because of the language difficulty and differences in training.
  (d) The men stated that they only took up arms because they felt under some obligation to the partisans for feeding them, and were intending when opportunity offered to return to western Italy.'

partisans, and Stump[1] led the party with a home-made compass belonging to me across thirty miles of country dominated by the Germans, into which no partisan would venture.[2]

The party crossed the Isonzo River to Circhina and passed into Yugoslav territory north of Idria; 40-odd men with poor footwear and equipment were detached to follow on more slowly. After moving south-east across the large plateau of western Slovenia, they kept broadly to the high country near the coast till they reached Otocac. There were often long marches in all weathers over difficult country, sometimes with German patrols on their heels, and food was poor in quality. On occasions they came under fire, and in the confusion of one hurried withdrawal a portion of the second party became scattered, though 22 of them later rejoined the main body and one or two came out with a later party.

In the course of their journey they met and were helped as far as possible by officers of the British military mission who had been smuggled into Yugoslav territory from April 1942 on. In late November they crossed the Kupa River into Croatia, and were taken on 140 miles by truck to Otocac, the seat of the Slovenian Liberation Government. After 18 days there, during which they were well treated and entertained at a sumptuous feast to receive the thanks of the Slovenian Government for the equipment sent by Britain and the United States, they were driven to the port of Senj. A fishing boat took them to the island of Vis, whence a landing craft brought them across the Adriatic to Bari on 23 December. They were the first party[3] to come out through Yugoslavia, and the information they brought helped in the organisation of what was to prove a most fruitful escape route.

A few British escapers from German prison camps had joined partisan units earlier in the war, among them a New Zealander[4] who had escaped in December 1941 while on a working party attached to Stalag XVIIID. Travelling hidden on the railways with the assistance of Yugoslav railwaymen, he and two companions

---

[1] Maj Gibbon.
[2] Capt Riddiford (6 Fd Regt). He commanded the New Zealand section of the party (26 all told) and also acted as interpreter in all the negotiations with the Yugoslavs. For his work with this party and his escapes he was awarded the MC.
[3] The party finished up with a strength of 62, including 26 New Zealanders. They were: Capt D. J. Riddiford, Pte J. A. Abel (25 Bn), Dvr W. F. Andrews (4 Res MT Coy), mentioned in despatches, Pte P. A. Burke (26 Bn), Pte H. Carson (28 Bn), Pte D. W. W. Chambers (24 Bn), Pte N. A. Gosling (20 Bn), Pte E. W. R. Hart (22 Bn), Pte J. A. Illston (22 Bn), Pte J. Hutton (20 Bn), L-Cpl R. D. Johnstone (20 Bn), mentioned in despatches, Pte H. J. Joseph (23 Bn), Cpl C. H. Kerse (18 Bn), Pte F. J. Laird (20 Bn), Pte J. E. Lockhead (19 Bn), Pte J. S. Lugton (27 Bn), Pte P. S. Mackay (23 Bn), Pte J. W. Mount (20 Bn), Pte H. Nicol (7 A Tk Regt), Pte R. M. Reeve (22 Bn), Pte E. M. Robinson (25 Bn), Pte B. M. Robson (23 Bn), Spr B. H. Smith (8 Fd Coy), Pte N. Smith (20 Bn), Pte A. J. Svenson (20 Bn), L-Cpl J. H. Wildman (22 Bn).
[4] Cpl J. Denvir (20 Bn). See pp. 134-5. For the destruction of a German train and its accompanying unit he was awarded the DCM, and he won the Soviet Medal for Valour for the whole period of his service with the Yugoslav partisans.

had made their way to Ljubliana, where Yugoslav patriots welcomed them and offered them service with the partisans then beginning to operate in the mountains south of the city. He had accepted this in 1941 rather than attempt the long and difficult journey to Turkey. During two years' steady fighting for the partisan cause Denvir was three times wounded; on the last of these occasions, when he commanded a partisan battalion against a large German attack in August 1943, his wounds caused him to be invalided back to Italy in January 1944. During his service with the partisans he had, to use the words of the British liaison officer in Slovenia, ' done much to enhance the respect of the British soldier throughout Yugoslavia '.

Those prisoners who were fortunate enough to be at camps in central Italy in September 1943, and who had the additional good fortune to be released or to be able to free themselves fairly easily, had little difficulty in deciding what to do. Some set out immediately to meet the Allied forces in the Naples area, and many of those that lay up for a day or two to size up the situation soon followed them; the remainder who decided to stay hidden and wait for the Allied forces to reach them were far enough south to make such an outcome seem only a matter of a few weeks. For by 27 September Foggia had fallen to British forces advancing from Taranto, and by 1 October Allied forces on the west of the peninsula had taken Naples and were advancing to the Volturno.

The break-out of 300 other ranks from the working camp PG 78/1 at Aquafredda, leaving behind only a medical sergeant and nine sick men, has already been mentioned. They were organised in parties of ten, equipped with a stock of Red Cross food, and told to make for the surrounding thickly wooded and rather precipitous hills. Unfortunately 4000-odd from the base camp at Sulmona had taken similar action, and the German military authorities had sent out strong patrols to recapture as many as possible. Many had taken shelter in the hill villages such as Caramanico and San Spirito, but had to leave when they were occupied by German troops. The Germans claimed to have captured 2000 escaped prisoners in the area around Sulmona, but many were soon in civilian clothing and either being sheltered by Italian families or living in the high country in caves, in both cases depending on the local population for their food. Numbers crossed the Maiella Massif to Pennapiedimonte and Guardiagrele, there to wait a more favourable opportunity of rejoining Allied forces.

Some of the early successful escapers avoided the area between Sulmona, Roccaraso and Castel di Sangro, where the German rounding-up patrols had been active, and kept in a south-easterly direction to reach the Eighth Army outposts near Bovino, Lucera, and San Severo in the Foggia area at the end of September and the beginning of October.[1] Others kept to the idea of making in the direction of Naples. One New Zealander[2] got within sight of the American lines south-east of Avellino a fortnight after leaving camp, only to be captured there by German troops. Taken back to Sulmona, he escaped from a train carrying 400 prisoners north to Rome, made his way back and brought 17 Indian troops through to an American division at Cereti, south of Letino, on 13 October.

In this early period, too, a number of men from camps in northern Italy successfully reached the Allied lines, covering the long distance by the simple expedient of getting on to southbound trains and travelling by rail as far as they could, thus obviating the disadvantage under which they had started. The trains in this period were packed with Italian troops and civilians returning to their homes, no tickets were required, and there was no check on who was travelling. For the first few days after the armistice trains were still running from as far north as Ancona down to British-held Bari. Then the Germans stopped them going much farther south than Pescara, and after a while they were roughly checking some of the trains in various parts of Italy; but it was not until mid-November that passenger traffic was strictly controlled. Using the trains four New Zealanders from Campo PG 107, north-east of Venice, were safe in Allied hands by 30 September, and another seven from the same camp, together with one from Campo PG 120/8, near Padua, in early October.

The stories of their dash southwards are similar. One party of six New Zealanders, after getting out of the camp, took a train as far as Pescara, walked and then took another train as far south as they could go, split up, and finally walked until they reached the Allies.[3] They came through to the British lines variously at San Severo, at Lucera, and at Motta, all in the area north and west of Foggia. The man from Campo PG 120/8 met British troops at Troia, a little to the south in the same area. Two others[4] from Campo PG 107, who had cut the wire and crawled out of the camp on the night after the armistice announcement, made a similar journey on foot and by train down the east coast and reached an

---

[1] As early as 19 September 327 British Commonwealth ex-prisoners had reached Allied lines.
[2] Sigmn J. A. Gaze (Div Sigs), awarded MM.
[3] Three of the party, Ptes E. Barnett (20 Bn), R. Kendrick (22 Bn), and C. L. Tayler (19 Bn) were mentioned in despatches.
[4] L-Cpl I. A. McK. Bond (ASC attached 5 Fd Amb) and Cpl J. Pullen (24 Bn), both mentioned in despatches.

American detachment. Among the first to reach the Allied lines near Naples was a New Zealand sergeant[1] from Campo PG 5, who had jumped from the train taking him to Germany and had wasted no time making his way south.

As the Allied armies advanced slowly north up the Italian peninsula, more men felt they were near enough to be able to avoid the German posts and reach liberated territory. But by mid-October the German forces had formed a defensive line astride the peninsula and their back areas were guarded. Civilian clothes were essential; roads had to be crossed by night and rivers forded. However, the British Intelligence organisation for extricating escapers and evaders (MI9) had field sections with both the Fifth and Eighth Armies, and their guides behind the enemy lines were encouraging and directing out large numbers of prisoners.[2] A few came down to the west of the Apennines to meet the American forces south of Venafro.

Many more made contact with Allied units near the Termoli-Campobasso road, among them 54 New Zealand other ranks (50 of them from Campo PG 78/1 at Aquafredda) and three officers from Campo PG 47 at Modena.[3] The last left the camp after the senior British officer had given permission but before the Germans had surrounded it, and after a few days in the fields made their way to Bologna in civilian clothes. They travelled by train to Pescara and then inland, finally sheltering with farmers in the Casoli area, with the intention of remaining until the Allied advance overran them. This was slower than expected, and the danger of being rounded up by German troops or betrayed by Fascists forced them into hiding in the hills. Having decided to try to get through the lines, they travelled cautiously southward, eventually crossed the Biferno River and reached a British outpost near Casacalenda in mid-October.

There were two New Zealanders in the Carcere Penale Badia at Sulmona serving long sentences that had been awarded them in Greece after their recapture in civilian clothing. After the armistice a British officer from Campo PG 78 came to the penitentiary and released everybody—twelve British Commonwealth troops, 50

---

[1] Sgt J. A. Redpath, DCM, MM (19 A Tps Coy). He had previously escaped from Galatas camp on Crete, made his way to Greece, and led a party of 17, which he brought back to North Africa. He then joined 'A' Force for operations in Greece, but was captured by Italians on the island of Antiparos. Involved in a tunnel escape at Campo PG 35, he was sent to Campo PG 5 and was there at the time of the armistice.

[2] The situation report of its No. 2 Section, based on Campobasso, as at 1 November 1943 states: ' . . . last 48 hours 46 E & Es brought out by my guides total since 22 October officers 24 other ranks 188. This figure only those brought out personally by our guides.' By 20 November the total claimed for all sections of the organisation was 1004.

[3] Lt-Col C. D. A. George (25 Bn), Capt J. D. Gerard (5 Fd Regt), and Flt Lt R. D. Campbell, all mentioned in despatches.

Greeks, and 400 Yugoslavs. Although one of the New Zealanders was recaptured and sent to Germany, the other[1] made a successful escape. He lived for three weeks in civilian clothes in the hill district near Pratola; then he and two others set off with a guide to get through to the Allied lines. In a little over a fortnight they met British troops at Castropignano.

By early November the Eighth Army had crossed the Trigno River and was advancing towards the Sangro; more prisoners came down from the hills to meet them at Palmoli, and later at Atessa and other places on the coastal slopes. Though they were nearly all from Campo PG 78/1, there was a sprinkling of men from Campo PG 70, from Campo PG 107, from Campo PG 120/5 near Padua, and three from Campo PG 145 at Campotosto, north of Aquila. There had been only a handful of New Zealanders at the last camp, from which about three-quarters of the prisoners had got away. Most of them made for Sulmona and then for the coastal plains; the three New Zealanders made their way south to Palmoli on 7 November.[2]

As the Allied forces advanced up the eastern Italian seaboard it became an obvious method of escape to secure a boat from a more northerly point on the coast and sail down the Adriatic to land on liberated territory.[3] A New Zealand officer,[4] who escaped by this means, got away from the camp at Modena after it had been taken over by German troops by remaining hidden for three days in a shallow trench under some tomato plants, and then dodging through the wire unobserved. With help from Italians in the neighbourhood he acquired civilian clothes and a map and travelled by various trains to Senigallia, whence he got a lift in a German truck as far as Ancona. He then travelled by bicycle and walked to Porto Civitanova, where he arranged with a fisherman to take him with a party of others to Termoli, announced over the radio as in British hands. They arrived safely on 14 November. Since the beginning of October an MI9 section based on Termoli had been landing agents on the Adriatic coast, and at the same time taking off escapers and evaders from the coast as far north as Ancona; fishing boats loaded with such parties had been regularly heaving to in the small harbour at Termoli.

At the end of November the Sangro was crossed and the New Zealand Division, in action once again, advanced as far as Palombaro and Castelfrentano. Numbers of prisoners[5] in hiding were then

---
[1] Sgt A. C. Barker (4 Res MT Coy), awarded MM for his efforts to escape.
[2] One of them, Pte W. G. Skinner (20 Bn), was mentioned in despatches.
[3] This method was first used in September 1943, when a boatload landed at Bari.
[4] Capt S. S. F. Goodwin (24 Bn), mentioned in despatches.
[5] A dozen or more New Zealand other ranks came out here in early December, among them Pte T. G. McCreath (20 Bn), mentioned in despatches, who had previously escaped from the Galatas camp on Crete.

able to reach safety at Palombaro and its environs. It was especially pleasing for New Zealand escapers, after a year or more of captivity, to be first greeted by their own countrymen. Among those who gained their freedom at this time were two New Zealand officers[1] from Modena who had hidden in the roof of one of the barracks after the German troops had taken over the camp. They left unobserved on 25 September and were for a while looked after by Italian peasants. Then they struck south and, walking all the way, crossed the Apennines into the Arno Valley; keeping for the most part to the high country, they passed through Gubbio, over the Gran Sasso, and finally over the Maiella Massif to near Guardiagrele. Here they waited for some five weeks before going to meet our advancing forces at Palombaro on 12 December.

A reference has been made to the establishment in Italy of field sections of MI9,[2] the British organisation for helping escapers and evaders, other sections of which had been operating for some time in Greece and Crete. Based on Algiers, the first elements of MI9 to land in Italy followed closely on the heels of the invasion forces, and by 12 October the responsibility for 'rescue work' (as it came to be known) was divided geographically as follows:

(*a*) The east coast of Italy, from fifty or sixty miles behind the enemy lines to the Po—the responsibility of a boat detachment with headquarters at Termoli.

(*b*) The west coast of Italy, from fifty or sixty miles behind the enemy lines to the Po and all territory north of it—the responsibility of main headquarters at Algiers.

(*c*) From the enemy front lines back to a depth of fifty or sixty miles—the responsibility of detachments with the invading armies.

The detachment of MI9 at Termoli was occupied at first with sea operations on the Adriatic coast, and main headquarters at Algiers with operations in Corsica and the western Mediterranean and with the dropping of agents in north Italy to carry out long-term plans.

It was the sections operating with the advancing armies which provided guides and gave men the encouragement, information, and aids[3] necessary to complete the last stage of their journey, a stage at which so many were recaptured through lack of guidance. There were three such sections: No. 1 working with the Fifth Army in the approaches to Cassino, No. 2 covering the central portion of the front but within the left flank of the Eighth Army,[4] and No. 5—

---

[1] Lts H. F. Flower (25 Bn) and R. M. Wood (19 Bn), both mentioned in despatches.
[2] The MI9 organisation worked in close collaboration with its United States equivalent and included Commonwealth, United States, and other Allied personnel.
[3] Money, maps, compasses.
[4] These two sections were in operation by mid-September, but the boat section not till October.

originally an offshoot of the boat detachment at Termoli—covering the eastern portion of the front. It was in the last sector that the majority of men came through in the period up to the end of 1943. By late October there were nearly a hundred British Commonwealth and United States personnel,[1] in addition to Italian agents, working behind the lines on rescue work—a number of them escaped prisoners of war, who were especially useful in this early stage because of their knowledge of conditions behind the enemy lines and of what escaped prisoners were likely to do.

Many of the escapers after coming through the lines were given meals and somewhere to sleep and were generally looked after by the field sections of MI9. But as these units were not equipped for this type of work, the men were sent south as soon as possible. The Allied Repatriation Unit, with forward sections to do this work, had not yet been formed, and transit camps were set up by the Armistice Prisoner of War Sub-Commission in this early stage only at Taranto, Naples and Algiers, though by 3 December there was also one in operation at Bari. After the collapse of the plan for a smooth evacuation of prisoners from their camps in Italy and the consequent scrapping of the large organisation set up to carry it out, the Sub-Commission took a little time to adjust itself to the new situation.

There was another factor working on the side of the escaper. In the months following the armistice, Italian underground 'Liberation Committees, had sprung up out of hatred for the German occupation forces in some of the Italian cities—Milan, Florence, Novara, Brescia, Como, and others. Many of them set up organisations for assisting prisoners to escape, operating mainly across north Italy to the Swiss border.[2] There were also 'rebel' bands of Italians in most of the mountain districts: in the Italian Alps, to the north of Biella, of Lecco, Bergamo, and Brescia, and of Udine in the east; in the Apennines, from Genoa to Monte Falterona and south to the Abruzzi. Many were soldiers from the former Italian Army and some were fairly well equipped; but equipment, numbers, and reliability varied a great deal. Nevertheless, Italian resistance to the Germans was such that as early as 13 October 1943 Italy was recognised as a co-belligerent by Britain, America and Russia. Escaped prisoners could usually find refuge with such bands, and often guides to take them on by the nearest escape route.

---

[1] The British and United States personnel consisted of guides and 'rounders-up', who were parachuted in or landed by sea, and beach parties. Most were sent in as part of a special operation mounted during October to bring off quickly as many ex-prisoners as possible. Later, British and US personnel were used sparingly behind the lines, as it was found to be more practical to employ Italian agents as guides.
[2] See p. 303 for a reference to such an organisation.

One escaped officer, in his interrogation, decribed the southward escape routes of prisoners of war from north and central Italy as forming a funnel at the southern end of the Apennines a few days' march from the Allied lines. Here in late 1943 were gathered men who had been forced up from the plains or deterred from making the last stage of their journey by the thickness of the German forces on the ground. Many of them had been compelled to live in hill caves and mountain huts, in order to avoid betrayal in a village and the consequent implication of the Italian family which sheltered them. With them in the high country were Italian rebels—soldiers avoiding conscription into the Fascist militia and civilians avoiding digging and other forced labour for the German forces. One estimate put the number of British escaped prisoners in these areas as high as 6000, and it is clear from the reports of escapers as they came through that the number was very large. For food they depended on the generosity of the local peasants, who however found the task of providing for increasing numbers very difficult. Some prisoners who had come long distances had worn out their boots, and to those with little clothing the cold of November and early December brought great hardship. Finally the snows became deep, and most of those attempting to get through the lines returned with the story that it was impossible. Sickness and the prospect of a winter under those severe conditions caused many to come down for shelter to the lower villages, hoping to make another attempt in the spring. But though many remained successfully hidden through the winter, others were caught and a few killed in the German round-ups that took place after the front became more or less static. One or two, undaunted by previous failures, pushed ahead over the mountains and reached the Allied lines by Christmas Eve.[1]

By Christmas 1943 the German Winter Line was stabilised, and the severe winter conditions made it likely to remain so until the spring; the Germans were accordingly able to devote time and men to clearing up their back areas. Regiments were set aside for searching out escaped prisoners, and many of these German troops began to operate in civilian clothes. With bribes and threats they persuaded some Italian civilians to inform, and Fascists were used both as spies and for the interrogation of any suspicious person arrested in civilian clothes. Ruthless reprisals, including death and destruction of property, were carried out against Italians helping prisoners. Some of the rebel bands were attacked and dispersed, and executions of civilians were carried out at villages in the

---

[1] Sigmn J. H. Byers (Div Sigs), Ptes N. H. Jones (5 Fd Amb), A. J. Halkett and R. S. Halkett (both 20 Bn), all did before Christmas, and Pte E. J. Morgan (27 MG Bn) in early January 1944.

neighbourhood of any place where German soldiers had been killed. This not only made Italian families careful about sheltering prisoners, but made those who did accept this risk chary of whom they let into their house and whom they talked to. One result was that the work of British rescue agents behind the lines became more difficult;[1] for until their identity was established, neither escaped prisoners nor civilian helpers would have anything to do with them.

IV: *New Zealanders captured in the Italian and Aegean Campaigns*

In mid-October New Zealand troops had landed in Italy to rejoin the Eighth Army, and by 14 November the New Zealand Division had taken over a portion of the line. In the attacks on Orsogna which followed the crossing of the Sangro, a number of New Zealanders fell into enemy hands. Fifty-three were lost in an ill-fated attack on the town by 25 Battalion on 3 December, and another 14 by 24 and 28 Battalions on 7 December. But the days of large-scale withdrawals were over for the New Zealand Division, and the number lost as prisoners was kept down to a hundred, only a fifth of the total number lost in action.[2] Some of these were lost in patrol activity against the enemy Winter Line.

As transit camps for new prisoners and for recaptured escapers, the Germans used some of the former Italian prisoner-of-war camps if the numbers were large enough; otherwise they used commandeered barracks and other buildings. Thus in the south some men were taken to the old Italian camps at Sulmona and Aquila, others to barracks at Aquila, Chieti, or Avellino. In the north, although there was a collecting centre at Trieste for those recaptured in the eastern provinces, the main transit camp was at Mantua and became known as Stalag 337. It had once consisted of an old garage and store-rooms; but if sleeping, washing, and sanitary facilities were primitive, the food was satisfactory, and prisoners were usually kept there for only ten days before going on to Germany.

---

[1] One was nearly shot by escaped prisoners. Many prisoners were helped and guided by Italians without knowing that their helpers had been dropped in by the MI9 organisation

[2] Comparative figures for this and the Battle for Egypt in the summer of 1942 are given below:

	Killed in action	Died of wounds	Prisoners of war
20 Jun to 31 Aug 1942	536	286	1819
12 Nov 1943 to 31 Jan 1944	298	101	100

In the later campaign losses in prisoners of war form only 20 per cent of the total, whereas in the Battle for Egypt they form 70 per cent. In the three earlier campaigns the percentage of losses in prisoners was higher still.

One of the many unpleasant thoughts that passed through the minds of prisoners transported northwards through Italy in the weeks following the armistice was the possibility of being bombed by our own aircraft. Though fortunately this did not happen on many occasions, there was a tragic occurrence of this kind on 8 December. Four hundred prisoners (including 57 New Zealanders) who had been collected in the old Campo PG 102 were being entrained at Aquila station. Some 260 had been locked in box-wagons, which happened to be in between a petrol and an ammunition train, when a heavy air attack was delivered on all the rolling stock at the station. Although the attack lasted only ten minutes over 200 were killed (including eight New Zealanders) and over 75 injured. In the ensuing confusion many of those uninjured were able to escape and some eventually made their way to Allied lines.

A few New Zealand airmen were captured in RAF operations over Italy in the second half of 1943. Before the Italian armistice those who fell into German hands were usually sent post-haste to Germany for interrogation; if they fell into Italian hands they were sent to the same prisoner-of-war camps as other prisoners. One New Zealander[1] brought down in July was sent to Sulmona. After being free after the armistice for 14 days, he was retaken but made another break shortly afterwards from a train. He lay up in the hills near Castel di Sangro for a while and, though wounded by a German patrol two days before, made his way to the British forces at Isernia on 7 November.

Another New Zealander, a Fleet Air Arm lieutenant,[2] who made a forced landing near Salerno on 9 September, had an even shorter period in captivity. He jumped from a German truck taking him to a prison camp and made his way south towards Naples, helped en route by local Italians. After spending ten days hidden with an Italian family, he and some companions climbed the slopes of Mount Vesuvius and crossed to the village of Torre del Greco, where he met British troops only three weeks after his capture.

On 14 September British forces took advantage of the Italian armistice to occupy Cos and Leros, two islands of the Italian Dodecanese. Included in the small occupation force on Leros was a New Zealand detachment of the Long Range Desert Group. Strong German airborne and seaborne forces eventually overcame the British garrison and occupied the island in November. Some of the British forces, including most of the New Zealanders, were able to disperse and evade capture, and many finally got away in small boats or were rescued by caiques of the MI9 organisation. But

---

[1] Flt Lt M. R. Head, RNZAF., awarded MC for his escape.
[2] Lt (A) D. Cameron, RNZNVR.

numbers were held prisoner, among them 22 New Zealanders, the majority of whom were captured while raiding the island of Levita in October. They were taken to Greece and so north to Germany.

V: *Protection of the Interests of Prisoners of War and Civilians*

Keeping track of the thousands of British prisoners who were one moment safely at camps in Italy and the next scattered over various camps in Austria and Germany, at liberty in Switzerland, or at large in Italy or Yugoslavia, suddenly provided all those agencies engaged in notification with an additional major task. Although nominal rolls were handed to the Germans for despatch to Geneva by many camp leaders, only a few names of those transferred to Germany had been received in London by early November, and the notification of these transfers had not been completed six months later. The names of several hundred New Zealanders were still outstanding at the end of the year, but these included men at large in Italy and Yugoslavia.

New Zealand prisoners of war and civilian internees were by late 1943 scattered over a good part not only of Europe but also of the Far East. The complicated task of maintaining up-to-date information about prisoners as well as escapers in Europe, and of obtaining any information at all about those in the Far East, made desirable the creation of a new central authority to receive and dissect all incoming information about New Zealanders missing or in enemy hands. At a meeting on 13 October 1943 of the appropriate service and civilian officials it was decided to set up a New Zealand Missing and Prisoner of War Agency within the existing structure of Base Records. The task of the new agency was to receive all relevant information, to verify and record it, and to distribute it without delay to the service departments concerned, for notification to next-of-kin. It was also to maintain an up-to-date card index of all New Zealanders who were missing, prisoners of war, or civilian internees. The Prisoner of War Information Bureau established at Army Headquarters was to continue to handle information regarding enemy subjects held in New Zealand.

The new agency began to operate immediately, and by the middle of the following year had taken over all its allotted functions. Thus the Prime Minister's Department, which had been acting as a clearing house for all notifications of missing and captured New Zealanders, was relieved of an ever-increasing burden of detailed work; and the delegation of this work to an already thoroughly experienced organisation assured the greatest possible speed and accuracy in notification of this type of casualty.

Negotiations between Germany and the British Commonwealth were still delicate in the latter half of 1943 on account of the reprisal incidents of the previous year. Although shackling had been relaxed to the extent of being symbolical, and although many German officials wanted to see it at an end, they had to tread very carefully when broaching the subject with their political leaders, who still maintained an uncompromising attitude. Moreover, such relaxations as had taken place had to be kept from the notice of these leaders, for fear of a strict reimposition of the order. The importance of this was realised by prisoner-of-war camp leaders, who asked prisoners to be especially careful not to refer to these relaxations in their letters. It was also realised by Allied governments, which maintained a strict control over publicity connected with the whole question of reprisals. On 21 July 1943 the Prime Minister of New Zealand made a statement in the House of Representatives, in which, although he could not mention that shackling had become merely symbolical, he indicated that it was not so serious as it had been. The statement provoked indignant protests from distressed next-of-kin, who were still receiving letters from prisoners giving no sign of any relaxation, and much care and tact were necessary in reassuring them.

Meanwhile the Swiss Minister in Berlin and the International Red Cross Committee never ceased their efforts to arrange for the shackling order to be rescinded. In August 1943 it appeared that Hitler was the only one needing persuasion that it was desirable to terminate shackling. In early November Dr. Burchardt of the International Red Cross Committee negotiated an assurance that it would in fact cease as from the 22nd of that month, even though the order might not be rescinded. From that date it did cease, though publicity concerning this was carefully toned down; for German officials had indicated to the Swiss Minister in Berlin that any 'malicious comment' in the British press might be prejudicial to the interests of British prisoners.

There were other indications that the German authorities (if not their political leaders) were prepared to be conciliatory on prisoner-of-war matters. Conditions for British prisoners undergoing judicial sentences in the German military prisons had for some time up to the middle of 1943 been so rigorous that few prisoners could have stood up physically or mentally to sentences of any length. It was usual to receive only one letter and to write only one every six weeks, to receive no Red Cross or private parcels, to have no books in English, and to be allowed only half an hour's walk in the open air every day. But by late 1943 conditions at the Graudenz military prison, at least, had been improved by the permission of three food parcels a month, as a result of representations by the

Protecting Power. British proposals for making the other restrictions less severe were under consideration by the German Government.

The most notable evidence of a change of heart on the part of the Germans was in the negotiations for the repatriation of sick and wounded and protected personnel. Since the fiasco of 1940, when an exchange had been stopped on the eve of its completion, Germany had remained adamant in her refusal to resume negotiations except on a basis of numerical equality. No effort had been spared by the Allied authorities through neutral channels to pave the way for a repatriation agreement. By the spring of 1943, as a result of successful operations in North Africa, the number of German prisoners in British and United States hands was sufficient to persuade the German Foreign Minister that it was worth while, and Germany made a proposal which became the starting point of successful negotiations. This time there was consultation between Britain and the United States[1] before the agreement was finalised. Britain wished the exchange to include protected personnel in order to make the German numbers nearly equal with the British, for fear that, if they were not, there might be as before a last-minute breakdown in arrangements; and the United States, though at first opposed to any additional complications, agreed. In its final form the exchange agreement also included civilians and merchant navy prisoners. Great care was taken to see that the success of the project was not prejudiced by premature or excessive press publicity.

The fact that no exchange agreement could be reached with the German authorities until 1943 had not prevented the examination at regular intervals by Mixed Medical Commissions in Germany of those cases put forward by Allied prisoner-of-war doctors as eligible for repatriation. These medical officers sometimes had a difficult task in selecting the most deserving cases, and in dissuading well-intentioned would-be escapers from trying to take a place in a repatriation draft which might give a very sick man his only chance of recovery. Over fifty of the men passed by the earlier Mixed Medical Commissions died in captivity before the end of 1942, and to many it seemed as if the whole business was doomed to failure. Prisoners selected for repatriation became more and more sceptical as the months dragged on without result, and they resigned themselves to seeing the war out in a prison camp.

But in late October 1943 camps received the order for these men to move. Some of them have recorded their incredulity and elation,

---

[1] Representatives of the United States Embassy and military authorities in the United Kingdom attended meetings of the Imperial Prisoners of War Committee Sub-Committee A from its twenty-eighth meeting on 29 October 1943 onwards. British representatives in Washington attended similar meetings there.

and have described the details of packing, farewells, final search by the German Abwehr, and the march to the railway station for those who could manage it. Then followed a journey by rail and sea to the ports of exchange, Gothenburg and Barcelona. Most of the New Zealanders travelled by comfortable hospital train to Marseilles and thence by the Italian hospital ship *Aquileia* to Barcelona, where the majority of the Dominion personnel were to be exchanged. The exchange took place there on 27 October, the sick and wounded leaving in the hospital ship *Tairea* and the protected personnel in the *Cuba*. During the voyage the repatriates were supplied with comforts by the British Red Cross, and after their arrival at Alexandria on 3 November the New Zealanders were looked after in that respect by the New Zealand Red Cross organisation in the Middle East. The 390-odd New Zealanders expressed their appreciation of the efforts of the Red Cross on their behalf since their capture by a donation of £1815 to the funds of the New Zealand organisation.

Further repatriation parties, mainly men from the United Kingdom and United States but including eight New Zealanders, were brought from Gothenburg in the *Atlantis*, the *Empress of Russia*, and the *Drottningholm*. The International Red Cross Committee had supervised the operations at both Barcelona and Gothenburg, which had taken place simultaneously and had involved the exchange of over 5000 British and United States prisoners for over 5000 Germans.[1]

The British repatriates brought practically the first eye-witness evidence of the treatment of prisoners in Germany, and Military Intelligence reports based on their statements added considerably to the information already collated from escapers, from letters, and from neutral reports. No time was lost in embarking the Army repatriates for New Zealand, since manpower conditions in New Zealand were such that every available man was required either for service with the Army or in some other sphere.

VI: *Relief Work*

Fortunately for the prisoners transferred from Italy to Germany, as well as for those already there, the British Red Cross between April and August 1943[2] had built up at Geneva and in the camps reserves of food parcels sufficient for twelve weeks. Not only, therefore, were existing camps in Germany able to cope fairly well in this respect with large additions to their strengths, but they were also able to send help to newly-established camps. In most cases it

---

[1] The total of New Zealanders exchanged at Barcelona and Gothenburg was 395 (169 sick and wounded and 226 protected personnel).
[2] 6,607,000 food parcels were sent from Lisbon to Geneva in that period.

Manacles used by the Germans on Allied prisoners of war as a reprisal for British action in tying the hands of German prisoners taken in the Dieppe raid

HUT INTERIOR AT STALAG 383

LUNCH FROM RED CROSS PARCELS

NO FOOD PARCELS FOR THIS WORKING PARTY
A hut scene after transfer from Italy to Germany, drawn by
A. G. Douglas during captivity

A CARTOON ON ESCAPING, drawn by *J. Welch*

THE PUNISHMENT FORTRESS OF CAMPO PG 5, GAVI, ITALY
Behind the bars is
Captain C. N. Armstrong, MC, who escaped from Germany in 1944

Brigadier James Hargest in his disguise as a French railwayman

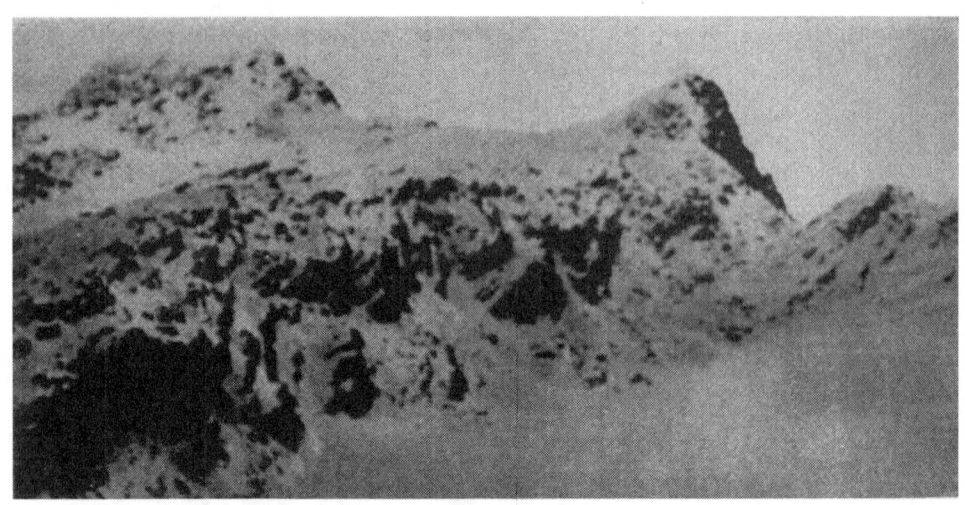

PASSO MORO, OVER WHICH SOME OF THE ESCAPERS FROM ITALIAN CAMPS CROSSED INTO SWITZERLAND

A SWISS FRONTIER POST
Many escaped prisoners of war passed through this post on first reaching Switzerland

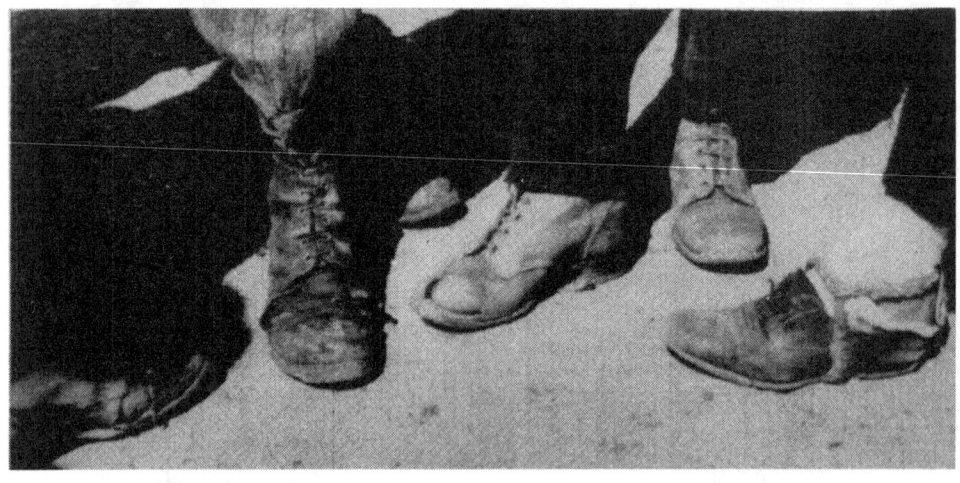

ESCAPED PRISONERS' FOOTWEAR AFTER REACHING SWITZERLAND

MEN FROM STALAG 383 AT ETEHAUSEN DURING THE FORCED MARCH SOUTH

A REST DURING A FORCED MARCH

Liberated prisoners waiting to be flown in American Dakotas from Landshut Airstrip to the United Kingdom

C. B. Burdekin, OBE, head of the prisoners of war welfare section of New Zealand House, London

PRISONERS OF WAR REPATRIATED FROM ITALY IN MAY 1942 READING MAIL AT MAADI

AT CRACOW, IN POLAND, BEFORE BEING TRANSPORTED BY THE RUSSIANS TO ODESSA
This group includes two New Zealanders

The ex-prisoner of war is swamped by his reception at 2 NZEF (UK) Reception Group—a cartoon by *J. Welch*

Outside the Sergeants' Mess at the Reception Group Wing at Folkestone

was only a week or two before supplies were received from Geneva, both of food and of other relief requirements.

Letter and parcel mail for prisoners of war, which was on hand in Switzerland or on its way there en route for Italy, was transferred to the International Red Cross Committee for redirection when new addresses should become available.[1] Meanwhile the despatch of letters and parcels from New Zealand was not held up for want of a camp address, on account of the time they took to reach Europe; letters were sent to the Prisoners of War Section of the High Commissioner's Office in London and parcels to the packing centre under its control. Although some prisoners lost most of their kit in transit from Italy to Germany, many others were able to take nearly all essential articles with them. An extra clothing parcel was sent from the New Zealand packing centre in London to any prisoner whose remaining kit was sufficiently meagre to warrant a request for one.

* * * * *

The seizure by Germany of some 50,000 able-bodied British Commonwealth prisoners was no doubt of threefold value to her war effort: it cut down British man-power by that figure, it supplied her economy with many thousand more potential workers, and it gave her much extra bargaining power in any future negotiations with her enemies. Moreover, British Commonwealth prisoners were not much of a liability, since their Red Cross organisations supplied them with the extra food necessary to keep them healthy, and their governments supplied them with clothing. The energetic German troops who quickly pushed these prisoners north over the passes into the Reich did a very good service to their country.

The possibility of a transfer to Germany had been a dark shadow cast over the lives of prisoners in Italy from the time that the collapse of the latter became imminent. Yet it is clear from many statements in New Zealand other ranks' letters, written after their arrival at a German camp, that (if they had to be prisoners) they at least preferred to be in German hands. Food was said to be more plentiful, mainly because of better delivery of Red Cross food parcels, and the feeling was that the German administration was more efficient. There seems to have been little lowering of morale as a result of the transfer: one man describes how his party, marching dishevelled from the train journey through the streets of Görlitz, ' sang down ' a party of Hitler Youth who passed them. For officers, NCOs, and other non-workers, on the other hand, the prospect of further wasted years as a prisoner cast a gloom

---

[1] More than 800,000 letters and 150,000 parcels were so readdressed.

over the whole period of transfer and transit camps, and time hung heavily for many of them until recreation could be organised in their permanent camps.

By the end of the year nearly 300 New Zealanders who had got free at the time of the armistice were safe in Allied hands or at liberty in Switzerland, and a hundred or two more were at large in Italy.[1] The latter, contrary to what most had expected before the armistice, found the majority of Italians friendly and hospitable, especially the countryfolk. Some have tried to see in this the purely selfish motive of ingratiation with the Allies, now obviously in the ascendant; and certainly Italian civilians were not loath to accept certificates from prisoners indicating the help they had given them. Some have even ascribed this friendly help to motives of immediate gain: the good woollen battle dress and underclothing of the prisoners, their Red Cross food, and other valuables. But there was clearly more to it than this. There was something of the traditional friendship for Britain and distrust of Germany; and there was also clearly much of the pure human kindness of simple, generous souls for a hunted, hungry, and sometimes sick fellow-creature. Whatever the various motives, many Italian people took great risks to help our men, and some paid for it with their lives and homes. The New Zealand officer who wrote, 'many of them have taken far greater risks for me than perhaps one could expect, even from our own people in similar circumstances,' was not alone in that view. Amongst ex-prisoners of war who were at large in Italy there is the highest regard for these people.

The news that most of our prisoners of war in Italy had fallen into German hands occasioned a great deal of anxiety among next-of-kin in New Zealand. It was weeks before most of the notifications of transfer to Germany were received, and months before the arrival of mail from those transferred. Although by mid-November some of the transferred men were beginning to receive mail and parcels readdressed from Geneva, it was much longer before fresh mail from New Zealand could reach them. It was only a short while before those who had reached Switzerland were again in touch with their homes, but those who were at large in Italy for some months remained almost completely cut off. Fortunately for next-of-kin in New Zealand, men who escaped were able on repatriation to reassure anxious wives and parents by relating the manner in which they had been looked after by the Italians while at large, and by explaining that though winter conditions made final escape very difficult, many of their comrades would only be waiting for the spring before going south to meet the Allied forces.

---

[1] Another 150-odd made good their escape. On available evidence it is only possible to estimate broadly how many men were at some stage at large in Italy.

CHAPTER 8

The Middle Phase of the War Against Japan

(June 1942—December 1944)

I: *The Turn of the Tide in the Far East*

ALTHOUGH the naval defeats in the Coral Sea and off Midway Island brought to a standstill the Japanese drive to the southeast, they did not prevent the Japanese holding stubbornly to the ground they had occupied nor destroy their hopes of future conquests. In early June 1942 they attacked the Aleutian Islands; their submarines made sorties as far as Sydney and Newcastle and for a long time remained a danger to shipping in the Pacific. The task of rolling the Japanese back the way they had come proved long and arduous. In early August Allied forces got a foothold on Guadalcanal in the Solomons, from which a Japanese assault in October failed to dislodge them. But it took six months to clear Guadalcanal, and it was not until the Japanese had been crippled by four costly naval actions in these waters that the way was clear for further Allied landings in the Solomons in September 1943. By then Papua had been cleared and the Japanese were being driven slowly westward in northern New Guinea; by that time, too, the Japanese had been driven from the Aleutian Islands. Before the end of the year the United States forces, by their attack on the Gilberts, had pierced the outer perimeter of the Japanese defensive system and forced in a wedge near the Equator that threatened to cut the now greatly elongated Japanese lines of communication to the south.

In 1944 the wedge was driven deeper. At the beginning of the year United States forces landed first in the Marshall Islands and shortly afterwards in the Carolines, and so secured the bases for the liberation of the Philippines and the carrying of the war a stage nearer to Japan itself. By the end of the year Leyte and Mindoro in the Philippines had been invaded, and the Allied aero-naval superiority was such that nothing seemed able to stop their inexorable advance in all sectors of the Far Eastern front.

The bulk of the New Zealanders who were held in captivity by the Japanese fell into their hands in the first few months of the war in the Far East, when the Japanese forces carried out their lightning conquest of South-East Asia. In the years that followed only a few Navy and Air Force personnel were added to those taken in this initial stage of hostilities. Two further naval officers were captured when the *Behar*, taking them to Colombo, was seized by the Japanese in the Indian Ocean in April 1944. A few New Zealand Air Force pilots continued to be lost over Japanese-held territory until almost the end of the war.

The largest additional loss of civilians occurred when the Union Steamship Company's vessel *Hauraki*, 37 of whose crew were classified as New Zealanders, was seized by a Japanese raider. While bound for Fremantle in July 1942 she was held up and boarded, and the crew were forced to sail the vessel to Singapore. They did their best to ruin the engines on this forced voyage and were able to conceal and get rid of nearly all documents which might have been of use to the enemy. On arrival at Singapore most of the crew were put ashore and interned in Changi Jail. The remaining 20-odd of the engine-room staff and senior officers were made to sail the vessel on to Japan, and were treated there as prisoners of war.

II: *Prisoner-of-war and Civilian Internment Camps*

The civilian internees at Singapore remained in Changi Jail during 1942 and 1943 and the early part of 1944. As time went on the supplies of food originally brought into the camp from stores in Singapore became exhausted, the Japanese ration scale progressively decreased, and the purchase of extra food outside the camp became more difficult owing to inflated prices, as well as continual uncertainty whether the Japanese would allow foraging parties to leave the camp and bring back the purchases. From April 1943 the Japanese allowed the Singapore agent of the International Red Cross Committee to supply the camp with extras and to pay for goods bought by the internees from a firm of Singapore merchants. Rice polishings thus obtained were added to the diet in time to avert a serious outbreak of beriberi. But if food was always a difficulty, facilities for recreation steadily improved, and many former internees mention excellent performances by the camp theatre and orchestra. Those who studied the *Shonan News* were able to glean something of the war situation by reading between the lines, and this was brought into focus by the reception of BBC bulletins from New Delhi on concealed radio sets.

An incident occurred in 1943 which showed that the Japanese Kempetai could be just as harsh in the application of their methods of investigation to civilians as to prisoners of war. The Japanese apparently became suspicious that the internees had established a spy organisation in Changi Jail, with contacts in the town of Singapore to stir up anti-Japanese feeling and commit sabotage, and with radio equipment which enabled it both to receive and to transmit messages. After a parade of all internees lasting from dawn until dusk in the jail yard, during which their quarters were searched (and looted), 57 internees, including three women, were taken for interrogation to Japanese military police centres in Singapore. They were crowded into small cells irrespective of sex or age, kept sitting at attention for some fourteen hours a day, and brutally beaten for any infraction of orders. Their food consisted of a totally insufficient amount of rice (occasionally vegetables and weak tea), their only water supply for all purposes was the one water closet in each cell, and bright lights were kept burning all night. Eventually they were all interrogated.

The following extract from the report of the commission[1] set up later to record the facts concerning this incident will show the actual methods of interrogation:

> The building occupied by the Japanese Military Police resounded all day and all night with blows, the bellowings of the inquisitors and the shrieks of the tortured. From time to time victims from the torture chamber would stagger back or if unconscious would be dragged back to their cells with marks of their ill-treatment on their bodies. In one such case an unconscious victim so returned died during the night without receiving any medical attention and his body was not removed until the afternoon.

Beating with iron bars or any other weapon offering, jumping on a stomach distended with water, burning the body with lighted cigarettes, electric shock, jiu-jitsu holds and various forms of mental torture—these were the principal types of savagery used by the Japanese military police in these investigations. Some of the internees spent months in their custody. Twelve, including the Changi Jail camp leader, died as a result. One man died after 55 hours' consecutive interrogation and beating; one died as a result of injuries received in an attempt to commit suicide; only one was executed. Among the conditions for which the survivors had to be treated in the Changi Jail hospital were extreme emaciation, dysentery, beriberi, heart strain, and various injuries to joints and limbs.

Many restrictions followed this investigation, mainly on contacts between the camp and the outside world. For several months this caused a drastic reduction in the extra food which could be brought into the camp. There was a general toughening in the attitude of the guards, and the forbidding of gatherings of internees put an end to educational classes and other camp group activities. In May 1944

---

[1] The commission, presided over by S. N. King of the Malayan Civil Service, sat from 30 August to 2 September 1945 at the Sime Road internment camp and took evidence from 36 survivors.

the internees were moved to the Sime Road camp, some twelve miles away. Here the accommodation was in somewhat dilapidated wooden huts with attap roofs, and though they were still overcrowded there was more space outside and, as one man put it ' more fresh air '. This, too, brought its problems, one of which was to keep down the incidence of malaria. Although those who worked for the Japanese received extra rations, the food in general deteriorated still further in quantity and quality. In an attempt to combat the protein deficiency in the diet, camp authorities set up a snail farm and made cooked snails available to those who desired them. The situation would have been much worse but for the competence of the camp medical authorities and the extra items received through the representative of the International Red Cross Committee.

Of the prisoners of war who were originally concentrated in the Changi garrison area of Singapore Island, those who remained quartered within the area improvised and adapted their living conditions to give them something approximating the regimental life they had formerly known. Spit-and-polish, saluting, and even drill for some time maintained their place in the daily routine. Those who were detached for work in some other part of the island and given new quarters there were chiefly concerned to maintain their health so that they could stand up to the constant physical strain of heavy coolie labour, and to study the best way of handling their guards in order to avoid the beatings and the other severe punishments with which the Japanese followed up their disapproval.

In the Changi area the water supply and electric lighting were in time restored to damaged buildings. Adequate sanitation was provided by properly sealed bore-holes, and the medical authorities did everything possible to prevent the spread of disease by explaining the danger to the men and encouraging them to pay more than usual attention to measures of hygiene. Even so there was a high death rate, caused mainly by malnutrition, beriberi, dysentery and diphtheria. The daily ration of poor-quality rice, reduced in quantity to an average of about nine ounces a day, would have needed the addition of a great deal more than the scanty and irregular supplies of fish and vegetables available at Changi to make it sufficient to maintain health. Red Cross supplies of food landed at Singapore from the exchange ships in September 1942 made little difference, as the portion which the Japanese authorities allowed to be distributed amounted only to some six pounds of food for each man. On medical advice rice polishings, a kind of palm oil, and a local type of lentil were added to the meals to combat deficiency diseases.

In the early months at Changi several parties of men had made unsuccessful attempts to escape. The Japanese took a serious view of this, and four men recaptured from one of the later parties were executed in the enforced presence of senior British officers. At the end of August the Japanese issued instructions that every man was to be asked to sign a document in which it was declared that he would not under any circumstances attempt to escape. Of 17,300-odd in the Changi area, all but about six men (at that time undergoing punishment) refused to sign. As a reprisal the Japanese ordered all prisoners except hospital inmates to move out of Changi into Selarang Barracks, about two and a half miles away. On 2 September the prisoners were herded with their possessions down the road and into the Selarang barrack square. This was an asphalted area, the former parade ground of 2 Battalion Gordon Highlanders, surrounded by seven barrack buildings which had formerly been their quarters. These were now called upon to accommodate seventeen to eighteen times the number for which they had been built, and many men had to sleep without shelter in the barrack square.

In the centre of the square wide and deep trenches were dug as latrines, and successive fatigue parties continued digging during almost the whole period they were there. Since large numbers of men had to sleep and eat a few feet away, it is not surprising that dysentery soon made its appearance, and a number of cases were taken into a small infirmary improvised in another part of the area. In spite of the appalling conditions and the fear of violence on the part of the Japanese, accounts of this incident speak of excellent discipline and high morale among the men, who held nightly concerts and sing-songs to show that the situation had not got them down.

Meanwhile the hospital at Changi with its 2000 or so inmates had been completely isolated, even the bodies of those who died in this period having to be buried inside the hospital compound instead of in the camp cemetery. After three days the Japanese, on orders from Tokyo, threatened to move all the hospital patients into the Selarang area, and it was realised that further negotiation with them regarding the order to sign the non-escape pledge was useless. The senior British officer took the responsibility of ordering all men to sign, at the same time explaining that it was parole given under duress and therefore need not be considered binding. Apart from the situation which would have resulted if the hospital patients had been moved into the Selarang area, a Japanese decision to keep the 17,000 fit men there for any length of time could only have resulted in much suffering and disease and a considerable death rate. Once the signatures were obtained the Japanese were satisfied and everyone was allowed to return to Changi.

All fit men were liable to be called out by the Japanese for working parties, apart from those required for camp fatigues. The clearing of bomb damage, the construction of the Changi aerodrome, the felling and stumping of trees, the construction of roads, the handling of bombs and other cargo at the Singapore docks or on Blakang Mati Island, and later the digging of trench systems and air-raid shelters, were tasks carried out almost entirely by prisoner-of-war labour. Where necessary detached camps were set up near the places of work, sometimes in thatch-roofed huts and sometimes, as on Blakang Mati, in vacant army barracks. Men in a small party were often able to make themselves more comfortable than they could have done back in Changi. Food was also sometimes more plentiful at these working camps. A New Zealander who worked on Blakang Mati speaks of 'unlimited rice with an ounce or two of meat or fish'. But as the war progressed the quantity of food supplied to all prisoners gradually decreased.

In mid-1942 the Japanese began to move numbers of prisoners from Changi to other areas. In June the senior officers (excepting lieutenant-colonels, mostly those formerly in command of battalions) were transferred to a camp on Formosa. Junior officers and men were moved to areas such as Korea or Borneo, where working parties were required and no Allied troops had been captured on the spot to provide them. Large numbers were required more particularly in Burma and Thailand, where the Japanese decided, for strategic reasons, to carry out the project for a railway connecting Moulmein and Bangkok, which had been begun before the war but abandoned by the countries concerned. Some 250 miles of railway between Thanbuzayat in Burma and Bampong in Thailand remained to be constructed, much of it through mountain country and dense jungle. Now, with a large reserve of prisoner-of-war labour, the Japanese authorities decided to push it through in the shortest possible time.

Small advance parties of prisoners were transported in June from Changi to Bampong, where they were given the task of getting transit camps in order for the reception of the main labour parties which were to follow. These were formed in Singapore as battalions,[1] each about 600 strong, from prisoners in working camps there or in the Changi area, many of the latter not long discharged from hospital. Some were told that they were going to a 'very fine camp in Thailand with plenty of food, running water and electric light'. Numbers took very little kit or even cooking

---

[1] They were designated by letters of the alphabet, for example, A Battalion. Several battalions formed a Group.

equipment with them on this account, but the more fortunate took everything. They were transported the 1200 miles to Bampong in steel goods trucks, 32 or more to a truck, so that there was room only for squatting. Intense tropical heat made the interior of the trucks like ovens, and one New Zealander speaks of the floor of his truck being at times 'awash with perspiration'. Under such conditions the six to eight days' journey left most men in a state of extreme fatigue.

Many of them, therefore, were not fit for the daily marches that followed. Eleven to thirteen miles over a muddy jungle track through torrential monsoon rains caused most of the prisoners considerable distress, especially those who endeavoured to carry their kit with them rather than leave it at Bampong. Stragglers often arrived at a staging camp at 3 a.m., having been beaten up on the way by Korean guards, but all had usually to be on the march again at 6 a.m. Staging camps had been established at Kanburi and other places on the route north to Tarsao, but the accommodation was inadequate. Often there was little more than an open piece of jungle with perhaps an odd hut, and men had to prepare their evening meal as best they could and then doss down in the open. Rations on these journeys were poor, and some who were at first thought fortunate in being taken part of the way by barge up the Kwei Noi River received no food at all while on board. The combination of poor food and physical exhaustion during these northward treks was the beginning of much illness that later ended fatally for the men concerned.

They now found themselves in areas where monsoon rains had been pouring down for five to six months and had converted any jungle clearings into quagmires sometimes knee-deep in sticky mud. These camp-site clearings were on the east bank of the Kwei Noi River, where the Japanese planned to lay the railway. They were usually at some height above the river and often had a precipitous, rocky approach, up which supplies such as bamboo for hut construction, water, and food had to be carried from the river's edge, where the bamboo grew and the cookhouse was usually placed. Exhausted though they were from the march, the men were set to work to build coolie-type huts or to put in order whatever huts already existed. These were bamboo structures about a hundred yards long and eight yards wide, roofed with attap palm leaves and fitted on each side for the length of the hut with six-foot-wide sleeping platforms of lashed bamboo. The task of building such a camp, making it habitable for one or two thousand men, and ensuring sufficient cookhouse and latrine accommodation was a big one. But the majority of prisoners in these parties were usually put on to road and railway construction work long before proper living accommodation for them was completed.[1] Some men had to live for long periods under tent flies and improvised bivouacs, and others still had at times no cover over their heads at all.

The water supply was the unfiltered river water, which was boiled and usually provided with each meal. But there was seldom enough and men often drank direct from the river, thus becoming victims of whatever infection was carried from camps further upstream. Food supplies were brought up by barge on the Kwei Noi or by lorry along a road that was merely a converted jungle track. Since by neither method was a consistent service maintained, rations were nearly always below Japanese official scales. Vegetables, long in transit, often arrived in a rotting condition. Rice was of a poor quality, often maggoty and mixed with all kinds of filth. Supplies of fish, meat, oil, salt, and sugar were on a minimum scale, and sometimes men had to live for two months or so on little more than a pound and a half of rice flavoured with salt daily. The fortunate, by trading with the Thais, were often able to obtain duck eggs, fruit, sugar, peanuts, and oil. Rice, together with vegetables and whatever else could be obtained to go with it, had to be cooked over bamboo fires in twelve-gallon shallow containers known as *Kwalis*. But there were often not enough of these for the numbers in camp, and all sorts of improvised clay ovens were made and successfully used. The Japanese kept cookhouse personnel to a minimum (one to four for a hundred men), and the heavy physical work of cutting bamboo and carrying all stores from railhead or barge mooring during long hours of work resulted in a high rate of casualties among them.

On the diet available the work demanded from the other prisoners was no less arduous. Jungle clearing, tree felling, making embankments, laying rails, bridging rivers and torrents, cutting through hard, jagged limestone rock which wore out boots in a few days and cut men's hands and feet: such tasks would have been hard enough for men adequately fed and working reasonable hours. But the Japanese railway engineers sometimes drove the prisoners from dawn till dusk, to a state of complete exhaustion. Moreover, they demanded from each camp a certain percentage of its strength for working parties, irrespective of the number of sick; and to make up the required quota, the Japanese camp commandants insisted on sick men quite unfit for work being driven out, sometimes carried out, to work. In some camps, in order to increase the percentage of men working, resort was had to systematic terrorising

---

[1] First priority was usually given to the construction of the Japanese guardhouse and accommodation for the guards; the fit prisoners' accommodation and the cookhouse came next; and last of all accommodation for the sick.

of the sick: hospital patients in general were not paid and were forbidden to read or smoke during working hours; some were on occasions kicked or beaten with sticks, and dysentery patients were sometimes dragged from the latrines. Japanese engineers who knew a little English boasted to prisoners that the line would be laid 'over [their] dead bodies'.

It was the practice during the first two or three months to send officers out with these working parties in the rough proportion of one to 25–30 men, in order to do what they could to safeguard the men's interests. But they were consistently ignored by the Japanese in charge of the work, and if they had occasion to remonstrate with the latter, were often made the object of especially spiteful treatment. Something has already been said of Japanese Army methods of enforcing discipline among their prisoners. On the Burma–Thailand railway beatings of varying severity, the holding aloft of heavy weights, standing to attention for long periods without cover and without food and water, being tied to trees or back to back with another prisoner, became accepted as part of the everyday routine. But, as one New Zealand ex-prisoner put it, beatings, although 'the usual thing', were 'worrying affairs' since one never knew when the guard might become berserk and carry on until the supposed offender died. In December 1942 the Japanese engineers in charge made their first attempts to persuade officer prisoners to work on the railway. By the New Year parties of officers had been forced out to work under the threat both of using firearms and of starving the sick, and by May 1943 they were being treated, along with the other ranks, as part of the prisoner-of-war labour force for the railway.

For those whose health broke down under these conditions of work, there were only the most inadequate medical facilities. Medical opinion regards the region through which the Burma–Thailand railway passes as one of the most unhealthy in the world. Tropical heat, monsoon rains, almost every kind of biting insect, and prickly bamboo, a scratch from which goes septic and produces an ulcer, created conditions which would have challenged an expert and well-equipped medical service. But not only were the available Japanese medical officers deficient in medical knowledge, but often a junior Japanese NCO or private soldier was in complete charge of the medical arrangements for a thousand or more prisoners. A 'hospital' was created simply by setting aside one or more of the crude jungle huts built to accommodate workers, and prisoner-of-war medical personnel accompanying the troops had to rely on whatever equipment they had been able to bring with them. In the areas occupied by prisoners there had been no malaria control or other hygienic measures before their arrival, and those undertaken by prisoner-of-war medical officers on their arrival were often rendered wellnigh impossible of execution by the refusal of the Japanese to free sufficient men from work on the railway to carry them out. Serious epidemics of dysentery and cholera were attributed to lack of facilities for sterilising water and failure to prevent available sources of supply from becoming contaminated. The drugs supplied by the Japanese to treat these and other diseases were ludicrously inadequate, though fortunately it became possible to obtain small quantities of essential drugs through a clandestine organisation. A great deal of essential medical equipment was improvised by such prisoner-of-war medical personnel as were allowed by the Japanese to care for the sick. But the proportion of these was in general only one per cent of camp strength, the remaining doctors and orderlies being forced to do manual labour on the railway.

Early in 1943 the Japanese authorities decided that progress on the railway was not sufficiently rapid, and orders were given for the bringing up of thousands of additional workers. Before the middle of the year 10,000 prisoners of war had come up from Singapore as 'F' and 'H' Forces, further parties had come from the Dutch East Indies, and tens of thousands of Tamils, Chinese and Malays, men and women, had been pressed into service as labourers. The latter, lacking any military organisation and, more important, any medical facilities, were soon decimated by tropical disease. Their situation became so appalling that even the Japanese recognised it by recruiting prisoner-of-war medical teams from Changi and sending them to the various coolie camps.

In addition to bringing up more workers, the Japanese increased their pressure on the whole of their labour force. From late April until November 1943, the 'speedo' period, each Japanese engineer officer drove his team of workers mercilessly so that his particular task would be completed on time. In April conditions on the railway were hot and dry, with thick layers of fine dust everywhere; but May saw the onset of the monsoon, which continued until October. Ceaseless rain and thick mud soon made conditions for the workers doubly hard and turned their pitiful encampments of huts and tents into evil-smelling quagmires. Little account seems to have been taken of this in the demands of the Japanese: the daily task for one man could rise as high as moving three cubic metres of soil a distance of 270 yards through mud and then up an embankment 25 feet high. Tools and equipment were often of the poorest and earth had to be carried in bags and baskets or on stretchers. Work went on in some places until 11.30 at night, and for two or three months some working teams hardly saw their camps in daylight. After a roll-call at dawn they were marched off immediately to work, and they did not return to camp until just before dark. No men were allowed to remain for camp cleaning and maintenance, and cookhouse and medical personnel were cut to a minimum.

A senior Japanese officer in charge of prisoners of war in Thailand stated in June 1943 the attitude that was general towards the sick: 'Those who fail in charge by lack of health is regarded as most shameful deed'. During the 'speedo' period, owing to exhaustion from overwork and semi-starvation, few of the workers were free from some kind of sickness. But as the sickness rate grew the Japanese increased their pressure. The threat to turn out all sick from the camp hospitals forced medical officers to admit only those who were seriously ill. Occasionally, men were forced to limp out to work on sticks and some were even carried on stretchers. Those who fell sick during work were liable to receive whatever savage punishment came into the mind of the guard or overseer. A prisoner stricken with a sudden attack of malaria might be stood up to his neck in a cold river; those who collapsed might be kicked or beaten with whatever implement was to hand; men with festering feet might be forced to work on sharp rock or in thorny jungle. Evacuation of the seriously ill was often not permitted for considerable periods, with the result that thousands accumulated in the various working camps dotted along the railway.

When it was permitted, evacuation took place by the haphazard means of hitch-hiking on a passing lorry or river barge. Since no fit men were allowed to accompany them, the weak were supported by the less weak, and they were often several days in transit with no medical attention and little food. Those who reached 'base hospitals', such as those at Takanun, Tarsao, Non Pladuk, Chungkai, and Tamarkan in Thailand or Thanbuzayat in Burma in mid-1943, moved into hopelessly overcrowded conditions and what one medical report describes as 'pools of infection and gangrene'. Only the devotion, skill, and enterprise of the prisoner-of-war medical staffs, with the aid of food and medicine clandestinely obtained, saved the lives of thousands of these sufferers and gradually evolved organisations which could control disease and mortality.

This reckless disregard by the Japanese of the health of prisoners and civilians alike decimated the labour force for the railway so quickly that for the final tasks of its construction there remained only the convalescent and the half-fit remnants of various groups, a small fraction of the original strength. In the space of a year the deaths among Allied prisoners on the railway amounted to something like a quarter of their number, or some 15,000 men out of a force of

60,000 or more; and groups working under particularly bad conditions had an even higher death rate than this. In addition large numbers of men were permanently disabled as a result of amputations or the after-effects of disease.

At the end of October 1943 trains of Japanese troops and supplies began to go right through from Thailand to Burma. The work eased, fine weather followed the end of the monsoon rains, and there was much-needed rest for those still up river in working parties as well as an opportunity for them to make their camps more habitable. At the end of the year most of the work on the railway had been completed and the Japanese began to move working parties down to base camps in the plains near Bampong. By March 1944 the bulk of the prisoners of war were concentrated in Chungkai, Tamarkan, Kanburi, Tamuan, Non Pladuk, and Nakom Paton in this area. At these camps accommodation was very much better than was possible at the working camps up river, notably that at Nakom Paton, built by Thais under Japanese orders as a sort of convalescent depot. At Chungkai the prisoners had built a hospital, a theatre and a church; there were gardens, recreation areas and canteens. While at the working camps up river it had occasionally been possible to obtain from local Thais duck eggs, fruit and nuts, at the base camps various canteen goods were in reasonably good supply throughout the whole period. By the time the prisoners from the railway were brought south, snack bars at these base canteens were selling omelettes, cakes, and peanut butter. The Japanese made a small issue of two-year-old Red Cross food. There were concerts and more elaborate stage shows at the camp theatre, and those whose physical condition allowed it could play volley-ball and basket-ball during the day. Guards had been instructed that Allied prisoners were to be better treated, and those men who had survived the dark jungle days of mid-1943 began to feel that the worst was behind them.

There appears to have been at this time some desire on the part of the Japanese to do something not only to prevent the terrible wastage of their prisoner-of-war labour force, but also to counteract the reputation for uncivilised treatment of prisoners of war which they were rapidly gaining all over the world. In May 1944 officer prisoners were required by the Japanese to write ' essays ' concerning their experiences on the Burma–Thailand railway. They were invited to express their opinion freely on such things as ' actual examples of most miserable, most detestable and most painful things or matter during the work '. The ' essays ' were to be used ' as reference on treatment of P.O.W. in future '. At Kanburi prisoners, most of whom were by 1944 reduced to wearing a very abbreviated loincloth known as a ' G-string ', were issued with clean uniforms.

These they were ordered to put on, then to sit round an improvised stage listening to the camp band, and even to smile and look happy while the official photographers of a Japanese inspection party took pictures of them. Similar photographs were taken at other base camps, always of the fitter-looking prisoners, dressed in clean uniforms and usually posing with Red Cross or other food. As soon as the photographs were taken, both clothing and food issued for the occasion were withdrawn.

Parallel with this effort to create propaganda for the outside world went attempts to present to prisoners and civilians within Japanese-occupied territory a picture of the war favourable to the Axis powers. But continued absurdly exaggerated claims in Japanese newspapers soon lost any power they might have had at first to impress prisoners of war. News from Allied sources was in any case available to discount such claims, for during almost the whole period of captivity radio receiving sets were operated by prisoners of war, and the gist of the broadcasts listened to was passed on to prisoners up and down the railway. Those who operated these radios risked almost certain execution at Japanese hands if discovered, and two of them were almost certainly beaten to death. There are many tributes to the courage of the men who thus kept open for thousands of their comrades this source of cheer and comfort.

There was another factor which gave the lie to the Japanese claims that events of the war were in their favour. As early as mid-1943 Allied reconnaissance planes began to make frequent flights over the territory of the railway; bombings followed and became more and more frequent. In some camps the Japanese allowed the prisoners to dig slit trenches, but they were seldom adequate and as often as not prisoners were forced to remain in their huts during the raids. Moreover, most of the camps were sited right alongside the railway track, some near bridges or other vulnerable points, and were therefore almost certain to suffer during aerial attacks against the railway. The camp at Tamarkan, for example, with not only a bridge but also an anti-aircraft battery nearby, had a considerable number of casualties as a result of raids. Non Pladuk camp was located among sidings holding petrol, ammunition, and stores trains, protected by an anti-aircraft post. In September 1944 a three-hour night raid on this area, during which no prisoners were allowed to leave their huts, resulted in 95 being killed and over 300 wounded.

Those who went 'up-country' in maintenance parties and were engaged on such work as bridge repairing also experienced Allied bombing. From May 1944 onwards there were many such parties, consisting for the most part of unfit or convalescent prisoners left behind when the fit were transferred to Japan in February. Besides maintenance work, these parties had the task of cutting wood fuel for the locomotives and of handling stores at dumps located at various points along the railway. Although at first the work was not too hard, a rising sick rate and the evacuation of the worst cases south to base hospitals caused a reversion to the long hours and the driving of the sick out to work which had been characteristic of the terrible 'speedo' period during the building of the railway. There were the same haphazard arrangements regarding feeding and accommodation and the same lack of proper medical attention. Conditions for some of these 'up-country' parties continued bad until almost the end of the war.

Besides those from Changi, the Japanese had used on the Burma–Thailand railway further large groups of British Commonwealth and Dutch prisoners shipped across in late 1942 from the Dutch East Indies. Fit prisoners in Java in excess of those wanted for aerodrome construction and other tasks were transported from Batavia to Singapore from April 1942 onwards, and taken on by ship to Moulmein for employment on the Burma end of the railway, though some shiploads in these convoys were sent on direct from Singapore to Japan. Similarly from Medan, in Sumatra, other ranks were taken to Mergui and Tavoy on the west coast of Burma and eventually on to Moulmein for use on the railway. Some of the officer prisoners on Sumatra went to Singapore and were taken north in the parties which worked on the Thailand portion of the railway. A certain number of prisoners were also shipped from the eastern port of Sourabaya to Timor, Amboina, and others of the more easterly situated islands of the Dutch groups. Some remained on Sumatra until their liberation.

Those who experienced the jungle camps of Burma and Thailand speak of conditions at the Bicycle Camp at Batavia as being 'reasonable' by comparison. Certainly Dutch barracks with tiled roofs and tiled floors, proper lighting and water supply were a considerable advance on the crude bamboo and attap huts the railway workers knew, though periodical severe overcrowding made life difficult for the occupants. The diet at Batavia settled down to a routine of rice, tapioca flour, occasional offal, vegetables, and a little salt and sugar, all in insufficient quantities. Officers worked the vegetable garden which, besides providing an essential element in their diet, gave them light exercise in the open air and sunshine. A canteen operated from the beginning of 1943, but its purchases were greatly restricted by the Japanese camp commandant. No Red Cross food was issued until July 1944, when each man received one-tenth of a food parcel. In the early days of the camp educational classes had been organised, but these and organised sport came under the ban on any kind of assembly later imposed by the Japanese. Provided the Japanese authorities saw no reason for

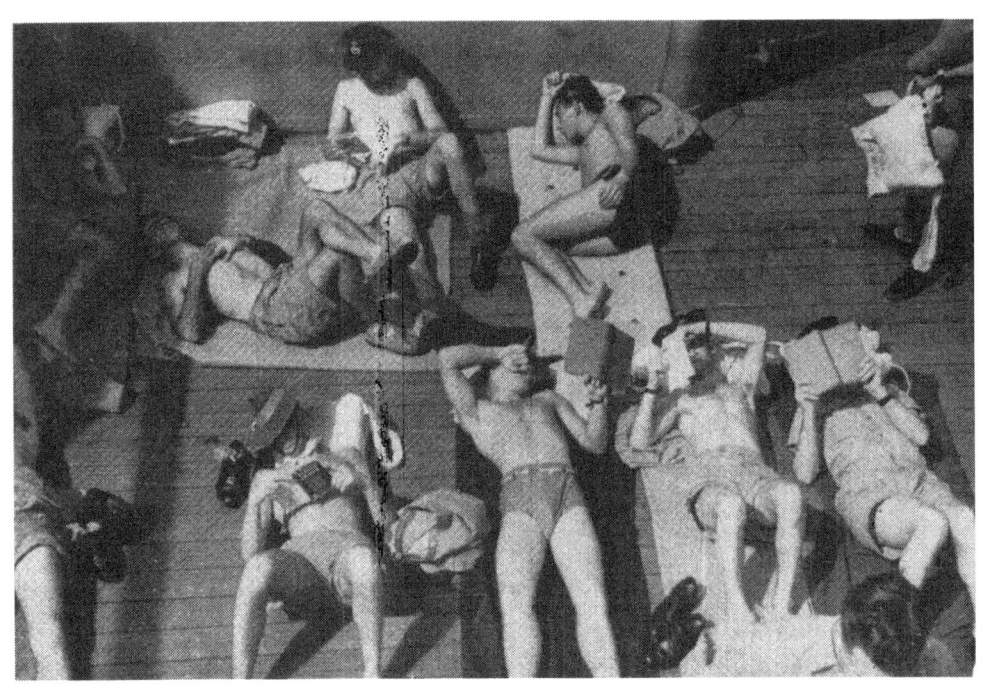

ON THE *ANDES* ON THE VOYAGE HOME

HOME AGAIN

A JAPANESE PRESS OFFICER
AT SHANGHAI INTERNMENT CAMP

THE ARGYLL STREET CAMP, HONG KONG

The Selarang Barracks, Singapore, crowded by the Japanese with 17,000 prisoners of war because they had refused to sign pledges not to escape

FOUR SCENES IN SELARANG BARRACKS: (from left to right) *top*—Signing the pledge not to escape—under British orders; filling in time: *bottom*—The cookhouse; a rainy day

CHANGI JAIL, SINGAPORE
This building housed civilian internees and, later, prisoners of war

WOMEN'S QUARTERS INSIDE THE CRYPT OF CHANGI JAIL
—painted by *Gladys Tompkins* during captivity

PRISONERS OF WAR WORKING ON A HILLSIDE IN JAPAN

UNLOADING SICK PRISONERS FROM SAMPANS AT CHUNGKAI—a painting by *J. B. Chalker*

The Kwei Noi River, seen from a north-bound train, Thailand, in October 1945. This is country traversed by the Burma–Thailand Railway

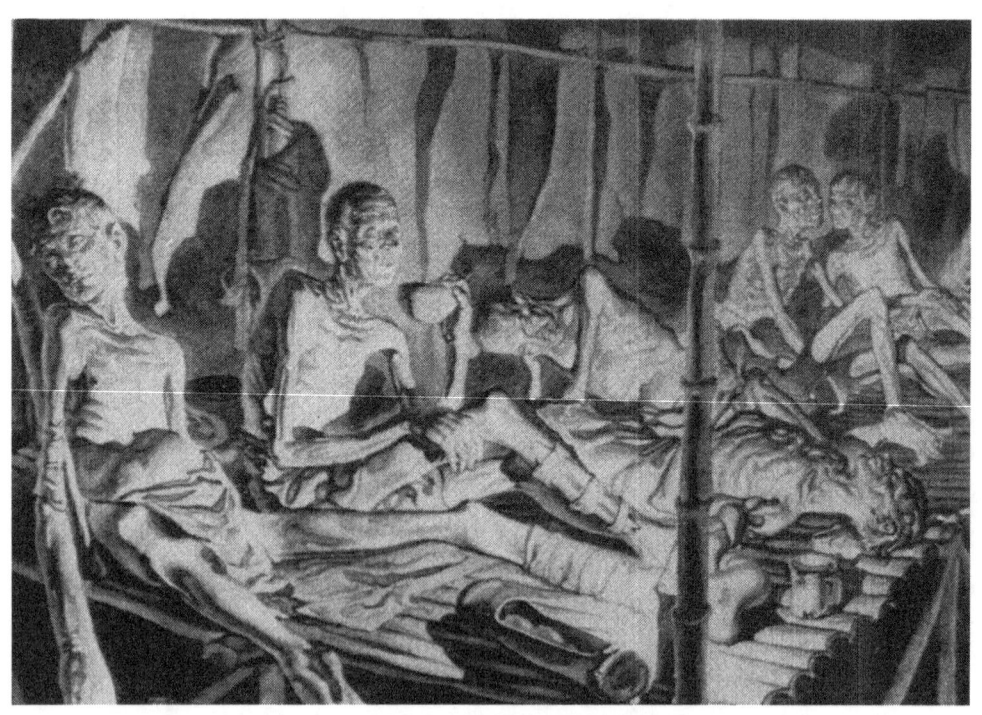

HOSPITAL WARD—THAILAND RAILWAY,
painted by *Murray Griffin*

A trestle bridge on the Burma–Thailand Railway

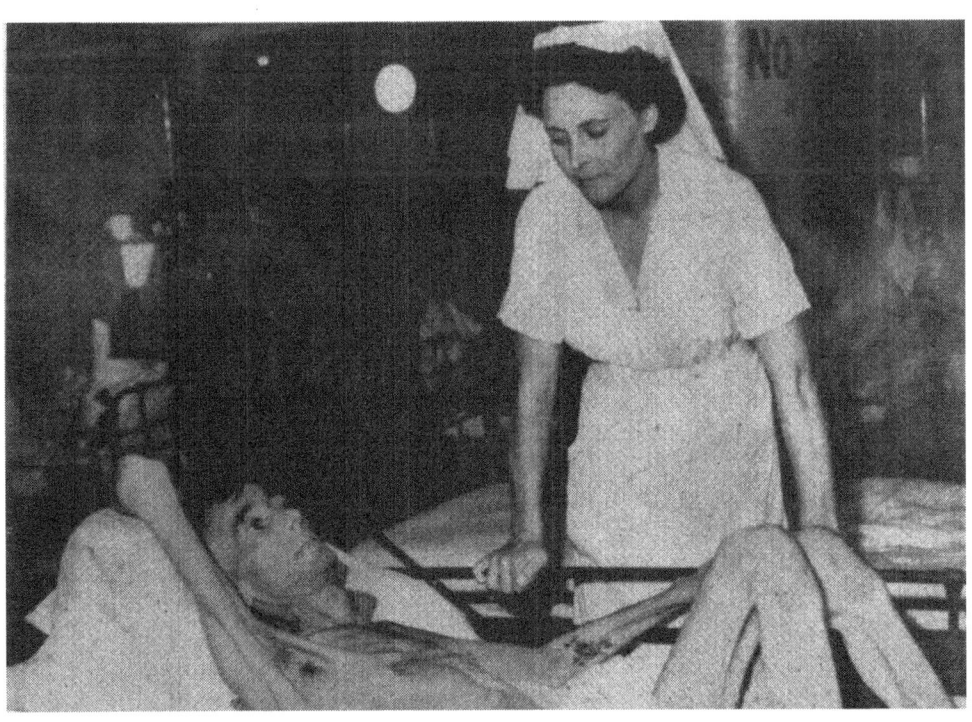

MALNUTRITION CASE FROM HONG KONG ON A HOSPITAL SHIP

A GERMAN INTERNEE IN NEW ZEALAND
He is working with paua shell

JAPANESE PRISONERS OF WAR IN THE WAIRARAPA, NEW ZEALAND

stopping it, a concert was allowed to be held every ten days. The worst feature of the camp was the haphazard infliction on prisoners of severe beatings (sometimes administered to Korean guards as well) by the Japanese camp staff. Morale, however, appears to have been high at all times, and a skilfully concealed radio kept the camp informed of war news. The general impression of prisoners who spent a period in this camp was that by comparison with others conditions were 'fair'.

The same overcrowding was evident in the camps at Sourabaya, which was a transit centre for prisoners going east, just as Batavia was for those going north. The Lyceum School built for 400 children was made to hold 2400 prisoners of war, and the Jaarmarkt camp with 5000-odd was little better off. In April 1943, however, drafts of prisoners were shipped off to islands farther east and others were moved back to Bandoeng for a few months, until at the end of the year nearly all remaining British prisoners were concentrated in the Batavia Bicycle Camp.

Small islands such as Haruku and Ambon, to which some of our men were sent, were by comparison with the main centres of Java primitive and ill-supplied. The Japanese High Command, however, wished to use them as bases for aircraft, and local Japanese commanders did not hesitate to send large numbers of prisoners of war there to construct aerodromes, although there were no adequate arrangements for their accommodation, their feeding, or their medical care. The treatment of a party of 2070 officers and men, which left Sourabaya in mid-April 1943 and spent some fifteen months on Haruku and Ambon, takes its place with the worst examples of treatment in Burma and Thailand. Many of the men were unfit before leaving Java, and a fortnight's voyage of the 'hell-ship' type described later further unfitted them for the heavy labour of unloading bombs and petrol to which they were set on their arrival in port. Long hours of work on Haruku, totally inadequate food, lack of medical supplies (the heavy kit and medical supplies of this party having been taken on to another island) sent the sick rate mounting rapidly. By 17 May there were 700 patients in the improvised hospital on Haruku, mainly with dysentery, beriberi, and other deficiency diseases. Besides reducing the rations for the sick, the Japanese periodically drove out to work all those who were just able to stagger from the wards, and a policy of general intimidation was carried out with great brutality by some of the guards. In a little over seven months some 400 of the prisoners were dead and another 650, very ill, had been returned by ship to Java. Conditions in the camp established on Ambon were also bad, but the temporary accommodation for the drafts of sick men coming from Haruku en route to Java was the worst of all. By September 1944 both Haruku and Ambon were cleared of Allied prisoners of war, and those who survived the sea voyage to Java were sent either to hospital or to further work there.

Those who had had the misfortune to be transferred to Macassar on the island of Celebes soon after their capture had a similarly hard time, although they were not decimated by disease to the same extent as those on Haruku and Ambon. After some six months in the Dutch barracks at Macassar described earlier in this narrative, many of them went out with working parties to small camps at Maros and Mundai, approximately twenty miles from Macassar. Here they were kept for about eighteen months. At Maros the accommodation consisted of bamboo and attap huts, with trench latrines ten yards or so away, and at Mundai of old and somewhat dilapidated buildings. Other camp arrangements were on the usual primitive scale. The food, which consisted for the most part of three cups daily of boiled rice and two helpings of vegetable soup, was cooked in the main camp at Macassar and sent out to the work-camps in boxes and tubs. Attempts by prisoners to supplement this diet by trading with the native population or by just taking what they saw while out at work were often successful but, if discovered by the Japanese, were savagely punished. The men seem however almost unanimous that the risk was worth it because outwitting their captors 'kept up morale' or was even 'the spice of existence'.

All 'who could crawl out of the gates' (to use the words of a New Zealander) were made to work seven days a week from nearly dawn until dusk, with perhaps five days' holiday a year. The tasks usually involved heavy manual labour: constructing aerodrome runways, building air-raid shelters, making roads, sawmill work, carpentry, powdering lyddite by hand. Some of the few 'rest-days' were filled in by compulsory labour in the camp gardens. Another New Zealander's account mentions that 'hardly a day passed but there was a beating'. These were sometimes with iron bars; the number of strokes often went as high as between one and two hundred and sometimes left the victim unconscious, with parts of his flesh almost pulped. Beatings were varied by standing to attention in the sun without a hat, hand-presses, holding heavy weights above the head, and the remainder of the Japanese Army repertoire for maintaining discipline. There was little relief for the prisoners from this brutish existence, since within a year of their capture there was a ban on sports, on meetings (which ruled out lectures, entertainments and church services), and even on singing and whistling. Some found solace in tobacco, and a New Zealander writes that if this was short 'most felt the lack of it acutely as nerves were highly strung through cruelty, air-raids, and overwork'. The air raids at least gave hopes that a favourable end to the war might not be too far distant.

Naval men captured in waters near Banka Island were eventually brought to Palembang in Sumatra, where a main camp for prisoners of war was established on the outskirts of the town. In the course of the next year or two the camp changed its quarters several times and was finally established permanently in an old orange grove a short distance from the town of Sungeron. The accommodation here was built by prisoners with bamboo and flax. About 1000 to 1500 prisoners were held here and used for working parties at the docks and in the neighbourhood. In general, more food and other supplies could be obtained at a camp near a large centre, but the rations at Sungeron camp, especially over the last period of its existence, were low enough to cause a large number of deaths from starvation. At first it was possible to obtain canteen supplies such as eggs and sugar, but this became more difficult and the rapid increase in prices soon made it impossible for prisoners to buy. Men had to rely for extras on what they could pick up while out at work in the docks or elsewhere, and take the risk of being caught.

One of the main working parties based on Palembang was the No. 1 Aerodrome Camp, far enough away to be established in its own quarters alongside the work. Here a draft of prisoners from Java brought the numbers to some 1500, but it was not long before bad living and working conditions had put about 600 of these in the camp hospital. Long hours of heavy manual labour on insufficient food and lack of medical supplies had the same result on the prisoners' health here as in many other Japanese prisoner-of-war camps. Here, too, there was no proper water supply, wells and nearby streams proving not always reliable. The position of the sick would have been much worse but for the purchase of extra food which was made possible through the sick fund set up from deductions from prisoners' pay. Eventually in May 1944 most of the seriously sick were sent to the main camp at Palembang, and a year later the remainder of the camp joined them.

The prisoners who had been held at Padang shortly after capture were moved in mid-1942 to an old military barracks in Medan. Here they were crowded, but the buildings were reasonably well equipped and properly lit. There was a garden in which they were allowed to cultivate vegetables for their own use; there was a library, though mainly of books in Dutch; there was a piano which made much easier the holding of sing-songs and other entertainments. A New Zealand naval man calls Medan a 'rest camp' by comparison with the 'jungle' camps in Sumatra to which he was sent later.

One of the latter operated for most of 1944 at Blanki Djeran, in the mountain and jungle area of northern Sumatra. Prisoners were engaged on heavy tasks such as road cutting, railway laying, and bridge building. Their quarters were crude huts, and a nearby stream had to serve for the double purpose of ablution and sanitation. During this period the ration of rice was reduced to 250 grammes daily for each man, and to a mere 100 grammes for those who were unable to work through sickness. Prisoners were able to barter with the natives for extra food, but as in other camps this entailed the risk of severe disciplinary action on the part of the Japanese guards. From here most of the prisoners were moved in late 1944 to another working camp in central Sumatra, where they were engaged on similar work constructing communications to a coal mine. Those who became too sick to work were eventually transported to a base camp at Pekan Bharu.

Civilians interned on Sumatra were not much better off. The women and children remained for 18 months in the area of disused houses in Palembang which had been allocated to all the internees on their arrival there. During this period the men had to build for themselves a separate camp of bamboo and attap huts, and their transfer to this new camp at Palembang eased the overcrowding in what then became the camp for women and children. The men, however, were again transferred, this time to Banka Island, and in September 1943 the women and children were all moved into the men's bamboo camp. Here leaking huts, mud floors, trench latrines, and drawing water from wells made life for the interned women and children one of great hardship. Finally in September 1944 the women were also transported to a camp at Muntok, on Banka Island. Rations here became worse than they had been on Sumatra, and lack of medicaments made it almost impossible to combat malaria. The death rate rose alarmingly and the hospital became filled with sick and dying women and children. In April 1944 the Japanese authorities moved the whole camp back to Sumatra.

A New Zealand nurse in this group comments on the appalling conditions under which the journey was made. The women and children were packed into the holds of a small ship and for long periods were unable to move from a cramped knee-to-chin position. Nine women were reported to have died before Sumatra was reached. Such conditions were typical of the voyages by 'hellship' on which Allied prisoners of war were transported in Dutch East Indian and Malayan waters, through the China Sea and as far north as Japan itself. The ships used were for the most part Japanese freighters, varying in size down to 1000 tons. There were often 500 prisoners in a hold, packed in with petrol drums, bombs, cases of supplies and other cargo, so that almost every account describes the space as insufficient to lie down. Sometimes they were battened down in spite of the terrific tropical heat, and on other occasions they were left unprotected from heavy tropical rains. Only meagre rations of rice and fish were provided, sometimes not properly cooked, and there was nearly always a minimum amount of water. The necessity of eating below decks and the siting of food distribution points near the few available latrines spread diarrhoea and dysentery. Most accounts speak of the filth, foul smells, lice and other vermin among which the prisoners were forced to live, sometimes for journeys lasting a month. As often as not separate accommodation for the sick was lacking, and it is small wonder that deaths occurred on the longer voyages.[1] Though some men were able to keep an outward show of cheerfulness, the revolting living conditions, the intense heat, the endless waiting for food and water, and the nervous strain when Allied aircraft passed overhead made these voyages seem like prolonged nightmares to most of those prisoners unfortunate enough to experience them.

Some twenty of the crew of the *Hauraki* were more fortunate in being able to travel to Japan from Singapore in their old ship at the end of 1942. The ship's senior officers had been sent on ahead in October for interrogation, and after an uncomfortable journey reached Yokohama. At the interrogation camp at Ofuna, about ten miles from the city, they were put into small cells and forbidden to speak to anyone. Here they were given 'just enough food to keep alive' and were subjected to an exhausting regime of physical exercise. They also experienced and saw the mass and individual beatings which helped to give this camp the title of 'torture farm'. After being softened up in this manner, they were interrogated several times in their six weeks' stay and were finally drafted out to a working camp in the Yokohama area.

Men from this working camp (Yokohama D1) were allotted to the Mitsubishi naval and merchant shipbuilding yards. They were accommodated in an old but large goods shed two miles away, and at first, when there were only 500 of them, were not overcrowded. The building, however, was filthy, and the straw of the wooden sleeping platforms soon became infested with rats, lice and fleas. There was a concrete floor and almost negligible heating, so that in the freezing winter months of early 1943 many men contracted pneumonia. Most of them had come from tropical climates, there were almost no medical supplies, and the camp diet consisted of a cup of grain and a cup of vegetable soup three times a day. These factors combined to make it difficult to resist disease. Sick men

---

[1] On one voyage from Ambon to Java 21 died in a draft of 217.

were often forced out to work, and nearly fifty of the camp strength died in the first year. Reveille was at 5 a.m. and, after a two-and-a-half mile march to the shipyards, the men began work at 7 a.m. They worked until 5 p.m., then marched back to camp; such lighting as the old go-down provided was extinguished at eight. There were the usual 'bashings' to maintain discipline, varied by making the whole camp stand to attention until midnight. At the shipyards the work consisted of all the heavy manual tasks connected with building and overhauling ships. The *Hauraki* herself came in for overhaul in January 1943 and went out again in September. At the end of 1944 Allied air raids began to be daily and nightly occurrences, and prisoners and guards were spending much of their time sheltering in snow-lined trenches.

Another group of prisoners was similarly employed at the Muroran Steel Works at Hakodate, in the south of the island of Hokkaido. They worked for thirteen days out of fourteen, shovelling coal and iron ore or in a large repair shop for railway engines. They were more fortunate than some in that the wooden one-storied huts of the camp had been specially built for prisoners of war and were therefore new and in good condition. There was ample water and they were able to get hot baths two or three times a week. In spite of the usual inadequate rice and vegetable soup diet, a New Zealander who had experienced some of the worst camps and hospitals of the East Indies before going to Hakodate thought the conditions were 'relatively good'.

New Zealanders also went to various camps in the group centred round Osaka, in the south of the island of Honshu. Conditions at the Tanagawa dock-construction camp, where the accommodation had a damp earthen floor and the diet was worse than the average at Japanese camps, caused much hardship and sickness. At other camps in this group accommodation consisted of the usual Japanese wooden huts, with sleeping platforms and straw mats. But although the rations at these camps were superior to those at Tanagawa, they were barely sufficient in quantity and, consisting as they did mainly of grain and vegetables, with meat and fish only occasionally, were seriously lacking in protein content. Even the calorific value, minimal for those on light tasks, was totally insufficient for men doing heavy work at a copper refinery or at a foundry manufacturing bomb cases.

Those who went to No. 6 sub-camp at Fukuoka were at first given temporary quarters in a disused railway shed, the worst feature of which was that there was no special accommodation for the sick. There was, moreover, no provision for heating during the first winter the prisoners were in Japan. They were employed for some eleven hours a day in a factory for making green carborundum, often working alongside high temperature furnaces. The diet was on the inadequate scale already described, and the guards at this camp were more than usually brutal in their punishments for trivial offences. During the winter of 1943-44 the death rate became serious and the following April they were removed into a camp of newly built huts.

At Zentsuji, on the island of Shikoku, the first of the prisoner-of-war camps set up in Japan, the treatment during the first year of its existence seemed to many prisoners who had experienced conditions elsewhere to justify calling it a 'propaganda camp'. However, the worsening conditions in Japan, and in particular the increasing shortages of essential foodstuffs and fuel, made themselves felt in Zentsuji, just as they did in the other camps in Japan to which men were sent from Malaya, Thailand, and the Dutch East Indies. Meat and fish were rarely seen at Zentsuji during the latter period of its existence, and there was no heating during the winter of 1943-44. Rest days from work, which had originally been on a scale of one in six, dwindled to one a month. At first prisoners had been employed on clearing mountain land for agriculture, but later they were working with coolie gangs on railway yards and docks, loading grain and heavy military supplies. Nevertheless, Zentsuji had better stocks of medicine and more clothing than most camps. A great deal more of the Red Cross food sent to Japan had been distributed in this camp than in most others, and the prisoners were able to add to their food supplies by raising chickens, rabbits, goats and pigs. The report of the neutral inspector who visited the camp in 1944 spoke of Zentsuji as 'considerably superior to other camps in many respects'.

Among the prisoners who filled the various camps in Japan were some three or four thousand from Hong Kong. The transfer of drafts of prisoners which began in September 1942 and continued throughout 1943 eased conditions at Shamshuipo camp a good deal by reducing the overcrowding. The second half of 1942 was probably the worst period in the camp's existence. Numbers were as high as 6000 to 7000, the diet consisted almost entirely of rice and poor quality vegetables, and for a considerable time, as a disciplinary measure owing to escapes, prisoners were forbidden to receive parcels from outside the camp. Before long there were a large number of cases of dysentery, beriberi and pellagra, and the death rate from malnutritional diseases as well as from an outbreak of diphtheria became serious. Visits from the representatives of the Protecting Power and the International Red Cross Committee in December 1942 were accompanied by the supply to the camp of a considerable quantity of tinned food. A naval surgeon in the camp notes that 'sickness decreased as a result', and it is thought that the husbanding of this bulk supply to supplement the Japanese rations throughout 1943 probably saved a good number of lives. Heavy labour required of working parties included unloading bombs and aviation petrol and enlarging the Kai Tak aerodrome. A redeeming feature of life in Shamshuipo was that the Japanese guards were for the most part confined to the perimeter and left the internal organisation and control of the camp to prisoner-of-war officers and NCOs.

The same could be said of the Argyll Street camp, to which nearly all officers were sent in April 1942. But it was some time before the camp could boast of even fairly simple amenities. Roofs leaked and there were at first no beds, most officers having to make good this lack by buying stretchers. It was a month or two before canteen facilities could be organised, but once they were it was possible to supplement the meagre Japanese rations to a certain extent, though at very inflated prices. By 1943 a fair library had been set up, and an officer speaks of 'reading, lectures and cards ad lib.' What the camp still lacked in material amenities could be forgotten if men were able to organise recreation and left reasonably free to enjoy it.

The conditions under which prisoners of war were transported from Hong Hong to Japan were similar to those (already described) for prisoners from the Dutch East Indies. A New Zealander among the draft of 1800 prisoners who left Hong Kong on the *Lisbon Maru* in late September 1942 described how they were 'cramped into the holds with little air and not enough room for everyone to lie down at once.' Many were suffering from dysentery and other diseases, but there was no provision for the sick, nor even any attempt to remove the bodies of men who died in the holds. On 1 October, when the ship was torpedoed, the first action of the Japanese on board was to batten down the holds and then to abandon ship. When the stern went down some 200 prisoners in the after-hold were drowned, but the remainder broke open the other holds. Once in the water, however, they were fired on by Japanese from auxiliary vessels near the sinking ship. Some 800 prisoners lost their lives, the remainder being eventually picked up by Japanese vessels. A few managed to reach Allied submarines and so escaped.

The value of news of the war and particularly radio news from an Allied broadcasting station in helping men to look beyond their captive state has been mentioned elsewhere. A regular service of such news was maintained in both North Point and Shamshuipo camps by operating old broadcast receivers, which had been either found in or smuggled into the camps and repaired in secret. A New Zealand naval officer[1] was largely responsible for this work,

---

[1] Lt H. C. Dixon, RNZNVR, awarded MBE for his work in constructing and operating radio sets in Hong Kong prisoner-of-war camps.

and the task of constructing a receiver for this purpose, partly from existing components and partly from components improvised from odd pieces of wire and other material, also fell to his lot. The radio finally went into operation in July 1943, after a year or more of solid effort to complete it, and BBC news bulletins were regularly received and distributed to the camp. Two months later it was discovered by the Japanese, and a number of officers were taken away for interrogation. Some were released after a month or more in local police cells, where they experienced, to quote the New Zealander, ' starvation, filth, thirst, torture, beating with boot, fist and stick or sword '. At the end of this period the senior naval officer had to be carried from the police station to Stanley Jail, where four of those implicated were to await execution in solitary confinement. The New Zealand officer received only a sentence of 15 years' imprisonment, which he began to serve immediately under conditions not much better than those just described.

In May 1944 the officers remaining in Argyll Street were moved to Shamshuipo, where a special area was set aside as an officers' camp. A considerable number of prisoners had got out of the camp in early 1942, and the Japanese had taken special precautions to prevent any further escapes, their security measures including an electrified perimeter fence. In view of this, of the strong likelihood of execution if recaptured, and of considerable feeling among certain prisoners against attempts to escape as they brought reprisals on those remaining in camp, the successful escape from Shamshuipo in July 1944 of a New Zealand naval officer[1] reflects the greatest credit on him, not only for his coolness and endurance of hardship but also for his strength of will in deciding to make the attempt. Having been prepared for some time in advance, he chose a dark night with rain and wind and reached a sea-wall just outside the camp after climbing an insulated post supporting electrified wires and crawling under two other fences. He then swam across the bay to the western side, climbed a cliff in heavy rain, and made for the hills. Five nights' travelling over rugged countryside and dodging Japanese brought him to Tolo Harbour. He skirted Mirs Bay as far as Shatau, swimming, wading, or scrambling over the coastal cliffs, and again struck inland. Eleven days after the night of his break, completely exhausted, his sight failing owing to malnutrition, he met Chinese guerrillas and found he was beyond Japanese patrolled territory. He was treated very well and passed from village to village until he reached Waichow, and thence Kunming. The British Military Intelligence report on this exploit describes it as ' one of the most remarkable escapes of the war.'

---

[1] Lt R. B. Goodwin, RNZNVR, awarded OBE.

Civilians remained throughout the war at the Stanley internment camp on the island of Hong Kong. Gradually the internees made good by improvisation the various deficiencies in the sleeping, cooking, and sanitary arrangements of the camp. They suffered, however, from a shortage of essential foods similar to that experienced in most camps under Japanese control. The excellent recreational and sporting facilities of the internment area have been described in an earlier chapter, but accounts of repatriates mention that after a while they became too weak to play football or softball or even to climb up the rather steep hill from the beach after sea bathing. The low diet of the first year of internment gave rise to some 1500 cases of malnutritional disease of varying severity. Supplies of Red Cross food received at the end of this year, and eked out for six months, did much to ease the situation and to eliminate the more serious conditions such as beriberi. Parcels from friends in Hong Kong and China, their own vegetable gardens, and attempts to raise pigs, fowls, and rabbits, all contributed towards alleviating the internees' food shortage in a way that was not possible for most prisoner-of-war camps. But besides the young children interned at the beginning of 1942, a considerable number of babies were born during the succeeding three and a half years; and the special requirements of the very young as well as the elderly, not to mention those of pregnant women and nursing mothers, made the requirements of a large camp for internees such as Stanley proportionately more difficult to fulfil. As in most internment camps containing men, women and children, many adults kept their diet down to an inadequate level in order that the children should have as much as possible, and their own health suffered accordingly.

The internment of Allied civilians in China began in November 1942, when between 200 and 300 men were confined under guard in Shanghai at what became known as the Haiphong Road camp. These men were evidently regarded as dangerous and suspect, and they were placed under the control of the Japanese gendarmerie. Early in the following year nearly all the remaining Allied civilians in occupied China, except a few of advanced years or in ill-health, were gathered into civilian assembly centres under the jurisdiction of the Japanese Consul-General. During 1944 internment was extended even to the elderly and ailing.[1]

Haiphong Road Camp was described by a delegate of the International Red Cross Committee as a 'camp for the detention of political suspects'. A New Zealander who was transferred from Stanley Camp at Hong Kong to Shanghai, and who managed while there to

---

[1] Upwards of 8000 British civilians, including some fifty New Zealanders, were interned in various camps in China.

transmit reports on internment conditions to the British authorities through the Swiss Consulate, was sent to Haiphong Road after imprisonment and torture at Japanese military police headquarters. The internees were accommodated in two large European buildings equipped with all conveniences, where, except for overcrowding, they were quite comfortable. They also had the use of a garden and a sports ground. Funds for maintaining the camp were at first supplied entirely by civilian members of the British and American Residents' Association of Shanghai, and for a while the meals were said to be superior to those served in the best Shanghai hotels. After the internment of most of the other civilians, the Japanese supplied some of the rations and the delegate of the International Red Cross Committee provided funds for buying meat and vegetables and other essential articles and services.

The Lungwha Civilian Assembly Centre, on the outskirts of Shanghai, housed some 1700 men, women and children, partly in the modern buildings of a Chinese university and partly in barracks enclosed in a 60-acre compound. In the Yu Yuen centre some 800 men, women and children occupied the Municipal School buildings and British Army barracks, and here too there was a large sports ground. At Pootung 1000 men lived in the former warehouses of the British American Tobacco Company, reconditioned so as to be suitable for living quarters. At the Great Western Road centre 400-odd men, women and children lived in British military barracks, most families having their own apartments; and again there was a large sports ground. Although overcrowded, another group of civilians of about the same size, interned in the building of the Columbia Country Club, were able to enjoy all the clubs' indoor and outdoor amenities.

The food at these civilian camps in China, at least in 1943, appears to have been on the whole better than that at camps in other Japanese-occupied territories, though still by our standards insufficient. Moreover, all of these camps had canteen facilities for the purchase of extras, though it became more difficult to get supplies as the war progressed. Many kinds of recreational activities were immediately available to the internees, since at nearly every assembly centre they had had the opportunity of bringing in with them as much sporting gear and other material as they wished. Quarters were nearly everywhere crowded, and internees usually had to improvise a great number of amenities which were lacking, but they were usually able to buy the necessary materials. Control by the Japanese Consulate-General ensured better treatment than they would probably have had at the hands of the Japanese military authorities.

New Zealanders working for missions in the Weihsien and Canton areas were also interned in early 1943. At Weihsien (Shantung) a civilian assembly centre was established in the former American Mission compound. At Canton the Oriental Mission compound on Honam Island became the internment camp. To the former went several New Zealand missionaries and teachers, who had up to that time been allowed to continue their work. At the latter the four New Zealanders from Kong Chuen saw out the rest of the war. The camp was under the comparatively mild supervision of a local Japanese consular official, and the Swiss Consul was able to visit weekly and arrange for grants in cash, a daily milk and egg supply, and other assistance.

The year 1944 saw conditions for the internees become more difficult, not only because of an increasing shortage of food and fuel, but because of a tightening up by the Japanese on all matters likely to affect their security. In the middle of the year some 350 aged and infirm British civilians were interned in the Lincoln Avenue Civilian Assembly Centre at Shanghai. The quarters consisted of houses formerly occupied by staff of the China Bank, but not all were in good repair. By this time the Japanese rations consisted mainly of poor quality rice and vegetables, and meat and fish that were sometimes hardly fresh enough for human consumption. Some, however, were able to get parcels from friends outside, and all benefited by aid from the International Red Cross delegate. The old people were expected to work at camp duties for half a day, but this was not compulsory for those over 60 years of age, and the strain upon those who had to attend to the needs of their more elderly comrades must have been considerable. It is probable that the camp diet, combined with lack of heating and general lack of sufficient comfort, hastened the deaths of many of the internees.

III: *Protection of the Interests of Prisoners of War and Civilians*

In their negotiations with the Japanese through neutral channels, the Allied authorities never ceased trying to obtain from them full information concerning the Allied nationals in their hands, regular facilities for the sending of relief supplies and mail, and permission for neutral inspectors to visit prisoner-of-war and internment camps. In spite of repeated requests for the regular forwarding of complete lists, not only of captures but of transfers and casualties, the Japanese never appear to have set up an organisation capable of dealing even with the notifications of capture of the 300,000 Allied nationals in their hands. The first British lists did not come through until May 1942; by January 1943 less than a quarter had been notified, and by September 1943 only 65 per cent of the British prisoners of war and only 20 per cent of the civilians. On the average New Zealand next-of-kin waited 18 months for the first news of their prisoner or internee relative; and the news even then was often only a card or a message over the Japanese-controlled radio. News of those held in the Dutch East Indies seems to have been withheld the longest.

The Japanese were similarly indifferent about mail. Besides that sent on exchange ships, mail for prisoners of war in the Far East was by July 1942 being transported across Russia to her Pacific seaboard and thence to Japan, under an agreement reached with the Soviet Government. The distribution of this mail among the prisoner-of-war and internment camps in Japan and Japanese-occupied territory was slow and haphazard. Censorship was a prime difficulty in the way of prompt delivery: piles of uncensored mail were found in some Japanese camp offices on liberation, and it seems probable that some was destroyed to avoid the work involved in censorship. The amount of mail received varied greatly and almost inexplicably. One New Zealander who worked on the Burma-Thailand railway received 126 letters, another only three. Prisoners in Japan on the whole fared better, especially those at Zentsuji (where one man received 80 letters), than men in the Dutch East Indies where the number seldom reached double figures. New Zealanders at Macassar received no mail at all. The average number of cards which the Japanese allowed to be sent out was from four to five for the whole period of captivity, and only some of these reached their destinations. Again those at Macassar fared worst: they were each allowed to write one letter only, which was not despatched but read out, often in a mutilated fashion, during a broadcast from Radio Tokyo.

While the attitude of the Japanese authorities regarding prisoners' mail seems to have been one of indifference, their attitude regarding visits to prisoner-of-war and internment camps was much more positive. In the first place they refused for the greater part of the war to recognise, except in Japan, Shanghai and Hong Kong, the right of representatives of the Protecting Power and the International Red Cross Committee to pay visits of inspection. The result of this was that International Red Cross Committee delegates were able to visit only 43 camps and Protecting Power representatives only 31,[1] whereas there were at the end of the war 102 camps in Japan, Formosa, Korea, and Manchuria alone. Moreover, for most of the war period it was estimated that some nine-tenths of the 300,000 Allied prisoners and civilians in Japanese hands were held in occupied territories, south of a line running roughly from Rangoon to the northern Philippines, in which not only were inspections of camps forbidden but no relief action of any kind could be undertaken without express permission from the Japanese

---

[1] Visits were allowed for the first time in March 1942.

authorities. Only in 1944 were the agent of the International Red Cross Committee in Singapore and the Swiss Consul in Bangkok able to work openly and effectively as distributors of Red Cross relief supplies.

Some ex-prisoners of war and internees have directly or implicitly criticised the neutral representatives who were able to visit camps, on the grounds that they accomplished nothing with the Japanese authorities. It should be mentioned that they had the greatest difficulty in obtaining the necessary permits for each visit, that during the visit they had to refrain from all reference to humanitarian texts in order not to anger the Japanese authorities, and that the latter always regarded them with suspicion and ill-will. The report of the International Red Cross Committee gives the best idea of how the visits were conducted:

> The duration of the visit of the camps was generally restricted to two hours, made up of one for conversation with the camp commandant, thirty minutes for visiting quarters, and thirty minutes for an interview, in the presence of the Japanese officers of the camp, with a camp leader appointed by them. No communication with the other prisoners was authorized, and negotiations undertaken with the object of altering this state of things were not successful. The camp commandants often refused to reply to questions put to them.[1]

A camp leader who openly criticised conditions and treatment was liable to be beaten after the departure of the visitor, and recourse was had sometimes to the passing of messages while shaking hands in order to convey the true situation. In 1943, when the International Red Cross agent in Singapore complained to a senior military official concerning his continued non-recognition, he was arrested and interrogated by the Japanese military police as a suspected spy. These men had no assurance that the Japanese would respect the persons of neutral nationals any more than they did those of the nationals of enemy countries. By taking too aggressive a stand they would have run a great personal risk and would probably at the same time have jeopardized what scant opportunities for relief work they had.

Negotiations with the Japanese for an exchange of sick and wounded prisoners of war produced no result, but those for an exchange of civilians made possible two repatriation operations, one in 1942 and the other in 1943. As early as February 1942 proposals had been made to the Japanese by the British Commonwealth and United States governments for an exchange of civilian officials, together with a certain number of non-officials. For Japanese from various parts of the Commonwealth there were to be exchanged Commonwealth civilians who wished to leave China, Japan, Thai-

---

[1] Report of the International Committee of the Red Cross on its activities during the Second World War, Vol. I, p. 451.

land, and Indo-China.¹ By July the details of the agreement with the Japanese had been finalised for the exchange to take place at Lourenço Marques, in Portuguese East Africa. In late August the *Asama Maru* reached Lourenço Marques with some 800 civilians from Japan, South-East Asia and the Philippines, and within the following fortnight the *Tatura Maru* and the *Kamakura Maru* arrived with a further 1000-odd from occupied China.² Besides returning with Japanese officials and other civilians, these ships carried back mail and relief supplies for Allied nationals held by the Japanese.

The Allied governments began negotiations for a second exchange almost immediately, but only the United States and Canada succeeded in reaching an agreement with the Japanese authorities. In September and October 1943 several hundred Americans and Canadians, including a number from Hong Kong, walked with relief from the *Teia Maru* on to the *Gripsholm* at Marmagao in Portuguese India. They expressed their thankfulness for having escaped from the semi-starvation of their internment camps, as well as their anxiety for the health of those they had left behind in Japanese custody. The information they provided gave urgency to the question of further exchange agreements, but in spite of unceasing negotiation, this draft was destined to be the last to be repatriated from Japanese custody until the liberation of the Philippines in February 1945.

IV: *Relief Supplies for the Far East*

Reports from the International Red Cross Committee on prisoner-of-war camps in Japan, received in London up to early 1943, showed that the ration issued by the Japanese authorities was 'insufficient in energy value for a man doing anything but light work'. It was, moreover, 'deficient in first class [animal] protein, fat, calcium, vitamin A and vitamin B'.³ Information gleaned from other Japanese occupied areas indicated that the ration of prisoners of war held there was even worse. This seriously deficient diet had created the conditions for the onset of many diseases resulting from malnutrition and for the weakening of resistance to other diseases normally encountered in those climates. In these circumstances and on the advice of the British Army medical authorities, first priority

---

¹The categories of civilians included in the lists submitted to the Japanese were: people imprisoned by the Japanese, people compelled to miss evacuation in the national interest, experts and technicians, missionaries, wives and families of the above categories, together with other women and children, the aged and infirm. These categories had equal priority.
²There were 13 New Zealanders in this contingent. No civilians were exchanged from territories occupied after 7 December 1941, which included Hong Kong, Malaya, and the Dutch Indies.
³Minutes of Imperial Prisoners of War Committee, Sub-Committee B.

in the despatch of relief supplies was given to drugs and dressings and second priority to concentrated foods such as dried meat, powdered whole milk, cheese and butter.

The problem of relief in the Far East resolved itself into finding ways of delivering the goods into the hands of the appropriate Japanese authorities and reaching agreement with them on their distribution to camps. From December 1941 until almost the end of the war, attempts were made to co-ordinate the arrangements necessary for a regular relief service by sea, either by deposit at and collection from a neutral port under safe-conduct or by delivery in Japanese waters on a neutral ship. In 1944 the Allied authorities had stored a considerable quantity of relief supplies at Vladivostok, and in November of that year the *Hakusan Maru* collected 2000 tons, which were distributed to areas containing prisoner-of-war camps in Japan and Japanese-occupied territory. But the *Awa Maru*, one of the ships carrying out the distribution in the southern occupied areas, was torpedoed on her return journey in April 1945, and thereafter Japanese co-operation in this field, such as it had been, came to a standstill.

Apart from this single voyage of the *Hakusan Maru* to the Siberian seaboard,[1] the ships used in the two civilian exchange operations of 1942 and 1943 were the only means by which relief supplies for Allied prisoners of war and internees were able to reach the Far East.[2] Little time was allowed for the loading of the exchange ships at Lourenço Marques in 1942, and of the 7000 tons of supplies gathered together from the Commonwealth under the supervision of the South African Red Cross Society, only 4000 tons could be loaded. At Goa in 1943, however, it was possible to load a large quantity of urgently needed drugs and other medical supplies. These three despatches spread over the whole war period allowed only a very thin distribution of relief goods to the 300,000 Allied nationals estimated to be in Japanese hands.[3]

There is plenty of evidence, too, that this distribution was far from satisfactory. Some packages were received damaged and incomplete; others had deteriorated through long storage at their

---

[1] The actual port of call was Nakhodka, adjacent to Vladivostok.
[2] Some packets of vitamins were sent by post via the Soviet Union and had been received in Japan at the beginning of 1945.
[3] The International Red Cross Committee estimate that during these exchanges the following quantities of goods were brought back by Japanese ships:

Exchange of August-September 1942
    Asama Maru 6993 parcels (to Japan)
    Tatuta Maru 48,818 parcels (to Singapore)
    Kamakura Maru 47,710 parcels (32,940 to Hong Kong)

Exchange of October 1943
    Teia Maru 48,760 parcels (to Singapore, Manila and Japan)

They estimate the total number of parcels received by the Japanese for distribution at 225,000.

destination. Very considerable quantities of food and essential drugs were even found to be still in stock at the time of the liberation. As might have been expected, the International Red Cross Committee had the greatest difficulty in obtaining satisfactory receipts showing that the prisoners or internees had taken possession of the goods.

It has been possible since the end of hostilities to gain some idea of how much prisoners and internees actually received over the whole war period. New Zealand prisoners in Japan seem to have received an average of four to five food parcels, except those in Zentsuji who received anything up to twenty parcels. Prisoners and civilians in China and Hong Kong also received about four to five parcels, in addition to a certain amount of bulk food which was used to augment the camp meals. Prisoners and civilians in Singapore received a fraction of a food parcel (sometimes as low as one-sixteenth) on three occasions, as well as bulk food. Those who were transferred to Thailand received during their stay there a fraction (anything up to one-seventeeth) on one occasion, in 1944. Prisoners in Java and Sumatra received fractions of a parcel on two occasions; civilians, a tiny fraction on one occasion. The men who went to Macassar received nothing at all.

It was fortunate that in some at least of the areas of the Far East where prisoners of war and internees were held, the Japanese permitted the local purchase of food and to a smaller extent of medicines. Once the pay of officer prisoners had been agreed upon, this provided an important source of camp funds for such purchases, and part of it was usually contributed towards a fund for other ranks[1] if they happened to be, as at Hong Kong, in a separate camp located in the same area. But, with the progress of the war, local currencies became greatly inflated and the prices of goods so high that in 1944 and 1945 these funds could not be made to go far.[2]

As early as March 1942 the delegate of the International Red Cross in Japan, foreseeing the difficulties in the way of Japan agreeing to regular relief shipments, asked to be supplied with funds for the local purchase of necessities. This was the beginning of the arrangements made by the British Government and the British Red Cross for the provision of large amounts of cash to representatives of the Protecting Power and to delegates of the International Red Cross Committee in the areas of the Far East where British Commonwealth nationals were held. The Japanese

---

[1] Working other ranks received between 10 and 30 sen a day according to the type of work.
[2] A New Zealand naval officer in Shamshuipo, Hong Kong, reports that in 1944 his monthly pay of 110 yen would buy only one tin of golden syrup.

were reluctant to allow this money to be spent on behalf of prisoners of war, as they considered that the latter were supplied with everything they needed. Prisoners of war working in Thailand on the railway had to be supplied by a clandestine organisation operating from Bangkok and at first financed from private funds. Medical supplies, eggs, chickens, fruit, soap, and cigarettes all found their way into some of the camps on the railway, in the face of Japanese opposition,[1] through the good offices of a small group of civilians in Bangkok and various intermediaries, all of whom ran a great personal risk. In October 1943 the Swiss Consul at Bangkok was officially allowed to send relief supplies to prisoner-of-war camps, and by late 1944 he was spending on behalf of the British authorities some £11,500 a quarter, as well as about £900 a week as pocket-money for prisoners to buy food on the spot.

Similar arrangements were made in other areas. In 1943 British authorities sent instalments of £10,000 to Singapore, increased in 1944 to £18,000. Hong Kong received as much as £10,000 a month, increased in 1944 to £15,000 a month. But of the latter only 25 per cent could be spent on behalf of prisoners of war in the area, and in Singapore as little as two per cent of the funds provided. It was not until 1944 that the Japanese would allow funds to be provided in the Dutch East Indies. A factor which may have contributed to Japanese complaisance in this matter as the war progressed was the fact that transfers of funds to the Far East had to be made in Swiss francs, and such transfers gave the Japanese Government additional badly needed European currency. Britain, on the other hand, had the greatest difficulty in finding Swiss currency, since not only did the vast sums required use up her reserves, but in time of war she was unable to supply Switzerland with the goods necessary to rebuild a credit. The authorities concerned realised that this would create post-war penury in respect of Swiss currency, but as this was the only means of regularly sending relief to British nationals in the Far East, who were in dire need of it, it was felt that the sacrifice was worth the consequences and the risk from the point of view of economic warfare justified.

V: *Japanese Prisoners of War in New Zealand*

Following the Allied landing at Guadalcanal and the subsequent actions against Japanese forces in the Solomons, some 800 Japanese prisoners captured on land or picked up at sea were brought to New Zealand. A camp to accommodate them was established at Featherston in September 1942 and the first batch of prisoners

---

[1] The Japanese allowed only the Catholic Mission to give relief on a small scale to prisoners there.

arrived shortly afterwards. The site of the camp was the piece of land used as a military training camp during the First World War, where an area of 60 acres was now enclosed by barbed wire. At first there was practically no accommodation other than tents, but the onset of spring weather alleviated any discomfort which might have resulted from this, and by March 1943 a good number of wooden huts were ready for occupation. There were also mess huts, shower huts, and covered latrines, and all the barracks were described by a neutral observer as 'airy and well-lit'.

Each prisoner was allowed five blankets and a full set of clothing, including an extra pair of trousers. Food was prepared by the prisoners' own cooks and included a daily ration of as much as six ounces of meat or fish, four ounces (later ten ounces) of rice, and twelve ounces of bread, as well as fresh milk, butter and fresh fruit. Many of the men arrived suffering from tropical and deficiency diseases, but after a few months in the camp many showed a gain in weight and nearly all a general improvement in health. There was full provision for medical, dental, and optical examination, and all medicines, dental work, and spectacles were supplied as needed. Most of the prisoners were required to work at camp duties, including clearing gorse and levelling, for which they were not paid, and at first 57 only were engaged on remunerative work, making concrete building blocks or cultivating vegetables. The latter were paid at the rates agreed by the Commonwealth governments for payment to German prisoners. Those who did camp duties only usually had their afternoons free and spent this and their other leisure hours playing outdoor sports, sketching and carving, beautifying the entrances to their huts, or playing Japanese card games. Although they had ample opportunity to write and send off letters, nobody availed himself of this privilege for fear that he might make an 'unfavourable impression' on his family.

Of the 600 to 700 prisoners, some 500 (No. 1 Compound) were members of work units of the Imperial Japanese Army; the remainder (No. 3 Compound, later No. 2 Compound) consisted of eight naval officers and a number of naval ratings, and regulars of the Japanese Army and Air Force. The former had created from the first practically no disciplinary problems. But the latter had on occasions disobeyed orders regarding hours of work and had even made difficulties about supplying a working party, had deliberately allowed their compound to become untidy, and had several times given evidence of insubordinate behaviour and even of concocting schemes for overpowering the guard. But such behaviour was not greatly dissimilar from that of many New Zealanders and other British prisoners in Europe. Moreover, the prisoners had in December 1942 voiced their appreciation of their food, accommodation, and general treatment to a neutral inspector, who had reported on the same occasion that relations between the prisoners and their guards were very satisfactory. The situation, therefore, seemed most unlikely to give rise to any incident as serious as that which took place on 25 February 1943.

It can be safely said that the New Zealand authorities responsible for Japanese prisoners of war at Featherston adhered strictly to the Prisoners of War Convention of 1929. In fact, in matters of general treatment and discipline they erred on the side of generosity towards the prisoners, in a way that would be normal in the treatment by the New Zealand authorities of their own depot troops. No immediate drastic action was taken, therefore, when on the morning of 25 February 1943 a working party from the compound containing naval and regular army prisoners, which had been ordered the night before, refused to parade for the New Zealand duty officer until an interview had been granted with the camp commandant. There was at first merely some parleying and repeated orders by the adjutant of the camp for the men to parade for work, and for two Japanese officers who had got into the men's compound to leave. All these were met by refusals, accompanied as time wore on by unconcealed amusement on the part of the prisoners. About 10.30 a.m., nearly two hours after the first act of disobedience, the orders became ultimatums, but threats by the camp authorities merely received the reply that force would be met with force. One of the Japanese officers having been forcibly removed, the adjutant threatened the remaining one with his revolver, fired a shot near him and then fired again, wounding him in the shoulder. There was immediately a shower of stones and other missiles from among the 240 or so prisoners, and a concerted rush towards the 34 armed men of the guard who were by this time in the compound. The latter opened fire when the nearest prisoner was seven yards away and the burst went on for 15 to 20 seconds. When it became possible to estimate the casualties, it was found that 48 Japanese had lost their lives and 74 had been wounded. One of the New Zealand guards died in hospital and six others were less seriously wounded as a result of ricochets.

In the subsequent investigations a number of hammers, meat forks, spanners, chisels, knives, and some implements improvised from sticks and nails—a secret collection with counterparts in hundreds of prisoner-of-war camps in Europe—were found in the possession of the Japanese prisoners. They were no doubt ready to be used as occasion demanded, and would perhaps have been used on the occasion described if it had been possible. It seems doubtful, however, whether the two Japanese officers who were considered responsible for the prisoners' resistance to authority would have instigated anything so futile as a mutiny backed by such crude weapons against the rifles and automatics of the guards.

A court of inquiry which met five days later to report fully on these happenings found that they arose from the failure of Japanese fighting personnel to appreciate the provisions of the Prisoners of War Convention[1] relating to compulsory work, from a mutual misunderstanding between prisoners and guards based on differences in language and mental outlook, and from the desire of these fighting troops (backed up by two Japanese officers and several NCOs) to continue the fight against their enemies. It should be remembered that among British prisoners in Axis hands the last two of these factors were usually present, but not the first, failure to understand the obligation to work being replaced in their case by determination to give as much trouble as possible to the enemy enforcing it.

Details of the incident were communicated to the Japanese Government, and a report of the proceedings of the court of inquiry was later forwarded. Subsequent exchanges with the Japanese Government consisted, on their part, of protests concerning the incident and rejections of the findings of the court of inquiry, and on our part, of repudiations of these protests, which at the same time drew attention to examples of flagrant disregard of humanity and international law by the Japanese in their treatment of Allied prisoners of war. It was feared that severe reprisals might be taken by the Japanese on New Zealand prisoners in their hands. But although the incident was brought to the notice of camps in which our men were held,[2] the only repercussions seem to have been that it provided Japanese guards with yet another pretext for making discipline for a time more severe and punishments for trivialities more harsh.

Meanwhile the New Zealand authorities continued to be meticulous in their observance of the Prisoners of War Convention and to supply the Japanese prisoners at Featherston with every amenity. The diet was improved still further from the Japanese point of view by the addition of fish and of more materials for seasoning, and the quantity remained such that some could not eat all their ration. Although the canteen received the same scale of allocation as other military canteens, its chocolate, biscuits, cigarettes, and toilet soap were quickly sold out to the prisoners, who were now

---

[1] Although copies of this Convention in English were always available, there was no translation in Japanese until after this incident.
[2] At the Jaarmarkt camp on Java, for example, a notice was posted stating that the New Zealand Prime Minister had announced that there had been 111 casualties, of whom 48 were killed by machine-gun fire, due to disobedience of orders in a prisoner-of-war camp in New Zealand. If satisfactory explanations were not forthcoming, reprisals would be taken.

earning more money. All prisoners were accommodated in wooden huts holding eight at a maximum, their recreation barracks were improved, sports grounds were made, and officers' quarters were equipped with easy chairs. Even men who were undergoing detention for breaches of discipline were confined in 'new, comfortable detention quarters' and assured a neutral inspector that they were being well treated. The hospital was fitted with the most up-to-date equipment, including an X-ray plant and an operating theatre, and prisoners received, in addition to routine medical and surgical attention, bone and skin grafts, orthopaedic treatment, and electrical and Swedish massage. A fulltime doctor and dentist attended to the needs of the sick, who received if necessary extra fresh milk and eggs. The prisoners were issued with two sets of uniform, those doing dirty work were able to draw still further items, and all prisoners could exchange any worn garments for a new one. They were able to buy slippers, wristlet watches, drawing materials, fountain pens, pictorial magazines and trinkets.

True, they were obliged to work for a maximum of 33 hours a week, but some of the work, in the joinery for example, was so congenial that it became difficult to make the prisoners stop work at the end of the day. Another popular form of work was market gardening at Greytown, where shelter sheds were built to protect them from the elements and to provide facilities for making morning and afternoon tea. Further parties worked at camp construction, pig farming, loading river gravel, making concrete blocks and (later) fireplaces, jute winding and stone crushing. At their request face-masks and sunglasses were provided to protect the workers from dust and sun. Naval and regular army prisoners, who had at first refused any work other than camp fatigues, were persuaded by mid-1943 to accept these paid occupations, although two whose consciences would not let them do so were allowed to work, one as an officer's batman and the other making wooden sandals for his fellow prisoners.

Reports by a neutral observer mention the 'mental suffering' of the prisoners, and there is no doubt that the end of the war seemed to hold little hope for these men, more particularly if it resulted in a victory for Japan. Since they had surrendered, they could expect no consideration from the Japanese authorities; to their country and to their families, they were 'dead'. Four men had to be kept under special observation for a considerable time to prevent their converting this fiction into fact by committing hara-kiri, and there was a comparatively high proportion of mental cases in the camp, although some were only temporarily affected. Everything possible was done to distract them from the hardships of their captivity. They received 500 dictionaries, as well as books from the New

Zealand Red Cross Society and from the Army Education Service. A New Zealand chaplain held lessons in English and a class for prospective converts to Christianity. They were supplied with cards and mah-jongg sets, ping-pong table, wrestling ring, sports grounds and equipment, radio and cinema shows. There was a fortnight's holiday from work at Christmas and a supply of ice cream to cheer them at New Year. By September 1944 a neutral inspector was able to say that their morale had 'improved': he had no difficulty in saying that they enjoyed 'very good material conditions', and that the 'spiritual side' was also 'very well cared for'.

* * * * *

The disparity between the treatment of New Zealanders and other British nationals in Japanese hands and of Japanese held prisoner in New Zealand is so obvious that it needs no restatement here. It is nevertheless as well to appreciate how wide was the gap between the treatment accorded their captives by the two countries, both of which agreed to observe the standards of the Geneva Convention of 1929. In mid-1944 'up-country' maintenance parties of British prisoners on the Burma–Thailand railway were dying in hundreds as a result of dreadfully long hours of work; of ruthless neglect of the sick, many of whom were driven out to work; of insufficient food, and of shockingly primitive and unhygienic general living conditions. At the same period in New Zealand Japanese prisoners were working a maximum of 33 hours a week; were supplied with sunglasses, eye-masks, and a third uniform if requested; were able to get bone and skin grafts, orthopaedic treatment and Swedish massage in their camp hospital; were being issued with more good food than they could eat; and were living in comfortable quarters, each compound equipped with a radio and the officers' mess with easy chairs.

It is true that all Japanese camps were not as bad as those of Burma and Thailand. In some there appear to have been elaborate arrangements for bathing and laundry, and in a few, adequate medical arrangements. Some camps, too, were allowed considerable facilities for keeping rabbits and other livestock. But these are overshadowed by the large number in which men were kept on the verge of starvation, were refused medical attention until beyond the point where they might have survived, and were denied medicine when there were unopened cases of Red Cross medical supplies within the camp area. In her shortage of suitable accommodation for prisoners of war and of material to build it, of European types of food and of drugs and other medical supplies, Japan was in a still more difficult position than Germany, when she, too, was suddenly faced with the custody of vast numbers of prisoners of war. But this does not explain nor justify her fanatical obstruction to the operation of relief schemes, nor her withholding of relief supplies after she had allowed them to enter her territory.

It has been estimated that the prisoner-of-war and civilian internment camps of the Far East stretched over an area of some 5,000,000 square miles. Treatment was worse, generally speaking, the farther captives were from Japan itself or from one of the sub-centres of occupied territory. Prisoners of war on the island of Macassar seem to have fared worse than most others from almost every point of view—notification, mail, relief supplies, and general treatment. It is understandable that the areas more remote from Tokyo would be less subject to whatever influence would be exercised by Allied negotiations or whatever humanitarian views were voiced by Japanese. By the same token these areas would be slower to reap the benefit of changes of policy, such as that which decreed in 1944 that the treatment of Allied prisoners of war should be improved. Unfortunately the majority of these prisoners of war remained in the more remote areas of the south-western Pacific for the greater part of the war.

Allied authorities had from the first carefully considered whether they should give publicity to the treatment of their prisoners of war and civilian internees by the Japanese. It was for some time difficult to decide whether such publicity, so far from influencing the Japanese to improve conditions, might not merely irritate them and be the cause of further hardship to those in Japanese hands, besides being a source of pain and sorrow to their relatives. On balance it was decided that, since the conditions of captivity could hardly be much worse in some areas, it was worth while testing Japanese sensitivity to world opinion, in case it might influence them towards the removal of possible grounds for criticism.

Official Allied statements at first covered the state of negotiations with the Japanese on various matters affecting the welfare of captives in their hands, and then became more outspoken on the inadequacy of the Japanese prisoner-of-war diet and ill-treatment such as that experienced by prisoners of war working on the Burma–Thailand railway. In January 1944 Mr Eden made a statement in the House of Commons setting out the serious situation in which our people in the Far East were placed; this was timed to coincide with similar statements at Washington and in various parliaments of the Commonwealth. Besides producing a violent reaction in Japan by way of denials and attempted refutations, these statements are thought to have had a salutary effect on the Japanese Foreign Ministry and perhaps even on Japanese Military Headquarters. There followed the Japanese press and radio anti-atrocity campaign to which reference was made earlier in this chapter. But evidence also points to some change of policy which brought about a general amelioration of prisoner-of-war conditions. There were improvements in conditions at some camps, concessions regarding the visits of neutral inspectors, and some progress in negotiations for sending relief supplies. Thereafter it became Allied policy to release reports of atrocities as soon as they were received, but to refrain from making them the subject of a government statement.

The anxiety of relatives for prisoners and internees in the Far East, aggravated by lack of communication and by occasional accounts of atrocities, proved much more justified than had similar anxiety for those in Germany and Italy. The special nature of the problem created by prisoners of war and internees in the Far East was recognised in the setting up of Far Eastern sections of governmental and welfare organisations, and even in the publication of a separate periodical by the British Red Cross. Intimidation of neutral agents and brutal repression of camp leaders made it difficult for Allied authorities always to gain an accurate picture of the situation. It was perhaps as well that relatives did not know the extent of underfeeding and overworking, of medical neglect and savage cruelty, practised in a large number of camps. But they would have been relieved had they known the apparently illogical but unshakeable optimism which permeated nearly all of them. The cruelty and neglect of the Japanese appear, quite understandably, to have had the effect not of destroying but of reinforcing the feeling of superiority to their captors with which a great number of prisoners were imbued. To them, therefore, it was just a matter of time before the Allies triumphed, and every effort had to be made to survive until that day came.

CHAPTER 9

The Year of the Allied Invasion of Western Europe

(January – December 1944)

I: *The Events of 1944 and German Camps from late 1943 onwards*

ALTHOUGH the beginning of 1944 saw a stalemate in Italy, there was much on the Eastern Front to indicate to prisoners of war that Germany's fortunes were on the wane and that liberation might come that year. Before March was out Germany was pulling back in Estonia and the north, had lost an army in the Kanyev 'pocket', and was desperately fending off an attack in the Ukraine. She occupied Hungary and Roumania just before the Russian drive into the latter that month, and by the spring she was withdrawing on the whole front. Prisoners following the course of the war had long expected the Second Front to come in the spring, and the news of the landing on 6 June was received with great jubilation.

For most prisoners in Germany the landing was the most significant event of the war; for as it became clear that it had been consolidated, they felt for the first time that they could see the end of their captivity. But the frustration of the plot against Hitler on 20 July, and the attempts of the propaganda machine to urge the German people, through fear, to greater efforts, precluded any thought of an early armistice. And though there were great advances on both the Eastern and Western fronts, and city after city was liberated from German occupation, the Allied forces in the West did not enter German territory until 12 September. After the setback at Arnhem, with the summer gone and the German leaders determined to fight on, nothing decisive seemed likely to happen by the 'fall of the leaves' (as had once been confidently expected)[1] and prisoners resigned themselves to another winter in Germany.

By the beginning of 1944 there were few prisoner-of-war camps in Germany that had not felt the influx of prisoners formerly in

[1] Many prisoners drew this conclusion from a guarded reference in a speech by Mr Churchill to what might happen in the autumn of 1944.

Italian camps. Of the officers' camps containing New Zealanders that existed before the Italian capitulation, Oflags IXA/H and IXA/Z both received sufficient of those transported from Italy to make them full to capacity. Oflag VIIB had been relieved by the transfer in the middle of 1943 of 300 to Rotenburg, but later received 200 of those captured in the operations in the Aegean. In order to maintain sufficient living space, it was necessary for the senior British officers and for neutral delegates to bring the danger of overcrowding constantly to the notice of the German authorities. Nevertheless, taking into account recreation space both indoor and out, their living conditions remained far less cramped than those of the stalags.

Oflag VIIB had a very fine sports ground, sufficient for most of the usual outdoor sports—football, cricket, tennis, athletics—and a large vegetable garden as well. Besides the temporary relief of overcrowding,[1] there had been some attempt by the German authorities to effect improvements in living quarters. Although the water supply still remained inadequate, it was arranged for the officers to have hot showers every fortnight instead of every month. The lighting was somewhat improved and by the middle of the year all barracks had electric light, though it was still weak enough to be a source of eye-strain to those trying to read at night. The camp had a fine library of upwards of 15,000 books, and all kinds of intellectual activity were highly organised. In the spring of 1944 parole walks became regular, there were occasional visits to cinema shows in Eichstaett, and in May there was a visit to a travelling circus. Apart from three mental cases in August 1943, the health of the camp remained good until the end of 1944 despite cuts in the German rations. By 1944 the supply of Red Cross food was regular enough to cover the deficiencies of the German diet, and Red Cross consignments and private parcels had built up adequate supplies of clothing, blankets, and the other more minor comforts that it was possible to send.

The conditions at the two other old-established officers' camps were similar. There was a constant struggle to avoid overcrowding,[2] with its resultant strain on sanitary and other facilities, poor lighting, and insufficient fuel for heating; an inadequate German supply of food and blankets was made good from Red Cross and private sources; and abundant recreational facilities were created by the prisoners themselves with material supplied through Red Cross channels. The more modern building at Rotenburg was

---

[1] The numbers fluctuated between 1650 and 1850, of whom between 1400 and 1600 were officers; between 90 and 100 of the total were New Zealanders.
[2] The numbers at Rotenburg during this period were upwards of 400 officers and 50 other ranks; some 40 of the total were New Zealanders.

spared the shortage of water which troubled other camps, but the shortage of fuel for a building with central heating and stone floors made winter conditions very comfortless. And the cold, combined with overcrowding which involved the use of study and recreation rooms for accommodation, deprived many prisoners of reading, study, and similar palliatives for the boredom and frustration of cramped indoor life.

The camp population at Oflag VA at Weinsberg remained more constant, for from the camp's beginning in late 1943 it had been of a higher density than that usual for officer prisoners.[1] As in most camps overcrowding was felt less in summer, when much time could be spent in the open air, than at any other time of the year. In the early part of 1944 the Germans had carried out a number of improvements. The water supply had been increased so that hot showers were available weekly, sanitation was better, the lighting had been made somewhat stronger, and facilities for sports were greatly increased. Parties of 120 prisoners at a time were allowed the use of a fine sports field amid the woods about half an hour's walk from the camp; and a generous supply of sports material from the World Alliance of YMCAs made it possible to use every yard of ground inside the small barbed-wire enclosure of the camp. Supplies of books and stationery from the same source had enabled the organisation of a wide variety of educational courses, and by early June more than 200 had applied to sit for recognised examinations. While many of the improvements in the camp amenities had been made possible by generous material aid from Allied sources, the appointment of a new German camp officer had resulted in much more reasonable relations with the German authorities and, in the opinion of the Swiss delegate, had caused the whole atmosphere to change for the better.

A matter which gave the prisoners in Oflag VA considerable apprehension, and about which it took a long time to persuade the Germans to take action, was the provision of adequate air-raid shelters. The trenches at first provided for this purpose were insufficient to accommodate all the prisoners and were inadequate in design to afford proper protection. As it transpired that there were in the immediate neighbourhood a factory for making aircraft wings and another for machine-gun parts, the necessity for protecting the camp from air raids was a real one. In 1944 the trenches were improved, and during a raid prisoners could use them or remain inside their barracks, whichever they preferred.

---

[1] The average camp population for 1944 was about 1130, of whom about 150 were other ranks. About 140 officers and ten other ranks were New Zealanders.

Relations between the 300-odd senior, elderly, and sick officers assembled in Oflag XIIB at Hadamar and the German staff of this camp also improved. By January 1944 the interior accommodation was satisfactory in almost all respects; and though the area for sport in the camp was too small, walks on parole did much to mitigate this. The transfer to this camp of all those of the rank of brigadier and above from other British officers' camps in May caused some crowding together, and it was soon obvious that officers of whatever rank at Hadamar would have to be prepared to share rooms.[1] Up till the time of the invasion they had had adequate supplies of Red Cross food and other materials, but there were the same troubles with German rations as in other camps. The potato ration was depleted through rotting, and there was the same difficulty as elsewhere in obtaining fresh fruit and vegetables, although, as the senior British officer pointed out, the German countryside was bursting with them. Ample sport, theatricals, and music were organised to keep everyone occupied and entertained. Apart from the conditions resulting from the Allied invasion, the camp remained satisfactory throughout the year.

Material conditions in Oflag VIIIF at Märisch-Trübau continued to improve during the early part of 1944: such shortages as there were (dentures, for example) were common to most camps in Germany, and the general impression made on a Swiss inspector in February[2] was a favourable one. There was in the camp, however, an active escape organisation, and the discovery in late April by German security personnel of plans involving civilians in nearby Czechoslovakia brought the camp into prominence with the German High Command. The latter, because of some successful mass escapes of prisoners of war, took a serious view of the matter and decided to transfer all the prisoners to another area. In early May they were divided into five parties and the move took place by train. All officers were handcuffed, deprived of braces, belts and boots, and packed up to eighteen in one-third of a cattle-truck, the remainder of which, fenced off by barbed wire, was occupied by German guards. The journey to Brunswick took from 42 to 48 hours, but no one was allowed to leave the trucks until arrival. Both before and during the move tempers were short on both sides, and there was some hitting with rifle butts during the march to the station. During the journey the prisoners soon found that the handcuffs were easy to remove; and some enthusiasts among them took advantage of their cross-country jaunt to distribute through the

---
[1] After this transfer the camp strength of 314 included : one major-general, ten brigadiers, 23 lieutenant-colonels, 80 majors, 93 captains, 53 lieutenants and 54 other ranks. The New Zealanders comprised 32 officers and five other ranks.
[2] At that date it contained a total of 1747 (1581 officers and 166 other ranks), of whom 39 were New Zealanders.

openings of the truck anti-German propaganda leaflets which they had run off on a home-made cyclostyle machine before leaving the camp.

The new camp at Querum (Oflag 79), on the outskirts of Brunswick, was situated only two kilometres from an airfield and was surrounded by military targets such as anti-aircraft batteries and factories. Two buildings inside the camp area had suffered in a previous air raid, and the location of the camp was considered by the Swiss representative so dangerous that a request was made to the German High Command on 9 May for its transfer elsewhere. Apart from this consideration, the accommodation, which was in four two-storied brick barracks, was quite insufficient for 1900-odd prisoners;[1] the same could be said of the modern bathing, toilet, and kitchen facilities, and provision for recreation both indoor and outdoor was practically non-existent. Although arrangements were in hand to increase the camp's accommodation in all these respects, the commandant of the new camp was described by the Swiss representative as 'petty and narrow-minded' and 'not at all fitted for his present post'. By the prisoners he was regarded as an obstructionist 'refusing all reasonable requests'.

As time went on relations between the prisoners and the German administration improved, and by August the accommodation had been doubled, there was more open space outside the barracks, and the educational classes, various forms of entertainment, and religious activities were all flourishing. On 24 August, however, the fears expressed when the camp was first opened were proved well founded, for during a daylight air raid a number of high-explosive and many anti-personnel and incendiary bombs fell within the camp area. The prisoner casualties included three killed, seven badly and thirty slightly wounded. Every building in the camp was damaged, one being rendered permanently uninhabitable; the cookhouse was destroyed, the electric-light system was dislocated, the entire water and drainage system, except for two barracks, was put out of action; and sizeable bomb craters largely nullified the recent additions to the outdoor games area. The German shortage of labour and material made the repair of the damage a much longer process than had been anticipated, to which continued raids in the Brunswick area no doubt contributed. There was no light for ten days, no proper drainage for three weeks, and no heating for three months, prisoners receiving on 2 December their first hot shower since the raid. In spite of these discomforts educational classes were increased, with some 500 officers preparing for examinations;

---

[1] These included 43 New Zealanders.

theatrical and musical entertainments were continued; and there was considerable interest in study groups on religious topics and other religious activity.

During 1944 New Zealand Army other ranks held prisoner in Germany numbered something over 6000. The majority of them were in Silesia, some 3000 in Stalags 344, VIIIA, VIIIB and VIIIC and their attached *Arbeitskommandos*. About half this number were in southern Austria at the farms and other satellite camps of Stalag XVIIIA. The remainder were in Poland, in central Germany, or in Bavaria.

By February 1944 the newly-established camp at Teschen (now Stalag VIIIB) was acting as an administrative base for many of the Silesian *Arbeitskommandos*, including 53 containing some 11,500 British prisoners, about a thousand of them New Zealanders. During the year the camp strength was gradually increased by another 2000 British, 200 of them New Zealanders. Teschen itself held only 250-odd of the British prisoners, together with about two or three times that number of prisoners of other nationalities. As in other British camps the prisoners' camp leader and his staff arranged all work parties, and the camp leader at Teschen was allowed frequent visits to all dependent *Arbeitskommandos*. Though the barracks and sanitary conveniences were very old and primitive, there was no overcrowding at this stage. Lighting, heating, bathing, and cooking facilities were all adequate, but there was little space for outdoor recreation.

Lamsdorf (now Stalag 344), on the other hand, remained very overcrowded in spite of the exodus to the new Stalag VIIIB and to Stalag VIIIC. At the beginning of 1944 the British prisoners alone numbered 10,000 in the base camp, with another 9000 spread among the 235 *Arbeitskommandos* attached to it. The sleeping accommodation, water supply, washing facilities, and latrines at Lamsdorf were all inadequate to cope with such numbers, and the German authorities planned to reduce the camp strength to about 6000 by transferring all Air Force, Canadian, and United States prisoners elsewhere. But in the first half of the year only some 500 were moved. This was enough to obviate the necessity of using the lowest of the three tiers of wooden bunks, but had no appreciable effect on the adequacy of the water supply and sanitary facilities. Shortage of water caused considerable discomfort, but pit latrines not emptied frequently enough to cope with the numbers using them caused an intolerable situation. Fortunately, the medical services of the camp were excellent. And the German authorities, perhaps realising the value of plenty of recreation in distracting prisoners' attention from physical discomfort and in compensating to some extent for their failure to provide a camp conforming to proper standards, began to openly encourage sport and theatrical entertainments. The latter, as well as special open-air carnivals, reached a standard hitherto unattained. For the rest Lamsdorf remained a huge, sprawling, changing prisoner-of-war community, ably but not too rigidly administered by the British staff, where a profusion of the world's languages was spoken and where prisoners seemed to be able to get away with almost anything provided they did not make it too blatant. It seems to have had something of the atmosphere of a European seaport city, with a good deal of the spit-and-polish of the regular British Army superimposed.

The other base camp for Silesia, Stalag VIIIC at Kunau, near Sagan, was much smaller than the two just mentioned. Here the British numbered about two to three thousand, with fewer than a hundred New Zealanders. Except for about 500, they were spread over some twenty *Arbeitskommandos,* most of them industrial.

Besides the *Arbeitskommandos* at the Silesian coal mines, there were others in factories of various kinds, on construction work, on lumber work in the pine forests, and on railway and general maintenance work. Most of the men at the factories were making their first acquaintance with the industries at which they had to work: cotton, sugar, cement, linseed cake, machinery and paper, to name a few. Occasionally an engineer might find himself operating a concrete mixer, his professional interest almost recaptured, until he remembered it would be better, in the interests of damaging the German war effort, to leave it to a fellow-worker completely unfamiliar with such work. For the majority of the prisoners there was at first a certain rather pleasant novelty about the jobs, and one man even said of coalmining that it was 'good experience'. At most jobs prisoners were working alongside civilian men and women of various nationalities. Not only was there interest in talking to civilians and finding out their views on the war, but the keener prisoners seized every opportunity to make good the lack of female society they had experienced over the previous years, sometimes with an astonishing disregard for conventional modesty.

Prisoners working at factories lived on the premises or in barracks close by, which were usually well heated in the winter. Their midday rations were normally supplied by the factory owner and cooked for them on the job. In any party of fifty or more the British stalag staff responsible for its organisation would include a medical orderly and an interpreter, so that its immediate medical and administrative needs were more easily looked after. All relied on consignments from the stalag of food, clothing, tobacco, and recreational material. Factory work was usually not too strenuous, and most men had plenty of energy for recreation in the evenings.

Often in summer the men would be taken to a nearby river to swim; in winter there were the usual card games, darts, and reading. A prisoner working in a coal mine writes of spending the evening 'talking, reading, arguing and eating in patches'. At the larger *Arbeitskommandos* there were games of football and cricket, concerts and theatrical shows.

Those on outdoor work, such as driving wedges in tree trunks or shovelling shingle, kept fit without the need of outdoor sports. The men from E588, a forestry party, left by train each morning at six o'clock, worked out of doors all day, and were back in camp by four in the afternoon. A party of three to four hundred, including 40-odd New Zealanders, at Mechtal were engaged in preparing excavations for a building which formed part of an electricity scheme. Another party of the same size, half of them New Zealanders, were doing similar work at Laband in preparation for the erection of a factory. In the spring of 1944 a prisoner wrote that he was the 'heaviest ever' due to his getting plenty of physical exercise and Red Cross food.

Some of the most pleasant work must have been that in the forest at a lumber camp. Even though it was sometimes loading heavy logs on bogies, the open air combined with Red Cross food and heavy workers' rations kept the prisoners in a camp such as this very fit. They were far enough away from military headquarters not to be forced to work too hard; and sitting round a roaring fire toasting bread at lunchtime almost gave the illusion of a camp holiday. Because of their remoteness the prisoners' living quarters, in old but snug farm buildings, were loosely guarded, especially in winter when it would have been very difficult for an escaper to get far without being detected. Prisoners often wandered alone to and from the work in the forest, and some were able in the evenings to visit Polish and German women living in the neighbourhood. A sympathetic German guard is even said to have been seen in the early mornings filling in the prisoners' return tracks in the snow.

One small party of 14 men, *Arbeitskommando* 243, was employed at the gasworks in Breslau, stacking and emptying gas purifiers. It was from this party that the first New Zealander[1] to escape from Germany proper made his successful break. He and another of the party got to know some Ukrainians in the factory and were able to obtain from them civilian clothes and a briefcase each in exchange for cigarettes. On 23 September 1943 they changed into civilian clothes, one a little later than the other, scaled a wall, and walked down the road away from the gasworks. They each went by tram

---
[1] Sgt B. J. Crowley (4 Res MT Coy), awarded DCM for his continued efforts to escape since capture in Greece in April 1941.

to the railway station and by train in various stages to Stettin, where they met again. French workers engaged in loading at the docks smuggled them on board a Swedish ship, on which they hid under coal in one of the holds. On arrival in Sweden they were handed over to the police, but were able eventually to report to the British Embassy in Stockholm at the end of September 1943.

The New Zealander was able to send back word to his companions of previous attempts that in his case the plan they had worked out together had succeeded. Two of these companions, New Zealanders,[1] and a British Army man got away on 23 December 1943 from the working party billets in a cement works at Oppeln. One cut the wire surrounding the latrines and the other two scaled over the main gate. All were experienced escapers, who knew the German language fairly well and had made careful plans and secured the necessary equipment before leaving the stalag. They all travelled by train to Breslau and to Berlin, showing false identity cards as Belgian workers. They went across Berlin by underground to a main station, but had to wait there for an Allied air raid to finish. Eventually they reached Stettin, where they stayed in a boarding house and managed to make contact with some Swedish sailors by going into a brothel. The latter agreed to smuggle them on board a Swedish vessel, which sailed on New Year's Day 1944. After five days crouched in a rope locker, they made their presence known as the vessel neared Sweden and were handed over to the police at Oselsund. They spent a month at Stockholm under British protection and were flown out to Scotland in early February.

The working party engaged on railway maintenance and construction at Oderburg put in a bad winter. They had to work in all weathers except heavy rain, and low temperatures made canvas gloves necessary to prevent their hands freezing on to the metal rails they had to carry. Though overcrowded until some of the men were transferred to a coal mine, their barracks were warm, for the surroundings in which they worked gave them ample opportunity to supplement their coal ration unknown to the guards. When undetected by the guard, they were also able to obtain fresh food from the Polish and Czech civilians with whom they worked in exchange for cigarettes, tea, and coffee. With only three slow-running taps, it would have been very difficult to keep clean if Red Cross soap had not been available to use instead of the German putty-like soap ration. By the spring they had completed the German firm's contract and were allocated to another working

---

[1] Dvrs E. J. A. Phelan and E. R. Silverwood (both 4 Res MT Coy). Both received the MM for their efforts to escape.

nearer Oderburg. The Czech overseers, who replaced the German they had previously worked under, shortened their hours of work and treated them more reasonably.

In mid-summer waves of Allied planes began to pass overhead and bomb the nearby industrial cities, and soon an air-raid alert became a daily occurrence. Oderburg was a railway junction of some size through which passed supplies to the Eastern Front, and it was too important to be missed. On 29 September the railway station, the yards, and main lines were heavily bombed. Five New Zealanders, together with a guard and a number of civilians, were killed when an air-raid shelter received a direct hit. The German authorities allowed them a full military funeral, with a guard of New Zealanders from the neighbourhood and the senior New Zealand chaplain[1] from Teschen.

Large numbers of prisoners had been employed since 1940 in the flat forest area south-east of Breslau, around Heydebreck and Blechammer, on the construction of a huge industrial centre. The scheme was under the control of the I.G. Farben group and was planned to realise the extraction of motor spirit and other by-products from coal. In late 1943 some 25,000 prisoners and other foreign workers of both sexes and of many different nationalities were being used there. British prisoners were organised into large construction groups of about a thousand men (known as *Bau* battalions), *Arbeitskommandos* of about the same size from which gangs could be drawn for work where required, and smaller *Arbeitskommandos* for more permanent tasks scattered about the area. By mid-1944 the stage of clearing and preliminary construction was over, and the demand was for skilled workmen to complete the detail of the giant project, and for more and more of the unskilled to go down the mines and hack out coal to feed into it.

A working camp of a thousand was large enough to permit the organisation of most of the amenities of the stalag—music, library, theatre, and even school—and small enough to be capable of an *esprit de corps* that the stalag lacked. A British camp of this size was allocated a British medical officer, and its well-being depended largely on the combined efforts of this officer and the camp leader. Insistence on adequate facilities for keeping clean and proper sanitation, apart from the treatment of minor ailments and the recognition of more serious ones, were all made easier by the presence of an officer skilled in a science which the Germans respected. His protected status and his visits to small outlying sub-camps, to neighbouring towns, and to stalag made it possible

---

[1] Rev. J. S. Hiddlestone, awarded MBE for his 'constant and untiring efforts' for 'the welfare of his fellow prisoners of war', particularly those in 'many and widely scattered work camps'.

for him to obtain articles of great value for the welfare and recreation of the camp; and his officer status enhanced his influence both with the German commandant and with his fellow prisoners. In E3 at Blechammer, the medical officer, a New Zealander,[1] was able over a period of two years not only to build up a very efficient medical service, but to play a large part in developing the general administration of a camp which earned a reputation for the well-being and high morale of those confined in it.

The working camp at the Gleiwitz aerodrome of some 300 British Commonwealth prisoners was typical of those *Arbeitskommandos* which acted as maintenance unit and light labour force for the surrounding district. The duties of the men in this camp varied from digging water-mains in the town and building barracks on the aerodrome to unloading and stacking on the nearby canal and carting loads of bricks or sand. They often travelled by train to work in Tost, Quellengrund, and other neighbouring towns. The change of scene and the variety of jobs, many of them in the open air, gave them a great advantage over prisoners not so fortunately placed. The German NCO in charge seems to have done his best to protect them against exploitation by civilian overseers, to help them in the organisation of recreation, and generally to see that they were reasonably treated. They were able to visit other camps for football matches, to go swimming, to run a band, to set up a 'beer bar', to give quite elaborate concerts. The festivities for Christmas 1943 included a mock court and a 'grand' concert, and the year 1944 came in with the band playing and the 'beer bar awash.' To offset the numerous searches, the locking up of trousers and boots, and other security measures in the new year, there was news of Allied success everywhere; and even before the spring brought its sunshine and wine-like air, the prisoners felt a certain elation for, as one man wrote, 'the days seem to fly when the griff is good'.[2]

All the men in this camp had been X-rayed in February, and about the middle of June some of the New Zealanders were transferred to E535, a coal mine at Milowitz, just over the border from Gleiwitz in south-western Poland. Here they were joined by small parties of other New Zealanders from various *Arbeitskommandos* in eastern Germany. They took the place of most of the British, Cypriots, French, and Spanish who had been there for some years. Milowitz may be taken as typical of a good number of the mining camps, though not all of them had such bad conditions.

---

[1] Capt J. Borrie (NZMC), awarded MBE for 'outstanding devotion to his fellow prisoners.'
[2] The quotations are from the diary of a New Zealand private at the camp.

Both on and off work conditions were rough and crude. The old mine shafts were in disrepair, the machinery was old, and there was a shortage of essential mining equipment such as lamps. The place lacked washing facilities capable of coping with coaldust and there was a totally inadequate soap ration. Near the mine shaft were the barracks—dirty, leaking, insanitary, bug-infested—on a piece of ground where every blade of grass had long since given up the unequal struggle against scoria. Discipline was in the hands of a German NCO of low mentality who was always threatening collective punishment and occasionally manhandling the prisoners. Their diet consisted mainly of swill soup, potatoes and bread, and the quantity would have been quite insufficient had it not been for regular supplies of Red Cross food parcels in the early stages. Fortunately they were able to trade regularly with Polish civilians for eggs and other fresh food, and occasionally for liquor of a kind. Fresh farm produce compensated for the unpalatability of the German rations, and occasional schnapps provided an escape from the ugliness and semi-animal atmosphere of the mine. This illicit trading the German guards tried to circumvent by searches at the camp gates.

As in many other camps, the arrival of newcomers with new ideas was resented by some of the old hands, and some clashes occurred. Gradually, however, most of the original occupants were transferred elsewhere, and more New Zealanders kept arriving until there were more than 500 of them. Old comrades who had not seen each other since the days of Crete met again and compared experiences.

Hours of actual work at the mine were long, usually eight and a half hours in the coal seam, preparations beforehand and cleaning up afterwards added another hour or two, and for a long time only one Sunday in four was a free day. This was later the subject of an official complaint when the International Red Cross Committee investigated all the German mining camps. Falls of stone and coal caused crushed and broken bones, and there were many cases of 'gassing' during work below the ground. Down in the mine prisoners were employed in pushing or shovel-loading trucks, working alongside Polish men and boys, sometimes ankle-deep in water. Above the surface they worked with Polish women 'separating', loading scrap-iron, coal and rations, and doing camp fatigues.

There was much threatening with pistols by both Polish-born overseers and German guards in order to keep the prisoners working. But constant bullying of this kind failed to make much impression on men who by this time had several years of prisoner-of-war experience behind them, had been screamed at by guards, snarled at by Alsatian police dogs, and threatened with firearms too often to be worried. They shovelled the required minimum of wagon-loads, less if they could deceive the overseer, and quickly learnt all the ways in which they could loaf on the job and get away with it. But work below was unpleasant and anyone who fell foul of a German guard was kept there for a long period.

The only accepted excuse for not working was incapacity through illness or injury, verified by medical examination. It is perhaps not surprising that there were a good many broken bones, 'rashes', burns, and sores self-inflicted by some of these forced miners in order to secure a spell from work. A few men became specialists in the infliction of these 'krankers'[1] as they were called, and some prisoners were able to avoid mining work for weeks or even months by this means. It seemed justified on the grounds of keeping men from working for the German war effort. But only five per cent of the camp strength was normally allowed off work at a time, and sometimes genuinely sick persons were forced down the mine to make up the work quota. The lot of the genuinely sick was made more difficult in any case if the Germans became suspicious of a succession of similar injuries. The British medical officer and many of the men felt, moreover, that the spells from work should have been shared evenly among those in the camp. The whole matter gave rise to some bitter arguments.

Among men working under such conditions and on various shifts throughout the whole day and night, it was unlikely that artistic and intellectual recreations would flourish as they did in other camps. There were almost no facilities for reading, and even letters were short in mid-1944. Football and boxing matches held on the rare free days and an occasional concert were the only light relief from the weariness and monotony of a life of continual dirt, hunger, and oppression.

Against this drab background there was the brightness of the war news—consistently good throughout this period on all fronts. To back it up there were increasingly severe air raids, and evidence of the approach of the Russian forces in the digging of tank traps in the neighbourhood and the evacuation of prisoner-of-war camps to the north and east. These things kept morale high, even when Red Cross food and cigarettes ran out and when the last quarter of the year brought rain and snow to add their share of discomfort. It was possibly through the inspiration of the good war news that the camp weekly newspaper *Tiki Times*[2] came into being in August and ran through 24 issues. It became the camp's chief artistic outlet and an enthusiastic meeting voted to publish it after the war, a resolution that has since been carried out.

---

[1] Derived from German *krank*, sick.
[2] The paper was edited by Pte J. Gallichan (22 Bn).

There was no lack of incentive to attempt an escape from Milowitz, but only two New Zealanders[1] were successful. They were in a party of four who got out in September through an old escape tunnel cut from a disused mine working. The break was made late on the night of the 12th, and the four men lost no time crossing into Slovakia. Here two of them were recaptured, but the two New Zealanders had the good fortune to meet in the hills near Mesto Slovakian partisans, who passed them on to the Allied military mission operating there. They were flown to Bari on 5 October.

As in other camps, the end of the year at Milowitz saw the Germans tightening up security measures for fear of concerted action by prisoners under the influence of the good war news. There were stricter searches at the gate to detect illicit trading, and searches of the camp by guards or Gestapo, in one of which a prisoner was caught with earphones listening on a secret radio. Some timely Red Cross food, a concert, and a pictorial issue of the *Tiki Times* helped to bring some cheer into Christmas, and some illicit schnapps contributed to a noisy New Year's Eve.

The prisoners began the new year with a strong complaint about the shortage of proper miners' boots, and many were allowed to remain above ground on this account. They followed it up by a concerted condemnation of the camp on letter-cards, in which almost everybody took part. The immediate result was the return of all the cards to the camp by the commandant in a fit of rage. Nevertheless, a film was shown shortly afterwards in the newly-built concert hall for the first time, and half the day shift were allowed to remain on surface work.

As the snow fell deeper in the first days of January 1945 the news became steadily better, and rumours of the close proximity of the Russians were confirmed by the feverish digging of defences nearby. On the 18th a pitiful rabble of Jews from the adjacent Auschwitz concentration camp was herded past on the road. Next day E535 was on the march, the first stage of a gruelling 1000-kilometre trek which in the next three months took them across Czechoslovakia and into Bavaria almost to Munich.

The British section of Stalag VIIIA at Görlitz, the other Silesian camp containing considerable numbers of New Zealanders, remained of moderate size compared with Lamsdorf. In 1944 its strength was about 3000, of which more than a third, mainly NCOs and including some 350 New Zealanders, were at the stalag, the remainder being spread over 40-odd *Arbeitskommandos*. As for the other camp

---

[1] Ptes W. S. Gilmour (27 MG Bn) and R. J. McKinney (26 Bn), both mentioned in despatches for their escape.

communities set up in Germany after the influx from Italy, 1944 was for Stalag VIIIA a period of consolidation and development. Prisoners were able to reap the benefit of the hard work put in while getting the camp in order following their arrival. Until the latter part of the year there were ample supplies of Red Cross food, tobacco, and recreational material. Camp routine was well established, and all the various departments of a properly organised camp, from post office to barber's shop, from library to theatrical rehearsal group, from church to escape committee, were put into smooth running order. In some ways they ran more smoothly than would be normal in civilian life, since in an NCOs' stalag or an oflag these were the only things to which the prisoner need devote his time.

At camps for non-working prisoners a full programme of recreational activities was essential if men were to have sufficient interests to occupy their time. A democratically constituted camp committee at Görlitz co-ordinated the work of a number of sub-committees for sports, education, theatre and the rest. While a large proportion of men engaged in outdoor sports as a means of keeping fit, the theatre was probably outstanding among indoor recreations in providing the most satisfying form of escape for the greatest number of prisoners. For at least the hour or two of the performance men could forget bedbugs, barbed wire, searches, police dogs, evening curfew, and the other annoyances that were all too insistent at other times. Towards the end of the year the theatre at Görlitz was closed by the Germans after a Gestapo search which disclosed, among other things, a radio set in full operation. But if they prevented a Christmas show, the Gestapo did little to eliminate traffic between prisoners and the outside world. For a few thousand cigarettes a group of New Zealanders bought a live sheep, which was in due course smuggled into the camp, slaughtered, and added to the Christmas menu.

The *Arbeitskommandos* attached to Görlitz were engaged in types of work similar to those already described: coalmining, quarrying, forestry, brick making, work in various kinds of factories, construction and maintenance work. Only a few, notably those at coal mines, had more than a hundred British prisoners; but they were kept up to strength by the German doctor, who ruthlessly drafted out prisoners from the stalag whether or not they were pronounced fit by the British medical officers. A group of about fifty were quartered in three rooms of an inn in the centre of Weisswasser, where they had to manhandle electrical equipment destined for German airfields. Such work was monotonous, and so was the stone-breaking done by another party at Greiffenberg. But in addition to outdoor sports at a village sports field, these men had opportunities of swimming and visiting the cinema already noted at other German *Arbeitskommandos*. Their surroundings both at work and at other times were freer and more pleasant than those of their fellow prisoners in stalags. A congenial party supplied with musical instruments, darts, and other equipment could pass their leisure hours pleasantly enough, and one man rates his time at a Silesian *Arbeitskommando* as the happiest of his prisoner-of-war days. But the disadvantages of a restricted community were accentuated in a small *Arbeitskommando*, and there were times when almost every prisoner of war could say, 'The monotony of the same faces, stagnant conversation, simulated cheerfulness and the deep longing for those we love make any conditions difficult, and the only really pleasant hours are those of sleep.'[1]

As in other parts of Germany, many men from these *Arbeitskommandos* made breaks from billets to attempt an escape. Such men had usually received information and equipment from the escape committee of the stalags they previously had been at. The only New Zealander[2] to succeed from a camp in this area left his billet at Munsterberg in the early morning of 14 July 1944. He made for the railway station wearing a civilian suit acquired from a Frenchman, and travelled by train to Breslau and on to Stettin. Here he met a Swedish sailor, who guided him while he swam out to his ship and boarded it by a rope ladder. He hid in the airshaft of the ship's main funnel until he could safely disclose his presence and was landed at Kalmar, in Sweden, at the beginning of August. Like most successful escapes from Germany, this was the last of a long series of attempts.

About 1300 New Zealand prisoners of war spent 1944 in southern Austria, the great majority of them in working camps. A good number of the latter, although they were recorded as being in Stalag XVIIIA at Wolfsberg, had never seen the stalag and knew it merely as the centre from which they were administered and obtained their relief supplies. The work of dealing with the needs of nine or ten thousand British prisoners working in more than 300 *Arbeitskommandos*, as well as the thousand or so at the stalag, was an administrative task at all times heavy, and in 1944 often very intricate. By the middle of that year some of the New Zealanders had begun their fourth year of captivity and some of the British Army prisoners their fifth. In spite of getting used to the routine, the length of captivity and the tension caused by anticipation first of the final Allied push and later by its completion began to tell on

---

[1] From an article contributed to *Interlude*, an illustrated account of Stalag VIIIA edited by ex-prisoners from the camp and published in England in 1946.
[2] Pte W. J. Siely (Div Pet Coy), awarded DCM for his persistent efforts to escape.

men's nerves. Fortunately by 1944, as in the camps already described, the organisation of Wolfsberg had reached a very efficient pitch.

There had been little change in the buildings of the stalag itself since the erection of a new barrack for 'disciplinaires',[1] a previous one on the same site having been burned to the ground just after its completion. The installation of a new drainage system had made sanitation much easier. The fittest of the German guards had been sent in late 1943 to one of the battle zones and their replacements were found to be susceptible to offers of cigarettes, soap, and chocolate. As a result, it gradually became possible to obtain almost anything desired in the way of fresh food or articles such as cameras, films, and radio valves, which had a special value in prisoner-of-war camps. Discipline became the easiest it had ever been, until a morning check parade mustered only about eighty prisoners and the guards had to be called out to clear the barracks.

If the discipline still continued fairly easy in 1944, the German security was considerably tightened. Representatives of working parties were restricted in their movements, chaplains were for a while prohibited from visiting work-camps except on entirely unacceptable terms,[2] and both the stalag and its *Arbeitskommandos* experienced more thorough searches than in any previous year. It still remained possible, however, for British prisoners liable to heavy sentences of imprisonment to be concealed in the stalag,[3] just as they were on a larger scale at Lamsdorf. It was possible also to maintain radio reception of BBC news bulletins and so continue the daily camp news service, which became of increasing interest to prisoners as they felt that their time of liberation was approaching.

The amenities of Stalag XVIIIA reached a high standard in 1944. There was a library of 15,000 books, besides large numbers in the *Arbeitskommandos* and a 'university' library of textbooks for serious students. A stalag school catered for the latter and especially for those wishing to sit examinations. There was a sports field inside the camp, besides ample facilities for outdoor games on Sundays at most *Arbeitskommandos*. A monthly cyclostyled stalag newspaper, the *Pow Wow*, published administrative instructions and information regarding Red Cross supplies in addition to topical articles, and the chaplains joined in the publication of the equivalent of a parish magazine. Both publications tried to help prisoners

---

[1] *Disciplinaire*, a prisoner who had escaped or committed some other offence warranting a jail sentence. He was usually sent to a special *Arbeitskommando* (See p. 137).
[2] The terms were that the chaplain would confine himself to the reading of one sermon previously vetted by the German censorship and one prayer; and that he would go immediately the religious service was completed without having spoken to the men before or after.
[3] Altogether some 27 such prisoners of war were concealed at various times in Stalag XVIIIA.

through the uncertainties and anxieties which succeeded elation over the Allied landings in Europe. On 19 December bombing of the stalag by Allied planes destroyed several barracks and killed a hundred prisoners. Whereas working parties threatened by bombing 'just made for the hills with the guards',[1] some of those in the stalag, in a kind of trapped panic, made a 'mad rush' for the slit trenches, in a manner which recalled to one eye-witness similar rushes for scraps of food in the early days at Marburg.

A majority of the men in the *Arbeitskommandos* in southern Austria had hitherto been engaged on farm work, but in 1944 the number used on industrial undertakings rose to 60 per cent: hydro-electric construction at Lavamünd and Unterdrauberg, quarrying at Trofaiac, road construction at Waldenstein and Egydi, railway work at St. Veit, Gross Reifling and Selzstal. Most men knew better than to refuse to do work permitted under the Geneva Convention. Such refusals had in the past produced savage sentences of three or four years at a military prison. A whole working party which refused to parade because an overseer had broken his promise of an extra day off was cleared out of its billet with rifle butts and police dogs. On the other hand, a party which made a firm stand against loading a tank onto a railway truck had its appeal upheld by a German officer. In general men found it better, where there was no legitimate ground for refusing to work, to loaf on the job, though this also was sometimes punished.

A good number of men attempted minor sabotage: breaking picks and shovels, putting sand in the oil-wells of railway trucks, inserting lighted cigarettes in truck-loads of hay. It was possible to get away with these. But anything more serious, such as throwing a hammer into a stone-crusher, was severely repressed by a heavy prison sentence; and one man who was caught jumping on a shovel handle received three years' imprisonment. It is impossible not to respect the spirit and courage of the men who thus defied their captors. But many prisoners held the same view as a successful escaper, who wrote that destroying picks and shovels was 'not worth the candle'. There certainly does not seem to be evidence that such minor, unorganised acts of sabotage as could be carried out by most prisoners of war had a sufficient effect on the German war effort to warrant their consideration as a duty incumbent on all. Oddly enough, sexual intercourse with German women was punished just as severely. It may have been regarded as an attempt at temporary sabotage of the German female labour force, or as permanent sabotage of the Nazi plan for a nation of pure 'Nordic' strain.

---

[1] From a prisoner's letter home.

Some of the *Arbeitskommandos* were large enough to be organised as sub-centres for the smaller parties in their neighbourhood; there were 400 in Klagenfurt and about the same number in the small camps for which it acted as base. By 1944 most Austrian working parties were fairly comfortably housed in barracks or farmhouses, though usually overcrowded. One party which was lucky enough to be billeted in a tourist guesthouse had mattresses, sheets and pillowslips, and three hot baths a week, but it is perhaps unnecessary to say that this was exceptional. Prisoners' rations were the same as those of the civilians who did the same work, but Red Cross supplies and fresh food exchanged for them made up any deficiencies. Though they received no working clothes (except wooden clogs) from their employers, nearly every prisoner had two suits of battle dress towards the end of 1944. Some camps, such as A945GW at Selzstal, were assured of recreation by having their own sports ground, musical instruments and library. But few men were able to concentrate sufficiently in the crowded after-work atmosphere of the billets to do any serious study. One man wrote bitterly that 'after numerous attempts over two years' he had had to give it up.

One of the members of the escape committee at Stalag XVIIIA estimated the number of known attempts to escape from the stalag and its work-camps at three thousand. Many were helped by this committee, which collected information, advised men on escape routes and methods, and where possible and needful provided maps, compasses, money and clothes. Many dozens of others made their own arrangements. Of the routes out—Switzerland, Hungary, Italy, and Yugoslavia—the last proved the most fruitful.

Some reference has been made in earlier chapters to the escapes of one or two prisoners of war from camps in southern Austria and to their subsequent movements south into Yugoslavia. In the spring of 1944 the British military mission in Slovenia reported that there was a 'steady, slow trickle' of escapers from these camps. They were being assisted by friendly Austrians in Graz and Marburg and outlying villages, and on contacting Yugoslav partisans on the general line of the River Drau, they were able to make their way with partisan guides to Slovene headquarters.

One such New Zealander[1] planned his final escape with some others while at the camp in Spittal. They managed to get transferred to *Arbeitskommando* 410L at Spitzendorf, near Graz, and on 8 April opened the doors of the farmhouse in which they were locked at night and went off. Having no civilian clothes, they

---

[1] Pte E. L. Baty (4 Fd Amb), awarded DCM for his attempted escapes. These included three attempts from Stalag XVIIIA: the first through a tunnel, another by climbing over the perimeter wire during a failure of the electric lighting, and a third by crawling through a drain under the perimeter wire. He subsequently walked away from two working camps in Austria before his final successful attempt.

travelled by night and hid up during the day. They improvised a raft to cross the Drau and entered Yugoslavia eight days after their break from camp. Their food exhausted, they stopped at the first house, which proved friendly. Shortly afterwards they met Yugoslav partisans who guided them to a post of the British military mission on 8 May. A month later they were flown to Bari.

In June 1944 the Allied escape organisation began to take an active interest in assisting escapers from camps in southern Austria and evacuating them through Yugoslavia. A post of the Allied mission in northern Slovenia had found that at St. Lorenzen, about 30 miles from Marburg, there was a working camp not well guarded from which a raid by Slovene partisans could free all the prisoners. About a hundred of the latter were transported from Marburg to St. Lorenzen each morning to do railway maintenance work, and returned to their quarters at Marburg in the evening. A British other rank, whose job it was to make hot drinks for the party, made contact with Tito agents in the neighbourhood, with whom he arranged for a small party of prisoners to leave the working party and meet Yugoslav partisans in a nearby wood. At the end of August a party of seven[1] was able to walk away past a sleeping guard at three o'clock in the afternoon, and at nine o'clock the men were eating and dancing with Tito partisans in a newly-captured village, five miles away.

Two British officers in the village arranged with the partisans for the rest of the camp to be abducted on the following day. Next morning the seven escapers returned with some twenty partisans to await the arrival of the work-party by the usual train from Marburg. As soon as work had begun the partisans, to use the phrase of a New Zealand eye-witness, ' swooped down the hillside and disarmed the eighteen guards '. In a short time prisoners, guards, and civilian overseers were being escorted along the route used by the seven escapers the previous evening.

At the first headquarters camp reached particulars were taken of the 132 escaped prisoners[2] for transmission by wireless to England. Progress along the evacuation route south was by no means uneventful, since German patrols were still very active. A night ambush by one such patrol caused the loss of two prisoners and two of the escort. Eventually they reached Semic, which had become a kind of advanced base depot catering for escapers. They were flown across to Bari on 21 September 1944.

---

[1] Including two New Zealanders, Ptes R. C. McKenzie (26 Bn) and G. M. Rendell (24 Bn).
[2] New Zealanders in the party were the two mentioned in the previous footnote and Gnr J. Hoffman (7 A-Tk Regt), Ptes L. W. C. Anderson (24 Bn), P. Hoffman (18 Bn), A. G. Lloyd (25 Bn), C. J. Ratcliffe (19 Bn), P. G. Tapping (25 Bn) and H. Turangi (28 Bn).

Besides those in the party from Marburg, one or two other New Zealanders from camps in Austria reached the Allied lines through Yugoslavia in the summer and autumn of 1944. From an *Arbeitskommando* at Radkersburg attached to Stalag XVIIIA, a New Zealand sapper[1] who had persistently tried to rejoin the Allied forces since his capture in April 1941 finally succeeded. When first rounded up at Kalamata he had managed to get clear, but after being in and out of enemy hands in Greece several times, he was recaptured with a party in a motor boat trying to reach Turkey. He was taken to Italy and was one of the few who escaped through a tunnel from Campo PG 57 in October 1942. Shortly after his transfer to Austria he escaped on 26 October 1943 from a working camp at Graz, and with others made his way into Hungary to join the group of escapers there, of whom some mention has been made elsewhere. Recaptured after the German occupation of Hungary in March 1944, he was injured while jumping from a train and was taken to Breslau hospital. He was later transferred to Austria again, and on 5 September 1944 walked off the farm at Radkersburg on which he was working. Having made contact with some friendly Austrians according to a prearranged plan, he reached a band of partisans north-west of Marburg. He and other escaped prisoners were taken south to reach Semic on 9 October and to Italy a fortnight later.

Two more New Zealanders left their Austrian working camps in September, to reach Ancona in Italy on the same day in late November. One[2] jumped, with two companions, on to a passing train while on the way to work at Graz. In this way the three escapers reached the outskirts of the city and walked on after dark, following the River Mur, which runs almost due south. After four nights' travel they met a Yugoslav who put them in touch with partisan forces. They were taken across the Drau and escorted by partisans to Metlika, whence their evacuation was arranged by the Allied military mission. The other New Zealander[3] to get away in September escaped a week later with six companions from *Arbeitskommando* 88HV near Marburg. After reaching Yugoslavia his evacuation was similarly arranged, and both parties travelled from Zara to Ancona on the same British naval vessel.

In October the escapes from Austria included two more New Zealanders, one[4] from *Arbeitskommando* 65GW at Thiesen and the other[5] from 11010GW at Kühnsdorf. The former was one of

---

[1] Spr R. S. Natusch (6 Fd Coy). For his many attempts and determination to escape he was awarded the MM.
[2] Dvr C. G. Le Comte (Div Amn Coy).
[3] Pte W. Wilson (25 Bn).
[4] Pte W. R. Harper (21 Bn).
[5] Pte R. J. Davidson (21 Bn).

a party who left their place of work near Thiesen, three miles south of Marburg, and hid in a wood. The local women fed them and brought partisan guides to take them south to Metlika. The other New Zealander was a member of an escape party which was also put in touch with the partisans through contact between one of its members and a local girl. The party escaped from the camp latrines while the guards' attention was distracted elsewhere, and made their way to a prearranged rendezvous with partisan guides. Both parties reached Italy from Zara in early December.

Another party containing two New Zealanders[1] got away from Kühnsdorf on 5 November. Shortly after six o'clock in the evening the camp lights were fused and the escapers were able to cut their way through the perimeter wire. An eye-witness account describes how the German camp police dog, well fed for some days before the break, was thrown a bone as the escapers left ' to keep it busy '. An Austrian-Yugoslav girl who worked in the same factory as the prisoners was waiting half a mile from the camp, and she led them to a rendezvous in the woods with two Yugoslav partisan officers. They were guided south to the Allied military mission at Metlika and finally evacuated from Zara in mid-December. These were the last New Zealanders from Austria to reach Allied lines before the end of the year; though several more broke camp in December, they were not able to get through until April of the next year.[2]

From 1941 onwards a few British prisoners had made their way into Hungary after escaping from camps in eastern Austria, some only a few miles from the Hungarian border. At first these men were held in a prison at Siklos, where conditions were bad, but later they were treated as military internees and housed in the Komarom camp for internees, where there were refugees from all the countries of German-occupied Europe. Later still they were given the rights of ' free internees ', corresponding to the status laid down in the Hague Convention for escapers who reach a neutral country, and were accommodated on the estate of a Hungarian count at Szigetvar in the south. They were allowed the freedom of the town of Szigetvar and its neighbourhood to a radius of six miles. By December 1943 there were some twenty British other ranks living there very comfortably and being well looked after, doing nominal work on the estate in return. It was inevitable, however, that in time some of them would become restive under the enforced inactivity. There was some dissatisfaction also among the local Hungarians, who worked long hours but noticed that, although

---

[1] Dvr E. V. Donnelly (ASC), mentioned in despatches for his escapes, and Cpl A. W. Brunet (24 Bn).
[2] Ptes J. C. Emery, W. A. Glasper, R. M. Wallace (all 21 Bn), H. W. H. Drawbridge (20 Bn), K. L. Clark (26 Bn), and Dvr L. F. Stringer (4 Res MT Coy).

the British escapers did not, they always had plenty of money to spend in the local taverns. To avoid this the men were ordered to work outside the estate, but relations with Hungarian employers and other workers were not always without difficulties.

There was in Hungary only one British officer escaper (a South African lieutenant-colonel), who was quartered in Budapest, where he was able to maintain contact with the British authorities. But a New Zealand sapper,[1] who had assumed the rank of captain to assist him in his escape plans, was on his arrival in Budapest sent down to the Szigetvar estate, as it was felt that his assumed rank would assist in maintaining discipline and preventing the occurrence of any incident likely to give the Germans an excuse for interfering. In early 1944 those at Szigetvar were warned that there were German officers in civilian clothes in the neighbourhood, and there is evidence that the Germans did their best to have the privileges accorded to British escapers restricted. In point of fact the Germans had good reasons to be suspicious, for two or three of the escapers had in late January 1944, by arrangement with British military authorities, prepared a landing strip and were ready to operate a system of ground signals for the reception of a British military mission. But its arrival was postponed, and before an attempt to land it could be made the German authorities had decided on the military occupation of Hungary.

This took place on 19 March 1944, and although the Hungarian authorities had given promises of protection for British escapers, they were for the most part not able to carry them out. The British at Szigetvar were taken over by the German troops on the following day; and although Natusch,[2] another New Zealander, and one or two others were able to break from their guards, they were recaptured later. A dozen or so other British escapers[3] (later arrivals) quartered on another estate at Lehervar were however removed to Zugliet prison without the knowledge of the German authorities, the plan being to arrange their escape when opportunity should occur. Later the German authorities heard of them and arranged their transfer to Germany. One or two broke out of the barracks before this happened, among them a New Zealander[4] who, with an

---

[1] Spr Natusch. See p. 384.
[2] He went to Budapest and, after being helped by an English woman living there, posed as a Dutch officer, but was later arrested by the Gestapo and closely questioned in both Budapest and Vienna. He was then sent as a Dutchman to Stalag XVIIA. While being transferred from there to Oflag 67 he jumped from the train, but injured his knee on a piece of iron. When recaptured he claimed his real name, rank and status, was taken to Breslau hospital and later to Stalag XVIIIA, from an *Arbeitskommando* of which he made his final escape.
[3] Including four New Zealanders.
[4] Pte G. E. Park (19 Bn), mentioned in despatches for his efforts to escape.

Englishman, was helped by an organisation in Budapest and contacted the Russians there in January 1945. Having assumed officers' rank, these two reached Debrecen and Bucharest, whence they were flown to Athens and Bari in late February.

The other New Zealander[1] who escaped from the round-up at Szigetvar headed for southern Hungary, but was caught after a few days and put in a camp at Zemun, near Belgrade in Yugoslavia. On 17 April 1944 heavy Allied bombing practically destroyed the camp and he was able to escape through the wire. He was taken by farm-workers to a village held by Yugoslav partisans, and shortly afterwards met an officer of one of the British military missions. He was moved with others through Yugoslav territory to a landing strip and flown to Bari in July.

Many of those escapers who were picked up in Austria as a result of border patrol activity or the suspicions of civilians spent some time, after their interrogation at Landek, at Stalag XVIIIC at Markt Pongau. The camp had on its strength between six and nine hundred British prisoners, mostly men from Italy and including about a hundred New Zealanders. They were not allowed to share the excellent theatre and sports ground of the French, and in spite of the Red Cross relief supplies, the general conditions and atmosphere of their section of the camp remained bad. One recaptured New Zealander records that it was a 'depressing place' and that the guards were 'tough'. A New Zealand medical officer observes that the huts were 'big, dark and damp', that the atmosphere 'got the men down', and that the camp 'stank always'. Some two to three hundred NCOs from Spittal who had refused to work were brought there in June 1944 in an effort to make them change their minds. They were crowded into one hut, segregated from the rest of the camp, and kept there under most unhealthy conditions. Though it was over seven months before any improvements were made, these men were reported as 'very cheerful' and they stuck it out to the end of the war. It was not surprising that most of the other ranks who were liable for work were only too keen to get out from such a camp to a working party. The first of them left in January 1944 and their conditions were reported as infinitely better. A Red Cross inspector reporting on Markt Pongau in October 1944 wrote that the camp made an 'extremely unfavourable impression.'

Among the prisoners of many nationalities assembled in Stalag VIIA at Moosburg, there had been New Zealanders since the time when those captured in the Greek campaign of 1941 had first reached Bavaria. New Zealanders had also formed a proportion of the thousands which had poured through the camp in late 1943

---

[1] Pte H. A. Hoare (23 Bn), awarded MM for his persistent efforts to escape.

en route from Italy to camps farther north. The majority had moved on, but for various reasons odd ones had stayed. These, together with airmen occasionally brought down in the district, escapers recaptured in Italy, and newly-captured soldiers from the Italian battlefront, brought the number of New Zealanders at Moosburg by the end of 1944 to over two hundred. About half the British prisoners on the camp strength were out working at *Arbeitskommandos*. Like the working parties from Markt Pongau, some were employed on digging and constructing air-raid shelters, others on a variety of jobs similar to those on which prisoners were used in Silesia and Austria. Conditions for the men were very much the same too. A large number of those who had been in other ranks' camps in Italy expressed their preference for the treatment they received in Germany.

Further north in Bavaria, the non-working British NCOs in Stalag 383 at Hohenfels were launched on a programme of educational and recreational activity which became one of the most extensive in Germany. In this they were greatly helped by material supplied under the scheme carried out by the World Alliance of YMCAs, and in particular by the interest taken in the camp by the delegate of the Swedish YMCA.[1] Among the 5000 or so NCOs there at the beginning of 1944, 330 of them New Zealanders, there was sufficient variety of talent and sufficient manpower to initiate and keep going almost every possible kind of camp activity. The 400 huts of the camp were organised into blocks and companies, each with its representative. The quartermastering and disciplinary side of the camp was run by the senior warrant officer, the welfare and other activities by an elected man-of-confidence. The German commandant was described as a 'very fair man', and there is ample evidence that the prisoners were given every opportunity to employ their leisure time profitably and pleasantly. Apart from the sports, theatricals, and other amenities common to many camps, there was a swimming pool in which over 200 men qualified for Royal Lifesaving Society certificates. In winter it became ice-bound, and with a hundred pairs of skates from the Swedish Red Cross the prisoners turned it into a skating rink. There were bee colonies and practical instruction in apiculture, one New Zealander passing the diplomas for the British Bee-keeping Society. An old stable was converted by the prisoners into a school to accommodate 2000, with separate classrooms and a reading room.

Where materials could not be obtained legitimately they could be purchased with British cigarettes on the black market by German guards. Many wireless-set parts, cameras, watches, and other

---

[1] Mr Erik Berg.

articles thus found their way inside Stalag 383, for the purchasing power of British and American cigarettes in the cities of Nazi Germany was in 1944 very considerable. The camp had not one but many radios. There were two well-equipped theatres and 15 varied music groups and orchestras. Stage shows like the 'Mikado' could run for three weeks. There was every conceivable kind of sporting event. Anzac Day began with a dawn service, followed on with a march past, and finished with a smoke concert. There were 22 exchange marts in operation, selling everything from a powder-puff to a set of false teeth. The latter might be thought to command a limited market but apparently, after remodelling, satisfied its purchaser. Some men had vegetable gardens; others kept rabbits. A New Zealander wrote, 'Nora has come along with her third litter'; and later, 'Knocked off five yesterday and had the best dinner in four years.' For those who did not care for set occupations or educational courses there was a library of over ten thousand books. One prisoner casually remarked in a letter, 'I think I've gone through most', and as an afterthought added (perhaps to avoid being thought ungrateful), 'but good books can always be re-read.' There is no doubt that there was ample scope in Stalag 383 for reading, extensive as well as intensive. One of the Swedish delegates who visited the camp on the occasion of the centenary of the YMCA in July 1944 stated that he had seen no better camp in Germany. In the latter part of 1944 Hohenfels experienced the food shortage and the attention from German security personnel common in other camps, and perhaps more mud than some; but it was better catered for than most in the way of materials and organised activities that could take men's minds off hunger and cold.

Two to three hundred New Zealanders remained during 1944 at camps in Saxony and on the northern fringe of Sudetenland. Most of them were prisoners who had come north from Italy; some were escapers who had been recaptured there after months in the hills or plains. They found well organised camps with ample supplies of Red Cross material, comfortable indeed after a miserable winter loose in Italy. Some described the conditions as the best they had experienced since their capture. There were vast numbers of men at these camps in *Wehrkreis* IV; during 1944 it was common for a stalag and its attached *Arbeitskommandos* to have a strength of 25,000 or more. The great majority of the men were at working parties in mines, on roads and railways, in the sugar industry or in a hundred and one different kinds of factories. There was always sufficient labour required in the crowded industrial districts around Leipzig and Dresden to keep this large additional prisoner-of-war population occupied. The mining camps as usual seemed to have worse conditions than the others, and a New Zealand doctor expressed his relief at leaving behind the 'gloom' of such a camp for the task of treating mental cases at a prisoner-of-war hospital. Many of the other working camps were out in the countryside, some 'in wooded hills', and though the hours of work were long, most men at these camps kept very fit and some were the 'heaviest ever'. The majority preferred the environment of the open country to that of a city such as Leipzig, where some were employed clearing up air-raid debris. One New Zealander obtained from Geneva a set of paints to record the landscapes and village churches he saw.

North-west in the region of Hanover, Brunswick, and Magdeburg were the camps attached to Stalags XIA and XIB, which still retained about 300 of the New Zealand prisoners sent north from Italy. Some of these too were recaptured escapers. Like those in *Wehrkreis* IV, these stalags had enormous numbers on their rolls, most of them out at working parties. *Arbeitskommando* 7001 at the steelworks in Halendorf has already been noted as one to which New Zealanders were sent. A prisoner records the work he did there: in winter 'standing in driving snow with a brush broom keeping electric points free of snow all day'; in summer 'pushing a railway line nearer to the edge of a slag heap'. This sounds very monotonous work, but the camp had a library, a concert hall where films were shown, and a sports field. There was less pleasant relief from monotony on the several occasions when the camp was bombed.

Not all the working parties in *Wehrkreis* XI had such dreary tasks. A few score New Zealanders were at *Arbeitskommando* 7005 at Salzgitter, felling trees, building a dam, and keeping roads in order. The hours were long, but as one man points out, it was nearly all pick-and-shovel work and 'mostly leaning'. There were others working in joinery and other kinds of factories, in quarries, and in sawmills. One of those at a rubber factory records how in August they were in 'very high spirits' and that their 'cheery faces and singing at work [had] become infectious'. There was usually some delay in the arrival of Red Cross supplies after a new working camp was established, but once the men received these regularly they were much happier there than in the stalags.

There were sixty or seventy New Zealanders in one or other of the forts[1] of Stalag XXA at Thorn, in Poland, until the camp was removed from the path of the Russian advance. Prisoners frequently went to Stalag XXA after completing a sentence at Graudenz military prison. The surrounding *Arbeitskommandos* employed prisoners mostly on farms, but also on forestry work, on the roads

---

[1] Fort VIII contained working other ranks and NCOs. Fort XIV was the camp infirmary. Fort XV contained over 400 non-working NCOs. Fort XVI held 40-odd prisoners undergoing punishment. New Zealanders were nearly all in Fort VIII.

and in factories. The stalag was one of the oldest established camps and was very efficiently run. Its escape organisation had been responsible for the first escape of a New Zealand officer[1] from Germany.

He had been recaptured after a previous attempt from Stalag XVIIIA/Z at Spittal-on-the-Drau only a fortnight earlier. On his transfer to Stalag XXA he and another British officer were given priority to escape, civilian clothes were arranged for them, and they were smuggled out as other ranks on 9 October 1943 to a working party at a rabbit farm. From there they and two other ranks were driven in a lorry to Bromberg, where a Polish factory manager put them up for the night and arranged their onward journey. They travelled by a closed van to Danzig and were each escorted by a Polish helper to a safe house in Gdynia. There they were smuggled onto a Swedish ship while she was loading coal. When she reached Sweden on 20 October they were handed over to the police, and were later looked after by the British Consul at Stockholm.

A New Zealander[2] escaped from a working party about two miles from Thorn in June 1944. He was able to walk past the guards in civilian clothes unnoticed. Moving mostly at night he made for Kutno, having given up the idea of making for Gdynia, where he had been recaptured on a previous attempt. After two weeks in Kutno and a longer wait outside it until the Polish rebellion in Warsaw was over, he entered the ruined city in October. He then moved south across the frozen Vistula, dodging German patrols, and met up with Russian forces in December not far from Praga. He was sent on to Lublin and eventually got out through Odessa four months later. His experiences are similar to those of a number of prisoners who made their escape to the Russian lines.

The setting up of a special camp for British non-working NCOs, Stalag 383, at Hohenfels in Bavaria in September 1942 has already been described. At the beginning of March 1944 the German authorities opened another such camp two miles from Thorn, to be known as Stalag 357. To it went British NCOs from stalags in various parts of Germany and Austria, but mostly from Stalag 344 at Lamsdorf. When the first drafts arrived the new camp was still partly under construction, and the wooden barracks that were up were overcrowded. But the camp had adequate bedding, lighting, heating and other facilities, a large sports field, and ample space between the barracks. Most of the NCOs were glad to be there after the conditions under which they had lived in other stalags.

---

[1] Capt C. N. Armstrong (22 Bn), awarded a bar to his MC for his attempts to escape. See p. 210 for account of his first attempt.
[2] Dvr A. G. Bloomfield (Div Pet Coy).

A New Zealander wrote that after a long train journey they went into a 'brand new NCOs' camp' where they could 'live more like soldiers'; another wrote that compared with his last camp he was 'really well off'.

For a while the camp held a thousand or so, but at the beginning of July it was enlarged by the formation of a further compound made necessary by the arrival of 3000 Air Force NCOs from Heydekrug. Some old army barracks were taken over, but they were insufficiently lit and had no heating, and the water supply in the new compound was bad. The camp was not adequate for the large numbers it now contained, but shortage of building materials slowed up the erection of the new barracks necessary to complete the accommodation. It was never completed, for the following month the whole camp was moved west to Oerbke, near Fallingbostel, where quarters previously occupied by Stalag 355 were taken over.

The German move to establish better camps for non-working British NCOs seems to have been part of a policy agreed on by the Wehrmacht and the German Foreign Office. Contented prisoners were far less likely to try to escape or give trouble than those for whom captivity involved continual hunger and boredom. Moreover it might be useful in the post-war world for Germany to have the friendship of these thousands of British who had the opportunity of seeing her at first hand. It was not practicable to feed them properly, but their own people were clearly too soft-hearted to allow them to starve. What could be done was to see that camp commandants gave them facilities for using their leisure so that they did not have time to think out trouble, and to appoint 'welfare' officers to some of the camps to encourage and assist such recreational activities. Several welfare officers were appointed to oflags in the autumn of 1943. Often they were secondary school masters given the rank of *Sonderführer* in the Wehrmacht; but later in 1944 they were civilian appointees of the German Foreign Office attached to the Wehrmacht staff of the camp. They obtained improvements in the amenities of the camps they were at: better walks, outdoor sketching parties, cinema shows, including some visits to town cinemas, costumes for dramatic shows, facilities for getting photographs of camp groups or theatre shows. The specific requests to which they gave effect do not appear to have amounted to very much, but they may have had a considerable influence on the general attitude of camp commandants.

German propaganda could obviously no longer dwell on British defeats, and it turned from a vain effort to make British prisoners see the faults of their own countries to a plea for British co-operation with Germany (that is, 'Europe'), more especially against the menace of Russian Communism. In 1944 *The Camp* still contained an occasional article designed to show that Britain's divorce rate was high and her birthrate low, but more to show that Britain was backing a wrong horse in fighting against Germany. From early 1942 a series of articles in this paper entitled 'The German Point of View' had endeavoured to prove what reasonable and civilised people the Germans were, in contrast to the British and other peoples they were fighting. But in 1944 the editorial staff seemed to be coming round more and more to the opinion that in their better moments the British were not so much impossible as misguided. In December there appeared an article on the British Navy, in January 1945 a description of how a mayor in Britain shook hands with a German prisoner, and in February 1945 a statement by repatriated German prisoners of war that 'the attitude of British camp officers and guards left nothing to be desired'. But if all this was clumsy enough not to deceive anybody, how much more so was the attempt in May 1944, and afterwards, to form a 'Free British Corps' to fight against the Russians? The circular[1] sent to prisoner-of-war camps, though patently false, was in unusually good English, but the time of launching the appeal could scarcely have been worse judged and the response was deservedly negligible.

A much more subtle idea was the setting up of 'holiday camps' and insistence that a quota of men from each camp should go to them. The 'holiday camp' at Genshagen, near Berlin, for other ranks was opened in June 1943 'to promote a better feeling between the opposing nations when the war is over'.[2] Not only was it to give men 'a better outlook' and 'relaxation from the tragedies of war' by 'educational, physical and social activities', but it was to be 'a spiritual centre where the men could be brought closer to Him

---

[1] The circular read as follows:

As a result of repeated applications from British subjects from all parts of the world wishing to take part in the common European struggle against Bolshevism, authorisation has recently been given for the creation of a British Volunteer unit. The British Free Corps publishes herewith the following short statement of the aims and principles of the unit.

1/ The British Free Corps is a thoroughly British volunteer unit conceived and created by British subjects from all parts of the Empire who have taken up arms and pledged their lives in the common European struggle against Soviet Russia.

2/ The British Free Corps condemns the war with Germany and the sacrifice of British blood in the interests of Jewry and International Finance, and regards this conflict as a fundamental betrayal of the British people and British Imperial interests.

3/ The British Free Corps desires the establishment of peace in Europe, the development of close friendly relations between England and Germany, and the encouragement of mutual understanding and collaboration between the two great Germanic peoples.

4/ The British Free Corps will neither make war against Britain or the British Crown, nor support any action or policy detrimental to the interests of the British.

Published by the British Free Corps.

[2] Quoted from an article which appeared in *The Camp* for 20 February 1944.

who alone can bring peace to this suffering world'.[1] Those running the camp had the good sense not to attempt any direct propaganda in it. There were 200 prisoners in each group and they were kept in the camp for four weeks. Apart from the entertainment provided by the prisoners themselves, they had music by German instrumentalists and opera singers, films, lectures, outings to Potsdam, facilities for sports, for indoor games and for dancing. Many of the men chosen were those who had been working in mines or on other unpleasant jobs for a long period, and it is not surprising that some at least found it an enjoyable break.

A similar camp for officers was set up in Berlin about the same time, and officers were detailed by the Germans to go to it. In 1944 the camp was moved to a schloss at Steinburg in Bavaria, near Straubing on the Danube, and though the Germans still insisted that a certain quota from each camp should attend, its selection was left to the senior British officer in consultation with the camp medical officer. In some oflags the choice was made from among those whose health would benefit from the change, or those whose long hours of work at some camp administrative task had earned them a rest. Almost every camp quota included one officer primed with information, for Steinburg became of great value to camps as a clearing house for news, intelligence, and ideas.

The camp at Steinburg was on the fringe of the Bavarian forest, a region of pine-clad hills and rich valleys dotted with neat, half-timbered villages clustered round onion-shaped church steeples. Ideal walks were easily accessible in this area, and inmates could stroll at any time in the forest meadows adjacent to the Schloss. There was accommodation for about forty, ten to a large bedroom, together with a large dining room and a comfortable reading room. An officer sums up the atmosphere thus:

. . . no wire, pleasant rooms, spring beds, soft mattresses, no petty restrictions, all the walks you want with small parties led by guides rather than surrounded by guards. . . .[2]

It goes without saying that the camp was amply supplied with Red Cross food, and that the cooking staff was efficient. The interpreters were men of university education. There was a good library, in which the Germans had however been unable to resist the temptation of sprinkling a few propaganda volumes for the gullible. More subtle was the inclusion in the staff of first-class photographers, from whom photographs were readily available to send home, and the plying of the prisoners with a liberal supply of letter forms.

Whatever efforts the German Foreign Office might make at the eleventh hour, the activities of the Abwehr and more particularly of

---
[1] *The Camp*, 20 February 1944.
[2] From the letter home of a New Zealand officer written at the Steinburg camp.

the Gestapo in prisoner-of-war camps made the creation of goodwill towards Germany an uphill task. The year 1944 saw them more active than ever. The experiences of escapers who fell into the hands of the Gestapo were bad, but so were the experiences of those who had the ill fortune to spend a period in the military prisons at Torgau and Graudenz.

Fort Zinna at Torgau, near Leipzig, was for the first years of the war the detention barracks to which British prisoners were sent after court-martial sentence for what the Germans considered serious offences: refusal to work, sabotage, assaulting a guard, sexual intercourse with a German woman. In this group of forbidding buildings prisoners of all nationalities served their sentences along with German soldiers, but anything up to a hundred British were kept in a separate building. Work gangs went from the prison to do navvying, harvesting, unloading railway trucks, and the other tasks of normal working parties. The food was insufficient and of poor quality and no Red Cross supplies of any kind were permitted. There were no books or any other kind of recreational material. The slightest breach of the prison regulations or timetable was punished with the utmost severity, on occasions by beating up and shackling. Prisoners under 'arrest' were crowded several into a small cell, where they lived on bread and water, with two blankets each and no beds or other bedding. A New Zealander who was there for several months mentions that everyone was 'under great nervous strain'.

The conditions at the prison forced men to take desperate measures to get away. Some inflicted wounds on themselves in order to be taken to hospital. A number who were able to escape from working parties took care to travel as far as they could from Torgau and to give a false name and number on recapture. Six New Zealanders had been sentenced, along with others, on 26 April 1942 to four years in this prison for refusing to work at an Austrian *Arbeitskommando*. Five of them got away in the same year and spent the rest of the war under assumed names in other prisoner-of-war camps. Two[1] were able to masquerade as Canadian corporals captured at Dieppe, and on recapture were taken to Lamsdorf. Three[2] were returned to Stalag XVIIIA under assumed names, one remaining undisturbed by the Germans, the other two being hidden until the hue and cry died down and then living on in the stalag like the other prisoners. The sixth, one of three who had made a dash from a moored barge on the Elbe while the guard

---
[1] L-Bdr T. A. Hitchens (7 A-Tk Regt) and Gnr E. C. Frederic (NZA).
[2] Ptes A. W. Birchall and J. A. Guilliard (19 Bn) and J. S. Hamilton (18 Bn). The unlucky member of the party was Pte F. J. Spry (19 Bn).

slept, fell exhausted and was recaptured at the edge of the wood which the other two were able to reach and so conceal themselves.

At the end of 1942 British prisoners were transferred from Torgau to another detention barracks at Graudenz, near Thorn. A high outer wall enclosed four stone buildings surrounding a large centre courtyard. Here in the winter of 1942–43 men were sometimes rushed out on parade without boots and with insufficient clothing. Between two and three hundred British prisoners were housed in small cells with bad ventilation and only the meagre light from a small high window. In the early stages many of the cells appear to have been allowed to remain verminous, and there were no proper latrines for the prisoners. Some officers were kept in solitary confinement. There was some brutal treatment of a similar kind to that at Torgau, and the same poor soup and bread diet. A New Zealand medical officer stated that after three months at Torgau, followed by another three and a half at Graudenz, he had lost four stone in weight and developed scurvy. As a result of representations to the German authorities conditions gradually improved, and by March 1944 the prisoners were permitted some Red Cross food, which was cooked by one of their number under German supervision. By the middle of the year many of the prisoners were digging air-raid shelters, and the allowance of Red Cross parcels was raised to four a month. Though discipline at the camp remained severe, the menace of serious malnutrition was thus removed.

Recaptured escapers were not usually sent to a military prison unless some other charge could be brought against them, such as sabotage or assault. But many of those officers who had come to be regarded by the Germans as 'habitual' escapers or as a source of continual trouble were sent to Oflag IVC at Colditz, not far from Leipzig in Saxony. This was not supposed to be a punishment camp, but merely one that differed from others only in being escape-proof. In point of fact conditions were extremely bad and, in spite of the heavy guard, there were no fewer than 21 successful escapes, eleven by British prisoners, to Allied or neutral territory, besides numerous other breaks from the camp. Several hundred prisoners of all three services of various Allied countries were housed in this ugly, old, castle-like group of stone buildings situated on a hill overlooking the River Mulde. These buildings were said to date back four centuries and to have been once used by a king of Poland as a hunting lodge. The camp was cold and ill-lit, had a poor water supply, primitive lavatories, and only a small cobbled courtyard for exercise. It had originally held French, Belgians, and Dutch and had been grossly overcrowded; but by the end of 1943 the camp population was mainly British.

In 1944 there were roughly 200 British, including half a dozen or so New Zealanders at various times.[1] In that year the German authorities collected at Colditz a number of prisoner relatives of highly placed persons in both Britain and the United States, presumably as a valuable bargaining counter if the German situation became desperate. They received the same treatment as the others; throughout the history of the camp this treatment had varied, even in the moderate phrasing of inspectors, from 'strict' to 'harsh'. By 1944 the camp had a library and a small orchestra, and the privilege of using a small nearby sports field; but on the slightest excuse all privileges and facilities for recreation were suspended. There was no let-up on attempts to escape, nor on the pressure brought by the senior officer of the camp on the German commandant. But such conditions are wearing; by October 1944 it was reported that sickness had increased and that men were suffering from 'nerves', insomnia, and dyspepsia.

In the latter half of 1943 and early 1944, the softening up of Germany by strategic bombing was well under way and Berlin was receiving some of its heaviest raids. Of the armadas of massed aircraft that attacked their cities, the Germans' flak and fighters were still able to exact a considerable toll. Among those who were able to bale out safely but fell into enemy hands were another 60-odd New Zealanders. There is almost no limit to the fantastic variations in circumstances under which airmen made their landings and were captured. Those of a New Zealand warrant officer shot down over Berlin are quoted as being less exceptional than some:

I landed on a rooftop in Berlin. I climbed down through the skylight and found the building apparently empty and the doors all locked. I sat on the stairs. One half of the building was blazing from incendiaries. At the finish of the raid, which was about half an hour after I landed, I went to the front door which was not locked. At that moment, the police arrived in company with a civilian and I was marched off to the police station where I spent the rest of the night.[2]

As the raids became more severe in the early autumn, civilian loss of life and property made captured airmen an object of hatred among the population. German newspapers fostered it by headlines and articles on the *Terrorflieger* and *Luftgangster* who 'murdered' their relatives and destroyed their possessions. There were cases of savage ill-treatment of airmen by civilians half-crazed with grief and shock, and it became necessary for them to be protected by police or troops.

---

[1] The only New Zealand combatant officer to go there was Capt C. H. Upham, VC and bar (20 Bn), who was mentioned in despatches for his attempts to escape in Italy and Germany.
[2] From his interrogation report.

In early 1944 the bombing of strategic centres built up to a climax at the time of the intense pounding of the Atlantic defences before the Normandy invasion. New Zealanders took part in the preparation for the landing, as well as in the support of land operations that followed, and had a share of the resulting casualties. At the end of the year another 90 had become prisoners and the total of our airmen in German hands was some five hundred. The difference in the type of aircraft and crew used in close co-operation with a land offensive is reflected in these casualties. Whereas total losses in prisoners had hitherto been in the rough proportion of one officer to two other ranks, in those for 1944 the proportion was reversed; from August to the end of that year the losses were 29 officers and only two other ranks. During 1944 the extension of the strategic bombing to Eastern Europe was responsible for the internment of a number of Commonwealth airmen in Roumania. But they were all liberated at the end of August by the Russian advance and immediately evacuated by air.

Auswertestelle West remained solely responsible for the interrogation of the additional thousands of Allied airmen taken prisoner in Europe, as well as those flown north from the Italian front. It was located at Oberursel until the end of the war, taking over the old quarters of the transit camp Dulag Luft when the latter was transferred in 1943 to a *Palmengarten*[1] in Frankfurt-on-Main. Modern listening equipment was installed in 50 of the 200 small cells it then contained, which enabled even whispered conversation to be heard if necessary and recorded on magnetic strip. By 1944 it had a staff of over 300, including 70 officers, which dealt every month with an average of 2000 prisoners and a peak of 3000 mixed airmen and paratroops in July. There were 55 full-time interrogators, carefully selected as native Germans of liberal background who had spent part of their lives in Britain or the United States, for violent Nazis were not a success at interrogation. Even so it became necessary to open branch offices in Holland, in western and northern France, and in Verona in Italy for the interrogation of the great majority of the airmen captured in these areas, only prisoners of special technical interest being sent to Oberursel.

The journey to the place of interrogation was usually by train in a carriage with civilians, from whom abuse (if nothing more) was common in spite of the endeavours of the guards. Sometimes both prisoners and their guards were attacked by infuriated civilians; one German local defence platoon boasted that not a single captured airman it had escorted had been killed or even injured. In October

---

[1] Public garden.

1944 a Luftwaffe order recommended that where possible such prisoners must be transported in closed vehicles if it was necessary to pass through parts of cities which had been bombed or attacked a short time previously. This was not necessarily as humane as it sounds, since it was in the interest of the Intelligence Branch of the Luftwaffe that newly-captured airmen should reach an interrogation centre with the fewest possible contacts in the shortest possible time. A German interrogator disguised in British or United States uniform and under guard was often put with prisoners on transport from the last railway station to the interrogation centre, to try to find out their unit numbers and other preliminary data, or to get an idea of their political views and general morale.

Interrogation methods reached a high standard of efficiency. On the one hand, in order to wrest information from a prisoner, his physical discomforts were studiously increased: 'lack of movement in his cell, of fresh air, of facilities for personal hygiene, of something to smoke, of adequate meals'. This was backed up over a period of some days by 'threats... sternness... sarcasm... even cynicism', and his 'resistance forced down by exhaustive interrogation.' On the other hand, in order to get the prisoner 'off his guard', he was encouraged to relax over a 'fully laden tea or supper table', 'in soft, deep club chairs', with cigarettes and even some alcohol, or on 'a short walk along a pleasant countryside'. 'A free conversation is started', 'friendly but not too friendly', and there are introduced 'jokes and humour', a 'sympathetic inquiry after his wounds' or his family, together with some apparent flattery.[1] In early 1944 *Auswertestelle West* had by virtue of its efficient organisation and its disregard of the Geneva Convention become a matter of serious concern to the Allied cause. The 'sweat-box' methods of overheating cells was the subject of strong protest through the Protecting Power to the German Government; and though cells were still being overheated (apparently deliberately) in June 1944, from then on it was usually stopped as soon as a prisoner protested.

The growth of Allied escape and evasion organisations and the mass breakouts, culminating in that from Stalag Luft III in March 1944, gave the German SS an excuse to interfere in the guarding of prisoners of war in transit from a police station to *Auswertestelle West*. Moreover the SS representative for the area in which the centre was situated made the 'good treatment' of prisoners at Oberursel a pretext for alleging anti-Nazi tendencies among the interrogation staff. The Luftwaffe was thus forced to agree to the

---

[1] Quoted from the report on *Auswertestelle West* by the German commandant in 1944.

posting of Gestapo personnel there, officially to assist in interrogation on political and economic affairs but really to check up on the staff. The latter were not slow to show their resentment: Gestapo interrogators received no co-operation from the staff and the commandant refused to have them in the Mess. They agreed to live in a separate building; but they did their interrogation in a portion of the premises of the centre known as 'the Shelter' and were able to insist that a proportion of all prisoners should be handed over to them for examination. Not long after their arrival they brought charges against some of the German officers of the centre, but these were refuted. The Gestapo men posted to Oberursel were poor linguists, and their methods varied between straight bullying and the provision of a luxurious hunting lodge outside Frankfurt for senior officer prisoners, with plenty of good food and liquor. They manacled one important British airman and questioned him for three weeks without getting any clue as to his mission.

As for the gleaning of information on the political and economic situation, the commandant of *Auswertestelle West* deplored the complete ignorance of most airmen on these subjects. In his experience airmen prisoners did not have any 'political knowledge superior to that of an interested newspaper reader'. Moreover, their reading of the newspapers was, he found, in the following order: '. . . First the puzzle corner, then the sports news, then the home news, and finally, if at all, the news from the various theatres of war and the news on international politics'. Whether it was due to the ignorance or the good security of airmen prisoners, the interrogators at *Auswertestelle West* do not seem to have extracted much political or economic information of value. If the regular staff had only very limited success, it is doubtful whether the Gestapo achieved anything at all. But their reputation for torture and brutality was such that most prisoners took care not to give them any excuse for using their well-known methods or for further delaying their being 'dumped' into the dulag.

In 1943 it was found that the compound at Oberursel was too small to act as a holding centre for prisoners after interrogation. Dulag Luft was therefore transferred in September from Oberursel to a new site adjacent to the *Palmengarten* in the centre of Frankfurt-on-Main. When the transfer took place the construction of a new camp was not complete, but those barracks that were finished were well heated and lit and reasonably comfortable. In some respects the camp was considered excellent; it had good washing and toilet facilities, a good kitchen, enough Red Cross food on hand for 20 months, extra 'fortifying' German rations, and good medical treatment. But, whereas Oberursel was in a safe location 15 miles out in the countryside, the new camp was considered by the International Red Cross Committee sufficiently liable to danger from air attack to contravene part of Article 9 of the Geneva Convention.[1] In spite of the air-raid shelter trenches with which the camp was provided, the British Government made an official complaint through the Protecting Power in December 1943 against the holding of prisoners in this camp.

A few months later, in the spring of 1944, a heavy bombing attack on Frankfurt destroyed the camp at the *Palmengarten,* and the prisoners had to be transferred to a location north of Frankfurt at Wetzlar-Klostenwald, the site of a former German Army camp in process of reconstruction. While awaiting new barracks prisoners were accommodated in tents. There was space in these for over 300, but as men seldom remained longer than eight days the new camp was rarely overcrowded. The only prisoners who had beds, however, were the permanent staff of the camp, those in transit sleeping on palliasses on the ground. By the middle of the year barracks had been completed to hold nearly 800 and most of the normal camp facilities were available. A library and other recreational amenities took longer to build up.

From late 1943 onwards officers went from Dulag Luft to Stalag Luft I at Barth or to Stalag Luft III at Sagan, and NCOs went to Stalag 344 at Lamsdorf, to Stalag IVB at Mühlberg, or to a new camp (Stalag Luft VI) at Heydekrug in East Prussia. In the latter half of 1944 some NCOs went to Stalag 357 at Fallingbostel, where some of the personnel from Heydekrug had been evacuated, and others to the newly formed Stalag Luft VII at Bankau, in Silesia.

Stalag Luft III had become the main prisoner-of-war camp for Air Force officers in Germany. Its East and North compounds continued to hold British officers, and by July 1943 United States officers had occupied the Centre compound, from which the NCOs had been transferred to Heydekrug. A few of the NCOs who had volunteered to remain as orderlies were moved in October to a newly-opened British compound at Belaria, three miles away, which had been established as an overflow from the main camp. This had been a training camp for German troops and was situated in the same pine forest near the town of Sagan as the other compounds of Stalag Luft III. By the end of the summer of 1944 there were some 3000 British officers in Stalag Luft III, including 152 New Zealanders, and the intake of the Belaria compound had risen to 300 prisoners a week.

The German authorities had taken some trouble to make the quarters in the north compound comfortable. Barracks were divided

---

[1] ' No prisoner may at any time be sent to an area where he would be exposed to the fire of the fighting zone. . . .'

into light, airy, separate rooms, each holding six to eight prisoners in two-tier beds. A theatre to hold 350 was built in nine months, a sports field was cleared, and a large educational programme launched. The German commandant encouraged all these activities in the hope of creating a contented camp from which serious thoughts of escape might be eliminated. By contrast the older compounds were the worse for wear: roofs were leaking, windows were broken, lights were bad. Throughout the whole camp neutral inspectors reported an 'intense intellectual life' and excellent health, especially in the summer months, when the small percentage of men in hospital were nearly all recovering from injuries sustained at sport.

Besides a number of individual attempts to escape, tunnelling operations continued in both the east and north compounds. In the former a tunnel dug under cover of the German check parades was completed by mid-March, but its use was temporarily postponed on account of shootings which followed a mass break from the north compound, and indefinitely postponed following the invasion a month or so later. In the north compound three tunnels were begun not long after its occupation by British officers, the work involving a large proportion of those in the compound.[1] One of the tunnels was discovered and one abandoned as a dumping ground for spoil from the other; but the third, undetected owing to the German listening apparatus having been disconnected on 19 December 1943 pending modifications, was completed by 14 March. A detailed plan had been worked out for a mass break of 200 through the tunnel. But on the night of 24–25 March, when it was put into operation, owing to falls of earth only 76 got out before the exit was discovered by one of the German perimeter sentries.

The escape caused not only consternation among the administrative and security staff at Stalag Luft III, but considerable alarm at German military headquarters. At that time the German Armed Forces were suffering reversals on every front, and the German High Command was apprehensive of an uprising among the millions of foreign workers and prisoners of war at that time in Germany. For the same reason the Gestapo had issued an order in early March that prisoners of war (other than British and United States nationals) who escaped from their camps and were recaptured were not to be returned to their camps but were to be shot; the International Red Cross Committee was to be informed afterwards that they had not been recaptured. Since a dozen or so of those who escaped through the Stalag Luft III tunnel were caught heading for Czechoslovakia,

---

[1] Six hundred were involved in the building of 'Harry', the tunnel 336 feet long, through which a successful break was made.

it was suspected that this escape was linked with the various underground movements there.[1] All civilians within a large radius of Sagan were warned of the escape and some 60,000 German Home Guard were called in to assist in apprehending the escapers. The matter was discussed at one of Hitler's conferences with his immediate chiefs, and there is evidence that Keitel was reprimanded for allowing the escape to become possible.[2]

Three of the escapers reached England, a few got to Danzig, the Czech, the Swiss and the Danish borders, but the majority of them were caught within 50 miles of Sagan. After recapture they were put in civilian jails, on the grounds that they were found in civilian-type clothing. They were taken out and interrogated singly. Orders were signed by Himmler and Kaltenbrunner for 50 of them to be shot, and by the middle of April the executions had been carried out by the Gestapo. In every case the victims had been driven to a lonely piece of country, ordered to walk away from the vehicles, and then shot as though in a further attempted escape. A German note to the Protecting Power on 12 June 1944 stated that mass escapes were a danger to public security in Germany, and that therefore special orders to guards were necessary in such cases; and also that weapons had to be used against 50 prisoners who had escaped from Stalag Luft III.[3]

The escape brought a swarm of Gestapo and Wehrmacht to the camp to investigate. As a result the commandant and several officers were relieved of their posts and later court-martialled. A new commandant had the unenviable task of informing the senior British officer of the shootings. The news came as a profound shock to the prisoners. There was considerable anxiety lest the Germans, once their military position became desperate, might decide to abandon any pretence of conformity to the international laws of war. If the punishment for attempted escape was to be shooting, the prisoners' policy in this matter would have to be reconsidered. In the summer of 1944, however, another tunnel was built, but like that in the east compound it was decided not to use it except for emergencies arising out of a sudden ending to the war.

The Air Force NCOs at Stalag Luft I at Barth were transferred to the new NCOs' camp at Heydekrug in November 1943, and the former became, like Stalag Luft III, an officers' camp. There was

---

[1] Oflag VIIIF was moved from its location near the Czechoslovak border for the same reason. See p. 367.
[2] Based on the report of an investigation of the affair over a period of two years by the Provost-Marshal's Department of the RAF.
[3] The victims included three New Zealanders: Flt Lt A. G. Christensen, RNZAF, Fg Off P. P. J. Pohe, RNZAF, and Sqn Ldr J. A. Williams, RAF, all posthumously mentioned in despatches.

little change in the conditions at Barth except that the camp rapidly became and remained very overcrowded. Living quarters were permanently congested and there were interminable queues for water taps. The Germans made unsuccessful efforts to expand the accommodation to cope with the increasing numbers. By the beginning of 1944 there were only some 800 British and United States officers, but the total increased in the course of the year to several thousands, mainly men from the United States and including only a dozen or so New Zealanders. The recreational facilities of Barth bore no comparison to those of older-established camps. Nor were there many in the camp who knew much about the technique of escaping, but numerous individual attempts were made and sixty tunnels were begun. After the invasion began the senior British officer decided, in view of the shootings following the break from Sagan, that there should be no further escape activity. But a tunnel was completed for use in case of emergency.

At the end of April 1943 batches of NCOs from the centre compound at Sagan were being moved to a new camp, Stalag Luft VI, at Heydekrug. These and others from Dulag Luft were joined in October by the NCOs from Barth, and by November 1943 there were 3000 British NCOs in the camp. By March 1944 it had four compounds, with a strength of 5000-odd, including airmen from most Allied countries and over a hundred New Zealanders. The camp was two miles south-east of Heydekrug, a town half-way between Tilsit and Memel in East Prussia. Its single-storied brick barracks were built on a sandy site amid flat, swampy country swept by strong winds. Like most other Air Force camps it became badly overcrowded during 1944, and marquees were being used for supplementary accommodation. Prisoners with records of escaping or other misdemeanours were segregated to a special barrack known as the 'black room'. During the year outdoor sports and educational classes became well organised, and several men refer to Heydekrug as the camp where they experienced the best recreational facilities of their captivity.

A committee controlled all attempts at escape, of which a considerable number were successful in getting out of the camp. But only those who followed the 'escape route' specially organised by the committee were able to reach Allied territory. A warrant officer made his way out of the camp in January 1944, established the necessary contacts and got word back to the camp through a Pole and a friendly German guard. Two RAF warrant officers reached Sweden, one in February and the other in April, before an investigation brought the whole affair to light. In the reprisals which followed two recaptured airmen were executed, as well as those Germans involved in the escapes.

In June 1944 word was received in the camp that all personnel were to be evacuated west, taking with them only what they could carry. One party of 2000 were transported under very bad conditions to Stalag Luft IV at Gross Tychow in Eastern Pomerania. They were taken by train to Liban and there jammed in the holds of a small tramp steamer bound for Sweinemunde. The journey took four days, during which the lack of air, water, and sanitation produced in the holds conditions comparable to those of the ships in which prisoners were transported by the Italians across the Mediterranean or by the Japanese across the seas of the Far East. Another journey in railway cattle-trucks brought them to the Kiefheide railway station, where they were awaited by a heavy escort and police dogs. The guard officer harangued the guard on the subject of Allied 'terror airmen' who had destroyed their towns and killed their wives and children. The last three miles to the camp had to be covered on foot, each man carrying his baggage, and the excited German guards drove the prisoners along at the run. Many straggled or fell exhausted, and some of these were stabbed with bayonets, clubbed with rifle butts, or bitten by dogs.

The second party from Heydekrug, consisting of the remaining 3000, had by comparison an uneventful journey by train to Stalag 357 at Thorn, where they occupied a separate compound in a camp already containing 7000 Army NCOs. The transfer of the whole camp six weeks later to Fallingbostel has already been mentioned. About the same time as the move to Gross Tychow and Thorn, another new camp (Stalag Luft VII) was established at Bankau, near Kreuzberg in Silesia, by the transfer of some NCOs from Dulag Luft. Soon afterwards all those from Stalag VIIA at Moosburg were moved to this camp, and it continued to receive further parties until January 1945.

In the autumn of 1943 the Air Force barracks in Stalag VIIIB at Lamsdorf contained about 2000 NCOs. Although not permitted to volunteer for working parties, many exchanged identities with Army prisoners and reached an *Arbeitskommando* in order to attempt a break. There were more successful escapes by airmen from Stalag VIIIB than from any other Air Force camp in Germany.[1] In June 1943 two Polish RAF sergeants from Lamsdorf had reached France and joined two other escapers to cross the Pyrenees. One of the latter, a New Zealander[2] who had also escaped from Lamsdorf, died of exhaustion in the crossing, but the others reached safety and eventually Allied territory.

---

[1] Eleven got to the United Kingdom or to Allied lines.
[2] Dvr F. G. Williamson (ASC).

In August 1944 a New Zealand warrant officer[1] made a successful escape to Sweden. He had exchanged identities with an Australian private at Stalag Luft III in July 1942 and had been returned to Lamsdorf with a party of orderlies. After several unsuccessful attempts, he made his final break from an *Arbeitskommando* at Olbersdorf on 17 August 1944 and travelled by train to Wismar. He hid aboard a Swedish ship and reached Stockholm at the end of the month.

In 1944 some of the newly captured or recaptured Allied airmen were taken for short periods to one or other of the horrible German concentration camps. Four of those recaptured after the mass break from Stalag Luft III were sent to the Sachsenhausen camp. A group of Commonwealth airmen shot down in June 1944 evaded capture and spent some time with the French resistance movement in an endeavour to get back. They fell into Gestapo hands and were taken to Buchenwald. There they stayed for two months before being transferred to Stalag Luft III.

Conditions in Marlag Nord, the camp for naval prisoners at Westertimke, 33 miles north-east of Bremen, had continually improved since its establishment. A great deal of what had once been a sandy piece of waste had been converted by the prisoners into turf and garden, planted with trees in appropriate places. The bombing of the interrogation centre at Wilhelmshaven in 1942 had caused it to be transferred to Westertimke, where a special building equipped with solitary confinement cells catered for new arrivals in a similar fashion to the Luftwaffe centre at Oberursel. Once clear of the interrogation building, naval men went into a well organised camp where, provided Red Cross supplies were coming in and provided there were no German restrictions on mail and movement consequent on an attempt to escape, treatment was said to be better than in most Army camps. Naval prisoners had a long record of escape activity,[2] and the searches of the camp by German security personnel were always severe. Naval ratings were used by the Germans in the construction of the camps and for a while in farming and forestry work in the neighbourhood. But gradually they were all transferred to Lamsdorf and other stalags.[3] In September 1944 400 civilians from Ilag Giromagny in the south of France took over a number of unoccupied huts adjacent to those of the remaining ratings.

---

[1] W/O G. T. Woodroofe, RNZAF, awarded MM for his escape.
[2] As early as January 1942 a tunnel at Sandbostel equipped with trolleys, lighting, and ventilation had enabled eleven officers and three CPOs to escape.
[3] Only five or six New Zealanders remained in Marlag Nord.

Milag, the Merchant Navy compound half a mile from the Marlag at Westertimke, became very crowded in late 1944.[1] By 1944 Milag contained nationals of 26 different countries, of all ranks from captains of ships to stokers, as well as a few passengers from sunken vessels. Beds and bedding became short and the huts dilapidated; the lighting and fuel supply, which had both always been poor, deteriorated still further. When the pumps for the camp water supply broke down, water had to be carried over half a mile. As one officer in the camp suggested, it demanded unfailing patience and tact on the part of the camp leader to make such a community run smoothly.

A detailed account of the part played by those members of the New Zealand Medical and Dental Corps who were detained in prisoner-of-war camps in Germany belongs properly to the histories of these two corps. It is sufficient to record here that there were in Germany 27 New Zealand medical officers and 359 medical orderlies, 11 New Zealand dental officers and 8 dental orderlies, and to note that their total effort towards the physical care of prisoners of war, spread over various main camps, *Arbeitskommandos,* and hospitals must have been very considerable. There is indeed ample evidence in reports, both by prisoners outside the medical and dental corps and by neutral inspectors, that very many of these men did outstanding work for their fellow captives. Their task was always difficult in that a compromise had to be made between being tactful and being firm with the German authorities, since the latter nearly always removed those who proved unceasingly ' difficult' to a camp or prison where they could no longer professionally help their prisoner comrades. Brief references have already been made to the medical and dental attention available in the sick-bay of a stalag or oflag and to the work of solitary medical officers or orderlies in larger and smaller *Arbeitskommandos.* A number of our prisoners had spells also in German military and civilian hospitals, and some of our protected personnel worked for a time in the prisoner-of-war sections of these hospitals.

Some of these hospitals were set aside entirely for British prisoners of war. The Lazarett at Lamsdorf in *Wehrkreis* VIII, for example, remained so from the time it opened in October 1941, and the large prisoner-of-war population in its neighbourhood kept it fully working. There were a dozen or so medical officers on the staff, including several specialists. In *Wehrkreis* IX the main general and surgical hospital for prisoners was at Obermasfeld, 90 miles south-west of Leipzig. It was well equipped for operating and also possessed a laboratory and dental and X-ray equipment. This was one of the few places where prisoner-of-war patients could receive

---
[1] There were 17 to 19 New Zealand Merchant Navy prisoners there.

full dental treatment and complete dentures where necessary. At Schmorkau in *Wehrkreis* IV a special barrack in the Lazarett was set aside for British patients. In the Lazaretts at Graz and Spittal in Austria and at Freising in Bavaria, there was similarly equipped hospital accommodation for the prisoners of war detained in these areas.

The Lazarett at Cosel, in Silesia, catered for prisoners of several nationalities and the staff contained French and Serbs as well as British. Among the last were several New Zealanders, and a number of our men working at various Silesian *Arbeitskommandos* were treated there. In 1943 it opened a new operating theatre equipped for major surgery, and most of the cases which had formerly to be sent to a nearby German hospital were operated on at the Lazarett. To cope with the increasing numbers in the mining camps of south-east Silesia, a prisoner-of-war hospital was opened at Tost in 1944 in the buildings just vacated by civilian internees. Many of the patients had to sleep on two-tier beds in large wards and, as in many other prisoner-of-war hospitals and sick-bays, had to help with the sweeping, bedmaking, and other light duties.

In the early stages of the war prisoners needing specialist treatment were sent to German hospitals, where they were segregated from the other patients. But the delay in organising repatriation exchanges of sick and wounded men necessitated the transfer of chronic cases elsewhere. For some types of treatment, where the numbers warranted it, specialist prisoner-of-war hospitals were organised. During 1943 the Lazarett at Elsterhorst, near the Elbe north-east of Leipzig, began to collect British tubercular cases from Königswartha and other hospitals. In 1944 it contained about 500 such cases. The hospital was well equipped and staffed and the diet was often enriched by a variety of supplementary delicacies obtained by trading with guards and civilians. Several batches left Elsterhorst for repatriation.

Reference has already been made to the orthopaedic work at Obermasfeld for limbless prisoners; the same hospital also set up a school for the blind. Later both types of patient were removed to Kloster Haina, near Hammelburg, which became the orthopaedic as well as the eye centre for British prisoners of war. A British eye specialist took charge of the eye centre, and a braille school was established at the hospital. Men learned to read and to write braille shorthand, as well as to type and play musical instruments. Many of those in Kloster Haina were repatriated, and the eye centre and school moved to Bad Soden in 1944.

A proposal for a second exchange of sick and wounded and protected personnel had been made to the German Government on

10 December 1943 by the United States and Commonwealth countries. The proposal was to include those from Italy passed there by a Mixed Medical Commission, those omitted from the October 1943 exchange, and all those since selected for repatriation. Although it was learned informally that the Germans were anxious for the exchange to be made, many of their services were disorganised by bombing, and it was not until the end of March that they notified their acceptance. Great care was taken to persuade the Germans to accept a Mediterranean port and not to insist on Gothenburg, without giving a hint of any strategical considerations. By late April an exchange at Barcelona on 17 May had been agreed upon. A number of administrative problems between the United States and Commonwealth governments had to be worked out before the operation took place.

Orders for repatriation came to those in German prisoner-of-war camps in the spring of 1944, when an atmosphere of intense expectation of forthcoming major events prevailed. The prisoners who had missed the exchange of the previous October, a number of others just examined, and some who were brought from Venice on the *Gradisca* made up the four trainloads which left Germany for Marseilles, to go on to Barcelona by sea. The *Gripsholm,* which brought 450-odd Germans from America, collected another 350 at Algiers and reached Barcelona on 17 May. She left two days later with a thousand-odd United States and British repatriates, of whom most of the New Zealanders were disembarked at Algiers. They comprised 52 sick and wounded, among them men of the Navy and Air Force, and 15 medical personnel, including a Merchant Navy doctor. One or two with next-of-kin in the United Kingdom went to Belfast on the *Gripsholm,* and then transhipped to the *Borenquin,* bound for Liverpool.

A little over a month after the invasion an approach was made to the German Government for a further exchange of seriously sick and wounded, surplus protected personnel, and civilians. The last alone were to be exchanged on a numerical basis, but though general agreement had been reached by the middle of August, by the end of the month the Germans were harking back to the idea of numerical equality for the prisoner-of-war exchange also. They declined to give any formal acceptance until they knew the approximate numbers of Germans to be repatriated, and they did not supply the figures of Allied nationals until 2 September.

They had, however, allowed Mixed Medical Commissions to examine prisoners of war and civilians in Germany, and had sent many of the approved cases to collecting centres such as Stalag IVD/Z at Annaburg. There they remained several weeks awaiting the final stages of their journey home. At the beginning of

September they were taken by hospital trains to Sassnitz on the Baltic, and on the 7th in Swedish ferry boats across to Trelleborg. A pleasant two days were spent in transit camps in Gothenburg, where the British Consul and the Swedish Red Cross did everything possible for their comfort. Our own men were looked after by a New Zealand medical officer supplied with gift parcels and other comforts for distribution.

The *Arundel Castle* and the *Drottningholm* had sailed for Gothenburg from the United Kingdom with German repatriates assembled there, and the *Gripsholm* brought others from the United States and Canada, to make a total of some 2100. The exchange took place on 8 September, and the three ships brought back some 2500 Allied prisoners and civilians. Among them were 129 New Zealanders, mostly 2 NZEF personnel, but a few of them RNZAF, Merchant Navy, and civilians. The repatriates received a special welcome at Liverpool. The *Arundel Castle* and the two 'mercy ships' docked to the sound of a military band, and a speech of welcome greeted the men after they had disembarked. A New Zealand party representing the recently formed 2 NZEF Reception Group and various welfare bodies was there to look after the interests of New Zealanders. A large number of our sick and disabled were admitted to English hospitals, and the remainder went to the headquarters of the Reception Group at Hartwell House, Buckinghamshire, before being sent on 28 days' leave. Various New Zealand welfare bodies in England looked after the comfort and other interests of those in hospital. On their discharge they went on to Hartwell House, and later to Dover after the Reception Group moved there on 3 October.

For some of those who took leave in England hospitality was arranged through various Empire societies, but many preferred to be left to their own devices. The majority were found to be in better physical condition than might have been expected in view of the fact that they had been prisoners for some considerable time and that each had some proved disability. From the psychological standpoint it was noticed that their reactions to freedom were in general favourable. Most of them are reported as taking things quietly, content to feel their way and realising that a return to health was the necessary first step towards rehabilitation. Amputees expressed anxiety to get artificial limbs quickly so that they could 'walk off the boat in New Zealand'.

II: *The War in Italy in 1944 and Escapes to Allied Lines*

The heavy snows of the winter of 1943–44 enabled the Germans to hold their defensive line across the narrowest portion of the peninsula with a comparatively small force. The containing of the Allied landing south of Rome at Anzio in January 1944 and the repulse of attacks on Cassino in February held up the advance until the late spring. In May, however, the fall of Cassino was the prelude to a rapid advance north, attacks from the Anzio bridgehead, and the fall of Rome. The end of the year saw the west coast of Italy cleared as far as the Apennines and the east coast as far as the Senio River, where the winter held up the Eighth Army's advance.

First with the Fifth Army and then back with the Eighth, the New Zealand Division was almost constantly engaged in either an attacking or a defensive role in the Italian fighting of 1944. The year's fighting cost us nearly a thousand killed[1] and 3600 wounded, but only a hundred or so prisoners. The battle for Cassino accounted for nearly half of the prisoners, most of whom were lost in the attack on the railway station by 28 (Maori) Battalion on 17–18 February and in the attack on the Continental Hotel by 21 Battalion on 20–21 March. Most of the remainder of the prisoners were lost piecemeal in the series of attacks which brought the Division to the Arno River[2] and later in the advance to Rimini. One or two were able to escape to our lines while in transit in Italy.

German policy was still to collect them at Stalag 337 (later Dulag 339) on the outskirts of Mantua and transfer them to Germany after a few days there. Not much trouble was therefore taken to improve conditions in the transit camp. Sleeping quarters remained unheated and the camp had 'practically no lighting.' In the latter part of 1944, however, when German transport was disorganised by air raids, men often had to stay several weeks. A kitchen, showers, and air-raid shelters were installed, and the camp managed to acquire indoor games and a library of 350 English books.

During the winter months and the early spring of 1944 while the German line remained static, only a trickle of escapers came through to the Allied lines in the south. It became exceedingly difficult for them to obtain sufficient food, especially when on the move, and enemy security had increased. Most of those who succeeded were helped by guides which the Allied rescue organisation[3] had infiltrated into enemy territory. The New Zealanders who came through in this period were nearly all from Campo PG 78/1, and had been living in and about the hill villages south and east of Sulmona since their break-out from camp.

---

[1] Including died of wounds.
[2] These included Brig K. L. Stewart who was captured while on reconnaissance. He was the third of three brigade commanders from the Division to be captured in the Second World War. The others were Brig J. Hargest, captured in November 1941 when his headquarters was overrun at Sidi Azeiz, and Brig G. H. Clifton, captured while on reconnaissance during the Alamein fighting in September 1942. The only other New Zealand brigadier to be taken was Brig R. Miles, captured while CRA 2 NZ Division during the Sidi Rezegh fighting of December 1941.
[3] See p. 314.

The only New Zealander to come through the lines in January was, however, from Campo PG 107.[1] He had wasted no time leaving the camp when a hole had been cut in the fence and had made for the south. When his companion became ill with malaria, he continued to walk on alone and by 20 October had almost reached the front. After spending some time hidden in a hillside tunnel, he was recaptured and taken to a transit camp. But he and five others escaped by cutting a hole in the roof of their hut, and he again went into hiding. When a plane dropped stores for prisoners one night, several of his companions were recaptured while trying to collect them, but luckily he was elsewhere. Finally he met a guide who had been parachuted in by the Allied rescue organisation, and joined a party of twelve which came out near Casoli after a strenuous 23-hour tramp.

In February there came through the lines the only New Zealand escaper to reach the Anzio bridgehead.[2] When the armistice was announced he had been recovering from an operation in Carpi hospital, which was taken over by the Germans next day. Four days later, by arrangement with one of the medical orderlies, he was wheeled out of the hospital, hidden in a box of rubbish, and tipped into a pit in the hospital grounds. At dusk he left the grounds, traded a ring for some civilian clothes, and set off for the foothills to the south. In the following weeks he made his way along the eastern slopes of the Apennines, where he was fed and sheltered by Italian households and occasionally by groups of Italian rebels. Skirting the Gran Sasso to the east, he and a British Army officer reached the village of Corvaro to the south of Rieti, where they stayed some two months, as the Englishman had fallen sick. Finally, with four Italian companions, they crossed a mountain range and made their way down towards Anzio. In their attempt to get through the German lines and no-man's-land several of the party were killed, but the New Zealander managed to get through with only an arm wound. He was able to give some valuable information about enemy dispositions.

The first two New Zealanders[3] from Campo PG 78/1 to rejoin the Allied lines in 1944 reached Casoli on 25 February. They had both lived near the hill village of Roccamorice; for part of the time one had lived in a cave and the other in an old barrack near a disused mine. Having met many of those who had tried to cross the mountains in late December and failed, they decided to remain hidden. Finally one of them met a guide, brought him to the

---

[1] Pte C. Galvan (21 Bn), mentioned in despatches.
[2] Capt C. Gatenby (26 Bn), awarded MBE for this exploit.
[3] Ptes L. N. Matthews (24 Bn) and F. Cameron (22 Bn).

hiding-place of the other, and the two joined a party of escapers who were brought down to Casoli two days later.

A week or so afterwards two groups of New Zealanders came out from enemy territory near Guardiagrele. One group[1] of three from Campo PG 78/1 had stayed in the Maiella Mountains for a fortnight after their release, returning to the camp for food when they required it. They had been discouraged by returning Italians from trying for the south and had stayed in their mountain hiding-place until November 1943. Snow had then forced them down to the village of Lettomanopello, where one had lived in a disused mine and the other two in a cave. At the beginning of March they made contact with two Italian guides, who brought them out two days later.

By April conditions for prisoners of war in hiding had somewhat improved. There had been a reduction in the number of German troops used for rounding up; and although some Italian clandestine organisations had been broken up, those which remained were better at looking after the escaped prisoners in their charge. The latter had learned whom to trust and whom not to trust among the population, but their distrust sometimes made the work of rescuers more difficult. The slow rate of evacuation of escapers was due partly to this, partly to a stricter control of documents, and partly to an increasing difficulty in obtaining civilian clothing and money. Many prisoners judged it wiser to wait for the Allied spring offensive which they felt was almost sure to come.

Four New Zealand other ranks[2] were guided out in April. They had belonged to parties which, on the break-up of Campo PG 78/1, had made their way to Caramanico. The local magistrate had instructed all the inhabitants to help escaped prisoners, and a New Zealand sergeant, before making his way to the lines in November 1943, had set up a small organisation to maintain contact with the various groups of escapers in the neighbourhood, supply them with money and information, and see that they were generally cared for. These four escapers moved along the hill villages during the winter, living as best they could, and made contact with guides in April 1944. With the latter they travelled across the Maiella Mountains to Fara San Martino, where they met British troops on 16 April.

Two[3] of the other group had left the camp at Aquafredda in separate parties, which established themselves in caves near each other. When the majority of those in each party left for the south

---

[1] Ptes A. E. Morrison (20 Bn), G. H. Logan (24 Bn) and C. R. Carolin (19 Bn).
[2] Cpl J. E. Broad (25 Bn), L-Cpl R. A. Tulloch (24 Bn), Ptes A. E. Bartlett (18 Bn) and J. M. Burke (20 Bn).
[3] Pte D. J. Pilcher (25 Bn) and Dvr T. D. McKay (4 Res MT Coy).

in November 1943, these two men (among others) had to remain, one because of a poisoned foot and the other because his boots had fallen to pieces. Those remaining behind went to the village of Roccamorice, but were betrayed by Fascists, captured, and taken to the old Campo PG 102 at Aquila. While they were being entrained for Germany, their truck had a hole blown in it during the bombing attack which has already been described.[1] There were no casualties in this truck and the two New Zealanders were able to get away with a third,[2] who had been captured near the Sangro only a month before. They made their way up to Roccamorice, where they stayed until the end of February, when they met a British-trained guide who brought them through near Guardiagrele.

Three others came out in March. Two of them,[3] after a period in the hills and in a cave, had joined a party which was being guided out. On the night of 2 March the party was split in two, and three days later their portion was recaptured in a village near Guardiagrele by a German patrol operating in civilian clothes. Together with a number of Italian civilians, they were set to work digging but managed to slip away. They found a cave in which they sheltered until they met a guide, who brought them out near Casoli on 10 March.

The last New Zealander[4] brought out in March had been recaptured in mid-October 1943 on the banks of the Trigno, south of Vasto, while still in uniform. But, with a companion, he had escaped from the old Campo PG 21 at Chieti, had reached Roccamorice, and had lived in the area for five months. Here the pair met one of the guides of the Allied rescue organisation and were brought out to Casoli on 21 March 1944.

The British generals from Campo PG 12, who had been sheltering in the Monte Falterona area, were evacuated in two parties by the boat section of the Allied rescue organisation. With the second of these parties on 9 May came two New Zealand other ranks[5] from Campo PG 120/8, the farming detachment at Fogolana. They had left in the large party conducted south to Ravenna by one of the Italian officers of the camp, but after making their way to a partisan band at Stabatenza, had fallen sick with malaria and had been cared for by an Italian family. At the beginning of April 1944 they were conducted to the coast and arrived at Termoli by fishing boat on 10 May.

Another section of the Allied rescue organisation had agents operating on the north-west coast of Italy near Genoa, whence

---

[1] See p. 318.
[2] Pte D. C. McLeod (23 Bn).
[3] Ptes R. E. Gain and I. V. T. Whitehead (both 24 Bn).
[4] Sigmn C. G. Burt (Div Sigs).
[5] Ptes K. C. H. Ellicott (21 Bn) and G. H. Ross (22 Bn).

parties of escapers were taken across to Corsica. A New Zealand officer[1] from Campo PG 29 came out by this route in February. After the armistice the British officers had all been able to move out from this camp into hiding and had been maintained by friendly Italians. Parties had been led into the mountains to the north-east of Genoa, and their evacuation by sea to Corsica had begun in October 1943, though it was soon slowed up by German and Fascist activity. During the winter the escapers were assisted by British agents operating in the area with the partisans, for whom supplies of money and other necessaries were dropped by air. On 19 February a party of 14, including the New Zealand officer mentioned above, left in a small vessel and reached Corsica two days later.

In May 1944 the breaking of the winter Gustav Line at Cassino and elsewhere and the attack from the Anzio bridgehead forced the Germans to retire rapidly north to their next belt of defence—the Gothic Line. The fall of Rome and the liberation of areas of central Italy where numbers of escapers had been sheltering enabled the latter to come out of hiding and meet the Allied forces, with whom they had originally been led to expect contact soon after the armistice announcement, eight or nine months earlier. Since October 1943 there had been an organisation in Rome supplying money, food, clothing, and accommodation to escaped prisoners both in the city and over a wide radius of country districts. From the beginning of December it had come under the control of a British major. In spite of the activity of German and Fascist police, the organisation continued to help large numbers of Allied prisoners, nearly 4000[2] having received help from it up to the time of the liberation of Rome.

From the beginning of June throughout the summer of 1944, numbers of Allied escapers[3] and evaders reported to the advanced elements of the Fifth and Eighth Armies. Most of the New Zealanders from Campo PG 78/1 had already come out or had been recaptured in the attempt, and the majority of those who came to meet the Allied advanced troops were men from camps farther north who had made their way south. Many had been sick and had had to lie up in a friendly house during the winter. Three of the first men out,[4] however, were from Campo PG 54 at Fara nel Sabina, on the western slopes of the Sabini hills; all three had lived

---

[1] Maj E. G. Kedgley (19 Bn).
[2] Of 3925 helped by the organisation, only 122 were recaptured and ten died from various causes. Of this total 40 New Zealanders were helped and one was recaptured.
[3] Forty-four were New Zealand ex-prisoners of war.
[4] Ptes H. C. Podmore (19 Bn), J. C. H. Adamson (5 Fd Amb) and R. A. Morris (5 Fd Amb).

in the Abruzzi Mountains since leaving their camp on 11 September 1943.

Another[1] had tried to get through near Cassino at the end of 1943, but had been recaptured and taken to the former Campo PG 54 at Fara nel Sabina. In January the train taking him north had been bombed while crossing a bridge near Orvieto and he and some companions had been able to escape. After spending some time with different rebel bands, he came through to Colfa to meet the Americans at the beginning of June.

Two officers[2] from Campo PG 47 at Modena were reached by the Allied forces on 5 June. Both had escaped from Campo PG 75 at Bari in August 1942 by cutting the wire and slipping out at night, but had been retaken a few days later by Italian civil defence personnel while making their way to Switzerland. They got away from Modena on 9 September, just before the arrival of German troops, made their way across the Apennines to Leghorn, and from there south to the Santa Lucia Valley near Rome. There they made contact with an organisation helping escaped prisoners of war and remained in the vicinity of Rome until liberated by the arrival of the Allied forces on 5 June.

Another New Zealand officer[3] cycled to meet the advancing troops at Arimazzo on 6 June. He had been one of eight who had made a break through a tunnel from Campo PG 29 in July 1943, but had been recaptured. On the release of the camp after the armistice announcement he and others made their way across the Apennines to the west coast and then decided to go south, skirting Florence and keeping to the hill country. He eventually reached Vallipietra, near Subiaco, and remained in the area for six months, during which time he was able to look after the welfare of other prisoners sheltering there by buying and distributing food, clothing and medicine.

Among those who regained their freedom in this period were another 13 from the work-camp 120/8 at Fogolana, from which a large party had been led south to Ravenna by the Italian camp chaplain. Many of these men, like others who had wandered in the marshy districts of Venetia, had contracted malaria and had been looked after by friendly Italian families during the winter. After reaching Ravenna most had made their way to the hills between Forli and Faenza, and though some had stayed for a while with rebel bands of Italians and Yugoslavs, they had eventually pushed south again to the mountain district north of the Gran Sasso. Some

---

[1] Pte L. H. Tong (26 Bn).
[2] Capt J. Burns (6 Fd Regt), awarded MBE, and Lt J. K. Phillips (6 Fd Regt), mentioned in despatches.
[3] Maj H. M. Evans, awarded MBE.

had tried to cross these mountains in December but were beaten by the snows; others had been lucky to escape from a disastrous boat party which had been supposed to leave from Ancona, but of which eleven out of 19 escapers had been rounded up by Fascists. After struggling through the winter with Italian help, these small groups of two or three men met the Allied troops in June near Spoleto, on the western slopes of the Apennines, near Aquila, and near Ascoli and Fermo in the east.[1]

A New Zealand officer[2] who escaped through the lines during this period had first regained his liberty near Verona by jumping from a train taking prisoners to Germany in September 1943. With a companion he had reached the central mountainous region and had worked his way south. He had made an attempt to get through the lines north of the Sangro in December, only to be recaptured by a German machine-gun crew. By posing as an Italian workman he managed to escape from a transit barrack at Aquila, and made his way again to the hill village not far away which had previously sheltered him. German search parties made it too difficult to stay there, and forced him to eke out a cold and hungry existence in a shepherd's hut higher in the mountains, and for some weeks to throw in his lot with a group of Yugoslav francs-tireurs. In mid-April he and a Canadian parachutist again tried to get through the lines, this time at Alfadena to the east of Cassino, but they stumbled into a German outpost when within reach of freedom. While being taken north he again broke free by diving into the Salto River, then in spring flood from the melting snows. Nursed back to health in an Italian household from the resulting pneumonia, he remained in the hills and came down to meet the advancing British forces near Aquila in mid-June.

The liberation of the area near Aquila in June enabled a number of other escapers to report to the Allied forces. Among the New Zealanders were men from prisoner-of-war camps in western Italy —one[3] from Campo PG 115 at Marciano, not far from Lake Trasimene, five[4] from Campo PG 145 at Poggio Cancelli, near Aquila. Others were from camps in the east and north: one man[5] who had got to Campo PG 70 at Monturano by exchanging identity with a Canadian; two officers from Campo PG 47 at Modena; and

---

[1] Cpl R. G. Sutton (20 Bn), L-Cpl R. L. Burbery (26 Bn), Ptes R. D. Barrett (20 Bn), W. Buchanan (20 Bn), S. Butson (20 Bn), J. A. Clarke (22 Bn), I. C. Dickinson (20 Bn), Gnr J. I. Flowers (14 Lt AA Regt), Pte F. C. V. Free (19 Bn), Gnr H. J. Gordon (7 A-Tk Regt), Ptes R. W. Pearse (27 MG Bn), J. A. Robinson (20 Bn), and Gnr H. C. Thompson (5 Fd Regt).
[2] Capt M. J. Mason (25 Bn), awarded MC for his escapes.
[3] Pte K. C. J. Ineson (LRDG), mentioned in despatches.
[4] L-Cpl W. J. Foy (24 Bn), Ptes J. McDowell (21 Bn), R. J. Marston (20 Bn), V. A. R. Trengrove (25 Bn) and Gnr D. J. Stanley (6 Fd Regt).
[5] Sigmn C. G. M. Cosgrove (Div Sigs).

several from Campo PG 120/5 at Abano, near Padua. They had all made their way south and had been forced into the hill country to wait for the advance of the Allies in the spring. Some had lived for most of the time with Italian families, others had spent part of it with mixed rebel bands in the hills or had lived a hermit existence in a mountain hut or cave. One[1] had been recaptured by Fascists, but had made a second break by slipping his handcuffs and dashing off under fire.

The two officers from Modena had both hidden up after the Germans took over the camp, one concealed inside a doorway through a two-foot-thick wall by locking the door on one side and fixing a false one on the other, and the other in a large empty lavatory cistern at the end of one of the barracks. They and their companions had escaped detection in the Germans' final search, had got out of the camp and had made their way south. The first[2] of the two officers walked for some 350 miles before the late December mountain snows near the Maiella Massif forced him back. He was pulled exhausted out of a snow-drift by two Italians on 1 January 1944 and was thenceforth looked after by Italian families until the Allied forces overran the area.

The second[3] of the two officers, with a companion, walked south into the Apennines, lived and worked on a farm north-east of Florence and finally had to live in a mountain cave. In late October they swam the Arno and, keeping to the hills and dodging patrols, reached by Christmas a hill village between Rieti and Aquila, where Italians provided shelter and food. From here they sometimes came down to raid German trucks for boots and clothing, and on such an occasion in February his companion was recaptured but he got away with a wound in the thigh. When the Germans pulled back north, he organised Italian working parties to get a portion of the road workable for the Allied advance. On 14 June he reported in to Aquila with three German prisoners.

Not all escaped prisoners had been able to find winter shelter so far south, for as time went on German and Fascist patrols made movement more and more difficult, and numbers of prisoners had spent their first months of freedom with rebels, or had been recaptured[4] and had had to make another break. As the Allied forces moved up to Rimini and to Florence, those who had survived the

---

[1] Pte W. E. Gundry (24 Bn), mentioned in despatches.
[2] Lt H. D. Slyfield (7 A-Tk Regt).
[3] Lt N. B. Mitchell (7 A-Tk Regt), awarded MBE for his work while an escaper.
[4] Without an inordinate amount of research it would not be possible to ascertain accurately what percentage of those who were at large in Italy were recaptured. But of the parties of escapers which have come to the author's notice more than half seem to have been caught.

German round-ups were able to come out of hiding.[1] Of the New Zealanders one[2] had been in the prisoner-of-war train bombed at Aquila, had kicked a hole in the damaged wall of his truck, and had made off. Two others[3] (from Campo PG 107/7) had joined a group of rebels at Piobbico and had stayed until the end of March, when they had fallen victims to the submarine trap.[4] But while being taken north by bus from the German transit camp at Laterina,[5] they got out at the back by night and walked to Siena, where they met British troops on 20 July.

One[6] of the men liberated in July had been a prisoner for only a little over three months. Captured at Cassino in late March, he had jumped unseen into a doorway while being marched from Campo PG 82 at Laterina to the railway station. He joined a rebel band until it was dispersed by a German attack, and then hid until the chance came to rejoin Allied forces. Another man[7] had got away from Torviscosa at the armistice and, before he met our troops on 22 July, had been recaptured and had three times made a fresh break. One of these breaks was from Verona hospital, where he had been sent wounded after the Germans had made an attack on the rebel band with which he was serving. Another still[8] had served with a rebel band at Vardo Bologna, but when this was broken up by Fascist attacks he joined a larger group at Monte Falterona, where he spent six weeks with their demolition parties. Finally, he joined another band at Arezzo, and was with them when the city was liberated in early August.

In July and August 1944 the bulk of the Eighth Army was moved back to the Adriatic sector to break through the Gothic Line and enter the fringes of the Po Valley. But although Ravenna was taken in December, the winter rains and desperate German resistance prevented further advance until the spring of 1945. The Fifth Army, too, which had advanced from the Arno Valley to attack the enemy's centre south of Bologna, was held up on the forward slopes of the Apennines. The liberation of another section of hill country meant the recovery of more escapers and evaders concealed in it, but the majority of escaped prisoners had been farther south and a

---

[1] L-Cpl T. I. Sangster (19 Bn) and Pte W. Wood (23 Bn).
[2] Pte F. A. Cumberbeach (26 Bn).
[3] Gnr D. W. Leonard (4 Fd Regt) and Pte F. C. Winter (18 Bn).
[4] This was one of the methods used by Germans and Fascists to recapture escapers. A woman or a man in civilian clothes would make contact with a prisoner or a group of prisoners and claim to be the agent for a scheme for evacuating escaped prisoners by submarine. A rendezvous would be arranged and the prisoners duly arrested. On one occasion a whole boatload was caught in this way at Venice. The same method was used by the Germans and Italians in Salonika and Athens.
[5] The old Campo PG 82.
[6] Pte J. A. Cleland (21 Bn).
[7] Gnr R. J. Lewes (6 Fd Regt).
[8] Pte R. R. Howard (26 Bn).

good number from this area had already been evacuated by sea operations on the Adriatic coast.

Only two New Zealanders were freed in this advance, one a medical officer[1] who had walked out of Lucca hospital thinly disguised as an Italian officer after the Germans had taken over in September 1943. He had later become ill and had been looked after by Italians in the hills north of Florence until the arrival of United States troops nearly a year later. The other New Zealander[2] had come from Campo PG 120/4 near Padua, had moved south and worked with partisans in the Monte Falterona area on railway sabotage, and finally had got through to the United States troops at Pracchia (west of Fossombrone) in late September.

The boat section of the Allied rescue organisation continued operations on the Adriatic coast, but there was only one further New Zealander[3] brought off by this means until the spring of the new year. He had moved south down the east coast from Campo PG 120/5 near Padua and had joined partisans in the hills south of Argenta. While here his evacuation was arranged by an agent of the escape organisation, and he and a party of others were escorted to Porto Corsini by partisans. They embarked on an American motor torpedo boat and reached Ancona on 25 November.

Comparatively few escapers from Italy tried to make their way into France, as it was merely exchanging one occupied country for another. One New Zealander,[4] who had joined an ill-equipped partisan band in the eastern Apennines, decided to attempt to enter France in the late spring of 1944. Moving west among the partisans in the Apennines, he reached Bobbio in July, and from there he continued alone until he crossed the French border south of Turin and was picked up by Free French troops. He was taken to Briançon, where he remained until the arrival of the Allied invasion force from the Mediterranean coast.

The liberation of southern France made possible the operation of a section of the Allied rescue organisation in the area north and north-east of Turin, where numbers of British Commonwealth prisoners were still living with civilians or fighting with partisans. In October three New Zealanders[5] from detachments of Campo 106 came out in a party of these escaped prisoners, guided over the passes into the Val d'Isère, which was by that time in American hands. It was not long before winter conditions made any more such evacuations impossible, and one party perished in a blizzard in

---

[1] Capt F. E. Webster (6 Fd Amb).
[2] Pte S. Stevenson (24 Bn).
[3] Gnr G. G. Speight (6 Fd Regt).
[4] Pte G. E. Heppenstall (27 MG Bn).
[5] Ptes P. G. Brown and J. W. McLean (both 26 Bn), and Dvr N. E. Burbery (4 Res MT Coy).

the Alps. There were several New Zealanders still with the partisans in the Biella area at the end of hostilities in Italy; others not so fortunate were shot by Fascists in February 1945.

Strong bands of partisans had been operating in the Bobbio area among the Ligurian Apennines for some time, helped by a British mission and by supplies dropped from the air. In the autumn of 1944 it was decided to organise an escape route through Pontremoli, which would bring the escapers out not far from Viareggio. Before the Italian campaign was ended 31 parties of escapers and evaders came out by this route. The first New Zealander[1] to use it had come south to the Etruscan Apennines from Campo PG 107/5, north of the Gulf of Venice. After living with a band of partisans, he was included in a party guided out near Barga on 19 November.

The other two New Zealanders to come by this route were from Campo PG 5, both having jumped from the roof of a train taking them to Germany in September 1943. Both were wounded and separated, and one,[2] after lying for three days in a ditch unable to walk, was finally found by an Italian and taken to his house. As soon as he could he hobbled his way south, but was laid up for three months and cared for by Italians near Piacenza. In March 1944 he joined a band of partisans in the Bobbio area and remained with them until they were dispersed by Fascists in May. He was with another group of partisans in the Apennines when, in November, he joined an escape party which reached the American lines at Pietrasanta. A week later his companion of the train jump[3] came out by the same route; he had been operating with another partisan band south of Pavia. This was the last party to come through on this route before the winter snows and increased German vigilance made it too dangerous to undertake further operations until the spring.

As well as those in the Apennines, there had still been at the beginning of 1944 a large number of ex-prisoners of war living either with partisan bands in the mountains of north Italy or with Italian families of the Lombardy plains. In the first months of the year the ' Liberation ' committees of northern Italian cities continued to help numbers of them to cross the Swiss border. The activities of the Milan committee may be taken as typical. This committee had organised a special branch, *Servizio Prigioneri di Guerra*,[4] which

---

[1] Dvr W. McKendrick (ASC).
[2] Lt E. H. Bishop (27 MG Bn), mentioned in despatches for his attempts to escape. He had evaded capture at Kalamata in the Greek campaign in April 1941, but was captured in May 1941 and taken to Italy. See p. 290.
[3] Capt J. W. C. Craig (22 Bn, seconded to 'A' Force). He had escaped from Greece in 1941, and returned there as a member of 'A' Force, but had been captured and sent to Italy. For his escapes and work while at large he was awarded the MC and bar.
[4] Service for Prisoners of War.

by means of its representatives in various localities, located prisoners who had escaped or evaded capture, saw that they were sheltered and fed, and in due time arranged their escort to the Swiss border. Civilian clothing and forged documents were supplied for the journey, and near the Swiss border a local guide, smuggler or partisan, was given the task of conducting the escapers to the frontier. Here they handed back the clothing and documents supplied them and signed a paper giving their name and number to indicate that they had been assisted into Switzerland. A British agent smuggled into Milan in February 1944 carried on the same work along the same lines.[1]

The New Zealanders helped by such organisations to reach Switzerland were almost all from Campo PG 107 and its satellites in the plains north-east of Venice. Several had at first attempted to reach Yugoslavia and some had been recaptured and had to make a second break. Two men from Campo PG 107 who crossed the frontier on 1 February had previously attempted to get through to Yugoslavia but had failed, one[2] being captured near the Trieste area by Fascists and the other[3] in the south during an attempt to reach the Allied lines. The former escaped from a German transit camp at Padua and was shortly afterwards taken in hand by a group of the National Liberation Party. He travelled by train to Milan and thence up the Tellina Valley to Tirano, from which a four days' walk with a guide took him over the hills to Campo Cologna. The second escaper was sheltered and fed by an organisation for a month before he was sent out by the same route.

Three men[4] from Campo PG 107/4, a farm at San Dona di Piave, entered Switzerland near Campo Cologna a fortnight later. They were part of a group of eight who had escaped from their barracks a few days before the announcement of the Italian armistice by sawing through the iron bars across a window opening. They later returned to the area of their camp and stayed with Italian families there, but were rounded up at the end of October by German troops acting on Fascist information. They managed to escape from custody in a crowd on the Verona station and made for the hills, where they obtained civilian clothing and were cared for by Italians. For a while they operated with a band of partisans, but found its methods a little too haphazard. Finally they made arrangements for a guide to take them to Switzerland and went by train to Milan.

---

[1] The committee and the British agent between them produced chits for 802 escapers assisted over the Swiss border. A number of others were lost during a round-up by Fascist and German security forces.
[2] Gnr M. A. Tyson (6 Fd Regt).
[3] Pte C. J. Maher (20 Bn).
[4] Cpl I. A. St George (24 Bn), Pte G. V. McLeod (20 Bn), and Gnr R. H. Ryman (6 Fd Regt), all mentioned in despatches.

On the way to Sondrio they were arrested for not having identity cards, but while being taken to Bergamo they kicked their way through the light boards of their cattle-trucks and were free again. They kept going east for six days over the mountains and then met a guide who brought them across a frontier pass near Tirano.

Although more carefully guarded, the Lake Maggiore-Lake Lugano portion of the frontier, being more populous and having more and easier places at which the crossing into Switzerland could be made, was favoured by the Italian escape organisations. And apart from those whose journeys were arranged from somewhere in the Po Valley, there were others who made their own way to the Lakes district and there stumbled on a friendly household which put them in touch with a guide.

One New Zealander[1] had this experience at Lecco, which he reached after walking and cycling across the plains from Gorizia, where he had been with a mixed band of Italian and Yugoslav partisans. After extricating himself with difficulty, he had had a narrow escape from arrest by a German patrol and a nerve-racking winter moving alone across northern Italy. Twenty-four hours after meeting his guide he was climbing up a mountain track, and the same night (1–2 February 1944) he crossed the frontier on the bed of a stream, near Chiasso.

Another New Zealander[2] who crossed in the same place had walked to the Como area after having been in the hills north of Verona with partisans. He paid a smuggler 1000 lire to bring him to the frontier fence and then burrowed his way under it with an old spoon.

When arrangements went well it took only one or two days to complete an escape into Switzerland from the eastern end of the Po Valley. A New Zealander[3] who fell a victim with numbers of others to a 'submarine' trap[4] and was recaptured at Venice, escaped from the transit barracks at Padua and later made contact with an organisation there. In less than forty-eight hours he had been fitted out with clothes and passport, had been taken by train to Milan and on to Como, and a guide had led him over the frontier near Chiasso on 13 March.

Two New Zealand airmen from Campo PG 47 at Modena came through together in the same way on 4 April. One[5] had reached Modena only on 4 September; shot down in Tunisia, he had spent the months following his capture in hospitals. Both got over the wall fence of the camp before the German guards took over, and

---
[1] Pte J. J. McCluskey (22 Bn).
[2] Pte S. N. Hamlin (22 Bn).
[3] Pte G. C. Loader (27 MG Bn).
[4] See p. 419.
[5] Flt Lt S. A. H. Short, RNZAF. The other was Fg Off W. Duncan, RNZAF.

lived with Italian families until the end of March, when they were put in touch with an Italian escape organisation.

Although some groups of Italian rebels had been reported in January 1944 as 'melting away', others reinforced by escaped prisoners of war had from the end of 1943 been causing sufficient trouble to outlying German forces and Fascist police for the latter to urge the shooting on recapture of all former prisoners of war. Many of those recaptured were thus denied prisoner-of-war status and were held in civilian jails, such as the Villaro prison in Milan, under deplorable conditions.

In May 1944 the German and Fascist forces in northern Italy carried out a large-scale round up, in the course of which some members of the liberation committee at Milan were arrested and a belt three kilometres wide along a part of the Swiss frontier was cleared of all inhabitants. This, combined with a lack of funds and the expectation that the Allied drive would sweep up to the north of Italy in a few months, caused the committee almost to cease its evacuation of escapers and evaders, though it continued to arrange for their food and housing. Most of the men who did get through to Switzerland after this period came through the mountain passes after long and difficult treks in almost inaccessible country.

Although the Tirano route had been used by some Italian organisations for assisting escapers, most of the prisoners who came out by mountain routes had joined partisan bands in the high country to the north and were led out by partisan guides. Two New Zealanders[1] had come through to Switzerland by this means as early as January. Both from farm detachments in the western Lombardy plains, they had joined partisan bands north of Biella. Their encampment was attacked by Germans on 17 January and they had to move to another area. Two days later they left with a guide for Switzerland; moving north to Domo d'Ossola and east to Santa Maria, they crossed the mountains north of Lake Maggiore into Switzerland on the 23rd.

Those coming from Campo PG 107 and its satellites tended to use the passes further to the east of the Swiss border. Two[2] from Campo 107/6 at San Dona di Piave, who had lived in the mountains north of Spilimbergo on the Tagliamento River, walked for three weeks, using the valleys and high country on the northern edges of the Dolomites, to Bormio, almost due west of Bolzano. From here they crossed through one of the passes to Santa Maria on 20 May 1944. Two others[3] who had been with them in the mountains near Udine came through by the same route to Bormio a fortnight later,

---
[1] Ptes D. M. Craib (26 Bn) and L. J. Read (24 Bn).
[2] L-Cpls P. E. Moncur (18 Bn) and E. O. Martin (22 Bn).
[3] L-Cpl P. W. Day and Pte E. C. Clarke (both 24 Bn).

but moved west up the Val Viola and crossed to Poschiavo. None of them had guides at any stage of this journey, but relied on maps and on the generosity of local inhabitants for food and lodging.

Another New Zealander,[1] who made the journey without a guide, had got away north of Verona through a hole cut in the floor of the railway wagon taking him to Germany from Campo PG 19. He lived with Italians until May, when Fascist activity forced him to leave. He too made for the frontier salient near Bormio, and after ten days' walking crossed into Scampf.

The last of our men[2] from the north-eastern camps to reach Switzerland had jumped from a train and joined partisans near Asiago in the Dolomites, with whom he remained until early August. He then tramped across the mountain country towards Tirano and crossed at Campo Cologna in the same month.

The other New Zealanders[3] to reach Switzerland were men from Campo PG 106 and its satellites in the Vercelli area, who had joined a partisan band and were supplied with a partisan guide. A few came through in May and June of 1944 and two[4] as late as January and February 1945. Altogether 110 New Zealanders escaped to Switzerland[5] and were there for varying periods before leaving to return to Allied territory.

It will be seen that many of those who eventually reached Switzerland or rejoined the Allied lines to the south had first made an unsuccessful attempt to get into Yugoslavia. A certain number, however, did succeed in crossing the border into partisan-held territory. The story of the party which made the journey in November and December 1943 has already been told,[6] but there were others at that time in Yugoslavia with partisan bands, usually in small numbers. Those of them who came out did not do so until the spring of 1944; some were recaptured and taken to Germany, and a few were killed.[7] It was not until late 1943 that Allied military missions were put into the country in large numbers, and could act (in addition to their normal duties) as rallying points, arrange safe accommodation, and generally provide help for escapers and evaders on their way south. And it was not until the spring that the Allied rescue organisation was able to drop in officers to work with these missions on purely escape work.

---

[1] Fg Off S. M. Hunt, RAF.
[2] Pte W. A. R. Churchouse (25 Bn).
[3] Ptes S. Barron (26 Bn), J. S. Skilton (22 Bn), and Gnr W. A. Choat (6 Fd Regt).
[4] Ptes R. R. Cameron (22 Bn) and W. Frost (24 Bn).
[5] This figure includes Brigadiers Hargest and Miles, who escaped before the armistice.
[6] See pp. 308–9.
[7] No New Zealanders, though some were very near to being shot after capture. Those who fell into the hands of the Ustachi in Croatia were regarded as lucky if they were handed over to the Germans and not tortured or murdered by their captors.

At the beginning of 1944 Tito and his National Army of Liberation, helped by British and American arms and supplies, were increasing their control over portions of Croatia, Slovenia, Bosnia and Herzegovina. Once routes for escapers were established, Allied military missions in northern Italy were told to send through to Yugoslavia all escapers and evaders encountered east of Verona.[1] But crossing the border was often made difficult not only by German patrols, no doubt intended to prevent the linking of Italian with Yugoslav partisans, but also by the mutual distrust and ill-feeling between Tito's Yugoslav partisans and some Italian bands of different political sympathies, who were alive to the objectives of Yugoslavs in north-eastern Italy and resented their presence. There was another difficulty once the escapers had reached Yugoslavia, for early in 1944 Germany gained a firm hold over the whole coastline and retained it until nearly the end of the year. This meant that escapers and evaders had to be taken across the Adriatic by air.

Two New Zealanders came out by this means from a landing ground at Petrovac in March 1944 in one of the first parties to be evacuated by plane. One[2] was from the group which became detached from Major Gibbon's second party during a German attack in late October 1943. For a while he was with some other New Zealanders who were attached to a partisan brigade, but became separated and travelled alone to Circhina. Here he remained to assist the British liaison officer to 9 Partisan Corps until the latter was recalled, when he went with him to Petrovac to await a plane.

The other New Zealander[3] in this early party had left Campo PG 107 with a small party for Yugoslavia in September 1943. With the help of a guide the party reached partisan-held territory near Gorizia, and moved with a group of partisans until scattered by a German armoured column while trying to cross a main road. He and one other New Zealander[4] continued on their way, trying everywhere without avail to make contact with a British liaison officer. Instead they were posted to a partisan brigade engaged in harassing German transport between Ljubliana and Nuovo Mesto, and for some weeks they had a lean and hazardous time as partisans. In January they were allowed to proceed south but did not reach the British military mission at Dvir until the end of February. They

---

[1] All the New Zealanders who came out through Yugoslavia were from Campo PG 107 or one of its satellites, except one or two from trains and those from Austrian camps.
[2] Dvr D. C. Thomas (NZASC attached 5 Fd Amb), mentioned in despatches. Of ten New Zealanders who became detached from Maj Gibbon's party, he was the only one to reach Allied lines.
[3] Sgt H. W. Kimber (20 Bn).
[4] Gnr A. H. Morrow (7 A-Tk Regt). While waiting for the plane at Petrovac he became ill with pneumonia, but was evacuated by air on 4 April.

were then sent off to join the party of escapers and evaders at Petrovac.

After the arrival in Yugoslavia of officers from the Allied rescue organisation in April 1944, landing grounds for the evacuation of escapers and evaders were established near Glina and Crnomelj. Near the latter a transit camp was set up, and clothing, food, and comforts were dropped in. The numbers to be catered for were considerable; not only were there ex-prisoners of war from Italy, but there were also numerous Air Force evaders who had baled out over Yugoslav territory.

At the end of April two more New Zealanders were flown out. They were both from Campo PG 107/2 at Prati Nuovi, where the prisoners had been sold to the Germans by the Italian padrone. When the German guards moved the prisoners, these two hid in the camp, got out later and then separated. One[1] joined the partisans at Castel Dobra and remained with other ex-prisoners in a machine-gun crew rather than join Major Gibbon's party, but decided in December to leave the partisan force on account of the poor food and the language difficulty. After being arrested by Germans and breaking free twice, he was taken to the transit camp at Trieste. Here, among 60-odd prisoners, he met his companion from Prati Nuovi, also recaptured. On the night of 9–10 March, the latter[2] picked the locks and cut the compound wire while others watched the sentries. Six got out of the camp and made for the hills, where they met partisan patrols. They were put in touch with a British mission, sent to Semic, and flown to Brindisi.

The work of the Allied rescue organisation in assisting escapers from camps in southern Austria and evacuating them through Yugoslavia has already been mentioned.[3] Sometimes parties from Austrian camps joined up in partisan territory with others from Italy and were moved south and evacuated together. Five New Zealanders[4] from Campo PG 107, who had lived in the countryside of north-east Italy until the summer of 1944 and then reached the partisans in the eastern hills, linked up with four other groups of escapers from Austrian *Arbeitskommandos*. The party was passed south along a chain of military missions and eventually flown across the Adriatic to Bari in mid-July.

Although individual ex-prisoners continued to come through from north-east Italy (one New Zealander[5] who had been with partisans north of Udine was directed out in August), the flow was not as

---

[1] Gnr D. W. Paul (5 Fd Regt), mentioned in despatches.
[2] Pte M. R. Hodge (27 MG Bn), mentioned in despatches.
[3] Page 383.
[4] L-Cpl W. J. Scott (26 Bn), Ptes T. O. Murtagh, J. B. Rice, and H. M. McGrath (all 22 Bn), and N. Petersen (25 Bn).
[5] Gnr J. P. Munro (7 A-Tk Regt).

good as was expected. At the beginning of September two officers of the Allied rescue organisation were dropped in, one to the north-east of Ljubliana and the other in the extreme north-east of Italy, to try to expedite the eastward movement of escapers and evaders. Their efforts were however hampered by the suspicion with which they were regarded by the partisans in these areas. Nevertheless parties were getting through, and one containing five New Zealanders,[1] all originally from Campo PG 107, was routed through from Pielungo and flown out on 10 September.

During August and September a New Zealand officer[2] came through in a party of fifteen or more British and United States escapers and evaders. After unsuccessful attempts to get away by hiding in the camp at Modena and walking off the Modena railway station disguised as an Italian, he had jumped from a train near Trevignano. On the way to Switzerland he met Italian partisans at Combai, and his and a number of other small groups of escaped prisoners spent the winter and spring in this area fed by the partisans or by local farmers. In early August he and five United States airmen set off for Yugoslavia with partisan guides, picking up other escaped prisoners on the way. Two of these were New Zealand other ranks, both of whom had taken shelter in the hills, one[3] with a party of Italian rebels operating near Tramonti di Sopra. The party reached an Allied military mission in Yugoslavia and was evacuated by air on the night of 17–18 September.

It has been seen that those ex-prisoners who joined Yugoslav partisan units found great difficulty in getting in touch with Allied mission officers. In the first stage they felt that they owed the partisans some service for the food and protection they had received from them. If they proved useful, the partisan leaders were reluctant to lose them and made it difficult for them to get in touch with an Allied mission. One New Zealander[4] joined the partisans north of Trieste in early January 1944, and spent eight or nine months operating with a battalion in the Gorizia-Trieste area until he met a British officer on 8 September. He was then guided through and flown to Bari on 24 October.

Towards the end of the year the German occupation forces were withdrawing north from Yugoslav territory, and first the port of Split and later that of Zara became available for sea evacuation of escapers and evaders. In November a vehicle was landed to run a service between Glina and the coast, and two New Zealanders[5] came

---

[1] Ptes L. J. Nixey, R. E. McEwan, W. W. Lowther, and A. T. Anderson (all 20 Bn), and C. F. Anderson (24 Bn).
[2] Capt W. J. Heslop (25 Bn), awarded MBE.
[3] Pte H. D. Sanderson (18 Bn). The other man was L-Cpl R. C. McKay (HQ 4 Bde).
[4] Pte W. M. Horne (19 Bn).
[5] Cpl W. A. Sharp (20 Bn) and Pte G. O. Johnstone (26 Bn).

out by this means on 23 November, just after Zara had been liberated. They had come through separately after getting guidance and help from military missions at Forame and Tramonti di Sopra, having had a difficult time up to August dodging recapture both on the plains and in the hills with Italian partisans. The general line of the evacuation route from Italy at this time, while avoiding towns, ran near to the following: Cividale, Gorizia, Postumia, then east to Nuovo Mesto and Metlika and south of Zagreb to Glina, thence by truck over the mountains to the coast.

Eight New Zealanders were among a large party which left Zara by British warship on the last day of the year. They had come through Yugoslavia in three separate parties, all of whose journeys had been arranged in November by military missions in north-east Italy. One group of five[1] had been together since the break-up of Campo PG 107, and had eventually been forced into the hills by German and Fascist activity in the district where they were being cared for by Italians. Others[2] had been operating with partisan bands until they were dispersed by a German attack. Another,[3] who had worked on a farm until August, had to undergo an operation for appendicitis, but was fit again in time to join a party for Yugoslavia which he heard was being organised.

The last group of New Zealanders to come out through Yugoslavia were set on their way in December. Several had been put in touch with a military mission by a New Zealand ex-prisoner lance-corporal[4] who was acting as an escape agent for a number of prisoners in this area. They[5] travelled south-east on the usual route and arrived at Bari from Zara on 11 February 1945. In late December the Germans began a drive against partisan forces in northern Slovenia to clear the way for the final evacuation of their forces. In early 1945 it was reckoned that the escape route from Italy was closed and Allied rescue organisation officers were withdrawn. Since the Italian armistice two thousand or more American airmen and several hundred ex-prisoners had regained their liberty by this route. Among these were 90 New Zealanders, 64 from Italy and 26 from Austria.

---

[1] Ptes A. W. Bassett (21 Bn), T. C. Green, G. A. Greer, and L. S. A. Mair (all 26 Bn), and S. D. Rutherford (20 Bn).
[2] Cpl D. J. Winter (ASC) and Pte W. M. Persson (19 Bn).
[3] Pte A. F. Chambers (26 Bn).
[4] L-Cpl D. Russell (22 Bn), shot in February 1945 and awarded a posthumous George Cross.
[5] L-Cpl L. J. Robinson and Pte D. Watts (22 Bn), Sigmn D. G. Marshall (Div Sigs), Ptes L. J. Powell and D. N. Watson (20 Bn), Ptes E. G. Kelsall and D. D. McLeod (24 Bn), and Dvr W. L. Tyler (ASC).

III: *Reception of Ex-prisoners of War in Italy*

Reference was made in Chapter 7 to the setting up of transit camps in Italy by the Prisoners of War Sub-Commission (of the Armistice Commission) to accommodate Allied escapers and evaders from enemy-held territory. The elaborate programme devised for the Sub-Commission was not carried out because the assumptions concerning post-armistice developments in Italy on which it was based were not confirmed by events, the situation demanding a much smaller organisation, with detachments up near the forward troops to receive escapers and evaders as they came through. Nevertheless, some of the ideas of the original repatriation scheme were put into practice. Its staff included, for example, detachments of New Zealanders and South Africans originally intended to assist in dealing with servicemen of the Dominions they represented.

The Sub-Commission was disbanded on 10 March 1944 and its work was taken over by the Allied Prisoner of War Repatriation Unit. At the same time the large stocks of welfare supplies built up for distribution to the ex-prisoners expected after the Italian armistice were, with the exception of a small residue, added to the general pool for the armed forces in Italy. For Allied Force Headquarters the accommodation and administration of escaped prisoners had become a relatively minor matter, to which it was not prepared to allocate more manpower and supplies than it felt to be absolutely necessary. The newly formed unit was therefore only too glad to retain Dominion personnel on its staff and to fill places on its war establishment with graded men available from 2 NZEF Base.[1] It thus became possible to have one New Zealander with each post handling ex-prisoners from the front line to the camp near Naples, where they were held while awaiting embarkation. The idea was that a New Zealand ex-prisoner would by this means always be able to consult one of his own countrymen at each stage of his evacuation. At the end of March the Allied unit had forward posts at Casoli, Torino di Sangro and Presenzano, and a staging camp at Foggia. The unit headquarters was at Naples, with a main camp at Resina nearby and an embarkation detachment at Taranto.

On arrival at one of these repatriation posts an ex-prisoner had his name checked against the War Office roll of prisoners previously located in Italy; he was also interrogated by a local representative of CSDIC[2] and warned about maintaining security concerning his

---

[1] At the end of May these New Zealanders were formed into No. 1 (NZ) PW Repatriation Unit, which while remaining under command of 2 NZEF, was seconded for duty with the Allied PW Repatriation Unit. Graded men were those medically unfit for front-line service.

[2] Combined Services Documentation and Interrogation Centre. This body was responsible for the interrogation of both Allied and enemy prisoners in the Middle East and the Mediterranean areas.

escape and helpers. He was accommodated and fed as well as circumstances permitted, and there was some attempt at providing the welfare amenities of a rest camp, including periodicals and a radio, but as soon as possible he was transported by road to the main camp at Resina.

Here he was able to have a hot shower, to get an issue of clean clothing, to have good meals, to sleep in reasonably comfortable accommodation, and to enjoy similar amenities to those of an army rest camp. As soon as possible he was given a medical and dental examination, and any inoculations and necessary dental work were attended to. Once he had passed through this routine, which came to be known as 'processing',[1] he was allowed to draw limited amounts of pay and to go on day leave to Naples. His subsequent disposal depended on how long he had been a prisoner; if for less than two months, a fit ex-prisoner was sent after three weeks' rest as a reinforcement to rejoin his former unit; if for longer than two months, an ex-prisoner was returned to New Zealand as soon as possible, though one or two of these (mainly officers) were allowed to rejoin the Division and serve with a unit in the field.

In May 1944 when the Allied advance north began, a collection post was staffed by the Allied unit and sent north to establish itself in Rome for collecting and evacuating the numerous prisoners who had been hiding in the neighbourhood of the city. Dealing with the two to three thousand Allied prisoners unearthed there, together with others recovered elsewhere, placed a strain on the limited staff of the unit.[2] The camp outside Naples quickly filled[3] and the overflow had to be found accommodation at army rest camps in the area. It was clear that more staff would be required, especially if to those Allied prisoners still to come from northern Italy were added the 50,000 in Austria and a proportion of those in Germany. But after the invasion of western Europe on 6 June the adoption of the SHAEF[4] plan to evacuate ex-prisoners from Germany for reasons of military expediency down the lines of communication of the advancing invasion forces was made known. Commonwealth ex-prisoners from Germany were to be evacuated to England, and the formation there of an organisation to receive them was begun.

At the time this was regarded in some quarters in Italy as a mistake. It was considered that, on the throwing open of prisoner-of-war camps following an internal collapse of Germany, the

---
[1] The whole 'process' included registration, identification, interrogation, disinfestation of old clothes, medical and dental examination, issue of clothing, and issue of pay.
[2] The commander mentions in a report compiled in June that 'three NCOs on the [processing] staff have collapsed from fatigue.'
[3] It was reckoned to accommodate 800, but on 21 June 1944 1250 ex-prisoners were being held prior to embarkation. The staff of the Naples camp was at that time seven officers and 58 other ranks, and that of the unit ten officers and 36 other ranks.
[4] Supreme Headquarters Allied Expeditionary Force.

prisoners would make for the nearest Allied troops (which would be in Italy), and that Dominion troops would 'probably do so instinctively because their homes lie in that direction'.[1] To anyone acquainted with the compelling attraction of a visit to the 'old country' for most New Zealanders, this makes strange reading. Yet it does not appear that the idea of New Zealand ex-prisoners from Germany being evacuated through the United Kingdom was viewed enthusiastically at that time even by 2 NZEF authorities in Italy. In view of the immensely greater amenities available in the United Kingdom, the operational considerations which caused these prisoners to be sent home by this route might, so far as concerned their welfare and ultimate rehabilitation, be considered almost providential.

Meanwhile it was clear that the staff and facilities of the Allied Repatriation Unit would have to be increased, for those existing in June and July 1944 were unable to cope adequately with the large numbers of ex-prisoners suddenly thrust upon them. A good deal of misunderstanding seems to have arisen during this period between the ex-prisoners and some at least of those in the Repatriation Unit. The latter seemed at the time ignorant of the fact that these ex-prisoners, whether they had come through the lines by their own efforts or been overrun by the Allied advance, had, in order to prevent their recapture and transfer to Germany, been living under considerable strain for some months.[2] They ignored, too, the inevitable dislike of combatant personnel for being handled by a purely Base organisation. The unit regarded some of the ex-prisoners as a 'hard resistant core which will undoubtedly present authority with many problems'. It records that 86 of them absented themselves without leave while waiting in Naples for a ship—some of them were known to have revisited the places in which they had been hiding before the German withdrawal. The desire of these men to return and thank the people who had risked their lives and homes for them, and if possible to see that they got credit for their help, was natural enough; and many ex-prisoners who were unable to do it were sincerely distressed. It was inevitable, too, that some of the men should have become affianced to Italian girls, and they were understandably concerned when they discovered that the ruling 2 NZEF order forbade such marriages.

---

[1] Report by Commander of the Allied Repatriation Unit requesting more staff.
[2] This was recognised in a memorandum circulated by the commander of the Allied unit to detachments in late December 1944: 'I notice that the attitude adopted by certain ex-prisoners of war whilst in our care is having its effect on the tempers of the staff of Detachments, Camps and Posts. A minority are troublesome . . . their behaviour is naturally remembered whilst that of the well-behaved majority is forgotten. . . . We must never forget that the nerves of these men have been kept taut for months or even years. . . .'

On the other hand the Repatriation Unit was honestly and conscientiously trying to carry out its orders, which were, so far as New Zealanders were concerned, to effect their repatriation without delay. The sudden influx in the summer of 1944 forced them to hasten embarkation, and the work involved in 'processing' and running the camps left them little or no time to listen to individual wants. There was perhaps too little realisation of these difficulties by the ex-prisoners and a natural tendency for them to draw comparisons with the efficient administrative organisations which had been evolved in some of their former prisoner-of-war camps. Perhaps they were not patient enough in explaining their point of view to the men who had been given the job of administering them. But it must have seemed to these ex-prisoners unlikely that members of the Repatriation Unit would be able in the short time available to understand their feelings after the physically exhausting and nerve-racking experiences that most of them had undergone. Many felt that few would see their point of view except those who had been prisoners themselves.

In August the need for some preparation of servicemen for the coming changeover to civilian life after the end of hostilities was recognised by the establishment in 2 NZEF of an Education and Rehabilitation Service (ERS), and provision was made for some of its facilities to be available in camps for ex-prisoners of war. By the end of 1944 the Repatriation Unit had handled over 18,000 Allied ex-prisoners of war, the number of detachments had expanded to eight, and another camp had been formed at Bari on the site of the former Italian prisoner-of-war camp.

A New Zealand interrogation section was operating at both camps to assist in coping with the large volume of such work. One of the difficulties of all interrogation organisations was that the newer members of their staffs did not have sufficient background knowledge of the situation behind the enemy lines, or of reports from other escapers, to know whether what they heard was true or false. One or two of those New Zealand ex-prisoners who had been working with 'A' Force or other clandestine missions very properly declined to give any information about these activities to any except the highest Allied Intelligence authorities. It was unfortunate that this sometimes resulted in misunderstanding between ex-prisoners and those given the task of receiving them. One escaped NCO, who later received the Military Medal for his escapes and work behind the enemy lines, was disbelieved and was sent to the Middle East under a cloud. Fortunately for such men, the Allied interrogation organisation possessed sufficient corroborative reports and other information to establish the authenticity of their stories.

IV: *Escaped Prisoners in Switzerland*

The New Zealanders who escaped into Switzerland after the Italian armistice remained there until October 1944. Owing to their status of *évadé*,[1] they were not placed in military internment camps but like the other British Commonwealth escapers had for the most part to remain in certain allotted areas. This was in accordance with the Swiss plan to maintain perfect neutrality while coping with the large numbers of Allied servicemen and Italians who had sought refuge within her borders. Except for the periods spent at winter sports areas, the living quarters for British escapers were in the north-east corner of Switzerland in the cantons of St. Gallen and Thurgau. The control of British Commonwealth escapers was vested in the British military attaché at Berne and a senior British escaper as executive officer with headquarters at Wil. In practice there was close liaison with the Swiss military authorities and strict control by the latter over all movements of escapers.[2]

It was to Wil that the escaper was sent after his preliminary period of quarantine and examination by the Swiss authorities. There he received a full-scale issue of British Army clothing released from the International Red Cross stocks at Geneva by authority of the British Red Cross and the War Office. From there he was drafted to one of a number of detachments of about 200 men located in nearby country districts, where they were billeted in vacant buildings such as schools or factories. The men slept on bedboards covered with straw and received the same food as the Swiss civilians. To the surprise of the ex-prisoner food was strictly rationed, for since the outbreak of war Switzerland had had to produce sufficient food not only for her own population but also for the thousands of refugees who crossed the frontiers. The rations, though not lavish in

---

[1] The Swiss term to denote escapers as distinct from military internees; not to be confused with an 'evader' in the British sense of a serviceman who avoided capture while in territory overrun by the enemy.

[2] In September 1943 the British Government had agreed through their Minister in Berne to the Swiss Government exercising some measure of military control over British escapers. A 'gentleman's agreement' on this point was understood between HM Minister at Berne and the Swiss Foreign Minister, and the Swiss thereafter admitted any British escapers who crossed their frontiers. In December the Swiss Government issued regulations for the control of escapers which, in the British view, were more appropriate for military internees than for escapers, the main point of difference being the presence of armed Swiss troops in the escapers' billeting areas to enforce obedience to Swiss regulations. In spite of many representations by the British Minister and the British military attaché in Berne, the regulations were never modified, though they were in practice somewhat relaxed. The result was a confusion in the minds of almost all the Swiss officers concerned between an escaper and an internee, and a good deal of irritation and resentment among escapers. It is clear, however, that the geographical position of Switzerland placed her in a most difficult situation, and it is by no means certain that her action in maintaining severe control on paper and leaving it to the discretion of the Swiss officer on the spot to relax it may not have been the most neutral action and in the best interests of all concerned.

quantity, were quite adequate[1] and very good in quality, and the senior officer at each detachment was allowed to purchase extra fruit and vegetables for the men. Officers were given an allowance and had to find their own lodging and food.

Part of the difficulty of catering for British Commonwealth servicemen in Switzerland was the limited amount of Swiss currency held by Britain, and the necessity of reserving sufficient for local purchases in the Far East in order to mitigate the appalling conditions of prisoners in Japanese hands. In lieu of pay it was necessary to issue pocket-money 'consistent with reasonable conditions'. Owing to the inflated prices in Switzerland the rates had to be raised three times to ensure that an adequate amount was available, especially to the lower ranks,[2] for the purchase of necessities. In addition to pocket-money there was a monthly allowance for postage.[3]

From the first it was realised that it was important to keep this large mass of men occupied. Those in detachments were restricted in their movements to certain areas, usually the perimeter of the village in which they were billeted, and had to be back in their barracks by ten o'clock each night; but they could obtain weekend leave on an invitation from the Swiss. Fortunately the 'hospitality and generosity of the Swiss people towards New Zealand escapees was nothing less than overwhelming'.[4] But there were dreary and boring periods for the detachments in lonely districts, and the continual presence of armed Swiss soldiers in the area, even though they acted more like military police than guards and even though most of them were relatively unobtrusive, was irksome to men who felt that they had earned their freedom.

Moreover, facilities for games of the kind to which the troops were accustomed were almost entirely lacking, and the winter in the lower parts of the country was usually foggy and wet. An unoccupied mountain hotel at Adelboden was therefore taken over, and large numbers of the men were sent there for a month at a time in rotation to enjoy the sunshine and winter sports. To meet the

---

[1] Approximate daily rations in June 1944:

Bread	260 grammes	Meat	22 grammes
Cereal	23 grammes	Eggs	2 a month
Peas, etc.	8 grammes	Sugar	17 grammes
Milk	11/30 litre	Chocolate	3 grammes
Butter	7 grammes	Sweets	3 grammes
Lard or oil	8 grammes	Coffee (or cocoa)	8 grammes
Cheese	12 grammes		

[2] Between 1 November 1943 and 5 February 1944 the rate for a private soldier had to be raised from 12s 3d to 17s 6d a week. All such advances were debited to the soldier's home pay account.
[3] Six Swiss francs a month (approximately 7s).
[4] *Report on New Zealand Escapees (ex-PW) in Switzerland* by Maj R. S. Orr (20 Bn) and others.

additional personal expenses[1] they incurred while staying at a luxury hotel (though not nearly up to peacetime standard), the men were given a 'winter sports' allowance of ten Swiss francs a day for the period they were there. One prisoner wrote: 'We are having such a pleasant life with ski-ing, tobogganing, dancing, etc., that I think it is almost as good as old New Zealand. . . .' This is high praise indeed from a New Zealander; and it is clear that these excursions to the mountains were of very great advantage to the men both physically and mentally.

In January 1944, by way of an experiment, a contract was let by the Swiss authorities to British headquarters for forest clearing and land drainage in Thurgau. There was no compulsion on escapers to work, but men were encouraged to volunteer for their own good and in order to earn Swiss currency for the British Commonwealth pool. The camp at Bornhausen, one of those set up under the scheme, contained 18 New Zealanders and was commanded by a New Zealand officer. The work was hard and dirty for 50-odd hours a week, sometimes in extremely cold weather; but the contract was completed up to time and some 70 acres of land were made available for crop-bearing. At Bornhausen and most of the other working camps the men lived in comfortable, specially built barrack huts.

A number of our men also volunteered for ordinary farm work, especially in the harvest season. Although the hours worked at this were longer, it was much more popular, for the soldier lived with the farmer and was in most cases treated as a member of the family; and so far as our men were concerned, the farmers were glad to have them, both for their work and for their good behaviour. For each day's work of any kind the soldier received two Swiss francs, and six Swiss francs were paid into the British Commonwealth pool for the expenses of escapers.

In addition to weekend leave, a scheme had early been arranged whereby each man could go on leave for ten days every three months, with a free rail fare to any part of Switzerland and a ration allowance of seven Swiss francs a day. But in March, for political reasons, further restrictions on leave were introduced by the Swiss Government. Weekend leave was cancelled and the quarterly scheme mentioned above was allowed to apply only to organised parties. Finally all leave was stopped after the Allied invasion on 6 June. It was a pity that the men were denied further opportunities of seeing a beautiful country; but the news of the invasion brought mental compensation, for as one man put it, 'every heart beat fast' in anticipation of final freedom.

---

[1] Beer, for example, was twice the normal price.

In mid-1944 conditions in billets were improved by the provision of palliasses from the Swiss authorities and of pyjamas from the International Red Cross stocks at Geneva. By this time camp amenities had been fairly well organised: there were canteens,[1] dance bands, a magazine for escapers, inter-camp sports, and cinema programmes. Summer camps[2] were opened at Arosa and Caux on a similar basis to the winter camp at Adelboden, and finally the smaller detachments were closed. University and trade training courses were made available, material and equipment for the latter being in some cases provided by Swiss firms. The men who attended had to wear civilian clothes and were given a special allowance to buy them. The mail service to Switzerland was good, though to avoid clogging the service to prisoners of war and internees no personal parcels were sent to escapers.

Not the least of the escapers' interests was the progress of the Allied invasion forces in the west. On 15 August 1944 the Allies landed in the south of France, and by the end of the month the blobs of red colour on the maps moved north and east until they were in contact with the Swiss border. It was thus at last possible for Switzerland to repatriate 4600-odd British Commonwealth escapers,[3] and arrangements were put in hand without delay.

On 23 September a special train started from Wil and picked up detachments of New Zealanders and Australians from Adelboden, Arosa, and Caux as it moved south, until at Geneva it transferred some 500 escapers (including a hundred New Zealanders)[4] to a French train which took them on to Marseilles. From there they were transported by tank landing craft to Naples and, after a short time in the Allied Repatriation Unit centre there, went by sea to Egypt and home to New Zealand in time for Christmas 1944.

Some of the repatriated men had spent nearly a year in Switzerland. In spite of administrative difficulties their stay had been of great benefit to them, both in shaking off the demoralising effects of prison-camp life by getting back to something like normal living, work and health, and also in gaining a broadened outlook through living among the people of a European country closely associated with international collaboration. All were high in their praise of the Swiss families who ' so generously opened their homes to us ',[5] and the senior New Zealand officer felt that the good conduct of our men had done much to foster friendship between their country and ours.

---

[1] From December 1943, 200 cigarettes weekly (or tobacco equivalent) had been made available from IRCC stocks at Geneva.
[2] A ' summer sports ' allowance of ten Swiss francs a day was paid to other ranks.
[3] Including 105 New Zealanders.
[4] For various reasons five New Zealanders were unable to leave at this stage but came later.
[5] Report by Maj Orr and others.

V: *Civilians in Europe*

Besides some twenty men of the Merchant Navy, there remained in 1944 about the same number of other New Zealand civilians in European internment camps. The camp at Tost had been cleared in late 1943 and had become a prisoner-of-war hospital in mid-1944, some of the internees being transferred to Kreuzberg in Silesia and others to Giromagny, near Belfort and close to the Franco-Swiss border. In Ilag VIIIH at Giromagny they were housed in several old French military barracks; stone-floored, cold, badly lit, and 'very uncomfortable'. In the winter following their arrival the men, a number of whom were elderly, had suffered considerably from these conditions, especially as it was some time before they were able to have a hot shower each week.

By comparison the 2000-odd men, women, and children at the St. Denis barracks in Paris were by 1944 well off. The quarters were well heated, and each internee had three blankets and could have three hot showers a week. One hut had been set aside as a restaurant, and food was sufficient to maintain good health in the camp. Flower and vegetable gardens, sports ground, library, orchestra, and school were all flourishing; there were even regular cinema shows and weekly excursions outside Paris by motor-coach.

At the end of 1941 a number of British internees had been transferred from Tost to form a branch camp (Ilag VIIIZ) at Kreuzberg, some 40 miles to the north and about the same distance from the Polish border. In 1944 the quarters, an old three-storied convent, were described by neutral inspectors as satisfactory, and recreational facilities as excellent. What sickness there was seems to have been due to the age of the internees affected. Nevertheless, a number were feeling the strain of long confinement, and there were four detachments of men who had volunteered to go out to work.

In 1944 there were New Zealanders from the Channel Islands at three camps in Germany: Ilag VII at Laufen for men only, and the two 'family' camps,[1] Ilag Biberach and Ilag Wurzach. Two of these had formerly housed prisoners of war: the hutted camp at Biberach and the old Bavarian castle at Laufen. The camp at Wurzach in Wurtemburg seems to have been the worst. There the internees were put into a broken-down old monastery, which was at first dark and damp, was infested with rats and mice, and was equipped with only the most primitive sanitary arrangements, which brought flies in summer. Considerable improvements were made during 1944, and by then indoor recreation was sufficiently well organised to provide some compensation.

---

[1] At Biberach men and women lived separately but could see each other all day. At Wurzach large families only were allowed to live together.

A proposal for the exchange of civilians between the European belligerents had been the subject of communications between them as early as June 1942, but no agreement was reached until early 1944. All civilians held by both sides who desired it were to be exchanged, except those serving common law sentences and those whose repatriation would be dangerous to the detaining power. The agreement provided for a series of exchanges on a basis of numerical equality. The first of these took place at Lisbon in late July 1944, when 900 British civilians were handed over in return for the same number of German civilians from South Africa. The *Drottningholm* brought the Germans to Lisbon on 11 July and took the British repatriates to England, among them a few New Zealand internees from Vittel and Kreuzberg.

Those who remained in Vittel and St. Denis were liberated shortly afterwards by the Allied advance. But those at Giromagny were evacuated to Marlag-Milag Nord, and they and the others in Germany had to see through another winter as internees. Shortage of clothing, overcrowding, and reduction in the amount of relief food all contributed towards making this last stage of a prolonged confinement[1] a very trying one. These conditions, combined with the disappointment at not being included in repatriation drafts, had not only most depressing effects on morale, but also a seriously detrimental effect on the health of some of the thousands of civilian men, women and children still interned at the end of 1944.

VI: *Protection of Interests of Prisoners of War and Civilians*

The administrative machinery for the protection of the interests of prisoners of war underwent practically no change in this period. Time and experience improved the co-ordination and efficiency of the various channels of inquiry and negotiation. Neutral inspectors knew what to look for when they visited a camp, and the form of their report was planned to cover all the points on which there had previously been complaint or controversy. By May 1944 arrangements had been made for them to meet the responsible German officials in Berlin and discuss outstanding matters. At the end of November officers from the prisoner-of-war branches of the British Foreign Office and the War Office were able to visit Berne and Geneva to discuss with representatives of the Swiss Foreign Office and of the International Red Cross Committee the matters with which they were all concerned, and possible further developments.

As many of the problems presented by interned civilians differed from those presented by prisoners of war, it became advisable to set up a separate committee in London to handle matters relating to

---

[1] Some of them had been interned since May 1940.

the former. An 'Inter-governmental Advisory Committee' met for the first time on 31 March 1944, and thereafter met regularly as the 'Commonwealth Civilians Committee'. It was composed of the High Commissioners for the Dominions and the Secretaries of State for the remaining portions of the Commonwealth, and was presided over by the Secretary of State for Foreign Affairs. In practice their places were occupied by representative officials, and meetings of the committee were also attended by technical advisers from the War Office and other British departments. The committee's terms of reference were:

> To exchange information and advice on matters affecting the protection, welfare and property of:
>
> (a) British Commonwealth civilians in enemy, enemy-occupied or recently liberated territories, and
>
> (b) enemy civilians in British Commonwealth territory,
>
> and to make recommendations for co-ordinating policy within the Commonwealth.[1]

When civilians were involved in exchange operations, the committee sat in conjunction with No. 2 Repatriation Committee to co-ordinate the necessary administrative arrangements.

A good deal of negotiation in 1944 concerned arrangements for the exchanges of prisoners of war and civilians taking place in that year and for future exchanges. Apart from the essential painstaking work of Swiss doctors on the mixed medical commissions who examined thousands of prospective repatriates in the preliminary stages, the agreeing of date and place, the provision of shipping, and the ensuring of medical facilities were some of the problems which involved an enormous exchange of messages over the weeks immediately preceding the operation. No less in their demands on the tact and patience of negotiating officials were the reconciliation of the sometimes differing attitude of the United States and the always unsympathetic attitude of Russia, whose consent was necessary for a safe conduct, though she disapproved of a measure which returned to Germany people who she felt might assist the German effort on the Eastern Front.

The arrival home of considerable numbers of exchanged prisoners of war demanded the fixing of a policy with regard to the personal pay accounts they brought back from the enemy country in which they had been detained. Some credit balances were found to be very large and to be due to profits derived from services rendered

---

[1] Commonwealth Civilians Committee paper dated 27 March 1944.

to fellow prisoners, from trading and sometimes from gambling. To avoid the difficult task of deciding which of the sources of income were fair and thus calculating how much of a prisoner's credit balance should be recognised, the New Zealand Government decided in 1944 that no deductions for German pay, or credits for savings of German pay, would be made against an ex-prisoner's service pay account. This decision was reinforced by the likelihood that insufficient documentary evidence would be available for accurate computation of balances, and by the desirability of treating ex-prisoners from Germany on the same basis as those from Italy.

The other matters affecting British prisoners and civilians in Europe which required close attention in this period arose mostly from the difficulties forced upon Germany by Allied operations on the Continent. No agreement was ever reached between belligerents for the exchange of information regarding the exact locations of prisoner-of-war and civilian internment camps, though in practice both sides received information incidentally in the reports on camps in which their nationals were held. This information was used by the Air Ministry in the briefing of aircrews before operations over the Continent, and no doubt prevented many casualties. But it did not include the locations of camps reported as containing only nationals of other Allied countries. Some thirty camps in Germany and occupied France were bombed, and notified loss of life among prisoners of war through this cause totalled about a thousand. There was a continual struggle with the German authorities to have camps removed from locations likely to be in danger from air attack, and also to allow sufficient air-raid shelter accommodation in all camps. By late 1944 it was apparent that the Germans did not have the material to build new camps, and effort was concentrated on securing adequate shelters. It was also thought at the time that they lacked sufficient rolling stock to move prisoners, but subsequent events showed that if necessary they could move them with or without transport.

The invasion of the Continent and the desperate military situation of Germany resulting from exhausting campaigns and destructive air attacks brought about an increasing tendency on the part of the German authorities to approximate the working conditions of prisoners of war to those of their own civilians. Working time at some *Arbeitskommandos* increased to ten or eleven hours a day, and men were sometimes forced to do overtime in excess of the period worked by German civilians. Conditions of work in coal mines and attempts to make prisoners work during air raids were two other matters related to Germany's desperate last effort on which representations had constantly to be made.

VII: *Relief Work*

It was as well that in the summer of 1943 a reserve of Red Cross supplies had been built up in Geneva,[1] for in the course of the following year there were serious dislocations of the system of transport to camps in Europe. The International Red Cross Committee's fleet operating between Lisbon and Barcelona had one ship sunk by a floating mine in October 1943, another bombed and sunk in March 1944, and a third bombed and damaged in May 1944. The last two incidents each caused a cessation of sailings of all such vessels for one month pending reassurance by the Allies that the Red Cross emblem would be respected. From June to November 1944 the route through southern France was out of action, for even after the Allied capture of Marseilles in August it was some weeks before the port was again workable. By June 24,000 tons of supplies had accumulated at Lisbon and ships were being diverted to Casablanca or sent directly to Barcelona, where their Red Cross cargoes were unloaded and stored. In September a northern route was opened, ships going direct to Gothenburg, where their cargoes were transhipped to Lubeck. But the Allied offensive in the west made German rail transport progressively more devious and difficult, and between September 1944 and February 1945 only 210,000-odd food parcels a month were received in camps for British prisoners and internees on the Continent, as compared with 640,000 a month for the year immediately preceding.

In June 1944 a German High Command order forbade the holding in prisoner-of-war camps in Germany of more than a month's reserve of food, and in September another order forbade any reserve whatever, as the Germans feared that the food might be used to supply invading forces or subversive elements inside the country. Under this order existing camp reserves were to be used up and new supplies were to be issued immediately on their arrival, the rule concerning the piercing of tins being strictly enforced. Camp leaders were not slow to protest, and in many camps agreement was soon reached with the Germans that a reserve might be held outside the prisoners' compound. In October the difficulties of getting supplies through made the maintenance of a reserve of any size virtually impossible and necessitated an instruction being sent to camp leaders that only one food parcel between two should be issued each week. There was, however, no slowing up at the parcel packing centres,[2] and a huge volume of supplies was built up ready to be used as soon as the problems of transport should be solved.

---

[1] The reserves at Geneva included large quantities of food in bulk instead of individual parcels, sent by the British Committee Council in the Argentine.
[2] Weekly figures: UK, 92,000; Canada, 80,000; New Zealand, 8000.

Although in 1944 there was need for a continual supply of replacements for uniforms and footwear, most men had received sufficient private parcels to prevent any serious hardship from a breakdown of supplies in clothing. Many men wrote requesting the maximum of chocolate and the minimum of clothing in succeeding parcels, and in October the despatch of private clothing parcels was temporarily discontinued. It was resumed in November and ceased finally in February 1945.

In late 1943, on the basis of recommendations of repatriated medical officers and of representations already received, the medical supplies for prisoner-of-war camps were replanned. Thenceforward the medical supply unit consisted of two packages, one medical and one surgical. By September 1944, 210 of these units were being despatched each week, as well as 10,000 invalid food parcels. Specially urgent supplies were sent by plane via Sweden. For limbless men still remaining after the repatriation of October 1943, materials were sent to hospitals in Germany for the making of artificial limbs on the spot. In spite of a shortage of dental supplies in the United Kingdom, a large quantity was sent to camps to cope with the vast amount of dental work necessary in prisoner-of-war camps, both fillings and dentures.

By 1944 there was ample evidence of the value in prisoner-of-war camps of the recreational and educational material distributed to them from bulk supplies sent from the United Kingdom to Geneva or bought in neutral countries with British Red Cross funds. The variety of entertainment provided by camp theatres at this time, from light opera to broad pantomime, would not have been possible without the librettos, the scores, the acting editions of plays and the make-up, either sent from England to Geneva for distribution by the World Alliance of YMCAs or bought by the latter with funds supplied by Commonwealth Red Cross organisations. The music festivals could not have been organised unless the instruments and sheet music had been sent. The art exhibitions depended on the supply of art materials. Sports would have been much more restricted and primitive but for the supply of footballs, team clothing, cricket sets, and the other items of sporting equipment that were sent. Even the camp gardens were largely the result of the seeds selected by the Royal Horticultural Society.

As a result of the books and courses sent to camps, thousands of British prisoners of war enjoyed educational advantages which would otherwise have been denied to them. Apart from the obvious gain to those who attended courses and passed examinations while prisoners, the effect of the serious reading that well-selected camp libraries made possible, though neither obvious nor measurable, cannot be otherwise than ultimately of great benefit to many individual ex-prisoners, and indirectly to the communities in which they live.

VIII: *Enemy Aliens in New Zealand*

Conditions at internment camps such as Giromagny and Wurzach were a contrast to those for the civilian internees at Pahiatua, where the camp continued to give a neutral inspector a 'very good impression'. Indeed material conditions continued to show improvement even on the high standard which they had previously attained. The numbers in the camp were reduced by the evacuation in September 1943 of nearly all the Japanese for exchange at Marmagao. The internees received more butter and meat than New Zealand civilians, who were rationed. The recreation barrack and workshop were completed and the furnishing of the camp buildings was improved. Radio, library, piano, billiard table, and other indoor amenities provided good facilities for passing the time. There was plenty of scope for outdoor sports, and walks outside the camp under escort were also permitted. The morale of the internees was described as very good.

Nevertheless there had been some difficulties. News of the Italian armistice had created strained relations between the Germans and the Italians, until in March 1944 the remaining 28 Italians left the camp to rejoin their families on conditional release. There had always been difficulties between the Germans and a small group of so-called 'internationals', consisting of some men of Jewish origin and others described as 'Communists'. Feeling became so high between the Germans and this group that arrangements had to be made as far as possible for them to keep out of each other's way.

In September 1944 the internees were moved back to Somes Island to make way for Polish refugee children whom New Zealand had agreed to take under her charge. They welcomed the return to their former accommodation as there was more freedom for them on the island, and this and the scenic beauty of the view more than made up, they considered, for any winter climatic drawbacks. By this time, too, a number of the Germans from Samoa and Tonga had been sent back on conditional release, and there remained only 87 on the camp strength. The accommodation, which had been improved, was therefore much less crowded, and the release of another 25 Germans to Samoa towards the end of 1944 made it possible for most of the remainder to go into separate cubicles. The internees were able to earn money by doing necessary carpentery and plumbing in the camp. For the rest, they spent most of their time out of doors, fishing, walking, or playing sports. A neutral inspector characterised the summer conditions on Somes Island as 'those of a picturesque, pleasant seaside resort', and the appearance of the internees bore testimony to the healthy life they were able to lead.

*****

The German High Command had just begun to adjust their system of prisoner-of-war camps to absorb the mass of prisoners transferred from Italy when the Allied offensive in the west burst upon them. It was not unexpected since it was heralded by intensive bombing, which continued to batter German towns of any economic or military importance throughout the year. Hampered and disorganised internally by air raids, blockaded by sea, and engaged in full-scale land operations to the east, south, and west as Germany was, it is perhaps surprising that she provided for her millions of prisoners of war and foreign workers as well as she did. She did not, of course, provide sufficient food or any clothing for British prisoners; but, knowing that their own authorities were able and willing to send both, with considerable realism she went out of her way to provide transport for British Red Cross supplies from Geneva to their camps.[1] In spite of the urgent calls on her building materials, she made an attempt, though an unsuccessful one, to build accommodation which would house properly the British prisoners of war in her hands and keep pace with the steady increase in numbers.[2] Only the devastating air attacks at the end of the year precluded the possibility of continuing such attempts, and so dislocated her transport system that she could not maintain her own low ration scale, let alone spare much rolling stock to supplement that of prisoners of war. That she spared any at all in her desperate situation might have been due partly to the value of prisoners in doing essential work and partly to the move towards conciliation with the Western Allies, of which some aspects have already been noted.[3]

It was chiefly on behalf of British prisoners doing heavy work that protests had been made regarding the inadequacy of the rations supplied by the German authorities. For in order to eke out the insufficiency of her labour force to cope with a last frenzied war effort, Germany had increased the working time of prisoners to as much as twelve hours a day for thirteen days a fortnight. Extracting

[1] The International Red Cross Committee estimated that an average of 900 railway box-wagons a month of relief supplies for British prisoners were transported on the German railway system between June and November 1944.
[2] The International Red Cross Committee added 10 per cent to the indents for supplies received from camps in southern Germany and Austria to allow for new prisoners transferred from Italy.
[3] See p. 392 et seq.

the last ounce of work from prisoners and still keeping them hungry might create a situation in which they became difficult to control, and the German High Command felt it necessary to pay special attention to their discipline. While moderate officials of the German Ministry of Foreign Affairs still did their best to patch up an Anglo-German understanding, the more ruthless Nazi Party members deplored any tendency towards lenience. Fear of organised violence among foreign workers and prisoners of war became the justification for increased interference by the Gestapo in matters relating to escape, especially in Air Force camps. Over eighty British prisoners were shot in the spring and summer of 1944, most of them recaptured escapers, and there were examples of extreme severity on the part of German officers and NCOs in control of detachments of prisoners.

The attempt on Hitler's life in July confirmed the fears of his subordinates that there was a real danger of a rising inside Germany, and gave Himmler and the police he controlled an excuse for asserting supreme control over all matters inside Germany, even of the Army. In August came the announcement of 'total war', orders for a six-and-a-half-day working week to meet its demands, and dire threats of punishment for defeatist talk. In the same month the Nazi salute took the place of the normal military salute among home troops. SS replaced Wehrmacht officers in posts of administrative control, except in the camps themselves. So far as British prisoners were concerned the German fears were exaggerated. Nearly all the plans being made by prisoner-of-war camp leaders were not for insurrection, sabotage, or guerrilla activities, since it was felt that the Allied military forces would have no need of such assistance and might find it an embarrassment, but for the protection of prisoners amid the chaotic conditions that would result from Germany's collapse. This was also the attitude of the Allied commanders, who saw no point in dropping arms by parachute to prisoners of war, but agreed on the issue of a solemn warning to anyone responsible for their custody not to ill-treat them and a declaration that the competent German authorities would be held responsible for their safety and welfare.

The effects of the invasion of France on the prisoner-of-war camps in Germany were in the first stage more psychological than material. It had been fairly obvious to most prisoners from the intensified bombing and the general progress of the war that the much talked of Second Front would come in the spring of 1944. When it did come, in June, the air of expectation that had preceded it gave way to unqualified optimism, and hope ran high that the war would be over that year. By November, however, this hope was seen to be false, and prisoners had to resign themselves to another winter in Germany. The disappointment brought a deep mental reaction, and in some respects the last winter for prisoners of war in Germany was the worst of the whole period of their captivity, a period which had already lasted over three and a half years for many of them. Food from whatever source was short and uncertain of delivery; fuel was equally short; lighting was poor. Existing accommodation was being more and more overtaxed by a constant trickle of new prisoners. Under these circumstances what would normally be considered trivial irritations, discomforts, and differences of opinion sometimes assumed a disproportionate size, and there was in many camps an atmosphere of considerable nervous tension.

This was more particularly so in officers' and NCOs' camps. In one officers' camp over half the officers had been in captivity for more than three and a half years. By November 1944 there was a waiting list of fifty for the German 'holiday camp' at Steinberg, all cases of strain through excessive study for examinations, of worry over domestic and private matters, or of a generally rundown condition. The number of cases sent to mental hospitals from this camp was large enough to be disturbing, and it was in such camps that the proposed repatriation of long-term prisoners (if it had been brought to fruition) would have had most beneficial effects.

Throughout this period, when fluctuations in food supplies, the weather, and the progress of the Allied armies had such marked effects on prisoner-of-war camp morale, there were a number of other influences that tended to maintain stability. Most camps had an excellent news service, which sifted material derived from both German newspapers and from the BBC heard over a concealed radio, and made its own, often cautious appreciation of the situation. This was an invaluable counter-agent against rumours and against excessive optimism or despair. In many camps prisoners had made large maps of the battle zones which were used to illustrate these summaries.

The progress of the war became the most engrossing interest of almost all prisoners. But those who were forced to work had little time or energy left for worrying about it. After long hours at their forced job, sometimes enlivened by air raids or by an argument with an oppressive guard, they were occupied with the business of feeding, keeping clean, and the other barest essentials of a decent existence. 'We live from day to day' is the summing up in one such prisoner's diary of this period.

On the other hand those in non-working camps had only too much spare time to think about the time and manner of their release and their subsequent activities. One man wrote, 'The waiting is almost unbearable'. Well-established camp activities, theatre, sports, and music continued with their existing momentum to distract large numbers of performers, helpers and spectators. A New Zealand diarist wrote of the camp theatre, 'It is a great help and keeps you from thinking.' Educational work, on the other hand, although it had reached a high standard of organisation and activity in the early part of the year, declined as the year wore on, material conditions worsened, and men found it more and more difficult to concentrate on reading and study. For those with little interest in these pursuits there were other distractions: at one camp gambling for large stakes and at another consumption of home-made spirits were sufficiently marked to warrant special comment in neutral inspectors' reports. Attempts to escape seemed pointless with liberation so near, and much thought went into the working out of possible plans of action for the period which would immediately precede it.

At the end of 1944 there still remained 6500 New Zealand prisoners of war and civilian internees in Germany, and others were still being captured both in Western Europe and in Italy. The work required to look after their welfare was as great as ever. Packing and despatch of food parcels by the Joint Council organisation in New Zealand had now become almost machine-like, and next-of-kin were just as experienced in knowing what to send in their quarterly clothing parcels. What information they lacked on this or other matters connected with those held in captivity was available from the Joint Council inquiry offices. To this body, to the British Red Cross which still supplied New Zealand prisoners with medicines, invalid foods, most of their books and educational material, and to the International Red Cross Committee, large sums of public money continued to be allocated.[1] It was obvious, however, that the war in Europe was in its final stage. Some repatriates and successful escapers had already arrived home, and people in New Zealand were getting ready to welcome home the remainder of the men they had farewelled anything up to five years before.

---

[1] The New Zealand Government voted £2500 to the funds of the International Red Cross Committee in September 1944. In 1944 the National Patriotic Fund contributed approximately £250,000 to the Joint Council, which settled with the British Red Cross for services supplied by the latter to each New Zealand prisoner.

CHAPTER 10

The Last Months of the War in Europe

(January–May 1945)

I: *Movements of Prisoners and Liberation in Germany*

AT the end of 1944 von Rundstedt began the unexpected counter-offensive which developed into the Battle of the Bulge; by late January 1945 it had petered out and the Western European battlefront had again become quiet. To prisoners in Germany this calm seemed merely a quiet interlude before the Allies struck again, and they could now feel with some confidence that the next Allied advances from West and East would end only with the occupation of all remaining German territory. The advance from the east began early in the new year. Just before the middle of January Warsaw fell and the Russians launched what was to be their final offensive from the Vistula. It drove with such momentum across East Prussia and Poland that the prisoner-of-war camps at Marienburg and Thorn were soon overrun and the prisoners who still remained in them came into Russian hands. These were for the most part the sick, since nearly all the others had been hastily evacuated to the west.

Military authorities in Germany had realised early in 1944 that prisoner-of-war camps situated in occupied territory to the east and west would be safer inside the German borders. In June of that year the Air Force prisoners in Stalag Luft VI at Heydekrug, in Lithuania, had been evacuated partly to Gross Tychow in Pomerania and partly to Thorn in Poland; and after six weeks the latter had been moved again to Fallingbostel in Hanover. Although conditions during transport were not always good, these were comparatively orderly moves in good weather by steamer and by train. But the speed of the Russian advance from the Vistula in January 1945 precipitated a decision by Germany on the advisability of further evacuations. The war had reached a stage when her transport was in a state of critical disruption and when her own defeat seemed not only probable but imminent. Nevertheless, the German High Command decided, on the pretext that Article 7 of the Geneva Convention required prisoners of war to be moved out of danger away from a fighting zone, that prisoner-of-war camps in Poland

and eastern Germany would be evacuated westwards if Russian forces appeared likely to reach them. Moves would be on foot if necessary; and for a great many camps this was going to be the only means of travel. The adding of hundreds of thousands of prisoners to the already large stream of evacuating civilians and troops was to place an additional burden on the already disorganised rationing systems of the areas through which they passed, and was to cause them tremendous additional hardship and numerous otherwise avoidable casualties.

The evacuation began with the camps in central Poland and those on adjacent German borders, which were transferred westwards into Brandenburg and onward in the direction of Brunswick. By 1 February, prisoners from Stalags XXB at Marienburg, XXA at Thorn, and the detention barracks at Graudenz were in northern Brandenburg. Almost at the same time, the many scattered working camps on the borders of Poland and Upper Silesia were threatened. A few of those near their parent stalags were brought in before the main exodus from these took place; others were merged with larger *Arbeitskommandos* or grouped together at the *Kontrol* centres for the sub-areas. It was originally intended that all these columns should be moved west to Stalag 344 at Lamsdorf or VIIIA at Görlitz, but the speed of the Russian advance and the severe overcrowding of the stalags forced many columns just to keep moving west and south into the 'Protectorate' of Czechoslovakia on what seemed an interminable and aimless journey. For a good number the move was to continue well into the spring and to end only with their liberation by the Allied armies. Among this mass of prisoners of war from Silesia there were between two and three thousand New Zealanders.

Thus the men at E535, the coal mine *Arbeitskommando* at Milowitz in Poland, where the prisoners were nearly all New Zealanders, set off on 19 January, and after traversing Upper Silesia, Sudetenland and the 'Protectorate', were to continue until they met the United States Army spearhead near Landshut, in Bavaria. They had only a few hours' warning of their move. Most of the men packed two blankets, warm clothing, and as much Red Cross and other food and personal possessions as they could carry. But many of the packs proved too heavy and cumbrous for long marches through snow, and much gear had to be jettisoned later by the wayside. The more enterprising managed to acquire or improvise sledges to carry their packs. For those who could not walk the Germans arranged transport, and men too sick to be moved were allowed to remain in the camp infirmary. The rest set off in the snow for a neighbouring *Arbeitskommando*, at a coal mine three or four miles away, and were glad when they reached it to rest their aching shoulders on the floor of a vacant room. There they joined up with another party, and the next day they became one of the many columns of prisoners moving west into Silesia along the secondary roads filled with civilian refugees and German military horse-drawn transport, to the sound of Russian gunfire not many kilometres behind them.

From then on they marched approximately twelve miles a day, sometimes in thick snow, often further in the early stages of the journey when the advanced Russian troops were almost on their heels and they could hear not only artillery but sometimes machine-gun fire as well. A 22-mile march on their second day in a temperature well below freezing caused some to drop out temporarily with bad feet or exhaustion. At the side of the road in the snow lay the wasted bodies of concentration-camp inmates who had fallen out and been shot to make sure they did not revive and escape. British prisoners of war were of course in far better health than these unfortunate people, and most of them managed eventually to struggle on to the goal set for the day's march.

Almost every night they were tightly packed into barns, which though they afforded some shelter were dark and cold. Men slept close together in pairs or in larger groups, to make more efficient use of the available blankets and body warmth; even so it sometimes took an hour or two for feet to warm sufficiently for sleep. To stop their wet boots freezing hard overnight they took them into bed with them. Even if there had been facilities for washing, few would have risked taking off their warm clothing. Men began to get frostbitten toes, and it was fortunate that a British medical officer marched with the column. On his evening rounds, as well as attending to the sick, he was able to keep up morale with news received on a radio carried in his pack. Those who reported sick at night were grouped together next morning to form a slow column, since only the most serious cases were allowed to remain in a local hospital.

Many of the guards, especially the older men, were in worse condition than the prisoners, and a number were left behind at various stages of the journey, unable to carry on. They were armed with rifles and hand grenades, and with some columns there were police dogs from the camps. Though some guards remained the bullies they had been in camp, others were disgruntled with the whole turn of events and were unusually friendly and helpful to the prisoners. Civilians, more particularly the Poles, were often willing to help with hot water and sometimes even with clothing and food. At almost every halt a few prisoners were able to escape from the column and hide up to await the arrival of Russian forces; many owed their success to fatigue or apathy on the part of the guards, as well as complicity on the part of civilians. But most prisoners were uncertain about the advisability of falling into Russian hands, and preferred in any case not to risk being caught by those SS troops whose task it was to clean up the area behind the battlefront.

In the bitter cold of late January the Milowitz column passed into eastern Sudetenland, where the prisoners found they could trade with the more approachable civilians. Chocolate, soap, clothing, and even watches and rings changed hands for bread, potatoes and other food, to solve the increasingly serious shortage of rations. Men stole and ate everything they could, even raw swedes and sugar-beet. There seemed to be no definite ultimate objective for the column, and the guards, lacking other instructions, merely moved on twelve miles a day and found quarters in what empty barns were available.

At the beginning of February the column was climbing up into the mountains on the Czechoslovakian border amid blinding wind and snow. One of the marchers wrote a description of this period:

> We crossed a mountain range with a wind of gale force lifting particles of ice into our faces. Soft snow piled up on the road in any place sheltered from the wind, made marching difficult. By afternoon the snow had become frozen and slippery. Many men had bad falls. One fall was worse than marching several miles. Usually a man who slipped on the snow and fell unexpectedly on the hard ground took some time to recover, having to be assisted to his feet.

He goes on to mention that after their arrival at the town where they were to spend the night they were kept standing for two hours, shivering in the snow, and when they were finally moved into billets they were so exhausted that they would gladly have lain down with packs and boots still on. More and more men were going down with sickness and falling out of the line of march, and more and more sledges were being reluctantly dumped. The thaw in the second week of February put an end to sledges and at the same time brought merciful relief from the intense cold, though boots were becoming so worn out that men's feet remained continually wet.

On 11 February the column crossed into the Czechoslovakian 'Protectorate'. The sun shone on a lovely countryside and the civilians were very friendly. Countryfolk supplied hot water for washing, hot soup and potatoes in the barns at night; townspeople threw food and cigarettes to the prisoners as they passed through their streets in the daytime. In one Czech town the populace showered them with loaves of bread, packets of biscuits, and other eatables of all kinds. Many prisoners broke ranks to retrieve what was thrown down, and the German *Feldwebel*[1] commanding the column gave orders to shoot any who did so in future. There

---

[1] Sergeant.

followed some rough use of rifle and pistol butts by way of intimidation. Two days later a New Zealander who stooped to pick up a piece of bread was shot through the back of the head by a brutal guard and fell dead on the line of march, but the column was kept going on as though nothing had happened.

It soon became the practice to have one day's spell from marching in every three. This gave respite to weary bodies and made washing, shaving, and mending possible. As February wore on, with less and less to eat and civilians forbidden to give them any food, and still no definite destination, more and more men succeeded in escaping. The Germans chose the last day of February to issue a propaganda pamphlet urging British prisoners to join Germany in the fight against Russia:

The Fate of Your Country is at stake ! ! . . . This means the fate of your wives, of your children, your home. . . . Whether you are willing to fight in the front line or in the service corps, we make you this solemn promise: whoever as a soldier of his own nation is willing to join the common front for the common cause, will be freed immediately after the victory of the present offensive and can return to his own country via Switzerland. All that we have to ask from you is the word of the gentleman not to fight directly or indirectly for the cause of Bolshevik-Communism as long as this war continues. . . . You will receive the privileges of our own men for we expect you to share their duty. . . .

Coming after the events of the previous six weeks, nothing could have been less calculated to achieve the object for which it appealed.

Other groups of *Arbeitskommandos* had similar experiences, and accounts of their marches draw attention to the same things: the forced pace at the beginning (often twenty miles a day) to get out of earshot of the Russian gunfire; the struggle through the snow feet deep along back roads and country lanes; the improvised billets in old leaking barns without heat or light; the blistered and frostbitten feet, the chills and stomach disorders, and eventually weakness from lack of sufficient food. One party had a dreadful night march through a blizzard in late January. Exhausted men had to be sustained by their comrades and some even drawn on sledges. Intermittent rifle and revolver fire in the darkness around them was a reminder that less fortunate Russian prisoners were being mercilessly killed because they could not continue the march. Our men were glad at the end of it to get into a barn, where the warmth of the farm animals helped to melt the ice on their garments and to soothe their aching bodies.

For most columns the rations received from the Germans were meagre and irregular issues of bread, tinned meat and potatoes, and there was a constant struggle to get enough food to keep going. Fortunately most of them benefited by gifts of bread and often of hot food and firewood in the smaller Czech towns and villages. Later groups coming on the heels of many thousands of other prisoners did not fare as well as the first parties to pass through the Czechoslovakian countryside, and eventually the Germans forbade the giving of food to prisoners of war since the Czechs refused it to German civilian refugees. But by then the weather was better and the pace easier, often slowed down by congestion on the road ahead. Even if little or no food was forthcoming, the columns received an enthusiastic welcome from the friendly Czechs, a pleasant change from the sullen manner of the Sudeten Germans whose territory they had not long since come through. A New Zealander's diary reads:

> Passing the town [Ostretin] crowded with civilians, we were greeted with cheers, salutes and cries of " Englander ". It made us feel like men again, and every man marched with his head up and shoulders back, though not a few had tears in their eyes; it was the first visible sign of friendliness (apart from the food) we had received on the march.

The first large camps in Upper Silesia to be affected by the evacuation were Stalags 344 at Lamsdorf and VIIIB at Teschen. According to the original German plan Lamsdorf was to send as many as possible to Stalag VIIIA at Görlitz, in order to make way for prisoners from Teschen and the Upper Silesian *Arbeitskommandos*. In fact, Teschen was too far south for its occupants to outpace the Russian advance in a move north to Lamsdorf, and was forced, as were most of its detachments, to turn west into Czechoslovakia. All prisoners except the sick left Teschen in a snowstorm on 27 January. Extremely severe weather conditions in the first stages of their march cost them many cases of frostbite, one hospital at Oberlangendorf having to treat 25 of them by amputation. Eventually most of the men reached Königgraz, whence they were taken on by train to Weiden. There the camp was overcrowded on their arrival, and though a few were allowed to remain, the majority were moved on to Stalag XIIID at Nuremberg which they reached on 10 March.

The general route of the column from Stalag VIIIB and its work detachments, as well as many of those from Stalag 344, was west through the southern tip of Upper Silesia, across the mountain ranges of eastern Sudetenland to Königgraz. Thence they moved in a general westerly direction towards Karlsbad. Plans had originally been made by the German High Command for these columns to form two groups, one to remain on the north-western frontiers of Czechoslovakia and the other to move into areas adjacent to Stuttgart, Nuremberg and Munich. Some of the columns were halted and put to work in Czechoslovakian territory, but the majority eventually found their way into Bavaria before being liberated by the advanced United States forces.

Prisoners in Stalag 344 at Lamsdorf received orders to move at two hours' notice on 22 January, and in the early afternoon columns of approximately a thousand men began to move out through the camp gates. Red Cross food parcels and German rations were issued to each prisoner before leaving. By evening the Commonwealth Air Force prisoners and Army NCOs, as well as all those of other nationalities, had gone, and there remained only the lightly sick and convalescent in a special compound. Fine, frosty weather with hard snow underfoot made for good marching conditions on the first day. In the distance could be heard the rumble of gunfire. A Red Cross inspector who saw the departure said that the prisoners 'were in high spirits, full of expectation to be overtaken by the Russians'. There is also evidence that some at least were glad to be on the move away from the Russian forces.

Only some six hundred of the column of one thousand RAF prisoners from Lamsdorf reached Stalag VIIIA at Görlitz a fortnight later. The remainder had been left behind on the way, sick, exhausted, or suffering from frostbite, though many of the last reached Görlitz on foot or by transport a few days after the main body. Though merely skirting the northern and eastern edges of the ranges in eastern Sudetenland, they had to march 150-odd miles in low temperatures and very severe weather generally. A week after their arrival they had to move on from Görlitz, and they spent February travelling west on a route that took them through Saxony into Thuringia. By the beginning of March they were at Meiningen, many of them suffering from stomach disorders, the result of poor and insufficient rations and the fatigue of long marches under difficult conditions.

Their story is largely the story of the other columns which made up the remainder of the 8000 men who left Lamsdorf at the same time, except that many of the Army prisoners who had been out at *Arbeitskommandos* doing heavy physical work were in better condition to stand the march. But even they were not proof against the bitter January weather in eastern Germany, nor against the incapacity of the German authorities, in the confusion of a rapid retreat, to provide food for large moving columns of prisoners.

The German rations, never adequate under normal conditions, reduced themselves to about four ounces of bread, a few potatoes, and a helping of soup each day. In the better-organised columns the Germans drew rations approximately each week from army dumps in towns they passed through, and brought them along on horse-drawn transport with the column. Some of these columns even had margarine, honey and sugar, but most seem to have been much more haphazard in their rationing. Sometimes only one of the staple items would be issued, and some columns went for days without any issue of rations at all. In spite of an effort by the International Red Cross Committee to bring food by lorry to them at various points on their line of march, their movements were so uncertain that only a small percentage of them were served. When their original Red Cross supplies petered out, the prisoners had to live on the German rations, together with what they could buy or take. They could not continue for long marching twelve miles a day on this fare without feeling the effects. By late February and early March they were showing the same signs of malnutrition as had marked for many of them the early stages of their captivity.

Back in Lamsdorf no further attempt had been made to move the two thousand or so who remained after the exodus on 22 January. Inside the wire the prisoners took over the ration and clothing stores, and camp life continued as before except that there was no German interference. Over the next three weeks there was increasing gunfire and air activity as the Russians advanced. By mid-February most men believed that they would be liberated by the Russian forces, as it seemed unlikely that the Germans would be able to spare rolling stock for their transport west. But on 21 February they were entrained, forty to fifty packed into each cattle-truck, and they began a leisurely ten-day journey across central Czechoslovakia and northern Bavaria. They were able to take plenty of Red Cross food with them, so that their most serious menace came not from malnutrition but from Allied air attacks. They reached Hammelburg unscathed, however, and were destined to stay some three weeks there in a crowded Stalag XIIIC before moving south on foot. Some of the hospital patients, including limb cases still in plaster, went by train (forty to a cattle-truck) to Stalag XVIIB at Krems, in Austria, a journey which took a week and was carried out under extremely bad conditions for the men concerned.

The second week of February brought such an influx of prisoners into Stalag VIIIA at Görlitz that they were sleeping on floors, tables, and wherever else there was available space. Cases of frostbite, some of them serious enough to necessitate amputation, and others with pneumonia and allied complaints filled the camp infirmary. Many of these would have been much less serious had the men been allowed to remain at the place on the route where they had first reported sick, instead of having to complete the march in a slower column.

In spite of protests to the Germans by the British man-of-confidence against a move in winter, in view of the large numbers in camp who had already undergone a gruelling march from the east, in spite of the scarcity of food and of the lack of transport for sick and disabled, parties of a thousand men began to leave Görlitz on 15 February. They were to continue marching twelve miles or more a day for four weeks, neither the prisoners nor the guards knowing where they were ultimately bound for. Issues of rations were made in the haphazard fashion that other columns had already experienced, and men had similarly to trade clothing and soup in the villages for bread and potatoes. A hot soup or stew would sometimes be issued at night to the men billeted in village barns. But it has been estimated that the average daily rations were not more than four ounces of bread and two ounces of meat. There was, moreover, no proper provision for drinking water on the road, and men had often to risk breaking the column to fill their water bottles in ditches and running streams.

Cold and wet weather in the first stage of the march turned many lightly sick into potentially serious cases. One column had a hundred of them at the end of a week; they were formed into a special party which was allowed to make its way as best it could behind the main body. A great many of the marchers developed intestinal troubles, sometimes caused or aggravated by eating raw sugar-beets. Fortunately, with one or two exceptions, every night was spent under cover, mostly in barns, but sometimes in factories or barracks. Usually, except for straw in barracks, there was no provision for bedding; nor was there any for drying wet clothes, which were 'usually dried on the body during the night, or semi-dried according to the weather conditions of the previous day.'[1] Two or three of the columns were forced to spend a night in an old stone quarry in rain, which later developed into sleet and snow, because the German burgomaster had complained to the guards that the prisoners had stolen potatoes.

By early March they had travelled nearly to Jena, following a line almost due west from Görlitz and running slightly north of Dresden. Although it had been intended that all these columns should be accommodated in proper prisoner-of-war camps, those camps near the line of march of the columns from Stalag VIIIA were full to overflowing and there was no alternative but to plod on further. Lack of knowledge of when the march would end had a demoralising effect on many men. Eventually most of them reached Duderstadt, not far from Göttingen, where they had been told they would be accommodated in 'Stalag XIC'. This turned out to be a large, three-storied brick factory, cold, draughty, and full of red brickdust. Access to the upper floors was by one narrow stairway, and there was one water pump and one primitive latrine

---

[1] Account by a New Zealand warrant officer who took part in the march from Görlitz.

for several thousand men. The whole building was infested with lice, and covered with refuse left by previous columns. Fires and lights were forbidden, men were not allowed out after dark, and strict supervision by jittery guards was responsible for several casualties among the prisoners. Although a hot meal was supplied once a day from a kitchen in the town, it sometimes did not arrive until after midnight, and the difficulties of proper distribution were very considerable. For the sick there was no suitable accommodation, and the impossibility of caring properly for cases of dysentery and pneumonia resulted in some fifty deaths in this area. It was only in the last week of March that the sending of a trainload of the less seriously ill to Fallingbostel made it possible for the medical officers to cope with the situation.

It was to Duderstadt also that the marching columns from Stalag VIIIC at Sagan eventually made their way. They had left Sagan on 12 February and had marched to Spremberg, anticipating that there would be rail transport to take them on. As it turned out they had to complete the 300 miles to Duderstadt on foot. They had to spend nights in the open exposed to rain or snow, and their days of rest were rare and irregular. Many became lice-infested through inability to wash properly. British medical officers who accompanied the columns did what they could to secure supplies and treat the sick. But many of the latter were forced out on the road unfit to walk far; and more serious cases (of pneumonia, for example) which should have been left at hospitals en route were brought along in open horse-drawn carts.

The large mass of Air Force prisoners in Stalag Luft III at Sagan was moved in the last days of January, and marched through the frosts, the snows, and the biting winds which beset the paths of the hundreds of columns at that period slowly making their roughly parallel ways west. Orders were given by senior officer prisoners not to attempt to escape, as it seemed that isolated fugitives who could not prove their identity might be an embarrassment to the advancing Allied forces. It was moreover impossible, owing to the weather, to travel across country and spend nights in the open; and German troops were streaming back through the villages and towns, many of them in an ugly mood. The Air Force prisoners had only three days on the road, for once they reached Spremberg they were entrained. Some went to Tarmstedt, near Bremen, and marched from there to Marlag-Milag Nord at Westertimke; another party went to Stalag IIIA at Luckenwalde, 40 miles south-west of Berlin, a camp which already contained some 16,000 prisoners of various nationalities; another party went to Stalag XIIIC at Hammelburg; and the remainder went to Stalag VIIA at Moosburg, in Bavaria.

Air Force prisoners from Stalag Luft VII at Bankau, in Silesia, were also moved to Stalag IIIA at Luckenwalde, but they set out at the same time as other camps in their neighbourhood on 19 January. They marched some 200 miles to Goldberg under the same conditions as the columns from Army prisoner-of-war camps, and then went on by train to Luckenwalde. The eight hundred or so British prisoners in Stalag Luft IV at Kiefheide, in Pomerania, left on 6 February and were marched west across the Stettin estuary to near Neu Brandenburg, where they were rested in barns for two weeks. But the number of unfit was so high that the German authorities decided to send them on by rail, and they reached Stalag 357 at Fallingbostel in early March. A party of five (typical of many), who escaped and tried to make their way back to the Russian lines, had to give themselves up through sickness after six days and were transported to Stalag Luft I at Barth.

So began and developed in early 1945 the vast trek of prisoners in Germany from east to west. At first the objectives were fairly definite: men from outlying work detachments were moved towards stalags, staging at previously emptied work-camps on the way; men from stalags were moved west to other stalags. Ultimately, as Germany became more and more disorganised, for those travelling on foot the goals became merely areas in central Germany: Hanover Brunswick, Thuringia, Bavaria. By late February there were approximately 100,000 Allied prisoners moving along a northern route towards the general area of Bremen, Hamburg and Lubeck; another 60,000-odd were moving westward through a central region bounded by Leipzig, Dresden and Berlin; in the south approximately 80,000 were moving through northern Czechoslovakia, some destined for western Sudetenland, others for Bavaria and southern Wurtemburg.

By March certain large stalags lying within a central belt straddling the Elbe and continuing through western Bavaria had become reception centres for displaced prisoners of war. Conditions in these camps were bad. At Stalag IIIA at Luckenwalde, to which part of Stalag Luft III had gone, all compounds were so badly overcrowded that when the three tiers of beds were filled there were still hundreds of men sleeping on the floor. Old disused and dilapidated barracks were brought into use. Washing and latrine facilities were totally inadequate. Rations were very short and Red Cross food parcels were lacking for nine weeks. There were nothing like enough medicines and drugs to make possible proper treatment of the sick.

Stalag 357 at Fallingbostel had received the prisoner evacuees from Thorn some seven months previously, but the continual arrival of new batches in 1945 produced conditions similar to those at Luckenwalde, and as early as February new arrivals had to be accommodated in tents on the sports field. To make matters worse, all British prisoners at Fallingbostel had been from 14 January onwards deprived of their palliasses, all but two blankets, and a large proportion of their stools and tables, as a reprisal for alleged British ill-treatment of German prisoners in Egypt. A neutral inspector ascribed the prevalence of bronchitis and chilblains to lack of bedclothing, and after enumerating the reprisal measures, including the suppression of all recreation, described Fallingbostel as 'a very bad camp'.

Two thousand Air Force prisoners from Stalag Luft III arrived at Marlag-Milag Nord at Westertimke on 5 February, and by mid-March the camp numbers had risen to 6500, a total which included Navy and Air Force prisoners as well as Merchant Navy and other civilian internees. The difficulties common to all these reception centres caused through insufficient bedding and rations were accentuated at Westertimke by the fact that, in the days following their arrival, a large proportion of the Air Force prisoners reported sick.

Accommodation in Stalag XIIIC at Hammelburg was equally cramped. The remnants of Stalag 344 at Lamsdorf who arrived by train on 2 March were crowded into a group of small huts that had once served as the camp's sick-bay. There was the usual shortage of rations and Red Cross supplies, but good weather made it easier to escape out-of-doors from crowded living conditions, and the German guards in Hammelburg appear to have made some attempt to alleviate the prisoners' conditions.

Other groups of evacuated prisoners had gone to Stalag XIIID at Nuremberg, others to Stalag XIA at Altengrabow, and others still to Stalag VIIA at Moosburg. While all these camps suffered from inadequacy of accommodation and lack of food, they were not nearly as bad as an improvised reception camp such as that at Duderstadt, which has already been described. Apart from these large collection centres, numbers of small columns were stopped where they were required for work and lodged in whatever accommodation was available in the nearest village. Thus *Arbeitskommando* 10503 left their camp at Hirschberg on 5 February, and found themselves 15 days later quartered at Christofsgrund, in western Sudetenland, working on railway maintenance. Other columns still found haven in neither reception centre nor work lager, but continued their wanderings without a break of any length until liberation.

Those camps in the western and central zones of Germany which had not become reception centres during the first three months of

1945 escaped the worst results of an inrush of additional prisoners into already overcrowded quarters. Their living conditions nevertheless showed a steady deterioration: Red Cross food almost petered out; the German rations were cut and the supply became more haphazard as Allied air activity increased; fuel was sufficient for perhaps three hours' heating out of twenty-four. In officers' and NCOs' camps the lack of food and heating and the increasing distraction of air raids made study and recreation extremely difficult. In March the Senior Medical Officer of Oflag VIIIF at Brunswick wrote:

. . . . a marked deterioration of the general condition of the camp during the last three months, most marked since the supply of parcels was exhausted. All officers have lost a considerable amount of weight and are very pale and anemic. Although at the moment there is no serious increase in disease, at any moment we may get an epidemic and with officers in their present low state of resistance, the disease would spread throughout the camp.

In early April there were cases of starvation and oedema and a great deal of bronchial trouble. Seven weeks on a bare minimum of 1300 calories a day had been sufficient to reduce everyone to an extremely poor physical condition.

One officers' camp suffered the same reprisals as Stalag 357 at Fallingbostel. On 15 January, on orders from the German High Command, a statement was read to the prisoners of Oflag VIIB at Eichstaett describing the conditions at a camp for German prisoners in Egypt, conditions to which (the statement went on to say) those at Oflag VIIB were now to be 'assimilated'. All palliasses (except those of the sick) and nine-tenths of all tables and stools were removed, and all public and recreation rooms were closed until further notice. In the freezing cold of a German January sleeping without a palliasse was a considerable discomfort, and shortage of food and fuel and lack of mail did not lessen the feeling of strain which most men were now experiencing. The fuel supplied was inadequate to keep ice off the frames and insides of the windows even during the day, and the dampness rising from the nearby river laid a depressing cloak over the whole camp area.

At the large NCOs' camp, Stalag 383, at Hohenfels, theatre and other recreation rooms were given up to accommodate new prisoners. During this period at Stalag 383, besides the same discomforts as those already noted in the accounts of other camps, the normal arrangements for emptying latrine cesspits broke down completely, with the result that there was a 'continuous overflow' and a situation reported by a neutral inspector as 'indescribable'. German daily rations for prisoners were estimated to yield an approximate average of 1200 calories a day in February and 800 calories a day in March.

It was with great relief, therefore, that the camp saw the first 'white angel' Red Cross lorry[1] arrive with an emergency supply of food parcels from Geneva.

The major concern of prisoners working at *Arbeitskommandos* in the industrial area of *Wehrkreis* IV and of those at the large stalags in this area was to make sure that they were adequately protected from the dangers of air raids. Casualties among prisoners both in main camps and at places of work, of which there had been a number in 1944, continued in 1945[2] as the Allied bombing concentrated more intensively on the heart of Germany. Fortunately, in many camps the German guards had been persuaded to allow prisoners a certain measure of freedom to seek shelter when an air-raid alert was signalled.

It will be clear from what has been said that, if living conditions in German camps in early 1945 were a severe hardship for fit prisoners, they were much more so for the sick and disabled. Fortunately nearly 2000 of the remaining British Commonwealth sick and wounded prisoners were spared the later stages of disorder in Germany by being exchanged at the end of January. Of the 89 New Zealanders in this party, the largest groups were sufferers from bad wounds and amputations, or from lung and related infections; the smaller groups were sufferers from mental conditions, from stomach disorders, and from blindness.

Many had been selected for repatriation in late 1944. Some had gone to the repatriation centre at Annaburg, Stalag IVD/Z, where they had been treated well, and the German commandant had sent them on their way, remarking that he hoped they would carry away a good impression of Germany. Hospital trains from this and other collecting centres went to Constance on the Swiss frontier, and between 22 and 25 January these trainloads of Allied repatriates passed into Swiss territory in exchange for trainloads of Germans who passed back into their own country. The British repatriates were housed for some days in Switzerland, where British officials and representatives of the International Red Cross Committee and of the Swiss Red Cross took good care of them. Most had borne the bitter disappointment of omission from former repatriation lists, and for a few who died in Switzerland while awaiting transport repatriation had come too late. But at least they were spared the additional hardships of Germany's last chaotic months of defeat.

---

[1] 'White angels' was the name given by prisoners of war to the lorries used by the International Red Cross Committee to distribute relief supplies in Europe during the last months of the war. They were painted white and had large Red Cross emblems on sides and roof.

[2] Although twenty New Zealand prisoners of war were killed in Germany in 1945, only one of these was in Wehrkreis IV.

At the beginning of February the New Zealand party went by train to Marseilles and thence on by the hospital ship *Tairea* to Alexandria.

On 7 March the United States forces crossed the Rhine at Remagen, and on the 24th there were large-scale crossings in preparation for the final drive into Germany from the west. In conformity with the policy of moving prisoners away from approaching Allied forces, the German High Command ordered the most westwardly situated camps to be evacuated eastwards towards central Germany and Bavaria. Several officers' camps containing New Zealanders, Oflag XIIB, Oflag IXA/H, Oflag IXA/Z and Oflag VA, thus found themselves on the move before the end of March. Other groups of prisoners who had already marched from the east to a reception centre such as Stalag XIIIC at Hammelburg were ordered out on the road again to move south-eastwards into Bavaria. Some columns, their move from the east still uncompleted, were forced to turn round and almost retrace their steps. But glorious spring weather had arrived, and with it the final stage of captivity. Within a month liberation came to most of these prisoners either at their new reception centre or en route.

Oflag XIIB at Hadamar, only 25 miles from the Rhine, was one of the first of these camps to be moved. On 21 March half the prisoners were taken on lorries 30 or 40 miles to a transit camp at Lollar to await rail transport further east. Before the remainder moved next day a New Zealand brigadier[1] took advantage of an air raid to cut the inner wire and slip through to concealment inside the outer fence. At dusk he climbed the gates and walked away disguised as a Dutch worker. After four nights' and three days' walking he reached wooded country near the Rhine, where he was able to contact United States forces. He was in England before the end of the month.

The special train waiting to take the prisoners on to Brunswick was bombed and they remained in the transit camp at Lollar, which a New Zealand officer describes in his dairy:

The whole scene is like a beehive. P.T., walking, toiletting, eating, brewing, sun-bathing, haircutting, playing, building, throwing, plane spotting—a mass of activity looked at by bored sentries, gaping foreign workers and women . . . and all the time the sound of battle in the distance.

The German commandant and guards seemed more anxious to be overrun by United States troops than to move to the east, and by the night of 27–28 March it was apparently too late for anything but the former. Next day the spearhead of the United States 7th Division, First Army, overran the village, and the German guards were dispersed and marched off. American infantry followed and

---
[1] Brig G. H. Clifton, DSO, MC, awarded a bar to his DSO for his attempts to escape while a prisoner of war. See also p. 194.

took over the area. For a few days the prisoners were billeted in German houses in the village and lived on the best food the countryside could supply (eggs, pork, milk, butter, cheese and bread) and French wines apparently brought to Germany for the Wehrmacht. An officer's diary for 31 March records 'champagne and porridge' for breakfast; from many viewpoints it was as well that evacuation was swift. The ex-prisoners were transported to Dulag Luft at Wetzlar, where they emplaned for Le Havre on 3 April and reached an aerodrome near Oxford in England next day.

On 28 March the prisoners from Oflag IXA/Z at Rotenburg were ordered out of their camp and forced to march east. Bed sheets sewn up to form the letters PW were carried and were laid out on the ground whenever a group of Allied planes seemed likely to pay attention to the column. The weather was fine, and by trading cigarettes and soap in the countryside for fresh food the marchers lived well. Moving some eight or nine miles a day, the column kept just out of reach of liberation by United States forces until after 14 days a swift thrust by the latter placed it in the middle of an artillery duel at Wimmelberg, near Halle. The German guards abandoned the prisoners and on the following day, 13 April, tanks of the United States Third Army overran the area. The prisoners were fortunate enough to be flown to England almost immediately.

The column from Oflag IXA/H at Spangenburg left a day later than that from Rotenburg, and had a pleasant seven days tramping through upland country towards the Harz Mountains before being liberated by an American jeep shortly after crossing the Werra near Eschwege, not far from Kassel. After a few days there they were flown to Paris, taken by train to Le Havre, and flown (as one repatriate saw it) 'through the spring sunshine across the Channel, over the coastline . . . and touched down—immortal moment —on Westcott aerodrome near Aylesbury.'

After a week of delaying by a commandant and guards who would clearly have preferred to stay, Oflag VA was evacuated by train from Weinsberg on the night of 31 March. The German authorities agreed to move only by night, to allow prisoners off the train into neighbouring fields by day, and to have the train marked on the roofs of trucks with the Red Cross emblem, a Union Jack, and the letters PW. It had been originally intended that the move should be to Oflag VIIB at Eichstaett, but the ultimate destination turned out to be Stalag VIIA at Moosburg. The 150-mile journey was made to take four nights' travelling by train and three days' pleasant picnicking in the fields. But the Allied advance proved unexpectedly sluggish in this sector and the transferred officers had to wait for their liberation at Moosburg.

Six New Zealand airmen fell into German hands in 1945, in time to go through the German Air Force reception organisation before its final disintegration. One of them[1] escaped from Dulag Luft at Wetzlar before it was completely evacuated.[2] He made his break on the last day of March and reached the Allied lines the same day. *Auswertestelle West*, the interrogation centre, remained at Oberursel until 15 April, when it moved to Nuremberg-Bushenbühl. Its various departments had earlier been dispersed over what then remained of Germany. When the American troops overran it on 25 April they found completely derelict what had been for five and a half years the headquarters of the German Air Interrogation Service. 'Its microphones had been disconnected, its records burnt or evacuated . . . the doors of its 240-odd solitary confinement cells hung ajar. . . .'

Stalag XIIIC was evacuated from Hammelburg on 27 March, a few hours before the American spearhead reached it. Marching columns set out in the early afternoon and kept going nearly all night to cover over 25 miles. In the next three to four weeks they covered some 230 miles in a south-easterly direction to reach Gutersberg, a few miles from Moosburg, on 22 April. During the march all manner of trolleys and handcarts had been improvised or appropriated to carry baggage; the prisoners' billets at night had been reasonably comfortable, and they had often done quite well for food from the surrounding countryside. Near Nuremberg they had received some Red Cross food sent out to them from the large stalag situated there, and loaded 'white angel' trucks were waiting at the farm at Gutersberg where they were billeted at the end of their march. By that time, too, the German ration officer was more than willing to co-operate; he ordered the killing of a pig and a steer, besides stocks of other food from the nearest large town. On 27 April an American tank column reached them, and in the next few days the prisoners scattered about the countryside, eventually making their way to a United States Army headquarters at Mainburg. They were evacuated from the airfield at Regensburg.

From the reception centre in the brick factory at Duderstadt the Germans persuaded several large parties to take the road in late March to find better billets, in return for which they would have to work. One party wandered north for a week to the outskirts of Brunswick, where they were billeted in two of the undamaged buildings. They had been able to get almost no food from the countryside en route, and their position was so desperate at Brunswick that the column leader was allowed to go to Lubeck to arrange if possible for Red Cross food parcels to be sent. One of

---

[1] Sqn Ldr K. F. Thiele, RNZAF.
[2] Its evacuation to Nuremberg began on 25 March 1945.

the prisoners remarks in his diary on the difference between themselves and some newly-captured paratroops: '. . . a startling contrast between these chaps and ourselves physically . . . we are so used to seeing thin, miserable specimens'. Since leaving Stalag VIIIA they had marched over 400 miles, and the same diarist records a loss of 40 pounds in his own weight. It was fortunate that a lorry of food parcels and cigarettes arrived from Lubeck, for on 9 April the prisoners were ordered out on the road again, this time to march away from the advancing United States forces towards Magdeburg. Four days later the Americans entered the village in which they were billeted 'to the excitement of all', and after a day or two they were flown off from Hildesheim. Those who had remained in Duderstadt were liberated when United States forces entered the town on 9 April.

The trainload of sick from Duderstadt, as well as another trainload which had gone direct from Görlitz on 17 February, reached Stalag XIB at Fallingbostel. By April this camp contained some 20,000 prisoners of war of mixed nationalities, and as new parties continued to arrive, organisation and supplies became more and more strained. Food parcels brought by Red Cross 'white angels' from Lubeck gave relief during the very hungry days. On 13 April the German commandant announced that the British forces were very close and that he proposed to move his guard company, leaving a token guard on the camp to avoid possible interference by SS troops in the area. Senior prisoner NCOs then took over the complete administration of the camp, even to issuing leave passes to the German guards. On the morning of 16 April British tanks arrived at the camp gates.

At the more recently formed Stalag 357 an attempt was made to move the Air Force NCOs north-east to Lubeck. They set out on 6 April, short of food but very cheerful, since it was obvious that the end could not be far off. In their weakened state many found the march strenuous, but foraging in the countryside enabled them to eat better than they had done for some months. They were well informed of the state of the war, for they carried several radio receivers with the column and circulated their own news bulletins several times a day. The German guards took little interest, and many men left the column. Those who remained with it had not long to wait before being overtaken by the spearhead of the British Army on 18 April near Lake Ratzenberger.

A similar attempt was made to retain control of naval and air force officers at Marlag-Milag Nord. After a period during which attempts were made by camp leaders to delay the move, they were marched off on 10 April. Good weather and the warning they had received of the move made possible a properly organised line of march: they were reported as moving in squadrons at 200-yard intervals with senior officers and interpreters in the rear. They marched north-east across the Elbe and went into billets on a large estate at Trenthorst, near Lubeck, on 27 April. Five days later they saw the first British jeep arrive, and they were evacuated to an airfield by a British Army lorry column a day or two afterwards. The other ranks and Merchant Navy prisoners who remained at Westertimke experienced the same fading out of German control which occurred at most camps. During the last week or two large numbers of prisoners continued to come in from the surrounding area, and a serious food situation was only prevented by the arrival of trucks of parcels from Lubeck. Finally, on 28 April fighting round the camp ceased and it was freed by a British armoured division.

As the military situation deteriorated, the German leaders tried to move prisoners they considered to be of the highest value into the Austrian 'redoubt' area around Salzburg. The collection at Oflag IVC of a number of prisoner relatives of high-placed Allied persons has already been mentioned. On the night of 12–13 April they were taken away under heavy guard to Laufen in Bavaria, and were to go on into the 'redoubt' area. But the efforts of a Swiss envoy and their own protests persuaded a senior SS officer to let the party go through to the American lines under Swiss protection. Those who remained in Oflag IVC were liberated on 15 April by the United States forces twenty-four hours or so after the 'hostages' had been taken away.

In the same way the Germans began to move camps in northern Bavaria south-east towards Moosburg, as the American advance approached them. Oflag VIIB at Eichstaett was paraded on 14 April (as one New Zealander put it), 'packed and loaded indescribably with food and belongings', and moved off on the road south. They had barely gone a few hundred yards down the road when they were attacked by Allied aircraft and suffered serious casualties.[1] The column returned to camp, did not move again until next evening, and continued to move only by night and to rest up by day. In their nine days on the road the prisoners lived well on what they obtained from the countryside, as well as on the food they brought with them, and they arrived in Stalag VIIA in good condition.

At Moosburg there were assembled some 80,000 to 100,000 prisoners[2] of almost every Allied nationality, and including a good number of New Zealand officers and other ranks. Like the other

---
[1] Seven killed, four seriously wounded, and 42 wounded. The serious casualties included two New Zealanders, one of whom died later.
[2] About 9000 British were actually in the stalag, of whom nearly 3000 were officers.

assembly centres, the stalag itself was badly overcrowded. Large numbers of men were sleeping on the floor, in some barracks with only a two-foot-wide sleeping space for each man, and sanitary and washing facilities were similarly choked. While the German ration was hopelessly inadequate, the dump of Red Cross food parcels established at the camp under International Red Cross Committee arrangements largely made good the deficiency except for bread and fresh vegetables. Until 25 April it was expected that officers at least would be moved to the Salzburg area, and the news of an agreement with the Germans for no further moves of prisoners was received with intense relief and excitement. On 28 April 1945 the German commandant handed over the internal administration of the camp to the senior Allied officer, and the majority of the German guard left. Next morning a minor battle swept past the camp and American jeeps drove in the camp gates soon afterwards. Bad weather held up the air evacuation of the prisoners, and some were billeted for a time near the airfield at Landshut not far away. By 8 May, however, the airfield was taking off several thousand a day to Rheims and Brussels.

The NCOs at the large Bavarian Stalag 383 were also moved towards Moosburg but did not reach it. All but 1500 of the 7000 NCOs left on foot on 13 April, and 1000-odd who could not make the march for medical reasons were brought along by road transport. Several hundred are estimated to have hidden up in the camp, escaped detection in the hurried German withdrawal, and waited till the United States forces arrived. The main party marched solidly for three days until they were south of the Danube. Then, after a three days' rest at Ingolstadt, all but a skeleton guard of Germans abandoned them and they were quietly overrun by the United States forces.

Some columns were kept on the move until the end, except for short breaks when they were forced to work. During March the Milowitz party, still some 1400 strong, continued moving south-west in western Sudetenland, where the not too friendly population gave them almost nothing and lost many potatoes, turnips, and even chickens as a result. An issue of half a Red Cross parcel to each man on the 17th relieved an almost desperate food situation. The appearance of Allied aircraft overhead also did much to cheer a by now weary and footsore band. By the end of the month they were halted in a small village 50 miles east of Nuremberg and billeted in an old pottery factory. Here some were 'chased' out to work several times, cleaning up bomb damage, but others were able to rest and sunbathe and try to get clean; all had the same constant struggle to get somehow enough food to keep going.

After nearly two weeks' 'spell' the party was suddenly moved south again, and hard marching brought them to the Danube near Regensburg on 16 April. Part of the column had barely crossed the river when a large formation of Allied planes came over and bombed the bridge. Some 25 prisoners[1] were killed and a larger number wounded. The whole party was scattered and some made off on their own account, though others returned in the course of the next day or two, preferring at this stage of the war to take advantage of the security afforded by a large organised party. The latter continued to move south, and on the 19th Red Cross food parcels again reached them. Eventually, on the 27th, they were put in a tented camp on the riverbed near Landshut, where they were scarcely under guard at all. A New Zealander's diary tells the story of their last hours of captivity:

It's rather peculiar the way things are going. We are just sitting round cooking and washing while a war goes on all around us. The Jerries just left a big ration cart along from us, and the Russians and our lads soon had it torn apart. The Jerry guards were also pitching their rifles and gear into the river and heading away. Tanks are not so very far from us now it seems.—(Two hours later)—THE FIRST AMERICAN TANKS AND RECONNAISSANCE CARS COME RACING DOWN THE ROAD TOWARDS US! Saw a lot of fellows break down and cry with relief. . . .

The column from Oderburg marched for some 720 miles before it was released. After two months on the road, these men were in the same condition as those in the other columns which had travelled long distances. Their boots were worn, their clothing lice-infested, their bodies tired and undernourished. The party went to Karlsbad and then down to the flatter country around Chemnitz, where they received an issue of Red Cross food parcels brought by 'white angel' trucks. From Weiden they were taken on by train in late April to Plattling, where they were billeted in an old grain store. The day after arrival they were put on railway construction work for a new line that was being laid in that area, but a heavy air raid on the railway station caused their labours to be diverted to the clearing of debris. After five days they were moved south again away from the United States forces, but the latter were close behind them. Eventually their guards abandoned them 20 miles from Moosburg, and here the Americans overtook them.

For some of those who were set to work inside Czechoslovakia the last stage of captivity lingered on into May. The party at Christofsgrund in northern Sudetenland, now attached to Stalag IVC, worked on at railway maintenance through March and April. Nearby at Brux there were still some thousands of prisoners of war

---

[1] Including four New Zealanders. Some 20 New Zealand prisoners in Germany suffered death in 1945 as a result of Allied military activity or enemy violence.

working in the coal mines. As the news got rapidly better, so the rations rapidly deteriorated. On 5 May the party was still doing railway maintenance, and the men received their pay for the previous month's work. They had the radio news, but the central area in which they were situated was one of the last to be reached by the invasion forces. One man wrote on 6 May, 'The war appears to be over, but there is nothing to prove it'. Within a day or so camps in the area were breaking up, and those who decided not to risk falling into Russian hands got on to refugee trains heading for the west. Eventually they were taken over by the United States forces.

Prisoner-of-war hospitals were among the few groups which were not made to move in one direction or the other across Germany in early 1945. But the days preceding their release were often none the less difficult and anxious. Medical officers were alive to the havoc that would be caused in a hospital full of patients by the bombing or shelling it might undergo when the fighting zone reached it. From the Bad Soden eye-centre the senior officers were able to get a letter to the United States forces asking them if possible to occupy the town without action; and this was done. Other hospitals not so well placed to make contact with the approaching forces had to accept the risk of being shelled by mistake and had to take what internal precautions they could. At Tost, in Upper Silesia, there had been barely time to get the bed-patients down into the cellar on 20 January before heavy gunfire made known the proximity of Russian forces, which overran the area later in the day. Fortunately it does not seem that any of the hospitals containing prisoners of war were mistaken by the liberating forces for military targets.

Among the camps liberated by Russian forces was Stalag IIIA at Luckenwalde. An attempt had been made on 14 April to move the RAF officers held there to Moosburg by train, but the latter was unable to go for want of an engine, and those who had been moved to the railway station had to return to camp. In the ensuing days the guards became more and more friendly, and several of them asked for certificates of good conduct to show to Allied forces. On 21 April the commandant formally handed over the camp to the senior Allied officer and the German guard marched off. Next day a Russian armoured car entered the camp, and a few days later fighting in the neighbourhood ceased. On 6 May a United States lorry convoy arrived to take away British, American, and other Allied prisoners, but the Russian commander refused to allow them to go and some lorries taking out prisoners had shots fired over them by Russian troops. Conferences with the Russians and further attempts to evacuate the camp proved fruitless until the arrival of a senior Russian officer in charge of repatriation. Nearly a month after their release, the rest of the prisoners were evacuated by Russian transport and handed over to the United States forces near Wittenberg.

The ten thousand or so Air Force prisoners in Stalag Luft I at Barth were more fortunate in their experience with their Russian liberators. German guards abandoned the camp on 30 April and Russian forces arrived two days later. By this time a section of the prisoners had taken over the nearby airfield. On 12 May British and United States aircraft arrived to evacuate the prisoners, and they were all transported to the United Kingdom by this means.

Release came to prisoners of war in Germany in such a variety of ways that a description of what happened to those at main camps and to a few of the hundreds of smaller parties cannot do more than cover some of the more typical aspects of liberation. Evacuation was a much more uniform affair. For, although a few of our men commandeered transport, most were willing to wait for instructions from those officers of the Allied occupation forces whose task it was to cater for released prisoners.

A plan had been made by SHAEF in the autumn of 1944 for this evacuation, and a central organisation known as PWX was set up at Supreme Allied Headquarters, with liaison groups at major headquarters which worked through contact officers. The latter were sent forward by every possible means to areas where prisoners were assembled. There were representatives from the Dominions and from all arms of the service in these contact teams. They carried instructions to the prisoners in camps to remain there, and for those outside to report to the nearest transit centre, in order to simplify maintenance and documentation and to avoid any uncontrolled movements of prisoners which might hamper operations. A chain of transit centres was set up on the lines of communication, and *ad hoc* units were formed to organise and maintain them. The latter were equipped with special disinfestation, bathing, clothing and medical facilities, Red Cross services, YMCA teams to organise amenities, and Army Education teams to give up-to-date information. The plan was to evacuate prisoners by air to the United Kingdom. In view of the bad physical condition of many prisoners resulting from the forced marches they had undergone, the air evacuation was pushed forward with all possible speed, and some of the services provided at transit centres on the Continent never had a chance to function fully.

Ex-prisoners either remained in their camps, or were taken to a transit centre, or were found billets until they could be evacuated from the nearest important airfield. Sometimes 'K' rations and other army rations were supplied to prisoners in billets. As soon as possible they were taken to the airfield by army lorries and organised into groups of 30-odd ready for emplaning.

Almost as soon as the flights of Dakota transport aircraft arrived they loaded, took off, and headed back towards the west. Only the prisoners from a few camps in north-west Germany were evacuated direct to the United Kingdom in British aircraft; most were taken to France or Belgium, where they broke their journey and spent a night, or a few hours only, at a specially prepared transit centre before going on. Most of our men seem to have gone to either Rheims or Brussels.

The transit centre at Brussels, which was the one to which it had been intended that the majority of British ex-prisoners should go, received and sent on some 40,000 of them in three weeks at the end of April and in early May. As the streams of Dakotas arrived from Germany and unloaded, lorries took the ex-prisoners to the transit centre; and at the same time streams of British four-engined bombers were taking on to England those who had already passed through. At the centre they were given showers, new uniforms, and an advance on pay. They could stay a night in an hotel run by the Belgian Red Cross Society; they had full use of recreation rooms run by the YMCA; and they could go on leave to take advantage of private hospitality, or to buy presents in the city, or just to look around. A liaison officer speaks of the prisoners being 'all in rocketing spirits'. But most of our men's spirits did not reach their climax until they arrived in England, for not until then were they back among people and in an environment nearly the same as their own. There was in England the additional thrill of seeing again (or seeing for the first time) the country from which the forbears of most of them had come during the last hundred years. At this point many consistently kept diaries finished abruptly. Here was an opportunity to be seized rather than written about; and most of the diarists no doubt had much the same feeling as the one whose last entry reads, 'Can't be bothered writing any more. Going to start out and enjoy myself.'

II: *Last Escapes to Allied Lines in Italy*

In Italy the year had begun for the New Zealand Division with reconnaissance patrols on the Senio River, and it was not until early April that there was set in motion the last swift offensive which took our men to Trieste by the end of the month. On 2 May the German forces in Italy surrendered. The few New Zealanders who were captured during this final sweep north were in enemy hands for only a matter of days, not long enough to be recorded officially as prisoners. With the exception of one airman shot down over Germany in the same month, they were the last New Zealanders to be made prisoners in Europe.

It was in March and April 1945 also that 29 of the New Zealand ex-prisoners who had been at large in northern Italy since the Italian armistice finally made good their escape to Allied lines. They were all from satellite working detachments of Campo PG 107, and they had spent their 19 months since regaining their freedom in the plains north of the Gulf of Venice and in the hills bordering them. After the first few months, when living among the Italian populace presented few problems, they had experienced a period when they had to be on their guard continually against German occupation troops and Italian Fascists.

Many worked on Italian farms and slept in the farmers' lofts. If that proved too dangerous for those who were sheltering them, they moved to improvised shelters in maize fields and vineyards, among piles of cane, or in the hollowed-out insides of haystacks. They were usually not able to stay too long in one place; and the report of one man speaks of 'moving almost daily, receiving only casual meals, and sleeping in any likely looking house.' They had all to depend entirely on the generosity of friendly Italians for their food, and those who became sick, for whatever nursing they received. Some were recaptured and were able to make a new break—by jumping from a German lorry for example. A number of their comrades who had been with them since the armistice were recaptured and taken north to Germany. For others the life became one of painful monotony: working as an Italian peasant in the fields, keeping a wary eye for search parties, and studying the news of the war for developments that might bring their final freedom nearer.

A New Zealand lance-corporal,[1] who had formerly been in Campo PG 107/7 at La Salute di Livenza, began soon after the camp gates were opened by the Italian guard NCO to find suitable safe accommodation for his camp-mates in the neighbourhood. This done, he gave himself the task of investigating escape routes which might bring them to freedom. From his contacts with the Italian population he heard of the partisan organisation in the hills east of Monfalcone, and in October and November 1943 he organised the moves to this area of 57 men who had been hiding in his district. There was of course at this early stage no organised escape route through Yugoslavia.[2] The Slovenian partisans at Ronchis, to whom the escapers reported, pressed them into their service and put them

---

[1] L-Cpl A. W. Scott (24 Bn), awarded MM for his work on behalf of fellow prisoners of war in Italy.
[2] See account on pp. 307–9.

under guard, and it was with some difficulty that they were able to make their way back to the plains.

The lance-corporal made several further attempts to find an escape route for his comrades: through the Communist headquarters in Udine, through the Padua organisation which sent people across to the Swiss border, and at Belluno on the Dolomite slopes, where he had heard in December 1944 of the arrival of British liaison officers by parachute. But those Allied military liaison officers who had been dropped were more interested in stimulating and aiding resistance to the Germans than in helping escaped prisoners. It was not until early 1945 that, in view of the large numbers of escaped prisoners and aircrew evaders reported in the area Verona-Brenner-Udine, the Allied rescue organisation decided to send in a mission by parachute. The New Zealand lance-corporal made contact with one of the officers of this, the 'Nelson', mission. The officer arranged by wireless the evacuation of four parties of escapers and evaders by motor torpedo-boat, and with his knowledge of their hiding places, the lance-corporal was able on four separate occasions to bring a party of New Zealanders to rendezvous with guides of the mission.

The first of these parties was taken off on the night of 9–10 March from a point on the coast near Caorle at the mouth of the Livenza River. From the rendezvous the escapers and evaders were led by a carefully reconnoitred track across canals and a piece of land recently inundated by the Germans, to a point among the sandhills near the beach. The six men[1] in the party were taken off by lifeboat to the waiting MTB and reached Ancona next day.

On the subsequent trips there were delays owing to bad weather and difficulties in crossing the canals, though this was made easier by a deflatable rubber boat which was part of the equipment of the mission. On one occasion a party had a narrow escape from running into a German patrol, but the members of the mission who acted as guides and guards for the escape party were well armed, and at that stage of the war it would have been unwise for a small German patrol to attack a party of Italian rebels of unknown size in the half light. There was always the difficulty of security, for the presence of strangers soon became a topic of local gossip. Four parties were successfully evacuated, and among those on the last trip was the New Zealand lance-corporal who had during his captivity contributed a great deal towards the safety of his comrades and towards their final evacuation.[2]

Another New Zealander[3] who had done similar work for his fellow prisoners of war since the armistice had the misfortune to

---

[1] Including three New Zealanders: L-Cpls F. T. Avery (21 Bn) and W. G. Morrish (26 Bn), and Pte R. Williams (21 Bn).

[For notes 2 and 3 see page 475

be recaptured by the enemy early in 1945. He had succeeded in the previous summer in making contact with the Allied military mission at Tramonti di Sopra, and later in arranging for several escaped prisoners to reach the mission and so be put on their way to Allied lines through Yugoslavia. After his recapture he and several others escaped from a prison camp near Udine at the beginning of February, but were pursued to Ponte di Piave, where they hid with Italian families. He then intentionally led the pursuit away from his companions, but was himself recaptured on 20 February and handed over to the German forces. Under severe interrogation he refused to give any information concerning his own activities or where his companions were sheltering. On the grounds that he was in civilian clothes and carrying a map and was therefore a spy, he was shot by a firing squad a week later. His courage in refusing to give information concerning those who were helping him and his companions was recognised immediately after the war by the members of the Italian local community, who erected a fine memorial over his grave, which they tended as that of one of their own.

There were many other examples of this quiet kind of courage on the part of escaped prisoners, fortunately not many with such a tragic sequel. A great many more Italians who helped and sheltered them, and even some who were merely suspected of doing so, were tortured or executed. Some of our men learned the language so well that in normal everyday life they could pass fairly easily for members of the Italian families with whom they lived. It was less easy to maintain the pose under long and close questioning by Fascist security officers and German Gestapo, with its accompaniment of kicking, punching, whipping, arm twisting, hanging by the arms, and the other skills of the trade by which these modern hired assassins served their governments. Some of our prisoners who had first broken free at the time of the Italian armistice were in enemy hands in northern Italy at the end of the campaign and had to wait for release by Allied troops or Italian patriots.

An Allied Screening Commission was early given the task of obtaining evidence concerning those of the local populations who helped Allied escaped prisoners and those who ill-treated them. The

---

See opposite page

[2]In the second party there were eleven New Zealanders : Cpls. S. J. Weir (20 Bn) and H. E. Wilson (18 LAD), Pte E. A. Eagan (25 Bn), Dvr R. P. Langley (ASC attached 5 Fd Amb), Gnrs S. G. Williams (5 Fd Regt) and H. R. McAllum (6 Fd Regt), Ptes J. A. Morrison (20 Bn), A. H. Pitcher (25 Bn), E. L. Ransley (22 Bn), W. F. Ross (27 MG Bn), and N. M. Sims (24 Bn). On the third trip there were nine New Zealanders : Sigmn M. N. Martin (Div Sigs), Ptes R. J. Anderson (5 Fd Amb), K. G. Key (19 Bn), A. C. S. Pearce, R. E. Ryan, J. M. Senior, D. M. Taylor and J. Waddington (all 22 Bn), and C. V. Wills (23 Bn). On the fourth trip there were six New Zealanders : Cpl T. E. Crack (24 Bn), L-Cpls A. W. Scott (24 Bn) and W. Wickliffe (18 Bn), Pte R. H. Johnston (22 Bn), Spr O. J. Locke (7 Fd Coy), and Pte R. V. N. Trayes (24 Bn).

[3]L-Cpl D. Russell (22 Bn), awarded George Cross posthumously. See p. 429.

section of the commission operating in Italy had a busy time in the spring and summer of 1945, examining the statements of ex-prisoners of war and investigating the circumstances of people to whom escaped prisoners had given certificates describing the help they had received from them. For the proven cases of ill-treatment there followed the more searching proceedings of the War Crimes Commission. For the proven cases of help there were certificates from the Allied commander, small monetary rewards, and sometimes more considerable compensation for loss.[1] This is no place to discuss the merits and demerits of War Crimes trials and of the punishments meted out to those found guilty. The allocation of rewards must also have been a difficult business. It seems likely that the small monetary rewards made to those who risked much and went without to feed and shelter escaped prisoners may have been received with mixed feelings. Many of our men who escaped have remembered those who helped them in their lean days and have made some return for the precious gifts of food, clothing, and shelter they then received. No doubt most of these Italian people chose the Allied cause and took some pride in doing what they could to help it, but many of them also liked and respected the men they sheltered and fed. There must be deep satisfaction to them in later receiving proof, in the form of letters and parcels, that what they did is not forgotten. There is scope for international understanding on this level that no scheme of official rewards and punishments can replace.

III: *Release and Evacuation of Camps in Austria*

Prisoner-of-war camps in Austria, which in early 1945 contained 1500-odd New Zealanders, experienced in this period many of the same discomforts and disadvantages of those in Germany proper. They suffered the same drastic food shortages until Red Cross convoys got through in late March. A New Zealander at Markt Pongau writes in early March: 'Our German rations are down to about 1500 calories per day . . . and men are getting very low . . . dozens have started stealing, fighting and not washing or shaving.' A month later the same man writes: 'Everything is rosy again . . . as food parcels are here in plenty. . . .' They also saw wave after wave of Allied aircraft come over to bomb targets in southern Germany and Austria; they were sometimes in the areas where Allied bombs fell, and there were further casualties among them from this cause. Fortunately they were spared the hardships of the winter marches

---

[1] For example, the head of a family whose members had helped many escaped prisoners received £205, and the members all received certificates. The widow of a man who died in prison as a result of helping escaped prisoners received £500.

suffered by those in camps in eastern Germany. As the months passed and the end of the war looked near, the attitude of the German guards towards British prisoners eased. In late April they opened the gates of the special compound in which the non-working British NCOs were held at Markt Pongau. The gates were soon smashed up and in use for 'brewing', and the Germans 'gave up in despair' when they found that the men had also torn down the inter-compound fence. What one man wrote was probably true of most camps at that stage: 'The boys are going to take a lot of holding now'.

The Germans had decided that as many British prisoners as possible should be moved from their camps in eastern Austria farther west into the Salzburg redoubt area. They were to move towards Markt Pongau or, if necessary, farther west towards Landek. On 13 April the Russian forces were in Vienna and some of the prisoners were already on the march. Towards the end of the month the sick and unfit left Stalag XVIIIA at Wolfsberg by train and nearly all the other British prisoners had already set off on foot. Those in the *Arbeitskommandos* to the south and east of Wolfsberg were also on the move. On 23 April a column of 400-odd from Wolfsberg arrived at Markt Pongau, and over the next few days hundreds of men poured into the camp. Some had come from as far as Graz and had been on the march for a week or two. Like those prisoners who had travelled south through Bavaria, they had been able to obtain a good deal of food from local farmers; they had found tramping across a pleasant countryside in the spring under such conditions a rather agreeable break from the routine of prisoner-of-war camp life.

Although some marching columns did not get as far as Markt Pongau, a sufficient number arrived to bring the numbers to nearly 13,000. Since the capacity of the camp was reckoned by the German authorities as four to five thousand, it needs little imagination to picture the overcrowding of sleeping accommodation and sanitary facilities. A medical officer comments that there were 'sick men lying on the floor in every corner of the hospital'. Though Red Cross supplies were on hand they were insufficient to cope with such a mass of men for any length of time, and the food situation could soon have become serious again. On 2 May the German guards were withdrawn, though fighting was still going on in the adjacent areas where the German forces had refused to capitulate. As in most camps, plans had been made months before for such a situation and a properly organised scheme was immediately put into operation. But by 6 May it was apparent that the controlling of the cosmopolitan mass of men then in camp was becoming increasingly difficult. On that day several hundred prisoners broke out of camp and looted a German goods train. A Swiss representative who had been stationed at the camp for some time reports that order was re-established by the camp leaders without any serious incident with civilians. But it would have been unwise to have risked a repetition. A medical officer was immediately sent up to Salzburg to contact the American forces, and a party of American troops arrived the following day.

From then on the food problem at the camp was solved by distributing supplies of American army rations, and arrangements were made for the speedy evacuation of the released prisoners, of whom some 700 were New Zealanders. British liaison officers, one of them a New Zealander, were in the camp by 17 May, and on the 20th the ex-prisoners began to move by lorry to the Salzburg airfield for the flight to France and on to England. Most of our men from Markt Pongau and adjacent *Arbeitskommandos* seem to have reached England by the end of the month.

It had been intended in the Allied plan that all liberated prisoners of war in Austria should go south to Italy and be repatriated from there. But unforeseen difficulties in securing the release of those who fell into Russian hands made it advisable for many groups of men to make their way to the American forces, and for the latter to transport them to the nearest available airfield for immediate evacuation west. Thus the camp leader of A945GW at Selzstal, a New Zealander, heard on 8 May that Russian and United States forces were both near at hand. After the German guards had abandoned the camp he managed to contact the nearest United States forces by telephone, and was told that although Selzstal was outside the American zone his men would be looked after if he could get them through. He managed to find a railway engine and two carriages and to persuade the engine-driver and his fireman to take them along the ten miles of railway to the American lines. Once there they were moved to an airfield near Linz and flown direct to England in Flying Fortresses.

Between three and four thousand British and some 15,000 other Allied prisoners were contacted by liaison officers from Allied Force Headquarters in Italy and evacuated south. As early as 8 May parties totalling about 4000 men were making their way through the Brenner Pass, and Liberator aircraft were over camps in the Wolfsberg area dropping food and medical supplies. On that date also MI9 personnel equipped with wireless were parachuted into Wolfsberg, and the German guards handed over the camp to the senior of the newly arrived officers. In the next few days men from outlying work-camps and others who had broken loose from the march columns poured into the camp. A guard of the most responsible prisoners was put on the perimeter to prevent men getting out and causing trouble with civilians.

It took a fortnight or more before all British personnel were evacuated from Wolfsberg and the hospital at Spittal. The Klagenfurt airfield fell into the hands of Yugoslav partisans, who were reluctant at first to make it available for British and United States aircraft. But by 24 May the bulk of the released British prisoners had been flown to Bari or Naples, and, after a day or two there, had been sent on by air to England. The men from some of the *Arbeitskommandos* made their way direct to the airfield. In response to a Russian request, Russian prisoners were transported north to Graz to be exchanged for those from the United States and the British Commonwealth. The exchange began on 24 May, but there were delays in getting our men south to the airfield, and some who should have come south to Klagenfurt were at first still being sent east to Odessa.

By the end of May the problem of evacuating prisoners from Austria, and from other parts of Europe as well, had almost resolved itself into a search for stragglers. Some men had stayed with Austrian or German girls and their families who had been good to them, in order to do what they could to protect them from the invading Russian troops. A few who had married or engaged themselves to do so were trying to get permission to bring their fiancees or wives out with them. New Zealanders in this predicament had to await permission from Base, but the War Office early agreed to evacuate the women as well, with the idea of getting the men out more quickly and sorting out the marriage problems later. The New Zealand repatriation unit sent a detachment to Klagenfurt to speed up the repatriation of New Zealanders, and it seems that the officer in charge handled a difficult task with a great deal of tact.

Apart from the men with wives or fiancees, there were others doing useful work as interpreters and guides with occupation units. Orders from New Zealand Base Headquarters were to evacuate any New Zealander as soon as possible, no matter what the circumstances, if necessary by placing him under arrest. There was at first little attempt to estimate the value of such a man as an interpreter or guide to the occupation troops, and a tendency to impute to him the worst motives for remaining. No doubt there were a few who might want to be 'last out and last to return to New Zealand', or who might just be indulging their appetites. But there were others who were glad of an opportunity to justify themselves by doing useful work (which only they, from their local knowledge, could do) after years of useless inactivity in a prisoner-of-war camp.

Although 12,000 British and other Allied prisoners came out in June, there were only 500-odd in July, and the Allied Repatriation

Unit was beginning to reduce its strength in preparation for final disbandment. Nine New Zealanders came out in July and four in August, and by that time there were fewer than twenty of our men still to be located in the whole of Europe. The task of tracking down the remaining missing was given to special contact teams in the various occupation areas. The disbandment of the New Zealand unit began on 1 September, when the main party moved to Taranto. Since its formation the Allied Repatriation Unit had received some 46,500 ex-prisoners, among them 1080 New Zealanders.

IV: *Evacuation of Prisoners released by Russian Forces*

The speed of the Russian advance in January 1945 did not allow the Germans time to move all the prisoners from camps on their eastern borders or in Poland. A good number of sick men remained in hospitals, together with the medical personnel attending them, and some of the smaller outlying working camps were overtaken by the Russian spearhead. One such camp came under Russian fire while being evacuated. Of its 40 men five were killed, including two New Zealanders, and 19 were released by the Russians. Men who had escaped either from camps or from marching columns were also able to make their way back to the Russian lines.

There was at first little organisation for the evacuation and eventual repatriation of these men, and they had for the most part to make their own way back, living as best they could while doing so. A New Zealander who reached the Russian front-line troops in December 1944, near Prague, stayed for a week with them, was quite well treated, and was then told to make his way back to Lublin. On the way he was picked up by some other Russian troops, who did not believe his story nor recognise his Army paybook. He was put into a civilian jail and kept there for three to four weeks with very little food and under very bad conditions. He was then taken under guard by train to Brest-Litovsk, where there was a second New Zealander in the same circumstances. Eventually, when a train came through containing other ex-prisoners of war, these two were put on it. The second New Zealander picked up at Brest-Litovsk was shortly afterwards shot dead by a Russian guard on the train.

A party of hospital orderlies from Tost, after receiving several incorrect instructions from Russian officials as to how to make their way back, were ushered into the local jail of a Polish town and told they were in a transit camp. Here men of different nationalities were being put to work crating up dozens of pianos, and at four o'clock next morning the British hospital orderlies were invited to assist. This they declined to do and spent a boring few days, until they were taken on foot the rest of the way to Czestokova, the nearest railhead, which had been made one of the assembly points for recovered prisoners of war.

In September 1944, when it had become apparent that prisoner-of-war camps in Poland and eastern Germany might soon be liberated by the Russians, negotiations for the welfare and evacuation of British prisoners while in Russian hands were initiated. There were in the areas likely to be affected some 3000 New Zealanders. A British Commonwealth approach to the Soviet Government asked the latter to notify the names of recovered prisoners of war and civilians, and to allow facilities for British officers to care for and organise them. The Soviet response was at first unsympathetic. But in October the British Foreign Secretary obtained from Marshal Stalin an assurance that every care and attention would be given to British Commonwealth ex-prisoners as soon as they were freed by the Red Army. In order to give what assistance might be possible towards the welfare of our men repatriated through Russia, the New Zealand Minister in Moscow kept in close touch with the British military mission there. Later, an officer was seconded from the New Zealand Reception Group in England and attached to the mission.

The British military mission to Moscow arranged with the Soviet military authorities for the earliest possible repatriation of released British prisoners, through Odessa. As early as December 1944 considerable British Red Cross supplies (food, clothing, medical supplies and tobacco) were sent to Russia, where the Soviet Red Cross and Red Crescent Societies had promised co-operation in distributing them to British Commonwealth prisoners liberated by Russian forces. In January the Soviet Government gave high-level assurance that provision would be made for the welfare and protection of British Commonwealth ex-prisoners. They wished, however, to have the right to make released prisoners work, in the same way as the large bodies of Russians released by SHAEF were being put to work by the latter. The New Zealand Government took up a position strongly opposed to this, and in the end the agreement negotiated on behalf of the Commonwealth provided that work other than camp maintenance should be only on a voluntary basis. It was not until 11 February that this agreement was concluded, at Yalta, between the USSR and the British Commonwealth countries, for the 'care and repatriation' of each other's ex-prisoner-of-war nationals. And it was not until it was concluded that the Russians would allow British liaison officers inside Soviet territory.

By February 1945 70 British Commonwealth officers and 2571 other ranks were on their way to Odessa, where a transit camp to hold 5000 was in preparation, medical officers and contact officers being sent from the military mission in Moscow. No official advice had been received, however, of the recovery of any New Zealanders by the Russians. The British Commonwealth party of contact officers waiting to go to Moscow had not yet received their visas. In order to contact New Zealanders in the forward areas, the Second Secretary of the New Zealand Legation in Moscow was attached to a party from the military mission which went to Lublin at the beginning of March. The party was not allowed much freedom of movement and almost no New Zealanders were seen. After a fortnight the New Zealand representative returned to Moscow. He was able to report that, although the Russians had established collecting points, there was no proper organisation. Thousands of prisoners were wandering about Poland, neglected by the Russians, some hungry and ill, others robbed of their possessions by Russian troops and threatened (but many, fortunately, well cared for) by the Poles. While there may have been no intentional ill-treatment or neglect on the part of the Russians, their lack of organisation under the prevailing chaotic conditions in Poland often made it seem as if there had been. By the end of March the holding camps in Poland were being closed and ex-prisoners were being directed back to Lwow and Volkovysk, whence they were sent on to Odessa. Teams of contact officers were allowed only at these points, and evacuation was slowed down because many prisoners preferred not to report until they contacted a British officer.

Conditions on the long train journey east to Odessa were poor, but do not appear to have been any better for the Russian troops and civilians travelling at the same time. One party took over three weeks to travel from Oels to Odessa. On 10 March an accident at Rudawa, near Cracow, to one of the trains, involving the telescoping of five cars, resulted in eight prisoners being killed and 30 injured.[1] The latter were taken to the Russian military hospital at Cracow, where they received excellent treatment and whence all except one who died of injuries were flown to Odessa.

In April and May a number of our men escaped to the Russian lines from German custody in Austria, either from the camp in which they were held or from a marching column moving westward. Some thirty of these men were evacuated to Odessa by the Russians. Some made their own way to Budapest and were then moved back through Roumania and the Ukraine. It would clearly have been more practical for these cases to have been repatriated across Western Europe, and representations were made on our side to

---

[1] New Zealand casualties were four dead and two injured.

have any British ex-prisoners in Hungary and Roumania either flown to Bari or moved overland to Graz for transfer to our forces. On 8 June the Russians announced that no further prisoners of war would be sent to Odessa.

At Odessa conditions appear to have been very good. A former school building had been set aside as a transit barracks, hot baths were provided for disinfestation, and the Russian authorities provided clean underclothing. Here many of the men met members of the British military mission for the first time. Red Cross food and other supplies were available and there was adequate medical attention. The men were allowed to move about under escort ('for their own protection') and one of our men records having been twice to the opera.

British ships repatriating Russians to Odessa were turned round almost immediately to bring back British and American prisoners of war from the transit camp there. The first drafts of New Zealanders sailed in early March, arriving at Port Said on the 12th and 13th. It had originally been intended that the New Zealanders from Odessa should arrive on one ship, which after a brief stay in the Middle East, would take them on to New Zealand. The first drafts were therefore held for 'processing' at Maadi, where it appears some of the men became a little restive and impatient. But further difficulties were avoided by deciding almost immediately to send them and later drafts on to the Reception Group in the United Kingdom.

By June 1945 all the New Zealanders[1] had been brought back from Odessa. Two-thirds of these were men from the camps and hospitals in Upper Silesia and Poland which had been swept up early in the Russian advance; another fifth were from camps in Austria, where the same thing had happened two months or so later. The remainder were stragglers who had made their way to the Russian lines in Poland or, perhaps unwilling to report to the Russians, had waited until they could contact a British liaison officer. Our men were (not surprisingly) indignant at being robbed of their possessions by Russian troops and at being kept under guard during their evacuation. Some realised, however, the problem which the Russian occupation troops faced in the masses of people of all nationalities who were wandering about Poland. Some realised, too, that they were being treated no worse than Russian soldiers and sometimes better, and that the standards of the Russian soldier in the matter of eating, sleeping, and washing were much lower than their own. Many men encountered friendliness; others said that so indiscriminate was the Russian use of firearms that they were glad to

---

[1] The total number of New Zealand ex-prisoners who passed through Odessa was 168, out of a British Commonwealth total of 4310.

reach Odessa without being shot. Some officials took the attitude that the Russian authorities were deliberately neglecting to fulfil their part of the agreement concerning our released men. Such recrimination is almost inevitable when two nations whose standards of living differ vastly undertake reciprocal obligations which involve such things as warfare and accommodation.

V: *Protection of Interests of Prisoners of War and Civilians*

By January 1945 there were about 40,000 British prisoners of war more than half-way through their fifth year of captivity. The idea of exchanging long-term able-bodied prisoners had been first brought to the notice of the belligerents in a letter by the International Red Cross Committee, circulated in August 1943, which suggested the accommodation in a neutral country, firstly, of 'those whose mental and physical condition appears to be seriously endangered by prolonged imprisonment', and secondly of 'aged prisoners who have endured long imprisonment'. The matter was considered at a meeting of the Imperial Prisoners of War Committee in March 1944, when it was decided to negotiate for the exchange of prisoners aged 42 years[1] or over, whose captivity had lasted 18 months or longer. No reply was received until the beginning of March 1945, when the Germans suggested that the numbers of such prisoners exchanged from each side should be 25,000. There were doubts as to the practicability of such a large exchange at that period of the war, and though there were efforts to make arrangements for a smaller number, no details were ever finalised. The rapid Allied advances of the ensuing weeks soon obviated the necessity of proceeding further with the negotiations. Thus the humane conception embodied in Article 72[2] of the 1929 Geneva Convention bore no fruit in the Second World War,[3] beyond raising hopes which were constantly deferred and adding yet another to the crop of prison-camp rumours.

The matter which gave the Allied authorities most concern in 1945, and which was the subject of most of the negotiations on behalf of their nationals in captivity, was the welfare of the latter during the large-scale transfers which the German High Command seemed determined to carry through until the end. As the first reports

---

[1] The total number of Commonwealth prisoners involved was 3351, and the New Zealanders totalled 78. The oldest New Zealand Army man then a prisoner of war was born in 1891 and captured in May 1941.
[2] 'During the continuance of hostilities, and for humanitarian reasons, belligerents may conclude agreements with a view to the direct repatriation or accommodation in a neutral country of prisoners of war in good health who have been in captivity for a long time.'
[3] In March 1918 the French and German governments negotiated such an agreement for men over 48 who had been over 18 months in captivity.

concerning the conditions for the marching columns came through, they were made the subject of protests to the German authorities through the Protecting Power. It was pointed out that the prisoners on the march were encountering far more danger and hardship than they would have done if left in their camps. The protests met with promises to take immediate steps to improve food and accommodation for prisoners of war, not only during transfer but also in the assembly centres at which they arrived. In particular there was a promise that sick and weak prisoners would in future be transported by train or lorry. Swiss investigations were able to reassure the Allies that no reprisals on prisoners of war would be taken by the Germans on account of the intense aerial bombardment of Germany and the devastation and loss of life it was causing. There was, it was considered, no intention on the part of the German authorities to ill-treat Allied prisoners.

It soon became apparent, however, that with the increasing disorganisation in Germany there was no guarantee of proper supervision of the marching columns, nor were the Germans capable of carrying out their promise to provide adequate food and accommodation. In the circumstances it was decided to attempt to get food and other supplies to the prisoners by lorry, and that representatives of the Protecting Power and the International Red Cross Committee should maintain the closest contact possible with lines of march and assembly centres in order to be on the spot to protect the interests of prisoners as need arose. The Swiss representative who arranged the release of the 'hostages' from Oflag IVC, and the one who remained at Stalag 317 during the difficult period at the close of hostilities are examples that have already been mentioned. The provision of relief supplies by lorry is dealt with in the next section.

In order to prevent further unnecessary hardship to prisoners of war, the British and American governments had early put forward a proposal that the Germans should be asked to leave them in their camps in eastern Germany if the Allies gave an assurance that they would not after recovery be again used on the battlefronts. To this the Soviet Government had not agreed. On 12 April the German Government made an almost identical proposal regarding prisoners of war in all camps, provided the Allies undertook not to return them to active duty. The offer was accepted on 23 April by the Governments of the United Kingdom, the United States, and the USSR. At the same time, in order further to safeguard prisoners remaining in enemy hands, the Prime Minister, the President, and Marshal Stalin issued this warning:

> The Governments of the United Kingdom, the United States of America and the Union of Soviet Socialist Republics, on behalf

of all the United Nations at war with Germany, hereby issue a solemn warning to all commandants and guards in charge of Allied prisoners of war, internees or deported citizens of the United Nations in Germany and German-occupied territory and members of the Gestapo and all other persons of whatsoever service or rank in whose charge Allied prisoners of war, etc., have been placed whether in the battle zones, on the lines of communication or in rear areas.

They declare that they will hold all such persons no less than the German High Command and the competent German military, naval and air authorities, individually responsible for the safety and welfare of all Allied prisoners of war, etc., in their charge.

Any person guilty of maltreating or allowing any Allied prisoner of war, etc., to be maltreated whether in the battle zone, on the lines of communication, in a camp, hospital, prison or elsewhere, will be ruthlessly pursued and brought to punishment.

They give notice that they will regard this responsibility as binding in all circumstances and one which cannot be transferred to any other authorities or individuals whatsoever.

The Allied forces were deep into central Germany from both east and west; Berlin was the scene of an artillery and infantry battle. Such a warning was calculated to make all but the most fanatical think of the future; and it seems probable that, in the period following, this combined with the cessation of further moves prevented much additional hardship and brutality. A fortnight later the German forces surrendered unconditionally.

VI: *Relief Work*

In October 1944 the first shiploads of relief supplies and mail to go to Gothenburg had been taken on by the *Lilli Mathiessen* (a Swedish vessel under International Red Cross Committee supervision) to Lubeck. A second trip was made in January 1945 and the route became well established. At the same time four vessels chartered by the British Red Cross Society were transporting supplies direct from Lisbon to Marseilles. The packing of parcels continued and huge reserves were built up in the United Kingdom.[1] The net effect of these arrangements was to bring forward food supplies for British Commonwealth prisoners and internees on a scale more than sufficient to restore full service to camps. The way was cleared for this by the agreement of the German authorities to the holding of reserve stocks in depots outside camps.

But whereas in the autumn of 1944 transport conditions inside Germany had again become fairly satisfactory, in January 1945 the

---
[1] In April 1945 there were 7,500,000 to 8,000,000 in stock.

German railways could provide only about one-eighth of the rolling stock necessary to make possible an adequate distribution to camps. By February the railways could no longer be relied upon at all; and to make matters worse, about one quarter of the Allied prisoners were on the march from eastern Germany to the west. In order to get some relief to the marching columns, the International Red Cross Committee sent food by German lorries from Lubeck on 12 February and distributed it to the prisoners making their way along the northern route to Neu Brandenburg. Dumps of food were made there and in the neighbouring region, and some 20,000 food parcels were given out to Allied prisoners at a time when they were in dire need of them. Another dump was established at Luckenwalde to serve those moving on the central line of march.

The severe shortage of food in camps used as reception centres for the columns of prisoners has already been mentioned. The International Red Cross Committee arranged with SHAEF for an experimental convoy of lorries loaded with food, each lorry painted white and marked with the Red Cross emblem,[1] to be driven by Red Cross drivers into Bavaria, where many of the prisoners were being sent. Such a convoy, consisting of 25 lorries provided by the Canadian and American Red Cross Societies, left Switzerland on 7 March. At the same time permission was obtained from the German authorities to move into Germany from Switzerland whole relief trains of Red Cross supplies, in order to establish quickly large dumps at suitable places. The first of these left Switzerland on 6 March and reached Moosburg 43 hours later with over 93,000 food parcels, medicines, and other relief. The state of the line, the difficulty of getting suitable coal, and the task of persuading anyone to drive the engine made the journey an eventful one for the accompanying International Red Cross official. Besides negotiating for the safe passage of the train, he had at times to set to and stoke the engine.

Meanwhile the lorries, after distributing supplies to camps and marching columns, had returned to Moosburg to reload. Four special convoys of twelve lorries, each driven by Canadian prisoners of war and accompanied by scout cars or motor cycles, left Switzerland between 12 and 18 March for southern and central Germany. A second train left for Moosburg on the 28th with 500 tons of food, and a third on 12 April; part of these supplies were taken on to Thuringia and adjacent areas which could not be reached by rail. The fleet of lorries had now reached a total of 150, of which 100 had been supplied by SHAEF, which also provided petrol and spares; and a portion of the fleet was based on Lubeck to serve the

---

[1] See p. 462.

northern area. Further relief trains established depots at Ravensburg above Lake Constance and at Landek in Austria, where large columns of prisoners were making their way.

In this final phase of the war in Europe the need for relief supplies became greater than it had ever been, while the means of conveying and distributing them became more and more difficult. Even with the co-operation of the German High Command, it was wellnigh impossible for the representatives of the International Red Cross Committee to contact the hundreds of columns of prisoners of war on the roads and supply them, since after a while only their general lines of march were known. The best results came from the supplying of reception centres where the arrival of food undoubtedly prevented much additional sickness and misery. The International Red Cross Committee pays a tribute to the camp leaders, who kept them informed of the numbers in their camps, and by negotiations with the local German authorities obtained concessions which made distribution easier. Rapid evacuation of British and Dominion prisoners of war soon eased the problem of supply, and left the Committee free to cater for the Allied prisoners who still remained in camps and with the more permanent problem of displaced persons.

VII: *Enemy Aliens in New Zealand*

The German civilians interned at Somes Island also presented an evacuation problem, since a number of them had expressed a wish for repatriation to Germany. Transport difficulties and the chaotic state of Germany in the immediate post-war period made it necessary to postpone any such moves. In the meantime the internees were kept in the camp on Somes Island. The subsidy of £15 a year which they had been receiving from the German Government had however ceased, and the complete defeat of Germany and their own rather hopeless position caused a serious deterioration in morale.

The New Zealand authorities finally decided that all these internees should have the option of remaining in New Zealand. When the camp was disbanded in mid-October 1945 they were permitted to take jobs in the civilian community. In his final report on the Somes Island camp, the New Zealand delegate of the International Red Cross Committee paid a tribute to the excellent conditions under which alien internees had been permitted to live in New Zealand, and to the ' humanitarian principles ' which had been the ' guiding factor ' in the attitude of the New Zealand authorities towards their treatment.

* * * * *

The way in which captivity would end had been for a long time for those held prisoner in Germany the subject of endless conjecture. The situation as it would affect the recovery of these men had been carefully studied by the Allied High Command. It was also the subject of careful consideration and detailed planning by camp leaders. An 'Operation and Administrative Order' issued in one of the large stalags made detailed provision for a situation in which the prisoners, in the event of an armistice, would have to march out under their own arrangements. Men's attention was called to the danger of leaving the camp independently and being at large in the country of a defeated enemy, where there might be no proper form of control. The plans at one of the larger oflags envisaged several alternatives to an armistice and covered the action to be taken in the event of a forced move of the camp, or its abandonment by the guards, or an attempt by SS personnel to use officer prisoners as hostages. Most of these plans were designed to secure the safety of the camp occupants and not to offer active military assistance to the Allied forces, since it was clear after the invasion that the latter did not require any. In the same way escaping was regarded in the spring of 1945 as not likely to be of help to the Allied cause, and some camp commanders forbade it.

Had it been necessary to put all the camp schemes into operation, it is problematical how many men would have carried out their instructions. Many of those who had been rounded up in their camps in Italy and transferred to Germany were resolved that, no matter what instructions were received about remaining in camp, they would trust their own judgment in a future emergency. As it turned out, the speed of the Allied advance precluded the necessity for most of the arrangements, but in some camps which were abandoned by their guards the planned organisations took over and seem to have functioned well.

The degree to which some elements of the German military organisation cohered until the very end was a matter of amazement to many prisoners of war inside Germany. As late as mid-April officers were moved from reception centres north towards Lubeck and south towards the Austrian redoubt. No doubt some of the guards and their commanders still believed that Germany would pull something out of the fire—some super-weapon—and save the situation. Others were more and more openly expressing the view that Germany was finished. Some prisoners mention that many guards became more 'lax' and 'friendly', more ready to take a 'reasoning attitude', and one man talks of a 'general softening up'; others found little change. But whether or not their attitude towards prisoners of war changed, most of the guards continued to the last to carry out orders to move, to prevent prisoners escaping, to send them out to work and even to pay them, as if the German military machine was intact and in perfect running order. An entry in a New Zealander's diary for 21 March reads:

> Definitely the end of our long, weary march; we start work at the factory tomorrow. We protested we were in no condition to work; it didn't mean a thing; we start tomorrow. . . .

It was only when they were near enough to the Allied forces to be overrun that the German guards ceased to care about carrying out their orders. Though some of the guards who had consistently shown brutality were pointed out to the liberating troops, there seems to have been little vindictiveness on the part of our released prisoners and no active measures of revenge. Some guards who had been considerate to the prisoners in their charge had been given certificates to present to the Allied forces when they surrendered. For many of these it must have been a relief to be able at last to present them.

Most prisoners seem to have expected their food situation to deteriorate in the period immediately preceding their release. The shortage of food in 1945 was of the same degree as that experienced by many prisoners in the transit period following their capture, but men who were just completing several years of captivity were probably in a less fit state to endure it. Besides the food shortage there was the mental tension created in the period of waiting for release. With the Allied forces so near, the uncertainty as to whether they would be moved, or abandoned, or handed over to the SS involved a strain on prisoners rather similar to that of a person playing a desperate game, who sees victory within his grasp yet does not know what last-minute moves his opponent may make to reverse the position. The tension was often relieved when a camp was moved; for men's minds were then distracted by the business of moving, and while on the move, of grimly keeping going. But the physical effort involved in the marches across Europe put a tremendous strain on the constitutions of many of those who took part in them. A New Zealander writes at the end of one of the marches:

> So here we are, after eight weeks on the road and covering 700-odd kilometres, marching from winter into spring, leaving many a comrade in his last sleep, destined to still exist until the end of the war, which, we pray God, won't be very long.

The long-term effects, both physical and mental, of captivity were recognised in the efforts made to exchange those who had been prisoners the longest. These effects and those which would be the inevitable result of the marches were at the time also being taken into account in the arrangements for the treatment of ex-prisoners of war in the reception centres on the Continent and in the United Kingdom.

The events of 1945 created an anxiety on the part of next-of-kin of prisoners and internees in Germany similar to that of people with prisoner-of-war relatives in Italy at the time of the Italian armistice. It was not for some time that the details of the marches across Europe became known. By the time that reliable information on these transfers was available, the war was in its last stage and camps were being liberated. Although provision had been made for the documentation of prisoners on the Continent, the Allied authorities judged that it was more important to evacuate ex-prisoners from the Continent to the United Kingdom with all possible speed rather than to delay their movement until certain ' processing ' had been carried out. A spell of bad weather at the beginning of May held up the air-lift, but when it ceased ex-prisoners were being flown to the United Kingdom at the rate of 10,000 or more a day; by the end of May more than 154,000 British Commonwealth ex-prisoners alone had been flown across. Many of our men sent cables to New Zealand from the Continent, but next-of-kin were understandably impatient to receive official confirmation, which was usually not possible until accurate lists had been compiled in the United Kingdom. It is clear from the statements of prisoners of war how much they appreciated the speed and efficiency with which they were evacuated from their camps and flown to the United Kingdom, and the absence of red tape and hard-and-fast procedure which might have caused delays. Besides military operations and the occupation of an enemy country, the Allied forces had to cope with 2,250,000 ex-prisoners of war, as well as a mass of displaced civilians. The promptitude with which our released prisoners and internees were evacuated is proof at once of the high priority accorded to their welfare and of the efficient co-operation of the various services whose task it was to handle them.

CHAPTER 11

The Reception of Liberated Prisoners in the United Kingdom and Their Repatriation

IT is of interest to record that in July 1942 the War Office set up a committee to prepare provisional plans for the repatriation and reception of Commonwealth prisoners of war following their liberation in Europe and the Far East, and that two months later the plans were under consideration by the Imperial Prisoners of War Committee. There was unanimity on two matters of policy: firstly that all prisoners of war should be repatriated with as little delay as possible, and secondly that adequate facilities should be provided for their comfort, welfare, clothing and feeding, until such time as they proceeded on leave, demobilisation, or further duty in the forces.

On this basis a detailed repatriation and reception scheme was worked out. As it seemed likely that both in Italy and Germany there would, before the end of hostilities, be a shortage of food and medical supplies, together with a fairly complete disruption of rail communication, it was thought advisable that prisoners should remain in their camps to await instructions, food, and medical supplies there. They would be moved as soon as possible to transit camps near their embarkation ports. The need for complete and accurate check lists of prisoners would be met by setting up existing lists in type immediately and keeping them continually up-to-date, so that when an armistice was imminent a complete register could be printed in a matter of days. The adaptation of this general scheme to cater for prisoners in Italy after the Italian capitulation, and the way in which things worked out in practice, have already been dealt with.

In 1942 it had seemed most practicable for men from the United Kingdom to proceed home direct from Italian and German ports, but for those from New Zealand and other Dominions to be collected at a transit camp at Trieste. This route, besides being geographically the shortest for our men, also took them through their already established base in Egypt. Nevertheless, it had been realised even at this early stage that transport difficulties on the Continent might make it advisable to evacuate all prisoners through the United Kingdom, in order to facilitate their immediate removal from the country in which they were held prisoners.

As the time of liberation began to seem nearer to those in prisoner-of-war camps their interest in their future movements quickened. By the end of March 1943 the New Zealand Military Liaison Officer in London had received a large number of inquiries from our men in prisoner-of-war camps as to the possibility of their returning home through the United Kingdom. The majority of these inquiries were from men who wished to complete studies and examinations in England, to gain special knowledge or experience in some branch of their occupation, to see parents and other near relatives, or to rejoin their wives and children temporarily resident there. Following the precedent set in 1919, the New Zealand Government decided to allow ex-servicemen special leave in the United Kingdom for family, business or educational reasons, but limited the first of these to exceptional cases and the two last to cases where the facilities sought were not available in New Zealand.

By the end of 1943 the staff of the Supreme Allied Commander in Europe and that of the War Office were agreed that it would be more speedy and generally practicable to evacuate all prisoners from northern Europe 'unsorted' straight down the lines of communication which would be set up following the invasion of Europe from the west. It was considered that to evacuate released Dominion prisoners on a special route through Italy would involve establishing and maintaining a third line of communication, a task which would take a considerable time and thus greatly delay evacuation. At the beginning of 1944, therefore, a new plan based on these operational considerations was submitted to the Imperial Prisoners of War Committee. It contained provision for the setting up in the United Kingdom of Dominion reception camps staffed by their own countrymen. Dominion Governments gave their approval and so set the stage for a repetition of the events of 25 years before, when large numbers of an earlier generation of Dominion servicemen also spent their immediate post-war period in the United Kingdom.

In early 1944 the only people with practical experience in catering for the needs of ex-prisoners of war were those in the United Kingdom and in the Middle East who had received the repatriation drafts of sick, wounded, and protected personnel, and the personnel of the Allied Repatriation Unit in Italy who had received escapers and evaders making their way to the Allied lines. From April 1942 onwards, however, successive exchange drafts of sick, wounded, and protected personnel had brought back information regarding the feeding and other conditions of those in enemy hands; and medical examinations, both physical and psychiatric, had provided data for a prognosis of the physical and mental condition of prisoners on repatriation. With the addition of facts gleaned from a steady trickle of escapers, those responsible for the welfare of British prisoners of war were able to build up a fairly accurate picture of prisoner-of-war life, though perhaps coloured a little too much with the viewpoint of the hospital inmate and the medical orderly. An experimental rehabilitation scheme for 1180 protected personnel repatriated in October 1943 was carried out at Crookham in England in December 1944, and the results of this and many other observations were embodied in a report by the Psychiatric Division of the War Office.[1] Its findings and recommendations became the basis for the treatment of repatriated prisoners of war from the psychological aspect. It summed up the problem thus:

Other things being equal, the difficulties of social readaptation on repatriation appear to be more severe in ex-prisoners of war than in any other body of men so far studied. . . . Emotional problems are disproportionately severe in men who have been prisoners for more than eighteen months. . . . Planning the rehabilitation of these men demands particular care—" Not soft handling, but *different* handling."[2]

The New Zealand Section of the Allied Repatriation Unit in Italy, whose difficulties in coping with large numbers of escapers and evaders have already been mentioned, took a different view:

Any ex-prisoner arriving in our hands should be treated as a normal soldier who has returned to duty after having had a slack time. He should be first 'processed', clothed, and documented and receive information on military matters to get him up to date, and his liability to Army orders made clear so that there is no doubt if he makes any breach of orders. He should be punished for breaches as a normal soldier. . . . Special treatment, leave or concessions such as UK leave on a big scale should be avoided.[3]

This was a viewpoint developed from dealing expeditiously with the administrative and material needs of escapers and evaders immediately after they reached Allied lines, and arranging to get rid of them to New Zealand as quickly as possible. Some of the Army administrative authorities in New Zealand also felt that there was a tendency on the part of the public to be over-solicitous regarding the mental and physical condition of ex-prisoners of war who had returned to New Zealand, and that some of them were inclined to play up to the sympathy of the medical officers examining them.

The Director-General of Medical Services took the view that a middle course should be steered between too much 'processing' and rigid discipline and too much fuss and emphasis on abnormal mental states. In the course of a visit to England in the spring of

---

[1] Lt-Col A. T. M. Wilson, RAMC: Report to the War Office on the psychological aspects of the rehabilitation of repatriated prisoners of war.
[2] The last phrase is quoted from the statement of an ex-prisoner.
[3] Report to HQ 2 NZEF by OC 1 NZ Repat Unit, 25 March 1945.

1944 he investigated from the medical point of view the accommodation requirements of the Reception Depot for New Zealand ex-prisoners there, with special regard to the psychological aspect. He recommended that the reception centre should be in the nature of a convalescent depot, with absence of pinpricking discipline, and that it should be near a town of reasonable size, as all ex-prisoners would be 'heartily sick of the country'. Once the ex-prisoner had been satisfied that he was medically fit (or alternatively that he needed treatment), his transfer to New Zealand should be a first priority, since most ex-prisoners had 'a strong desire to get home and . . . mingle with the civilian community'. Fortunately for all concerned, it was this enlightened viewpoint that was adopted by the Reception Group in the United Kingdom.

In March 1944 the Military Liaison Officer in London produced an estimate of accommodation, staff, and other requirements for the 8400 or so New Zealand Army ex-prisoners of war who would be received in England pending their transport home to New Zealand. In a report to Army Headquarters in New Zealand he drew attention to the importance of efficient handling of this side of the problem, preferably by a staff of New Zealanders.

These [ex-prisoners] . . . will tend to be unduly critical of any mismanagement and intolerant of even apparent blunders, no matter what the circumstances might be. They will not only be news, but a very wide political capital, and press and public will be even more critical and less understanding. . . .

On the basis of this and already discovered requirements for handling repatriates and escapers, a detailed plan was worked out in consultation with the War Office. With little change this was the blueprint from which the 2 NZEF Reception Group was built.

The plan suggested that senior Army staff officers should immediately begin work for an organisation which would consist of a headquarters and four 'Wings' (with a possible increase to eight), each to accommodate about 50 officers and 1000 men. The Pay and Postal sections of the organisation should be ready to function well in advance, the Pay Corps staff being already available in the United Kingdom. As no ex-prisoners should be used on the staff of the Reception Group until they had taken their 28 days' special leave (regarded as a necessary mental relaxation for the majority), the organisation should be complete before the arrival of the first draft. Onward passage of repatriates to New Zealand was not expected to be possible for six months, and to fill in the waiting period educational and recreational facilities would be organised for the unfit, and all-arms training for the fit majority.

If the last item sounds strange in retrospect, it must be remembered that in March 1944 a sudden end to the war with Japan was not foreseen, and the future operational employment of fit ex-prisoners could not be neglected. For the same reason the ultimate importance of the Education and Rehabilitation Service was not recognised, and the minor part it was expected to play is reflected in an establishment of twelve all ranks out of a Group total of 930. At this stage, too, the evacuation of German prisoner-of-war camps by air had not yet been considered, and the influx of prisoners was not expected to be other than a gradual process extending over a period of twelve weeks from the date of the armistice. Neither the extent of the food shortages of the last months of the war, nor the forced marches across chaotic Germany, were then foreseen, and a camp reception hospital of only 50 beds was considered sufficient for the 8000 or so repatriates.

At first it was thought by the service authorities concerned that the most convenient and economical way of catering for the 450 or so Air Force and the handful of Navy repatriates, and at the same time ensuring that they were handled by New Zealanders, would be to make use of the extensive accommodation and organisation arranged for the larger numbers of repatriated Army personnel. But senior officers of all three services in London foresaw in this plan difficulties based on differences between the services in pay and administration. In early July 1944 it was finally decided that New Zealand airmen repatriates should go to an RAF station, which would include a New Zealand reception centre, staffed with a considerable percentage of men from the Dominion. Naval airmen would go to this centre, and the remaining Navy personnel would be catered for in Royal Navy transit camps.

After the invasion of the Continent had been launched on 6 June 1944, there were no longer any security reasons for postponing the setting up of reception centres for repatriated prisoners of war. A nucleus of eleven officers[1] who could be spared from Italy arrived in England to make preliminary arrangements. Brigadier James Hargest[2] was appointed to command the New Zealand Reception Group, but he had hardly time to meet his officers and discuss general policy when he was killed in France while on a farewell visit to the division with which he had been serving as observer. The Group moved into temporary quarters in Hartwell House, Aylesbury, Buckinghamshire, and it was there that it received 89 of the 116 New Zealand repatriates included in the exchange of

---

[1] Under the command of Lt-Col L. F. Rudd, former Military Secretary, 2 NZEF.
[2] Brig Hargest took part in the D Day landing in Normandy as New Zealand observer. He was killed in action on 12 August 1944, on what would have been his last day in the field before taking command of the Prisoner of War Reception Group.

September 1944. The staff were thus able to gain their first practical experience of catering for the needs of ex-prisoners.

It was expected that it would be some time before transport would be available to take the repatriated prisoners of war to New Zealand, and provision was now made in the reception scheme for facilities to enable them to fill in the period of waiting. It was decided that each ex-prisoner would receive 28 days' leave, with 4s 6d a day subsistence allowance and a free railway warrant to anywhere in the United Kingdom. In addition he would be allowed to take in the United Kingdom all except a fortnight of his discharge leave, while awaiting transport to New Zealand. To provide the men with purposeful and congenial occupations during this period and to help them on the road to rehabilitation, approval was given to set up a complete Education and Rehabilitation Service in the United Kingdom.[1] In addition to funds and goods supplied from the National Patriotic Fund, the Government passed a vote of £10,000 to provide special comforts, entertainments, and conducted tours for ex-prisoners during their stay. Provision was also made by the Red Cross, the YMCA, and the Church Army for canteen and recreational facilities.

The Education and Rehabilitation Service aimed at giving the men a chance to take advantage of their presence in the United Kingdom by securing educational courses and professional experience not otherwise available to them. Its work was planned to cover a period of six months and to give three kinds of facilities: firstly, information to fill the gaps created by captivity in knowledge of the progress of the war, of New Zealand from all aspects, and of world affairs generally; secondly, vocational training, including university courses, trade training, and attachments to factories or offices for gaining further specialised experience; and thirdly, advice concerning facilities provided by the Rehabilitation Act of 1941 and readjustment to civilian status generally, especially for those who had been too young when they joined the armed forces to have properly started on a career. Textbooks, libraries, and films would be provided, and advantage would be taken of local educational facilities. Short courses and attachments to factories and offices, as well as longer university and trade courses, were to be awarded only after consideration by a special committee. The whole scheme was to be on a voluntary basis, but each man was to be fully informed of all the facilities available to him.

On 25 September the Government approved the appointment

---

[1] An initial grant of £9500 was made, mainly for the purchase of library and textbooks.

of Major-General H. K. Kippenberger,[1] then convalescing in England, as Commander of the Reception Group.[2] He took over his duties at the beginning of October, just before the Group moved to permanent quarters in part of the Old Park Barracks, Dover, a group of buildings erected in 1939 but in constant use during the war and somewhat damaged by bombing. This was to be the Group's headquarters and the centre for receiving and partially 'processing' all repatriates before they were distributed to their appropriate wings. The latter were to be located partly in these buildings, partly in the Duke of York Military School at Dover, partly at the Turnpike Camp at Hythe, and partly in requisitioned buildings, mainly large hotels, at Folkestone, Margate, and Westgate. Had the war in Europe ended with an armistice in late 1944, it is probable that our repatriates would have arrived in Dover Harbour in ships and been received and distributed according to this plan. But Dover was on the line of communication of the British Liberation Army, and the accommodation there had to be evacuated in February 1945 to provide a leave centre for British troops from Europe.

This meant a second move for the Reception Group staff at a time when Germany was obviously nearing cracking point, and therefore it entailed the risk of their not being ready in time to receive released prisoners. But there can be little doubt that the requisitioned buildings they now occupied had far greater possibilities for the creation of the type of rest centre visualised for repatriates. The Turnpike Camp at Hythe, the only barrack accommodation retained, later produced such an unfavourable reaction from repatriated officers that it was decided to abandon its use. The new accommodation included fifty buildings, most of them hotels a hundred yards or so from the sea and thronged by tourists in peacetime. Their temporary shortcomings in respect of electrical fittings and plumbing and their shortage of furniture in April and early May were more than outweighed by their pleasant situation and lack of barrack atmosphere. From the psychological point of view the new accommodation had a high potential value for the rehabilitation of released prisoners of war.

By mid-March the Reception Group headquarters was established at Westgate, with wings at Folkestone, Cliftonville, and Broadstairs, and the Group hospital at Haine. Provision was made to

---

[1] Maj-Gen Sir Howard Kippenberger, KBE, CB, DSO and bar, ED, m.i.d., Legion of Merit (US); Wellington; born Ladbrooks, 28 Jan 1897; barrister and solicitor; 1 NZEF 1916–17; CO 20 Bn Sep 1939–Apr 1941, Jun–Dec 1941; commanded 10 Bde, Crete, May 1941; 5 Inf Bde Jan 1942–Jun 1943, Nov 1943–Feb 1944; 2 NZ Div 30 Apr–14 May 1943 and 9 Feb–2 Mar 1944; Prisoner of War Reception Group (UK) 1944–45; twice wounded; Editor-in-Chief, NZ War Histories.
[2] Col Rudd was appointed second-in-command, and Brig J. M. Twhigg ADMS.

receive well over one thousand ex-prisoners at each of the infantry wings, and a total of 6600-odd, including some 370 officers and some 440 senior NCOs in the whole Group. Puttick Wing[1] was organised to act as a transit reception wing through which all repatriates would pass for preliminary equipping and processing before going to their permanent quarters. The welfare side of the organisation had been thoroughly developed, and now included a residential club[2] in London staffed by New Zealand Women's Army Auxiliary Corps personnel.

As the war had progressed prisoners of war had become the object of increasing public interest and sympathy; and now that their liberation seemed near, everyone was alert to ensure that they received the best treatment on their arrival in England. In October 1944 the War Office had circularised all United Kingdom next-of-kin with a list of suggestions for handling their ex-prisoner relatives, based on ideas obtained from those already home. Broadcasts and press releases for the public generally followed, emphasizing the same points:

> Don't be hurt if he does not come and see you for a bit. . . . Don't give him too much of a party when he does come to see you. . . . Be a good listener. . . . Answer all his questions carefully. . . . Don't pity him. All he wants from friends and relatives is understanding help until he finds his feet.

Similar advice was published in New Zealand not long afterwards.

In his broadcast talk of 21 February the Commander of the New Zealand Reception Group, speaking of its forthcoming task, said that he was glad of ' an opportunity of being of service to so many old friends and comrades '.

> All the time I intend to treat these men as soldiers. There will be discipline in the camps of a sort that, I think, will be calculated to maintain self-respect and to restore or keep high their morale.

The problem of maintaining order in such a large and rather amorphous body of men might well have been a serious one. There can be little doubt that any attempt at strict regimental discipline would have been disastrous with men who had spent the previous year or two doing their best to thwart a system of military discipline notorious for its severity, and some of whom had suffered sufficiently to regard almost any future eventuality with indifference. Further, the European conflict over and an assault on Japan imminent, the emphasis should obviously be on rehabilitation. On this point the Commander stated simply: ' We will do everything we can think of . . . to get them ready for return to civilian life.' Ex-prisoners

---

[1] Wings were named after senior 2 NZEF officers: Freyberg, Puttick, Miles, Hargest, Barrowclough, Crump, and Park.
[2] The Fernleaf Club in Lowndes Square, Knightsbridge.

of war in general regarded it as fortunate that the Reception Group was commanded by a man who saw their problems with such clarity and understanding.

The arrangement for the reception of New Zealand Air Force ex-prisoners followed similar lines. A large waterfront hotel as accommodation for No. 12 Personnel Distribution and Reception Centre of the RAF station at Brighton had been made available for them. There was provision for transport to the centre, cleaning and pressing of uniforms left in England before capture, comforts and free cigarettes, and private hospitality. The 2 NZEF Reception Group supplied two complete dental units, a postal unit, a YMCA officer to run a canteen, and all the facilities of the Army Education and Rehabilitation Service. The Prime Minister summed up the policy of the New Zealand Government regarding the reception arrangements in England:

> No expense will be spared and no avenue overlooked by which the organisation can be perfected and the men made to feel that New Zealand herself is welcoming them on the shores of England.

On the last days of March, three weeks after the move to the Isle of Thanet, Brigadier Clifton,[1] who had escaped a few days before his camp was liberated, arrived at the Reception Group headquarters at Westgate. He was followed on 5 April by the first draft of released prisoners, 31 officers and one other rank. By the end of the month some 100 officers and 1100 other ranks had been received, of which a large number had been processed[2] and were already on leave. The effects of lack of food and long marches had been noticed in the condition of many of the repatriated men,[3] and about 250 of them had been admitted to Haine Hospital. But many of those not seriously affected quickly showed improvement as a result of the rest, sea air, and good food they enjoyed at the reception centre. There was a great spirit of cheerfulness, and many men expressed their pleasure at being with fellow New Zealanders.

---

[1] Brig G. H. Clifton, DSO and bar, MC, m.i.d.; Auckland; born Greenmeadows, 18 Sep 1898; Regular soldier; CRE 2 NZ Div, 1940–41; Chief Engineer 30 Corps, 1941–42; commanded 6 Inf Bde Feb–Sep 1942; p.w. 4 Sep 1942; escaped Mar 1945; NZ Military Liaison Officer, London, 1949–52; Commandant Northern Military District, Mar 1952–Sep 1953

[2] 'Processing' was not to take more than three days for each man and consisted of: (1) short address of welcome; (2) recording of name, etc.; (3) preliminary medical and dental examination ('fit for leave'); (4) pay; (5) mail; (6) interrogation; (7) interview with ERS; (8) issue of kit; (9) issue of comforts; (10) interview for officers with A Branch.

[3] The report of the ADMS for April states: 'As a result of recent privations and hardships the general condition of returned prisoners of war has been poor and a high proportion has been found to be suffering from varying degrees of malnutrition and avitaminosis. Of the number reporting to the NZEF (UK) Reception Group, approximately 18% have required hospital treatment.' (In the first two weeks the proportion was as high as 30 per cent.)

Local people were sincerely generous in offering hospitality, and many ex-prisoners were taking advantage of this to get in touch with the atmosphere of home life again. The English inns with their pleasant environment and sensible drinking hours were also contributing in no small way towards restoring men to normality by their homely atmosphere and convivial company. Dances were proving very popular, and there was a general keenness on the part of repatriates to take part once again in the normal life of a community.

At the beginning of May the intake from the Continent slackened off a little because of bad flying weather. But the excellent weather which followed made it possible to bring the total number of New Zealanders 'safe' in the United Kingdom to over 5500 by the end of the month. On the whole the health of the later arrivals was better, for the majority of them were from camps in central and southern Germany which had not had to march long distances, which in any case had not had to march until the winter was over, and some of which had not had to march at all. The percentage of hospital cases from the May intake was only 4.7, and a very small number of men were suffering from deficiency diseases. Nevertheless, at the end of May there were still 368 of the repatriates in hospital in England.

The majority of the New Zealand Air Force ex-prisoners arrived at Brighton in May, most of them landing at Dunsfold airfield and being brought down by special buses. The Women's Voluntary Service of Brighton helped to make the hotel in which they were billeted comfortable: by making beds, by putting flowers in the bedrooms, and by organising a club[1] for Australians, New Zealanders, and South Africans near their hotels. The messes for both officers and other ranks were described by the men as excellent, waiting and cooking being done by the Women's Auxiliary Air Force personnel.

Naval repatriates went to Royal Navy depots such as Lee-on-Solent and Goscourt, where they were rekitted and processed, much in the same way as Army and other liberated prisoners. They were placed on three months' leave, at the end of which they were cared for either by 2 NZEF Reception Group or by the RAF Reception Centre at Brighton. They had all left by sea transport for New Zealand by the end of July 1945.

In late May a draft of 500-odd ex-prisoners, mostly from Austrian camps, arrived from Italy, and a similar number arrived on 10 June. Men who had been repatriated via Odessa and small

---

[1] The Southern Cross Club.

numbers of men from the Continent continued to arrive in June, and by the middle of the month it was estimated that all except about a hundred ex-prisoners had been transferred from the Continent to England.

No attempt was made by the Reception Group to force repatriates to take their leave immediately on their arrival; on the contrary they were encouraged to wait anything up to 14 days with the Group so that they could derive more benefit from leave when they did take it. The food supplied by the British Army Catering Corps was of a very high standard, and this was supplemented by delicacies from the National Patriotic Fund stocks. While the men remained at their reception centre there were organised tours to Canterbury, Chatham, Dover, Windsor, and other nearby places of interest. The canteen worked long hours to serve the two to three thousand repatriates who were not on leave, and in the evenings there were ENSA concerts, cinema shows and dances.

Although hardly anyone failed to spend some time in London during his leave, full use was made of the free rail warrants to anywhere in the United Kingdom, and repatriates were soon spread from Inverness to Land's End. Diaries mention not only Madame Tussaud's, the Battersea Power Station and Saint Paul's, but also Fort William, Loch Lomond, and the Glasgow shipyards. An enormous number of free tickets were available throughout the country for almost every kind of entertainment, as well as special facilities to visit important places of interest. Accommodation was at this period difficult to find in London, and that provided by the Fernleaf Club, as well as the meals and canteen service that accompanied it, saved a large number of men a good deal of money and a good deal of trouble of various kinds. There were several other servicemen's clubs in London which served meals and provided sleeping accommodation.

These also existed in the other large towns to which repatriates made their way in the course of their leave, but few men did not at some stage of their journeying receive an invitation to private hospitality. Apart from the welfare organisations which arranged such hospitality, the British people were lavish in extending the freedom of their homes to our men. A young New Zealand private soldier records drinking champagne with a retired British Army officer in his Berkeley Square flat as a result of a conversation in a railway compartment. Later in Edinburgh a kind old lady with whom he is billeted insists on making him rest in an armchair and giving him cough-mixture for his smoker's cough.

As to the extent of the repatriates' travels, one leave diary begins with London and goes on to Epsom, Southampton, Winchester, Salisbury, Edinburgh, Linlithgow, Aberdeen, Inverness, Fort

William, Glasgow, Carlisle, Newcastle, Northallerton, York, Bristol, Cheddar and Bath. But there were no doubt many unrecorded tours which surpassed this. Apart from the mental recreation of seeing new places, the returned men were able to mingle freely with the civilian population and begin their own social readjustment in their own time and in their own way. In early June one man says he is 'shyer than ever of women' and he leaves a dance to spend 'over an hour in a pub'. Three weeks later there is evidence that his shyness is disappearing. An evening in the company of a young Englishwoman which ends with 'vows on both sides to write', passes so quickly that he is locked out of the YMCA in York and has to spend the night at 'the best hotel.' There is no doubt that leave in the United Kingdom did much to break our repatriates in to the normal life of a community once again.

Their leave completed, many men set about taking advantage of the ERS facilities. By early June a large number had applied for individual study courses, and about one hundred for special attachments to offices and factories for further experience in their own vocation. The latter were of anything up to six months' duration and covered a wide variety of places of work. They ranged from the photographic section of the London Polytechnic to the office of a large firm of accountants, from the workroom of a tailor's cutter to the wards of a hospital specialising in some branch of medicine. Altogether between two and three hundred men took up one or other of these attachments. Fifty more were granted bursaries for university and other long courses of one or more years. Whereas the man on attachment remained in the forces on service pay, the bursar was discharged and received £250 a year and other special allowances. By the time that the majority of men were on the way home and the ERS was closing down, nearly a thousand men had used individual study courses, 130 had attended short 'leave' courses at English universities, and 30 had taken special wool courses at Bradford. The Director of Army Education visited England in July to report on these activities, and in particular on the attachments to factories and offices. He visited representative men at their work and found that the senior officers of the firms were taking a personal interest in the welfare and progress of the soldiers on attachment to them, and that in addition to the professional and vocational advantages, these attachments were greatly assisting the men in their readjustment to normal civilian life.

For those not wishing to take courses there were, during their period of waiting for a ship home, all the amenities of the wings at the Reception Group. There was a little marching and organised sport, but the men on the whole were left free to rest and find their own recreation. Discipline was very light, and short overstaying of leave was generally disregarded.

One of the problems with which the Reception Group was faced was how to discourage repatriates on release from reckless spending, or loss by other means, of their accumulated pay. Rumours of the limitation of drawings which reached prisoner-of-war camps in 1942 had caused many to transfer balances to trading banks, private firms and individuals. Assurances from pay officers that there would be no such limitation caused a great reduction in such transfers. Even so, as early as November 1944, the amounts so transferred totalled £107,000, and this total was at that time increasing at the rate of £4650 a month. To avoid a breach of faith and a discrimination which would hinder the policy of reabsorbing ex-prisoners of war as normal members of the forces, no restrictions on drawings of pay were imposed. But every effort was made to foster among repatriates by pamphlets, by personal interviews, and by unit talks the idea of limiting their spending in the United Kingdom to actual necessities, in view of the unduly high prices of all unrationed goods and the advantage of arriving in New Zealand with ample funds.

Those who were sick enough to have a spell in hospital were well looked after in the New Zealand Military Hospital at Haine and in a number of British hospitals equipped to treat specialised cases. The unexpected influx into Haine and its conversion from a 50-bed to a 250-bed hospital placed a severe strain on the staff. The average stay, however, proved to be about ten days only. For the men whose main requirements were special feeding and rest, the quiet situation and pleasant grounds at Haine were admirable. Over 90 per cent of the repatriates required dental treatment, of whom more than half needed dentures. The enormous work of getting 6000 men dentally fit continued on the ships taking ex-prisoners home, and in some cases was not completed until after their arrival in New Zealand.

Transport to New Zealand proved speedier than had ever been anticipated. On 30 May a first draft of 500-odd left Liverpool in the *Dominion Monarch.* Just under 1000 left on 18 June and another 200 on the 28th; in July a draft of 1400-odd sailed on the 3rd and another of 1000-odd on the 25th; and in August there were another two drafts, one of 1400 on the 7th and another of 400 on the 30th. By the latter date, not four months after the cessation of hostilities, there remained only some 600 repatriates in the United Kingdom, and over 4000 were already back in New Zealand.

At the beginning of August it was decided to contract the Reception Group to the Headquarters at Westgate and Puttick (reception) Wing at Cliftonville, and that even these should gradually decrease their staff and accommodation. Haine Hospital was closed at the end of the month. In September there remained only some 300 repatriates[1] still in the care of the Reception Group in England, and the majority of these left for New Zealand in October. Those who were on attachments were able to complete the full periods for which they were seconded and went home by later sailings with drafts of other returning servicemen.

It is clear from what ex-prisoners have said of the reception facilities in England, both Army and Air Force, that what was most appreciated was the minimising of service routine and the provision by ample leave of an opportunity to get away for a while from service life altogether. Men did not fail to note the 'freedom from irksome restrictions' and the small amount of 'form filling and red tape', as well as the 'friendly cooperation of reception staffs' and their 'real desire to help'. They spoke highly also of the good food, the 'spacious' quarters, and the service provided by ERS. Their comments show that the authorities were right in approaching the problem of receiving ex-prisoners mainly from a psychological angle. What many found most helpful was 'being left alone'. A naval airman sums up the opinions of many repatriates in his appreciation of:

The good sense and helpfulness of all who had any contact with us and the quick and expedient way in which the necessary formalities were disposed of, so that in record time we were free to do as we wished, which was to get peace and quiet.

The first large draft arrived back in New Zealand on 3 July. They were welcomed home by the Deputy Prime Minister, the Hon. Walter Nash, and transported expeditiously to their homes. It was noticed that in general they looked fit and healthy; no doubt both the period in England and the sea voyage had helped to restore their physical well-being. But many had emotional and domestic problems still to solve. Few could have been unmoved at finding themselves, after so many years overseas, once again in places and among people familiar from their youth but altered, sometimes markedly, with the passage of the years of absence. It remained to be seen how well these gaps could be bridged.

---

[1] A number of men, including those awarded bursaries, were allowed to take their discharge in the United Kingdom for various reasons.

CHAPTER 12

Liberation in the Far East and Repatriation
(January—September 1945)

I: *The Last Months of Hostilities and the Capitulation*

IN late 1944 the Philippines had been cut in two by the invasion of Leyte and Mindoro. Luzon was invaded at the beginning of 1945 and a month later Manila was liberated. The same month the drive north to Japan began with assaults on the Ryukyus and Iwojima and continued with another on Okinawa. On the Burma front the Allies had consolidated their positions in 1944, and in 1945 a drive south through Arakan brought them to Rangoon, which fell in May. In June the Australians landed on the coast of northern Borneo. By the middle of the year the Japanese were in full retreat throughout the Far East.

At the same time the air assault on the Japanese islands had begun, and a naval bombardment in mid-July demonstrated the overwhelming superiority of the Allied aero-naval forces. Yet as late as the 27th of that month the Japanese Government rejected the Potsdam ultimatum, and it seemed that their armed forces would fight on until Japan itself was completely overrun. A week later an atomic bomb fell on Hiroshima, and a few days later another on Nagasaki. Under the threat of an unknown new weapon which promised something approaching national annihilation, the fanatical determination of the Japanese military leaders to fight on was overruled. On 11 August the Japanese Government ordered their forces to surrender.

The New Zealanders captured during the last months of the war in the Far East were Fleet Air Arm or Air Force pilots shot down in territory still held by the Japanese—Burma, New Britain, the Dutch East Indies, or Japan itself. It is probable that the Japanese treatment of prisoners immediately after their capture and during interrogation improved on the whole during 1944, though not so markedly as it did in the last few days of the war.

In late 1942 a New Zealand airman who had been shot down in Burma and badly burned had been fortunate enough to be treated by a Japanese doctor, who had put on proper dressings; but his interrogators, in a rage at their lack of success after four hours of questioning, had torn them off and dragged their victim away for execution. The intervention of a senior Japanese officer had saved him, the same doctor had redressed his wounds, and he had been flown to Rangoon in a semi-conscious condition. Several more of our airmen crashed into the Burmese jungle in the later stages of the war, but they did not experience brutality matching this. In 1945, however, captured aircrew were still being told that they were not ordinary prisoners of war but criminals awaiting sentence. Certainly, too, it was exceptional for prisoners' injuries to be properly attended to by the Japanese, though no doubt partly because the Japanese themselves were desperately short of medical supplies. Nor did these injuries deter the Japanese from imposing on prisoners temporary spells without food or water during interrogation, from preventing their sleeping, nor from administering the usual beatings.

Thus two New Zealanders who baled out over Japan in August 1945 were 'set on by the local population and given the customary beating' with hoes and sticks, and were kept without food until their interrogation at Sendai was completed. But though beating accompanied the questioning, they were 'not kicked around after that'. On the other hand, in more remote areas there were brutalities almost to the very end. A New Zealander who crashed on an island in the New Britain group was taken to Rabaul and confined for two months by himself in a dark cave, the entrance to which was so small that his broken leg had necessitated his being dragged through the opening. Luckily he had not long to wait for liberation. Some prisoners had the misfortune to meet their death in the last few weeks of the war. A New Zealand airman, captured in Sumatra in early 1945 and taken to Singapore, was executed by the Japanese a fortnight before the capitulation.

It will be recalled from an earlier chapter that there were a number of New Zealanders among the 3000-odd civilians interned in the Santo Tomas University camp at Manila in the Philippines. The overcrowding at this camp was increased in the middle of 1943 when some 800 aged, sick, and mothers with young children, who had previously been released conditionally, were reinterned. A number of families, in order to achieve something approaching family privacy, had built themselves primitive shanties in the courtyards or grounds, and there did their cooking, washing, ironing, and other household chores. Food, which had always been in short supply, became still more scarce. For the first year it had been possible to buy eggs, fruit, and vegetables at a camp canteen, though at excessive and rapidly rising prices, but latterly these supplies almost disappeared. Many internees grew vegetables and a few had fruit trees. There was a marked loss of weight among all internees and a considerable number died from malnutrition or through lack of drugs.

During 1943 a number of civilian men were moved from Santo Tomas to a camp at Los Banos, some twenty miles south of Manila on the other side of Lake Laguna. They were joined in the following year by more civilians of both sexes, until the numbers reached over 2000. Here there were crude barracks with thatched roofs, most of them without doors or flooring, and still cruder sanitation arrangements. The camp lacked a proper water supply, and after three weeks of extreme shortage fatigue parties were allowed to bring it from the nearby hills. Rice was fairly plentiful until the last few months of captivity, and it was possible to buy fruit until late 1944. In the weeks preceding liberation supplies of all kinds became increasingly scarce—a situation which played into the hands of the black marketeer. Recorded prices include 75 dollars for a packet of native tobacco, and a jewelled tiepin for eight ounces of rice.

As an assault by the United States on the Philippines became imminent, the Japanese evacuated as many prisoners as possible to Japan by ship. But when the invasion had begun they did not try to move camps from the path of the invading forces, and for the most part handed over prisoners correctly, with the exception of a number of those on Palawan, who were horribly massacred. Civilian internees were left in their camps but were extremely apprehensive as to what action their guards might take. The attitude of the latter seemed to have become bitter or, as one internee described it, 'sullen and ominous'. It was known that the Japanese had adopted towards the pro-Allied Filipino population a policy which did not stick at wholesale butchery.

Fortunately both camps were liberated without any barbarity on the part of the Japanese. On 3 February American planes flew over Santo Tomas dropping messages of good cheer, and twelve hours later the first American tank drove into the camp. The liberation of Los Banos three weeks later was more dramatic. Six men who had escaped a week before led in Filipino scouts and American paratroops close to the Japanese guard posts by night. Next morning carriers dropped more paratroops over the camp, and the Japanese guard was accounted for in less than an hour. Since the camp was in what was still a battle zone, the internees were ferried across the lake to Manila in amphibian vehicles. They were quartered in the former Bilibid prison, converted into an emergency hospital, and plied with good food and medical attention. After a short stay at Manila most of the New Zealanders left for Australia and were back in New Zealand by the middle of April.

A number of New Zealand airmen captured in operations over Burma were confined in the former British civilian jail at Rangoon. The treatment of prisoners in this camp, more especially of the aircrew captured in 1944 and 1945, was bad and at times inhuman. In 1943 it was possible to buy eggs, tomatoes, and sugar fairly regularly; but as time went on this became impossible, and men had to exist on little else than an inadequate rice ration and vegetables grown in the camp garden. Medical care was hampered by lack of supplies and sometimes by obstruction on the part of the Japanese. It was only after some time that books were allowed in the camp, and a ban on all gatherings made it impossible to carry out any organised recreation, to set up educational classes, or to hold religious services. It was exceptional for a day to pass without someone receiving a beating with bamboo, steel golf club or other weapon, and beatings into unconsciousness were not uncommon. Aircrew received worse treatment still. They were kept sometimes five to a filthy cell measuring five yards by three, were given no bedding except old sacks, received half the rations of the other prisoners, and were beaten if caught conversing with one another. Those who came in wounded were almost without exception denied the services of a medical officer.

Some of the inmates of the cells were in time moved to another part of the camp and were able to improvise some kind of medical treatment for their sick and wounded comrades. Over the whole period of its existence the camp had a death roll of more than 40 per cent of its strength. In the last week or two before liberation some prisoners noticed a slight improvement in the general treatment, but others record that some of the guards were 'nastier than ever'. Perhaps in this camp more than in others prisoners had good grounds for wondering whether they would survive until liberation came.

As British forces approached Rangoon the Japanese attempted to transfer fit prisoners to Moulmein, but the rapidity of the British advance compelled them to release most of their prisoners while on the move. Thus on 25 April about half the prisoners in the Rangoon area were marched off towards Pegu, and two days later they were abandoned by their guards. The last Japanese abandoned the Rangoon jail on the night of 28-29 April, leaving behind them a message informing the prisoners that they could regard themselves as free and saying that they hoped to meet them again on the battlefield. Four days later units of the British Army marched into Rangoon, and liberated prisoners were sent by air or by hospital ship to Calcutta.

By June 1945 sufficient prisoners of war and civilian internees had been recovered from Japanese captivity during military operations to assess the extent to which Allied nationals were in special danger as liberating forces approached them, and to determine what measures could be taken to protect them. Apart from the resiting of camps close to military targets which the Japanese wished specially to save from bombing, there was evidence that the Japanese were tending to secure their prisoners in strategically safer areas rather than move them to areas where they could be more usefully employed. Movements of senior Allied officers from Formosa to Manchuria, and of all kinds of prisoners from the Philippines to Japan, from Malaya to Indo-China, from western to eastern Thailand, and from Shanghai farther inland to Fengtai, all pointed to this and to their possible use as hostages. It was conceivable that the Japanese might still try to move more prisoners north from the threatened southern areas. In order to omit no step which might save Allied lives, it was proposed to attempt to negotiate with the Japanese an agreement to cease further withdrawals of prisoners of war; and if no response was received, to give Commanders-in-Chief discretion to issue solemn warnings similar to those given to Germany. In view of the Japanese rejection of the Potsdam ultimatum it seems doubtful whether these measures would have been effective; but the swift advent of the armistice obviated the necessity of putting them to the test.

II: *Recovery and Evacuation after the Armistice*

Planning for the evacuation and repatriation of released prisoners from the Far East, like that for prisoners in Italy and Germany, had been begun by the Imperial Prisoners of War Committee in late 1942. Towards the end of 1944 a draft directive was submitted to the Combined Chiefs of Staff and detailed planning began. Commanders-in-Chief in the Pacific were made responsible for the protection, maintenance, and evacuation of all United Nations prisoners of war within their respective operational zones, but were to co-ordinate their plans. These were to ensure provision for prisoners of war in any armistice agreement made with the enemy, to take control of prisoner-of-war camps, to see that liberated prisoners were properly cared for, to send back nominal rolls, to preserve enemy records concerning prisoners and to apprehend enemy personnel charged with their maltreatment. Governments of countries to which prisoners belonged were made responsible for informing the War Office and the War Department[1] of the numbers[2] and locations of their nationals held by the Japanese, as

---

[1] For transmission to Supreme Commander South-East Asia Command, to Commander-in-Chief South-West Pacific Area, or to Commander-in-Chief Central Pacific Area respectively.
[2] There were approximately 130,000 British, 15,000 United States, and 30,000 Dutch.

well as of any special requirements for their handling after recovery. Members of the forces to which prisoners belonged were to be used as repatriation personnel at the earliest possible stage of evacuation. Priority in repatriation was to be given to sick and wounded, but no other distinction was to be made among United Nations servicemen in respect of either rank or arm of the service.

The surrender terms imposed on the Japanese made it obligatory on them to preserve the safety and well-being of all prisoners and civilian internees in their hands and to supply adequate food, shelter, clothing, and medical care until the Allied forces took over. Until this occurred, prisoner-of-war and civilian internment camps were to be handed over to the command of their camp leaders. The Japanese were to prepare complete lists of all those in their hands, together with their camp locations, and, when required, to transport them to places where they could be conveniently handed over to the Allies.

To bring relief immediately after the armistice to prisoners of war and civilian internees, information leaflets, food, clothing, and medical supplies were dropped into camps from the air. In the area covered by the South-East Asia Command alone about one and a quarter million pounds of Red Cross stores were thus distributed to some 250 camps. These air drops, by bringing badly needed information and relief, benefited especially those isolated camps whose evacuation might take time. By 12 September all known camps had been flown over and assisted in this way.

As soon as it became possible, recovery teams were organised and sent to known camp locations and to areas where prisoners were thought to be. Owing to the sudden collapse of Japan the only recovery teams immediately available were drawn from the Australian forces operating under the command of General MacArthur; and the Australian authorities agreed that they should be available for dealing with all Commonwealth prisoners of war until the arrival of United Kingdom and other Commonwealth teams. Eighteen of them were established, as well as staff for a large reception camp at Manila. It was these teams which had the task of carrying out the initial responsibilities of Commanders-in-Chief regarding prisoners of war and civilian internees in their respective areas.[1]

On 17 August a flight of RNZAF transport aircraft, each fitted with bunk accommodation for sixteen, left New Zealand for duty under the South-East Asia Command, to assist in the return of our released prisoners of war and civilian internees to New Zealand.

---

[1] The operation was given the title RAPWI (Recovery of Allied Prisoners of War and Internees) and the teams were known as RAPWI teams.

Based on Singapore, this RNZAF flight was responsible for the evacuation of most of our people from the southern areas. A New Zealand Army RAPWI team followed in early September to accompany the land forces of South-East Asia Command into recovered areas and assist with documentation and other tasks affecting New Zealanders. Since reliable news of the latter was at this stage a matter of the greatest interest to an anxious New Zealand public, a senior Army officer[1] was also sent on 13 September to work with the Australian recovery organisation in the northern area, including the Philippines, China, Hong Kong and Japan. In practice the work of all three components of this rather uncoordinated piece of organisation tended to overlap. But in the upshot New Zealand was promptly informed about our nationals in the various areas, adequate attention was given to obtaining news of the missing, and arrangements for the care and speedy repatriation of our people gave general satisfaction.

When the civilian internees at Singapore were transferred to the Sime Road camp in 1944, the prisoners of war from the Changi area took their place in Changi Jail. There they remained for the last year or more of their captivity, some 6000 prisoners crammed into a prison designed to hold 600 peacetime criminals. The officers and the camp hospital were housed in attap huts outside the building, but living conditions generally were much worse than they had been previously. Over the last months of the war the rice ration became smaller than ever, and other food almost negligible in quantity. Some prisoners noticed a more conciliatory attitude on the part of a few of the guards, especially after the collapse of Germany; but others saw no change, and there appears to have been no change in treatment until almost the time of the capitulation. This was not announced to the prisoners until some days after it occurred, and in that period generous quantities of food, including Red Cross food parcels, which had evidently been in store for a considerable time, were poured into the camp. Shortly afterwards, on 28 August, Red Cross supplies were dropped by Allied planes, followed by RAPWI officers equipped with wireless. Finally, on 5 September Allied forces landed on Singapore Island to take over control of the area and arrange evacuation.

Civilians in the Sime Road camp noticed an appreciable change of attitude on the part of their guards for a month or more before the capitulation. On 26 August the camp leader was informed by the Japanese that the war was over, and the internees then took over control of the camp until the arrival of Allied recovery teams. Liberated New Zealanders, both military and civilian, spoke highly

---

[1] Brig G. H. Clifton.

of the welfare work and the efficient arrangements for their evacuation, for which the RNZAF flight stationed in Singapore was responsible. Many of our people were flown all the way to New Zealand, though a number also went at least part of the way by sea transport. The majority were home by September.

Some account has already been given of the siting of prisoner-of-war camps in Burma and Thailand near military objectives during the last year of the war, and of the resultant bombing and casualties. During 1945, in addition to the railway maintenance parties whose hardships have already been described, the Japanese sent into Thailand large parties of prisoners to cut roads through virgin jungle and to construct defence works in the north. Treatment of these parties followed the pattern of the worst experienced by those who had worked on the construction of the railway: in a little over a month one party of 1000 had 50 per cent sick and 18 per cent dead. In the base and more settled camps, however, some noticed 'more latitude', especially on the part of Korean guards, who were beginning to show anti-Japanese feeling. Other men reported that many of the Japanese guards became even more severe and petty than usual.

Not long before the armistice the Japanese decided to move officer prisoners from Kanburi, where they had all been gathered into one camp, to another location some seventy miles north-east of Bangkok. They were at Bangkok in transit when the capitulation was announced. In many camps work ceased a few days before any announcement to prisoners by the Japanese, who first distributed long-stored Red Cross parcels, just as they had done in Malaya. So far as food was concerned, those in Bangkok were well looked after by the Swiss and Swedish representatives there, and most other camps were able to obtain ample supplies from the local Thais. As in Malaya, Red Cross supplies were dropped from the air, and this was followed by the parachuting in of RAPWI contact officers. After a journey to Bangkok by truck or train, liberated New Zealanders were flown to Singapore and from there to New Zealand.

Most of the British prisoners in Java were by April 1945 gathered in a native jail outside Bandoeng. The strength of this camp rose to nearly 6000 prisoners, and overcrowding became similar to that experienced in the early days of captivity. Here the attitude of the Japanese guards towards their prisoners seems to have hardened as Japan suffered more and more from Allied air raids, and seems to have shown little sign of relaxing until almost the end of hostilities. Then suddenly beatings stopped, and food, clothing, and medicines were brought in. Shortly afterwards contact officers arrived by parachute and arranged for prisoners to be evacuated to Batavia. From there our men went by RNZAF transport planes to Singapore, and home by the routes already described.

A number of our men had been moved by ship from Palembang to Singapore at the end of 1944. For those who remained on Sumatra the food became steadily less. In one camp in central Sumatra workers were receiving in 1945 only 150 grammes of rice a day and sick men only 100 grammes. One New Zealander records how prisoners were driven to supplementing this with coconuts and bananas, edible fungi, and even cobra flesh. The number of prisoners in camp hospitals or in special camps established for those too sick to work rose rapidly in the last months before liberation. In the main camp at Palembang from May to August 1945 there were approximately 260 deaths out of a camp strength of 1150; 70 of these died in the fortnight immediately preceding the armistice. As elsewhere the Japanese made a last-minute effort to retrieve the situation before the arrival of Allied troops, by sending into the camps quantities of food, clothing, and (in one prisoner's phrase) 'anything our authorities demanded'.

Most of the men in the Macassar area were moved in 1944 to a makeshift bamboo camp on the outskirts of the town and were used as dock labour at the port. They were subjected to regular bombing attacks from Allied aircraft. The last stages of the war brought little change in the treatment received from their guards. On the capitulation, however, they were moved to a better camp, and food became more abundant and varied. It was not until 21 September that British naval units arrived with Australian troops and evacuated the prisoners to Australia, en route for home. Australian troops also liberated the neighbouring territory of Sarawak, and New Zealanders held there also went home via Australia.

In the Shamshuipo prisoner-of-war camp at Hong Kong, news of the armistice was received on 17 August from outside the camp before the Japanese camp commandant had decided to announce it. The camp leader immediately demanded an interview and, receiving an admission that the Japanese had capitulated, insisted on the withdrawal of Japanese guards and the complete transfer of camp administration to himself and his staff. Forage parties were sent out for fresh meat and milk, and the camp began to live comparatively well. Most of the civilian internees at the Stanley camp remained there after the announcement of the armistice, though the Japanese guards, who thereafter kept to themselves, did not interfere with their liberty and supplied them with large quantities of food. At the end of August a British naval squadron arrived, and evacuation took place by plane or ship to Manila and home.

The last months of captivity for people in the civilian assembly centres of occupied China were hardly less rigorous than those of internment camps properly so called. In mid-July all civilians from the Yu-Yuen and Colombia Club centres were suddenly transferred to the Sacred Heart hospital, which had been evacuated the day before by the Japanese Army and left filthy and verminous. Besides trying to exist on very bad and inadequate food, these people had the anxiety of suddenly finding themselves in the middle of an industrial area which had already been severely bombed. Reports from most of the centres indicate that there was little change in the attitude of Japanese guards, except perhaps a certain hardening when the news of the bombardments of Japan filtered through.

When the capitulation came the guards were immediately marched off, leaving the civilians to themselves. People who were at the Lincoln Avenue centre describe how their leader, who had been to see the Swiss Consul on 15 August, came back with the dramatic news that the camp was to be 'dissolved at noon'. In point of fact, owing to the danger of rioting and violence in the city, most Allied civilians in the Shanghai area found it wiser to remain in their camps until liberation forces arrived. They were well looked after for food and money by the Swiss Consul. United States troops were flown in within a week, and those who chose to do so returned to their former work in Shanghai, while the others were evacuated to Hong Kong.

United States contact officers did not arrive in Northern China until the end of August, and in some places it was more than a month later before evacuation became possible. But food and other supplies were regularly parachuted in to these camps until their inmates too could be moved to Hong Kong.

The pattern of events as they affected captives in Japan during the last phase of the war differed from that in other areas only in the degree to which conditions and treatment worsened. Apart from the strain on her economy imposed by the years of war, Japan became the principal objective of Allied bombardment. Not only did prisoners and civilian internees held there experience personal danger and the shortages and discomforts that follow destruction, but they bore the brunt of the increasing resentment and nervous tension among the Japanese who guarded them.

A New Zealand merchant navy man, who was imprisoned at Omori, describes the mud floors, the lack of heating during the winter of 1944–45, when temperatures went well below zero, and the poor quality of the food, which his weakened digestion caused him sometimes to vomit up while attempting to swallow it. But the deterioration of conditions within Japan brought no relaxation in the amount of heavy work demanded of prisoners. At Omori they had to load heavy sacks of rice into railway trucks or work in the holds of filthy tramp steamers discharging pig-iron. Those at Sendai were employed long hours in a pig-iron and carbide factory or clearing land of dense scrub with crude farm implements.

Some prisoners had the comparative good fortune to be moved from industrial centres to camps in the country; a number went, for example, from the Muroran steelworks near Hakodate to lumber and mining work in the hills at Nisi Asibetu. Others, including some New Zealanders, who had to remain in what had become military targets, lost their lives in the terrible naval bombardments of Japan by the Allied fleets. At the beginning of August the Kaimichi steelworks, some 300 miles north of Tokyo, was bombed and shelled on two occasions and practically demolished. A considerable number of prisoners working there were killed or injured, and a few succumbed later to burns. It is one of the war's cruellest paradoxes that men who have survived battle with the enemy, and later as prisoners, enemy ill-treatment, should thus helplessly find death at the hands of their own comrades.

Some of those who came in contact with Japanese civilians at their work noticed a change in their morale and a more conciliatory or even 'friendly' attitude on their part towards Allied captives. But in almost every prisoner-of-war or civilian internment camp the discipline imposed by the guards became more strict, right up to the time of the armistice. The complete reversal of attitude which then took place was all the more striking. Thus, in the last winter of the war, men at Hakodate were being made to stand for long periods on one of the guard towers in the snow as a punishment for having brought firewood into the camp in excess of the amount permitted. At one of the camps at Osaka a New Zealander reports that in this period the guards 'knocked us around just the same and even worse'; another mentions that as the war took its decisive turn against Japan they 'became very sullen and quiet'.

Liberation in varying degrees came to nearly every camp in Japan soon after the armistice, and the Japanese home forces seem to have made every effort to carry out the Allied instructions regarding prisoners of war and civilians. Camps at Tokyo, such as Omi, were handed over to the prisoners on 15 August, and at other centres the capitulation was announced to the prisoners and internees by the commandant in the course of the next day or two. Local Japanese authorities plied some camps with so much food that there were resultant cases of sickness and stomach pains. At the same time large quantities of food and other supplies were dropped from Allied planes: at Nisi Asibetu, for example, 40 parachute loads at a time. It took a little longer—up to a month in outlying districts

—before the arrival of United States troops. But swift evacuation to Manila followed, by hospital ship when necessary.

As in Europe, it had originally been intended that repatriation should be a gradual process, but when capitulation became imminent there was a change of plan. It was thought best for recovered personnel to be repatriated to their home countries as quickly as possible, with the exception of those unfit for the voyage. The use of hospital ships where possible substantially reduced the latter; and the use of transport aircraft speeded up evacuation of ex-prisoners of war and internees both from camp areas and also from reception centres on part at least of the journey home. In general, those from Japan, Korea, Manchuria, and Formosa went to the reception centre at Manila before going on; those from China and Hong Kong went home direct from Hong Kong; and those from Thailand, French Indo-China, Malaya, and the East Indies went to Singapore.

The Australian Reception Group, under whose care came the fitter New Zealanders evacuated to Manila, had two camps some 18 miles from the city. Each had sleeping accommodation for 4000 in tents, as well as dining halls, canteens, and recreation huts built of wood and iron. These had been provided and were kept supplied by the United States Forces. Red Cross welfare workers served in the canteens and gave other services at all hours. Those who required hospital and convalescent treatment before onward routing went to a United States general hospital on the outskirts of Manila. At Hong Kong a reception camp was established under British arrangements to handle ex-prisoners recovered on the China coast. Prisoners and civilian internees released in the Changi area at Singapore were catered for by a RAPWI centre established there. New Zealanders passing through Singapore also benefited from a welfare centre set up in the Cathay Building by the RNZAF party established there to undertake their evacuation.

From these reception centres New Zealanders went by sea or air, or partly by each, to Australia and on to New Zealand. While in Australia they were well looked after by the Australian Red Cross Society, which provided welfare facilities at various points on the routes followed. Comforts were supplied to them after their arrival in New Zealand by the Joint Council. They were provided with accommodation at their port of arrival, were subjected to only essential 'processing' and sent on almost immediately to their homes. Generous arrangements were made for the supply to them of pocket-money and, if necessary, further financial assistance. Most of our people from the Far East were back in their homes by the middle of October.

III: *Protection of the Interests of Prisoners of War and Civilians*

There were signs in 1945 that the previous three years' negotiations with the Japanese authorities regarding prisoners might at last begin to bear fruit. In January the Swiss Minister in Tokyo was able to say that the notification of lists of prisoners had improved, and that he was continually receiving fresh lists of considerable size. The head of the Japanese Prisoner-of-War Information Bureau announced that he hoped to be able to make regular returns of camp strengths. The Imperial Prisoners of War Committee decided that Japan might be offered similar regular returns on a basis of strict reciprocity.

Similarly, a survey of mail to and from the Far East revealed that by February 1945 the position had greatly improved. In the summer of 1943, when the Arctic convoys had been suspended, a new route for forwarding mail to Moscow had been established through Persia. This became the normal route for all correspondence from New Zealand, as well as from Australia, South Africa and India, and for air mail from the United Kingdom. From Moscow it went on through Korea to Japan, air mail completing the journey in seven and a half weeks, and surface mail taking nearly twice as long. There were also signs that delivery to the prisoner-of-war camps in Japan had been speeded up, though there were still long delays in delivery to distant areas. The delivery in Japan of an accumulation of very old mail, and statements by Japanese officials that there was no objection to letters of one page in length,[1] seemed to indicate that the Japanese had to some extent improved their censorship arrangements. But the Japanese still made censorship difficulties their excuse for not permitting a regular quota of outward letters or postcards from prisoners and civilian internees.

However, in view of the slowness of mails, the Japanese Government had proposed in late 1944 an exchange of telegrams through the International Red Cross Committee between prisoners of war in their hands and their next-of-kin. The scheme began in December, and by February 1945 completed forms were being sent to Geneva at the rate of 2000 a week; but Radio Japan proved unable to absorb more than 500 or so telegrams a day. And, though in three months some 40,000 British Commonwealth messages were received by the International Red Cross Committee and about 29,000 were retransmitted to Japan, by the end of April fewer than 200 had been received in the United Kingdom and only about sixty in Australia.

---

[1] A strict limit of 25 words had previously been imposed.

The International Red Cross telegram scheme having proved disappointing, it was decided that broadcasting should become an officially recognised method of communicating with prisoners of war and internees in Japanese hands, and that it should be made available to next-of-kin through the Commonwealth. Previously it had been regarded as a danger to security, since it involved direct communication with the enemy and since the Japanese would certainly use it for transmitting propaganda. But the state of the war in 1945 had largely removed these objections. Broadcasts from Australia had begun in August 1944, under an arrangement with Japanese-controlled Batavia Radio for an exchange of messages between prisoners and their relatives in Australia. New Zealand was included under this scheme in early 1945. By May messages were being sent from Australia at the rate of 300 a week, and the scheme proved of considerable value in establishing contact with camps in southern areas increasingly cut off from seaborne mail.

During 1944 there had been some extension of the facilities for neutral inspectors to visit camps in Japan and in Hong Kong, and the Japanese authorities had granted visas for four more delegates of the International Red Cross Committee to proceed to the Far East. The Swiss Minister in Tokyo, however, considered that the Japanese would never allow neutral delegates to speak to prisoners without witnesses, and that it would be useless to make further representations on this matter.

Unfortunately, neither in their visits to camps nor in their other opportunities for negotiations with the Japanese authorities were these neutral agents able to accomplish very much. The Swiss Minister in Tokyo, after numerous representations concerning the dangerous location of certain prisoner-of-war camps, received the reply from the Japanese Foreign Minister that his Government was always careful to site these camps outside danger areas. The casualties at Non Pladuk and other camps on the Burma-Thailand railway mentioned in an earlier chapter were sufficient to disprove this statement. And there followed further bombing at camps in Japanese-occupied territory and, especially in 1945, in Japan itself. Moreover there was evidence in February 1945 that the Japanese were deliberately siting prisoner-of-war camps in order to protect vital targets. Although it was not possible on this account to divert air attacks from them, the Allied air forces received instructions to exercise all practicable care. Since the Japanese broadcast details of every such attack, the Allied authorities decided to publicise the facts in such a way as might influence the more responsible Japanese.

IV: *Relief Work in the Far East*

It is to be expected that in the months immediately preceding a country's defeat the supply of relief goods to the enemy captives she holds will deteriorate. In 1945 such relief transport arrangements as it had been possible to make with Japan came to an end. The danger to her external sea communications from the Allied fleets and to her internal communications from the Allied air forces would have made this inevitable, even if there had been a strong initiative on Japan's part to maintain them. Not only were no relief supplies arriving in Japan, but the inflated prices and the shortages resulting from bombardment made local purchases more difficult than ever. The Japanese made small distributions of old stocks of Red Cross parcels to some camps, but this brought little improvement to a situation which, in respect of food at least, became worse than it had ever been.

Only after the Japanese capitulation in August did relief supplies again become available, and so urgent was the need by then that large-scale parachuting operations were necessary to get them to camps where they were needed to save further loss of life. Neutral delegates were immediately able to visit all camps, even in the southern area of Japanese-occupied territory, and to send out word of their requirements. As the Allied authorities received the messages giving each camp's food and medical position, the numbers of seriously and dangerously ill, and the prevalent conditions, packages of supplies were made up to meet each situation. Besides food, clothing, and medical supplies, medical teams and specialists, including psychiatrists, were dropped where they were urgently needed. Two British hospitals were flown into Bangkok. The immediate fall in death rates, and the vast improvement in the condition of many captives in the few weeks before their evacuation, serve to indicate how much disease and death might have been avoided had only a fraction of these supplies been regularly available throughout the war.

V: *Japanese Prisoners of War in New Zealand*

Although the 800-odd Japanese prisoners of war at Featherston remained under excellent material conditions until the end of their captivity, their anxiety concerning their future increased as the end of the war became imminent. In September 1944 they told a neutral inspector that unless some arrangement could be made by which they could either return to their native country as 'honourable citizens' or find asylum in some other territory such as an island in the Pacific, they would probably only be able to end their unhappy position by mass suicide. Their hopes lay in the possibility of the neutral observers who visited them in their camp being able to explain their predicament and negotiate on their behalf.

Once they had heard the news of the cessation of hostilities, their questions took a more precise form. They were anxious to know whether they were covered by the Imperial Rescript to the Japanese Armed Forces ordering them to lay down their arms; whether reprisals would be taken on them in New Zealand on account of the bad conditions in the prisoner-of-war camps for which their countrymen were responsible; when their repatriation would take place, and whether they would be able to take their possessions and accumulated pay with them. They were assured that no reprisals would be taken on them in New Zealand, that their repatriation would take place as soon as shipping difficulties were overcome, and that representations were being made to the Supreme Commander in the Far East so that on their return their future might be assured and they might be given credit in Japanese currency for the money they had earned in New Zealand.[1]

By the end of 1945 arrangements were in hand for them to leave on two large American tank landing craft. The New Zealand authorities went to a great deal of trouble to ensure that conditions on this voyage would be as comfortable as possible. Although it did not prove possible for the New Zealand representative of the International Red Cross Committee to accompany the repatriates (as the latter had requested), a detachment of the New Zealand guard from Featherston Camp who were acquainted with the prisoners was placed on each vessel in order to facilitate dealing with them during the voyage. A stock of comforts purchased by funds of the New Zealand Red Cross Society was placed on board the vessels for distribution on disembarkation. Special bunk accommodation for the prisoners was installed in the vessels, special rooms were built to accommodate the sick, and extra ventilation and steam heaters were fitted to adjust the interior temperature both to the tropics and to the northern winter. All the prisoners were embarked on 30 December 1945, and the vessels left for Yokohama on the same day.

So ended New Zealand's first experience of housing and guarding on her soil enemy prisoners of war. Before leaving on their repatriation voyage the senior officer among the prisoners wrote to the General Officer Commanding the New Zealand Military Forces thanking him for the 'just and considerate treatment' they had received. There can be no doubt, as the International Red Cross

---

[1] A total of approximately £5500 was credited to the Japanese prisoners during their period in New Zealand.

representative said in his final report, that the Geneva Prisoners of War Convention of 1929 was applied 'in every respect'. By most standards the treatment was extremely generous. It is tragic that an incident such as that of February 1943 should have happened at a prisoner-of-war camp whose administering authorities were so humane and well-intentioned. The whole experience serves as another illustration of the fact that guarding prisoners is not always the simple task it seems. It also suggests that those negotiating on behalf of prisoners of war could, if their zeal to ensure humane treatment were allowed to overrule all other considerations, make control of prisoners by detaining guards almost impossible without the use of firearms.

* * * * *

In March 1945 it became Allied policy to use the Japanese treatment of their prisoners of war as a weapon of political warfare. By this time sufficient was generally known about camps in Burma and Thailand and in the recently liberated camps of the Philippines to make it clear what kind of conditions had existed there. It was felt that the Japanese in retreat would realise that their future in the world would depend largely on their external relations with the Great Powers, and that further ill-treatment of prisoners of war would count heavily against them. No suggestions of reprisals or revenge were made, and no imputations that any improvements in treatment which did occur were due to the deterioration of their military position. But it was made clear that unless local commanders responsible for ill-treatment were punished the Japanese Government would be held responsible.

Accounts of the last months of captivity by prisoners of war and civilian internees do not show that their treatment improved; but neither do they show that it deteriorated in a way or to an extent that could be attributable to definite Japanese policy in that direction. Most important of all, the Allied fear that the Japanese might in a last resort use their prisoners as hostages, and that wholesale massacres might occur, was confirmed by subsequent events in very few places. If Allied policy contributed to this result alone it was amply justified.

The capitulation of Japan concluded New Zealand's first experience of the hostility of a major Asiatic Power in aggressive mood. The threat to their own country reminded many people, who had in the past thought of it only as an outpost of European culture, that it was geographically situated much nearer to Asia. Those who came into direct contact with the Japanese found out that in spite of outward similarities they differed fundamentally from

Europeans and ourselves in their standards of diet and living in general, in their conditions of work, in their military discipline, in the value they placed on human life, and in their regard for humanitarian considerations that we in our tranquil and prosperous isolation have sometimes tended to regard as inherent in human nature. If we are really to think out for ourselves more of our international relationships, we need to see more of the world through the eyes of our own people. However short our pre-war contacts with the peoples of the Far East may have fallen of what was appropriate to our position in the Pacific, there are now numbers of New Zealanders who have had close contact with them both during the war and since. Those of our men and women who suffered captivity in the Far East have first-hand knowledge of the mentality of one of these peoples at war. To take account of this knowledge does not necessarily imply continued rancour towards a former enemy; to neglect it is to be unrealistic.

Conclusion

THE mobile type of warfare practised in the Second World War often made it impossible for outnumbered land forces to be extricated, and left them no alternative to destruction but surrender. It was thus that numbers of able-bodied soldiers far exceeding those of previous wars, in addition to seriously wounded,[1] were taken prisoner between 1939 and 1945. The initial lightning campaigns of the German Army brought these numbers to more than two million by late 1940, and the later campaigns of both Allied and Axis Powers in Europe, Africa, and the Far East added further hundreds of thousands. It is safe to say that more than one person in every thousand of the world's population was held captive for some period during these six years of war.

For New Zealand's population the proportion was much higher. More than one person in every two hundred suffered captivity; and the majority of these for three years or longer. The proportion is large enough to justify some examination of the effect of such losses on the New Zealand Armed Forces during the war, and the possible effects on the New Zealand community as a whole in the post-war period of having had such large numbers in enemy hands.

By far the greatest number of those taken prisoner belonged to the New Zealand Army. With the expedition to Greece the New Zealand Division began a series of four campaigns belonging to that desperate middle period of the war, which did not end until the victorious breakthrough at Alamein. Two withdrawals followed by sea evacuations from Greece and Crete, what was at best a very costly victory in Libya in 1941, and a narrow escape from annihilation during the retreat into Egypt in 1942 were ordeals which might be expected to weaken any division. By the close of the fourth of these campaigns at the end of August 1942 the Division's dead amounted to 2641 and those taken prisoner to 7897—a total loss of 10,538 men.[2] The number of men to be replaced totalled nearly a whole division.

In fifteen subsequent actions during the remaining years of the war, although the Division's dead rose by 2736, those taken prisoner increased by no more than 425. Thus nearly 90 per cent of the 9000-odd New Zealanders held captive in the Second

---

[1] About one-seventh of the New Zealanders taken prisoner were wounded.
[2] This takes no account of wounded (other than prisoners who were wounded), many of whom were not again fit for active service. The dead include killed in action and died of wounds.

World War were soldiers who fell into enemy hands during a period of little over a year between the spring of 1941 and the summer of 1942. The bulk of them were to spend in captivity the three to four years that dragged on before Germany's final defeat, to which they had contributed a great deal in a most critical period.[1] By the nature of their operations Air Force personnel fell into enemy hands in only small numbers at a time, but over the whole period of the war. They made up six per cent of the New Zealanders in captivity. Naval men and merchant seamen made up less than one per cent each.

It is not easy to attempt an assessment either of the effects of captivity on individuals or of the influence on the community as a whole of having had such a considerable proportion of its population held captive in enemy countries for several years. At the end of the war the fact that an ex-serviceman had been a prisoner of war was not regarded officially as of significance for his rehabilitation, and no special records of ex-prisoners of war were maintained. A comparison of the post-war histories of ex-prisoners of war with those of a like sample of other ex-servicemen would therefore involve a major piece of research. All that is attempted here is an analysis of the replies to questions concerning the physical and mental after-effects of their experiences, put to a selected sample of ex-captives from Europe and the Far East.

The enormous variety of camp conditions and of individual experiences makes difficult any wide generalisation about the physical condition of prisoners of war and internees on their release. Conditions varied in different countries and, inside these countries, in different camps at different periods of the war, quite often according to whoever was the enemy camp commandant. Clearly a man's physical condition on release depended on the length of his captivity and on his own personal experiences as a captive. If he had worked in the Silesian coal mines or on the Burma-Thailand railway at its worst, if he had been in one of the less fortunate columns that marched across Europe or subjected to severe exposure and privation while attempting to escape, if he had served a spell in a German military prison or been beaten and tortured by the Kempetai, he would probably be in a worse state than if he had not had one or more of these experiences. The local supplies of food, water, and medicine and local conditions of heat, cold, and dampness all had an influence. In general it may be said that prisoner-of-war conditions in the Far East were more damaging to health than those in Europe. If the latter had turned

---

[1] Except for the casualties in Greece and Crete, the figures used are those of the *Statement of Strength and Losses in the Armed Services and Mercantile Marine in the 1939-45 War*, presented to both Houses of Parliament in 1948. The Crete casualties are the revised figures published in the official history of that battle.

out to be better than most prisoners had expected, the former had turned out generally worse. Yet some men were released from captivity in Europe in worse condition than some from the Far East.

Many repatriates from Europe were below normal weight on their release; many found that they tired easily and lacked their former 'punch' and endurance; a considerable number, more especially the older men, had digestive troubles and rheumatism or fibrositis in some part of their bodies. They generally found, however, that these effects wore off after some months of good food and healthy living.

Generally speaking, repatriates from the Far East were suffering from the effects of malnutrition and tropical diseases such as malaria; their condition varied from merely being somewhat underweight to extreme emaciation; some still had dysentery or beriberi, and the more fortunate had got off with digestive upsets; many found their eyesight had suffered; a number had contracted hernias, and others had a variety of aches in muscles and joints. Some found it took them a year of care and good feeding to get back to normal physical condition and to build a reserve; the worst cases were still receiving medical or even hospital treatment eighteen months after repatriation. Some were prevented by resultant physical handicaps from again taking up their pre-war occupation; others, on medical advice, did not return to the country of their pre-war employment in the East. A number of those whose medical examination immediately after repatriation revealed no serious defects succumbed, after a period of normal life and work, to ailments that could have been attributable to their conditions of captivity. In some of these cases a medical re-examination resulted in the grant of a war pension.

It was probably the mental effects of captivity which were the most difficult to gauge, especially from the necessarily somewhat brief and standardised type of medical examination that was given to all returning servicemen. Here again the individual's reaction to captivity depended on the length of his term, the strain of the work he had to do, the facilities for recreation and further education, and any specially drastic experiences he might have undergone during interrogation or disciplinary punishment. There can be little doubt that the often very fine musical and dramatic performances given in prisoner-of-war camps helped to reduce the strain of living in cramped and sometimes squalid conditions amid an atmosphere of irritability; and that the often excellent educational facilities enabled men to offset the demoralising effects of inaction and frustration. Occasionally men drove themselves so hard at their studies that they became nervous victims of overwork; but in general the effect of so occupying the mind seems to have been beneficial. Some men felt deeply what they imagined to be the disgrace of capture, and regular soldiers sometimes felt that their career had been ruined by it. To many of the younger men lack of freedom of movement was a greater trial than it was to those whose mental resources had had more time to develop before their capture. A good number of men had worried during their captivity as to whether physical deprivations would not leave behind some permanent impairment of their bodily functions: respiratory, digestive, or sexual. To them a reassuring medical report on their physical condition was nearly always able to eliminate one element of the nervous tension which accompanied their release.

Many repatriates from Europe speak of restlessness and inability to settle, impaired powers of concentration and memory, a tendency to be easily affected emotionally (notably by a pathetic film or music), a feeling of awkwardness in meeting strangers, a strong dislike of crowds and queues, and an overpowering desire to be quiet and alone. Many men were inclined to resent and oppose restrictions on their freedom of action. 'If anyone tries to order me round I take strong exception to it', wrote one repatriate. While such an attitude could easily derive from situations other than captivity, no doubt the latter tended to accentuate it. For most of these men such after-effects tended to disappear after some months of normal living.

Repatriates from the Far East described themselves as 'nervous and emotional' or 'wrought up'; lethargic, unable to concentrate, and content to just sit and dream; depressed; unable to sleep; easily irritated; 'mentally tired'. While they mentioned that these symptoms had become less severe with the passage of time, it was clear that those men who had spent three years or more as prisoners in the Far East or had had especially bad experiences would need a long time to recover.

Where, among United Kingdom repatriates, for one reason or another these mental effects were severe, but not severe enough for hospitalisation, they were dealt with in England at a special prisoner-of-war rehabilitation centre.[1] Here a 'new but transitional society' was formed under the guidance of people who had made an expert study of prisoner-of-war conditions and their effects. In order to make the transition to civilian life more gentle, factors such as drama work were introduced into the routine, since they provided a link with prisoner-of-war 'tradition'. At the same time the local community near the centre was drawn upon to help the repatriate in finding suitable and satisfying work and in getting

[1] See, for example, Dr. Maxwell Jones in *British Medical Journal*, 6 April 1946, Vol. I, p. 533, and in *Journal of Neurology*, etc., Vol. XI, No. 1, February 1948, p. 53.

himself used to normal social life. Within a few months of leaving the centre 60 per cent of these men had found the former, and all but 12 per cent were well on the way to the latter, as a follow-up study showed. While nothing similar to this appears to have been done in New Zealand, our repatriates from the Far East were few enough in numbers to receive more than usual individual care, and many of those from Europe were greatly helped on the road to rehabilitation by their stay in England and by the long sea voyage that followed.

The variation in official attitudes to returning prisoners of war has already been noted.[1] Enough has been said above to indicate that a rehabilitation scheme which did not take prisoner-of-war experience into account might well be psychologically unsound, at least for that proportion of the ex-prisoners of war whose experiences had been prolonged and severe. The type of official attitude which regarded ex-prisoners of war as just ex-servicemen who had had a slack time for a year or two found its counterpart among a few members of the public, who asked repatriates why they had not managed to escape and presumed that they would be immediately ready to start work where they had left off five years before, to make up for such a long period of idleness. But publicity over several years, especially for stories of hardship and atrocity, had tended to steer public opinion in the opposite direction. The romanticising of the state of captives in enemy countries and the lionisation that often attended the arrival home of repatriates (usually born of a desire to assure them that they had not been forgotten) were justly felt to be unfair to those other ex-servicemen who had had a hard time but of a different kind. It is understandable that there would be a reaction against this public attitude among both ordinary ex-servicemen and among military officials. The pity was that such a reception was desired by few, if any, of our ex-prisoners of war. The vast majority of them wanted no brass bands nor functions in their honour, no strings of solicitous questions as to how they had been treated, no notoriety as some kind of modern Rip Van Winkle. They merely wanted to be alone and quiet and to be allowed to feel their way back into the community to which they had belonged before the war, a community they found different, just as they themselves were different from the men who had left several years before.

Most of these men had been away for four or five years; they had experienced battle and the shock of defeat and capture; they had known real hunger and other kinds of misery; they had known the frustration of being cooped up behind barbed wire, at the

---

[1] See pp. 494–5.

mercy of an underling with a lethal weapon. To meet their situation they had developed an aggressiveness against anyone who further threatened their freedom of action; a resourcefulness in improvising the necessities and amenities they lacked, coupled with an ever-increasing helplessness in dealing with the real world outside the wire; a high regard for the virtues of self-restraint, thoughtfulness for their comrades, and unshakeable integrity in those holding positions of trust, without which the crowded life of a prison camp community became intolerable. It is of interest to record their impressions of the civilian community they found on their return.

Many of them were keen to get back to some kind of work as soon as possible, to make up for the time they had lost; and those who quickly got themselves into suitable work found it, as one man said, 'a joy and a tonic'. Some of those who had seen 'orderly civilian communities replaced by the chaos of war and its aftermath' in Europe were resolved to enjoy civilian life 'while it lasts'. A good many others could not help noticing that the average civilian seemed 'self-centred' and 'out for himself'. This came as a shock after years in prison camp communities, where those who 'pulled up the ladder after them' regardless of anything but their own welfare were despised and sometimes rudely disciplined. A number were depressed by what they saw of the civilian attitude to work; by a tendency for each civilian 'to give as little as possible' and 'take as much as he can'; and by what they saw as a 'disinclination to accept responsibility'. Some felt that the moral fibre of the civilian community had deteriorated during the war years, and, according to their temperament, they felt 'amused' at what they found, or 'disillusioned' or 'irritated' or 'disgusted'.

Those from the Far East especially found it hard to understand what civilians had to 'growl about' in the 'green and pleasant land' of New Zealand, where material conditions seemed to repatriates little short of 'perfect'. They might be excused for listening unsympathetically to the occasional civilians who told them of the long hours they had worked during the war, or of the difficulties they had had in getting silk stockings or new suits. Nor is it surprising that these men commented on what seemed to them the waste of food which they found to be the normal accompaniment of civilian life. They detected, moreover, what they felt to be 'complacency' and 'self-satisfaction' with our way of doing things, and an 'intolerance' of those who thought and lived differently.

No doubt much of this was reaction to the contrast between the reality as repatriates found it and the enchanted picture of their homeland which they had built up in their minds, and which had buoyed them up during the blackest days in their distant prison compounds. It might be tempting also to dismiss any such criticisms as the by-product of the more or less abnormal state of mind in which ex-prisoners remained until they got used to normal civilian life again. But it is perhaps open to doubt whether post-war civilian life is normal. It must be remembered too that nearly all these men had seen something of the normal life of peoples in other parts of the world, and some had lived among peasant communities in Europe for considerable periods. These experiences provided them with some kind of a yardstick. And if nearly all of them left the country of their captivity thankful for British standards of living and British forms of government, they could not help feeling on their return that their civilian compatriots, who had seen only their own environment, did not appreciate these advantages at their full value. 'The people of New Zealand are more dissatisfied and disobliging than in countries where life is more of a struggle' was the way one man summed up his impressions.

It is no part of the present task to try and evaluate these opinions, but merely to record them. Their interest lies in the fact that they form a picture of how we seemed in the immediately post-war years, not to visitors from other countries but to our own brothers, husbands and sons, from varied walks of our national life, on their return from several years of the chastening experience of imprisonment and forced labour among other peoples in Europe and the Far East.

While a few men discounted their period of captivity as pure loss, the vast majority regarded it as an experience which taught them much. It is natural that those who spent a long captivity slaving at manual labour for the enemy and struggling to keep alive under appalling conditions, only to return broken down physically if not mentally, would feel that not only were their years of captivity wasted years, but years whose effects would hamper them all the rest of their lives. For these men it was a 'waste of time', a period in which they 'lost everything materially'. But the majority, especially of those in Europe, experienced long periods during which conditions were bearable and during which they had the strength and urge to look about them and make good use of their time. These men, who returned to normal health soon after repatriation, were as definite that they gained from their captivity knowledge which might never otherwise have come their way. They say that they 'benefited vastly', and that the experience of captivity was worth 'a four year college education' or 'twenty years of ordinary life'.

In some camps, especially those for prisoners who were not forced to work, there were educational and cultural opportunities such as civilian life might never have afforded. Libraries, dozens of trained minds from almost every profession, musical instruments and scores, the raw material for dramatic production, the essentials for pictorial art: all these, together with the amazing improvisations for which captivity provided the stimulus, formed in some camps a background to a vigorous intellectual and artistic life. There were few inmates of these camps on whom such an atmosphere did not have its impact. Within the small area of their compound they were able to listen to authoritative lectures and to read widely; to find fellow prisoners with special qualifications willing to discuss religion, philosophy, history, and indeed almost any aspect of human knowledge; to see competently produced drama; to get to know good music; and to attain some degree of skill in various arts and crafts. So that, quite apart from those who seized upon their enforced leisure to further their professional training, there were thousands whose intellectual and emotional life was enriched by activities for which they could not have found in civilian life either the time or the opportunity.

Prisoners who were in working camps had neither the facilities nor the opportunities for study and recreation on this scale. But they travelled, sometimes widely, in enemy and enemy-occupied countries, and they made contact not only with local foreign populations but with fellow prisoners from many of the Allied countries, either at work or in the large holding camps from which working parties were drawn. Living together in the British compounds of these camps there were usually men from a number of Commonwealth countries, and the close intimacy of crowded prison-camp life gave them an almost unrivalled opportunity to learn something of each other's characteristics and foibles.

Apart from sharing captivity with their Commonwealth colleagues, there was more or less close contact with a majority of the peoples of Europe and the Far East. Among New Zealand ex-prisoners of war one could find large numbers who lived and worked among Austrians, Germans, and Italians; others who, while captives or fugitives from captivity, spent periods of time with Belgians, Dutch, French, Greeks and Cretans, Poles, Russians, and Yugoslavs. Most of our nationals who were captives in the Far East had been living there before the war, but captivity often widened or intensified their contacts with the varied populations: with the Burmese, the Thais, the Malays, and the Chinese of South-East Asia; with the Dutch and the indigenous peoples of what is now Indonesia; with the Chinese and the Manchurians of the mainland; and, above all, with the Japanese. It is not surprising that New Zealand ex-prisoners speak of having lost for ever the 'insularity', which some regard as one of the less fortunate but almost inevitable consequences of our geographical position, and to have gained not only an increased knowledge of languages but a 'broadened international outlook'.

An ex-prisoner priest wrote in 1947 that he had learnt more of human nature in three years of captivity than he could have done in thirty years of normal life. The majority of ex-prisoners hold a similar opinion, and it may be of interest to examine briefly what it was about the prison camp environment which made men feel that they had learnt so much about the mentality of their fellow humans. One man explains it by saying that he was able to observe 'a cross-section of all types of men under duress'. If physical discomfort and chronic shortage of what most people regard as the essentials of civilised life provide tests of men's unselfishness, then there was ample opportunity for prisoners to observe how their fellows stood up to these tests.

But most repatriates would say that on occasions the tests went deeper, and that intense hunger, or the threat of death by some other means, showed the 'heights and depths' of which human beings are capable. Some men noticed 'how easily one can die, yet what a terrific amount the human body will endure'. Under conditions where men were 'just striving to exist', prisoners of war saw the 'thin veneer of civilisation' being shed to reveal men 'in the raw'. Some of them, on occasions men of apparently impeccable probity and respectability, showed themselves 'almost beasts' or 'little removed from animals'; others, often those 'from whom one expected nothing', 'did things of great kindness and bravery', and some of them showed 'leadership, courage, generosity, patience and self-control'. A judge found that the effect of 'hunger with a capital H' on 'humanity in the mass' was 'salutary but somewhat terrifying'. A majority of men felt that in the prisoner-of-war community the effect was on the whole salutary, and that the better aspects of human character predominated. There were few who did not speak rather nostalgically of the 'real comradeship' of their days of captivity; and the ex-prisoners of war associations which have been formed since 1945 are no doubt born of a mutual understanding that grew up from the common experience of captivity and a desire to continue the mutual help which so many men found to be its main redeeming feature.

Some of these men admitted to being chastened by their own first reactions to fear and hunger, and there were few who did not feel that they came out of the experience with a better sense of their own worth and of life's values in general. Nearly all spoke of entering civilian life again with a better appreciation of the ordinary things of life, especially freedom and food. Some spoke almost ecstatically of the joy of clean sheets, clothes, water from a tap, privacy, books. At the same time they knew that they could easily again do without many things which others regarded as necessities, that they could 'rough it with anyone'; and some felt that they could have 'no fear of the worst', and even that they could 'never be unhappy again'. Having tasted the misery of hunger, cold, and lack of those comfortable things which insulate civilised man from the world of nature, many felt a great understanding with the 'poor' and a sympathy for 'those who suffer in the world—the homeless, hungry, naked, sick and dying'. But they realised that wealth and material possession were not the secret of happiness. 'These things matter little, but the state of one's mind matters a lot' was one man's summing up; and a woman internee felt that the 'human soul transcends one's possessions—one is freer without them'. It is not the first time in history that captivity, with its attendant privations and persecutions, has led people to rethink their philosophy.

These are the things which our men and women who were prisoners of war and internees feel they have learnt from their captivity. Except for professional training, they are in the main intangible, and describing them in some detail does not make it any easier to estimate their carry-over into the life of the New Zealand community. Yet, if a large number of our people of middle years, amounting to one in every two hundred of the population, have gained a knowledge of and sympathy for people of other countries; if they have probed deeper than most beneath the surface of human beings in general and have seen more of their psychological make-up; if they have learnt contentment and patience and tolerance above the average, then many may feel that, whatever the loss New Zealand suffered by their capture, she has been repaid with interest by their return. During their captivity it was New Zealand's policy to ensure by the expenditure of money and effort that these people were kept as physically healthy and as mentally alert as circumstances allowed, so that they might after repatriation again become useful citizens. There is no reason to suppose that this policy has not been amply justified. There is, on the contrary, a good deal of evidence to show that the majority of repatriates are on balance mentally the richer for their experience of captivity. And, while their influence as individuals may vary, what they have gained individually should, in the long run, enrich the New Zealand community as a whole.

Editor-in-Chief	... ...	Sir HOWARD K. KIPPENBERGER, KBE, CB, DSO, ED
Associate Editor	... ...	M. C. FAIRBROTHER, DSO, OBE, ED
Sub-Editor	... ...	W. A. GLUE
Illustrations Editor	... ...	J. D. PASCOE
Archives Officer	... ...	R. L. KAY

THE AUTHOR: W. Wynne Mason, MC, went overseas with the Second Echelon and served with the 2nd New Zealand Division in Greece, Crete, and the Western Desert until capture in the Second Libyan Campaign. Born in Wellington in 1910, he was educated at Scots College and Victoria University College, where he graduated BA (Philosophy) and later MA (Modern Languages). Before the war he spent some years in law, farming and language teaching. After repatriation in 1946 he worked on the present history with the War History Branch of the Department of Internal Affairs and later joined the Department of External Affairs. He served from 1949 to 1951 as Second Secretary at the New Zealand Legation in Paris, and is now on the staff of the High Commissioner's Office in London.

Index

ABEL, Pte J. A., 309
Adamson, Pte J. C. H., 415–16
Adelboden, 435–6, 437
Admiral Scheer, 35, 37
Aerodrome Camp, No. 1, 341
'A' Force, 229, 232, 312, 433
Africa, North, v, vi–vii, 21, 39, 52, 61, 104–5, 139, 153–4, 190–3, 249, 268, 274, 280, 317, 321
  Camps, 40, 105–10, 144–5, 194–202, 255, 266
  Escapes, ix, 40, 106–7, 109, 193–4, 195, 198, 200–1
  Evacuation to Italy, 107, 109, 110–11, 147, 196, 201, 202–3, 223, 266
Africa, South, 44
  Red Cross Society, 354
Air Force Prisoners, v, vii, 1–6, 10, 12, 20–35, 36–7, 39, 40, 42, 83, 85, 88, 90–2, 108, 126, 138, 139–45, 160, 166–7, 182, 191, 233, 234, 236, 249–54, 255, 261, 272, 276, 280, 291, 305, 318, 326, 369, 388, 392, 397–406, 409, 410, 423–4, 449, 455, 458–9, 460, 465, 466–7, 470, 471, 496, 500, 501, 505, 506–7, 509, 525
Akhaia, 111–12
Aleutian Islands, 325
Aliens, enemy, xxiv–xxv, 6, 10, 11, 15–18, 49–51, 146, 265–6, 440, 444–5, 488
Allied Prisoner of War Repatriation Unit, 315, 430, 431–3, 437, 479–80, 493
Allied Screening Commission, 475–6
Amboina, 338
Ambon, 339, 340
American Red Cross Society, 487
Amos, Sigmn F., 233
Anderson, Pte A. T., 428
Anderson, Pte C. F., 428
Anderson, Pte L. W. C., 383
Anderson, Pte R. J., 475
Andrews, Dvr W. F., 309
Aquila, 317, 318
Aquileia, 322
Arbeitskommandos, 31, 96, 101–2, 133–4, 260, 262–3, 268–70, 441, 445–6, 453
  Austria, 85–6, 87–8, 133–4, 136–8, 243, 244–8, 369, 379, 380, 381–2, 477, 479
    A945 GW, Selzstal, 381, 382, 478
    65 GW, Thiesen, 384
    88 HV, 384
    410 L, Spitzendorf, 382
    11010 GW, Kühnsdorf, 384, 385
  Germany, 89, 129, 131–2, 138, 240, 242–3, 295–7, 298, 299, 369, 370–1, 372–4, 377, 378–9, 388, 389–90, 407, 450, 462
    E 3, Blechammer, 373, 374

Arbeitskommandos—continued
  Germany—*continued*
    E 243, 371
    E 588, 371
    7001, Halendorf, 296, 299, 390
    7005, Salzgitter, 390
    10503, Hirschberg, 460
  Poland, 390–1
    E 535, Milowitz, 374–7, 450–3, 468–9
    E 596, Jaworzno, 298
Arezzo hospital, 224
Argentine, 184
Argyll Street barracks, 170, 171, 346, 347
Arkadia, 72
Armistice Commission, 274, 279
  Prisoner of War Sub-commission, 274, 315, 430
Armistice, Italian, 274, 277, 279
  Release of prisoners, plans for, 274–81
Armstrong, Capt C. N., 210, 391
5th Army, 312, 314, 411, 415, 419
8th Army, 104, 190, 191, 280, 311, 312, 313, 314, 317, 411, 415, 419
Arosa, 437
Arundel Castle, 410
Asama Maru, 353, 354
Atlantis, 300, 322
Aumale, 40, 144
Australia, 44, 185, 186, 258, 517
  Red Cross Society, 517
Australian Reception Group, 517
Austria—
  Camps, 85–8, 132–8, 243–8, 291, 292, 296, 369, 379–82, 387, 476–9
  Escapes, ix, 86, 134–5, 137–8, 247, 292, 309, 382–5, 427, 429, 482
  Repatriation, 478, 479–80
Auswertestelle West, 139–41, 249–51, 398–400, 465
Avellino barracks, 317
Averoff prison, 230–1
Avery, L-Cpl F. T., 474
Awa Maru, 354
Ayto, Capt J., 192

BAD SODEN, 408, 470
Ballentine, Maj, 308
Bampong, 330, 331, 336
Bandoeng, 180–2, 339, 513–14
Banka Island, 165, 183, 341, 342
Bangkok, 163, 330, 356, 513, 520
Barce, 107, 196
Barcelona, 322, 409
Bardia, 104, 105, 107–8, 110
Bari hospital, 112, 124, 223, 224, 225
Barker, Sgt A. C., 312–13
Barnett, Pte E., 311
Barnett, Flt Lt M. B., 255
Barrett, Pte R. D., 417

Barron, Pte S., 425
Barrow, Dvr R. S., 69
Bartlett, Pte A. E., 413
Bassett, Pte A. W., 429
Baty, Pte E. L., 382-3
Behar, 326
Belaria, 401
Belcher, F/Sgt C., 40
Belgian Red Cross Society, 472
Belhamed, vi, 105
Benghazi, 105, 107, 108-9, 110, 198-201, 223, 280
Berg, Mr E., 388
Bilibid prison, 508
Birchall, Pte A. W., 395
Bishop, Lt E. H., 290, 421
Blackler, Pte R. T., 81
Blakang Mati Island, 176, 330
Blanki Djeran, 342
Bloomfield, Dvr A. G., 391
Blunden, Pte P. R., 81, 83
Boei Glodok jail, 182
Bond, L-Cpl I. A. McK., 311-12
Borenquin, 409
Borneo, 159, 164, 187, 330, 506
Bornhausen, 436
Borrie, Capt J., 374
Bowen Road hospital, 172
Bowerbank, Sir F., 494-5
Brand, Pte J. McR., 81
Brewer, Pte O. V. T., 80
Brighton Reception Centre, 500, 501
Bristow, Sgt W. H., 69
British Red Cross Society, 2, 7, 9, 10, 11, 12, 13, 14, 15, 18, 26, 28, 42, 44-5, 46, 49, 99, 100, 101, 125, 150, 151, 153, 158, 186, 262, 263, 322, 355, 363, 434, 445, 448, 481, 486
    Educational Books Section, 47-8, 152, 264
    Fiction and Games Section, 47, 152
    Invalid Comforts Section, 13
    Middle East Commission, 151
    Next-of-kin Section, 46
Broad, Cpl J. E., 413
Broadstairs, 498
Brown, Pte P. G., 420
Browne, Sgt S. F., 255
Brunel, Dr, 56, 58, 76, 99
Brunet, Cpl A. W., 385
Brussels, 472
Brux, 469-70
Buchanan, Pte W., 417
Buchanan, L-Cpl W. T. F., 81
Buchenwald, 406
Bukom Island, 176
Bull, Lt-Col W. H. B., 65, 66, 89
Burbery, Dvr N. E., 420
Burbery, L-Cpl R. L., 417
Burchardt, Dr, 320
Burdekin, Mr C. B., 47, 100
Burke, Pte J. M., 413
Burke, Pte P. A., 309
Burma, 159, 160, 330, 361, 506,
    Camps, 183, 338, 509, 513, 522
Burma-Thailand railway, 330-8, 351, 356, 361, 362, 519

Burns, Capt J., 416
Burt, Sigmn C. G., 414
Butler, Pte J., 138
Butson, Pte S., 417
Byers, Sigmn J. H., 316

CAMERON, Lt D., 318
Cameron, Pte F., 412-13
Cameron, Pte R. R., 425
Camp, The. 102, 271, 393-4
Campbell, Sgt H. P., 198, 290
Campbell, Flt Lt R. D., 312
Campo PG—
    5, Gavi, 209, 210, 212-13, 282, 287, 288, 305, 312, 421
    12, Vincigliata, 118-19, 213, 414
    19, Bologna, 276, 282, 293, 295, 425
    21, Chieti, 208, 414
    29, Viano, 305, 415, 416
    35, Padula, 118, 124, 209, 276, 312
    38, Poppi, 114, 116-18, 124, 149-50, 154, 209, 210, 224
    41, Montalbo, 118
    47, Modena, 209, 210-12, 214, 276, 277, 278, 281, 282, 287-8, 293, 295, 305, 312, 313, 314, 416, 417, 418, 423, 428
    51, Altamura, 206, 208, 215, 216
    52, Chiavari, 114, 119-22, 123, 214-15, 219, 288
    54, Fara nel Sabina, 415, 416
    57, Gruppignano, 114, 122-3, 124, 154-5, 205, 206, 208, 214, 215-18, 219, 221, 222, 224, 275, 277, 281, 282-3, 287, 288, 289, 292, 296, 298, 301, 384
    62, Bergamo, 302
    65, Gravina, 115, 123-4, 215, 277
    66, Capua, 112-14, 119, 120, 208, 276-7
    70, Monturano, 313, 417
    75, Bari, 112, 115-16, 202, 203-5, 208, 277, 416
    78, Sulmona, 39-40, 112, 118, 119, 149, 205, 207, 208-9, 223, 231, 276, 310, 317
    78/1, Aquafredda, 207-8, 223, 232, 281, 284, 286, 310, 312, 313, 411, 412, 413, 414, 415
    82, Laterina, 419
    85, Tuturano, 112, 114-15, 116, 123, 205, 206-7, 208, 223, 277
    102, Aquila, 318, 414
    103/6, Ampezzo, 223, 283, 296, 299
    103/7, La Maina, 223, 296, 299
    106, Vercelli, 222, 284, 286, 302, 303, 305, 420, 425
    106/19, 222
    106/20, Arro (Salussola), 222, 275, 281
    107, Torviscosa, 215, 219-21, 277, 281, 283-4, 286, 302, 306, 311, 313, 412, 419, 422, 424, 426, 427, 428, 429, 473
    107/2, Prati Nuovi, 284, 427
    107/4, San Dona di Piave, 221, 422
    107/5, Torre di Confine, 284, 421
    107/6, 424

Campo PG—*continued*
  107/7, La Salute di Livenza, 284, 419, 473
  115, Marciano, 417
  120, Padua, 222, 286
  120/4, 420
  120/5, Abano, 305, 313, 418, 420
  120/8, Fogolana, 286, 311, 414, 416
  129, Macerata, 222
  145, Campotosto (Poggio Cancelli), 313, 417
  148, Bussolengo, 221-2, 276, 283, 287, 288
Canada, 44, 97, 99, 185, 259, 262, 353
  Red Cross Society, 45, 487
Canton, 161, 350
Cap Saint Jacques, 227
Capture cards, 36, 42, 58-9, 66
Carcere Penale Badia, Sulmona, 312-13
Carolin, Pte C. R., 413
Carson, Pte H., 309
Carson, Spr S. E., 76-7
Carter, Pte B. B., 69
Caserta hospital, 112, 124, 223, 224, 225
Cassino, 410-11, 415
Caux, 437
Celebes, 165
  Camps, 166, 183-4, 340-1
Chambers, Pte A. F., 429
Chambers, Pte D. W. W., 309
Changi Garrison, 164, 165, 173-7, 328-30, 334, 512, 517
  Jail, 177-9, 326-7, 512
Channel Islands, 256
Chieti barracks, 317
China, 160, 161-2, 353, 512, 517
  Camps, 169, 348-50, 355, 515
Choat, Gnr W. A., 425
Christensen, Flt Lt A. G., 403
Christofsgrund, 460, 469
Chungkai, 335, 336
Churchouse, Pte W. A. R., 425
Clark, Pte K. L., 385
Clarke, Pte E. C., 424-5
Clarke, Pte J. A., 417
Cleland, Pte J. A., 419
Cleverley, Sgt G. G., 198
Clifton, Brig G. H., 194, 411, 463, 500, 512
Cliftonville, 498, 504-5
Cochrane, Capt A. L., 78
Collins, Pte G. G., 70
Columbia Country Club, 349, 515
Combined Chiefs of Staff, 510
Combined Services Documentation and Interrogation Centre, 430
Commonwealth Civilians Committee, 439-40
Connelly, Tpr A., 58, 81
Cook, Capt C. C., 78
Cook, Thomas and Sons, 39
Cooper, Mr B., 37-8
Cooper, 2 Lt E. F., 74
Coral Sea, Battle of, 189, 325
Corinth, 54, 55-9, 77, 78, 81, 203, 228
Cosel, 408
Cosgrove, Sigmn C. G. M., 417-18

Crack, Cpl T. E., 475
Craib, Pte D. M., 424
Craig, Capt J. W. C., 73, 74, 209, 229, 290, 421
Crete, vi, 59, 61-4, 79, 98, 101, 103, 104, 106
  Camps, 64-6, 67, 69, 71, 72, 77, 95, 99, 110, 233
  Escapes, vi, ix, 60, 66-71, 72, 74-5, 312
Crossley, Plt Off E. D., 170-1
Crowley, Sgt B. J., 371-2
Cuba, 322
Cumberbeach, Pte F. A., 419
Cumberlege, Lt C. M. B., 70
Curley, Pte I. C., 233
Cycle camp, 182, 338-9
Czechoslovakia, 450, 452-4, 459, 469-70

DABA, 193, 194-5
Davidson, Pte R. J., 384, 385
Dawson of Penn, Lord, 13
Day, L-Cpl P. W., 424-5
Denvir, Cpl J., 134-5, 309-10
Derna, 105, 107, 196
Dickinson, Pte I. C., 417
Dieburg, 92, 138
Dieppe raid, 190, 233, 238, 258
Dittmer, Lt-Col G., 107
Dixon, Lt H. C., 346-7
Dodecanese Islands, 318-19, 365
Dominion Monarch, 504
Donnelly, Dvr E. V., 385
Donovan, Sgt J. T., 81
Dover, 410
Dragonfly, HMS, 165
Drawbridge, Pte H. W. H., 385
Drottningholm, 322, 410, 439
Dulag Kreta *see* Galatas camp
Dulag Luft, Oberursel (later at Frankfurt-on-Main and Wetzlar-Klostenwald), 3-4, 5-6, 21, 23-9, 30, 31, 37, 85, 88, 91, 102, 139, 142, 143, 251, 253, 254, 398, 400-1, 404, 405, 464, 465
Dunant, Henri, xxiv
Duncan, Fg Off W., 423-4
Dunlop, Lt-Col E. E., 180, 181

EAGAN, Pte E. A., 475
Ecumenical Commission for Assistance to Prisoners of War, 43
Eden, Rt Hon R. A., 362, 481
Education, International Bureau of, 43
Egle, Dr, 186, 187
Egydi, 381
Ellicott, Pte K. C. H., 414
El Mreir, 191, 193, 194
Elsterhorst, 408
Emery, Pte J. C., 385
Emirau Island, 37
Empress of Russia, 322
Empson, Sgt A. H., 69, 229
Encounter, HMS, 165-6
Ermland, 37
Escapes, ix, xi, 21, 82-3, 86, 157, 255
  Africa, North, ix, 40, 106-7, 109, 193-4, 195, 198, 200-1

Escapes—*continued*
  Austria, ix, 86, 134–5, 137–8, 247, 292, 309, 382–5, 427, 429, 482
  Crete, vi, ix, 60, 66–71, 72, 74–5, 312
  Far East, ix, 163, 170–2, 173, 176, 180, 182, 184, 329
  France, ix, 37–8, 90, 94, 213, 255, 288, 301, 420
  Germany, ix, 28–9, 33–5, 84, 90, 91, 92, 102, 129, 142–3, 144, 157, 236, 238, 240, 252–3, 254, 293–4, 367, 371–2, 379, 395–6, 397, 399, 402–3, 404, 405–6, 446, 463, 465
  Greece, vi, ix, 54, 58, 59, 72, 73–5, 76–7, 79, 80–2, 227–33, 384
  Italy, ix, 116, 121–2, 205, 209, 210, 211, 213, 217, 220, 222, 232, 277, 278, 281, 282, 283, 284–8, 289–90, 301–17, 318, 324, 384, 411–29, 473–6
  Poland, 92, 253, 254, 377, 391
Evans, Maj H. M., 416
Exeter, HMS, 165–6
Eysines, 36

FAIRMILE, 310, 165
Falun, 40
Featherston camp, 356–61, 520, 522
Federated Malay States Volunteer Force, 164
Fernleaf Club, 499
'F' Force, 334
Filipino Red Cross Society, 179
First World War, v, xxiv, xxv, 10, 12, 14, 16, 17
Flavell, 2 Lt N. R., 75
Fleet Air Arm prisoners, 31, 39, 254, 318, 506
Flower, Lt H. F., 314
Flowers, Gnr J. I., 417
Foley, Dvr E. F., 75
Folkestone, 498
Foote, Pte A. S. R., 75
Foreman, Capt H. M., 138
Formosa, 330, 351, 510, 517
Fort Bismarck, 291, 293
Fort de la Revere, 145, 255
Fort Zinna, 395, 396
Fortune, Maj-Gen Sir V., 83–4
Foy, L-Cpl W. J., 417–18
France—
  Camps, 35–6, 37, 94, 144, 145–6, 255–6, 438, 439, 441
  Escapes, ix, 37–8, 90, 94, 213, 255, 288, 301, 420
Fraser, Rt Hon P., 320, 500
Frederic, Gnr E. C., 395
Free, Pte F. C. V., 417
Free British Corps, 393
Freising, 408
Friends, Society of, 17
Frontstalags—
  121, Vittel, 94, 145–6, 255–6, 439
  142, Besançon, 94
  183, Salonika, 55, 59, 77–80, 81, 95, 101, 228
  221, St Médard en Jalles, 35–6, 37, 51
Frost, Pte W., 425

Fukuoka, No. 6 sub-camp, 344–5

GADSBY, Tpr W. A., 81
Gain, Pte R. E., 414
Galatas camp, 64–6, 67, 69, 71, 77, 95, 110, 233, 312
Gallichan, Pte J., 376
Galvan, Pte C., 412
Garian, 109–10
Garoet, 166, 167, 180
Gatenby, Capt C., 412
Gaze, Sigmn J. A., 311
Geneva Convention, 1864, xxiv
Geneva Convention, 1929, xxiv, xxv, xxvi, 7, 8, 9, 12, 13, 23–4, 26, 32, 35, 36, 41, 43, 46, 61, 87, 92–3, 95, 96, 101–2, 122, 148, 150, 184–5, 186, 226, 247, 258, 359, 401, 484
Genshagen, 393–4
George, Lt-Col C. D. A., 312
Gerard, Rt Rev G. V., 227
Gerard, Capt J. D., 312
German Club, Auckland, 16
German Government—
  Camps, location of, 96
  Clothing, 26, 33, 46, 95, 156, 263
  Communications with, 11, 41, 96, 97, 146
  Foreign Office, 7, 41, 95, 96, 127, 234–5, 259, 392, 394
  Geneva Convention, 1929, adherence to, 7, 91–2, 95, 101–2
  Internees, xxiv, 6, 38–9, 146, 256
  Pay, 148, 149, 150
  Protected personnel, 147, 261
  Repatriation, 38, 93, 102, 125, 147, 261, 300, 321, 408–9, 484
  Reprisals, 91, 102, 258, 259–60, 268, 320
German High Command, 4, 5, 23–4, 29, 79, 235, 238, 239–40, 241, 247–8, 249, 259, 291, 367, 368, 402, 442, 445, 446, 449–50, 454, 461, 463, 484, 486, 488
Germany—
  Camps, 1–6, 23–35, 37, 51–2, 83–5, 88–91, 92, 95, 96, 102–3, 126–32, 138–44, 149, 150, 152–3, 155–7, 233–44, 248–53, 255, 262–4, 268–71, 291, 292–9, 323–4, 364–74, 377–9, 387–90, 392, 393–5, 396, 398–07, 441, 442, 445–8, 449–71, 488–90
  Escapes, ix, 28–9, 33–5, 84, 90, 91, 92, 102, 129, 142–3, 144, 157, 236, 238, 240, 252–3, 254, 293–4, 367, 371–2, 379, 395–6, 397, 399, 402–3, 404, 405–6, 446, 463, 465
  Internee camps, 8, 38, 94, 138, 145, 146, 256, 438
  Movement of prisoners, 1945, 377, 449–60, 463–70, 484–5, 490–1
  Red Cross Society, 9, 289
  Repatriation from, 43, 93, 102, 261, 321–2, 408–10, 462–3, 471–2, 484, 491
  Transfer of prisoners to,
    From Greece, 55, 59, 79, 82–3, 85, 86, 88, 92, 101

Germany—*continued*
  Transfer of prisoners to,—*continued*
    From Italy, 275, 279–80, 281, 283, 287, 288–91, 299–300, 301, 305, 317–18, 323–4, 364–5
Gestapo, 21, 377, 378, 394–5, 399–400, 402, 403, 446, 486
Gibbon, Maj E. H., 308, 426, 427
Gibbs, Cpl D. J., 304–5
Gilbert Islands, 159, 160–1, 167, 325
Gill, Pte H. W., 70
Gilmour, Pte W. S., 377
Gilroy, Pte D. P., 81
Glasper, Pte W. A., 385
Gleiwitz, 132, 243, 270, 374
Goodwin, Lt R. B., 171, 347
Goodwin, Capt S. S. F., 313
Gordon, Gnr H. J., 417
Goscourt, 501
Gosling, Pte N. A., 309
Gothenburg, 322, 409, 410, 486
Gradisca, 77, 80, 92, 125, 227, 409
Grasshopper, HMS, 165
Graudenz, 320–1, 390, 395, 396, 450
Gray, Capt W. G., 305
Graz, 408
Great Western Road centre, 349
Greece, v–vi, 39, 53, 63–4, 98, 103, 104, 106
  Camps, 54, 55–9, 72–3, 77–80, 99, 101, 111–12
  Escapes, vi, ix, 54, 58, 59, 72, 73–5, 76–7, 79, 80–2, 227–33, 384
  Germany, transfer of prisoners to, 55, 59, 79, 82–3, 85, 86, 88, 92, 101
  Red Cross Society, 56, 57, 73, 76, 78, 99, 231
Green, Pte T. C., 429
Greer, Pte G. A., 429
Gregory, Spr W. A., 201
Greiffenberg, 378
Gripsholm, 353, 409, 410
Gross Reifling, 381
Guilliard, Pte J. A., 395
Gundry, Pte W. E., 418
Gutersberg, 465

HAGUE CONVENTION, 1899, xxiv
Hague Convention, 1907, xxiv, 184, 302
Haine hospital, 498, 500, 504, 505
Haiphong Road camp, 348–9
Hakodate, 344, 516
Hakusan Maru, 354
Halkett, Pte A. J., 316
Halkett, Pte R. S., 316
Hamilton, Pte J. S., 395
Hamlin, Pte S. N., 423
Hargest, Brig J., vi, 107, 119, 213, 411, 425, 496
Harper, Pte W. R., 384–5
Hart, Pte E. W. R., 309
Hartwell House, 410, 496–7
Haruku, 339–40
Hauraki, 326, 343, 344
'Haw Haw, Lord', 10, 90, 102, 271
Haycock, Cpl F. B., 73, 74
Head, Flt Lt M. R., 318
Hedgehog, HMS, 70

Heppenstall, Pte G. E., 420
Heslop, Capt W. J., 428
Heydebreck, 373
'H' Force, 334
Hickton, Sgt H. T., 255
Hiddlestone, Rev J. S., 373
Hill, WO II D. B., 74
Hinton, Sgt J. D., 54
Hitchens, L-Bdr T. A., 395
Hoare, Pte H. A., 387
Hodge, Pte M. R., 427
Hoffman, Gnr J., 383
Hoffman, Pte P., 383
Hohemark hospital, 4, 22–3, 25, 26, 141–2
Holloway, Lt R. A., 165
Honam Island, 350
Hong Kong, 159, 160, 165, 186, 187, 353, 512, 517
  Camps, 163–4, 169–73, 345–8, 351, 355, 356, 514, 519
  Escapes, ix, 170–1, 347
Hong Kong News, 173
Hong Kong Volunteer Defence Force, 163, 169
Hooper, Sgt R. A., 232
Horne, Pte W. M., 428
Howard, Pte E. A., 81
Howard, Pte R. R., 419
Hungary, 137, 247, 364, 382
  Escapers in, 86, 134, 384, 385–7
Hunt, Fg Off S. M., 425
Hutton, Pte J., 309
Hymettus, 72

ILAGS—
  VII, Laufen, 256, 438
  VIII, Tost, 94, 138, 145, 256, 438
  VIIIH, Giromagny, 406, 438, 439
  VIIIZ, Kreuzberg, 438, 439
  XIII, Wülsburg (later Zweiglager XIIIA), 8, 38, 51, 94
  Biberach, 256, 438
  Liebenau, 94, 146, 256
  Wurzach, 438
Illston, Pte J. A., 309
Imperial Prisoners of War Committee, 7, 11, 97, 103, 146, 184, 256, 261, 279, 484, 492, 493, 510, 518
  Sub-committee A, 321
  Sub-committee B, 148, 150, 151
India, 44, 97
Indo-China, 159, 517
Ineson, Pte K. C. J., 417–18
Inter-governmental Advisory Committee *see* Commonwealth Civilians Committee
Inter-governmental Committee on Prisoners of War, 10, 44, 96
  Sub-committee A, 44, 96–7
  Sub-committee B, 44, 96
Interlude, 379
International Red Cross Committee—
  Appeal to belligerents, Sep 1939, 8
  Camps, visits to, 9, 41–2, 95, 96, 351
  Central Agency, xxv, 8–9, 10, 36, 42, 148, 184, 257
  Finances, 42, 43, 95, 257
  Internees, xxiv, 6, 7, 8, 9, 15, 39, 42–3

International Red Cross Committee—*ctd*
  Orthopaedic mission, 263
  Permanent delegations, 9
  Protection of interests of prisoners of war, xxiv, xxv, 8–9, 15, 18, 36, 41, 97–8, 146, 147, 148, 184, 185–6, 241, 257, 258–9, 263, 320, 439, 485
  Relief, xxv, 8, 13, 28, 42–3, 45, 46, 48, 57, 76, 95, 99–100, 101, 151, 152, 154, 156, 186, 187, 241, 257, 263, 323, 351–2, 355, 442, 445, 448, 456, 462, 485, 486, 487, 488
  Repatriation, 8, 43, 92–3, 125, 322, 384
  Special missions, 9
  Telegram scheme, 518–19
Internees—
  Europe, xxiv, 6–8, 9, 10–11, 12, 13, 15, 18, 35–9, 41, 42–4, 47, 93–5, 100, 138, 145–6, 150, 157, 158, 255–6, 319, 321, 406, 409–10, 438–40, 441, 448, 460
  Far East, 160, 161–4, 167, 169, 172, 177–80, 183, 185, 319, 326–8, 337, 342–3, 348–50, 351–3, 355, 507–8, 511–17
Interrogations, 3, 4–5, 21, 22–4, 55, 61–2, 91, 106, 139–42, 164–5, 166, 194, 247, 249, 250–1, 326–7, 343, 398, 399, 400, 506–7
Italian Government—
  Germany, transfer of prisoners to, 275, 280
  Notification of capture, 148
  Pay, 148, 149, 150
  Protected personnel, 106, 125, 147, 226
  Release of prisoners at Armistice, 275, 279
  Repatriation, 93, 147, 226, 261, 300
  Reprisals, 260
Italy, vii, 39, 41, 272
  Camps, 39–40, 52, 100, 112–24, 139, 148–50, 154–5, 203–23, 262, 263, 266–8, 274–9, 281–4, 286, 287–8, 315, 317, 411
  Escapes ix, 116, 121–2, 205, 209, 210, 211, 213, 217, 220, 222, 232, 277, 278, 281, 282, 283, 284–8, 289–90, 301–17, 318, 324, 384, 411–29, 473–6
  Germany, transfer of prisoners to, 275, 279–80, 281, 283, 287, 288–91, 299–300, 301, 305, 317–18, 323–4, 364–5
  Hospitals, 124, 223–6, 277, 300
  Liberation committees, 315, 421–2, 424
  Rebelli, 307, 315, 316
  Reception of ex-prisoners, 274–5, 430–3
  Repatriation from, 124–6, 147, 226–7
Itzehoe, 2

JAARMARKT, 339, 359
Jantzen, 110–11, 147, 215
Japan—
  Camps, 167–9, 343–5, 351, 355, 515–17, 518, 519
  Prisoners of war, attitude towards, 188–9
  Surrender, 506, 511
  Victories, 153, 159–61, 163, 164, 165, 166

Japanese Government, 258, 271
  Allied warnings to, 362–3, 522
  Camps, visits to, 351–2, 519
  Geneva Convention, 1929, adherence to, 184–5, 186
  Internees, 185
  Japanese prisoners in New Zealand, 359
  Mail, 186, 351, 518
  Neutral agencies, 185–6, 187, 351–2, 519
  Notification of capture, 185, 350, 518
  Relief, 186–7, 351–2, 355–6, 362
  Repatriation, 352
  Telegram scheme, 518–19
Java, 159, 165, 166–7, 187
  Camps, 167, 180–2, 338–9, 355, 513–14
Jennings, Mrs M. A., 163–4
Johnston, L-Bdr B. W., 70
Johnston, Pte R. H., 475
Johnstone, Pte G. O., 428–9
Johnstone, L-Cpl R. D., 309
Jones, Dr M., 527
Jones, Pte N. H., 316
Joo Chiat, 164
Joseph, Pte H. J., 309

KAIMICHI steelworks, 516
Kai Tak aerodrome, 346
Kalamata, v, 53–4, 55
Kamakura Maru, 353, 354
Kampong Toh, 162–3
Kanburi, 331, 336–7, 513
Karikal camp, 164, 177
Kedgley, Maj E. G., 415
Kelsall, Pte E. G., 429
Kempetai, 171, 326–7
Kendrick, Pte R., 311
Kennard-Davis, Pte J. S., 288
Kerr, L-Cpl W. T. W., 80
Kerse, Cpl C. H., 309
Key, Pte K. G., 475
Kildare, 145
Kimber, Sgt H. W., 426–7
King, Mr S. N., 327
Kippenberger, Maj-Gen Sir H. K., v–viii, 107, 497–8, 499–500
Klagenfurt, 136, 270, 382, 479
Kloster Haina, 153, 408
Kobe, 167
Kokkinia, 54, 56, 63–4, 72–3, 74, 75–7
Komarom, 385
Komet, 36, 37
Kong Chuen, 162, 350
Königswartha, 408
Korea, 330, 351, 517
Krappitz, 242–3
Kuching, 164
Kwei Noi River, 331, 332

LABAND, 371
Laghouat, 144–5, 255
Laird, Pte F. J., 309
Lamia, 55
Lamond, Flt Lt H. W., 144
Lamsdorf hospital, 92, 263, 407
Landek, 247, 387, 477, 488
Landshut, 469

Langley, Dvr R. P., 475
Larissa, 55, 231-2
Lavamünd, 87, 136, 137, 246, 381
Lazaretts—
　Bad Soden, 408, 470
　Cosel, 408, 470, 480
　Dieburg, 92, 138
　Elsterhorst, 408
　Freising, 408
　Graz, 408
　Hohemark, 4, 22-3, 25, 26, 141-2
　Kloster Haina, 153, 408
　Königswartha, 408
　Lamsdorf, 92, 263, 407
　Obermasfeld, 138, 153, 407-8
　Rottenmunster, 92
　Schmorkau, 408
　Spittal, 408, 479
　Stadroda, 138
　Tost, 408, 470, 480
Le Comte, Dvr C. G., 384
Ledgerwood, Mr J. H., 247
Lee, Fg Off K. L., 305
Lee-on-Solent, 501
Lehervar, 386
Le Lievre, Pte W. A., 81
Leonard, Gnr D. W., 419
Lewes, Gnr R. J., 419
Library Associations, International Federation of, 43
2 Libyan Campaign, vi-vii, 104-7, 112, 139, 153-4
Lilli Mathiessen, 486
Lincoln Avenue Centre, 350, 515
Lisbon Maru, 346
Llandovery Castle, 125
Lloyd, Pte A. G., 383
Loader, Pte G. C., 423
Locke, Spr O. J., 475
Lockhead, Pte J. E., 309
Logan, Pte G. H., 413
Logan, Lt J. D. K., 195
Lollar, 463-4
Long Range Desert Group, 318-19
Los Banos, 508
Loveridge, Dvr S. N., 70
Lowther, Pte W. W., 428
Luftwaffe, 2-3, 4, 5, 21, 22, 28, 62, 139, 143, 249, 399-400
Lugton, Pte J. S., 309
Lungwha Civilian Centre, 349
Lyceum School, Sourabaya, 339

McAllum, Gnr H. R., 475
Macassar, 166, 183-4, 340-1, 351, 355, 362, 514
McCluskey, Pte J. J., 423
McConchie, Sgt P. A., 109
McCreath, Pte T. G., 313
McDonald, Sgt C. C., 109
MacDonald, Lt K. M. W., 305
McDowell, Pte J., 417-18
McEwan, Pte R. E., 428
McGrath, Pte H. M., 427
Mackay, Pte P. S., 309
McKay, L-Cpl R. C., 428
McKay, Dvr T. D., 413-14
McKendrick, Dvr W., 421

McKenzie, Pte R. C., 383
McKinney, Pte R. J., 377
McLean, Pte J. W., 420
McLeod, Pte D. C., 414
McLeod, Pte D. D., 429
McLeod, Pte G. V., 422-3
MacNab, Sgt D. G., 74
McQuarrie, Pte D. N., 69
Maher, Pte C. J., 422
Mair, Pte L. S. A., 429
Malaya, 159, 160, 164, 173, 353, 517
Manchuria, 351, 510, 517
Margate, 498
Marks, Miss O., 94
Mark Time, 181
Marlag-Milag Nord, Westertimke (formerly Sandbostel), 234, 254, 255, 406-7, 439, 458, 460, 466-7
Maros, 340
Marshall, Sigmn D. G., 429
Marshall, L-Bdr F. S., 76-7
Marshall, Pte W. S., 81
Marston, Pte R. J., 417-18
Martin, L-Cpl E. O., 424
Martin, Sigmn M. N., 475
Martin, Dvr O., 200
Mason, Capt M. J., 417
Massautti, Miss Ariadne, 56
Matthews, Pte L. N., 412-13
May, WO II E., 284
Mechtal, 371
Medan, 166, 338, 341
Meiningen, 455
Merchant Navy prisoners, v, vii, 32, 35-8, 94, 145, 160, 234, 255, 321, 326, 343, 407, 409, 410, 438, 460, 467, 515, 525
Mergui, 338
Mersa Matruh, 191, 194, 195, 223
MI9, 68, 71, 74-5, 80, 81, 201, 229, 279-80, 286, 301, 312, 313, 314-15, 317, 318, 478
Midway, Battle of, 189, 325
Miles, Brig R., 119, 213, 411, 425
Millar Flt Lt R. D., 181
Minqar Qaim, vii, 191, 192-3, 208
Mitchell, Lt N. B., 417, 418
Mixed Medical Commissions, 43, 93, 125, 226, 300, 321, 409, 440
Moir, Sgt T., 70, 71, 229
Moncur, L-Cpl P. E., 424
Morgan, Pte E. J., 316
Morice, Dvr J. B., 74
Morigi di Piacenza hospital, 224
Moro Pass, 303-5, 306
Morris, Pte R. A., 415-16
Morrish, L-Cpl W. G., 474
Morrison, Pte A. E., 413
Morrison, Pte J. A., 475
Morrow, Gnr A. H., 426-7
Morton, Gnr R. M., 75
Moulmein, 330, 338, 509
Mount, Pte J. W., 309
Mundai, 340
Munro, Gnr J. P., 427
Muntok, 342
Murtagh, Pte T. O., 427
Myers, Col B., 49, 100

NAKOM PATON, 336
Naples, 112
Nash, Rt Hon W., 505
National Patriotic Fund, 14, 43, 47, 49, 99, 151, 153, 157, 448
    Board, 14, 47
Natusch, Spr R. S., 384, 386
Nea Hellas, 228
'Nelson' mission, 474
Neu Brandenburg, 459, 487
Neuhammer, 138
Newfoundland, 227
New Zealand
    Aliens, enemy, xxiv–xxv, 11, 15–18, 49–51, 146, 149, 265–6, 444–5, 488
    Japanese prisoners of war, 356–61, 520–2
    Relief, 14, 15, 49, 99, 100–1, 103, 150–2, 157–8, 186, 262, 264, 323, 448
    2 NZ Division, v, 524–5
        Crete, vi, 60–1, 103
        El Mreir, 191, 193
        Greece, v–vi, 53–5, 103
        Italy, vii, 313, 317, 411, 472
        2 Libyan Campaign, vi–vii, 104–7, 112, 139
        Minqar Qaim, vii, 191, 192–3, 208
        4 NZ Infantry Brigade, vii, 105, 191
        5 NZ Infantry Brigade, vi, vii, 104, 105, 191
        6 NZ Infantry Brigade, vi, vii, 105, 191
        Ruweisat Ridge, vii, 191, 193, 194
        Units—
            18 Battalion, 193
            19   ,,   , 191, 193
            20   ,,   , vi, 105, 191
            21   ,,   , 104, 105, 411
            22   ,,   , vii, 191, 193
            24   ,,   , 105, 191, 317
            25   ,,   , 191, 317
            26   ,,   , 105, 191
            28   ,,   , 317, 411
    2 NZEF, 95, 160, 161, 191, 430, 432, 479
    NZ Dental Corps, 54, 107
    NZ Education and Rehabilitation Service, 433, 496, 497
    1 NZ General Hospital, 54, 125
    NZ Medical Services, 105, 106–7, 125, 407
    1 NZ Prisoner of War Repatriation Unit, 430, 433, 479, 480, 494
        Reception Group, 410, 495–500, 501, 502, 503–5
New Zealand Forces Club, London, 47
New Zealand Government, 40, 259, 272
    Aliens, enemy, 15, 16, 17, 50
    Base Records, 157
        NZ Missing and Prisoner of War Agency, 319
    Internal Affairs Department, 15, 44
    International Red Cross Committee, grants to, 95, 257, 448
    Internees, 6, 7, 11, 44, 146
    2 NZEF Reception Group, 497–8, 500
    Prime Minister's Department, 11, 98, 157, 319
    Prisoners of War, protection of interests, 11, 44, 97, 98, 184–5, 259, 441, 481
    Repatriation, 493

New Zealand High Commissioner's Office, London, 6, 7, 11, 44, 47, 97, 98, 142, 148
    Prisoners of War Section, 100, 101, 145, 152, 153, 264, 272, 323
New Zealand Joint Council of the Red Cross, 14, 15, 17, 28, 47, 49, 99, 100, 151, 157, 158, 262, 448, 517
    Prisoners of War Inquiry Offices, 100, 103, 157–8, 264, 272, 448
New Zealand Military Forces, 11, 15
New Zealand Women's Army Auxiliary Corps, 499
New Zealand War Services Association, 47
Nicol, Pte H., 309
Nielsen, Pte R. J., 232–3
Nino Bixio, 202–3
Nixey, Pte L. J., 428
Non Pladuk, 335, 336, 337, 519
Norderney Island, 1
Northover, WO II L. N., 232
North Point camp, 163, 169–70, 346

OBERMASFELD, 138, 153, 407–8
Oderfest, 243
Oderburg, 297, 372–3, 469
Odessa, 481–2, 483
Oerhingen, 132
Oflags—
    IVC, Colditz, 34, 92, 234, 396–7, 467, 485
    VA, Weinsberg, 291, 293–5, 366, 463, 464
    VB, Biberach, 83–4, 88
    VIB, Warburg, 84, 85, 92, 126–9, 143, 152, 234, 236, 237, 253
    VIIB, Eichstaett, 236, 237–9, 258, 365, 461, 464, 467
    VIIIF, Märisch-Trübau, 295, 299, 367–8, 403, 461
    IXA/H, Spangenburg (formerly IXA), 2, 3, 5–6, 29–30, 31, 91, 92, 128, 129, 143, 234–5, 236, 257, 268, 295, 365, 463, 464
    IXA/Z, Rotenburg, 235, 236, 291, 365–6, 463, 464
    XC, Lubeck, 84–5, 91, 143
    XIIB, Hadamar, 291, 295, 367, 463
    XXIB, Schubin, 236, 251, 253–4
    67, 386
    79, Querum, 368–9
Ofuna, 343
Oldnall, Able-Seaman H. R., 165
Old Park barracks, 498
Omori, 515–16
Omi, 516
Oppeln, 372
Orama, 94
Orion, 36, 37
Orr, Maj R. S., 305, 306, 435, 437
Orsogna, 317
Osaka, 344, 516
Ospedales—
    PG 201, Bergamo, 224, 225, 277, 300
    PG 202, Lucca, 209, 224, 225, 226–7, 420

Ospedales—*continued*
  PG 203, Bologna, 224, 225
  PG 204, Altamura, 224, 226, 277
  PG 206, Nocera, 224, 277
  PG 207, Milan, 277
  Vescovile, 224

PADANG, 166, 182–3, 341
Pahiatua Camp, 265–6, 444
Palawan, 508
Palembang, 183, 341, 342, 514
Palm Tree Camp, 196–8, 201
Paravicini, Dr, 185–6
Park, Pte G. E., 386–7
Parma hospital, 224
Parole, 30, 235
Pasteur, 257
Patras, 112, 231, 232
Paul, Gnr D. W., 427
Pearce, Pte A. C. S., 475
Pearse, Pte R. W., 417
Pekam Bahru, 342
Peking, 161
Percival, Lt-Gen A. E., 164
Persson, Pte W. M., 429
Peters, Gnr R. P. A., 67
Petersen, Pte N., 427
Phelan, Dvr E. J. A., 372
Philippine Islands, 159, 160, 187, 325, 353, 506, 510, 512
  Camps, 164, 179–80, 507–8, 517, 522
Phillips, Lt J. K., 416
Piacenza hospital, 225
Pilcher, Pte D. J., 413–14
Pilos, 111
Pitcher, Pte A. H., 475
Podmore, Pte H. C., 415–16
Pohe, Fg Off P.P.J., 403
Poland—
  Camps, 91–2, 138, 253–4, 298, 369, 374–7, 390–2, 449–50, 480
  Escapes, 92, 253, 254, 377, 391
Polkinghorn, Lt S., 169
Polytechnic School, Athens, 56, 63–4, 72, 75, 76
Pool, Lt-Cdr F. G., 68
Pootung, 349
Port Hobart, 35, 36, 37, 255
Powell, Pte L. J., 429
Pow Wow, 380–1
Prince of Wales, HMS, 159
Prisoners of war—
  Enemy, 10, 44, 52, 91, 92, 96, 97, 103, 125, 149, 227, 235, 238, 239, 257, 258, 259, 260, 321, 356–61, 410, 520–2
  Europe—
    Camps, inspection of, 9, 41–2, 95, 96, 146–7, 439
    Capture, notification of, 9–10, 14–15, 36, 42, 45, 97–8, 148, 157, 271–2, 319, 324
    Clothing, 26, 33, 46, 95, 156, 262–3
    NCOs, compulsory work, 131, 248, 260–1
    Pay, 31, 43, 44, 85, 96, 114, 119, 120, 148–50, 440–1

Prisoners of war—*continued*
  Europe—*continued*
    Protection of interests, xxiii–xxvi, 7, 8–11, 18, 41–2, 43–4, 52, 95–8, 103, 138, 146–50, 157–8, 256–62, 285, 319–21, 439, 440–1, 481, 484–6
    Rations, 32, 95, 99, 115, 130, 150, 224, 241, 262, 434–5, 440–1
  Far East—
    Camps, inspections of, 351–2, 519
    Capture, notification of, 185, 350–1, 518
    Mail, 186, 351, 518
    Protection of interests, 184–6, 319, 350–3, 518–19
    Rations, 353
    Repatriation from, 352–3, 510–17
    Telegram scheme, 518–19
Prisoner of War News, The, 267
Prisoner of War Relatives' Association, 158
Propaganda, German, 10, 90, 102–3, 247–8, 268, 270–1, 392–3
Protected personnel, 8, 105, 106, 124–5, 147–8, 226, 227, 261–2, 321, 322, 408–9
Protecting power, xxv, 6, 7, 10, 11, 15, 40, 41, 45, 95, 96, 145, 146, 147, 184, 185–6, 248, 256, 294, 321, 351, 355, 485
Pudu jail, 173
Pullen, Cpl J., 311–12
Puttick Wing, 499, 504–5

QUELLENGRUND, 374

RADKERSBURG, 384
Rangitane, 36, 254
Rangoon jail, 509
Ransley, Pte E. L., 475
RAPWI teams, 511, 512, 513, 517
Ratcliffe, Pte C. J., 383
Ratibor, 243
Ravenstein, Gen von, 104
Read, Pte L. J., 424
Red Crescent Society, 481
Red Cross form, 23–4, 61–2, 139, 140, 250–1
Redpath, Sgt J. A., 69, 209, 229, 312
Reeve, Pte R. M., 309
Reid, Pte J., 81
Relief—
  Europe, xxv, 7, 8, 11, 13–14, 15, 18–19, 28, 41, 42, 44–5, 51, 52, 100–1, 125–6, 153, 154, 241–2, 257, 264–5, 445, 448, 481, 485
  Cigarettes and tobacco, 13, 47, 101, 153, 264, 437
  Clothing, 12, 13, 33, 46, 49, 156, 241–2, 262–3, 323, 434, 443
  Food, 11, 12, 13, 26, 32, 42, 44, 45–6, 47, 48–9, 99–100, 103, 130, 150–2, 155–6, 157–8, 186–7, 262, 264, 322–3, 442, 456, 462, 486–8
  Educational material, 13, 43, 47–8, 101, 152–3, 264, 443–4
  Medical supplies, 12, 13, 45, 92, 100, 153, 186, 263, 443

Relief—*continued*
  Europe—*continued*
    Recreational materials, 43, 47, 101, 152, 187, 264, 443
    Far East, 185, 187, 351–2, 362, 511, 520
    Food, 186, 354–6
    Medical supplies, 353–6, 520
Rendell, Pte G. M., 383
Repatriation, 8, 92–4, 261–2, 272–3, 440, 492–5
  Austria, 478, 479–480
  Far East, 352–3, 510–17
  Germany, 43, 93, 102, 261, 321–2, 408–10, 462–3, 471–2, 481, 491
  Internees, 6, 11, 38, 256, 300, 409–10, 439
  Italy, 124–6, 147, 226–7, 261, 274–5, 431
  Russia, 480–4
  Switzerland, 437
Repatriation Committees, 261–2, 300, 440
Reprisals, 35, 51, 77, 91–2, 102, 171, 212, 233–4, 235, 238–40, 248–9, 256, 257–60, 261, 268, 271, 298, 320, 404, 460, 461
Repulse, HMS, 159
Resina, 430, 431
Rice, Pte J. B., 427
Riddiford, Capt D. J., 292, 308
Robinson, Pte E. M., 309
Robinson, Pte J. A., 417
Robinson, L-Cpl L. J., 429
Robson, Pte B. M., 309
Robson, Pte T., 306
Rolfe, Dvr R. W., 70
Ross, Pte G. H., 414
Ross, Pte W. F., 475
Rosson, Pte L. S., 70
Rottenmunster, 92
Royal Navy prisoners, v, vii, 10, 30, 36–7, 59, 83, 144, 160, 163, 165–6, 169, 182, 183–4, 233, 234, 254–5, 272, 280, 326, 341, 406, 409, 410, 460, 466–7, 496, 501, 525
Royal New Zealand Air Force, 511–12, 512–13, 514, 517
Rudd, Lt-Col L. F., 496, 498
Russell, L-Cpl D., 429, 474–5
Russia, 153, 190, 258, 271, 364, 440, 449, 485
  Repatriation from, 480–4
Rutherford, Pte S. D., 429
Ruweisat Ridge, vii, 191, 193, 194
Ryan, Pte R. E., 475
Ryman, Gnr R. H., 422–3

SACHSENHAUSEN, 406
Sacred Heart hospital, 515
St. Denis, 94, 145, 255, 438, 439
St. George, Cpl I. A., 422–3
Saint Hippolyte-du-Fort, 145
St. Lorenzen, 383
St. Veit, 381
Samoa, 16, 17
Sanderson, Pte H. D., 428
Sangster, L-Cpl T. I., 418–19
Santo Tomas University, 164, 179–80, 507–8
Sarawak, 159, 164, 514
Sark, 238, 258
Schmorkau, 408
Scott, L-Cpl A. W., 473–4, 475
Scott, L-Cpl W. J., 427
Selarang barracks, 329–30
Sendai, 507, 516
Senior, Pte J. M., 475
Serang, 180
Serbian Red Cross Society, 82
Servizio Prigioneri di Guerra, 421–2
Sfakia, vi, 60, 64
Shackling, 238–40, 248–9, 257, 258–9, 271, 298, 320
Shamshuipo barracks, 163, 170, 171, 345–6, 347, 355, 514
Shanghai, 161–2, 186, 187, 348, 349, 350, 351, 515
Sharp, Cpl W. A., 428–9
Shearer, Pte T., 69
Short, Flt Lt S. A. H., 423–4
Sick and Wounded Convention, 1929, 147, 184
Sidi Azeiz, vi
Sidi Hussein, 108
Sidi Rezegh, vi, 104–5
Siely, Pte W. J., 379
Siklos, 385
Silverwood, Dvr E. R., 372
Sime Road camp, 327–8, 512–13
Sims, Pte N. M., 475
Sinclair, Lt R. B., 74
Singapore, 159, 164, 166, 187, 352, 355, 356
  Camps, 164–5, 173–9, 326–30, 512–13
Singkep Island, 165
Skilton, Pte J. S., 425
Skinner, Pte W. G., 313
Slyfield, Lt H. D., 417, 418
Smith, Spr B. H., 309
Smith, Pte N., 309
Smyrna, 125, 227
Solomon Islands, 325, 356
Somes Island, 17–18, 49–51, 265, 444–5, 488
Soviet Red Cross, 481
Speight, Gnr G. G., 420
Spittal, 408, 479
Spry, Pte F. J., 395–6
Stadroda, 138
Stalags—
  IIIA, Luckenwalde, 458, 459, 470–1, 487
  IIIE, Kirchhain, 91, 142, 143
  IVA, 299
  IVB, Mühlberg, 275, 295, 296, 299 401
  IVC, 469
  IVD, 299
  IVD/Z, Annaburg, 409, 462
  VB, 92
  VC, Offenberg, 291
  VIIA, Moosburg, 138, 291, 292–3, 296, 387–8, 405, 458, 460, 464, 467–8, 487

Stalags—continued
 VIIIA, Görlitz, 270, 291, 292, 295-6, 297, 298, 323, 369, 377-8, 379, 450, 454, 455, 456-7, 466
 VIIIB, Teschen, 298, 369, 454-5
 VIIIC, Sagan, 298, 369, 370, 458
 IXB, 92, 138
 IXC, Badsulza, 91, 102, 138, 143, 239
 XB, Sandbostel, 37, 38, 51, 94, 145, 254, 255, 406
 XIA, Altengrabow, 296, 299, 390, 460
 XIB, Fallingbostel, 296, 299, 390, 466
 XIC, Duderstadt, 457-8, 460, 465-6
 XIIA, Limburg, 29, 30, 31
 XIIIC, Hammelburg, 138, 456, 458, 460, 463, 465
 XIIID, Nuremberg, 454, 460
 XVIIA, 386
 XVIIB, Krems, 456
 XVIIIA, Wolfsberg, 85, 86-7, 135-6, 137, 243, 244, 245, 247, 369, 379-81, 382, 384, 386, 395, 477, 478-9
 XVIIIA/Z, Spittal-on-the-Drau (formerly XVIIIB), 133, 243, 244, 291, 292, 296, 300, 387, 391
 XVIIIB, Wagna, 244, 251
 XVIIIC, Markt Pongau, 247, 291, 292, 387, 476-8, 485
 XVIIID, Marburg, 85, 132-3, 243, 244, 309, 383
 XXA, Thorn, 91-2, 138, 234, 262-3, 390, 391, 449, 450
 XXB, Marienburg, 449, 450
 337, Mantua (later Dulag 339), 287, 288, 317, 411
 344, Lamsdorf (formerly VIIIB), 29, 30-1, 37, 88-90, 92, 129-32, 143, 152, 239-42, 243-4, 251, 258, 261, 263, 291, 293, 295, 296, 297-8, 300, 369-70, 391, 401, 405, 406, 407, 450, 454, 460
 355, 392
 357, Fallingbostel (formerly at Thorn), 391-2, 401, 405, 449, 458, 459-60, 466
 383, Hohenfels (formerly Oflag IIIC), 239, 243-4, 248-9, 251, 258, 261, 296, 388-9, 461-2, 468
Stalags Luft—
 I, Barth, 31-5, 85, 90-1, 142-3, 251, 401, 403-4, 459, 471
 III, Sagan, 142, 143-4, 234, 251-3, 254, 291, 399, 401-3, 404, 406, 458, 460
 IV, Gross Tychow (Kiefheide), 405, 449, 459
 VI, Heydekrug, 392, 401, 403, 404-5, 449
 VII, Bankau, 401, 405, 459
Stanley, Gnr D. J., 417-18
Stanley internment camp, 163, 172-3, 348, 514
Steinburg, 394, 447
Stevenson, Pte S., 420
Stevenson-Wright, Capt E., 138
Stewart, Brig K. L., 411
Stott, Sgt D. J., 75
Straker, Maj T. W., 290, 305

Stringer, Dvr L. F., 385
Stronghold, HMS, 165-6
Student, Gen K., 61, 62
Student Relief Fund, European, 43
Suani Ben Adem, 202
Sumatra, 159, 165, 166, 338
 Camps, 182-3, 341-2, 355, 514
Sungeron, 341
Sutton, Lt H. B. J., 75
Sutton, Cpl R. G., 417
Svenson, Pte A. J., 309
Swedish Red Cross Society, 388
Swinburne, Dvr W. H., 71
Switzerland, 43, 137, 145, 147, 184, 258-9, 263, 301, 320, 356, 382, 439
 Escapers in, ix, 301, 302-3, 304, 306-7, 324, 425, 434-7
Szigetvar, 385-6, 387

Tairea, 227, 322, 463
Takanun, 335
Talamba, 227
Tamarkan, 335, 336, 337
Tamuan, 336
Tanagawa, 344
Tapping, Pte P. G., 383
Tarawa, 161
Tarhuna, 108, 201-2
Tarmstedt, 458
Tarsao, 335
Tasik Malaja, 166, 167
Tatura Maru, 353, 354
Tavoy, 338
Tayler, Pte C. L., 311
Taylor, Pte D. M., 475
Teia Maru, 353, 354
Tempo, 121
Tennent, Lt-Col A. A., 115
Termoli, 313, 314, 315
Thailand, 159, 162-3, 361, 517
 Camps, 330-8, 355, 356, 513, 522
Thanbuzayat, 330, 335
Thiele, Sqd Ldr K. F., 465
Thomas, Dvr D. C., 426
Thomas, Lt W. B., 80, 81
Thompson, Pte (28 Bn), 67
Thompson, Gnr H. C., 417
Thomson, Maj G. H., 54, 85
Thrasher, HM Submarine, 68
Thurgau, 436
Tiki Times, 376, 377
Timor, 338
Titmoning, 84
Tjilatjap, 166, 167
Tjimahi hospital, 180
Tobruk, 107, 190, 195, 196, 223, 262
Tokyo Draft, 1934, xxiv-xxv, 8, 16
Tong, Pte L. H., 416
Torbay, HM Submarine, 68-9
Torelli hospital, 110, 201
Tost hospital, 408, 470, 480
Trayes, Pte R. V. N., 475
Trengrove, Pte V. A. R., 417-18
Trenthorst, 467
Treviglio, 300
Trofaiac, 381
Tulloch, L-Cpl R. A., 413
Turangi, Pte H., 383

Turnpike camp, 498
Twhigg, Brig J. M., 498, 500
Tyler, Dvr W. L., 429
Tyson, Gnr M. A., 422

UNITED KINGDOM GOVERNMENT, 40, 106, 159, 184
  Air Ministry, 10, 12, 26, 441
  Escapers, 285, 302–3, 434
  Foreign Office, 6, 10–11, 96, 97, 146, 256, 280
  Geneva Convention, 1929, adherence to, 7, 185, 186
  Home Office, 10, 11, 146
  Inter-departmental Committee, 10, 43–4, 96
  Internees, xxiv, 7, 8, 10–11, 146
  Pay, 148, 149
  Prisoners of war, protection of interests, 10, 11, 43–4, 96, 97, 138, 146, 147–8, 184–5, 186, 256, 275, 320–1, 401, 439, 481, 485–6
  Protected personnel, 106, 125, 147–8, 226, 321
  Relief, 13, 241, 355, 356
  Repatriation, 93, 146, 226, 321
  Reprisals, 258, 259, 320
  Treasury, 10
  War Office, 11, 12, 46, 146, 241, 259, 263, 434, 439, 492, 493, 499, 510
    Directorate of Prisoners of War, 43, 61, 256
    Italian armistice plans, 275, 278–81
    Prisoners of War Branch, 10, 43
    Prisoners of War Information Bureau, 17, 97, 98
    Psychiatric Division, 494
United States of America, 7, 40, 41, 95, 101, 145, 147, 153, 159, 321, 352, 353, 409, 440, 485, 510
  Berlin embassy, 6–7, 7–8, 9, 10–11, 97, 127, 132–3, 147
Unterdrauberg, 381
Upham, Capt C. H., 397

VATICAN, 148, 226, 272
Visp, 306
Voyce, Gnr G. E., 69

WADDINGTON, Pte J., 475
Waldenstein, 381
Wallace, Pte R. M., 385
War crimes, 61, 62, 116, 189, 203, 257, 476
Watson, Pte D. N., 429
Watts, Pte D., 429
Webster, Capt F. E., 420

Wehrkreis IV, 296, 299, 389–90, 408, 462
  VIII, 407
  IX, 2, 138, 407
  XI, 299, 390
  XVIII, 296
Wehrmacht, 3, 21, 28, 61–2, 143, 144, 392, 403, 446
Weiden, 454
Weihsien, 350
Weir, Cpl S. J., 475
Weisswasser, 378
Wesermunde, 1–2
Westgate, 498, 500, 504
Westgate, Cpl J., 81
'White angels,' 462, 465, 466, 469, 485, 487–8
Whitehead, Pte I. V. T., 414
Wickliffe, L-Cpl W., 475
Wil, 306, 434
Wildman, L-Cpl J. H., 309
Williams, Sqn Ldr J. A., 403
Williams, Pte R., 474
Williams, Gnr S. G., 475
Williamson, Dvr F. G., 405
Willibaldsburg Castle, 238
Wills, Pte C. V., 475
Wilson, Lt-Col A. T. M., 494
Wilson, Lt F. E., 305
Wilson, Cpl H. E., 475
Wilson, Pte W., 384
Winter, Cpl D. J., 429
Winter, Pte F. C., 419
Witting, Sgt R. R., 69
Wood, Lt R. M., 314
Wood, Pte W., 418–19
Woodlands, 176
Woodroofe, WO G. T., 406
Woollams, Cpl F. I. A., 232
Woosung, 169

XILOCASTRON, 231

YEOMAN, Lt A., 210
Yokohama D1 camp, 343–4
Young, Capt R. R. T., 195
YMCAs, World Alliance of, 13, 26, 43, 90, 95, 152, 187, 216, 241, 366, 388, 443
Yugoslavia, 137, 247, 301
  Escapers in, 86, 134–5, 307–10, 382, 383, 384, 387, 425–9
Yu Yuen, 349, 515

ZAAFRAN, 105
Zannas, Mme, 76
Zentsuji, 167–9, 345, 351, 355
Zindel, Dr, 186
Zugliet prison, 386

www.ingramcontent.com/pod-product-compliance
Lightning Source LLC
Chambersburg PA
CBHW080528300426
44111CB00017B/2644